'This account of the party from 1922 to 1997 [...] like a novel: lucid, entertaining and beautifully written ... This book is a feast of excellent writing' *The Times*

'This is a highly idiosyncratic work ... it is compulsively readable and abounds in perception and witty insights ... The reason this book deserves serious study is not because of its celebrity author, or his jokes (always good), or even his splenetic rants against the self-satisfaction of the Tory Wets as they complacently managed our 20th century decline. It is because its central thesis, however quirkily presented, points to the ultimate reason why the Conservatives will revive, or why they will die' *Evening Standard*

'*The Tories* by Alan Clark tells it like it was, and he sure knows how to tell it' *Spectator*

'Makes for livelier reading than the earlier dogged accounts of the various tergiversations in Conservative economic policy' *New Statesman & Society*

'Alan Clark's work is reckless, contrarian and a cracking good read' *Express*

'Clark is the master of anecdote ... [he] is a romantic nationalist, a brilliant entertainer, and a good popular historian. Buy this book' *Scotsman*

'Although he has a roguish reputation, one should not forget that Clark is an accomplished historian ... His new book could well become the classic history of Twentieth-Century Conservatism' *Publishing News*

'A wonderfully entertaining book ... He is a serious historian and he has a case' *Sunday Times*

'As befits one of the most sensational diarists since Pepys, his survey of modern Toryism (that, rather than mere Conservatism) is full of colour and passion'   *Independent*

'Clark has the rare ability to make the dry bones of political history leap up and dance. *The Tories* is as good as a novel . . . The last chapters are instant narrative history of the highest class. This is a book to be devoured, relished and argued over. There is something to be savoured on almost every page'   *Daily Telegraph*

As a historian Alan Clark sprung to prominence in 1961 with his highly controversial account of the battles and commanders of the British Expeditionary Force in 1915, *The Donkeys*. His other books include *Barbarossa*, the classic account of the Russo-German conflict, 1941–1945.

From 1974 to 1992 he was MP for Plymouth (Sutton), served as Minister of Trade, 1986–89, and Minister of State, Ministry of Defence, 1989–92. At the 1997 General Election he was elected MP for Kensington and Chelsea. He is married, has two sons, and lives at Saltwood Castle, Kent.

In 1993 he published his *Diaries*. Covering his years as a junior minister in Mrs Thatcher's Government, it had *The Times* commenting in a leading article: 'The best diaries, from Pepys and Boswell, to "Chips" Channon and Harold Nicolson, have been souls of indiscretion. But none so indiscreet as Mr Clark ... for its deadly candour, it is one of the great works of the genre.'

The Donkeys: A History of the BEF in 1915

The Fall of Crete

Barbarossa: the Russo-German Conflict, 1941–45

Aces High: the War in the Air over
the Western Front 1914–18

A Good Innings: The Private Papers of
Viscount Lee of Fareham (edited)

Diaries

The Tories

Conservatives and the Nation State
1922–1997

ALAN CLARK

PHOENIX

A PHOENIX PAPERBACK
First published in Great Britain
by Weidenfeld & Nicolson in 1998
This paperback edition published in 1999
by Phoenix, an imprint of Orion Books Ltd,
Orion House, 5 Upper Saint Martin's Lane
London, WC2H 9EA

© 1998 Alan Clark

A CIP catalogue record for this book
is available from the British Library.

ISBN 0 75380 765 3

Typeset by Selwood Systems, Midsomer Norton

Printed and bound in Great Britain by
Clays Ltd, St Ives plc

For my grandsons
Albert, Angus and Archie,
in the hope that History may
give to them that same solace
and enlightenment which it
has always provided for me.

CONTENTS

Between pages 168 and 169

The Lord Chancellor's mistress. Portrait by Sir William Orpen.

On stage at the London Coliseum 'to hear Mr Baldwin's declaration of the future policy of the Conservative and Unionist party.'[1]

Stanley Baldwin in Windsor High Street on his way to dine at the Castle.[1]

Churchill in 1932, after falling into the path of an American taxi.[1]

Sir Kingsley Wood leaves Downing Street, 30 August 1938.[1]

'Rentamob' 1938 at the Oxford by-election.[1]

Neville Chamberlain in Downing Street, 30 September 1938.[1]

Bomb-site electioneering in 1945.[1]

Churchill speaks at an open-air meeting, Wolverhampton Wanderers football ground, 1949.[1]

Lord Camrose's *Daily Telegraph* party at the Savoy, election night 1951.[1]

Between pages 424 and 425

The Chairman of the Party (Lord Wootton), the Prime Minister (Anthony Eden) and his successor (Harold Macmillan).[1]

Macmillan in his prime.[1]

Alec Dunglass, as Neville Chamberlain's PPS, 1938,[1] and a quarter of a century later, as Prime Minister and now known as Sir Alec Douglas-Home.[1]

Margaret Thatcher, with Edward Heath and Quintin Hogg, June 1970.[1]

1975 Conservative Party Conference: Mrs Thatcher rouses the faithful.[1]

Mrs Thatcher displays poise with a bunch of 'monkeys' at very close quarters.[1]

A propaganda postcard from Conservative Central Office.[1]

The European Community Treaty of Accession has just been signed.[1]

Michael Heseltine.[2]

Michael Portillo.[2]

Douglas Hurd, John Major and Jacques Delors at the 1992 Birmingham European Community summit.[1]

In John Major's final two years as Prime Minister, Michael Heseltine was Deputy PM and First Secretary of State.[1]

Sources
The author and the publishers thank the following for permission to reproduce photographs:

[1] Hulton Getty Picture Collection

[2] 'PA' News

For those who expect to find a proper reference made to every significant episode in the political history of Great Britain over this century, and its importance assessed, this is not the book. Nor does it make any claim to be an account of British, still less of European, or of world events over that period.

But the plain fact remains. For eighty years of the twentieth century, from its underwriting of the Lloyd George Coalition in 1916 until it was put to rout by New Labour in 1997, the Conservative Party was the dominant political force in Britain – even when, for short periods, it was in Opposition. How did it conduct itself? Were things different in the engine room from the wheelhouse? What were the moments of equipoise, when even a gust of wind might have caused it to alter course? Too often, under the stress of crisis or with the excuse of immediacy the party may be thought to have turned aside from its real duty – the nurturing, protection and advancement of the British nation state. And of all – *all* – within its borders. The excuse, and a tacit article of faith among serious Conservative politicians, being this: That the interests of the British nation state are best served by contriving the perpetuity of a Tory administration whatever *apparent* sacrifices of principle or policy this may entail.

My narrative is linear, in the sense that the story is told from the Carlton Club meeting in 1922 up to the catastrophic defeat of May 1997. But as successive Cabinets, and episodes, and personalities within their period are regarded, the focus will alter. Sometimes it is narrow; sometimes panoramic. I make no claim to have marked what more punctilious authorities would regard as 'significant milestones'. It is the detail, often the apparent triviality, of *politics* that I illuminate. And it is here, I believe, that the reader will detect a pattern of repetition in both events and individual conduct. The motivation of the Conservative Party at all times and in both the corporate and the individual context, is their appetite for power. When this is controlled, and directed, the party flourishes. But when it is frustrated the party reverts, all too predictably, to cannibalism.

As to my sources, I enjoyed in the last quarter of the century the advantage (although I must recognise it, in terms of objectivity, also to be a handicap) of being a direct participant. Not so senior, though, as to have had direct access to much documentation. There are notes of meetings and correspondence that I did not see and which will be restricted for another thirty years. And conversations whose substance (or even whose setting) the participants may forget or distort. I have long believed the proper place for bibliography to be at introduction and make mention of the most significant below.

As a chronicler I believe that the very first book to which in all humility but in the highest esteem I should refer is Lord Beaverbrook's *The Decline and Fall of Lloyd George*. Here is the scene set for the great Tory coup of 1922, with which this narrative starts. And at the outset is written that most durable of all political aphorisms, substantiated at so many points across my own text:

> Yet he could not ... [stand down]. The driver's seat was as he believed his rightful place. He clung to the wheel, guiding the vehicle of state until he was rudely flung forth – the fate of every politician who stays too long.

With Lloyd George out of the way (although, as will be seen in other cases also, former colleagues are often the last to recognise that a contemporary of whom once they stood in awe and deference is now in permanent eclipse) there would follow a period of Conservative domination. This is almost unbroken, and during its course, at an interval of twenty years, Beaverbrook himself twice edged towards the very centre of power (and on the second occasion, indeed, contemplated seizing it by *coup de main*). A strange and irresistible historian is Lord Beaverbrook. A man of immense power and wealth – yet already almost forgotten, and his empire in ruins. Flawed judgement, huge energy, a mellifluent and observant pen – all this is reflected in his writing, as in his political career.

Lord Blake's own history, so dry, so meticulous and yet written with that certain *hauteur* that hints at a disdainful wit, has to be at the core (even if buried deeply) of any treatise on the party. While both John Ramsden and Anthony Seldon have assembled great banks of data, presented in a fluent and congenial style, from which those of a more eclectic taste may pick and choose. The inseparable linkage between political aspiration and economic reality – and the manner in which all who sought to ignore this came to grief – is beautifully illustrated by Edmund Dell in his seminal work, *The Chancellors*.

Memoirs I treat with some reserve, particularly those of the 'I - discussed - the - situation - with - the - Permanent - Secretary; - together - we agreed - that - while - circumstances - might - give - grounds - for - concern - it - would - not - have - been - appropriate - to - take - action - immediately' kind. Although the very fact that they have in the majority of cases been so obviously composed to justify the career and attainments of the author can, to an observant reader, reveal much. Diaries are of a far higher value. As a diarist myself I am sensitive to traces of hindsight editing, and like to think that I can detect them. But diaries, on account of their immediacy, are the best of all indicators as to motive and mood – and not just those of the author. If I were to single out one only it would be Leo Amery's remarkable *The Empire at Bay*, over one thousand pages and not a single one of them dull.

Approved biographers do, of course, have access to their subject's private diaries. And, as Ben Pimlott has noted, will declare that while enjoying complete and uninhibited access to family papers have 'never at any time acceded to pressure . . .' etc. I'm not so sure. The ideal remains when the diary, in bulk, is deposited in a university library, and the curious student may travel there to confirm or embellish some entry in the published selection that may have caught his eye.

None the less it is true that political biographies, in which English literature is particularly blessed, have become richer as the century passes and the *mores* of restraint slacken. I have drawn help and inspiration – mentioning them in no particular order – from John Campbell's life of Birkenhead, as also from his compelling work on Edward Heath – a model combination of scholarship, sympathy and detachment. Sir Robert Rhodes James has written the best single book on Winston Churchill, his *Study in Failure*; although in saying this I would not seek in any way to understate my gratitude, shared by all students, to Sir Martin Gilbert for his extraordinary and meticulous compendium. Sir Robert has also produced an absorbing study of the life of Anthony Eden – and it is a tribute to both authors that it can, indeed should be, read simultaneously or in sequel to David Carlton's work on the same subject. Anthony Howard's biography of Rab Butler should also be read between the lines, and is certainly an exception to the general rule that only those who belong to the Conservative Party can properly understand the way in which it works. Some of the lightweight instant biographies – particularly those rushed through at the coronation of a new leader, Thatcher, Major, Blair – are worthless. But two of the most interesting recent works, John Charmley's *Chamberlain and the Lost Peace*, and Andrew Roberts' biography of Halifax, *The Holy Fox*, are under three hundred pages. And this is also true of certain books that illuminate particular aspects of the period yet stand as worthy histories in their own right – Paul Addison's *Churchill on the Home Front*, Richard Cockett's *Twilight of Truth* and Scott Newton's interesting monograph, *Profits of Peace: The Political Economy of Anglo-German Appeasement*.

Additionally I must acknowledge a debt to all those who have, either by correspondence or in conversation, shared their recollection of events in which they participated; I should add that I have not always rejected hearsay evidence if I feel it to be important. I would also wish to pay a particular tribute to Dr Graham

Stewart, formerly of St John's College Cambridge, whose own PhD treatise has been of great use, and who has worked with me throughout, both researching material and correcting texts as well as stimulating my interpretation of events with his own lively and eclectic opinion.

One curious phenomenon, to my mind, emerges. Practically every Tory leader, with the possible exception of Stanley Baldwin – and even he said that leading the Conservatives was like driving pigs to market – came, in their different ways privately, but quite strongly, to dislike the party which had put them at its head.

Neville Chamberlain, bemused and full of chagrin. Churchill, replete with memory of what the Conservative Party had done to his father, its long attempt to exclude him from power, and its deep personal mistrust even at the height of the war. Anthony Eden, mindful of his ostracism in the thirties; uncomfortable in the company of back-benchers, looking constantly over their heads to a more distant prospect. Harold Macmillan, whose absolute cynicism would have caused him to enjoy rather than resent Cuthbert Headlam's judgement that 'Macmillan is a megalo-maniac, and a bore with it ...' And Alec Douglas-Home (often referred to as 'Hume' in Central Office memos, even after becoming Prime Minister), the last of our Premiers to be endowed with a feeling for history, sensing the alteration in substance and content that his displacement would bring.

As for Edward Heath, it is more than arguable (though not specifically asserted in this text) that neither he nor his successor were by instinct Conservatives at all. They were, from their different angles of approach, *modernisers*. And the party, responding to their management, did in its own time consume and destroy each one of them.

Finally, at the very end of the century, came John Major. The party had in sequential order brought down an aristocrat, a pragmatist, and an ideologue. It must have seemed only natural for Major to be wary of this sullen Hydra; to have concluded that neither loyalty, nor even gratitude, were to be expected for one instant longer than its own endemic life-support system would allow. And only his inner self will recognise the real feelings that drove him, on the first morning of his election defeat on 2 May 1997, to resign instantly, absent himself from Westminster, and go to watch cricket.

BOOK ONE

Evolving
Appeasement

ONE

The Carlton Club
and the New Conservatives

The state of the nation – Disgruntled partners –
Personalities manoeuvre – The 'Second XI' – A
surprising victory – Bonar Law in the saddle.

IN THE MONTH of October 1922 the appearance of Great Britain was indeed majestic. Her enemies had been vanquished, all of them, and were out of sight. Her Empire was at its widest extent. Quite truthfully it girdled the globe. So that a coal-burning steamship could, with the single exception of the three-day stint across the South Atlantic from Ascension Island to Trinidad, be sure that at every nightfall on a voyage around the world it could berth safely under the lee shore of a British dependency where the Union Jack did fly.

The Royal Navy was enormous; so ordered and disposed that it was capable, simultaneously, of fighting major fleet engagements in the Mediterranean, the Pacific Ocean and the North Sea. Sixty-one battleships, one hundred and twenty cruisers, and four hundred and forty-three destroyers carried the white ensign – a tonnage strength never exceeded before or since by any other navy. It was only two years since the mighty *Hood*, the largest, fastest, and most heavily armed warship in the world had, brand new, gone through her acceptance trials in the Minches. Against which foe, at that time, was it envisaged that she should do battle? No matter. *Hood* symbolised the absolute dominance by the Royal Navy of the world's trade routes; and, by the mother country, of the commerce that flowed across them. Her vicissitudes, and ultimate fate, will mirror the course of events and fortune that affected Great Britain in the first half of the twentieth century.

The theme of maritime supremacy percolated into surprising and unconnected areas of the nation's life. Railway staff, postmen – even museum attendants – carried uniforms of a suggestively naval pattern. It was the preferred dress of the King, and his princes. Even the penny, a handsome coin of solid copper, more than twice the size of its equivalent in the specie of less fortunate lands, depicted the naval theme. Britannia looked out beyond a lighthouse and across the water, on which sailed a British ironclad. On the obverse side, the monarch's profile gazed without expression; and around the rim were engraved those acronyms, at the same time hubristic and reassuring – *Fid Def*, and *Ind Imp*.

And yet . . . appearances deceived.

A strange pallor, of countenance and enthusiasm, far from indicating serenity or discretion was the consequence of a most fearful and prolonged haemorrhage. One that had left the country, and the whole of society, chronically anaemic. The brutal attrition of the Flanders battlefield, continuing over four years, had been suffered particularly by the infantry regiments. And in those regiments by the subalterns; boys – for they were given no chance to grow up – in their teens who had gone straight from public school to the Ypres Salient, stopping only for a few weeks' training at Shorncliffe camp. Their life expectancy during a 'push' was ten days, four months if they survived the first battle. Twenty-nine thousand small country estates scattered across the realm would come on the market during the decade 1920–30; sold by their occupants now childless and, from age, barren and without heir. No one can calculate the loss – in terms of gifts aborted – poets and designers, farmers, industrialists and inventors of the future. But the effect on middle-class society, particularly in the rural areas and the market towns, was profoundly disturbing. With rupture of continuity came loss of faith. It has been said that 'The remainder felt themselves to be a small generation, and the many gaps broke the cohesion, the subtle cumulative power of the survivors . . .'[1] A whole generation, or what was left of it, were disgusted (in the majority of cases subconsciously) by politicians, whose cowardice and double-dealing they blamed for the loss of friends and brothers. An ageing second team remained on the field.

And so the Government, from some aspects, had a strange appearance. It was a coalition, but although the Prime Minister was a Liberal, David Lloyd George, he depended for his acceptance not on a disciplined band of followers in Parliament, responsive to a Whip, but on personal magnetism and his record of wartime leadership. These are not hard currencies in that bazaar where party-political advantage is traded.

Lloyd George was not the leader of the party with the largest number of seats in the House of Commons. That advantage was enjoyed by the Conservatives. Their leading lights, men of distinction and achievement, warily eyed each other across the dinner table, and sideways along the green leather of the front bench in the House of Commons. There was Austen Chamberlain top-heavy with *gravitas* – 'he always played the game, and always lost it'. Winston Churchill, nominally a Liberal but 'more conservative than a Conservative' and ceaselessly manoeuvring for personal advantage. F. E. Smith, now Lord Birkenhead but referred to always by his initials – '... tall, dark, slender and a little overdressed. His eyes and hair were lustrous; the first from nature, the second from too much oil ... a fox-hunting man who could swear elegantly in Greek ...'[2] And a walking illustration, it must be added, that there is such a phenomenon as an *over-endowment* of charisma. No one trusted FE, though many loved his company. While others in the party, denied that pleasure, were unforgiving. A back-bench colleague later observed that:

> ... these two political adventurers [Birkenhead and Churchill] are anathema – they sold the principles of Unionism to LlG and they possess no principles of their own. They are out to have the plums of office for themselves – nothing more and nothing else – but they have brains and brains are power – especially when their game is to beat your opponents by any means that are possible, however dirty and unprincipled.[3]

Last and, certainly in terms of his appearance and manner, least, was Bonar Law. Subdued and mouse-like he never made jokes, seldom laughed. He smoked a great deal and smelled of tobacco. But Law had a very retentive memory and an unerring sense of political timing. His intervention at a meeting, in a low Scottish accent, was listened to always with respect.

So the finesse required of Lloyd George was that these colleagues, and a good proportion of back-benchers, should believe that their seats and political prospects were dependent on the personal status and prestige, above party, of the Prime Minister. This, though, tends to be a wasting asset. Even two years before, soon after his victory in the 'coupon' election, Lloyd George had found it impossible to formalise – that is to say formally *perpetuate* – the Coalition by merging 'his' Liberals* with the Coalition Conservatives into a new 'Centre Party'. At that time, ominously, while the Conservative Chairman had agreed, it had been the Liberals in government who refused. Thus it was the Conservatives who were keeping Lloyd George in place – but from calculation rather than altruism. Who would be the first to call the other's bluff?

From then on, Lloyd George remained uneasy about the Tories; and particularly about 'BL'.† If they walked out on him Lloyd George was done for. He and Tom Jones‡ would talk over possibilities late into the night. On occasion they would fall somnolent in their chairs and then, abruptly coming to, lapse into their mother tongue. Yet of one thing the Prime Minister was confident. He knew how to manage men. Cajolery, inducement, the subtle exploitation of personal weakness – these techniques would, or should, ensure that Lloyd George kept his balance.

But the year had gone badly. A short inflationary boom had

---

* Those who had abandoned Asquith when the Lloyd George Coalition was formed in 1916.
† The initials (BL) by which Bonar Law was referred to in both notes and conversation.
‡ The Deputy Secretary to the Cabinet.

run for the previous twelvemonth on private war profits and servicemen's gratuities (a new Rolls-Royce would command £6,000* on the 'free' market) but had petered out as confidence faltered and the scale of the country's indebtedness both to its own people and to the United States Treasury began to seep through. Industrial discontent festered, and a rail strike was called. In Ireland a full-scale guerrilla war was raging. There were violent pitched battles and ambushes at company strength. From a contemporary record a typical two days (30 and 31 March) shows:

> An officer murdered leaving his hotel in Dublin, a bomb explosion in Amiens Street, a military lorry seized, a retired officer shot in County Cork, rioting in Belfast, a Royal Irish Constabulary patrol ambushed and one man killed, an armoured car attacked, an attempt to derail a train, a raid by rebels on a farmer's house in Monaghan, a telephone office burnt and one man killed in Killiney.[4]

The number of police killed in the first six months of the year was 223, and of soldiers 94. On 22 June the recently retired Chief of Imperial General Staff, Sir Henry Wilson, was shot on the doorstep of his own house in Eaton Square.

None of these things predicated a government properly in control of events, although they will have been at the back of Lloyd George's mind when he coined that durable epigram – 'a change of nuisance is as good as a holiday'. With the Liberals still crotchety and muddled, Lloyd George's best bet for survival remained the emergence of a 'Centre Party', a device to legitimise, in party-political terms, the continuance of the Coalition. This concept (known at the time to sophisticates as 'fusion' and destined in the future, and with a different title, to reappear on these pages) was never going to be easy, as experience in 1920 had shown. By now the Chairman of the Conservative Party, Sir George Younger, had changed his mind. Churchill, an essential part of it, had been

---

* Slightly more, it is interesting to note, than the 'adjusted' cost – either of that car or its modern equivalent – in 1998.

talked out of the idea by that great broker of power in the constituencies, Alderman Salvidge of Liverpool.

The Conservative Chief Whip, Freddie Guest, was more encouraging. On 16 January 1922 he wrote privately, and most indiscreetly, to Lloyd George:

> At the risk of appearing importunate, I want to place on record my opinion that – given the desire – this is the supreme opportunity for the formation of the Central [*sic*] Party and for the establishment of the great triumvirate [that is Lloyd George, FE and Winston] . . .
>
> Is not the Conservative position at the moment rather a counterpart to the one which you tackled so boldly in 1916? FE should do now what you did then.* I have spoken to him in this sense, but, if this is to be brought about – and I believe it to be in the National interest – it will require more pressure and more argument . . .[5]

By now the mood in the party had slipped. Bonar Law was their favourite. Of FE the Chairman wrote: 'He is as usual looking after "No. 1". I see his game quite clearly. He would like to keep the Coalition alive to go to the country again as we are. That would give him a better chance in the future than he has at present of securing the leadership.'[6]

The Prime Minister was well aware that the Conservative Party was divided. But, as many of his Tory successors would also find in the years to come, Lloyd George mistakenly attached a higher significance to the support of senior figures than of discontented (and more numerous) back-benchers. Lloyd George was also convinced that, just as in the 'coupon' election two years earlier, he could, if he got into serious difficulty, again play the patriotic card. He contrived an international 'crisis'. Its substance is now forgotten and obscure. But its ingredients included a supposed threat from the Turks against the Dardanelles shoreline, which had been demilitarised under the terms of the Versailles Treaty, and against the district of Chanak where a small British 'peace-keeping'

---

* i.e., split his own party.

force had been established. Lloyd George stoked the Chanak crisis for all it was worth. He believed that whatever personal reservations Tory MPs might feel, they would, at weekends, come under pressure from their constituency activists.

No such thing happened. Quite the reverse, in fact. The Chanak crisis offered an early illustration that the British people had lost their taste for military adventures in Europe. People had closed their minds to the war. The soldiers themselves were too shocked, or too imbued with the ethic of the stiff upper lip, to speak – except occasionally with their old comrades. It was a mood epitomised by a couplet in that saddest of all wartime ballads:

> And when they ask us . . . we'll never say;
> We just whiled away our time, drinking in a street café . . .

And here, indeed, were the first traces of a public mood which was to affect the interplay of foreign and domestic policies for the next two decades. All were aware, even if (in rare cases) only through their subconscious, that something really frightful had happened. The mind must not be allowed to dwell on this, of course; nor any word of doubt be allowed in print or picture. That would be 'letting the side down'. But just occasionally the pretence would falter a little. The decimation of whole villages and districts, the unnatural age-gap between the venerable and the very young, a void really, in pubs and clubs where formerly the 'pals' had sat or stood about laughing. And everywhere there were the *mutilés*, the 'Not Forgotten' Association with wounds that needed to be dressed daily. Gaunt and shocked and still, many of them, undergoing the pretence of treatment, they trailed around on 'outings' where they would spend their time sitting, in their strangely white shirts and hospital blue serge, glazed with morphine and fatigue, on special benches painted a lurid blue so as to forewarn ordinary members of the public out for a stroll, in parks and gardens, of the disturbing sight which the occupants might present. And in any case we had recently fought the Turks, and been defeated, had we not? Folk-horror tales of Gallipoli had run by word of mouth through Wiltshire, South London, Manchester, home ground of battalions shredded at Suvla Bay. Far from seeking revenge, the mood was – stay away.

Politically, this took a wider form than the simple expression of dissent over foreign policy. Many MPs in all parties, and not a few ministers of middle rank, were sick of the Coalition, which was stuck in its ways and whose senior ranks seemed united only in obstructing the advance of their juniors. Dangerously late, the Prime Minister came to realise this. And in his confusion he was not alone. The heavy dignitaries of the Tory Party were aware, of course, that their own back benches were discontented and restless. But the mechanism for counting heads and assessing opinion was imperfect. A strict count of malcontents on the back benches might have shown less than a third still committed to the Coalition. But few of the old guard seemed to realise how they were out-numbered – even if they could rely on the loyalty (itself doubtful) of their personal protégés. The calculations of the Chief Whip were not reliable, neither could they include the feelings of prominent office holders in the National Union. Yet they could console themselves, these very senior Tories. In addition to weight they had status; experience; access to, and pledged support from, most of the daily press. Chamberlain,* Birkenhead, Churchill.† These were 'big names'. Who had heard of anyone – excepting those sophisticates who knew the name of Bonar Law – among the Conservative back-benchers?

J. C. C. Davidson‡ raised a complaint – not for the first, nor certainly the last, time in the history of the party – about the quality of the 'new intake':

> The first thing that struck me on entering the House of Commons was the high percentage of hard-headed men, mostly on the make, who fill up the ranks of the Conservative Party. [They are] ... modern and unscrupulous ... The old-fashioned country gentle-

---

* Austen Chamberlain. His brother, Neville, will cross the stage later.

† Although still nominally a Liberal, Churchill at this time was a prominent member of the Coalition administration.

‡ J. C. C. Davidson was elected for Hemel Hempstead in 1921.

man and even the higher ranks of the learned professions, are scarcely represented at all.[7]

As for the unfortunate Law himself, he havered and dithered and faltered. For a lot of the time he was feeling 'mouldy'.* Soon he settled, though with no very great appearance of comfort, for being Lord Beaverbrook's glove puppet. Law was in and out of Beaverbrook's residences – Cherkley in Surrey, 'The Vineyard' in Fulham – on most days. He submitted, at Beaverbrook's insistence, to a comprehensive medical examination from Lord Horder.† And Lord Beaverbrook, as will be seen at many different points in this chronicle, had no residual loyalty or attachment to the Conservative Party whatever. His fondness was for mischief. For crisis and confusion whence he could derive personal profit and aggrandisement.

Such a situation was not far off. And its impending arrival had been for some time apparent to most Tories who fancied themselves as contenders for enduring office, if not for the premiership itself. Their conduct became erratic. From time to time it might have been termed 'disloyal' – were it not for the fact that loyalty is a barely recognisable quality where party politics is subordinated to the concept of coalition. Most of these figures overestimated Lloyd George's primacy at the same time as they coveted his job. Winston Churchill had been the first, characteristically, to consider breaking ranks. He began to look round for an excuse to detach himself and thought that to do so in protest at Lloyd George's intention to recognise the Bolshevik regime in Russia would earn him a substantial following on the Tory back benches. Birkenhead, however (still nurturing his own plans for the future), talked Churchill out of such foolish action:

> this ... [would make you] ... the hero of the *Morning Post* and the
> leader of some thirty Tories in the House of Commons who would

---

* Law was pre-cancerous. A malignant tumour of the oesophagus was to be diagnosed seven months later.
† See p. 23 below.

disagree with you on 90% of all the subjects about which you feel really deeply. Moreover you would cut yourself adrift, perhaps permanently, certainly for a very long time . . .[8]

Churchill thought it over, and backed off. At that time he conferred regularly with 'FE'. The pair commanded in the House of Commons a mixture of awe and resentment. But there was an undercurrent, not just confined to the Conservative back benches, that they (and several others) had 'got too big for their boots'. Viscount Rothermere,* with his uncanny sense of public mood, wrote to Bonar Law exhorting him to: 'Stick your toes in . . . George [sic]† and Chamberlain haven't one chance in a thousand of winning the election, while the Conservative party might, and I think would.'

In the first fortnight of October the Cabinet met almost every day. The atmosphere was fractious in the extreme. Discussion of the urgent need for a general election, and how it should be handled, occupied much time. Hastily scribbled notes were passed across the table.[9] The problem was urgent: how to get the Tories to fight as part of a coalition. The idea shared, if not articulated, between Lloyd George and the Tory luminaries was that a Carlton Club meeting would show up the dissidents. MPs would be addressed, *en masse*, by their leaders. They would then (as current parlance now has it) have to 'stand up and be counted'. The watchful eye of their superiors, and those who allocate junior ministerial responsibility, would concentrate the mind. Even so, nothing was left to chance. The meeting was fixed for the day on which the result of a key by-election, in Newport, would be announced. An 'anti Lloyd George Conservative' was standing, in open breach of the electoral pact between Tories and Liberals, and the results would show Labour getting in, with the Coalition vote split. In the Commons itself the Whips were untiring. 'Between Sunday 15 and Thursday 19 [October] . . . every man's political

---

* Harold Harmsworth, Viscount Rothermere, 1868–1940, controlled Associated Newspapers (*Daily Mail, Evening News, Sunday Dispatch*). Air Minister 1917–18.
† Many of his derogaters would refer to David Lloyd George thus.

soul was required of him. Promises and promotions and honours were sprinkled from Downing Street on the green benches with a hose.'[10]

It was to no avail. The unexpected victory of the maverick Conservative at Newport removed at one stroke the single fear with which the Tory back benches might have been disciplined – that their seats were in jeopardy. They could afford to cheer Bonar Law when he said that he 'attached more importance to keeping our great Party united than in winning a general election' – enjoying the pretence of piety while eagerly looking forward to the contest. And more of them (than, from the point of view of Curzon's own prospects, was healthy) saw through his tactic in staying away from the meeting – 'I could not vote against my colleagues'. The final tally was 185 for the 'new' Conservatives, only 88, including ten ministers, for the old guard.

Bonar Law returned from the Palace with all the authority that attaches to a Premier just appointed; even one so hesitant and pessimistic ('I know well that our troubles are only beginning,' he wrote to Sir Robert Borden★). The Tories had now returned to power. Personalities barely mattered. The party had shown that, in the present climate, it was strong enough to discard the prominent and 'carry' the feeble.

It is never safe, of course, for a leader (particularly a new leader) to have a lot of distinguished and self-regarding former ministers on the loose all at the same time. But in the immediate aftermath of the Carlton vote their power base in the party rested on little more than meeting, and grumbling, one with another. And Law's Cabinet-making seems, with one exception, to have been unassertive to the point of hesitance:

> I drew up for Bonar, rather like an application form, all the vacant offices on the left hand, and on the right hand side the various candidates in order of preference. We then started off interviewing

★ Canadian Prime Minister 1911–20.

people.. It was really very awkward because Bonar always had in
his hand the paper with the names written in ... I particularly
remember ... [the case of] ... Derby. After I had shown him in I
went back to my room. The bell rang; I went into Bonar's room
and Bonar said, 'David, where did you send Derby ...?'[11]

In fact, as is invariably the case, most nominees were content,
and glad to be included at all. Except, that is, for Viscount
Rothermere. He had moved in on the Prime Minister promptly.
And insisted on an earldom as the price of his newspaper's support.
More than that, he wanted his back-bencher son Esmond to be
advanced to a seat in the Cabinet. Law made no comment on the
topic of the earldom, but offered to make Harmsworth (as he was)
a Parliamentary Secretary at the Department of Education. A
row followed. Curses were audible in the first-floor corridor at
Number 10. But Rothermere still supported (as Law knew he
would) the 'new' Conservatives at the election. The 'old' ones
were carefully left in limbo, and Law instructed that they should
be unopposed from within their own ranks. Plainly this made it
easier for face to be saved, and denials issued, later on when the
wounds started to heal.

One key figure, though, 'came over' and lent his special *tone* to
Law's Cabinet. Greatly to the disgust of his senior colleagues, the
Marquess Curzon decided to stay on in the post of Foreign
Secretary. 'There he was, an impeccable Conservative, a great
aristocrat, a hallmarked Tory leader, born in the purple, believed
to be in possession of a big American bank account ...' as
Beaverbrook witheringly declared. 'Just the sort of material with
which the Conservative shop window has always been dressed.'[12]

Law wasted no time before dissolving Parliament, and presenting his new – and exclusively Tory – team for endorsement.
Not a few of their number (even some who had voted in his
support at the Carlton Club) tried to hedge bets during the
campaign; and to save their seats by private deals with the Liberals
'so as not to split the anti-Labour vote'. Freddie Guest, the Coalition Chief Whip, who sat as a Conservative (but whose record in

prediction had already been shown as highly defective) went so far as to hang portraits of Lloyd George *and* Bonar Law side by side in his Committee Room. This particularly irritated Beaverbrook and provoked his sense of mischief. Beaverbrook accordingly found, and 'ran', a maverick Tory candidate against Guest, who defeated his own former Chief Whip by a majority of more than 5,000. Whatever may have been the feelings in Guest's rocksafe Lloyd George seat of East Dorset, the general mood of the country was caught by Law's manifesto slogan: 'Tranquillity'. As so often, the electorate wanted nothing radical – simply a change of personalities. Neither this attitude, nor any lack of confidence in the outcome, had been apparent in the ranks of the grandees. They were replete, still, with mutual recognition of their wartime achievements and dignity. Least of all were there any traces of doubt on election night at Number 100 Park Lane, where Sir Philip Sassoon had convened a special party to eat delicious food and enjoy an orchestra while the results came in. The fashionable portraitist Sir William Orpen who, a few years back, had painted Sassoon as Haig's ADC, safely behind the lines at the White Chateau, observed the scene and wrote a little ditty (although some critics might have preferred him to use a brush):

> . . . we were almost all quite tight
> 'Mid beauty' and the flowing wine
> With clouds of nicotine divine
> We sat
> And watched
> And waited
> Till lo! The small machine began
> To 'Tic Tic'. Then the little band
> Ran smoothly out in Philip's hand
> Curling, curling like a snake
> Till Philip's hand began to shake
> Impossible!
> 'Twas like the writing on the wall
> That told of old King Nib's sad fall

> When in the dawn we learnt it all
> Old England's choice, we clearly saw
> Was Max!
> I beg pardon! Mister B. Law.[13]

The muddle into which the Liberal Party had descended caused their share of seats to split almost exactly between Asquith (60) and Lloyd George (57). Labour effectively became the Opposition, but with only 138. While Tories, 'old' and 'new', scored an imposing 344.

This was a far better result than could have been predicted. Truly a 'new' Conservative Party appeared to be installed. There now existed, probably to a greater degree than at any time later in the century – although there was to be an attempt at recovering this after the defeat of 1997 – an identity of personnel and outlook, a congeniality, between the Members of Parliament, squires or 'small' businessmen with bucolic pretensions, and the party activists in their various positions of authority. All should have been set fair. A great country, its strength depleted by prolonged exertion in a noble cause, now in need of a tranquil period in which its spirit and self-confidence would recover, had acquired exactly the kind of administration – headed by an unadventurous nonentity – most likely to bring this about.

Writing afterwards, though, and with his view coloured from disappointment at the premature failure of his protégé, Beaverbrook warned:

> But disaster pursues us. Disaster pursues us with a step as steady as time and an appetite as keen as death.[14]

TWO

Bonar Law
Comes to Grief

Set fair for the Government – Trouble with the
Treasurer – Bonar Law disappoints – is sent on holiday –
and dies – Davidson's role – The conspiracy to thwart
Curzon.

LADY (RUTH) LEE WAS A very rich American of great beauty
and charm. Her husband, Arthur, had entered Parliament as Conservative Member for the Fareham constituency at the turn of the
century and had survived the Liberal landslide of 1906. Lady Lee
had bought for Arthur a house in Abbey Garden – being as close
a residential location to the Palace of Westminster as it is possible
to find – and a beautiful country estate near Princes Risborough
called Chequers. Lee himself can be regarded as personifying in
the most acute form the travails of the Coalitionists. He had
performed with distinction in both wartime administrations.
Then, attaching himself to Lloyd George, and convinced that
his patron was to all intents guaranteed the premiership for the
foreseeable future, Lee decided on a grandiose gesture. One that
should, at a single bound, allow him to overtake in favour those
other senior Tories who clustered around the Prime Minister. The
culture of the country-house weekend dominated, at the upper
reaches of government, both the transaction of business and the
evolution of policy. But here was a Prime Minister who did not
possess a country estate; and in all likelihood he would be followed
by others in the future who were similarly handicapped.

Suffering a sudden brainstorm (which caused his less volatile
wife considerable, and lasting, anxiety) Arthur decided to make

over Chequers as a permanent country residence for the Prime
Minister. Barely, though, was the ink dry on the conveyance than
'LlG' was out – for ever. While Lee, overattentive to the great
Liberal, was thought to be 'a bad Party man'. And although there
was talk of Lee becoming Viceroy he, like his hero, never was to
hold ministerial responsibility again.

In the early twenties the Lees entertained generously. And
shortly after the election result a group of disconsolate senior
members of the Coalition, including F. E. Smith and Austen
Chamberlain, were present at dinner. Lady Lee has recorded the
mood of general agreement that the retired members of the late
Government should simply 'go away and play.... No one wants
to hear anything from the late Government – not even the most
God-given wisdom – and their best course is to fade out of the
public recollection as completely as they can.'[1] Thus, for the new
Cabinet, the early prospects were favourable. But almost at once
the upper echelons of the Conservative Party found themselves
distracted by a tiresome episode which had overtones, in the
parlance of the late 1990s, of 'sleaze'.

In January of 1923, to the considerable dismay of the Chairman
of the National Union, and other managers, the Party Treasurer
refused to sign a cheque for £20,000, drawn on the Central Office
account, for the payment of salaries and other expenses incurred
during the election. His excuse was that some of the monies had
been collected for the Coalition, and did not belong to the
Conservative Party. This was a thin argument, and it did become
immediately apparent that all was not well. The individual concerned, Lord Farquhar, was known as an intimate friend of the
Prince of Wales. On becoming His Majesty, King Edward VII on
accession made Farquhar Master of the Household. From 1915 to
1922 he was Lord Steward. Farquhar had been originally a Unionist
MP, and had been promoted first to a baronetcy, then through
successive stages in the peerage, until in autumn 1922 he received
an earldom – an unusually high level of preferment – from Lloyd
George in the Resignation Honours List.

Lord Farquhar was generally thought to be 'a man of considerable wealth and much financial acumen'[2] – itself a reputation which can often merit scrutiny. Now it would appear – *might* appear – that he had been using party funds not simply for his own advantage and enrichment but to purchase ennoblement directly from the leadership of the Liberal Party. After some tentative inquiry, necessarily cautious, Younger (the Chairman) wrote to the Prime Minister:

> I am not in a position to state definitely that he did collect money for the Election expenses and handed that money to the Lloyd George Executive, but I have every reason to believe that he did so, and hope to be able to prove this one of these days.[3]

It was a situation that needed to be discussed 'bilaterally'. The Prime Minister with great reluctance conducted, a week later, an interview with Farquhar. The Party Treasurer blustered. His memory failed him. At times he was 'incoherent'. What was to be done? Bonar Law wrote a conciliatory memorandum about 'poor old Farquhar':

> I have seen him twice and there is now no question of his hesitating to sign cheques for the actual Party funds, but *I have still a strong suspicion that he has handed sums – perhaps large sums – to L.G. for his party, while acting as our Treasurer.** He is so 'gaga' that one does not know what to make of him, but among the many statements he made to me was one which he repeated several times – that he had given no money to L.G.'s funds that was not earmarked for that purpose. Hicks, the accountant, has been seeing him and he has now become sane enough to realize that this was not a wise thing to say; so that he has now said to Hicks that he has given no money to L.G. except £80,000 from Astor. He spoke to me also about this and said that at the same time he handed over £80,000 to you. This he did, so he tells me, on the ground that Astor had left him a perfectly free hand to deal with it as he liked. I said that in that case, provided you as representing our Party knew what had been done, I had not a word to say against it . . .[4]

* AC's italics.

As so often when inquiring into a situation of potential embarrassment, the interrogation was not pushed to the limit. In fact Farquhar was already in some personal difficulty. He died in the autumn, bequeathing large sums both to members of the Royal Family and to senior courtiers. But his estate proved to be insolvent. Tiresome and distracting though this mini-drama may have appeared at the time, the situation had been dealt with according to the customary techniques of the established order. Two other crises, both occurring in the New Year and both with an international dimension, were less amenable.

The Conservatives very soon had to face a broader problem concerning Bonar Law. He lacked vigour. During the election campaign Law had set out his view of the burdens of Prime Ministerial office:

> My idea is that of a man at the head of a big business who allows
> the work to be done by others . . . and gives it general supervision.
> That is my idea of the work of the Prime Minister.[5]

Gone now, it seemed, was even the dour stubbornness which had characterised Law's ascent in the party, and his dogged resistance to Lloyd George during the years of Coalition. He had difficulty in making up his mind on even the smallest issue. In April he developed a 'summer cold' and a bad sore throat which, his physician told Law, was in all probability accounted for by his 'lowered resistance' – itself due to overwork and living on sandwiches. At first it was thought that the Prime Minister's health would recover if he took a 'proper' (his physician's phrase) holiday over the Easter recess. His family booked him into a Torquay hotel. Sir Frederick Sykes, who had married Law's daughter Isabel, and Law's two sons Richard and Tony, made up the party. Law played a certain amount of golf, occasionally went onto the tennis court.

In an attempt to raise the morale of the Prime Minister, Beaverbrook had been running eulogistic essays, and headlines, in his newspapers. Now he got to work on Lord Rothermere. Between them they should be able to 'carry' Law for a year or so. Rothermere had been sulking since his clumsy request for an earldom had been turned down.* Now, with singularly maladroit timing, Rothermere allowed himself to be persuaded that Law would hold on to his position for many years. A note to Beaverbrook on 26 April indicates that the concept of an earldom had not, in Rothermere's mind at least, receded very far:

> If Bonar places himself in my hands I will hand him down to posterity at the end of three years as one of the most successful Prime Ministers in history, and if there is a general election I will get him returned again. This may sound boastful but I know exactly how it can be done.[6]

Beaverbrook acknowledged and set about, for the time being at least, his own promotional schemes.

Law's recovery, though, will not have been helped by a letter from Curzon. On the last day of the previous session the Prime Minister's voice had been so weak that he had delegated Stanley Baldwin to answer questions in the Commons while he had sat at the Chancellor's side and whispered suggested replies. Rumours of Law's ill-health were circulating.

> My dear Bonar [Curzon wrote]
> I write against the possibility – which I *devoutly* hope not to be the case – that the succession to the Premiership may soon arise ... there should be no need to remind you of my own claim to this. My record and reputation ... my own years of experience of high office ... What I must make clear at the outset ... is that I could not surrender [*sic*] these claims or consent to serve under any of my present colleagues ...

Tersely, Law replied. He had not been well recently, it was true. But he was now fully recovered, and had no intention of resigning.

But once back in the Commons although, the *Daily Express* claimed, he was 'looking tanned and fit', Law found that he could not sustain his voice for more than a minute or so. Baldwin had

---

* See p. 14 above.

to answer, the two men now regularly appearing on the bench
side by side. Beaverbrook suggested a Mediterranean cruise in the
month of May. A stateroom suite was booked on the *Princess
Juliana*, a Dutch liner of modest luxury.

A week before leaving, and most aggravatingly, there was more
trouble from Curzon. And on this occasion Law's own behaviour
would hardly have got past the 1997 Committee on Parliamentary
Standards. On 25 April the Prime Minister had written to his
Foreign Secretary:

> Lord Winchester called to say that he had been invited to form a
> syndicate to develop Turkey in various ways including a loan, and
> wished to know if there was any objection on the part of the
> Government to his doing this before peace was declared. I see
> none, but would be glad to have your confirmation before writing
> him definitely.

The Foreign Secretary's retort had been crisp:

> If I may say so I think the right thing would be for your private
> secretary to say that Lord Winchester should address himself to the
> F.O. and not to No. 10. As a matter of fact, I know all about Lord
> Winchester who was Lord Lieut. of my present county, Hants, and
> whom I have known for 30 years. He ran away from his wife – a
> most charming lady – with another woman: he had to resign the
> Lord Lieutenancy: he became involved in some very shady financial
> transactions: he had to sell his place, and is wholly discredited.
>
> That anyone should offer a loan to Turkey before peace is
> concluded would be very doubtful policy. But that that person
> should be Lord Winchester renders it quite out of the question. I
> am sure you did not know all this.
>
> When these persons go to No. 10 instead of here they are really
> reproducing one of the least admirable features of the L.G. regime.[7]

Law was greatly offended by this rebuke. Although he did
still make Curzon his deputy before leaving, six days later, for
Southampton where he was to board the *Juliana*. And he wrote to
the King that Curzon would be presiding over meetings of the

Cabinet, while Baldwin led in the Commons. But Law was not alone among Conservatives in 1923 (and at other times) in finding such 'prissiness' discordant. Curzon, too arrogant to subordinate his vice-regal principles to the overall party consensus of what was, or was not, 'helpful', had irritated the Prime Minister. Curzon had caused uneasiness to many around him; and (as he was shortly to find) still further imperilled his own claim to the succession.

Eight days out of Southampton the *Juliana* put in at Genoa. Her next port of call was to be Algiers, and Law, in considerable pain – now from the side of his face – and taking 100 grains per day of analgesic, decided to leave the ship. He and his son Dick travelled, an uncomfortable rail journey, to Aix-les-Bains. On arrival the two ran into the Rudyard Kiplings, old friends. Kipling, who had not set eyes on Law for almost a year, was horrified by his appearance. He telephoned to Beaverbrook, telling him that his old friend 'looked like death' and should be attended immediately. Post-haste Beaverbrook travelled south in the Blue Train. As soon as he set eyes on Law Beaverbrook, too, realised that the Prime Minister had deteriorated – but attributed this to the 'depressant' tablets. None the less, Beaverbrook took the precaution of sending for Sir Thomas Horder, paying the doctor's fare to come directly to the Crillon Hotel in Paris, whither this little itinerant coterie, attached to the Prime Minister of the most powerful country in the world, next set its steps.

Horder only ten days before had charged Law for a consultation. At the conclusion of this he had recommended 'a warmer climate, sea air and a month's rest from duties'. Now Horder re-examined his patient in the hotel bedroom on 17 May and immediately afterwards took Beaverbrook aside. This time Horder said that the Prime Minister was afflicted by an inoperable throat cancer and would be dead within three months.

The impending departure of a leader always makes for instability in the upper reaches of the party. All at once the question of the succession had become urgent. The 'Magic Circle' was in disarray. Was it to be one of the senior dignitaries, still in exile after the break-up of the Coalition? Could Baldwin, in spite of his mishandling of US Treasury negotiations, at least 'caretake' until things had settled down? Or must it, as all the indicators seemed to predict but as many racked their brains to try and prevent, be Curzon?

Beaverbrook, greatly to his chagrin, was to go 'out'. He would be excluded from the inner loop of high politics – though often, as will be seen, trying to hijack one or another vehicle within it – for seventeen years. Only a week before the débâcle in the Crillon, and sensing probably that things were going to move outside his grasp, Beaverbrook had written an *aide-mémoire* for Borden (and the reader will note his pre-emptive disclaimer in the last paragraph). The document remains as good a survey as can be found of the state of play in the Conservative Party in its first summer after recovering that political dominance which it was to enjoy – with but one short interruption – for the next seventy-five years.

Here we have (1) Curzon with his claim supported by the senior members of the Government who are not competing with him, but handicapped by his personal unpopularity (2) Baldwin with the younger members of the Government who are influential, and closer in touch with the machine and the constituencies, and then (3) the possibility of a dark horse winning if Curzon and Baldwin cannot come to terms. The dark horse is Lord Derby – who would bring Austen Chamberlain back to the Government as his contribution.

If Curzon is to succeed, he must come to an accommodation with Baldwin. If Baldwin is to oust Curzon, he must work the Press in his own interest – an art for which apparently he has no inclination or talent . . . Baldwin is in fact in the position of a man who has a stronger hand than he realises. For Curzon could not be premier if he resigned; while Baldwin could be if Curzon went. Only however in the event of a complete disagreement between these two principals and some sign of fear of a party rupture, would Derby's candidature become a serious possibility.

This is the situation as I see it today, and it obviously calls for an honest broker. You may be inclined to ask why I do not undertake the role. My answer is that if you back a man for the Premiership, you are more or less [*sic*] obliged to support him afterwards and I should prefer the chance of regaining a complete independence for my own policies.[8]

The thwarting of Curzon, and the assemblage of a tacit coalition of rivals, back-benchers, senior civil servants, 'modernisers' and courtiers to achieve this, shows the Conservative Party at its most implacable. Just as his treatment afterwards, and early death, illustrate its callousness.

On Friday 18 May Davidson, Law's PPS and inscrutable party fixer, waited in Paris just long enough to draft the text of that kind of press release which can only be issued after the markets have closed: 'In spite of his rest the Prime Minister's voice is still unsatisfactory. We are unable to promise improvement within a reasonable time . . .' And, in case the import was still unclear, '*The state of the Prime Minister's health is not good*'. His instructions, or so Davidson alleges, were to 'prepare the way at the Palace and with some of his senior colleagues'.[9] But for what? Law himself was weakening by the hour. Unlike Harold Macmillan forty years later, who recovered his vitality and urge to meddle within hours of coming round from the anaesthetic, Law did not want to be bothered about anything. Least of all by queues of suppliant notables lining up outside his bedroom door. In sickly disregard of both precedent and protocol Law asked Davidson to tell the King that 'the [Prime Minister] would prefer not to be consulted'.[10]

This could hardly have suited Davidson, who had his own plans, better. As soon as he was back in London Davidson sent Baldwin a telegram telling him to come to London immediately. Next he telephoned Stamfordham, the King's private secretary, told him of the impending resignation, and revealed that Bonar Law was not prepared to make any recommendation about his successor.

The conversation seems to have been somewhat one-sided. Stamfordham was nobody's fool, and could see at once that

Curzon's position had weakened – perhaps fatally. 'Who should the King consult, then?' Balfour* and Salisbury†, retorted Davidson, naming the two grandees personally coolest – whether from jealousy or other resentment – towards Curzon. Davidson then added, most improperly, that the day when a peer could be Prime Minister had passed. Resistance to Lord Curzon would not only come from the Labour Opposition, but from a very large percentage of the Conservative Party also.[11] This argument, although it may look respectable, even 'progressive' at a distance of half a century, was spurious. There were only 138 Labour MPs, and the identity and station of the Tory Prime Minister was hardly at the top of their concerns. As for the Conservatives, with an overall majority of 89 the back-benchers' principal aim would be to ingratiate themselves with, rather than 'resist', whoever was leading their party. In fact Davidson's objective was clear. He had for long been close to Stanley Baldwin; more intimate, indeed, than he was with Law himself. With Curzon, though, Davidson had nothing in common; nor any prospect of promotion, nor even of keeping a job in government at all.

On the Saturday Davidson was already halfway into a memorandum setting out *the views of the normal* [sic] *back-bencher on the Government side* (which he afterwards claimed that Stamfordham had asked him to submit). Baldwin had arrived in London and that evening the two men met for dinner in the Argentine Club. Baldwin feigned – or at least expressed – reluctance. The conversation went on for two hours. Davidson concluded with the conventional plea that if Baldwin were sent for by the King he must accept 'as a duty to his country and his party'.

Davidson's skill and experience in drafting is well displayed in

---

* Arthur James Balfour, KG, 1922; Earl; Conservative Prime Minister 1902–5. Foreign Secretary 1916–19. Lord President of the Council 1919–22 and 1925–9.
† Fourth Marquess of Salisbury, eldest son of the Third Marquess (Conservative Prime Minister 1885–92, 1895–1902). Tory 'diehard' and opponent of continuing with the Lloyd George Coalition. Lord President of the Council 1922–4, Party leader in the House of Lords 1925–31. President, National Union of Conservative and Unionist Associations 1942–5.

his memorandum. Only those with long experience of Whitehall will have recognised, from its opening line – '*The case for each is very strong . . .*' that the first name to be mentioned will be the individual *against* whom the recommendation is to be made. So the opinion that 'Lord Curzon has, during a long life' (too old) 'held high office almost continuously' (is exhausted) and 'his grasp of the international situation is great' (is completely ignorant of domestic considerations) was but an introduction to a highly developed argument in favour of Baldwin. Nor was Curzon's case helped by Salisbury's somewhat equivocal verdict that he would recommend the Foreign Secretary 'whose faults were improving'. Balfour, predictably, expressed reluctance to 'discuss the merits' of the candidates, but in a long meeting with the King emphasised the difficulties of having a Prime Minister in the Lords.

The fatal wound, though, was inflicted in Davidson's memorandum with that one assertion which invariably and in any context causes the Conservative Party to lose its nerve:

> Lord Curzon is regarded in the public eye as representing that section of privileged Conservatism which has its value but in this democratic age . . .

Throughout the weekend, while these various machinations proceeded, the hapless Curzon remained at Montacute. He did nothing, spoke to no one. In the entire house there was not one single telephone (which, grandly, Curzon had declared to be 'a disastrous invention'). It was, after all, only ten days since the Chairman of the Party had told Curzon that his succession was inevitable because Baldwin lacked both experience and authority. In the warm May sunshine of the Whit weekend the Foreign Secretary was in shirt-sleeves. He was at ease. He cut one of the lawns, and strolled among the voluptuous curves of the great yew hedges.

On the evening of Whit Monday the village policeman cycled up the drive, bearing a telegram. Stamfordham wanted a meeting. While the policeman waited, Curzon wrote out his reply. He

invited attendance at Carlton House Terrace on the following
afternoon.

In the train, the press was reassuring. His wife Grace, the
Marchioness, although recorded as having considered the premiership to be 'a detestable office', was with him. They chattered
comfortably about plans. He would, Curzon thought, continue
to live at Carlton House Terrace rather than move to Number 10.
And would combine the responsibilities of Foreign Secretary with
those of Prime Minister. He turned his mind, also, to the question
of ecclesiastical appointments.

When the couple drew up at their own front door Curzon's
valet told his master that Lord Stamfordham had warned that he
would be delayed, and not arrive until half past two. Curzon 'smelt
danger'. But Grace reassured her husband: 'if the King was going
to pass him over he would not send his private secretary to
apologise'.[12] An hour later the interview started. From the outset,
Stamfordham was not comfortable. He made matters almost
unbearable by telling Curzon that 'the monarch recognised the
superiority of his claims to those of any other candidate'.

Why . . .? How . . .? Surely, though . . .? Curzon said that it was,
and would be seen as, a slur on his long career; that it would force
his retirement from public life; that many had told him that only
he could reunite the party; that it would not be understood 'in
the chancelleries of the world'. Stamfordham listened. He had
managed, whether from tact or moral cowardice, to avoid saying
that the decision was irrevocable. Curzon begged him to put these
considerations to the King. Miserably Stamfordham took his leave.
He could not bring himself to tell Curzon that Baldwin had
already kissed hands at noon.

Very large numbers of ministers, and political appointees, make
these pleas when they are told of their rejection or displacement.
Yet there is not one single example in history of it having made
the slightest difference to the superior decision, or of moderating
in any way the disappointment to which those protesting have
been subjected.

THREE

Stanley Baldwin
Finds His Feet

Baldwin to 'heal' Tory divisions – His political strategy –
and miscalculation – A Cabinet divided – A precipitate
dissolution – and unexpected defeat.

CURZON'S DESPAIR AT BEING OVERTAKEN by Baldwin must
exceed – excepting possibly the pain and incomprehension
suffered by Margaret Thatcher when she was deposed in 1990 –
the misery ever felt by any Conservative politician. Winston
Churchill, in 1945, had suffered a shock of equal dimension but
remained, or so at least he was led to believe, personally popular
in the country – 'Good Old Winnie'. But in the year 1923 the
Foreign Secretary and former Viceroy of India had no broad
constituency from which he could draw comfort. He will have
recognised the private dislike of colleagues having combined to
reinforce a trend in the party – social? modernist? pragmatic? – all
too apparent from the Carlton Club vote the previous year. By
abandoning his old colleagues, the Coalitionist grandees, when
the first Conservative Government had been formed by Bonar
Law in October, Curzon had hoped to pre-empt this trend. But
it was no use. Balfour's own treachery illustrated to perfection the
manner in which the excuse of party cohesion and advantage can
so often give cover to the indulgence of personal prejudice. 'No.
It will not be "dear George".'[1]

For some weeks Baldwin fumbled about trying to heal the
wounds, such as they were, and to give additional 'bottom' to the
Cabinet. Austen Chamberlain had been on holiday at Baden-
Baden and returned over-hastily. The new Prime Minister had

been minded to offer Chamberlain, who was, after all, one of his predecessors as Leader of the Party, the post of Lord Privy Seal. But Baldwin was deterred from doing so by the threatened resignation of Leo Amery and others.[2] Baldwin then offended Chamberlain by offering him the Embassy, first at Paris, then Washington. Chamberlain refused, and wrote a letter to *The Times* saying that although he was anxious to assist the reunion of the Conservative Party he 'had not, so far, been invited'. Next, Baldwin was rebuffed by Sir Robert Horne to whom he suggested the Treasury. Horne would not abandon Chamberlain. And, in any case, Horne 'felt that' F. E. Smith should also be invited back, which Baldwin quite understandably thought was none of Horne's business. Besides, to do this would, as the Prime Minister knew, induce a number of resignations from colleagues who were already installed. Only Sir Laming Worthington-Evans crawled back – to the lowly rank (he had been Secretary of State for War from 1921 to 1922) of Postmaster-General. Worthington-Evans, though, had seen the point. 'It's now or never,' he wrote, defiantly apologetic, to Austen Chamberlain, 'there will be no cry for help later on.'[3]

There was in fact little need for Baldwin to try and placate these grandees. His government, and he himself, were riding the wave. And only 'events' could displace them. But on a level higher than the immediate preoccupations of party management or day-to-day political controversy there were great issues that required immediate attention. The questions of Tariff Reform (protection); and the gold standard.

The nation and Empire, though terribly depleted by its experience in war, was still so huge an agglomeration of asset value and military strength that, as in physics, mass endowed inertia, and inertia served to preserve momentum. But that momentum, albeit very slowly, was running down. Britain was no longer the world's leading manufacturing nation. Nor (although the linkage between the two was not widely perceived) could her Bank, and her currency, any longer dominate the world's trade and rates of exchange. Here, at its very earliest stage, was a malign condition which if not addressed would within a decade or so make the task of reasserting and maintaining the *Pax Britannica* impossibly difficult.

And certainly, as Lord Curzon slides gently into oblivion, the question must be put: Would he, drawing on instinct, training and experience, have been better suited to address these issues than Baldwin? The answer has to be 'yes'. If only because Curzon's limitlessly high opinion of himself as a world statesman required for its fulfilment that British power be sustained at nineteenth-century levels. But the corollary – that achieving this within the context of maintaining party unity and keeping political opponents off-balance was quite outside Curzon's natural disposition – affords an excellent example of the Conservative Party's *instinctive* (because there cannot be many who will have thought it through) preference for their own cohesion over the political uncertainties attendant on a wider grasp of the national interest.

For the decision to break the Coalition, and Bonar Law's subsequent sweeping endorsement at the polls, had marked the onset of a new strategy which Baldwin, with his particular loathing of Lloyd George, was to take over and make his own. And for the next ten years Conservative high politics would seek to accelerate the free-fall of the Liberal Party between the commanding heights of Tory and Labour domination. Four more decades were to pass before this strategy had advanced so far as, in certain seats, to threaten Conservative tenure. Another ten years before the whole policy was stood on its head and approved Central Office tactics became the encouragement of Liberal survival in seats where the Labour Party had attained an ascendancy.

Baldwin's objective of discrediting the Liberal Party had both a personal and a strategic dimension. Deliberately he emphasised the contrast. Lloyd George was 'dynamic' (not yet, in the early 1920s, a compliment), devious, and corrupt. Baldwin went out of his way to articulate the merits of decency, fair play, and transparency. It was to be expected that, by inference, the listener would associate these virtues with he who was expounding them. Baldwin had been educated at Harrow and Cambridge. Plainly

he was of the governing class; and this stood in the way of too
overt a pretence of ordinariness. But Baldwin would talk much
in cricketing metaphors, about the straightforwardness of the
Englishman, a nationality to which (conveniently) neither Lloyd
George nor the Leader of the Labour Party belonged.*

The sporting metaphor worked for Baldwin because it conjured
up the supposedly English notion of 'fair play'. When in 1929 he
would broadcast his electoral message appealing for support, he
prefaced his remarks about the unsoundness of Lloyd George's
public-works schemes by reminding listeners poised to vote:

> Now in choosing a team for cricket or football to represent the
> country in international matches you pay great attention to the
> records of the players and no less attention is necessary in choosing
> a government in noting and comparing the records of the men
> who ask for your support. I want, for four or five minutes, to
> examine the record of the Conservative Government which will
> be appealing to you to renew your confidence in them and to
> show how they have fulfilled the pledges which they undertook
> in 1924.[4]

Conceding that he knew of no miracle cure for unemployment,
Baldwin continued: 'I am not going to make reckless promises to
you which I know full well cannot be carried out and when you
hear such promises being made by the other parties I want you
to examine them carefully to see if they are really sound and
businesslike.'[5] (There was no need for Baldwin to remind his
audience that Lloyd George had never delivered his promise of
'homes for heroes' when he had been in office.) Baldwin's chosen
method of insult in concentrating on deviousness and disreputable
character was aimed more at Lloyd George than at Ramsay Mac-
Donald. He took the view that the Labour Party, regionally
concentrated and resting on the allegiance of a working-class vote

---

* In fact Baldwin was only half English, his mother, Louisa Macdonald, being
of Welsh and Highland Scottish stock, but this ancestry was not from where he
developed his cultural sustenance.

that, in Baldwin's estimation, was 'biddable', formed no threat to Tory hegemony. His decision to eschew any prospect of anti-socialist alliance with the Liberals in order to prevent the Labour Party from forming a government in 1924 and 1929, without a parliamentary majority, was certainly instinctive as much as strategic.

Bonar Law's snap election triumph the year before had been achieved despite the all too apparent division within his own party. For the old Coalitionists the passing of the succession to Baldwin had only confirmed their belief that they were beaten by the 'Second XI' (a cricketing metaphor which in different circumstances would have been the sort of analogy to have tripped off Baldwin's own tongue). The new leader had none of the commanding mind or intellectual grasp which the old guard (or 'toffs' in the parlance of political commentators of the 1990s) had long detected in their own make-up. Baldwin seemed to lack the human delicacy and understanding which might have soothed their bruised egos.

Like Curzon, Austen Chamberlain remained conscious – overly so in the eyes of some – of having been snubbed. Nor was he alone. One must pay attention to his background. Bonar Law had inherited the leadership of a party every bit as gripped in schism as the Liberals. That party, while still under the nominal leadership of Asquith, was in busy contention over how to cope with the troublesome Lloyd George and his refugees from the collapsed Coalition. And a seventy-five-seat majority in the Commons should have given Law a clear five-year period in which to rebuild. But with their new leader's sudden exit from the stage the Conservative Party had been faced with the awkwardness of a fresh leadership 'contest' while still sore from its recent internal bruising. Yet the very extent to which the old Coalitionists had been reduced in status had been demonstrated by the fact that none of their number was considered a serious contender when the leadership contest took place. Indeed, the recollection that Curzon had been both tardy and unconvincing as a convert to the cause of party independence will have been yet another nail in what, as has been seen, was to become a decidedly airtight political coffin.

For the moment, the revulsion against the old Coalition was sufficient within Tory ranks for Baldwin to rule without regard for the 'toffs'. But to exclude them permanently risked stirring up trouble. If they did no more than stay around and grumble within the Conservative Party, it was containable.*

A more serious threat hung in the air – that instead these venerable and respected figures might seek political remuneration by reverting to their previous master in coalition, Lloyd George. Amid a plethora of converging indicators this will have been foremost in persuading Baldwin that he should act. He did so by springing a surprise. On 12 November 1923, less than two years into his premiership, Baldwin dissolved Parliament.

The full rationale behind Baldwin's decision to call a general election in 1923, only a year into the sizeable majority that he had inherited from Bonar Law, remains unclear. In 1922 Law had pledged that if re-elected he would not introduce any major provision of Tariff Reform without consulting the electorate. Thus Baldwin's stated reason for going to the country in 1923 was in order to seek a direct mandate from the electorate for this very purpose. Unemployment, it is true, particularly in the old staple industries, was high. The Unemployment Committee of the Cabinet had, just before the summer recess, reported their concern and their (scarcely helpful) view that '. . . there is no easy solution'. Protectionism could be held up as the antidote to this ominous development. J. C. C. Davidson, at the time Chancellor of the Duchy of Lancaster and a close confidant of the Prime Minister, has recorded:

> Throughout the summer of 1923 I had grown increasingly pes-
> simistic about the European† situation. I had for some time thought
> that we should pay more attention to the development of our
> Imperial resources . . . SB realised that it was essential to relieve

---

* And cf. Lady Lee, p. 17 above.
† (Trade.)

the American exchange* of purchases of raw materials which could well be produced within the Empire.[6]

Baldwin and Davidson took their summer holiday at Aix-en-Provence. Before his departure Baldwin had listened to a gloomy forecast from his Minister for Labour, as a result of which he 'began to think seriously of tariffs both as a means of reuniting the Party as well as dealing with the unemployment situation'.[7] Before the war, Baldwin had supported Tariff Reform although he had no more articulated its case forcefully than he had any other great issue of the day. Nor had his subsequent tenure at the Treasury been marked by a particular advocacy of protectionism as a tool of policy. Indeed Baldwin had even considered offering the free-trade Liberal, Reginald McKenna, the Chancellorship. This hardly pointed to a deep-seated commitment to the lessons and teachings of the late prophet, Joseph Chamberlain. But in concentrating the Prime Minister's mind, the importance of two other developments played a part. Lord Beaverbrook undertook that his newspapers would support a protectionist campaign – without equivocation. And the Bradford Chamber of Commerce came out with a request for protection for the woollen and worsted industries.

This notable turnaround, by an industry hitherto noted for its devotion to free-trade principles and from a region where many constituency results were finely calculated, pointed to a fundamental shift. The balance of international economic advantage was now moving against the manufacturing industries of the United Kingdom. Whether or not Baldwin grasped its full dimension he preferred, or affected, to see the resolution simply as indicating 'a change of heart in the country' and was encouraged.

There was also the Imperial dimension. In the debate on the Colonial Office vote on 23 July (at that time an important occasion in the Conservative back-bencher's diary) the Under-Secretary of State† told the House that at the autumn Imperial Conference the

* i.e., the balance of payments.
† William Ormsby-Gore.

topic of protectionism would be 'discussed'. In other words, that its advocates – who were many, and usually discouraged from too forcefully expressing their viewpoint – would be given a free rein.

A crudely protectionist policy was not feasible, of course. The interdependence of manufacturing, agricultural and financial interests required that it should be addressed with high circumspection. But within the countries and dependencies of the Empire the basic framework was in place. For Imperial Preference to function effectively was required, first, some equilibrium on trading account between the partners; and second (if only because the former would not be sustainable indefinitely and without variation), a high degree of public acceptance and enthusiasm. This was as important in the Dominions and the colonial territories as it was in the motherland. In 1923 the battle-cruiser squadron had set off on a round-the-world tour. 'Trade follows the flag'. And certainly at this time the white ensign was flying above some formidable cannon. That array of dual fifteen-inch guns in their armoured turrets could have reduced most ports of call, within an hour or so and had the command been signalled, to smoking rubble. But to friends they gave reassurance. When *Hood* drew alongside the quay at Melbourne on St Patrick's Day 1924 there were 100,000 people assembled to view her, and apply for boarding passes. At a civic dinner the Admiral in command of the squadron, greatly exceeding, it may be thought, his remit, although his audience were delighted, promised that 'there will always be capital ships to defend Australia; but she should be building* her own cruisers'.[8] The voyage of the battle-cruiser squadron, the political climate in the Dominions, the language of their press, the hard arithmetic of their own separate trade balances – all came together in a powerful mixture to supplement the gradual change in mood of so many manufacturing lobbies in the United Kingdom. Nevertheless Baldwin's announcement, coming from one so self-evidently un-ideological on the issue, surprised many and encouraged speculation about other motives.

* i.e., 'paying for'. The ships were always built in British yards.

As can often happen, the distinction between real party advantage and supposed national interest was cloudy. As to the former, Baldwin's mind ran as follows. The old guard Coalition Conservatives were protectionists. Being led by Austen Chamberlain, they could hardly be otherwise. Although personally Chamberlain seemed to have lost drive on the issue, no longer putting it above other considerations. But Baldwin's strategy – demolition of the Liberal Party and bringing about an effective two-party political culture between Labour and Conservative – was threatened by anything that might drive the old Coalitionists into the arms of Lloyd George. The old war leader was drifting. Watched with a mixture of curiosity and apprehension by his former colleagues. But Lloyd George was (understandably) regarded as capable of any somersault if it meant bolstering his own position. Free trade had never held the same centrality to Lloyd George's beliefs that it had for the official Liberal leadership under Asquith. Indeed in 1910, whilst a free-trade Chancellor, he had contemplated deals with the Unionists. Lloyd George, as Baldwin knew, and feared, never ruled anything 'out'.

Now, in July, Baldwin had got wind of a notion that Lloyd George, just as soon as he had returned from a trip to the United States, would declare his conversion to protectionism.[9] This could turn into a disaster. Lloyd George would at once become the focus of attention. And the Tories would be faced with a major policy dilemma whose divisive potential spread far wider than the personal grievances of a few grandees who thought themselves to have been slighted. The Conservative leader's response, therefore, was to beat him to it and announce his party's intention to fight a fresh general election immediately on that very issue. This would, or should, strike Lloyd George's feet from under him, forcing him back into the Liberal Party which would fight united for free trade. It would also disqualify his future appeal to the Tory old guard. While they, with this danger removed, could be welcomed back into the fold of high and honourable office.

But it would be a mixed blessing to engineer the reconciliation of the Tory factions on an issue which could, equally, reunify the

normally schismatic Liberal Party. To strengthen the Liberals as
the non-socialist alternative to Labour was the opposite of what
Baldwin had set out to achieve. Given the speed with which he
took his decision to call an election, the observer is forced to the
view that Baldwin may not have thought through all these variables
very closely. In the meantime the broader strategic march of events
was being neglected for tactical party advantage. A legitimate, and
common enough Conservative failing. But only excusable when
it worked.

In fact it was not just the ex-Coalition grandees that Baldwin
had to worry about. If humoured ideologically, Amery could be
counted upon. But beyond the likes of William Bridgeman and
J. C. C. Davidson, Baldwin had few genuine cronies in his Cabinet.
And even those who were content to serve with him like Sir
Philip Lloyd-Graeme* and Neville Chamberlain (his eye on the
succession) had originally presumed towards an administration led
by Curzon. The rest of the Cabinet had no particular personal
regard for the new Prime Minister.

Baldwin will have realised that he needed some tangible
achievement both for himself and for the Government if his
authority was going to be properly recognised as a leader rather
than a mere referee of self-motivated factions. (The very fate which
would overtake his successor, in not dissimilar circumstances, at
the end of the century.) And this was especially important before
any consideration could be given towards adding further hostile
faces around the Cabinet table.[10] Whatever protectionism's appeal
to the majority of grandees, abruptly to espouse it was a gamble.
Not least because three members of his existing Cabinet, the *super-
grandees* – Devonshire, Salisbury and Derby – were free-traders.
Thus even the sort of cautious protectionist programme Baldwin
had in mind commanded the active support of only four ministers
and was disliked by at least half of the rest of the Cabinet.[11]

Just as in the great disputations of 1992–7 each side of the

---

* Later Cunliffe-Lister, later still Lord Swinton.

argument declaimed their own case to be the only way of reuniting the party. In all probability Baldwin would have maintained this balancing act, as best he might, for at least half the life of the 1923 Parliament. But, uncharacteristically, he had allowed himself to be 'bounced' by the political opponent of whom still he was most in awe.

> The Goat [Lloyd George] was in America. He was on the water when I made the speech and the Liberals did not know what to say. I had information that he was going protectionist and I had to get in quick. No truth that I was pushed by Amery and the cabal. I was loosely in the saddle and got them into line in the Cabinet. Dished the Goat, as otherwise he would have got the Party with Austen and F. E. and there would have been an end to the Tory Party as we know it. I shall not forget the surprise and delight of Amery. It was a long calculated and not a sudden dissolution. Bonar had no programme, and the only thing was to bring the tariff issue forward.[12]

The Prime Minister's announcement to the National Union in Plymouth on 25 October 1923 that he intended to fight for the introduction of the tariff had only been put to the Cabinet two days previously. Sprung on it, indeed, without even being put on the meeting agenda, although Baldwin had been working out the details with Amery, Lloyd-Graeme and the Chancellor, Neville Chamberlain, over the previous fortnight. Cabinet had agreed that the announcement should not be accompanied by any immediate declaration for an election. This, it was implied, could be delayed well into the following year. On this latter point pro and sceptical protectionists were united in agreement. Then, to the surprise of all concerned, and against the (expressed) personal inclinations of the King, Baldwin announced to the Cabinet on 13 November that Parliament would be dissolved for a snap election.[13]

In the run-up to the Plymouth speech, Baldwin had been worried not only by Lloyd George's next move but just as importantly by Ramsay MacDonald's advocacy of a Capital Levy. Baldwin was now finding himself increasingly unsure of the temper of the new mass electorate. He realised that the Conservatives needed to be seen to be proposing an active remedy to unemployment, the issue which was so much at the heart of the Labour Party offensive. It was clear that the political and financial stability of Germany was now outside Britain's control alone (if it had ever been inside) and the German economy, reeling under reparation demands, had been still further disrupted by the abrupt and unilateral French occupation of the Ruhr. Clearly the looked-for upturn in the European market had been postponed *sine die*. But these were not factors easy to explain – even for one habituated to the technique of being 'bluff', or 'down to earth' – to an electorate who remained sick of Europe and all its unpredictabilities.

In fact, what Lloyd George had been pondering on boarding the ship for Canada – as he told his former Chancellor, Sir Robert Horne – was not so much tariff as subsidy. The promotion of 'active intervention by the State both to develop our resources and to extend our markets'.[14] This was not intended to centre upon a protectionist tariff policy, although the two are not easily separated. But in any case, as soon as Lloyd George got back to England he found that Asquith was now willing to do a deal.

Beaverbrook convened a meeting at Cherkley, his country house in Surrey, with Churchill, Austen Chamberlain and Birkenhead. Here, assembled once more, were the old Coalition heavyweights. They were far from happy with the running of the Government. To consolidate their position as natural arbiters in the event of an uncertain outcome, as much as to reassert their own 'indispensability', they agreed to back both sides in the forthcoming election. Austen Chamberlain and Birkenhead would back the Conservative campaign for tariffs; whilst Lloyd George and Churchill would back the Liberal campaign for free trade and work closely with Asquith.

The fact was, Baldwin had, in great haste, dug a trap, then blundered into it. As Lord Blake subsequently pointed out, if Baldwin had seen ahead the need for such a call, then why did he not give himself time to mount a proper campaign to soften up the electorate in advance? Indeed, many of the tariff measures necessary to confront the areas of structural unemployment most in need of tackling could have been achieved by extending the scope of tariff mechanisms already in existence, without the need to fight an election on a platform that presented so many hostages to fortune.[15] This line had been argued by the Chancellor, Neville Chamberlain, and others.

Baldwin's protagonists have suggested the possibility that he called a snap election so that the Liberals, although suddenly reunited, would not have time to get their campaign running.[16] But the same applied to the Conservatives who also had to adjust themselves to this abrupt – though to many congenial – change in policy. Even if his decision made both economic and politico-strategic sense (in itself debatable), the manner of Baldwin's tactics was such as to lend credence to the grumble – now often heard – that he was in the habit of taking a leap in the dark, looking round, and then taking another. The fact remained that by his sudden change of tack, opportunist and ill thought out as it was, Baldwin muffed the chance to align the Tories with their traditional standpoint, and that to which most of those back-benchers at the 1922 Carlton Club meeting believed themselves committed. The attempt to revive the gold standard, the General Strike, the Slump, were all to intervene before, masquerading as a 'National' government, the Tories would belatedly put Tariff Reform back in place.

Aware of this floundering direction the Conservative Party, in its higher reaches, became restless in the extreme. Derby and Salisbury, (his brother) Lord Robert Cecil, Wood (the future Lord Halifax) and Devonshire were among those who now threatened to resign. Deftly Baldwin raised the stakes. He intimated to the former Coalitionists that they could be invited back into the Cabinet. Notwithstanding their posture, the idea appealed to them – both collectively and as individuals. Word of this got about. It was plain that if so drastic a change of guard should happen at the same time as the Salisbury group resigned, then much of the effect of the Carlton Club revolt would be instantly reversed – although with Baldwin still in charge.

The position was further complicated by the fact that several Cabinet ministers were (or claimed to be) so disgusted by Birkenhead's vigorous private life that they regarded his return as a resignation issue in itself. He had seduced, then found himself infatuated by, Mona Dunn – a school friend of his daughter. She was a great beauty. Orpen painted her portrait. With her racy friends she would dance until dawn in, and sometimes on the tables at, the Criterion Restaurant. This aroused considerable jealousy among senior Tories. But the private lives of public men being at that time 'respected' by the press, the critics had to rationalise their protests as founded in indignation at the brutality with which Birkenhead would express his political opinions. (He had just delivered the notorious 'glittering prizes' speech as Rector of Glasgow University which in its stark expression of *realpolitik* was felt to be offensively out of keeping with the banal platitudes of the times.)

All this mutual recrimination between would-be colleagues will have further encouraged Baldwin to get the election over and done with as quickly as possible. He was quietly confident. On the eve of poll the Prime Minister had told Stamfordham that Central Office 'had been through all constituencies with a tooth-comb' and were sure of a majority of 30 over Labour and Liberals.[17] But in its outcome this election, so hastily and ill-foundedly called, was a serious defeat.

FOUR

An Unhappy Ship

Grandees uncomfortable in defeat – Illusory strength of
the Liberals – Winston Churchill tacks to leeward – and
is rewarded – The new Cabinet takes shape – Neville
Chamberlain perplexed – Final humiliation of Curzon.

THE WORKINGS OF THE ELECTORAL system during this tran-
sitional period of three-party politics had disproportionately
rewarded the Conservatives in 1922 despite their gaining only a
little over 38 per cent of the poll (interestingly, 5 per cent less than
the party had secured during their notorious landslide defeat of
1906). When this distortion came closer to being ironed out in
1923 the minimal faltering in the Conservative vote (which fell
by only 0.1 per cent from the result in 1922) was enough to sweep
away a host of seats.*¹ Thus was demonstrated the precarious
nature of electoral politics so long as there were three principal
mainland parties in contention. Baldwin's gamble had led to new
life being breathed into the Liberal Party just at the time when (as
he himself had originally observed) the sensible strategy was to
squeeze it out of the system so that a two-party conflict could
more profitably fill the stage marked out by the first-past-the-post
rules.

So a sizeable Conservative majority with four years to run was
needlessly thrown away. The Liberals took or held 159 seats; taking

---

* However, the national share of the vote percentages were slightly misleading
because the Tories had far more unopposed returns – 42 in all – than their
opponents who, combined, had 14 in 1922 as against 35 and 14 in 1923.

constituencies from the Conservatives in Wales and Lancashire, a net gain of 43. But Ramsay MacDonald's Labour Party was confirmed as the larger of the two free-trade parties with a total of 191 seats, doing particularly well in the industrial areas which were clearly far from convinced that protectionism was an antidote to unemployment. Lloyd George and Asquith had even appeared together on the same platform at Paisley on 24 November, an occurrence which had not happened since before Lloyd George had ousted his own leader from the premiership in December 1916. The election had been fought, in effect, as a referendum on tariffs. Thus the route to keep Labour out by a Tory–Liberal pact was blocked, since no arrangement could be put in place between the two parties diametrically opposed on this fundamental issue.

Nevertheless, there were those who saw reason to propose it. Former Coalitionists such as Austen Chamberlain and Birkenhead had assisted Baldwin's Conservatives at the election. Given their support for protectionism they could hardly do otherwise. But they had done so with a minimum of good grace. Now confusion reigned. Birkenhead took it into his head (joining that small but self-perpetuating group of senior Conservatives, around a half-dozen in number who, at any given moment, feel that they personally ought to be leading the party) that he had strong claims. He sent his emissary, Oliver Locker-Lampson, to seek an audience with the King's private secretary, Stamfordham. He, Birkenhead, the message ran, would be ready, or else gladly fall in beside Arthur Balfour or Austen Chamberlain.[2]

In no time a rumour started that Chamberlain was going to be called. Balfour – his last throw of the dice on the big board – 'let it be known' that if Baldwin were to resign he, Balfour, 'would be available to form an administration'. Quite quickly though, and characteristically, Balfour changed his mind.[3] Austen Chamberlain was too old, Birkenhead too strongly disliked. None of the Big Three could rely on back-bench support to any greater degree than they had at the Carlton Club meeting eighteen months earlier. Like several of his successors in office Baldwin would enjoy a substantial prolongation of his life expectancy because none of the potential claimants appealed widely enough.

Additionally, just as Edward Heath tried to do in March of 1974, Baldwin wanted to hang on as Prime Minister until voted out by the new Parliament; thus retaining residual authority, of a sort, that would help his defence against malcontents.

The election result was being interpreted in Liberal circles as a triumph for free trade and the beginning of the fight-back of Liberalism. But on such terms, a deal with the Tories against the free-trade Labour Party simply did not fit. In crowning Labour (and in performing the ceremony without first extracting any contractual returns of favour) the Liberals thereby asserted their nuisance value to all non-socialist voters, but marginalised their future relevance and electoral appeal.

Baldwin, though, was lucky not to be ousted. Most of his senior colleagues said, on or more typically off the record, that he should resign the leadership. However, there being no agreement as to who should replace him and to what end, and with his opponents from the Salisbury wing of the party now adrift from his opponents from the Birkenhead wing and all regarding the hostile noises of Beaverbrook and Rothermere with resentment, Baldwin's immediate prospects had improved. The alternatives were, by the bulk of the party establishment, regarded as suspect. Neville Chamberlain's enthusiasm for protection was thought to have been a bad influence on recent events. It had made the encouragement of emigration from the Liberal Party more difficult. Balfour was by now infirm. Austen Chamberlain, Curzon (even Curzon's name was being bandied about at dinner parties) and Birkenhead had an unacceptable number of enemies.

Baldwin immediately set about retrenchment, and reconstruction. High-minded theory, even homely chats about cricket, were for the time being at least, old hat. By 11 February 1924, a mere three weeks since losing office, the cornerstone of policy on which the party had fought the last election, protection and subsidising of agriculture, had been dropped. In its place came a

negative campaign of anti-socialist scaremongering. For the first
time an effective 'shadow cabinet' (then known as the Consultative
Committee) was established on an official basis as distinct from
the rather haphazard convocations of displaced statesmen which
had previously sought to give an impression of coherence whilst
in Opposition. Policy-forming sub-committees were set up to
undertake the detailed work between meetings of the Shadow
Cabinet. This process led in June to the launch of a Conservative
Party statement of intent, *Aims and Principles*, overseen by Neville
Chamberlain and duly approved. Baldwin took this respite from
the cares of office to present the party as a modern outfit, restruc-
tured internally to the realities of a new Britain. And his articulation of this 'new Conservatism' was an early example of a titular
prefix used in similar circumstances and to good effect by a leader
of the Labour Party in 1997.

The likelihood of a Labour government had created unease.
MacDonald himself, who was not even a privy councillor and had
been most controversially an opponent of war in 1914, was viewed
with concern. However J. H. Thomas, displaying the Labour
Party's congenital awe of power and status, had hastened to reassure
a worried Stamfordham that all would be well if MacDonald was
called to kiss hands. The existing (Tory) Budget's framework
would be retained; the idea of a Capital Levy shelved; and an
attempt likely to abolish the dole – the 'pernicious' effect of which
was to ensure that youths 'were growing up to dislike work and
to live upon the State'.[4]

As it transpired, MacDonald and the King got on better than
could ever have been expected. Labour's first months of office
were far from being the national disaster so long predicted. A
figure of quite Gladstonian financial rectitude, Philip Snowden,
was installed at the Treasury. While the parliamentary majority
was itself dependent on the whim of a Liberal Party led by H. H.
Asquith. Many of the key decisions were plainly at the Liberals'
behest (the very last time in the twentieth century that the Liberal
Party was to have significant influence on policy or legislation):
the protectionist tariffs which had been introduced during and

since the war years were swept away; even the tentative under-takings concerning Imperial Preference which Baldwin had so recently made to the Dominion Premiers were reneged. And the building of a reinforced naval base at Singapore to guard the eastern Empire and Dominions was cancelled. (This short-sighted and highly significant act being dressed up, predictably, in the liberal baloney of the time as 'representative of the fresh mood of international conciliation'.) None the less, contrary to expect-ations, Labour had occupied office and done little worse than its Conservative predecessor. Red revolution appeared no nearer a possibility.

Almost immediately the Government got into difficulties. This raised the spectre which Baldwin sought to avoid, a new com-bination (possibly with ex-Coalition Tory assistance) and Asquith as Prime Minister. Baldwin formed the view that he should avoid bringing MacDonald down at the first opportunity. When the moment was right to strike, the Government's fall must be so terminal as to bring about not just its resignation (out of which all manner of dangerous hybrid intrigue might spring) but a fresh general election for which the Liberal electoral machine was unprepared and under-funded. Thus when the new Government suffered its first Commons defeat on 13 March, the Conservative division lobby arithmetic was redrawn in the evening so as to prevent the Government being defeated by a hostile Liberal onslaught. Whilst the Tories opposed Labour's attempts to reduce the scale of the spending on the naval programme, all the same they backed the decision to scrap building the Singapore base.[5]

Given this state of affairs, the Conservative task was to paint the most lurid picture possible from the palette offered them. Deci-sions taken by MacDonald to bolster markets for British trade such as the recognition of Soviet Russia (of which his party's left wing were passionately in favour) thus provided opportunity to imply the worst possible intentions. When Baldwin was ready and the election came, one of the Conservatives' posters under the heading 'So THIS is SOCIALISM!' displayed a cartoon of

MacDonald shunning a handsome upright-looking chap from the Dominions in order to accommodate a couple of unshaven, shifty-looking Bolshevik soldiers conveniently standing in front of a blazing inferno. Combined with the faked 'Zinoviev Letter' published in the *Daily Mail*, which purported to show that the Bolsheviks were looking to kick-start revolution in Britain on the back of the Labour Government, and the failure to press for the prosecution of a communist journalist, J. R. Campbell, the nine-month period in which MacDonald had striven to show that a Labour government was capable of behaving in a responsible way could be presented as a façade covering the real sympathies of the Labour Movement.

The decision to bring down the Labour Government over the Campbell case was Baldwin's. Asquith realised too late that it could be a trap to destroy the Liberals at an ensuing general election. While MacDonald also seemed acquiescent, having little stomach for holding on in a situation increasingly impossible once Asquith had deserted.

Of course Baldwin did not believe that MacDonald was the precursor to Bolshevik upheaval in Britain. And his fingerprints were nowhere to be found on the Zinoviev forgery. Indeed the Conservative leader had been happy (for his own reasons) not to force parliamentary defeat on substantive Labour measures until he thought the time was right. Baldwin's preference was for November to aim to fight and win an election; hence the decision to combine with the Liberals over the Campbell case debate in September. Labour was defeated by 364 to 198 and MacDonald sought a dissolution immediately.

As Baldwin had worked for, and predicted, the electorate was this time polarised. The Liberals were squeezed out of existence, declining from 158 seats to 40. Labour, now and henceforth the Opposition, held their own citadels with a strength of 151. While Baldwin, with 419 Tories and allies, found himself leader of the first independent and united Conservative majority Government since 1905. Jubilation abounded, and not a little anxiety about who would be 'in' and who 'out'.

With an eye, perhaps, on his own credentials, Birkenhead wrote that:

> If we do not miss our opportunities, we have the chance of rendering the greatest service which the Conservative Party has ever rendered to the nation. By stable, orderly and resolute government, combining economy with the sympathetic consideration of real grievances, we may at last get over the difficulties and bitterness of the war.[6]

Now came the question of Cabinet appointments. The Coalitionists had behaved moderately (in both senses of the word) well throughout the period of Opposition, and during the campaign itself. Whatever may have been his private inclination Baldwin could no longer ignore their claims. But his own loyalists, too, expected reward. As so often, balance, if not duplicity, was required of the Prime Minister. Of the three great grandees Austen Chamberlain was the least contentious. In an age when the self-confidence of politicians allowed them to disregard the assessment of 'image' he did in fact possess the personal advantage of *looking* like a Foreign Secretary. And it was to this position that he was promptly appointed. Yet even this move was fraught with tension and anxiety. Curzon, who had not 'behaved badly' since his rejection, assumed his prescriptive right to occupy the post until he saw fit to stand aside of his own volition. No sooner, though, had the polls closed than ugly rumours began to reach him:

> I cannot believe that you would propose to put such a terrible slur upon my administration [of the Foreign Office] which was conducted amid extreme difficulties but not without success in the closest and pleasantest cooperation with yourself and your predecessor, and as I have always been led to think, with your just approval. It would be too much to expect me to accept such a situation.[7]

The meeting was painful. The Prime Minister spoke (how unwelcome to the suppliant must be that phrase, with its aura just faintly evocative of some future memorial service) of the 'need for a fresh start'. Curzon sobbed.[8] He was offered Lord President of the Council and – which hardly could have been denied him – Leadership of the House of Lords. It was, or certainly it seemed to Curzon, a great, undeserved, and additional humiliation. Grace, though, insisted that her husband accept; rightly anticipating (as she told Lord Crawford two weeks later at a dinner party) that not only was it his duty to the State but that George 'would be intolerable at home' with nothing to do.[9]

If the placing of Curzon was uncomfortable, dealing with FE was awkward. He had done his best, though in characteristically abrasive style, during the campaign to signal his good intentions towards the Liberals:

> Let us at least see to it that ... cut-throat contests are avoided in the constituencies between men who are in fundamental agreement, with the result of handing over constituencies to minority Socialists...
>
> Do not let us demand that [the Liberals] shall come to us on humiliating terms, making public recantation of things in which they have long believed...
>
> There is room in the army to which we belong for another wing...[10]

Unfortunately for FE these, and kindred declamations, were not enough to rid him of widespread personal disapprobation – as a right-wing loudmouth and drunkard enviably enjoying the favours of his 22-year-old mistress. It had been only a year since Baldwin, primly rejecting the former Lord Chancellor's claims, murmured that 'We are a Cabinet of faithful husbands, and I think we will remain so'.[11]

Birkenhead's own biographer, John Campbell, believes that if he had really insisted, FE could have returned to the Woolsack.[12] This may be underestimating the power as well as the obstinacy of the Prime Minister. A low opinion that was certainly shared by FE himself who wrote, only two days after the election victory, that it was 'a great tragedy that so great an army should have so

uninspiring a Commander-in-Chief'.[13] Following some consultation with colleagues Baldwin hit on a solution that would
best suit both men. He drew Birkenhead out of the wilderness,
but at the same time showed him the cities of the plain. The post
of Secretary of State for India offered proximity (but not too close
or too frequent) to the centre of power; not much by way of
'leverage' in either Parliament or press; and the social temptations
of dabbling in viceregal splendour where Rufus Isaacs, Marquess
of Reading, was at Government House. It will none the less have
been with some relief that Baldwin could note:

> [FE] ... was pleased. He said he had a sharp tongue and had said
> bitter things about me. He hoped that was past. He would help all
> he could, and if any action of his hurt me, in future he hoped I
> would tell him so, have it out, and be done with it ...[14]

Having accommodated Austen Chamberlain and FE, Baldwin
turned over in his mind the question of Winston Churchill.

The Liberal leadership's decision to put Labour in power had
been the last straw for Churchill, that most untiring of Anti-
Socialists. He now had his reason for seeking to leave that sinking
ship he had joined in the more seaworthy days of 1904. (Although
some might, and did, say that he had already walked the plank
when defeated as a Liberal candidate for West Leicester in the
1923 general election.) It had at that time been Churchill's expectation that Asquith would form a government with Conservative
support. Instead he had been disconcerted to find the Liberal
leader, with whom Churchill had in any case suffered poor relations since 1915, proceed to put Labour in office. The result,
Churchill accurately predicted, would be the recovery of the
Conservative Party into whose ranks his ex-Coalition colleagues,
Horne and Birkenhead, strongly urged him to return.

At first Churchill resisted these blandishments. His ambitions
were for leadership, and he believed that with the winding-up of
Lloyd George's Coalition Liberal group he, Churchill, now could
form a nucleus of Liberals prepared to work with cross-party
coalitions against Labour in the future. Given the belief that the

electoral trend had been set by the three- and four-party confusion of 1918, 1922 and 1923, this was not an unreasonable strategy. But the whole mechanism of the Liberal Party was hostile to Churchill; and his hostility to socialism stood to embarrass the position of the leadership. Churchill realised that he might have to wait for an eternity before being given a Liberal seat to fight. By then the landscape could have changed out of recognition.

From a combination, therefore, of impatience and caution, Churchill decided to attempt a comeback on a non-aligned ticket while looking to the Tories for sympathy. In March 1924 there arose a by-election heaven-sent for such a tactic. The Abbey (Westminster) constituency had one of the most politically sophisticated electorates in the kingdom. Standing as an 'Independent Anti-Socialist' Churchill polled more than the Liberal and Labour candidates and came within an inch of unseating the Conservative. For someone whose career had been written off so many times, not least by his own hand, this was an enormous vote of confidence. And Baldwin, ever the realist, took note.

The Exchequer, usually the first post to be filled, was still vacant. Neville Chamberlain had the strongest claim. But he was also the likeliest successor to Baldwin in the long term. Both men had their motives for preferring that a 'neutral' Chancellor be appointed. The assumption was that it would be Sir Robert Horne. Baldwin, though, remembered that Horne had refused the post in 1923, and did not want to be snubbed two years in succession. If he gave it to Churchill this, surely, would anchor the highest-calibre loose cannon on the scene?

Yet the Prime Minister needed to be circumspect. On the afternoon of 5 November he saw Neville Chamberlain in the Leader's Room at Central Office.

'Needless to say, I want you to go back to the Treasury.'

Chamberlain said nothing. (And in parentheses it may be noted that in the whole of this chronicle there must be very few senior Conservatives who, when offered the Treasury, said nothing.) Baldwin went on,

'Horne is not as well thought of in the City as he imagines. I've offered him Minister of Labour.'

At that moment a letter was brought in. It was from Horne. Baldwin tore it open, said, 'He won't take it.' A further pause ensued. 'I'm going to have to take Winston back in. He would be more under control inside than out. Perhaps he could go to Health?'

This drew the desired reaction from Chamberlain. 'I have given the matter full consideration, and *I* would wish [to go back to] Health.'

'Well, who is to be Chancellor? I suppose if it was Winston there would be a howl from the party?'

Chamberlain knowing, in all probability that Baldwin would brush the suggestion aside, mentioned his own distant, but long-term, rival – Sam Hoare. 'There will be a howl about Winston wherever you put him.'

The two men talked for a little while about junior appointments. Then Baldwin said he had another visitor. Chamberlain noted that the Prime Minister showed him out of the room by a side door. However, on the landing who should Chamberlain see but Churchill himself coming up the stairs arm in arm with Sidney Herbert* '... and so deep in conversation that he never even noticed me'.†[15]

With the announcement even Churchill's friends found their breath taken away. 'SB is mad!' declared Austen Chamberlain. 'FE is as much disturbed as I am, and feels that W[inston]'s appointment in place of H[orne] will rouse great antagonism *and is not good for W*.'‡[16] Horne himself rang Sam Hoare at 3 a.m. and complained for an hour 'in a state of dementia'. Hoare, too, fell into 'a state of despair'. He told Neville Chamberlain that·

... S.B. had made every mistake possible. He had never said a word

* Baldwin's private secretary.
† Chamberlain's diary entries for 5 and 6 November 1924 are reproduced in full in Appendix I.
‡ AC's italics.

to any of the peers he was leaving out in the cold – Balfour, Devonshire, Derby or Peel. The City would be intensely alarmed over Winston's appointment. 'Anyone but him' they would say, and all over the country confidence would be shaken.[17]

Chamberlain shared in the disappointment. He recorded that:

For myself I feel thoroughly depressed. By his incredible bungling S.B. has already thrown away much of what we had gained by the election. Why on earth he should be in such a desperate hurry to rubbish his Cabinet at once I can't think. Why he should act on his own initiative in such delicate affairs without a word to people like Austen is a mystery. He is unfit to be leader, that is the long and short of it and I foresee splits in the Cabinet, resignations and the destruction of our great power before long![18]

But the fact remained that once again Churchill had demonstrated his extraordinary political resilience. Henceforth, although often subject to derogatory comment and (to unsympathetic editors) background briefing about his 'maverick' tendency and the risks he carried, Churchill remained a serious presence on the political scene. Disliked, distrusted by the more orthodox of his colleagues. But one whose attitude had always to be considered when political decisions were at the formative stage.

FIVE

The Gold Standard
and its Consequences

Churchill at the Exchequer – is charged with reverting
to the gold standard – His doubts – Keynes's hesitations –
A rapid deterioration in confidence – Alternative courses
of action are considered – A mismatch with party trade
policy – The deed is done, but half-heartedly.

ALTHOUGH THE GREAT WAR HAD thrown into disorder the
international co-operation necessary for the effective operation
of the gold standard, the criterion itself had not formally been
suspended in Britain until 1919. In that year an Act of Parliament
had made illegal the British export of gold coin and bullion other
than under licence. But this suspension was only ever regarded as
a temporary measure. And it was intended that it should lapse at
the end of 1925. As Chancellor, Churchill now had to decide
whether there were grounds for going against the presumption of
a 'return to normality'.

After the gold standard's suspension, the Cunliffe Committee*
had argued for its return once a 'normal' pattern of world trade
appeared to be in place. In the meantime, whilst Britain sought
to rebuild its war-distorted economy, deflation should be pursued
in order that British prices, which had soared during the war,
could fall back into a competitive position with the United States.
In 1924 a further committee was appointed to look into the
issue by the short-lived Labour Government. This concluded
unambiguously in favour of the gold standard's readoption on the

---

* Headed by the outgoing Chairman of the Bank of England.

assumption that British prices continued to fall (the target being
by 6 per cent).

Thus Churchill was able to announce in his Budget speech (and
even at this stage it is clear that he is guarding his back):

> A return to an effective gold standard has long been the settled
> and declared policy of this country. Every Expert Conference since
> the War – Brussels, Genoa – every expert committee in this
> country, has urged the principle of a return to the gold standard.
> No responsible authority has advocated any other policy . . . It has
> always been taken as a matter of course that we should return.[1]

Unable by their own record to oppose Churchill's return to the
gold standard in principle, Labour were reduced to intermittent
sniping at its 'undue precipitancy'.[2] The measure passed, without
great difficulty, and Churchill continued – though with unchar-
acteristic lack of conviction – to shore up his position:

> it is remarkable that no formal challenge should have been made
> against the principle of returning to the gold standard by any
> political party . . . no member of either branch of the legislature
> voted against it.[3]

The arguments, though, were many of them technical. 'Members
of the legislature' (and not, certainly, for the last time in this
century), being limited in their economic expertise, took refuge
from arcane disputation by turning to accepted wisdom. This, as
is invariably the case, rested in the experience of what had gone
before, coloured by the personal prospects – as they saw it – of
those giving their opinion.

In the distance, but no more than the middle distance, was
the brilliant young economist whose devastating analysis of the
disorder and turbulence inseparable from the provisions of the
Versailles Treaty★ was already ruffling Establishment feathers and
who, in the fullness of time, was to become the supreme guru

★ *The Economic Consequences of the Peace.*

of mid-twentieth-century economic planning, John Maynard Keynes.

Keynes was frail, bisexual ('most men only marry in order to have a wife to boast to'), raffish and crushingly intellectual. He enjoyed the company, and adulation, of that 'set' of artists – Roger Fry, Vanessa Bell, Duncan Grant – who worked, none too strenuously, under the name 'Bloomsbury' but were in fact settled in a property on Lord Gage's estate at Firle in Sussex – Charleston Farmhouse. His touch was not always sure, for Keynes was that most dangerous of mixed personalities – half academic, half compulsive gambler. In 1920 he had been touring Italy with Duncan Grant and Vanessa Bell, whose money he was 'managing'. 'Maynard has been speculating brilliantly on the fluctuating European exchanges. Every day he announces that we are richer than the day before.' This early failure to distinguish between real and 'paper' profits allowed Vanessa joyfully to acquire 'seventeen pairs of gloves and a great many stuffs in the Piazza dei Fiori' but soon led to nemesis. On their return to London it appeared that

> Maynard's speculations on the fluctuating currency exchange had miscarried; the syndicate he had formed, and in which Vanessa and Duncan [Grant] had placed all their capital, was suddenly bankrupt.[4]

Sir Ernest Cassell duly came to the rescue, but Keynes's blithe attitude to exchange rates remained his weakest point.

In any case, whatever Keynes may have been preaching, the advice that Churchill was receiving from the Treasury and the City was such as no prudent politician – certainly not one still conscious of carrying the responsibility for Gallipoli – would have overridden.[5]

Critics of his policy, including Keynes and even, ultimately, Churchill himself, came to see the decision as one forced by the orthodox financial establishment. Churchill chose to rely on the advice of the Controller of Finance at the Treasury, Sir Otto Niemeyer. His calculation was simple. Niemeyer could back Churchill's decision to return to gold with 'irrefutable arguments to support it'. But if the Chancellor opted to stay off gold he would be faced with criticism from the City authorities, against which he would not have any effective answer.[6] Churchill neither was, nor ever would become, at ease in the company of economists. As he once remarked of Treasury civil servants: 'after a while these fellows start talking Persian. And then I am sunk.'*[7]

The evidence does indeed show that Churchill made as much investigation into alternatives to the Treasury view as could reasonably be expected of him, given the limited amount of contrary evidence available. In January 1925 he drew up the so-called 'Mr Churchill's Exercise' which posed the Treasury questions about the reasons for returning to gold and the other options available. The intention of the paper was as much to lay out a brief on the charges which might potentially be laid against a decision to return to gold, as to ascertain whether that decision should be taken in the first place, but the text does show that Churchill was fully versed in what was to become the Keynesian critique. He seemed particularly apprehensive that the proposed objective, as set out by the Chamberlain–Bradbury Committee, of reducing prices might necessitate a 6 per cent bank rate. This would be a 'very serious check' on 'trade, industry and employment'.[8] Certainly in correspondence with Niemeyer, Churchill displayed little of the respect which a supposedly deferential Chancellor might have been expected to adopt. On 22 February 1925 he wrote:

> The Treasury have never, it seems to me, faced the profound significance of what Mr Keynes calls 'the paradox of unemployment amidst dearth'. The Governor [of the Bank of England, Montagu Norman] shows himself perfectly happy in the spectacle of Britain possessing the finest credit in the world simultaneously with a million and a quarter unemployed. Obviously if these

---

* It should be said, though, that Churchill's private secretary at the Treasury, James Grigg, felt that Churchill was 'less malleable' than his two predecessors as Chancellor, Sir Robert Horne and Philip Snowden. (Diary entry, 17 May 1925, in Keith Middlemas (ed.), *Tom Jones, Whitehall Diary*, vol. 1, 1916–25 (1971), p. 315.)

million and a quarter were usefully and economically employed, they would produce at least £100 a year a head, instead of costing us at least £50 a year a head in doles. We should have at least £200 millions a year healthy net increase . . .

The community lacks goods, and a million and a quarter people lack work. It is certainly one of the highest functions of national finance and credit to bridge the gulf between the two. This is the only country in the world where this condition exists. The Treasury and Bank of England policy has been the only policy consistently pursued. It is a terrible responsibility for those who have shaped it, unless they can be sure that there is no connection between the unique British phenomenon of chronic unemployment and the long, resolute consistency of a particular financial policy. I do not know whether France with her financial embarrassments can be said to be worse off than England with her unemployment. At any rate while that unemployment exists, no one is entitled to plume himself on the financial or credit policy which we have pursued.

It may be of course that you will agree that the unemployment would have been much greater but for the financial policy pursued; that there is not sufficient demand for commodities either internally or externally to require the services of this million and a quarter people; that there is nothing for them but to hang like a millstone round the neck of industry and on the public revenue until they become permanently demoralised. You may be right, but if so, it is one of the most sombre conclusions ever reached. On the other hand I do not pretend to see even 'through a glass darkly' how the financial and credit policy of the country could be handled so as to bridge the gap between a dearth of goods and a surplus of labour; and well I realise the danger of experiment to that end. The seas of history are full of famous wrecks. Still if I could see a way, I would far rather follow it than any other. I would rather see Finance less proud and Industry more content.

You and the Governor have managed this affair. Taken together I expect you know more about it than anyone else in the world. At any rate alone in the world you have had an opportunity over a definite period of years of seeing your policy carried out. That it is a great policy, greatly pursued, I have no doubt. But the fact that this island with its enormous extraneous resources is unable to maintain its population is surely a cause for the deepest heart-searching.[9]

This was forthright to an unusual degree (at that time or later) in the relations between ministers and very senior officials. And certainly it showed that Churchill had recovered his confidence and equilibrium. Lacking in economic expertise he may have been, but the clarity of Churchill's prose and the compulsion of his imagery required a considerative response. In any case a familiarity with the terms and language of the science – the 'Persian' tongue – was not, in the 1920s, as indispensable as it came to be thought in the 1970s. Whether that was Churchill's intention or not, the document remains one of the most lucid as well as one of the most beautifully expressed of all arguments for protectionism ('Tariff Reform' in one shape or another). And it illustrates how formidable Churchill would have been on that platform. Particularly considering the powerful allies – Beaverbrook and his papers, together with the majority, still, of 'natural' Conservatives in the country.

But Churchill's personal ambitions lay elsewhere. He had only just returned to government. In no time he reverted to those standard country-house tactics which usually served well in helping ministers to get their way, or stay out of trouble by finding reverse gear.

In March, a month before his Budget announcement, Churchill convened a dinner party at which he pitted those Treasury hierarchs Niemeyer and Lord Bradbury against the two public figures best known to have reservations about returning to gold, the former Liberal Chancellor, Reginald McKenna, and John Maynard Keynes. Neither of the latter two were in unqualified opposition to a return to gold 'in principle'. But Keynes in particular stated his view that the Treasury, by believing there was only a 2.5 per cent discrepancy between British and American

prices, would recommend a return at the fixed-rate parity of
£1:$4.86.[10] This would be to overvalue the pound and cause
deflation. Such deflation might contain prices, but it would aggravate the already debilitating unemployment figures; and cause yet
more industrial strife. According to Keynes, the British/American
price differential* was not 2.5 per cent but 10 per cent. McKenna
agreed with this analysis but admitted that there was no escaping
a return to gold, concluding to Churchill that 'you will have to
go back; but it will be hell'.[11]

Still things hung in the balance. Unexpectedly, Keynes himself
then faltered. Before the Budget announcement, he covered his
tracks by writing in *The Nation*, a pro-Liberal Party journal:

> If we are to return to gold, and in the face of general opinion that
> is inevitable, the Chancellor and the Treasury and the Bank have
> tried to do so along the most prudent and far-sighted lines which
> are open to them.[12]

It must be acknowledged that Churchill received no significant
advice against returning to the gold standard. The view of established finance was very much in favour of returning at a relatively
high rate on the not unreasonable, though far from sophisticated,
assessment that the lower the rate the faster would the reserves
drain away. Nevertheless, as his correspondence with Niemeyer
shows, Churchill could see that the good of the financial sector
and of industry might not be one and the same. Sir Robert Horne,
who had expressed such bitter disappointment at being overtaken
by Churchill when Baldwin formed his second Cabinet, was now
in the 'private sector', a respected Conservative financier. He had
been Chancellor of the Exchequer during the Lloyd George
Coalition. And that would leave him no room for manoeuvre.
In speeches before City livery companies and other congenial
audiences, Horne expressed the orthodox view that the two sectors
were in fact inseparable:

* i.e., the gap in the real-purchasing-power equivalent.

industry benefits enormously from the position which we occupy
as the centre of the world's finance. These loans which London so
often has to grant to other parts of the world have, in the past, as
everyone knows, been the means by which British pre-eminence
in industry has been built up ... If the financial fabric be now
imperilled, it will equally be to the detriment of our industries,
because it will take away the very means by which industry has
been fostered...[13]

Churchill, though, was uncomfortably aware of the existing
ascendancy of the United States in international finance. The
Americans had been implacable in their pursuit of debts arising
out of the Great War. And in the majority of cases had insisted on
repayment in gold. Would not this course of action play into their
hands, still further postpone the date when Britain might recover
her primacy?

On 2 January, Churchill had suggested to Niemeyer that:

The United States has accumulated the greater part of the gold in
the world and is suffering from a serious [sic] plethora. Are we sure
that in trying to establish the gold standard we shall not be favouring
American interests? Shall we not be making their hoard of gold
more valuable than it is at present? Shall we not be relieving them
from the consequences of their selfish and extortionate policy?[14]

(It was to be less than twenty years before the validity of this
prediction was, on Churchill above all people, to press most cruelly.
Yet nowhere in his papers at that time, nor even in those records
of his private conversations,★ is there any sign that he recalled his
period at the Treasury, or its lessons.)

By the time Churchill had to present his case to the Commons,
he had settled at least on the consolation that although the United
States had accumulated half of the world's gold in circulation, it
was the British Empire, with 70 per cent, that was the main source
of the world's gold supply.[15] This is a fairly specious argument. As

★ e.g., with his doctor, Lord Moran.

was its *sequitur*; although with the latter can be detected the spectre which drove all decision making at this time and, indeed, persisted in one form or another up until the Bretton Woods Agreement of 1944 – 'the whole rest of the British Empire would have taken it without us, and it would have come to a gold standard, not on the basis of the pound sterling but of the dollar'.[16]

Thus did fear that the rest of the world was bent on returning to a financial system which had previously been centred in London, but now quite possibly without Britain's participation at all, underpin Churchill's positive decision. Sir Robert Horne kept up the pressure:

> When we find that Sweden has already been a year on the gold standard, that Germany is now linked to gold, that Austria is linked to gold, that Holland has taken the same action as we are taking and at the same time, and that all our great Dominions are taking the same action along with us, it surely would be an extraordinary confession of weakness if we, who regard ourselves as the centre of the world's financial system, were to declare that we were not ready to take this momentous step. I feel that it would do us more harm, certainly as a financial centre, than anything else could do.[17]

The key passages in the former Chancellor's argument are: '. . . *all our great Dominions are taking the same action along with us*'; and, '*we who regard ourselves as the centre of the world's financial system . . .*'

Yet it remains debatable to what extent, in reality, the City's international influence was determined by sterling's convertibility into gold as distinct from its general financial expertise. Were not the Dominions prepared to return to gold because they anticipated the coherent and unbroken assumption of the British policy-makers since 1919 that the sovereign would reassert its primacy when the time was right?

Even twenty-five years later the readiness of nations, English- and non-English-speaking alike, to adhere to the radically different departure in British financial policy post-1931 – against gold, and with the creation of the Sterling Area, without dollar par-ticipation – should be noted. These were not questions around which the 1925 debate (insofar as there was one) revolved. A party-inspired editorial in *The Times* expressed the unsophisticated view: 'Not only financial pursuits, but the great majority of common-sense men in business will rejoice in the announcement that the gold standard is restored in international dealing. Expert opinion has always agreed that this step was indispensable to the recovery of our position in the markets of the world.'[18]

The critical decision was the sterling/dollar exchange rate. If this was miscalculated, no amount of backing could save the pound. It would be sold short by American speculators until all the gold in the vaults of the Bank, and in the Rand, and still unsmelted, would be used up. To take sterling back on to the gold standard at a rate of £1 = $4.86 was a clear indication of Churchill's desire to recover the City's international position, it being the rate at which pounds had been exchangeable before the outbreak of the Great War. Illuminated by hindsight it can be seen as a huge and unsustainable overestimate. But at the time it was almost impossible to find any authority (with the exception of Keynes) arguing for a lower rate.

As with subsequent and, insofar as British interests are concerned, equally damaging agreements, Bretton Woods and the European Exchange Rate Mechanism, those who supported them at the time changed their tune later on. And the explanation for ultimate failure was centred not in terms of a problem with the mechanism itself but upon that rate at which sterling was fixed within it. Sterling would be seen as overvalued within the post-1945 fixed exchange systems. Just as with the ERM. In each case ultimate suspension was inevitable when London proved unable to sustain its parity against the collective selling power of the markets. This has also become the charge levied against Churchill's decision to return sterling to a parity of $4.86, despite the fact that its purchasing power was supposed to have decreased since 1914. The result of this overvaluation, according to the received wisdom, was to make British exports comparatively expensive compared with foreign imports, exacerbating unemployment and further worsening the inter-war slump. The price squeeze that the decision to return to gold at $4.86 involved has also been seen as the source of the industrial unrest in the mining community which brought about the General Strike in 1926.

But the portrayal of Conservative policy as 'a brutal and exploitative orthodoxy' (the harshest condemnation was to come not from the Socialists but from Oswald Mosley and his New Party) does less than justice to both the weight of expert opinion and to what an objective, non-ideological assessment of the national interest suggested.

Keynes maintained that returning to the pre-war parity in 1925 overvalued the pound by around 10 per cent. In fact, the free-floating pound had dived in the aftermath of the gold standard's suspension, but by February 1923 it had climbed back to $4.73, almost regaining its pre-war parity. Subsequently it had slid to $4.34 before rising to within 2.5 per cent of the dollar's pre-war value during early 1925. The successful attainment of a mere 2.5 per cent differential between Britain and the United States led the Treasury quite naturally to argue that 'we were so near the old parity that simply tinkering at the margins would create a shock to confidence and endanger our international reputation for so small and so ephemeral an easement'.[19]

Keynes's forecast may subsequently have proved closer in the longer term, but this was not the evidence upon which the policy decisions were made at the time. British interest rates had been kept relatively subdued before 1925 whilst the exchange rate with the dollar had strengthened because of the United States' expansionary international monetary policy at the time. (American policy here was not put into reverse until 1928.) The appreciating exchange rate from October 1924 and the bank rate rise of March 1925 had not stimulated any immediate deflation in the British economy. This suggested that such a course did not necessarily inflict serious domestic hardship.[20] Given their belief that American and British prices were almost running parallel, the Treasury would in any case have been expected to want a higher-bank-rate policy in the second half of the 1920s (and well beyond if it was realistic to do so) regardless of whether or not the pound was on gold. The Chamberlain–Bradbury Committee's judgement of 1924, as summarised by the Treasury in 1929, was that 'only a small additional strain would be entailed by the restoration of the gold parity, as compared with the strain [*sic*] required to hold sterling at its then exchange value'.[21]

It was the old staple labour-intensive industries which were hit hardest after 1925. But without productivity gains it was hard to envisage these industries ever regaining their predominance. And it was increases in productivity which the Treasury viewed (just as in 1981 and thereafter) to be a product of promoting a dearer money policy. In fact, and contrary to the uniformly depressing picture painted of the 1920s, industrial production in Britain rose by 2.8 per cent and its productivity by 3.8 per cent per annum. Between 1924 and 1930 efficiency in the coalmines increased 18 per cent and (1923–30) iron and steel production rose by a quarter. If the effects of sterling's overvaluation were damaging, then they were certainly not comprehensively crippling. Furthermore, a strong pound meant that the cost to the consumer (domestic and industrial) of food and raw material imports was much reduced. Given that Britain could not even remotely become self-sufficient in some of these areas, this reduction in cost produced corresponding economic savings for all. As a classical liberal free-trader of mid-Victorian outlook with all its Peelite associations with the cheap loaf, Churchill was well aware of this. The gold standard, like free trade, was a natural self-adjusting mechanism – an economic principle he had always fully digested.

Then again, the post-war economic upheavals and uncontrolled monetary policies which had led to inflation in countries like Germany had seemed to put in jeopardy their entire social and political fabric. In Churchill's mind, as in the majority of his colleagues', at most university high tables and on the editorial board of *The Times*, the gold standard helped to suppress the inflationary spiral whatever government was (or might be) in power.

Churchill defended it, at an exchange rate which made essential imports of foodstuffs and raw material cheaper, with the same style of language he used in defence of free trade:

> We are not a self-supporting country. We have this immense
> working-class population ... These people are dependent mainly
> on overseas food and our industries are dependent on overseas raw
> material. What is one of their principal interests? It is surely stability
> of prices.[22]

It can also be argued that the $4.86 parity may not have damaged
Britain's trade very much. Partly because so many Empire currencies were pegged to the pound sterling and partly because
France, stabilising after Britain, might well have chosen a still
lower value for the franc if Britain had fixed the pound at a
figure lower than $4.86. While as far as the financial sector was
concerned, Britain resumed her pre-war role as an earner of
current-account surpluses and as an external lender both on short
term and on long term. But the country's short-term obligations,
most obviously to France but also to Empire countries and to
other authorities and persons who kept their foreign balances in
the form of claims on London, grew.

Here detectable are the first signs of that incipient weakness
which would make even the far looser mechanism of the 'Sterling
Area' unworkable. The disciplines of the gold standard were, for
Britain, unsustainable without the imposition, in however benign
a form, of a regulated siege economy. Thus the paradox that a
device which should have allowed the 'market' to set the pattern
was in fact unworkable without the support of measures designed
to thwart that same market.

In the meantime the falling value of Britain's assets abroad
was a constant anxiety. Had British overseas property income
maintained its late 1920s levels during the 1930s, then Britain's
cumulative current-account deficit would have been wiped out.[23]
As it was, government policy was hesitant. The Conservatives
attempted to combine the freedom of the market with bouts of
intermittent, and panicky, intervention. It was characterised
neither by the *laissez-faire* (founded on immense strength) of the
American economy, nor the totalitarian control (founded on

police repression) with which Hjalmar Schacht, President of the Reichsbank, was to cure inflation in Germany.

For all these reasons the policy was a compromise. It was one which would bring about the financial crisis of 1931 and the formation of the National Government in Britain.

SIX

The General Strike

Bourgeois apprehensions – The plight of the
coalminers – 'Red Friday' – The Samuel Committee –
Equivocal position of the Trades Union Congress
(TUC) – The mood in Cabinet – Loss of control by
the principals – Working-class solidarity – The forces of
conciliation – The changed face of labour relations.

THERE NOW EMERGED ONTO the stage the Conservatives' traditional adversary. One who was to assume, for the middle decades
of the century, immense symbolic importance as the elite force of
trade union militancy. The coalminers.

It must be realised that the propertied class – and this category
extended deep into the humbler reaches of the bourgeoisie – had
been, for the last one hundred and fifty years, haunted by the
spectre of 'the mob'. Most of the kingdom's larger cities contained
districts of Hogarthian squalor, overcrowded jerry-built slums and
what are today termed 'no-go' areas. Urban architecture, while
not on the scale of Haussmann's grapeshot enfilades, included
many discreet devices such as angles and railings to obstruct the
assembly, or even the individual presence, of beggars or, as the by-
laws described them, 'meanly dressed persons'.

This shadow was never, it seemed, far distant. 'Boney', it was
true, had been smashed by the Iron Duke – but not before the
entire French aristocracy had their lands appropriated and their
heads chopped off in public. In 1848 the European governing class
had moved ruthlessly but only in the nick of time to forestall a
series of 'popular' (that is to say founded on riot and the street

barricade) insurrections. In 1870 it had been Paris, again, that had fallen into the hands of the Communards following the defeat of the army in the Franco-Prussian War. And only eight years previously the Tsar, cruellest and most secure (it seemed) of all tyrants, had been deserted by his own guards, kidnapped and, with his wife and children, butchered.

Nor could nervous bourgeoisie find comfort in reassuring one another that these phenomena were mainly 'foreign'. There had been unwelcome examples, dealt with 'firmly' but none the less alarmingly, in recent years, where disputes at dockside or colliery had taken on a violent flavour which had spilled over to the adjoining urban district.

During MacDonald's minority Labour Government in 1924, the miners had been awarded higher wages. European competition had been depressed, blighted by the Great War's legacy of destruction, occupation and dislocation. But as normal conditions returned, the recovery of the German and Polish coalmining industry cast a shadow over the pitheads. By July of 1925 losses were running at £1 million per month. (In 'real terms' this compared only to the losses of British Steel in the late 1970s.) The mine-owners sought to cut costs by applying that traditional solution of the nineteenth-century employer – longer hours (at the coalface) and reduced pay. While the return to gold in 1925 and the policy of maintaining a strong pound ensured that there could be no deliberate boost to coal export competitiveness.

Frank Hodges, Secretary of the Miners' Federation of Great Britain (MFGB), moved towards adopting an uncompromising stance. The Government's desire was to avoid involvement in the dispute. Their prime concern being to evade any further subsidy whose principal effect – or so they believed – would be to postpone the sector's reorganisation. The TUC, on the other hand, was less concerned to co-ordinate the miners' desire for a sympathetic general strike than to establish its own primacy by negotiating directly with the Government over the miners' heads. Their objective was to evolve a compromise package to force on miner and mine-owner alike. Reduced miners' wages would accompany the state-sponsored reorganisation of the industry in which the Council would play a continuing, and assertive, role.

It is hardly surprising that the miners should see things differently. Their refusal to accept lower wages ensured that a lock-out would take place a month later – 31 July 1925. With the TUC endorsing the prevention of all movement of coal, the Government – as was to become the habitual Tory tactic in the first round – folded. With only twenty-six hours to go before the lockout was due to begin a fresh subsidy was promised, estimated at £10 million (but eventually costing £23 million) in order to maintain wages and profits for the next nine months whilst a Royal Commission under the former Liberal Home Secretary, Herbert Samuel, would make recommendations for boosting efficiency in the coal industry. Baldwin undertook to lend the Government's support to the Commission's findings if both the miners and the owners accepted them.

Cuthbert Headlam, a Conservative MP in the coalmining area of County Durham, recorded in his diary the split feelings some Tories had over dealing with the unions in this fashion:

> a strike should be avoided – because it would be such a costly drain on our financial resources and its consequences could not be gauged – at the same time, I am convinced that if Parliamentary Government is to be retained in this country, a stern fight will have to be fought against Trade Union dictation.[1]

But when the 'Red Friday' coal subsidy was announced, Headlam noted:

> Baldwin was mildly cheered after he made the announcement – the Party is clearly divided – the Government has not managed the business cleverly – and a subsidy is a subsidy by whatever name you chose to call it – still a *subsidy will cost less than a strike* and one could not have risked a general upheaval of labour (and presumably that was inevitable) without being convinced that the great mass of public opinion was against the miners. Thanks to the [owners'] tactless stupidity it was not.[2]

Whether 'Red Friday' was, as some saw it at the time, an unfortunate precedent set for trades unions to regard governments as malleable at the flexing of their muscle is debatable. Ministers were divided. The Home Secretary, Joynson-Hicks ('Jix'), thought it a surrender. But others who would today be regarded as on the Left, including Walter Bridgeman, the Lord Chancellor Viscount Cave and the (as seems inseparable from the job) conciliatory Minister of Labour, Arthur Steel-Maitland, were also uneasy. It was the support of Churchill and Birkenhead – later seen as anti-union demons – as well as of Baldwin, Austen and Neville Chamberlain that saw the policy adopted.[3]

Without exception, though, the Tory grandees were biding their time. Whether or not Margaret Thatcher had, before her own great war to the death with the National Union of Miners (NUM) in 1984, browsed in Lord Birkenhead's papers has not been disclosed. Had she done so she would fully have understood and approved his strategic thought and prediction:

> I am myself of opinion ... that we shall have no peace until the matter has been fought out to a victory ... We shall have to set our teeth just as we would have done if six months more war had been necessary, and carry the matter once and for all to a conclusion ... which will involve a complete reconsideration of the exceptional legal status conceded to Trades [sic] Unions...[4]

At first the railway and transport unions refused to take the brunt of preventing the movement of coal alone. But soon the other unions decided to support the miners. While the way in which the mine-owners had handled the assault on their employees' wages and conditions had been badly received by the public. Baldwin quickly saw that if the miners were to be attacked head-on, then it would be better to wait until their own pig-headedness had tipped the scales of public opinion back at least into equilibrium.[5] As Headlam noted:

> The Hof C full of gossip – apparently a lot of our people are furious with the Government for surrendering to the extremists,

etc., etc. I had a long talk with the PM ... His line was a very obvious one – a General Strike could not be faced on an issue on which the Party itself was divided, the miners' case a fair and reasonable one, the owners' case ditto but their tactics bad. I asked him whether he meant to fight Trades Union domination when the issue was a straight one – he said he certainly meant to do so – so there it is.[6]

Plans had been drawn up by the Lloyd George Government to face the threat of industrial unrest in 1920. These were enhanced by the Cabinet's Supply and Transport Committee and supplemented by the work of the party's Policy Unit run by Colonel Lancelot Storr. This body, since its establishment in February 1924, had concentrated much of its energy on preparing suggestions as to how a general strike could best be beaten.[7] Most of these arrangements had in fact already been made by 'Red Friday'. The Board of Trade had started collecting data on food stocks and established a Food Advisory Council of the major foodstuffs traders with local committees set up throughout the country to ensure distribution. The RAC and AA gave lists of drivers to the Ministry of Transport and local committees were established to supervise the best distribution of vehicles made available. The majority of these were provided on a regional basis by the major road hauliers. To supplement the Government's direct initiatives, an 'Organisation for the Maintenance of Supplies' (OMS) was also established, of registered helpers who would contribute during the early stages of the strike whilst the Government's plans took effect.

Central to the administration of the anti-strike provisions was the Government's appointment of ten 'Commissioners', all junior ministers of which nine were MPs and one a peer – so as to maintain the notion of reference to Parliament – to preside over their respective districts. It is interesting to note that these plans survived in Whitehall into the 1950s. But when they were revived, as the basis for an administrative structure, the 'Commissioners' were all designated senior civil servants who abrogated to themselves priority allocation of 'fall-out' shelters in the event of a nuclear attack. During a general strike the Commissioners were to supervise the distribution of supply and transport and take '*appropriate measures*' according to circumstance, in the name of the Government, although without needing to wait for direct orders from it. Joynson-Hicks controlled an overview of their responsibilities from London while the GPO and the Air Ministry co-operated to guarantee communications between him and the divisional HQs. The paralysis with which rail strikes had threatened the Edwardian capitalist order was mitigated by the spread of cars and road transport in general, ensuring that supplies could get through. Judged by results and the limitation of 1920s communications, the Government's ability to preplan the best ways of keeping supplies circulating is highly impressive.[8] The complexity, and reach, of these arrangements is remarkable. But they are an uncomfortable reminder also of how quickly democratic societies can degenerate into totalitarianism when the governing order feels itself to be under threat.

The Samuel Commission reported on 11 March 1926. But its nod towards the miners (better working conditions and the nationalisation of royalties) was outweighed by its reinforcement of the main point at issue, a reduction in wages – as was claimed by the coal-owners – 'to aid international competitiveness'. The employers then reasserted their claim for increasing miners' working hours. Such a move would require legislation, and therefore the abandonment of the Government's desire to involve itself in the details of the dispute as little as possible. Baldwin and the TUC next attempted, though without much enthusiasm, to get the MFGB to start the compromise ball rolling by agreeing to reduced wages. This at once hit the brick wall of Herbert Smith's announcement that the miners had 'nowt to offer' in return.[9] The Prime Minister then turned to Lord Weir, the Honorary President of the National Confederation of Employers' Organisations. After a long meeting Baldwin issued a statement. He 'thought' that the mine-owners' request would be 'helpful' to the miners if their reduced wages were compensated by increasing their working day to eight hours.[10]

Events were now moving at a fast pace. The same day as the miners were officially locked out for refusing their bosses' offer, a specially convened conference of the TUC gave its General Council the go-ahead to launch a nationwide strike two days hence, on 3 May, by an overwhelming 3.5 million votes to 50,000. Although the miners did not recognise the TUC's right to bargain away their position (regarding the TUC's only *raison d'être* as to cause national havoc on their behalf), the General Council now focused on committing the Government to enforce the findings of the Samuel Report, including its call for the reduction in miners' wages as a way of solving the dispute.

Certainly it is unsurprising that the Government were prepared to proceed on the basis of the Samuel Report. But the TUC then swayed back towards the miners and insisted on a further subsidy being needed to retain coal wages until the promised reorganisation took place. Government strategy proceeded along the lines of trying to disentangle the TUC negotiators like J. H. Thomas who wanted to avoid a strike and the miners who were wholly ·irreconcilable.

However, when the negotiators arrived at the Treasury the Cabinet Secretary recalled how:

> I showed them into a waiting room where a fire had been kindled for them. Cook* asked me, could he have a wash as he was very tired. I took him to the Treasury lavatory and plunged at once into a discussion as to how far he was prepared to go in the matter of wages. He said ... the word 'revision' would ease matters if he used it instead of reduction.[11]

Some further discussion took place of a technical kind, regarding piece rates and the hewers, before A. J. Cook 'felt that he could not stay any longer away from his executive'. Brief though this exchange had been, the fact that it took place at all was an indicator of weakness, or at least lack of unanimity, among the miners.

* A. J. (Arthur James) Cook. Secretary, Miners' Federation of Great Britain, 1924–31.

Accordingly the Government insisted that it would only negotiate with the TUC if it had the support of the MFGB for lower wages. The TUC believed – or affected to believe – that it had already won such an acceptance when in fact it had not. The Government negotiators, Baldwin, Birkenhead and Arthur Steel-Maitland (Minister of Labour), seemed prepared to extend the subsidy for a fortnight on proposals drawn up by Sir Horace Wilson.★ This met with disapproval from a majority in the Cabinet. Especially from Churchill who was, typically, ready and eager for action. The formula, being based on reduced wages, was in any case unacceptable to the MFGB, at least while they were discussing the matter among themselves.

Cabinet hostility, and confidence, intensified when the GPO revealed that it had intercepted precautionary strike orders. The anti-strike supply and transport organisation was put on alert. On the afternoon of 2 May, Joynson-Hicks, with Cabinet backing, sent out telegrams with instructions to the vital supply distribution units on whom the Government was relying to circumvent the feared strike. The final trigger was the action of *Daily Mail* compositors (without TUC sanction) in refusing to print an editorial endorsing a government advertisement for volunteers. This led the Government, urged on by Churchill, to break off negotiations.

The mood around the Cabinet table was excitable:

> At the [*sic*] moment [around midnight] Jix came in with a message and dramatically announced 'The *Daily Mail* has ceased to function. The men have refused to print its leading article entitled "For King and Country".' 'Thank God,' shouted FE & was immediately & hotly attacked by Winston. 'A great organ of the press is muzzled by strikers & you say "Thank God".' FE said it was only a joke & moreover a joke which Winston himself had made the day before. Thomas had said to him 'There'll be no papers tomorrow' & Winston had replied 'That'll be a comfort anyhow.' 'Yes, but I said that to Thomas,' said Winston. 'Well I

★ At that time Permanent Secretary at the Ministry of Labour but who reappears a decade later as Neville Chamberlain's *éminence grise*.

say it to you,' shouted FE. But Horace Wilson who has a cool head said 'This changes the whole situation & I think it gives you a way out.' FE instantly seized on the idea & reversed his attitude, the PM gave way & in a few minutes we were revising our ultimatum so as to make this 'overt act' the main reason for breaking off ... About 12.30 the Cabinet intensely relieved at its release from a most awkward situation dispersed.[12]

The discussion had gone on far into the night. And so when the King's private secretary, Clive Wigram, was telephoned with the news he seemed unable to take it in, admitting that he was 'in his pyjamas'. Nor could he quite grasp the (alleged) significance of what had happened at the *Daily Mail*. 'We don't take the *Mail*, or the *Daily Express*, at Buckingham Palace,' he said.

The TUC negotiators did in fact return to Downing Street. But by then Baldwin too had gone to bed. Ernest Bevin tried to get the process restarted but met with a refusal from those ministers remaining, who would only consider it if orders for the General Strike were cancelled. Bevin was a skilful negotiator, but he had his pride. The strike was made official to begin on 4 May.

Generally, union members obeyed TUC instructions and there were few abstentions from the call to lay down tools. Called out on strike immediately were transport, iron and steel, printing, building, electricity and gas workers. Engineers and shipbuilders were not called out until 11 May.[13]

The Government's line was set out by Churchill:

There are two disputes on. There is the General Strike which is a challenge to the Government, and with which we cannot compromise. Strike Notices must be withdrawn unconditionally. There is also a trade dispute in the coal industry; on that we are prepared to take the utmost pains to reach a settlement in the most conciliatory spirit.

However, even Baldwin was now privately convinced that:

We shall have to find some way to deal with all this Trade Union business [*sic*] and revise its powers and machinery so far as the

Government is concerned in the light of this tremendous centralising ... We must get some way by which the voice of the rank
and file can be made effective.[14]

Thus, in characteristically homespun terms, did the Prime Minister first articulate the motivation which, when they tried to give
it effect, was to cause both Wilson and Heath governments to lose
a general election; but which would be put in place by Margaret
Thatcher.

There were 4,000 prosecutions for violence or its incitement
which ended in gaol sentences even though the great majority of
strikers stayed firmly within the law. There was never any threat to
parliamentary order. Nothing remotely reminiscent of Mussolini's
March on Rome occurred. Only in the London Docks were
troops deployed for action, the recollection of which measure
lodged firmly in docklands mythology and was to blight industrial
relations in that sector for the next fifty years. It rapidly became
clear that there were not enough police on the Metropolitan
strength. The recruitment of temporary 'special' constables from
volunteers proved to be insufficient and of uneven quality. After a
while the Government became fearful of a serious 'incident'. They
looked with apprehension at the volunteers' constant reliance
upon the military to make the presence of authority felt. In
London by 12 May there were seven battalions, one cavalry squadron and two armoured car companies on top of other sprinklings
of troops at key points.[15] On 8 May the Government had used the
presence of troops and 500 volunteers to move essential foodstuff
supplies out of the heavily-picketed London Docks. And supplies –
of all kinds – were kept in circulation without confrontation of a
kind that could degenerate into concerted violence. What might
have happened if the trade unionists had stood their ground is
another matter. But by behaving lawfully they caused much of the
fear, and the urgency, to dissipate.

Beyond some throwaway rhetoric, there was relatively little
evidence of co-ordinated Communist subversion. Although the

Communist Party doubled its membership during 1926 there was no long-term gain, with membership sliding back soon afterwards.[16] Yet even a moderate northern Tory MP like Cuthbert Headlam made clear the extent to which the strike was seen as a revolutionary measure, writing in his diary that: 'the Labour people triumphant ... clearly the whole thing has been cleverly prepared and they mean revolution', and the following day that 'the attempt to hold up Society and bring revolution is the thing the country is interested in'.

In fact, as Baldwin had initially suspected and very soon came to realise, this view was far from universal. A Midland parson wrote to the Deputy Secretary, Tom Jones:

> As to the miners I am all with anyone who will fight for the maintenance of their wages. Our men are a decent quiet lot, by no means wanting a fight for the sake of being nasty. They simply cannot live on less. They feel – and I fully agree with them – that much of the subsidy was grabbed. They see the wasteful luxury of some owners. Our men are not hotheads like some of the Celts may be, but I am convinced they are going to keep up their end desperately ...

Two days later, though, Headlam was still writing that 'it is obvious now to almost anyone that it is a definite bid by the TUC for political power'.[17]

Government strategy went to plan. The stopping of cheese production ensured there was no shortage of milk. Volunteer drivers and special constables from the ranks of the ex-officers and the universities kept the flow of goods moving – an act which represented to left-wing thinkers not the patriotism they saw in the strikers but rather 'class war in polite form'.[18] While under Churchill's direction, the *Morning Post*'s press was used to produce the *British Gazette* which far outshone the feeble TUC alternative, the *British Worker* (which was, in any case, banned from printing ordinary news or issuing propaganda). The BBC, which Churchill and Birkenhead wanted to commandeer for the duration of the strike,[19] contrived to retain its independence by failing to report anything contrary to the Government's image.

Not all the Establishment were as partisan. Religious leaders and, in particular, the Archbishop of Canterbury publicly called for a compromise solution – in effect endorsing the original position of the TUC General Council. Lloyd George, nostalgic for his old roots, also sounded his trumpet. The Presbyterian Central Assembly spoke out sympathetically towards the miners. The Archbishop of Canterbury issued a 'message' calling on the Government and the mine-owners to climb down in order to get the peace process negotiations moving again. Its tone being in fact milder than that urged on him by the Archbishop of York (Gordon Cosmo Lang), three Bishops and an assortment of Nonconformist churchmen who had convened with him at Lambeth for a joint statement. As is their wont, the basic premiss of these churchmen was that securing industrial peace was of more importance than the constitutional issue. However, when the Archbishop asked for permission to broadcast his appeal on the BBC, Baldwin, who was harder-headed, refused.[20] And even after the General Strike ended and attention turned to ending the miners' dispute, Church leaders were preaching in favour of a further four months' subsidy, an 'incredible effrontery', according to Birkenhead, which 'probably prolonged the strike for three weeks'.[21] Lloyd George's particular and personal sympathy with the strikers was out of step with the other Liberal leaders. Especially Asquith who would be disagreeing with Lloyd George as a matter of principle. The former Liberal Attorney-General, Sir John Simon, instigated a walk-out of the Commons chamber by Labour MPs[22] when he declared the General Strike to be outside the remit of the 1906 legislation and therefore illegal – advice on which the Government wisely chose not to act. However, most of the Asquithite Liberal leaders, including Sir John Simon, began to swing round to opposing Baldwin's terms of unconditional surrender when they heard the Archbishop of Canterbury's opposition to it.[23]

Not that this was unwelcome to Baldwin. Since he could not reopen negotiations directly with the TUC, which would have conceded both momentum and the argument that the unions' actions were unconstitutional, it was via Liberal politicians that the Government kept open channels to the Council. It was a logical development from Baldwin's initial strategy. He had reduced the Liberals from being a primary to an ancillary Opposition. Now, in this crisis that was to set the fault lines of British politics for the next half-century, he had effectively neutered their own role. Herbert Samuel was particularly useful and the Cabinet gave him to understand that they were supportive of what he could achieve although could not promise to be bound by it.

Whilst Baldwin was making these conciliatory overtures (although based on the premiss of unconditional surrender by the strikers), the Cabinet began to consider proposals of the Lord Chancellor, Viscount Cave, to introduce legislation to reverse that of 1906, allowing for the freezing of union assets and the right of employers to sue the strikers for losses incurred by their action. Sympathetic strikes would become illegal. Churchill, meanwhile, was telling anyone who came within earshot that 'we are at war. We must go through with it. We must hold our nerve.' Any suggestion of a moderate approach was overwhelmed, as the Cabinet Secretary noted, by 'a cataract of boiling eloquence'.[24] Indeed Churchill rapidly became such a nuisance to the staff and sub-editors of the *British Gazette* that, after refusing a highly inflammatory article on the need to embody (mobilise) the Territorials, they tried by various devices to keep him away from their office.

For a few days there was stalemate, or so it appeared. In fact the sands were running out for the TUC. Baldwin's calmness, little different, as at times it seemed, from torpor, could only be disturbed by a further escalation. And short of concerted violence, and its unpredictable consequences, the unions had nothing left. The Prime Minister broadcast, his tone at the same time melancholy but reassuring, on the evening of 8 May. (And certainly his text should be compared with the petulant indecision of Edward Heath's own broadcast during the miners' strike of February 1974.*)

* See Chapter 29 below.

The following day, at lunchtime, Baldwin, his younger son and
Tom Jones 'squeezed into the back of a little Bean car'. It carried
a heavy load, this small twelve-horse-power saloon, as it ground
up Haverstock Hill in second gear, for the front seats were occupied
by the chauffeur and the personal detective. They parked by the
Whitestone Pond, walked to Kenwood, then over Hampstead
Heath to Parliament Hill Fields. A considerable distance that took
more than two hours. No reference whatever was made to the
crisis, although in the car Baldwin had pulled out of his pocket a
letter from the Prince of Wales congratulating the Prime Minister
on his broadcast, and read out extracts. A strange episode. Thera-
peutic, possibly. But was the Prime Minister also hoping to be
recognised, with his pipe and walking stick, his demeanour radi-
ating that all was well? It is very typical of Baldwin and somewhat
disarming. But bizarre none the less.

After some days' deliberation Samuel offered Thomas, who had
by now subsumed the role of chief TUC negotiator, a package.
This being not far from what the TUC had originally demanded
before the General Strike commenced, Thomas wanted to accept.
The package involved miners' wage reductions (as defined by a
National Wages Board) once the Government had given swift
assurance in favour of mine reorganisation. The problem, though,
remained. The MFGB would not accept the terms. Not even
Thomas's threat to end the General Strike and leave the miners
to fight their own battle would shift the dogmatic position of the
miners' leaders who were aggrieved at what (with some reason)
they saw as a Samuel/Thomas carve-up over their heads. While
the TUC saw themselves as unable to break the Government's
supply lines yet tied in the public mind to a group of militants
who were not going to agree to anything which was remotely
acceptable to the Government.

Baldwin now decided to apply further pressure. He did so by
the time-honoured means of the 'arranged question'.

> Q: Does the Government intend to deal with the position of Trades Unions?
> A: The Government are not now contemplating any modification in existing trade union legislation, but they are considering the desirability of making clear what they believe now to be the Law, namely that a General Strike is illegal.

'Not now contemplating' was enough to endow the TUC moderates with the upper hand. So when on 11 May, in the Chancery Division, Mr Justice Astbury ruled that:

> the so-called General Strike ... was contrary to law and those persons inciting or taking part in it were not protected by the Trades Disputes Act 1906. No Trade Dispute has been alleged or shown to exist in any of the Unions affected except in the Miners' case. No Trade Dispute could exist between the TUC on the one hand and the Government and Nation on the other.

– they had both reassurance and excuse.

Thus, on 12 May, the TUC General Council unilaterally and without the support of the miners, called off the General Strike.

In fact there had been little difference between terms of the pre-strike Samuel Report and the post-strike Samuel offer. Each was on the outer limits of how far either the Government or the TUC could go together towards a settlement. At the outset the TUC believed that it could not renege on its threat of a general strike and leave the miners to their lonely fate without causing a serious split in the trade union movement. But their commitment was always suspect, while Baldwin's own amiable, though vulpine, *gravitas* was perfectly suited to maintaining a broad level of middle-class support in a dispute where, all too obviously, '... it would be possible to say without exaggeration of the miners' leaders that they were the stupidest men in England if we had not had frequent occasion to meet the owners'.[25] J. C. C. Davidson wrote to Lord Carson that 'the vast majority of the public and the vast majority of the strikers themselves are not only good citizens but very patriotic'[26] and these were sentiments shared even by the Executive

Committee of the National Union of Conservative Associations where the tradition of Tory paternalism quickly reasserted itself. Baldwin in 1935 was still telling the Party Conference of the 'Englishness' of trade unions and how their spirit was 'the bulwark of popular liberty'. Without unions, Baldwin lectured his audience, there 'would be chaos, and chaos would lead to disaster' and the road to Communism and Fascism.[27] Even Walter Monckton* never went as far as this; although the theme, or something very like it, was to colour Harold Macmillan's approach to 'industrial relations' during his own premiership.

There were two further consequences which flowed from the Conservative Government's steady nerve in 1926. When the economic and financial crisis of 1931 arrived and the time came to cut wages, it was the Labour Party which split rather than the subdued trade unions, many of whose members (particularly in the unionised heavy-industry side) either found themselves out of work or feared that they might soon be. With a more moderate trade union membership to deal with, the National Government would cautiously bring the unions into the governmental process. By the outbreak of the Second World War the TUC had their presence in the machinery of government recognised through a process which had accelerated during the 1930s, with their membership of Government committees rising from seven representatives on five committees in 1931 to twenty-nine representatives on eleven committees in 1938.[28]

Deprived of sympathetic strike action, the miners surrendered six months later in a worse position than when they had started. And in May 1927, the Government carried by closure the Trades Disputes Act, outlawing any strike defined by the courts to be 'designed or calculated to coerce the government'.

Yet the 1927 Act did not go so far as reversing the legislation passed by the pre-war Liberal Governments, which Conservatives saw to be at the heart of the subsequent poor industrial relations. Birkenhead had told the Central Unionist Council, in the imme-

* See p. 339 below.

diate aftermath of the strike, that strike ballots, abolishing the closed shop, curbs on picketing and a reversal of the Taff Vale decision – i.e., that unions could be sued for damages caused by strikes – were all essential.[29] But it was already too late. The party preferred a partnership whose essential element was compromise. It was an arrangement that would work well enough while the union barons functioned within the Establishment. But as the doctrinal extremists began to reclaim territory the Trades Disputes Act came to look mild; and certainly inadequate compared to what was finally reclaimed from union monopoly by the Thatcher Government in the 1980s.

SEVEN

Stanley Baldwin Survives

The hunger for scapegoats – The intrusion of Lord
Beaverbrook – Winston Churchill is unreliable – The
economic climate worsens – as does the position of
Stanley Baldwin – The Rothermere–Beaverbrook axis –
The Party Chairman 'resigns' – The Topping Report –
An impulsive decision – is soon corrected.

ALTHOUGH THE GENERAL STRIKE HAD at first the appearance
of an earthquake; then, as its tremors subsided, had been seen to
have left few dead; the event had in fact brought about a huge
realignment of the political landscape.

The election which followed, of May 1929, had been fought
by the Conservatives in dispiriting circumstances. The slogan
'*Safety First*' was typically Baldwinian, combining lack of inspiration (it was little more than a rewrite of the successful 1924 slogan
'*Peace and stability at Home and Abroad*')* and torpor. It was fought
against the background – at the same time familiar and unwelcome – of a bungled reform of the rating system and a systemic
paranoia concerning sections of the press. J. C. C. Davidson
(whose role in blocking Curzon's accession to the premiership,
and the Conservatives' abrupt flirtation with protectionism in
1924, will be recalled)† was now Chairman of the Party. Davidson
disliked Lord Rothermere, and the feeling was mutual. Well before
the election Davidson had prepared an analysis of the *Daily Mail*'s

---

* See p. 32 above.
† See pp. 25–6 above.

attitude to the party over the previous two and a half years, concluding with the assertion that 'Today's leading article is an attack on the Conservative Party of a very virulent nature ... obviously was dictated by Lloyd George'.[1]

An attempt to mediate was put in train, through the good offices of Esmond Harmsworth, Rothermere's son who remained in the administration, although still at a junior level. Harmsworth said that his father was

> ... terribly hurt and offended by a series of snubs and open rebuffs from Baldwin, but that he was prepared to have a bridge built as easily as possible from Baldwin's point of view.

Davidson was lukewarm, although 'Esmond put it very nicely and frankly'. The Chairman minuted that:

> The support of the Rothermere press is important, and if the purchase price is a platitudinous utterance, then I feel it should be paid.[2]

It was to no avail. The public continued to agree with the *Daily Mail*, while small businesses were thoroughly resentful at their increased rate burden. For the first time the Labour Party secured the largest share of seats. Once the final tally had been counted, Labour had won 287 contests, the Conservatives had won 260 and (whilst disappointing compared with the Herculean scale of the effort) Lloyd George's campaign had pushed the Liberal parliamentary party back up to a complement of 59 in the Commons.

'It cannot be pretended that Baldwin's leadership ...' as one of our most distinguished political historians has written '... was notable or energetic.'[3] To a close (female) friend the Prime Minister wrote during the campaign that at a huge meeting in Lancashire 'a few wise and cunning words ... met with warm approval ... I do hope it has done good and my trainers will be pleased. *It was pretty tiring*, but I have had a bath, put on clean things and am just going to have dinner. Off first thing to Scotland in the morning. And all the time the divine Spring is going on ...'[4]

This time though (unlike his behaviour after the 1923 defeat) the

Prime Minister acknowledged the country's verdict immediately. Ramsay MacDonald was thus again called to form a government. And, just as in 1924, he was again denied a parliamentary majority, albeit by a tantalisingly small margin. Baldwin's party-political strategy, in the furtherance of which so much of wider importance had been overlooked or deferred, appeared to be in ruins. It was Lloyd George who now held the balance of power.

At first the bulk of criticism was directed at Davidson. The Chairman had made many enemies. Not least from his assault on 'sleaze'. Davidson was none too tactful in his exchanges with prominent industrialists or back-benchers whose demands ranged from knighthoods and peerages to (for example) acceptance of tenders for the Singapore construction contract. Sometimes their overtures were rejected at the outset. On several occasions there is a threat to sue the party organisation for a sum of money – often huge – to be returned. Nor was the traffic one way only. Some colleagues nearing the end of their time in the Commons were asking for titles *and* cash as consideration for vacating a safe seat. In Davidson's papers is a note, dated 1 May 1929:

> I saw Mr … (MP) at 12 noon. He is prepared to resign from his constituency for a Knighthood and £15,000.
> In 1922 Bonar offered him a Baronetcy and £10,000.[5]

Davidson had also been closely involved in fixing irregular payments to FE when he was short of cash and threatening to write revelatory articles for the press; and of spiriting Maundy Gregory★ out of gaol, and installing him in France, where Gregory was to subsist for the rest of his life on a 'confidentiality' retainer.†So chequered a record of intervention, whether tactful or otherwise, can often endow a kind of immunity. But in Davidson's case,

---

★ Maundy Gregory was the go-between for those ready to bankroll Lloyd George's campaign fund in return for honours.
† See, in particular, *Memoirs of a Conservative: J. C. C. Davidson's Memoirs and Papers.*

as soon as he began to slip, there were many who had scores to settle. And the situation can hardly have been helped by a preemptive eulogy in the *Agents' Magazine*, in the immediate aftermath of the election defeat:

> The sniping in the press and elsewhere of [*sic*] a much-loved Chief has given exquisite pain to those at Headquarters familiar with Mr Davidson's sterling worth. So far from de-throning him in our affections, these cruelly unjust attacks on one who has given his very life-blood to the cause ... have merely served to increase the admiration in which a gifted leader and splendid sportsman is held.[6]

At a fast pace the Conservative Party galloped past those ritual beacons that mark the route towards an open attack on the leadership. First, the 'presentation' of policies. 'I am not sure that our advertising department was all it should have been, or that we advertised quite as effectively as we might have done' (Amery). Next, the indirect attacks on the Chairman at party groups convened 'to gather together all those who felt aggrieved over the conduct and outcome of the General Election' (the host on this occasion being Colonel Gretton MP, a 'big' brewer). Then, the personal rebukes from grandees: 'I have received your letter this morning ...' (wrote Lady Londonderry on a subject that matters not):

> ... and it is exactly the kind of letter I expected from you. If you do not realise yourself how rude the whole thing is, it only confirms to my mind how hopeless the management of our Central Office is. If you treat *me* in this very off-hand fashion, I hardly like to contemplate what occurs elsewhere.[7]

The contagion spread. Those unpleasant toxins that affect all political parties – and especially the Conservatives when in, or threatened by relegation to, opposition – ran through the parliamentary party and the former Cabinet. Mistrust, backbiting, urgent calculation of personal advancement. The fault lines could be delineated as free trade versus protectionism. This may have been convenient – but it ignored a deeper reality. Baldwin was on the 'Left' of the Conservative Party. He opposed, wherever feasible, the reactionaries. Worse (in their eyes), Baldwin within a very short time of MacDonald assuming the premiership assured him that he would not *worry* MacDonald in office, but would 'give fair play'.

What was at the back of Baldwin's mind we cannot know. Often he was ambivalent, and calculated tactically. But he was faced very soon with dangerous pressures, and they came not just from personal rivals for his job – who were numerous and each in their different way (and own view) well fitted to succeed. The lure, still, of Lloyd George and the majesty of Coalition was felt by most of those who had been worsted at the original Carlton Club meeting (a distance no further, let it be noted, than would separate the challenge of Sir Anthony Meyer in 1989 and Mr John Redwood in 1996). The polls had not even opened before a memo from Davidson was on Baldwin's desk:

> The main point about Winston is that he is not to be trusted in the Party because he is always out for office and never prepared for opposition, . . . people suspect he is already in negotiation with Lloyd George to secure a post as second man on the new ship if it is ever launched.[8]

Although Churchill also had his own claque on the Conservative back benches his threat to Baldwin was founded more on the prestige – or 'credibility' as is the current expression – that would attach to a rival of the old Coalition personalities. Lord Irwin (later to play a more significant role as Lord Halifax) remained supportive. His judgement is central to the Tory ethic – 'I still believe that SB has got a bigger hold on the country than is always realised and after all elections are not decided so much by the convinced adherents of either party, as by middle, unattached opinion which does not care greatly about high politics, but forms an impression of men.' But that last phrase was a let-out. Irwin could transfer his support at any time, if one 'man' should become preferable to another.

This, then, was what made Baldwin's position precarious. He had long made a conscious decision to resist leading the party in the direction – measured at least by the views of activists in the country and a majority of its own back-benchers – in which it wanted to go. Baldwin was not, nor ever would be, of the Right. Nor was he, by instinct, a protectionist. Although it is usually true that free-traders are drawn from the Left and protectionists from the Right it is no more valid to see this schism, which plagued the Conservative Party, particularly when in Opposition, as an exact Left–Right split than that between Euro 'phile' and 'sceptic' in the 1990s. Had it been, Baldwin might have sought relief by attaching himself to the growing advocacy of a 'National', that is to say centrist, administration. But to flirt with this Baldwin was too traditional a Tory; too wary of the traps that lay concealed in such an arrangement – not least of which was his suspicion that it was the old Lloyd George Coalition repositioning itself behind a smokescreen.

To bring this latter circumstance about there was certainly no lack of meddlers and enthusiasts: 'Figures on the fringes of political life, tied loosely to party or not at all. They included the editors of some of the quality newspapers, businessmen of various kinds, journalists, fixers, pundits and retired politicians or senior civil servants.' Exactly the company, in other words, to which the majority of Prime Ministers of all parties soon find themselves deferring, and whose esteem they seek. As Dr Stuart Ball has so percipiently observed, '. . . their parallel voices could give the impression of an emerging consensus'.[9] To this tiresome combination there was soon added a most unsettling new element. While the Conservatives appeared to have run out of steam the problems that pestered the country, in particular unemployment, had not.

The loss of marginal seats had ensured that, proportionate to the whole, the ratio of right-wing Tories returned in 1929 had increased in the parliamentary party. Some of the more vocal from this group now believed that the time had come for a concerted effort to place protection back at the forefront of Conservative economic policy – as it had been in the years before the war and, so briefly, in 1923.

Now that the free-trade Churchill had gone from the Treasury there were many who hoped that Neville Chamberlain, son of 'Radical Joe', the great prophet of Imperial Preference, would take the lead in articulating a new forward policy. Baldwin was, of course, well aware that Neville Chamberlain was his likeliest successor. He would have to be cautious in what he said. But Baldwin would still not be moved into a rash policy review. He shared with Churchill the fear that a commitment to food taxes would smash all hope of the Conservatives capturing the middle-ground liberal vote. It remained an awkward dilemma. To win back marginal constituencies in a future election, the case for resisting measures which involved taxing the basic necessities of the consumer was as powerful as ever. But to fail to make moves – or at least be seen to make moves – in this protectionist direction was to try dangerously the patience of the majority of his party.

The situation deteriorated. The rival owners of the *Daily Express* and the *Daily Mail*, Lord Beaverbrook and Lord Rothermere, buried their differences in order to rally the tariff wing of the party. Now the traditional protectionists could enhance their technical arguments with a powerful dose of populism. Baldwin's comfortable hopes that the contentious issue could be left to drift for the time being were shattered.

A variety of motives lay close to the heart of Beaverbrook's initiation of his 'Empire Crusade'. 'Empire Free Trade' was a nicely phrased expression for the abolition of free trade with the rest of the world and the introduction of food taxes. But it was firmly grounded in Beaverbrook's certainty that the creation of a common market of Britain and her Dominions could be the precursor to the vision of a more politically united Empire. This concept, geostrategic in scope, brightens, fades, and recovers at a number of points in the party's twentieth-century history. With each revisitation its credibility diminishes. Because as the century progresses Britain becomes weaker, and her centripetal strength – both military and economic – diminishes. Until, in its last stages, the policy would be cited (still, in his old age, by Beaverbrook) as a form of refuge rather than a springboard. But in the year 1929 the opportunity was yet to be grasped (although the deterioration of the world economy would, for some years, distort all national asset values). It remains a dilemma of central importance. Had the right course been followed, the possibility of staying out of a European war takes on a different credibility.

Aside from this major policy divide, personal antipathy towards Baldwin was also a potent incentive. And in this Beaverbrook was guaranteed the assistance not just of Lord Rothermere but of many others who for their own reasons had become either resentful or impatient of his cautious, not to say stagnant, approach. No effort (nor, with these affluent supporters, expense) was spared in drumming up support for the Empire Crusade. Many aspects of the campaign foreshadow in impact and technique the extravagant intervention on the British political scene, sixty-seven years distant, of Sir James Goldsmith. Only those Conservative candidates who declared support for Empire Free Trade would not, as it was threatened, have an Empire Crusade candidate fielded against them. And 'coverage', particularly by the Beaverbrook papers was, to say the least, tendentious. Three days before the (unofficial Conservative) candidate it was supporting won the Twickenham by-election of 8 August 1929, the *Daily Express* was found to be carrying the news headline '*Canada joins the Empire Crusade*'. Only very small print made clear that the reference was to a favourable comment in the *Alberta Farmer*.[10]

Yet the fact remained that the British free trade arrangements were only good and well in a reciprocal world. Such an environment was fast disappearing. The protectionist siege economies which were becoming the hallmark of so many of Britain's major foreign competitors meant that they were free to dump their exports on the British market without the British being able to retaliate on the same terms.

The record of the Conservative Party between 1929 and 1931 is not creditable. It was the official party of the Opposition, yet for most of the period it expended its principal energies in internecine squabbling and spent too little time focusing its sights on the Government.

Baldwin's failure to take a decisive lead for fear of marginalising any one wing of the party inevitably meant, just as it was to do for his successor in 1992, that colleagues would take it upon themselves publicly to try and 'bounce' him into adopting their own desired position. If he did not espouse Tariff Reform then he faced Conservative candidates losing votes to the 'Empire Crusade' Party launched by Beaverbrook. And this was an apprehension felt by a majority of his front bench, as well as most Tory back-benchers. They drew confidence from the expressed views of the extra-parliamentary party in the constituencies where the consensus was by now strongly protectionist. But Baldwin seems to have thought (just as with John Major each side believed that he was *instinctively* on theirs) that if he bowed to this pressure then he stood to lose from his team certain key heavyweights; including Churchill and the Leader in the Lords, Lord Salisbury, a devout free-trader. Such was his fear of Lloyd George and the Welshman's magnetic pull on his former ministers that Baldwin could not bring himself to let Churchill resign from the front bench for fear that Lloyd George would make work for idle hands.

Faced with these conflicting options, Baldwin had recourse to fudged compromises which pleased no faction. His position on food taxes was a primary case in point, with him moving incrementally from foodstuff to foodstuff and from referendum to 'free hand'. Each shift appeared not to come from any deep-seated command of the issues involved but as a result of a fresh bout of pressure applied on him. Detractors soon realised that the more they sat on the Party Leader, the greater the impression they made upon his subsequent articulation of policy.

In May 1930, Baldwin's outer defence ring finally collapsed. His long-time ally and confidant the Party Chairman, J. C. C. Davidson, fell on his own sword. Davidson was a scapegoat for the division and disorder in the party created by the pro-tariff movement in the wake of electoral defeat. But the Right, who had never trusted the Chairman, now tasted blood. The final straw had been an article (unsigned) by one of their number in the *Weekend Review.*

> The present chairman does not possess what must be regarded as the bare essentials of fitness for the task ... There is only one way, compatible with the well-being of the Party, out of this most unfortunate situation. The Chairman must take the necessary step himself.

The piece continued in this vein at length, with a clear message at the end: 'It must be frankly stated that in the opinion of the Party he has not "made good", that —

> The ultimate danger is that those who are never weary of intriguing against the Conservative leader may find in the question of the Chairmanship a weapon with which to strike him down.'[11]

This, of course, was perfectly clear to Baldwin. And at first he had decided to fight it out on Davidson's terrain. He convened a private party meeting at which he said, shrewdly linking the identity and status of the Chief Whip to their joint fate, that '... those who attack Mr Davidson and Sir Bolton Eyres-Monsell attack me, and if one goes, we all go'. (Just the faintest trace here of the style in which Kenneth Clarke was to 'defend' his own leader at the Conservative Party Conference in 1994.) No sooner had Baldwin made this statement than convincing evidence was proffered that the Chief Whip did in fact dispose of only small authority over the parliamentary party, and was disinclined to assert it. A highly critical Early Day Motion attracted 140 signatures.

The subject of the motion was the damage inflicted on British naval supremacy by overenthusiastic adherence (on instruction, principally, from the Treasury) to the limits on new construction imposed by the Washington Treaty. It had become apparent that the other signatories were 'cheating'. Now it seemed to the mass of Tories that not only were we ignoring the possibilities, the imperatives as the Empire Free-Traders argued, of Imperial commitment; but we were also deliberately running down the naval capability essential for its defence.

The signatures on the motion covered every 'wing' and faction in the party. Baldwin decided he could hold out no longer. Davidson was allowed to go. And in his place now arrived Neville Chamberlain, the heir presumptive.

But the problem remained. By trying to stay 'on side' with the floating voter with a non-contentious platform, Baldwin was deepening division in his party. As this found public expression so did the floating voter come to regard the Conservatives as irrevocably divided. After a while that familiar device of political leaders unsure of their authority, the referendum, made its appearance. In June Baldwin called a party meeting to endorse his policy of staging a referendum on 'food taxes' immediately after a general election. He carried the day. But proving good health by survival through continued spins at Russian roulette is a dangerous form of recreational medicine. And by October 1930 the situation was so bad that one MP, William Ormsby-Gore, admittedly a free-trader, found himself writing to Lord Salisbury that 'the Party is simply rotting before our eyes'.[12]

In the nick of time the situation was stabilised by an announcement from Richard Bennett, the Canadian Prime Minister, who had arrived in London for the Imperial Conference. To the surprise of his audience, and the deep mortification of Beaverbrook, Bennett made clear that the sort of Empire Free Trade policy which Beaverbrook was championing was 'neither desirable nor possible'.[13] Beaverbrook always maintained that Bennett acted out of pique because his old friend had sat on the fence (as indeed he had done, for reasons never made clear) in the recent Canadian general election. In all likelihood Beaverbrook had assumed that Bennett could not do without his goodwill, and his money, anyway.

It was a serious tactical miscalculation, and offered a golden opportunity for Baldwin to seize. But even now Baldwin could not move. Chamberlain, already showing his mettle, acted fast, pronouncing the 'free hand' as the new party policy and virtually guiding his leader's hand over the declaration to that effect. Baldwin's listless approach can be gauged from Amery's diary entry for that day:

> What is really rather comic about the whole business is that the idea of a statement should come not from S.B. but from others, that it should be drafted without him, taken across to the Travellers for him to sign and evidently signed after less than ten minutes' discussion, and as far as I could see without alteration.[14]

Next, Baldwin called a second party meeting to endorse the new line – and his leadership with it. This time the vote in his favour was by a clearer margin (462 to 116) although the loyalty of at least a quarter of his parliamentary party in the Commons remained questionable. This group now found fresh avenues of concern in Baldwin's support for the Labour Government's proposed constitutional reforms for India. Their stated intention was to guide the path towards the subcontinent's attainment of Dominion status. Beaverbrook had no particular interest in the Indian issue beyond a general hope that it would damage Baldwin. But Rothermere was genuinely incensed at what he took to be the impending surrender of the brightest jewel in Britain's Imperial splendour. On the front bench Rothermere found a ready ally in Winston Churchill who, following the death of Birkenhead, now took up the principal role in resistance to what was presented as a gradual relinquishment of British responsibility in government to Indian politicians.

At this time the natural feeling of most Tories was to regard with fear and suspicion Labour's aspirations for constitutional reform for India. Little wonder that many of them were aghast that far from executing his task as Leader of the Opposition, Baldwin should now speak out in favour of Labour's intentions. Baldwin's actions may to some extent have been motivated by his personal regard for the liberal-minded Viceroy, Lord Irwin. But he calculated also that resisting Indian Home Rule for partisan advantage would take Westminster politics back down the divisive road along which the protracted Irish Home Rule debate had led

the political generation before 1914. When Irwin released Gandhi
from gaol without the latter giving any guarantee to end his illegal
campaign of civil disobedience against the law, the Tory Right
were furious. But Baldwin made no move. Indeed, he spoke in
defence of the Viceroy's tactics and in favour of the general Indian
policy of the MacDonald Government.

Churchill, scenting personal advantage, leapt in. The ex–Chancellor now publicly dissociated himself both from Baldwin's
comments and from his 'Business Committee' which was making
do as a co-ordinating forum for front-bench speakers. This was
the equivalent, today, of resigning from the Shadow Cabinet. In
language wholly contrary to the mood expressed by his Party
Leader, Churchill proceeded to tell his area constituency council
that:

> It is alarming and also nauseating to see Mr Gandhi, a seditious
> Middle Temple lawyer, now posing as a fakir of a type well-known
> in the East, striding half-naked up the steps of the Vice-regal palace,
> while he is still organising and conducting a defiant campaign of
> civil disobedience, to parley on equal terms with the representative
> of the King-Emperor.[15]

In the meantime, the Empire crusade had won the South
Paddington by-election. Next, having split the Tory vote and
let in a Labour candidate at East Islington, the Beaverbrook–
Rothermere axis decided to field a candidate in one of the safest
Conservative seats in the country, Westminster St George's.

The confidence of the press lords should be seen in the context
of the utter demoralisation afflicting the Conservatives in those
first months of 1931. If there is one thing which, inevitably, gives
rise to a total failure of nerve in the parliamentary party it is by-
elections 'going wrong'. And at this point the already selected
Conservative candidate for the seat, J. T. C. Moore-Brabazon,
announced his intention of standing down rather than defend
Baldwin in public. Worse was to come. The party's principal
agent, Robert Topping, had been gathering opinion in the constituencies. His report necessarily, and for reasons of discretion,

was prolix. But it could not avoid the conclusion that 'there has grown a very definite feeling that Mr Baldwin is not strong enough to carry the Party to victory'.

When Topping started on his quest for opinion the Party Chairman (to whom he was obliged under the constitution to report) was Davidson, who would have muffled it. Since May, though, it had been Neville Chamberlain. Chamberlain was the heir presumptive. Now, it seemed, he had been handed the dagger. Canny enough to realise that he could not use it himself Chamberlain set about showing the report to, and talking it over with, selected Cabinet colleagues one by one: his brother Austen, Cunliffe-Lister, Hoare and Hailsham. Last in line was the Chief Whip, Eyres-Monsell. Then, when the news of Moore-Brabazon's defection was published, Chamberlain sent the report round, by hand, to Baldwin, accompanied by a short covering note. The Chairman apologised for adding to the Leader's anxieties at a difficult time, but went on that he would 'no doubt wish to consult regarding the contents, with colleagues'.[16]

It was Sunday 1 March. Icy cold, with snow on the ground. Baldwin was in the depths of depression. The previous day he had received an anonymous, but offensive, letter on Carlton Club headed writing paper. He telephoned to Chamberlain, 'come round at once'.

When the Chairman arrived he was told that the Leader would be resigning immediately. In all probability he would be retiring from the Commons before the election. Chamberlain said very little. He expressed neither consolation nor encouragement. But as soon as he had left, Chamberlain made contact with Geoffrey Dawson, editor of *The Times*, who set up both its front page, and the leader article, for the following day – '*Mr Baldwin Withdraws*'. It so happened, though, that Davidson had been in the house, although he had not been in the room. After Chamberlain had left, Davidson did his best to cheer Baldwin up, then departed to hold a meeting with Willie Bridgeman, a great Baldwin supporter. That evening, after dinner, the two men went back to Baldwin's house. They persuaded him not to retire meekly, but to go out with a grand gesture. The idea, ludicrous in retrospect, that *he* should fight the St George's by-election, first resigning his Worcestershire seat, began to take shape in Baldwin's head. It did not last long, and soon he allowed himself to be dissuaded. Within days a new candidate, Alfred Duff Cooper, was brought forward, and when Baldwin went to speak for him he minted one of the great political aphorisms of the century – that the press were pursuing 'power without responsibility, the prerogative of the harlot throughout the ages'. The tactic worked. Now the 'establishment' press, suddenly eager to distance themselves from their 'yellow' confrères, connived to distort the position as much to Baldwin's advantage as the Beaverbrook and Rothermere press were determined to condemn him. On the orders of Geoffrey Dawson, *The Times* always remembered to put DSO after any reference to Duff Cooper. The *Daily Telegraph* likewise put itself at the disposal of the Conservative candidate.[17] The majority was slashed, but Duff Cooper was returned.

Ironically, but as can often happen when a personalised campaign backfires, it had been the press lords' excesses which had saved Baldwin's bacon; kept him in place, indeed, for another six years. Whereas feeling in the party could well, if left to mature without outside interference, have brought about his peremptory removal.

EIGHT

Economic Crisis and 'National' Government

THE TIME THAT BALDWIN BOUGHT or, by courtesy of Rothermere and Beaverbrook, had been granted, was well spent. Neville
Chamberlain negotiated a pact with Beaverbrook, which in effect
ended the 'Empire Crusade's' by-election antics. And Gandhi, by
agreeing to call off his civil disobedience campaign in India, did
much to lower the internal temperature of the Conservative back
benches. More importantly, it was becoming clear that the Labour
Government was running into serious trouble and that a general
election might not be far off. Despite the internal havoc in the
party, all the indications now pointed to an outright Conservative
victory. The familiar argument that the 'boat' should not be rocked
so close to such a contest focused the minds of the Conservative
leadership and consolidated, for the time being, their personal
position.

It was the seemingly irreversible rise in unemployment which
acted as a constant attrition of Labour's claim to be the party best
able to help the working man. Protectionist arguments now began
to gain ground in that party also. Each month's figures signalled a
further lurch into deficit of the country's visible balance of trade;
while the Exchequer bill for unemployment benefit was plain for
all (particularly foreign bankers) to see. Yet such are the bonds of

orthodox expertise that no politician from any party could be found seriously to suggest stimulating trade by taking Britain off the gold standard and letting sterling float to a more sustainable level. Doctrinal and economic orthodoxy were at one. And Snowden, as Chancellor, let it be known that he regarded such a possibility as unthinkable.

At the end of July 1931, the May Committee revealed (conveniently, but in accordance with standard Whitehall practice in handling contentious statements), the day after Parliament had risen for its summer recess, that the expense to the Exchequer of unfunded unemployment liabilities was contributing to a projected £120 million Budget deficit for the existing financial year. From there, the position was expected to deteriorate further and to meet the situation cuts were recommended of £96.5 million. This news was serious in itself, but its timing was to be disastrous. London had misguidedly tried, and ultimately failed, to prop up collapsing German and Austrian banks in the previous months. Many City institutions had become overexposed. Reports of the Budget deficit now encouraged a concerted attack on what was left of the gold reserves by foreign and, through their overseas bank accounts, some British speculators.

This international speculation threatened to drive down sterling – still pegged in the gold standard at $4.86. To prevent this, loans were sought from France and the United States. Not unreasonably, the response was conditional on the British Government getting its own financial house in order. And this could, in effect, only be done by cutting spending – spending out of which unemployment assistance was by now taking the lion's share.

Consider at this point the unfortunate position of the Labour Prime Minister, Mr Ramsay MacDonald. At times of acute economic crisis it is usual for Prime Ministers to find that their friends are confined to that small group entirely dependent on the leader's patronage. Others, sometimes openly, more often through the medium of the background briefing, will be distancing themselves.

MacDonald's plight was worsened by the fact that he could not, even in the good times, guarantee a majority in Parliament. The allegiance of part of his own party was in doubt. Although dole money was more generous than it had been during the previous Labour Government, a large swathe of Labour's parliamentary party were deeply unhappy that meeting the crisis by 'hitting the jobless' appeared to be official policy. There were many in the Cabinet who agreed with them. Not to make the cuts, however (or so they were told), would be to invite financial collapse. The suddenness of the speculative onslaught meant (as, again, ran the received wisdom) that there was no time for a long-term strategy to meet the crisis. Something had to be done quickly to quell the outflow of reserves and attract foreign loans. This meant being seen to 'balance the books' as soon as possible.

Gladly MacDonald now shed some of his load by acceding to the Bank of England's suggestion that the leaders of the Conservative and Liberal parties be informed of the dangers of the situation. Baldwin, having so recently weathered his own storm, was on holiday. He had to be recalled from Aix-les-Bains. Neville Chamberlain was in Scotland fishing and, taking the sleeper train from Inverness, got to London first. On 13 August they had their first meeting with MacDonald and Snowden at Downing Street. Chamberlain took the lead. He conveyed (but did not say) that if the Government recalled Parliament to approve emergency measures, as recommended by the May Committee, then it would probably have the support of the Conservative Party but that further increases in taxation might not.[1]

This was hardly a specific commitment. But neither man fancied joining a government so obviously on its knees. Their ploy was to contrive the minimum association consistent with avoiding (and if possible to take credit for preventing) national collapse. After the meeting Baldwin, out of his depth in 'Persian', wisely returned to his holiday destination and left Chamberlain to monitor briefings from Bank and Treasury officials and to keep an eye on the situation.

Over the next few days, the drain on the gold reserves continued. Snowden was full of fears that the currency might collapse and Britain would suffer Weimar Germany's disastrous experience with hyperinflation. (An indication, it may be suggested, both that the Chancellor was being deliberately misled by officials who wanted to be rid of him; and that theory of the relationship between inflation and the money supply was still in its infancy.)

The cross-party discussion resumed on 20 August. Sir Herbert Samuel led for the Liberals in place of Lloyd George who was convalescing after a serious operation, although whether his presence would have made much difference seems unlikely. Baldwin saw no point in returning a second time from the south of France so for the Conservatives Chamberlain was joined by the ambitious (and thus highly conformist) figure of the young Sir Samuel Hoare, who was Lord Beaverbrook's new favourite. Snowden revealed that the estimated Budget deficit of £120 million would now have to be revised upwards by a further £50 million. The economies he proposed still left a yawning deficit in the Government's finances of more than £90 million and, after the Cabinet had whittled down Snowden's proposals further the following day, the deficit rose to £114 million.

Chamberlain and Hoare weighed up the situation. If the Government was in fact going to survive then they must not be seen to have withheld their support. On 22 August both men thought they liked the look of a revised Government scheme – on the condition that the Bank of England considered it would be sufficient to meet the immediate emergency. Chamberlain believed that MacDonald would receive the support of his Cabinet in pushing through these measures and that the crisis would pass.

The proposals however, which included a 10 per cent cut in unemployment benefit, caused grievous dissension around the Cabinet table, with a group informally centred around the Foreign Secretary, Arthur Henderson, refusing to agree. Wearily MacDonald informed King George V, after compelling him to cut short his stay at Balmoral, that his Government was on the verge of breaking up. This news brought Baldwin back to London. Could there be an opening? Straightaway he dined with his friend Geoffrey Dawson. But the *Times* editor, ever Establishment-minded, played 'a straight bat'. Dawson expressed the hope that the Conservative Party would support the Labour Government's efforts.

Baldwin listened, but was unconvinced. Clearly he thought that MacDonald's position was irretrievable and that within days he himself would be kissing hands at the Palace. The following morning he discussed tactics with Chamberlain. The Shadow Chancellor* was less sanguine. He told Baldwin that until a dissolution occurred (and this was hardly possible in the middle of an imminent financial collapse) a Conservative administration could not survive in the Commons without offering places to Liberals and, if they were interested, securing MacDonald and Snowden as well.

Then, on the evening of 23 August, the Government collapsed when half of the Cabinet refused to accept the economy proposals. MacDonald tendered his resignation to the King.

The royal mood had been somewhat affronted by MacDonald's peremptory intrusion on the Balmoral holiday. The King was fretting at Windsor, and pining for the heather. None the less His Majesty urged MacDonald to try and mould a new temporary government with Conservative and Liberal support. Still fresh in the royal memory, and in the mind of those to whom the King looked for immediate advice, was the 'close shave' of 1926. What might be the mood of the working class if 'the Bankers' were seen to have brought down their very own government?

This royal suggestion was not what Baldwin had been hoping for. His whole policy and deportment over the preceding seven years had been conceived to illustrate his own centrist and healing credentials. However, when his monarch put it to him formally,

---

* Although the post did not yet officially exist, Chamberlain's replacement of Churchill as chairman of the Conservatives' Finance Committee in April 1931 ensured that he was the party's chief spokesman on economic policy and, in effect, the Chancellor-in-waiting.

along with Samuel and MacDonald, at Buckingham Palace on the morning of 24 August, he could hardly turn aside.

Thus, conceived as a temporary measure for a proposed duration of a matter of weeks, the force which was to dominate British politics for the rest of the decade, the National Government, came into being. It having been created in such a hurry, the component figures in this administration now had to seek endorsement from their parliamentary parties. The Conservatives had gone into the summer recess aware that Labour's minority Government was tottering and expecting an outright Tory success in an autumnal general election. Instead, MPs returned for the reconvened Parliament on 8 September to a situation in which Baldwin had joined a Cabinet headed by Ramsay MacDonald. Despite the fact that the new Government was overwhelmingly dependent on the massed ranks of the Parliamentary Conservative Party, of the ten seats in the emergency Cabinet only four went to Conservatives. Neville Chamberlain went back (perhaps shrewdly) to the Ministry of Health, the post he had held with distinction in the 1924–9 administration; Hoare went to the India Office, and Sir Philip Cunliffe-Lister became President of the Board of Trade. Baldwin opted to become Lord President in Council, an office which conferred on him the air (and reality) of an *éminence grise*. More than a handful, it is true, of Conservatives on the Right, like Leo Amery, were unhappy about this sudden metamorphosis. But the atmosphere was one of crisis. And hardly any Conservative MP now spoke up against their leader's decision. The attributes of courage, statesmanship and 'country before party' were now showered upon the man so many had wanted rid of only months before. That same individual whose resignation had been specifically recommended in the memorandum to the Party Chairman. The party's commitment towards the National Government, being unavoidable, became, almost overnight, total and resolute.

This position was markedly in contrast to that adopted by the Parliamentary Labour Party who were aghast at the manoeuvres of MacDonald and suspected (wrongly) that events had a pre-planned air about them. The Prime Minister's decision, along with those Labour MPs who joined him in the new Cabinet, not to attend a party meeting convened to discuss their future finished any lingering hopes that they might be allowed to stay within the Labour Party. Instead, MacDonald and Snowden headed the list of those expelled from the party and only eight back-bench Labour MPs declared support for the new Government, one of which was MacDonald's own son, Malcolm. J. H. Thomas, a Labour minister who joined the new Cabinet, found that his own trade union, the National Union of Railwaymen, which he had served as political secretary, now pronounced him ineligible to claim his pension from them.

All these actions took place on the assumption that the new alignment was to be of interim duration. Perhaps of no more than a few weeks in length. It seems unlikely that when reluctantly they agreed to take up the King's Commission, MacDonald and Snowden realised that they would be permanently cutting themselves adrift from the Labour Movement they had nurtured to manhood.

This expectation of a short administrative life also affected, but in a very different way, the attitudes of those Conservatives who in contrast were now endorsing their leader's behaviour. The new Government had two stated aims: to save sterling and balance the Budget. These aims were, in any case, regarded as complementary to each other. Once an emergency Budget had been passed to bring this about and the run on the reserves had been halted, it was seemingly clear that there was no Tory motive in staying in the administration.

Conservatives were convinced that Britain could not be put back onto a sure economic footing without the protective tariff measures to which Baldwin had been forced to commit himself. Since these could not be introduced by a National Government which included such staunch free-trade figures as Snowden and the Liberal, Sir Herbert Samuel, a general election on the old party lines was promised soon with the Tories fighting it on a platform of commitment to tariffs. This was made explicit at the time and seemed not just logical but inevitable.[2]

★   ★   ★

There now occurred one of those episodes of which examples can often be found in the long run of history – whose significance is hugely magnified by their timing and the context in which they take place.

The mass of the Royal Navy's capital ships – what in former times would have been called the Grand Fleet – was assembling at Invergordon, prior to setting sail for the autumn Atlantic exercise. From the outset a number of malign coincidences accumulated, setting the scene for national humiliation. The Admiral, Sir Michael Hodges, was taken suddenly ill with pleurisy. He was put in hospital ashore and his flagship, *Nelson*, remained at Portsmouth. The commander of the battle-cruiser squadron was appointed to take Hodges's place. This was Rear-Admiral Tomkinson, who at once transferred his flag to *Hood*, but was barely senior to two other candidates for the temporary overall command, E. A. Astley-Rushton and Wilfred French.

Just before Tomkinson sailed north from Portsmouth the Admiralty had transmitted a signal:

> For the Navy the sacrifice involves the acceptance of the recommendations of the Report of the Committee on National Expenditure [the May Committee] and these include placing all officers and men at present in receipt of pay on 1919 scales on the revised scale introduced in October 1925 and reducing all standard rates of pay of officers by 11 instead of eight per cent, as previously decided to come into force in July last...[3]

– but this was sent not to Tomkinson but to the *Nelson* where Hodges's chief of staff drafted an acknowledgement for his signature, then locked it in the safe pending the Admiral's return from hospital. The topic was mentioned 'in passing' to Tomkinson, who agreed with this course of action. But by the time *Hood* reached Invergordon the whole anchorage was alive with rumour. Launches and small craft were running from ship to ship distributing newspapers, while many of the crew had heard on the BBC details of Snowden's emergency Budget. The Admiralty, sensing trouble, had sent all squadron commanders an 'explanatory' note. But Tomkinson's, once again, went to the wrong ship. Both Astley-Rushton and French had received this note, but neither of them advised their flag officer.

It was thus both with alarm, and some incomprehension, that Tomkinson found his own crew becoming first sullen, then boisterously unco-operative. On Sunday 12 September, a large contingent from the Fleet (not all with shore passes) had attended the Invergordon Games. In the evening there was rowdiness; impromptu meetings were addressed by 'troublemakers'. And some officers, frequenting the canteens in civilian dress, were roughly handled. The longboats bringing back libertymen were late, and noisy. Bawdy and disrespectful shanties echoed across the harbour. All this was hardly surprising as an able-seaman's pay was being cut from four to three shillings per week. And the *Daily Worker*, *Daily Herald* and *Scottish Daily Record* were freely circulating with inflammatory predictions of still more savage cuts in pay. On the Sunday *Nelson* turned up, having left Hodges on his sick-bed, and Tomkinson finally received his letter.

That same day two of the capital ships – *Warspite* and *Malaya* – sailed on time for the exercise, their crews drawn up in perfect order on the forecastle and quarter-decks. Tomkinson recovered his poise enough to signal the Admiralty that:

> There was a slight disturbance in the Royal Naval canteen, Invergordon on Sunday evening, caused by one or two ratings endeavouring to address those present on the subject of reduction in pay. I attach no importance to the incident from a general disciplinary point of view, but it is possible it may be reported in an exaggerated form by the Press. Matter is still being investigated.[4]

Within twenty-four hours, though, a 'slight disturbance' had become a mutiny. Crews were refusing to man the winches and unshackle cables so as to allow the remaining ships to put to sea. Only *Repulse* left the harbour in good order. Both the new 16-inch battleships *Rodney* and the absent C-in-C's *Nelson*, together with a half-dozen cruisers and many smaller craft, were in a state of indiscipline. Lusty singing of 'The Red Flag' could be heard.

Tomkinson's signals to the Admiralty now issued thick and fast, all of them classified as 'Immediate':

> Further disturbances took place ... there is considerable unrest among the lower ratings ... considerable proportions of ships' companies have absented themselves from duty ...

The Admiralty made only cursory response. Tomkinson raised the stakes, insisting that some concession should be made to these grievances.

> I would urge a very early decision should be communicated by their Lordships. Until this is received I regret that, in my opinion, discipline in the Atlantic fleet will not be restored and may still further deteriorate.[5]

For all of Tuesday 15 September the Admiralty remained silent. Although, as records subsequently showed, there were those who made the case for turning guns on the mutineers. Then, at 7 p.m., came an appeal for 'loyalty' coupled with a meaningless assurance that 'The Board of Admiralty will always give their earnest and immediate consideration in representations of hardship ...' By now Tomkinson was not merely alarmed (reports indicated that few ships' companies were abed, but roaming the decks and communicating with each other by flag and loud hailer), he was angry. At 1 a.m. Tomkinson signalled:

> I must emphasise that the situation at Invergordon will not [sic] be met until definite decisions have been communicated. A continuation of the exercise programme is out of the question in the present state of mind of a considerable proportion of the crews.[6]

Throughout Wednesday the entire Fleet remained, effectively, inoperable. Tomkinson played his last card, signalling for 'Most Immediate' response his fear that crews would soon begin to sabotage machinery, or break out of their ships.

And that night their lordships caved in. The Atlantic exercise was cancelled, and Fleet units were instructed to sail to their individual home ports. Thus *Rodney* and *Nelson* returned to Portsmouth; *Hood* to Devonport. Much shore leave was granted and, predictably, ratings preferred the company of their families to the rantings of agitators in temperance halls. The mutiny petered out. Although as an effective military force the Royal Navy remained for many months gravely diminished. Tomkinson himself was, in the fullness of time, censured and dismissed; learning the news from a BBC bulletin while at sea *en route* for the West Indies spring cruise.

The Invergordon mutiny, in terms of bloodshed, violence or even dislocation, was relatively unimportant. But it came at the end of a month-long period of alarm and turbulence in world financial markets. 'As safe as the Bank of England' had been seen already as a hollow claim. Now it was joined by 'as strong as the British Navy'.

News of the mutiny straddled the world's headlines over the very same days that the confidence debate, and Snowden's emergency Budget, preoccupied the House of Commons. Hourly the reserves drained away and the exchange rate against the US dollar shrank. Had not insurrection in both Germany and Russia started, little more than a decade earlier, in their navies? 'Our Navy is us', had pronounced Ramsay MacDonald himself.[7] And so it was. On that very evening that the Fleet slowly and separately steamed out of Invergordon harbour on a southerly course the gold sovereign abandoned for ever its historic dominance of the global exchanges.

On 21 September a Bill had been rushed through Parliament, suspending all sterling payments in gold. The currency could now float freely on the foreign exchanges. There was an immediate dive in value, but it eased off and soon the pound began a more gentle climb back. Thus the decision to let sterling float, one that had been resisted by all members of the Cabinet until the very last moment, clinging to the hope – as would their successors on many such occasions in the future – that their mere resolute presence would drive off the speculators, eased the situation.

There were many who resented the blow to national pride that the speculators had dealt to sterling. It was something for which there was no precedent in living memory. But the international financiers, demonised at that time as the 'Bankers' ramp'; on a later occasion as the 'Gnomes of Zurich'; later still as 'the Forex dealers' – even, by no less a person than the President of the United States as the 'Bond Markets' – could not be resisted. Running for them in harness were the three strongest forces in the financial arena – a troika of greed, fear and rationale. (Ironically the speculators had done as much as any number of Cabinet decisions to foster Britain's subsequent economic recovery.) The beneficial effects of a floating currency were to be profound but not immediate – although it was not long before the Bank and the Treasury were busy attempting to transform a floating currency into a managed one.

The weeks following sterling's uncontrived exit from the gold standard were difficult ones in which the Establishment, at Westminster, at Whitehall, and in the City, held its breath as sterling continued to fall and unemployment continued to rise. Sterling, which had been fixed at $4.86, at one point fell as low as $3.23. This, it was now argued, was no time to cause further uncertainty by breaking up the National Government.

The Conservative leadership now had to consider the position carefully. It was not in the national interest to seek party advantage in the narrow sense by breaking up the great Coalition. But how long could they continue in a government whose broad character would not endorse the exclusive protectionist doctrine which the Conservatives had come to regard as their only sure means of redemption? Desperately short of funds, the Liberals were not keen to hold a general election, and from his bedside the invalided Lloyd George was ordering his lieutenants in the Cabinet on no account to concede on this point. While certain Labour ministers in the Government, including Ramsay MacDonald and J. H. Thomas, were now known to have lost faith in free trade and were, at least at the edges, amenable to Tory pressure. Furthermore, because they had been rudely expelled from their own party, these Labour ministers had no political future should the Government break up. Personal motivation may not have been the main force at work here, but it was asking a lot of human nature (and MacDonald was famously vain) not to identify it in the background.

As with so many of his decisions, the apparently ruminant Baldwin acted suddenly and decisively in opting to force upon the Cabinet a general election which the parties within the National Government would fight (supposedly) together as separate parties but under a joint appeal. Many of the non-Conservative members of the Cabinet were reluctant. But Baldwin knew, as did each one of them, that a Conservative withdrawal from the administration, and its resulting collapse, would leave them nowhere to go. It was a reminder of the first democratic truth – that no argument succeeds without a parliamentary majority at its back.

The Liberals seemed destined to lose whatever the outcome, but Samuel's attempt to keep the Liberal contingent under the National umbrella so infuriated Lloyd George that the latter withdrew his personal support from the Government and went into Opposition. Like the Labour Party, they had split. But unlike Labour, it was mortal.

Not always obliquely, Conservative electoral addresses on the campaign stump made abundantly obvious that the party favoured protection but the official line of the 'National' message was merely to ask for a 'doctor's mandate' on the issue. Promising an impartial and scientific examination once re-elected to take – or avoid – whatever (unspecified) measures on tariffs it found to be necessary. This was of course a deliberate compromise framed to stop the non-Conservative ministers in the appeal creating undue discord. Not that this was necessary. Power beckoned at last. Disputation (if any) could come later.

The election itself was a mosaic of confusion. For the most part, constituency associations were prevailed upon to withdraw candidates of rival pro-National parties so that there was only one candidate standing on the National ticket in each constituency. As a result, there were 409 straight fights as against 102 at the previous election in 1929. The notion being that the National candidate selected to fight would be the one who (on the basis of the last election) could best be expected to retain the seat or gain it from the Labour Opposition. This reduced the number of Liberal candidates markedly, to the chagrin of Samuel, but given the state of the party's finances the sacrifice was more symbolic than real. In all too many cases, there was no sacrifice at all, and rival National Liberal and Conservative candidates fought each other for votes in the same constituency against a Socialist. A Conservative even stood against Samuel himself, to the scarcely concealed smirks of many around Westminster who could not abide 'Slippery Sam'.

Whilst a number of scare stories put out (largely by Liberals, then, as always, past masters in the art) about what the Opposition would do if returned to power were fanciful to the point of being deliberately misleading, this was indeed an election in which the Labour campaign was openly founded on socialism and class conflict. But besides being unpopular this was in many cases personally inconsistent. The – former – self-appointed scourge of the plutocrat and rentier (a category rather broadly drawn), Snowden now had the temerity to describe in an election broadcast the Labour Party in which he had so recently been a leading light as 'Bolshevism run mad'. Yet, if this was a little colourful, it was the sort of abuse that the Labour campaign was bound to generate. Its appeal to the masses to overthrow the classes misread the mood of the moment. The claim that the crisis was manufactured by a 'Banker's ramp' was scarcely credible – indeed if the Bank of England and opinion in the City was suspect, then it was because in advising the Government they underestimated the stringency of the measures needed to restore confidence. Sloganeering against the 'rich', a category which on closer inspection seemed to include anyone not actually down a coalmine, only further reduced Labour's appeal.

Inevitably, the first-past-the-post system magnified the electoral swing against Labour, but even without this, the result was an enormous vote of confidence in the forces making up the National Government. In 1929, Baldwin had gone down to defeat on the supposedly complacent slogan of 'Safety first'. In 1931 the situation was more grave and thus entirely different: faced with the prospect of putting the country in the hands of the radical detritus of a Labour government which had clearly failed was far less appealing than clinging to the reassuring image of unflappability of which Baldwin was the living embodiment. The year 1931 saw also the final consummation of Baldwin's game plan of squeezing the Liberal vote: the reduction in number of Liberal candidates ensured that many Liberal voters switched to the Conservatives (despite Lloyd George's advice to vote for the candidate – usually Labour – who promised to preserve free trade).

When all the results had been tallied, the scale of the landslide became apparent. It was the only election of the century in which a government was returned with more than 60 per cent of the vote. Combined, the National forces claimed the return of 521 seats, the cumulation of results in which even some of the most unlikely and depressed industrial wastelands of the north returned pro-National candidates.

They may have styled themselves as 'National'. But when their colours were shown, party allegiance broke down thus: of the new MPs, 473 were Conservative, 13 were 'National Labour' supporters of MacDonald, and the rest were divided between the two factions of the pro-National Liberal Party, one led by Samuel and the other by Sir John Simon. The anti-National faction of Liberals loyal to Lloyd George saw only four successful returns, three of whom were relations of the old man. But the end of Lloyd George as a serious force in politics was nothing compared to the destruction visited on the Labour Party. Humiliated by its own divisions, Labour were reduced to fifty-two MPs. None of its senior figures were returned. George Lansbury, whose political career had peaked in the office of First Commissioner of Works, was the only member of the late Labour Government to be returned. This honourable and muddled man now found himself Leader of the Party by default. But concern for the poor and a pacifist commitment to abolishing Britain's already inadequate means of self-defence are not a credible specification for a national leader.

MacDonald retained the premiership, although his credentials for royal sponsorship had markedly diminished. Baldwin felt it prudent to stay on as Lord President. But possessed now of a parliamentary majority on a scale unprecedented in British history, he could have taken – for himself and his followers – any job in government that he fancied. The rigorous Neville Chamberlain now took over at the Treasury, and all was in place for the Conservative domination of national life. The Opposition was irrelevant. From the other side of the Chamber, at least. And also, for the time being, from within the Tories' own ranks. Surrounded by new faces who owed their seats to the circumstances of recent months, and the moderate appeal with which he associated himself, Baldwin no longer needed to bother about his ever critical right wing. Nor was there any need to offer office to free-thinking mavericks like Winston Churchill who might (Baldwin's analogy had moved across from 'dry bob' to 'wet bob'*) *rock the boat*.

For the Tory Party which had emerged from the debris of the Carlton Club meeting ten years before had finally attained full status. Nothing now could stop the introduction of protection. Nothing now could prevent the means of confronting the desperate economic situation by orthodox balancing of the Budget and reductions in state spending. With unemployment heading towards three million, the immediate issue was the cut in payments to the jobless and to those on state salaries. While the universal public desire for disarmament surrendered to the Treasury grounds for shaving off yet further cuts from defence spending. The pattern of politics for the 1930s had been set.

---

* Cricket and sculling, in the parlance of Etonians.

NINE

Foreign Affairs

Problems with the Versailles settlement – Mussolini is
troublesome – The Hoare–Laval Pact – The arrival of
Anthony Eden – The Rhineland – Appeasement, a
respectable policy – Baldwin's days are numbered.

STUDENTS WHO TURN TO THE diaries of Lord Balniel in August
of 1914, remembering that he sat in the House of Commons as
the elder son of the Earl of Crawford and Balcarres, and was Tory
Chief Whip at the time, may be surprised by the subject matter
for the entry of Thursday the 4th. On this day the uhlan lancers
were storming across Belgium, and Sir Edward Grey had finally
succeeded in ... forcing? shaming? his colleagues to go to war.
These subjects are not touched upon in the Chief Whip's notes.
Balniel was preoccupied with the notion that certain regiments in
the British Army, at the Curragh barracks in Ireland, might mutiny
if ordered to go in and discipline the Orangemen, and about the
effect that this might have upon Conservative back-benchers and
thus on the passage of parliamentary 'business'. A similar insouciance concerning events in Europe can certainly be found in the
letters, and in the business papers of members of the Government
in the early months of 1933.

Adolf Hitler – who was he? Something of a rabble-rouser, it
seemed. And not overscrupulous in his use of violence. At one
point in the past he had attempted to stage a coup; had, indeed,
served a stint in gaol. But in January of this year he had come to
power 'democratically'. Insofar as any official appreciation of what
this implied can be traced at all, Hitler is seen as an improvement

on the various Freikorps thugs who had wandered on and off the disorderly stage of German politics since the war's end. 'The German Chancellor' as he was punctiliously, and without exception, described henceforth was soundly anti-Red, and was setting about the Spartacists and their ilk with enthusiasm. He was 'sensible' in his relations with industrialists. Had, indeed, murdered (on the Night of the Long Knives in June of 1934) the leading figures in his own, Nazi Party* who were committed to socialism.

None the less, at the start of the thirties there could be detected a subtle, but unwelcome, change in the climate of international affairs. Most portentous had been the Japanese invasion of Manchuria in 1931. Japan was a formidable military power, undefeated in battle, and with an enormous navy: ten modern battleships, thirty-four cruisers and 123 destroyers. Frail and delicate did the elegant, white-painted sloops and cruisers of the Royal Navy's China Squadron look beside this armada. Already Japanese experimentation with airborne torpedo bombers was far ahead of any other navy, and their carriers exceeded the combined total of British and US Pacific Ocean strength.

A fleet of this size was far beyond the needs of protecting seaborne trade. It completely outclassed the few remaining hulks of the Soviet Far Eastern fleet at Vladivostok, the survivors of the rout at Tsushiba some twenty-five years earlier. Japanese new construction could have only one objective – a trial of strength with the Royal Navy. And then, once the South China Seas had been cleared and the British trading stations and colonial outposts annexed, there would be a sufficient tonnage of guns and armour-plate to deter the United States from sailing west of Hawaii.

If this contingency was distant from the strategic planners in Whitehall, from the electorate at large it was utterly remote. On 14 October 1933 the random, inchoate Disarmament Conference in Geneva, largely – even from the outset – presentational in character, had been jolted by a German walk-out. Far from arousing a feeling that some measure of cautious rearmament might

* National Socialist German Workers' Party.

now be prudent this had the effect, greatly exaggerated by the manner of its reportage in the 'yellow' press, of starting a 'war scare'. The incident came in the middle of a by-election campaign in the East Fulham constituency. The Tory candidate, a local alderman, was defending a majority of 14,000. Against him stood an Independent Labour Party (ILP) agitator who campaigned on an 'anti-war' ticket. The unfortunate alderman found himself daily being heckled as 'demanding armaments and war' even though he was resolute in avoiding the topic altogether. A special message from George Lansbury was distributed with every ILP election address: 'I would close every recruiting station, disband the army and dismiss the air force. I would abolish the whole dreadful equipment of war, and say to the world -"Do your worst".'[1] This kind of maso-pacifism does sometimes break surface within the Labour Party, nearly always causing damage to its authors. But not in East Fulham in October 1933. The ILP won the seat with a majority of 5,000.

The lessons of this result were to dominate policy; attitude to, and presentation of, 'news'; and the speeches and deportment of most performers in public life until – not even the Munich 'crisis' – the annexation of Prague more than five years later. The Labour Party, anxious not to be outflanked on the Left, now adopted 'disarmament' (occasionally, but not often, linked to 'collective security') as Opposition policy. The press, while ready always to make mischief, traded without scruple on the rejection of 'warmongering'. Whatever strategic decisions a government might in the future have to consider, public utterance would henceforth be confined to platitude and reassurance – with the inevitable result that these sentiments soon invaded the area of private discussion also.

The ten-year rule (under which there was a running assumption, in all matters of equipment and supply procurement, that a major war was unlikely for at least ten years) had been revoked. But a Defence White Paper, most tentatively approaching the topic of rearmament, had to go through several drafts in order to play down any possible inference as to the identity or source of future threats, which might (or so the Foreign Office advised) have damaged our diplomatic relations. Which made it less easy to defend against Attlee's charge, when debated in the Commons under a vote of censure, that 'we deny the proposition that an increased British Air Force will make for the peace of the world'. Or the attack from the Liberal benches led by Sir Archibald Sinclair (later to have a place in Churchill's War Cabinet) on the 'folly, danger and wastefulness of this steady accumulation of armaments'.

In fact public apprehensions, such as they were, focused more on Mussolini than on Hitler. The Italians had been asserting themselves as a colonial power, quite openly subjecting British citizens to insult and provocation.* Their campaign against the Abyssinian tribesmen was brutal as well as clumsy, and involved the first use of poison gas from aircraft. While the reaction of the League of Nations – impotence; of our French allies – corruption, (the French Foreign Minister, Pierre Laval, of whom more will be heard, had actually accepted a huge bribe from the Italians in order to dissuade – which did not prove difficult – his British counterpart from pursuing oil sanctions against the aggressor) compounded our humiliation.

As details emerged of the agreement between Baldwin's Foreign Secretary, Sir Samuel Hoare, and M. Laval, which actually 'awarded' more Abyssinian territory to the Italians than that which they had conquered, and which amounted to a shameless abandonment of the principles of the League of Nations, its 'Covenant' and the concept of Collective Security, a political storm blew up. Hoare was sacked. The young and politically acceptable Anthony Eden was put in his place.

'Foreign affairs' now dominated the news. The League of Nations Union staged a 'Peace Ballot'. A quarter of those polled answered 'No' to the question 'Should an aggressor be stopped by

---

* An example that aroused great indignation was carried in the *Daily Herald* in June 1935. While traversing the Suez Canal the crew of the Italian battleship *Cavour* lined her decks in order better to urinate on a British lighter that was passing alongside.

economic, or if necessary military, measures?' Another 20 per cent were 'Don't know's. The whole mood was irrational. None thought to question the validity of an answer that did not first put the question: ' "Aggressor" against *whom*?' And yet slowly, but ominously, there were threats against the British Empire gathering critical mass. The sooner that the whole issue of strategic priorities could clearly be addressed, the sooner could the Conservative Party unite in its traditional role.

The majority of MPs, as of the public at large, felt that the Versailles Treaty was now 'over'; that it had been needlessly puni-tive; and that Germany's period of penitence could quietly draw to a close. So when, in March of 1936, German troops marched into the demilitarised Rhineland attention was focused on Hitler's accompanying statement, with its talk of guaranteeing peace for twenty-five years and general disclaimer of warlike intention. The Establishment attitude is well illustrated by the substance of a memorandum addressed privately to the Prime Minister* by a former Cabinet Secretary:

1 Welcome Hitler's declaration ['guaranteeing' peace] whole-heartedly.

2 Condemn entry of German troops into forbidden zone. Palliate offence, as the last and least of the breaches of Part V of the Treaty, of which German rearmament was the chief. Treat this as relatively *de minimis*, and not to be taken tragically in view of the peace proposals which accompany it. Versailles is now a corpse and should be buried...

3 *Treat entrance to zone as assertion, demonstration of recovered status of equality and not as act of aggression.*

4 Go on with our rearmament programme ... No friend of European peace wants a weak and undefended England. Germany will not object and any other course would be entirely mis-understood ... This does not exclude consideration of dis-armament later.

* Baldwin succeeded Ramsay MacDonald as Prime Minister in June 1935.

5 Accept Hitler's declaration as being made in good faith ... If he
plays false you are no worse off and you put him wrong in the eyes
of the world and particularly of USA.
6 Summon a conference in London as soon as ever possible to
examine Hitler's peace programme. He is alarmed by the Franco-
Russian pact. He wants above all to be accepted by England as
respectable ...
7 Invite Germany over here at once to partake in the conclusions
of the Naval Conference ...
8 This is the last 'bus' and all turns on SB catching it tomorrow.[2]

Here, complete in every aspect, are the practical recommendations for implementing appeasement policy. From the
fatuous – 'palliate offence'; to the realistic – 'Go on with our
rearmament programme'. From the hypocritical – 'Accept Hitler's
declaration as being made in good faith'; to the delusory – 'He is
alarmed by the Franco-Russian pact'. Unsettling, too, for Baldwin
was the verdict that 'this is the last bus'. It was also premature. But
the fact remained that with each successive attrition by Germany
of the Versailles settlement that was to go by without a 'general
understanding' (if necessary by secret protocol) the risk would
magnify of war by accident.

Baldwin had by now become insecure in his position. The Prime
Minister had suffered something of a nervous breakdown, no less
troublesome for being both mild and intermittent. And his touch
in the field of foreign affairs was becoming increasingly unassertive,
if not hesitant. The Prime Minister had been here before, of
course. Twice, at least, over the last decade he had been on the
point, or so it seemed, of being forced from office. But on each
of those two occasions there had been no obvious successor. This
time it was different. Neville Chamberlain was waiting in the
wings, cool, self-assured and with seemingly limitless reserves of
stamina. Baldwin was, on his own admission, 'dreadfully weary'
and suffering from dizzy spells.

On the weekend of 22 May 1936 fell the Whitsun Bank Holiday.

Neither House of Parliament was in session; and a gathering of Tory notables assembled as guests of Lord Winterton at his country house, Shillinglee Park, in Sussex. The composition of this group was significant notably on account of its including – apparently at random – a good cross-section of grandees. Among the guests were Austen Chamberlain, still formally respected but now, in terms of his prospects for the highest offices, safely neutered by the passage of time and the eclipse of reputation; Sir Henry Page-Croft, rich and 'reliable', widely respected on account of his readiness to declaim concerning such abstractions as principle or conscience. Only a couple of years before, Page-Croft had circulated every constituency association ahead of the Party Conference with his opinions concerning Indian Home Rule. A row followed, with Central Office complaining of improper conduct. Page-Croft, unrepentant, issued a statement: 'What I have written, I have written, and I will never hesitate personally to address any communications to Conservatives at any time when I consider that there is danger to British or Imperial interests.'[3]

It was at conclaves such as this that the strategic direction of party policy was discussed. There would be no agenda – save what the participants carried each in their own head; no officials would be present; no minutes would be taken; there would be no sitting around a table save one which was heavily laden with silver-lidded dishes and decanters of wine. But Baldwin knew what was up. This was an execution squad; and they were preparing for action at the customary time – just before the summer recess. Tetchy from fatigue, thirteen years in the job and recently – or so some authorities claim – near to a complete nervous collapse, the Prime Minister, goaded at Question Time, told the House of Commons that it was '... the time of the year when midges come out of dirty ditches'.[4]

As the time for recess approached, more trouble, of a purely local nature, pressed in on the Number 10 office. Jim Thomas, the Colonial Secretary, had leaked some of the contents of the Budget in April of that year. Promptly he was sacked. But now there was gossip about his intentions. In return for a large sum he had been persuaded to contribute to the *Daily Mail* articles of 'personal and political reminiscence'. This could mean anything. On 16 July Baldwin's private secretary had received an unwelcome letter:

> I've had a rather frightening talk with Jim on the telephone. He really seems to be going under – no work, no companionship, etc, and his family are also rather fussed. He's terribly anxious about the money problem and is quite convinced that this delay means that nothing is coming.
>
> I didn't have much success in calming him so I wondered if it is in any way possible to hurry on – and come to a quick decision...[5]

As Lord Davidson's biographer delphically notes, '... the matter was discreetly and efficiently organised, and ... Thomas was saved from complete penury' (nor, of course, did the *Daily Mail* carry his 'reminiscences'). The sickly atmosphere persisted, though. Baldwin withdrew to Chequers, with the intention of walking the countryside, then moving on to Gregynog, the great house in mid-Wales owned by Tom Jones's two friends and supporters, the Misses Davies.

But the Prime Minister felt too exhausted to walk much. In his pocket he carried a letter, marked by the semblance of affection, from Davidson. It warned of a 'vague feeling', 'even among your most devoted supporters, that there is some truth in the accusation of "lack of cabinet control by the PM" '. Unsubtly shifting blame, Davidson then mentioned 'that the inactivity of your colleagues in your support confirms the criticism'. The customary sporting analogy followed with the image of '... a very tired fox ... gone to ground at Chequers, with no fight left in him'.[6]

Just before leaving for Wales Baldwin had submitted to a medical examination. Naturally it was conducted by Lord Dawson who, whatever may be thought of his narrow diagnostic powers, was adept at telling distinguished patients what privately they wished to hear. After subjection to what sounds like a very early adaptation of a cardiometer – 'I sat as if I were going to be electrocuted, in a chair with wires attached to both arms and one leg ...' – the Prime Minister was told to *go very easy and try to lose sense of time* for the next three months.[7]

This, from the country's point of view, was unfortunate advice. The Government had, in the judgement of one of its most percipient historians,* already had a 'bad' nine months. Partly this may be explained by Baldwin having to pay the price in terms of irritation and even, periodically, of instability for his failure better to balance party factions in constructing the administration after victory in the 1935 general election. Yet, the paradox remains that all of the factors whose convergence were causing loss of confidence were outwith the normal band of domestic preoccupation. Earnings, production, employment – especially in the South-East – were in recovery and heading for a better pattern than would be seen again at any time until the mid-eighties. This was baffling for Baldwin, upon whose claim to understand and interpret the feelings of ordinary electors rested his reputation – and his usefulness – to the party.

But the decade of 1930–40 was a period when most unusually the interpretation of 'news' and the standing of governments was measured largely within the context of international affairs and diplomacy. There was much violence; abroad but distant. And a subconscious impression widened its spread to include – as was one of the period's more durable clichés – 'the man in the street', that there were forces ready and gaining strength to assault, with every intention of subjugating, the amiable and placid democracies of the West.

The question was still unsettled. To what extent, and when, would this feeling start to displace the longing for Peace at Any Price? And as this shift gathered momentum, who would be best placed to take from it party or, more particularly, personal advantage? In the normal course of events such questions could be expected to come to the forefront when Parliament returned.

* Robert Rhodes James.

The month of November is often critical in the history of the Conservative Party. But natural evolution would shortly come to a full stop as a strange and unprecedented catastrophe took shape.

TEN

The Abdication

A badly behaved Prince – The Establishment is
apprehensive – HRH becomes infatuated – A dilemma
is posed – The temperature rises – Stanley Baldwin takes
his opportunity.

IN THE LATE SUMMER OF 1936 the behaviour of the King could
no longer be ignored. It was erratic, careless of protocol, intermittently – and unpredictably – rude. And by the lights of the
majority of his subjects of the middle class (most of whom were
Conservative voters as well as most of the ministers in the Dominion governments), redolent of impropriety.

All this could, of course, be accepted by the Government of
the day, socially unsettling though it might have been, were it not
accompanied by sporadic interventions – unpredictable, both as
to style and content – in the field of domestic, and of international,
politics, no doubt attributable to King Edward having had too
long in his unfulfilling attendance as Prince of Wales. There were
plenty who argued that with the coronation 'out of the way'
and the King's regal duties firmly in place in a full and formal
engagement diary he would 'settle down'.

Six years earlier, in the winter of 1929, King George V had
fallen ill. Lord Dawson of Penn, royal physician, whose abilities
seem to have been no more than comparable with those of his
colleague and rival Lord Horder,* was going round the London

---

* Horder's equivocal role in caring for the Prime Minister in 1923 is chronicled
on p. 23 above.

drawing rooms shaking his head and telling anyone who might be
listening that he feared for the King's life as there was an infection
in his left lung that was 'resisting treatment whatever we do'. The
Prince of Wales, who had been on a safari tour in Kenya, was sent
a cipher telegram by Baldwin couched, it may be thought, in less
than respectful language (which would, of course, have been
shared among those charged with its decoding):

> We hope that all may go well. *But if not, and if you have made no
> attempt to return, it will profoundly shock public opinion.*

The Prince, showing exactly the kind of political sophistication
that was already making Conservative politicians apprehensive,
said that he did not believe a word of it . . . 'It's just some election
dodge of old Baldwin's.' At this 'Tommy' Lascelles, his secretary,
flew into a rage. 'Sir, the King of England is dying. If that means
nothing to you, it means a great deal to us.' Edward 'looked at
him, went out without a word and spent the remainder of the
evening in the successful seduction of the wife of a local British
official'.[1]

In fact, the King did not die. And by the time that his son
returned was out of danger. Dawson was telling people that '. . .
never in all his experience had he known any patient, old or
young, be so ill and yet survive'. Edward, though, told Lady
Mount Stephen that 'I have never got on with my father but
when, on getting back, I found a little shrunken, old man with a
white beard, the shock was so great that I cried'.[2]

The Prince was thirty-four years of age. He was intelligent,
energetic and courageous. And had he ascended the throne in that
year, of 1929, it is more than possible that he would have matured
into a responsible monarch; and one, moreover, well suited to the
altered post-war world of the twentieth century. But he was kept
waiting. His father the King again fell ill in January 1930 and again
Dawson could be heard muttering the incantations of the witch
doctor – 'a dead bone in the King's wound which will have to be
opened up . . . dangers of another anaesthetic . . . heart [*sic*] poi-
soned . . .' George V, though, was tough. The royal lungs, deeply

impregnated over many years with nicotine, recovered and the King was to live for another six years.

During this period the Prince's frustrations mounted. He was aware of problems, both at home and abroad, that would be susceptible, surely, to an incisive and free-thinking solution. To his cousin, Louis Ferdinand of Prussia, the Prince of Wales wrote, soon after the Nazi electoral victory in 1933:

> Dictators are very popular these days, and we might want one in England before long...

And to the Austrian Ambassador, that

> Of course it [National Socialism] is the only thing to do ... we will have to come to it, as we are in great danger from the Communists too.[3]

Yet the Prince was very far from being a reactionary in the conventional mould. Had he been, it would have presented something recognisable, familiar and easily contained. It was his populism – an affinity with his subjects founded on mutual affection – which so alarmed the English Establishment, and with which they felt quite incapable of dealing. With Robert Bingham, the American Ambassador, the Prince shared his opinion that there had to be

> a change in conditions here, and a correction of social injustice among the English people which would relieve poverty and distress; that this must come and that it would come either wisely, constructively and conservatively, which would save the country, or it would come violently, which would destroy it.[4]

Here was a dangerous paradox. The Prince hated the Communists, whom he regarded as traitor puppets of those Soviet assassins who had murdered his uncle and would, if they could, put the entire House of Windsor before a firing squad. But he felt a compelling duty to communicate with the British working class. He invited a notorious trade union agitator, the Clydesider David Kirkwood, to an audience. When Kirkwood protested that he had no formal dress the Prince told him that 'It is you, not your clothes that I want to talk to'. Kirkwood was transfixed. Afterwards he wrote: 'I felt, as I feel when I see an expert engineer at work, that I had been in the presence of a man who had a big job to do, and is earnest, and determined to do his job well.'[5]

Equally threatening, from the corporate standpoint of the Establishment, was the Prince's attitude towards the Empire. He was intensely proud of the 'Possessions', but ominously sympathetic towards the 'natives'. To one of his lovers he had written that the tedium of official duties would have been scarcely supportable were it not for the fact that he was having '. . . a real success here. I think I've managed to *get* these natives.' The Viceroy of India, reporting on the Prince's post-war tour, commented: 'The Prince . . . by his unaffected manner and simple heartiness and friendliness to the people, won his way right into their hearts.'[6] And when there was talk of a *Durbar* to mark his assumption as King-Emperor he chilled the blood of officials by declaring that

> I can not contemplate holding a bazaar with applauding troops, police, and civil servants, with a sprinkling of the public carefully selected inside the ring and a disdainful and angry mob outside it.

As for international diplomacy, the Prince's views were both consistent and at complete variance with the official line at the Foreign Office. In June of 1935 he had fulfilled a long-standing engagement to address the British Legion. 'To loud cheers . . .' reported *The Times* (with whose editorial policy the Prince was, in this instance at least, in complete conformity) '. . . His Royal Highness suggested that a group of its members should visit Germany. "There would be no more suitable body . . . of men to stretch forth the hand of friendship to the Germans than we ex-Servicemen."'[7] The Cabinet were made angry by this. They 'concluded' that the Prime Minister or Foreign Secretary should have been consulted by the Prince of Wales before making his speech. And they agreed that the Prince (who was not normally allowed to see Cabinet minutes) should be shown this 'conclusion' by his father.

For those in authority in Britain all this, in combination, made up an unwelcome prospect. In foreign, in domestic, and in colonial policy the heir to the throne had clear ideas. He was 'up to date'; he was populist; and he was practical. 'His personality is amazing. His gift of keen appreciation of every situation in a flash – of the perfect word to say and the perfect way to say it – struck me tremendously.' And there was no way out. The King, surprising though his powers of recovery had proved to be, was in his late sixties. The Prince, dissolute though his lifestyle often appeared, was full of manic energy. Succession was inevitable, and the need then to 'manage' royal impetuosity was going to impose great strains. What a pity it was, some must privately have thought to themselves, that the next in line to the throne was not the amiable and orthodox Albert, Duke of York.

Was this idea ever mooted? Surely it must have been, though starting (as do many radical concepts) as a 'joke'. Once when the Prince of Wales had returned hurriedly from abroad a letter from his brother awaited him.

> . . . a lovely story going about . . . that I am going to bag the Throne in your absence!!!! Just like the Middle Ages.[8]

Objections to the way in which the Prince indulged his various private weaknesses could never accumulate sufficient weight to offer any realistic likelihood of displacement. He was often tipsy; he was grossly unpunctual; he was promiscuous. All that was irritating for those involved in ceremonial, and aroused disapproval among churchmen. But in his lineage it was far from unprecedented. In many respects the social behaviour of the Prince of Wales was more decorous than had been that of his grandfather Edward at the same distance from ascending the throne. It was his propensity to interfere with the process of government – and in an unpredictable manner – that aroused so much apprehension among the governing class.

Then, in the early spring of 1934, the Prince became infatuated. And his deportment soon altered, from day to day, in accordance with whether the object of his desire was complaisant or – as intelligent and ambitious women may so often become in relation to their devotees – shrewish. Sometimes the Prince would look bored and uninterested. He would be irritable. On a visit to the Royal Infirmary he kicked the little dog which, belonging to the Superintendent, had amiably and expectantly jumped up at the royal guest. At other times, and particularly when in the company of his loved one, he would be 'as utterly charming as only he can be'.[9] Generally, though, the impression began widely to spread of 'a moody and irresponsible egoist, wholly involved in his own personal problems, unable or unwilling to carry out even the minimum of the duties associated with [his] role'.[10]

As the Prince's 'personal problems' intensified so did the realisation spread, quite covertly in the beginning, that these problems had, built within them, the opportunity for a wider political solution.

First, the role of London 'Society'. This meant, in the thirties, several different things. By tradition and usage it included everyone who could get an invitation to the Royal Enclosure at Ascot. The 'smart' end, though, subsumed many whose conduct and marital record disqualified them for the approval of the Lord Chamberlain's office. This was a sector where the distinction between gossip and conspiracy was marked. By contrast the 'heavy' end of Society – the press lords, the big landowners, the remains of the existing court – affected to hold in contempt the fashionable set, regarding them as flappers and 'lounge lizards', who commanded the attentions of the gossip columnists but had no real access to power.

Yet now, at the very pinnacle of café society the idol, and the arbiter, was the Prince of Wales. And the Prince's fancy woman had every quality appropriate to this setting. Wallis Simpson came from Baltimore; the Warfields were a grand family but a cadet branch and with very little money. She was chic, thin and witty. She had been presented at court as a debutante. So far, so good. But already she was on her second husband. She admitted to affairs, also, with Aly Khan and a notorious Argentine diplomat. These were acceptable characteristics for a paramour and the mistress of a *salon*; but likely to prove an impediment to wider acceptance.

Sir John Aird wrote that the Prince's friends 'of his own selection . . .

> are awful and one of the worst examples . . . a couple called Simson [*sic*], she is an American 150 per cent . . . he is a very unattractive and common Englishman . . . They seem terrible at first and this feeling does not decrease as one sees them more often.[11]

The Prince himself had little taste for this kind of attitude, even if it had not been so personalised. All his life he had rebelled against that Society, the ethic of his father who had even banished a little visiting German princess from the tea table because on a summer afternoon she was wearing tennis shoes. Who, now, was rejecting whom?

Nothing was too good for Wallis Simpson; while her husband, Ernest, gradually faded from the scene. A house was found for her, at Number 12 Northumberland Gate. Mrs Syrie Maugham, the fashionable interior decorator, was put to work on 'creating' a set of interconnected White Rooms. The Prince bought great quantities of modern jewellery, so extravagantly that Mrs Belloc Lowndes, looking at Wallis, expressed surprise that someone so chic could wear so many 'costume' pieces. Sometimes he drew £10,000 in cash from the Duchy account (which greatly upset the Comptroller but could not, legitimately, be prevented).

An American! And a divorcee! A most scandalous consort for the heir to the British throne, certainly. It was arranged and agreed that wherever possible Mrs Simpson's name should not appear in the press, certainly never in BBC broadcasts, and that at no time should there be the faintest suggestion that some kind of a liaison was being enjoyed. After some little while, though, word got back to the Prime Minister that, in total disregard of her present matrimonial status, the Prince intended to *marry* Mrs Simpson. She was planning to divorce her husband. 'Plans [are] already afoot to liquidate Simpson (matrimonially speaking) and to set the crown upon the leopardess's head.'[12] A major constitutional crisis would then be in prospect. And it was urgently necessary that the Prince be talked out of it, made to realise the intolerable damage that this would surely inflict on Church and Empire, on the country's prestige, on his own status; how in truth it would be incompatible with his role as King.

'*Incompatible with his role as King*'. Here, surely, it seemed as if an irresistible force was to collide with an immovable object. Then gradually it began to dawn on a small inner circle, at court and in Downing Street, that the object might not, after all, and *in extremis*, be 'immovable'. Tragically, and for the best possible reasons (as did the formula of excuse take shape), it could become necessary to consider circumstances where this erratic personal threat to the stability and effectiveness of politicians' monopoly power might be neutered.

Others saw the opportunity in a different light.

Lord Beaverbrook was frustrated. His taste was for mischief. His objective to sell newspapers. Beaverbrook was restless under that ordinance of self-denial which the other press lords had agreed when, at the Prince's earnest command, he had first approached them. Moreover Beaverbrook was restless for a return to the mainstream of political action; where decisions were formulated by the inner circle over brandy and cigars at late-evening dinners, and implemented the next day. He had been 'out', effectively, since the death of Bonar Law. Now a new court and a new Cabinet (for there was intermittent talk of *en bloc* resignations if the King, once installed, did not mend his ways) offered the possibility to Beaverbrook of returning to the role for which he pined.

Winston Churchill was in the same boat. The 'Focus' group* had not yet been launched as a national crusade for 'Arms and the Covenant'. Baldwin wanted him nowhere near the Government. But Churchill was impatient. The eligible time for his return to high office was running out. He was, too, a natural Cavalier, and saw Baldwin as an archetypal parliamentary Roundhead. Soon he was to become more deeply involved and harangue his cronies:

* See Chapter 36, p. 525.

What crime has [he] committed? Have we not sworn allegiance
to him? Are we not bound by that oath? Is he to be condemned
unheard? Is he seeking to do anything that is not permitted to the
meanest of his subjects?[13]

These were indeed explosive ingredients. And throughout 1935
the conduct of this fashionable and wayward couple had grown
daily more scandalous, their antics most gleefully reported by the
French and American papers, the resentful misery of the Prince's
parents more acute.

Then King George V died.

The Prince of Wales was now King Edward VIII. Although,
on a St David's Day broadcast, he inserted in the official text his
own sentence, '*You know me as the Prince of Wales and that is who I
shall always be.*' All too soon it became plain that the new King's
attitude to many questions was, to say the least, untrivial. His
kinsman the Duke of Saxe-Coburg Gotha, and an ardent Nazi,
was over immediately for the funeral of George V and asked the
King if it would be 'useful' for Hitler and Baldwin to meet. 'Who
is King here?' came the reply. 'Baldwin or I? I myself wish to talk
to Hitler . . .' Saxe-Coburg's report, quite possibly intercepted by
British intelligence, declared that '*The King is determined to concentrate the business of Government on himself*'.*

With gusto the King set about asserting his authority. Elderly
courtiers were dismissed or ignored (the King's temper not having
been improved by discovering, at the reading of his father's will,
that, although each of his brothers and the Princess Royal had
been left £750,000 in cash, he had been left nothing) and the
clocks at Sandringham, showing half an hour fast for the last
forty years, were corrected. When Cosmo Lang, the newly
inducted but bloodless incumbent of the See of Canterbury, paid
a courtesy call Edward fidgeted restlessly throughout and, as talk
turned to the subject of the King's 'moral welfare', concluded the

---

* Although doubt has been cast on the reliability of Saxe-Coburg's testimony by
Viscount Norwich, the son of Duff Cooper, this report is to be found in *Documents
on German Foreign Policy, Series C*, vol. iv, pp. 1062–4.

interview before its time. The Archbishop recorded that '... it was clear that he knows little and, I fear, cares little about the Church and its affairs'.[14]

Predictably, at the new court sycophancy was competitive. Winston Churchill (in keeping with an American verdict that 'his bombast always reached its heights when he could not deliver the goods') uttered a characteristic dedication:

> and heartfelt wishes that a reign which has been so nobly begun may be blessed with peace and true glory; and that in the long swing of events Your Majesty's name will shine in history as the bravest and best beloved of all the sovereigns who have worn the island Crown.[15]

For some months there was great public euphoria and Baldwin's dilemma seemed to abate. It was still not too late to save the King. Scandal there was, to be sure, in huge degree. But scandals recede. The instigators lose the attention of the media; they disperse. The King, and the throne, remain. It was plain that the King was unshakeable. So it was towards the Simpsons that the Prime Minister ought to have directed his efforts. And indeed, had it been to correct the situation rather than exploit it to remove the individual, this would, for the Prime Minister, have been perfectly possible. Ernest, the husband (still), was amiable, unambitious. His price would not have been high. Wallis, though, was made of steel. She wanted to be Queen. Only a combination of threat and cajolery, behind the back of the King, might get her to change. Who could administer this medicine? Not, certainly, Walter Monckton, Attorney-General to the Prince of Wales since 1932. His oblique phrases and courteous style would have been interpreted as weakness. The emissary would have to be brutal, carrying authority, but not so redolent of the English governing class as immediately to put Wallis's back up. There was a man who answered to this specification. Max Beaverbrook, moreover, would in his gravelly New Brunswick accent, have been speaking to Wallis in her own tongue.

'Look,' Beaverbrook could have said, 'you've nearly made it.

You can never have it all. Don't think you can ever be *crowned* in Westminster Abbey – forget it. But everything else is within your grasp. Just leave it to me. You won't be Queen, but you will be as near *wife* as makes no difference. London Society will still be at your feet. In Baltimore they'll be naming whole districts after you.' And then the threat, 'But if you go for broke – you'll end broke.' It would have been a deal – but in a language and of a kind which the British governing class seem always inhibited from touching.

There was, though, another approach; and one less confrontational. Ernest Simpson's divorce was *decree nisi*. The judge had been unhappy about the evidence. And the divorce would not become absolute (thus allowing remarriage) for six months. It would not be granted if in the meantime any proof came to light of collusion between the couple seeking to divorce, or of misconduct by the innocent party. Quite by chance, and some days later, a young Conservative lawyer, John Foster,* was at dinner with Ernest Simpson and his brother. They talked about the divorce, and Ernest disclosed that he had admitted to a completely fraudulent adultery with the wife of a friend in order to 'give Wallis Simpson her freedom'.[10]

Here indeed was information which could prevent the divorce going through. Immediately Foster sent a message to Baldwin. Surely this was a heaven-sent gambit for delay. For time in which Wallis could formally be installed as the King's mistress – like the Duchess of Grafton in the seventeenth century or even Nell Gwynne – and allow passions to cool. Time for further impediments to be set in place.

Quite soon Baldwin's answer was received. 'Do nothing,' he said.

From this reaction (ignoring all the other abundant, but inferential, evidence) it is plain that Baldwin, encouraged by a few others, was set on driving Edward from the throne. But it could only be done by stealth, not through confrontation. At each step

* Later MP for Northwich, 1945–74.

the King must himself be encouraged to go deeper into his own grave. In the autumn Mrs Simpson's name appeared on the Court Circular as a guest, on her own, at the September holiday at Balmoral. There was constant flouting of social orthodoxy. Rumour in London abounded, often exceeding, as can soon happen, reality – scandalous though in fact that was. At any moment a newspaper might renege on the joint agreement.

The Prime Minister now judged that the time was ripe for him to apply pressure. 'I happened to be staying in the neighbourhood of Fort Belvedere about the middle of October ...' he was subsequently to tell the Commons in the debate on 'The Message from the King', and from that time on he made several visits, soft-spokenly intractable and talking of the constitution. On one occasion, and to the King's considerable alarm, Baldwin brought a suitcase with him in case he needed to stay the night.

Gradually, the Prime Minister and the King's own advisers wore him down. Incapable of communicating with any freshness or lightness of heart, they dwelt always on duty and obligations and morality and discipline. Was there no other world? The King loved his subjects, and his Empire. It was his wish to connect with them directly and in a language that they both understood. Here, though, was this dark and towering conspiracy to chain him, for the rest of his life, to a giant caulk of teak in the prison yard. How best should he resist?

For Baldwin there remained one contingency of acute peril. The King was searching, still, for a formula that might allow him to marry Mrs Simpson but without her assuming the title of Queen. Reasonable as this may have seemed as a compromise it was doomed from the outset. The Cabinet, aware now that their prey might at the last moment elude them, judged it too perilous. Neville Chamberlain opined that 'it would only be the prelude to the further step of making Mrs S Queen with full rights'. And in any case Baldwin was no more interested in accommodating Mrs Simpson than was, three years later, Hitler concerned about ethnic Germans living in the Polish Corridor. What the Prime Minister wished to do (though shedding no more blood than was necessary) was to eliminate his opponent.

So it greatly aroused Baldwin's anxiety when the King suggested that he might broadcast to his people and put the idea of a 'morganatic' marriage to them. Sometimes the King said this was best done directly; sometimes he proposed that he should absent himself for a little while to allow free discussion of the possibility. In Cabinet there was speculation that the King might approach Lord Reith personally and, citing the BBC charter, insist on his right to do so. As most ministers were by now tacit conspirators in what was afoot and thoroughly alarmed, it was minuted that '... the urgency was great, and must not be allowed to drag on indefinitely'.

Lord Beaverbrook, in the meantime, had decided on his own initiative that Mrs Simpson should, albeit temporarily, be removed from the scene as she was in the way, and affecting the King's judgement. He organised poison-pen letters, and threats, to be written by staffers on the *Daily Express*. Mrs Simpson duly moved from Regent's Park – but only as far as Fort Belvedere. The next day a mob gathered outside her house and pelted the windows. The police had to be called.

The Times had for some while had a leader set up in type deploying that most favoured of all Fleet Street smears – the publication of charges under the pretext of offering an opportunity to answer them. So only two days after her arrival at the Fort the King agreed that Mrs Simpson should leave the country altogether, and Lord Brownlow was detailed to accompany her in a new Buick, across France to the Riviera.

But as the temperature rose, so did expressions of loyalty to the King multiply. Churchill, who on 4 December had dined alone with him at Fort Belvedere, issued a long statement the next day: 'I plead for time and patience ...' This was by now the recognised code for those who were declaring their allegiance to the King; while 'the need to prevent the crisis dragging on ...' was the preferred formula of the abdicationists. The sting, though, was to be found halfway through Churchill's text:

If the King refuses to take the advice of his Ministers they are, of course, free to resign. They have no right whatever to put pressure upon him to accept their advice by soliciting beforehand assurances from the Leader of the Opposition that he will not form an alternative administration in the event of their resignation, and thus confronting the King with an ultimatum.[17]

And it was common knowledge that Churchill's own alternative administration was taking shape – at least in his head. Duff Cooper and Philip Sassoon were going to the Exchequer. Hore-Belisha and 'Shakes' (William) Morrison were getting key departments and 'weight' was coming from Hoare – notoriously ready to pledge his support to whichever side appeared to be in the ascendant.

On that last Sunday of Edward's reign, 6 December 1936, more pressure was put on Baldwin by General Sir Ian Hamilton, who said that 'there would be an ex-servicemen's revolution if the King abdicated'; and there was even talk of young hotheads, junior captains in the Household Brigade, taking up arms and putting the Prime Minister under arrest.[18] But by the Monday morning the atmosphere – particularly in the House of Commons where it can change so dramatically and so fast – had altered. Margesson told Baldwin that no more than forty back-benchers were of the 'King's Party'. A huge postbag had come in and, as respectable church-going constituents tended to be keener correspondents with their MPs than the more feckless sort, the great majority of those letters expressed distaste for the King and at his conduct.

So it was that when the subject again came before the House of Commons that afternoon, and Churchill intervened with his pleas for 'careful consideration', he was shouted down, and stalked from the chamber, shoulders hunched. In the space of five minutes he had undone, as Harold Nicolson pointed out and as he himself realised, the patient reconstruction work of two years.[19]

By now the King was worn out. And without Mrs Simpson he had become increasingly nervous. He had come to the point when for most of the time he wanted simply to be shot of the whole rigmarole and join Wallis on the Continent. His statement, no longer an appeal for 'understanding', would be unequivocal and terse. Lord Reith, Director-General of the BBC, who was to introduce him, did so as 'His Royal Highness Prince Edward'. The text is principally remembered for its reference to 'the help and support of the woman I love'. But when heard on audiotape the snarl in his voice '... unable to rule in the manner that *I* would have wished' is the more remarkable. And gives as good a clue to the reasons for his enforced departure.

And so the deed was done. To themselves many Tories will have been thinking, in the words of a footman at Fort Belvedere as, four weeks before, he had watched Mrs Simpson walk across the lawn to her waiting car for the last time: 'Well that's that, then'. Nothing, now, could 'go wrong'. A compliant, orthodox and public-spirited monarch was to be substituted for an erratic princeling. And the Crown, with all its residual authority of prerogative, would revert to a subordinate role. Subordinate, that is to say, to *advice*. And the advice coming to it would, over the next decade, be that of the Conservative Party.

Proceedings in the House of Commons were, or were intended to be, a formality. Baldwin's performance, although acclaimed at the time and by historians since as 'masterly', was a shameless concoction of hypocrisy and untruth. The Prime Minister made great play of his friendship with the King. 'I know that he would agree with me in saying to you that it was not only a friendship but, between man and man, a friendship of affection.' Poor Edward who, all too soon, was going to need 'friends', may have cast his mind back to the assurance, given in the opening minutes of Baldwin's address, that:

> ... when we said 'Good-bye' on Tuesday night at Fort Belvedere
> we both knew and felt and said to each other that that friendship,
> so far from being impaired by the discussions of this last week,
> bound us more closely together than ever and would last for life.

Touching on the one occasion which, had he wished to keep the King, or even to buy time, he might have exploited, Baldwin said no more than 'I was aware also that there was in the near future a divorce case coming on, as a result of which, I realised that possibly a difficult situation might arise later'.[20]

As for Churchill, he now blamed himself bitterly for his earlier intervention, believing, or so he told friends – whose numbers, all of a sudden, seemed fewer than in the weeks preceding – that his career had been irreparably damaged. Yet he showed his resilience by returning to the subject in the House; speaking briefly and tritely for eight minutes. Certainly in London Society there was much fast footwork to be seen, and 'distancing'. But this was no more than the conditioned reaction of those who trade in the superficial. Did anyone realise the enormity of what a Conservative Prime Minister, acting (at least nominally) at the behest of his Cabinet, and his party, had done?

Because Baldwin could have saved the King, could have kept him on the throne. But he chose not to. Here then were the Tories, the King's party since the seventeenth century, conniving at the monarch's displacement for their own supposed political convenience. Always ruthless in the treatment meted out to their own leaders the Conservatives had now extended the principle – that party stability and prospects justified any breach of honour or integrity – to the Crown itself. And in so doing had buried a seed of long and resilient germination, that was to lie below the surface of the soil for nigh on fifty years – and would grow to illustrate that the whole institution, and the persons of all those who were themselves *of* the monarchy – were *disposable*. The very contingency which Baldwin had, in his long agonising with the King, warned against, he had himself brought about: '– the respect that has grown up in the last three generations for the Monarchy . . . it might not take so long . . . to lose that power far more rapidly than it was built up, and once lost I doubt if anything could restore it'. It was left, paradoxically, to the Communist Willie Gallacher to point up the essential aspect of the whole affair.

> . . . the ruling class knew no loyalty. As long as the King served their interests they would keep the King. When the King failed to

serve their interests, out the King would go ... At the time when there is the greatest need for loyalty, it is not there. It is not there because he ceased to serve the interests of a particular group that surrounds the Monarch, the Cabinet at the present time. Their loyalty goes, and the King matters nothing, and you cover it all up by talking about the Constitution ...[21]

And Churchill's career – what, anyway, was left of that? It matters not whether his attachment to 'the King's party' was genuine; founded, that is to say, on a romantic loyalty, a commitment to the strictness of primogeniture in a dynastic system; or whether it was simply opportunist. Another device, like Indian Home Rule, or German aircraft production, or his posturings during the General Strike, that would give him personal publicity, and thereby leverage on the administration of the day.

Churchill's relations with Baldwin were now damaged beyond repair. Not that this mattered. For the Prime Minister's own days in office were numbered. And of one thing his chosen successor, Neville Chamberlain, was determined – Winston Churchill was insupportable as a colleague in Government. Never again should he be allowed to approach the levers of power.

ELEVEN

Diplomatic Disappointments

Chamberlain now Prime Minister – First hint of
problems with Churchill – Old Baldwinites purged from
the Cabinet – Resentment – 'Bouncing' Hore-Belisha –
International affairs, the 'Establishment' view – Lothian,
Lloyd George – The Spanish Civil War – The pressures
of *Lebensraum* – The Sudeten dilemma –
'Peace in Our Time'.

NEVILLE CHAMBERLAIN'S ACCESSION TO POWER was seamless
and smooth. Of all the change-overs in the party's twentieth-
century history it was the least contentious. There had not been
the disappointment visited on Curzon or Butler; the impugned
sleight of hand that characterised Macmillan and Douglas-Home;
the frustrations attendant on Anthony Eden; nor of course any of
the rancour to be felt so bitterly by Edward Heath and Margaret
Thatcher. The shock of that back-bench *attentat* which was to
displace Chamberlain in 1940 being, by the political scale of
measurement, far distant. Indeed Winston Churchill, its motivator,
had proposed the speech of welcome at the 1922 Committee
meeting on 31 May 1937.

Two very slight notes of warning might have been audible to
Chamberlain. First the sheer resilience, and powers of recovery,
which seemed to be vested in the persona of Winston Churchill.
An erratic Home Secretary, a reckless First Lord of Admiralty, a
failed Chancellor, a career concluding – surely? – with his espousal
of the die-hard case in India and, emerging from that affair, the
alternative royalism of Edward VIII. And yet there he was –

certainly the least predictable, if not the most dangerous of Chamberlain's rivals, comfortable in the role of a new Cassandra and scarcely attempting, even in that first speech of welcome, to moderate a reference − was it sarcastic, or was it patronising? − to his own preoccupation and declaring that 'no one ... [*no one?*] ... was so active in pressing forward the policy of rearmament' as Chamberlain. This was greeted with applause. And there was a further growl of approval for Churchill's hardly less far-fetched assertion that Chamberlain was 'a Parliamentarian who would not resent honest differences of opinion'.[1]

Of course it was − by tradition − Churchill's duty, as senior Privy Counsellor, to undertake this task. But it would have been entirely possible for Lord Derby (who had formally requested Churchill to do so) and the Chief Whip, David Margesson, who would never reject a chance to 'take Winston down a peg', to have in combination made some other arrangement. They could have marked up Churchill's isolation by delegating the speech to a respected elderly stalwart, if they had thought the Committee would accept it. There, at the very outset of Chamberlain's premiership, could a distant storm-cloud be seen.

The Prime Minister now set about constructing his Cabinet applying, as was his nature, little more than the technique of shuffling that which he had inherited, while evicting some of Baldwin's favourites. Several of those excluded did not take their fate kindly. Leo Amery whose (not unjustified) high assessment of his own qualities had already, on an earlier occasion, caused him to make a scene, made a direct approach:

As there was some time before lunch I went down to Neville's room and had a short talk with him about his own future arrangements, both with reference to myself and with regard to the kind of Cabinet he is making. I told him that ... I was prepared to [take office] if it were ... a piece of work that was really worthwhile ... I did not think that I should care to go back to the Dominions or the Colonial Office where I had already made my name and where there was nothing specially important to be added to what I had

already done. On the other hand I could reorganise the Army and
there were many things I could do at the Board of Trade or at the
Treasury ... better still, if he did create a policy Cabinet, membership of that.[2]

Amery says that at the start of their conversation he told Chamberlain that he 'need not reply' to the specific points. Which
Chamberlain didn't.

Some time later the list was published.

That absurd creature De la Warr is made Privy Seal and a Member
of the Cabinet and bouncing Hore-Belisha put into the War Office.
The Admiralty is inflicted with Duff Cooper while Sam [Hoare]
moves on to the Home Office of all places. Jim Stanhope is to
preside over education and worst of all, Oliver Stanley is put at the
Board of Trade.

I think [in a later holograph note added to text] N's idea is that
he wants to impress on the public that he is not swinging to the
Right and then pursue his own policy, the civil servants keeping
ministers straight on detail and he on general policy. With such a
mixed team and with one who unlike S.B. or J.R.M[acDonald] is
incapable of dodging issues in a cloud atmosphere, trouble may
not be far ahead![3]

A few days later Amery took a stroll with Hoare '... who
professes to be as bewildered about the shuffle ... as I was'. But
Hoare was on the way up. Amery, it must have seemed, was
becalmed. As much (one must suspect) to shut Amery up as from
any genuine concern, Hoare expressed sympathy and said he was
'vexed by' Amery's exclusion. But (never an easy line with which
to placate a disappointed colleague) '... there would not have
been much point in ... [you] ... being in a Government so
constituted'. After the two men parted Hoare wasted no time in
relaying Amery's discontent to the Prime Minister. Chamberlain,
realising that Amery still had his own following, made a perfunctory effort to smooth him down.

I had a silly little line [2 June] from Neville the general tenor of which was that he was sorry he had not been able to 'fit me in'.

I have not answered yet, though I think I must at any rate make it plain to him that I do not consider myself as an ordinary candidate for Office, and that if he doesn't realise what a difference I should have made to his Government both in fact and in public estimation . . . so much the worse for him.[4]

Almost immediately after sending this, another note from Chamberlain was placed in Amery's pigeon-hole in the Members' Lobby. The Prime Minister deployed the customary technique of 'quite misunderstanding what I had said and thinking that I had suggested that he had accused me of self-seeking'. Rather than 'misunderstanding adding to misunderstanding' Amery button-holed Chamberlain in the Aye lobby at the evening vote and – doubtless to the Prime Minister's considerable relief – told him that 'I had no desire for office as such, but would gladly have helped if a real live policy had been his object'.[5]

This *resumé* of frustrated ambition and slighting – real or imagined – can be replicated a hundred times in the papers of senior ministers who feel themselves to have been denied a proper recognition of their administrative talent and other, personal, qualities. And it may be borne in mind when, less than three years later, Amery himself was to unsheathe the first dagger to be plunged between Chamberlain's shoulder-blades.

At the time, the omission of Amery was understandable – certainly in terms of party 'balance' (even though, in constructing a new Cabinet, the weighting of this commodity above talent usually ends with trouble). But the promotion of 'bouncing Hore-Belisha' was an error of calculation by Chamberlain. And this was to become apparent with the passage of events. 'Leslie' as he was known by colleagues, 'H-B' by officials and his pertinacious military adviser B. H. Liddell Hart, 'Horeb Elisha' by public school boys in the 1922 Committee, was a politician ahead of his time. Not since Horatio Bottomley had anyone been quite so trans-parently on the make; and none had attained so early a mastery of the 'photocall' and the 'soundbite'. Everything that is today

subsumed under the heading of 'Public Relations'. Smiling, smir-
king; booming, braying; lifting lids, peering into cupboards or
under (motor-vehicle) bonnets; asking useless questions and
making conversation of the most banal kind, Hore-Belisha had
already established a reputation with the press for being wholly
amenable. He would, that is to say, do anything, assume any pose,
for a picture or 'story'.

But there was more to him than that. As an administrator at the
Department of Transport, Hore-Belisha had been clipped and
efficient. He introduced the driving test. He banned the sounding
of motor horns at night. He drafted the first edition of the
Highway Code, and he made free of such populist phrases as 'Mass
Murder on the Roads' in his drive to reduce accidents. Especially
did he address the safety of pedestrians (in 1935 a more electorally
significant category than car owners) with the introduction of the
striped 'safe area' of tarmac on which even to set one foot could
endow the walker with instant and statutory priority over an
approaching vehicle. 'Belisha crossings' they were instantly chris-
tened, and the black-and-white poles, at the top of which glowed
a large orange sphere, were known and described, even in magis-
trates courts, as 'Belisha beacons'. Road casualties in one year,
notwithstanding an increase in the number of cars produced and
delivered, fell by almost 14,000. And the Belisha beacon motif was
transposed into 'novelties' such as pencils, ashtrays, and cigarette
holders. Furthermore, 'H-B' had delivered to his own civil servants
the highest gift of which a minister can hope to dispose – elevation
of their department to Cabinet status.

Hore-Belisha was at this time the only Conservative★ who
could match Churchill's gift for opportunist publicity. His appeal
to the public, in 1937, was in reality stronger than that of Churchill.
Belisha seemed possessed of the common touch, but without the
contentious past or doom-laden style of the Member for Epping.

★ As a National Liberal MP, his future was tied to the coalition with the
Conservative Party. From 1942–5 he changed his official affiliation to 'Independent'.

Naturally this aroused the jealousy of colleagues, none the less acute for their being at the same time obliged to sustain the admission that 'Leslie got things done', and was bringing credit to the party. But for Chamberlain 'Leslie' carried also an attribute of inestimable value – there were absolutely no circumstances (or so it seemed at that time to everyone except Hore-Belisha himself) that the party could choose him as leader.

To more than one commentator this dimension was apparent:

> [Hore-Belisha's appointment] . . . reduces definitely the chances of Mr Winston Churchill. The Belisha record at the Ministry of Transport shows that he can supply the drive and the ideas which have been urged as Mr Churchill's special contribution. The Churchillians 'forgot Belisha'.* Disappointed die-hards say that 'Winston called off his opposition too soon'.

Chamberlain was well aware that he owed his own position in large measure to Baldwin's perceived indolence in the whole field of international affairs, and the restlessness which this had aroused in both country and party. He knew, too, that a level of military strength was inherent in the ability to assert Britain's perceived 'rights', still more – as was the subject of demands steadily more insistent as the concept of Collective Security lost repute – of effective 'arbitration'.

But for Chamberlain financial stability, and the industrial power from which it was inextricable, was not simply the fourth arm of Defence, it was the precondition:

> If we were now to follow Winston's advice and sacrifice our commerce to the manufacture of arms, we would inflict a certain injury on our trade from which it would take generations to

---

* A reference to Churchill's father, Lord Randolph, who resigned as Chancellor of the Exchequer in the mistaken belief that he was irreplaceable and therefore indispensable, having forgotten that George Goschen was available to take his place.

recover; we should destroy the confidence which now happily exists, and we should cripple the revenue.

Immediate testimony to the extraordinary difficulties attendant on combining rearmament and financial orthodoxy came with the abrupt fate of the National Defence Contribution. This well-conceived and sensible measure would have fulfilled what was to become the favourite, and later the orthodox, role of taxation – namely to combine the raising of revenue and the constraint of inflation. In essence it amounted to a form of excess profit tax on the different firms that would be taking advantage of the steady proliferation of defence contracts. Chamberlain had announced the measure in his Budget of 20 April 1937, while still nominally Chancellor but in attendance on Baldwin's formal stepping-down. Some four weeks later the Conservative Finance Committee (normally attended by eight or so back-benchers but on this occasion swollen from indignation, at so flagrant a levy on profit, to over 150) passed a strong resolution urging its withdrawal. Then, on 1 June, came the Budget debate.

Already a change was apparent from Churchill's eulogy of welcome at the 1922 Committee:

> I take a friendly interest in this Government. I do not quite know why I do. I cannot go so far as to call it a paternal interest, because, speaking candidly, it is not quite the sort of Government I should have bred myself...

Churchill then went on to make a wholly opportunist and shameless attack on the whole idea of the 'Contribution'. It would not help the revenue; it would be a 'check to enterprise'; it would be 'opening up a whole vista of doubtful, superfluous and troublesome new matter'. And if this dose of verbiage were not sufficient, he continued, '... if the Government cannot maintain a mental and moral relationship with those who are producing arms, they may be confronted with the gravest difficulties.' So much for any idea that Churchill might be relied on for constructive help in

framing a rearmament policy that would not dangerously ᳕
the bonds of orthodoxy. (It was, after all, only six years since
panic of 1931 and 'the Bankers' ramp'.) It must have been clear t
Chamberlain from this time that Churchill, whenever he felt the
mood of the House running with him, would take the maximum
of personal advantage. Chamberlain was forced to drop the
scheme. And his temper will not have been improved by hearing
his rival appeal (Churchill knowing by then, of course, that this
was going to happen) that the Prime Minister show 'the flexibility
and resilience of mind, and the necessary detachment from personal and departmental aspects'.

It is always desirable to be strong, of course. A proper responsibility of Government though one often neglected or deferred.
But who, in 1937, was the enemy?

If it had not been for the anxieties of the French, to whose
unstable succession of administrations Britain was tied by treaty,
there was no obvious reason to be concerned about Germany.
The Anglo-German Naval Agreement, although already it was
apparent that its detailed provisions were being broken, did allow
Admiralty intelligence to keep a check on the number, and class,
of hulls under construction. Raeder, the Nazi Grand-Admiral,
might be (in fact systematically was) cheating on limitations to
armour, ballistics and displacement. But the treaty had made it
impossible for a new High Seas Fleet (the only instrument that
could, as Churchill had observed in 1915, cause us to 'lose the war
in an afternoon') to take shape; except on a very long notice of
intent, and were that to be served British yards, it was assumed,
would always have the capacity to outbuild German ones, just as
they had in 1912–14. While claims for restitution of the African
and Pacific colonies were, rightly, dismissed as no more than
formal negotiating postures.

Most visitors to Germany concluded, much as had Lord
Lothian, that they

are very anxious to be friends with us if they can but that if we
allow things to drift and don't help the solution [sic] of the Central

European question they will solve it by force, in which case we are likely to climb down ignominiously.[6]

Lothian's judgement of Nazi personalities was idiosyncratic. But not unfriendly. Hitler was 'essentially a prophet'. Goering was 'a genial buccaneer of the FE type'.[7]

And certainly this was a tribute to the Reichsmarschall's broad-spectrum appeal to the landed British aristocracy. Goering had commanded the Richthofen Staffel in 1918, flying in combat without a parachute. He had been Prime Minister of Prussia, Chief of the Berlin police, and original founder of the Geheime staatspolizei whose acronym – GESTAPO – was to assume prime position in the demonic lexicon of the twentieth century. Yet Chips Channon on first meeting him at a dinner party (in 1936) was pleased to find Goering 'flirtatious, gay and insinuating'; he 'exchanged German banter with Honor',[8] seems all vanity and childish love of display. While Halifax, after a visit to Karinhalle, Goering's hunting lodge in East Prussia, in the autumn of 1937 was to describe him approvingly as part 'overgrown schoolboy', part 'head gamekeeper at Chatsworth'.[9]

Goering, on the basis of these assessments, was to become the repository, among Conservative politicians, of much faith, hope and wishful thinking in the years to come.

Nor was it only among Conservatives that the Nazis enjoyed approval. In September of 1936 Lloyd George who, five years on, was to be seen (and may well have seen himself) as a 'British Pétain', had accepted an invitation to visit Germany. To his friends he confided that Hitler had made a deep impression on him ... 'a mixture of mystic and visionary. He likes to withdraw from the world for spiritual refreshment; that he has no vices, or indulgences or ambition; and that he is blindly worshipped by the German people.'[10]

The changing conventions of political correctness are well illustrated by a further approving note starting with Hitler's 'greatest respect for England and, like most Germans, he cares what we think and craves our good opinion ...'

Apart from prestige, LlG does not believe that they care much about regaining their colonies, provided that they can get the raw materials they need elsewhere. They feel too strongly about 'purity of race' to be anxious about scattered possessions with black inhabitants. They look with horror at the way in which French blood is being mixed as, in their view, the negro only becomes formidable when he has a touch of white . . .[11]

In any case the main centre of critical tension, for Britain, remained the Mediterranean and the leading 'bogeyman' was not Hitler but Mussolini. It was Italy that had flouted the League of Nations with violence, broken its treaties and placed in ridicule the concept of Collective Security. Italy had used poison gas on the luckless Abyssinian armies, murdered their prisoners and annexed the entire territory. And it was Italy that straddled our Imperial commerce routes at their most vulnerable and congested point. In strategic terms, as numerous Chiefs of Staff papers made plain, the 'threat' to British interests in Central Europe barely existed; and where it did there was nothing that we could do about it. But Gibraltar, Malta, Suez, the Arabian oilfields, Aden – these were pressure points on the great Imperial artery that ran from the open Atlantic to the Indian Ocean, the ViceRoyalty and the riches of Malaya. Here, if no 'accommodation' could be reached, force, whether defensive or pre-emptive, would be justified.

This geo-strategic truth was complicated by political cross-currents. Most notably those affected by the war in Spain. At its outset, in the spring of 1936, the issue had seemed plain enough. General Francisco Franco was a 'strongman'. He had set himself the task of dealing with 'the Reds'. And certainly Franco's disciplined army seemed at first to be having little difficulty in dispersing 'workers' battalions'. Communist irregulars, the public were told, had been soaking nuns in petrol and setting fire to them. Or had they? In any case it was plainly undesirable that the Spanish Left, manifestly extreme and in close association with Moscow and with the Communist element of the Popular Front

Government in France, should get the upper hand. Many Tory back-benchers would have agreed with that doyen of the 1922 Committee, Sir Henry Page-Croft, that 'I recognise General Franco to be a gallant Christian gentleman, and I believe his word.'[12]

Then, however, the Italians began to send 'volunteers', and heavy equipment and aircraft. Two British merchantmen carrying civilian cargoes were attacked off the Balearics by 'pirate' (Italian) submarines. Quite soon the Russians, having been active from the outset politically and with small military contingents, raised the stakes with the despatch of interceptor aircraft and their crews, artillery and, in some sectors, a full-scale Commissar hierarchy. Alarmed, and aware that in combat the Italians were often running away and abandoning their equipment to the 'workers', Franco now sought help from the Germans.

For a month or so Hitler had hesitated. This was a theatre outwith his strategic planning, itself framed around a phased expansion in the East. Intervention in Spain would be a diversion – both of force and international attention. Two things decided him. A 'Communist' victory would affect the balance of power in the Mediterranean and must be prevented. And an extensive 'exercise with live ammunition' was needed by the Wehrmacht, which had not fired a shot since the Freikorps battles died down in 1919. The Kondor legion, a balanced expeditionary force complete with Stuka dive-bombers, was speedily assembled and despatched to Málaga. Thereafter the military outcome in Spain – short of more extensive Great Power intervention – was not in doubt.

Politically, though, the arrival of the Germans in the western Mediterranean still further complicated attitudes. That of France altered, diametrically. The original likelihood of a troublesome, Left-inclined neighbour dabbling indirectly in their domestic affairs had faded. First to the probable emergence of a Fascist associate of Italy; then, still more alarming, to the likelihood of a battle-hardened German military machine standing on their southern as well as on their eastern borders. The destruction by the Luftwaffe of Guernica, a town less than 40 kilometres from the French frontier, and a target selected plainly for its intimidatory effect, had the result of simultaneously raising French anxieties and diminishing their resolve.

Thus for Neville Chamberlain, just as for his predecessor Baldwin, the ramifications of the Spanish war were three-dimensional. Domestically the party-political divide was clear enough. 'Reds' in the *Daily Mail* were 'Loyalists' in the *Herald*. The original demarcation lines which *The Times* had drawn in 1936 between 'Government forces' and 'Insurgents' were quietly dropped. Conservative orthodoxy, as well as instinct, strongly inclined towards Franco. While the intelligentsia, the trade unions, the articulate Left were all, many passionately, 'Republican'. The more gullible among them hailed the war as part of a crusade against Fascism. Some enlisted in the International Brigade where they were able (if allowed to stay alive) to form an early impression of Communism's endemic treacheries. This raised the temperature of debate. And, particularly, the controversy was unwelcome to Chamberlain where it overflowed into the broader arena of foreign policy.

The policy of non-intervention, perfectly sensible at its inception, became rapidly discredited. And the flagrant disregard which the three totalitarian countries and, to a lesser extent, the French were displaying indicated a level of commitment which might, in the immediate future, break out into general conflict. Lloyd George, seventy-three years old, still waiting for the 'call' and always ready to declaim for a journalist, predicted 'the seeds of a third World War'. Merchantmen flying the red ensign were intercepted on the high seas and the Royal Navy did nothing. A number of incidents occurred where Britain seemed to have been 'humiliated' – a condition inseparable always from electoral deficit. While the whole experience was soon cited as further evidence, not welcome to Chamberlain, busy trying to find acceptance for his own placatory approach, that 'the dictators can't be trusted'.

Finally there was the strategic aspect, as measured purely from the standpoint of Imperial security. Certainly this was the sole factor that was causing concern to the Conservative back-benchers. Would our interests in the eastern Mediterranean be better served by a weak, unstable Spanish democracy of Weimar pattern? By a well-armed and disciplined regime taking its orders from Moscow? Or by a Fascist dictator strongly behoven to Mussolini? And, in any case, what leverage could we apply?

The dilemma between Communism and Fascism was well illustrated by an exchange in the House of Commons debate on 14 April 1937:

> *The Rt. Hon. Member for Epping (Mr Winston Churchill)*: I hope not to be called upon to survive in the world under a Government of either of these dispensations.
> *The Hon. Member for Glasgow Cathcart (Mr James Maxton)*: You would not.[13]

This, in the 1930s, was one of the few strategic questions where Chamberlain arrived at completely the wrong answer. To what extent his calculations were objective; to what extent influenced by memories of the Italian role at Stresa and Locarno; his own personal dislike of Anthony Eden and intention gradually to prise the Foreign Secretary off his perch – or even, perhaps principally, by the letters and 'intelligence' which Lady Ivy Chamberlain, his sister-in-law, admirer of Mussolini and personal confidante (although those confidences do not seem to have been spontaneous) of the Italian Foreign Minister Count Grandi, cannot be known.

Chamberlain believed that he could have a relationship with Mussolini of mutual understanding, and that the Italian dictator could be deployed as an arbitrator between Britain and Germany. But there were no territorial disputes between Britain and Germany – except those in which the British chose gratuitously to interfere. While Italy had a perpetual vested interest in maintaining tension, and asserting claims to British Imperial possessions, in the Mediterranean and the Red Sea.

Simultaneously with this pressure from Italy, and its appease-ment, the steady expansion of Nazi German frontiers proceeded north of the Alps. First, as has been seen, the recovery of the

Rhineland. Then, the Anschluss. Although in both these cases the evident delight of the 'host' population hardly made it an easy task to sustain complaints of aggression. Next, the declared intention to liberate all those ethnic Germans who lived in the Sudetenland, the border territory allocated – as much from reasons of drafting and cartological convenience as any other – to Czechoslovakia under the Treaty of Trianon (Versailles).

Quite how Britain found herself being slowly drawn into a position where the blood of her own servicemen (and civilians) might have to be shed in defending the borders of an artificial Central European state created less than twenty years earlier is, to say the least, contentious.

The geo-strategic factors were complex. France had been defeated in 1870 by the German Army, and in 1917 bled to the point of mutiny, saved only by a prodigious expenditure of British lives. The French believed that some kind of Balkan alliance – a 'Little Entente' – was necessary to divert, and if possible contain, German power in the east. While the Soviets wished to keep the German Army as far away from their own borders as possible. They too had an interest in preserving the 'independence' of the small states on Germany's eastern frontier. Yet Russian capacity to intervene militarily was inhibited by the fact that none of these small countries would consider giving rights of passage to the Red Army. It was a situation that demanded patient negotiation, and considerable readiness to concede to German demands.

The atmosphere was not congenial to this. Emotions were highly charged and Hitler's inflammatory language, and constant citing of 'atrocities' (all, as is now known, staged by *agents provocateurs*) raised first the possibility, then, as the autumn progressed, the likelihood that the Germans would invade Czechoslovakia. Gunfire, dead and wounded, a dozen Czech Guernicas – the situation would be out of control. In order to prevent this, British statesmen had practised for several months what came later in the century to be known as 'shuttle diplomacy'. And in the end Chamberlain went to Munich himself.

Without Britain, the Germans could get what they wanted.

But Britain's position was based on bluff. Chamberlain realised that his principal objective could only be to minimise the damage – to British prestige, and to what was left of international order and the concept of Collective Security. How could we intervene? A Chiefs of Staff paper made the point that 'distance and inaccessibility make it impossible for us to intervene directly'. Furthermore,

1) The Czech army has excellent equipment, but is subject to considerable ethnic tension and some of its units are unreliable.

2) The fortifications along the old Austrian frontier are incomplete and rudimentary and the main German thrust can now be expected from this quarter.

3) The Czech airforce is small, and its effective combat life estimated in days only.

4) Even if the French Army were to attack in the west on any scale this would be unlikely to take effect on German dispositions before the Czech campaign had been successfully concluded.

Feelings of great bitterness were generated by the argument. The Conservative Party split – although the two parts were far from being in balance.

It was a division between romantics and realists. On the one side, a huge bank of cultural commitment – to 'honour', sportsmanship, 'not letting the side down', saving a weakling from the playground bully. On the other, a cooler calculation. The country squire, and the balance sheet of his estate. The romantics tried to rationalise their case. The Germans would 'climb down'; or (inconsistently) – better to fight them now before they got any stronger. The realists tried to back their arguments with a higher morality. As Chamberlain privately commented – *before* setting off on his mission – 'Englishmen should not kill Germans in the wastes of the Atlantic because the district of Eger had been given to Czechoslovakia by the Treaty of Trianon.'[14]

Thus the conclusion of the Munich Conference was foregone. The Germans were going to get what they wanted because no other power had the combination of strength, nerve and opportunity to prevent them. Could the Czechs have fought on their own? Not for long. The one danger, though, which both Chamberlain and the French Prime Minister Edouard Daladier feared, was that a prolonged, or 'heroic' resistance on the fortress line might cause a drastic change in domestic, perhaps even in 'world' (which meant, of course, the United States) opinion. So it was on the Czechs that pressure had to be applied. And after a few days they folded. And the 'brokers', Britain and Germany, could each claim a triumph, and leave the details of forced territorial cession – the brutalities, theft and evictions – to be worked out by their officials.

Some Conservative MPs were furious. Others simply felt dejected. Harold Macmillan talked wildly of resignation, of forming a Centre Party with 'anti-Fascists' from the Labour side. Although not a few of these Tories, as Hugh Dalton sagely observed, were now alarmed at the prospect of losing their seats if a general election were immediately called on the Peace-in-Our-Time platform, when they might have found an 'official' Central Office candidate running against them.

As for the electorate they, like the King who on the Prime Minister's return welcomed Chamberlain onto the balcony at Buckingham Palace the better to acknowledge the greetings of the crowd, were delighted and relieved. 'The Government had to choose between war and shame,' growled Churchill. 'They chose shame, and they will get war too.'[15] Most people, though, preferred the judgement of Lord Halifax.

> [Winston's view is] ... when Germany has done this that and the other in Central Europe, she will in overwhelming might proceed to destroy France and ourselves. That is a conclusion which I do not believe myself to be necessarily well-founded and, if you do not necessarily believe this, it makes you look jealously at the remedies that are immediately proposed to forestall it.[16]

Could a line now be drawn? Was there in prospect a new golden age in international relations? In the last months of 1938 there was much wishful thinking around, most of it in the voluntary ranks

of the Conservative Party. And not a little resentment also –
directed at those who had behaved in a manner 'likely to bring
the Party into disrepute'.* 'Bobbety' Cranborne, a prominent
anti-appeaser, did not find that the deference due to his rank or
lineage (or the fact that he was landlord of most of his own South
Dorset constituency) offered any protection from being attacked
as '(a) a Socialist (b) a warmonger and (c) a poison-pen about the
PM'.[17] While Churchill faced a motion for his deselection
couched in the strongest terms, and carrying the heavy fingerprints
of Central Office and Sir Joseph Ball:

> Mr Churchill's ... [behaviour] ... was shocking. Loyal Con-
> servatives ... have been placed in an intolerable position ... unless
> Mr Churchill is prepared to work ... for the Prime Minister he
> ought no longer to shelter under the good will and name of such
> a great party.[18]

In some cases the feeling was mutual. Dick Law blamed his
Women's Advisory Committee. 'The brutes, untouched as they
are by any but the most crudely material considerations, they have
brought nothing but degradation and dishonour to politics.'[19]

Most Conservative MPs, though, settled back comfortably into
the *status quo*. Some turned their minds to the inevitable general
election – now not many months distant. One pillar of the Manifesto had been well expressed by Nevile Henderson† in a note
to Halifax: 'I love my country more than Czechoslovakia, or
Sudetendeutsche or Austrians or Poles or even Frenchmen. As for
Germany ... I am only too glad that she should look eastwards
instead of westwards.'

In any case the strategic realities had altered not one jot. If we
could do nothing to save the Sudetenland, then surely we had
neither the reach nor the weight to do anything about the still
more distant countries of Eastern Europe or the Balkans.

---

* The very phrase, it is interesting to note, resurrected and inserted into the
rule-book by the party leadership in 1998.
† The British Ambassador in Berlin.

*   *   *

Some ten days after the Munich Agreement was signed, Cadogan*

> ... tried my hand at a skeleton draft of a paper on future policy.
> But it's very difficult, as I don't know what it's to *be*. I only know
> the one we have followed is *wrong*.[20]

* Sir Alexander Cadogan, permanent under-secretary at the Foreign Office,
1938–46.

TWELVE

Munich to Outbreak
of War

A sigh of relief – Economic overtures – Hitler annexes
Prague – Popular outrage strengthens Churchill – Polish
(and Romanian) frontiers are guaranteed – 'Managing'
the press – The Nazi–Soviet Pact – Invasion of Poland –
Waverers (and turncoats) – Declaration of war.

IN THE YEARS THAT FOLLOWED THE Munich debate the occasion
became endowed with a historical importance that was certainly
not deserved or even, at the time, apparent.

Churchill's own speech was magnificent. The phrases, the
imagery and the nobility of his text and its delivery were truly
Roman, unmatched by any other speaker. But on that evening its
impact was less certain. The number of Tory MPs actually voting
against the Government was 'containable' and a close examination
of their names and constituencies* indicates that the Chief Whip
would not have been greatly surprised, nor the party in the country
much impressed.

The mass of people was hugely relieved. Not so much because
England had 'gained another year in which to prepare' (although
this justification was much put about after hostilities broke out),
but because a completely unnecessary and pointless conflict had
been avoided.

It should be recalled that there had, in any case, been no war
plan. The Royal Navy was charged, though with no specific
instruction other than an improvised reference to the blockade

---

* These are shown in Appendix II.

dispositions of 1916, with intercepting German shipping. But at
the Air Ministry there were no detailed contingency plans. Royal
Air Force bombers were no more capable of penetrating German
air space from their bases in Lincolnshire than was the Luftwaffe
able to reach London from its own home territory.

As for the Army, it was minuscule, still perilously under-equip-
ped and ignorant of what was expected of it. Of discussions at
Staff level with the French there had been practically none. In any
event the French Army itself had little idea as to how it should
react – save that there could not be a frontal attack on the German
West Wall. That lesson at least, learned in the Vosges in August
1914, had not been forgotten.

In the days immediately preceding the settlement, though, an
ominous symptom had made itself felt (something that was not,
outside the columns of the financial press, remarked on) – the
dollar value of the pound sterling was sold down from 5.12 to
4.67. A covert reminder of Britain's altered status as a world power,
and of how the financial centres assessed her economic, if not her
military prospects. For in 1914 the traffic had been the other way.
As the threat of conflict gathered momentum it was the royal
sovereign that had magnetised the currencies of Europe.

Equally significant had been the attitude of the Dominions.
The High Commissioners in London had all been urging, through
their own channels, that Chamberlain compromise:

> ... surely the world can't be plunged into the horrors of universal
> war over a few miles of territory, or a few days one way or other
> in a time-table?

More elegantly reasoned was the counsel of Lord Tweedsmuir*
who will have been articulating the private views of many of his
former colleagues in the House of Commons:

> I am wholly of *your* mind† ... that if trouble in Europe does come

---

* The novelist and Governor-General of Canada, John Buchan.
† AC's italics. Tweedsmuir was addressing Mackenzie King, the Prime Minister
of Canada.

to a head, if possible we must keep the British Empire out of it. The situation is wholly different from that of 1914 . . .

Canada has no interest in this miserable struggle of [sic] Communism and Fascism in Europe, and no more has Britain. I am very clear that except for a direct threat to the Low Countries, which are an external British interest, or an unprovoked attack on France Britain should not accept any challenge.

Whether or not the Empire could be counted on for 'credits', for the extension of debt that is to say, in the acquisition of raw materials, there seemed little likelihood of direct military assistance on the scale of the Great War. Or even, it must have seemed to Chamberlain, of belligerence.

There now followed a period of some months in which great efforts were made, with government encouragement and support, to strengthen economic relations between Britain and Germany. Perhaps, in the 'new' atmosphere, a huge sterling loan would consolidate relations between the two?

In December Hjalmar Schacht, President of the Reichsbank, came over to visit his counterpart, Montagu Norman. With him he brought several of his co-directors, at least one of whom was a Gestapo agent who had been placed on the board by Goering to monitor the negotiations, ostensibly as *rapporteur* to the governing committee of the Five-Year Plan. The visit was described as a 'private' one to be concerned principally with the 'question of German refugees'. As almost all of these were Jewish and many of them, wealthy in their own country, were keen to expatriate assets which the Nazis had confiscated when their owners had hurriedly left, the 'talks' started from a point of imbalance. Moreover the British Government's approach to the question of a broad trade settlement was characteristically ambivalent. At the same time as an expressed readiness to allow Germany additional credit for imports from the United Kingdom a carefully structured scheme (also backed by sterling credits) was being set up to *contain* German trade expansion in the Balkans by offering 'favoured nation' status to Romania,

Hungary and what was left of Czechoslovakia in certain commodities.

Thus on the one hand economic pressure – often cited as a desirable discipline on Nazi adventurism – was being eased at the centre; while Germany was being irritated, and British commercial interest raised, in a region that was regarded by all parties as her natural protectorate. As so often, the Foreign Office instructed Norman to indulge in irrelevant homily also. Schacht wanted from Britain enough credit to cover the Reichsmark's transition to convertibility. Norman said that this would depend on German agreement to cut expenditure on armaments.

Thoroughly alarmed by what appeared to be happening in London the commercial attaché in Berlin signalled that the Reichsbank only wanted hard currency to fund raw materials for their weapons programme. Mason Macfarlane, the military attaché in Berlin, supported the argument that 'the Nazi regime is deeply hostile to Britain and there was no chance of détente'. Roger Makins, in the Central Department of the Foreign Office, cautioned strongly that the Germans were directing their newly acquired subsidies only into strategic raw materials – 'copper and other non-ferrous metals, all kinds of scrap, especially iron, other metals, rags, paper and rubber'.[1]

The date of Makins's paper was 9 March 1939. Less than a week later the German Army in a carefully co-ordinated manoeuvre moved into Bohemia and Moravia. Within a few hours Prague had 'fallen'. No shots were fired, the cession of the Sudeten fortress ring under the terms of the Munich Agreement had, as was foreseen by all the signatories at the time, left the country defenceless. Now German industrial strength would be still further augmented by Czech factories and, in particular, the great Skoda foundries, historic suppliers of heavy ordnance to the whole of the Hapsburg Empire.

In the press there was uproar. Calls for Chamberlain to resign. The entire Government. An immediate general election. Ladies paraded in Whitehall and Oxford Street carrying sandwich boards

bearing the single name – CHURCHILL. Was this spontaneous?
Unlikely. So who was paying them?

Only Dawson held the line. The *Times* editorial opened with
the reassuring comment that 'Developments in Central Europe
... [were] ... following along a course which had been long
foreseen'. The paper's City correspondent (in fact, financial
markets were not much moved) uttering the dismissive comment
that '... as this development had in some quarters been predicted as
inevitable its occurrence can be said to have removed uncertainty'.[2]

But for Chamberlain this was a catastrophic blow. It marked a
widening of his separation from Halifax. And the likelihood,
stronger than probability, that the country would find itself forced –
by political pressure, public expectation, and ill-thought-out Alliance commitments – to go to war with Germany. Worse, it began
to look as if this war would entail, once again, the need to put an
army on to the continental land mass. The very contingency, the
inner, *core*, contingency which Chamberlain's whole carefully
structured rearmament policy had been designed to avoid.

Was it still possible to jerry-build an Alliance structure that
might deter Hitler? As yet no blood had been shed except, as it
were by proxy, in Spain. Perhaps a realistic prospect of major
conflict in the centre of Europe, if by urgent diplomacy we could
contrive its likelihood, might yet concentrate the minds of 'wiser
counsels' (the phrase had been Halifax's) around the German
Chancellor. But who were they? 'Deter' Hitler from what?

Any close observer of this period will be struck by the remarkable inadequacy of the British intelligence services. Telephone
tapping and the interception and decoding of telegrams – what is
today loosely embraced by the term Sigint – was haphazard, and
without central co-ordination. Too much reliance was placed on
'agents', many of whom were not 'spies' in the professional sense,
or even glamorous amateurs as depicted by Mr John Buchan.
Some were not even British subjects and, more often than not,
had their own fish to fry.

One such was Count Tilea, the Romanian Ambassador in
London. This figure, dapper and rich, and with a perfect command

of English, had been 'taken up' by fashionable society whose accents and mannerisms he affected to the limits of caricature. Out of his personal fortune he had bought Number 1 Belgrave Square,* the most imposing and, with its corner site, the most valuable address in that quarter, only a stone's throw from Number 5 where Sir Henry Channon would once or twice a week play host.† On 16 March, the day after the annexation, Tilea asked for an 'urgent' appointment with the Foreign Secretary. At first Halifax tried to fob him off with Cadogan; but Tilea insisted and, his tale having doubtless matured overnight, went in for a personal meeting on the morning of the 17th.

Tilea warned Halifax that a full-scale *démarche* by Germany against the Balkans was now imminent. He embroidered the story. German armoured divisions were to be allowed passage through Hungary. Some of the Balkan governments were weak, or even (like Hungary and Bulgaria) sympathetic to the Nazis. Prince Paul, acting Regent of Yugoslavia, was 'unreliable'.

Most of this was balderdash. And it is some measure of how muddled and indecisive the Government had become that the Foreign Secretary instead of listening, gravely but without commitment, convened a special meeting of Cabinet that afternoon. At this the mood was 'bellicose'.[3] But of practical suggestions there were few. It was decided to send a telegram, couched in much the same language, to all the threatened states 'asking them, more or less, what they are going to do about it'. Almost at once Sir Reginald Hoare, Ambassador in Bucharest, came on the telephone. He was sceptical. But Halifax, instead of letting the whole thing drop and the temperature cool down, sent again for Tilea. What were his sources?

Tilea was evasive. He *knew*.

---

* Number 1 remains to this day the residence of the Romanian Ambassador.

† Even as late as 1940 Tilea continued to entertain: 'a dinner which began with masses of caviare and vodka . . . gradually we all got intoxicated and seldom have I known such a high pitch of gaiety, wit and fun. It was 1.25 am when we left the dining room' (Channon diary, 10 January 1940, Robert Rhodes James (ed.), *Chips: The Diaries of Sir Henry Channon* (1967), p. 231).

It should have been apparent after a moment's scrutiny that Romania was simply putting in a bid for British protection – since this now seemed to be available to all and sundry. Not so much from Hitler (although his 'threat' was to be the excuse), but against her traditionally hostile neighbours, Hungary and Bulgaria. And indeed this is corroborated by the discovery, after the war, of a German intercept in which Tilea boasts that 'he made the utmost possible use of his instructions'.*

The meeting of Cabinet called to consider the 'crisis' was a gloomy occasion. The Chiefs of Staff warned that there was 'little' chance (i.e., none) of helping Romania 'directly'. They then went on to outline the dangers in 'allowing' Germany access to the Ploesti oilfields, warning that this would completely negate the effects of a naval blockade. The following day, 19 March, although a Sunday, saw yet another morning Cabinet convened.

> By then replies came in from various capitals where, in spite of R.H.[oare]'s hold-up [sic] our Representatives had taken action. All of them, in reply to our question 'What will you do?' said 'What will *you*?'[4]

– which, it could be thought, might easily have been foreseen. Namely, very little indeed. Enough to irritate Germany and fuel the pretence of 'encirclement' with which Hitler embellished his domestic speeches, but not enough in any degree to deter. The text of a joint declaration was agreed, to be issued on behalf of Britain, France, Poland and Russia, that their governments '... would immediately consult together about joint resistance to action threatening the independence of any European State'.

The Tilea affair, its irrelevance to British security and the futility

---

* An alternative contemporary explanation, linking Rob Bernays, the Parliamentary Secretary to the Ministry of Transport, 'an excitable, pleasant youth, sensitive and semitic, left-wing and intensely anti-German ...' with Princess Marthe Bibescu, a noted *demi-mondaine* given to dabbling in intelligence matters, can be found in the diary entry of Chips Channon for 18 March 1939. Whichever version is preferred, the episode offers additional evidence concerning the febrile and unco-ordinated nature of government foreign policy in 1939.

The Lord Chancellor's mistress. When, at the age of 26, she died of 'peritonitis'
Birkenhead composed a sonnet;

> *Eyes frosty blue, which still could warmly melt;*
> *Some Northern legacy of golden hair;*
> *Inapt dissembler of the things she felt,*
> *Of gay and reckless temper, yet in reticence how rare.*

– and asked Max Beaverbrook to run it in the Sunday Express. But Max declined.

Main picture The contemporary caption reads: 'Great meeting on stage at London Coliseum to hear Mr Baldwin's declaration of the future policy of the Conservative and Unionist party.' In this bizarre setting every face repays study. Halifax sits one place to the right of Baldwin. Churchill on the extreme left of the front row.

Below left Baldwin in Windsor High Street on his way to dine at the Castle. SB's claim to affability is not entirely supported by features hinting at that cunning which David, the King's son and Prince of Wales, was soon to experience.

Below An extraordinary phenomenon of the 1930s was the remarkable durability of Winston Churchill. Here he is in 1932, back in London and on the way to recovery after falling into the path of an American taxi.

Right Sir Kingsley Wood who, in common with many others, fancied himself as Prime Minister, shields his right profile as he leaves Downing Street.

It is 30 August 1938, and the next two years will be turbulent for Wood.

Below 'Rentamob' 1938 at the Oxford by-election. The gang leader will have been given 2s 6d (12_p).

Edward Heath backed Lindsay, the 'anti-appease-ment' candidate, who was defeated by Quintin Hogg. Once he was returned to Parliament, Hogg changed sides and voted against Neville Chamberlain in the Confidence debate.

The night of 30 September 1938. The caption, headed 'The Man of the Moment', reads: 'Mr Chamberlain tonight is the foremost man in the British Empire. Here he is seen smilingly talking to the crowds in Downing Street from a window of No. 10. He advised them to go home and have a good sleep in peace.'

Bomb-site electioneering in 1945. A well-dressed crowd in the strongly Labour area of Bethnal Green is addressed by Lord Buckhurst (calling himself on the poster 'Bill') from a moderately safe distance. The second poster reads 'Demand Democracy, not Bureaucracy'.

Open-air meetings could still attract enormous crowds in the forties. Here is Churchill speaking at the Wolverhampton Wanderers football ground, August 1949.

Lord Camrose's Daily Telegraph party at the Savoy at 4am on election night 1951. The Liberal tally is counted in the same column as the Conservatives. The christian names of the unsuccessful candidate for Dartford are Margaret Hilda.

of its conclusions offered a perfect endorsement, at little cost, of Chamberlain's determination to avoid entanglement in Eastern Europe. But no lesson was drawn therefrom. The press, or large sections of its tabloid readership, were strident. Churchill was issuing warnings of impending doom on a weekly basis. Many with a vested interest in aggravating relations between Britain and Germany were becoming bolder. While Hitler, himself and through Ribbentrop who was now Reich Foreign Minister, seemed to be paranoiac, unpredictable and hostile.

On 31 March 1939, unable any longer to hold out against the clamour, Chamberlain made a statement to the House of Commons. The Prime Minister took care, even then, over his choice of words:

> In the event of any action which clearly threatened Polish independence ... His Majesty's Government would feel themselves bound at once to lend the Polish Government all support in their power.[5]

And 'for the avoidance of doubt' Chamberlain telephoned that evening to Geoffrey Dawson. The day before, Leo Kennedy, the *Times* chief leader writer, called round at the Foreign Office where Cadogan gave him (to use the Permanent Secretary's own expression) 'the lowdown'.[6] When the editorial was printed the following day Churchill was the first to spot, and warn in the House of Commons against, 'a sinister passage ... similar to that which foreshadowed the ruin of Czechoslovakia':[7]

> the new obligation which this country issued does not bind Great Britain to defend every inch of the present frontiers of Poland. The key word is 'independence' [rather than 'territorial integrity' which might have meant a guarantee of all existing Polish frontiers].[8]

A cacophonous chatter broke out immediately among that class which is prone to it, in addition to *The Times*'s own rival newspapers. For a minute, Dawson wavered. But on 3 April Halifax invited him in to lunch, and congratulated him. 'He and the PM thought the article was just right.'⁹

Churchill will have known that this briefing (or 'spin' as the technique is presently known) will have been put out by Number 10. So, more significantly, will Hitler. It is thus hard to avoid the conclusion that the Polish 'guarantee' was of little more than demonstrative value – for domestic political consumption: '*PM Gets Tough with Nazis*'. Within a twelvemonth, as he was well aware, Chamberlain might have to fight a general election. He had missed the opportunity to dissolve Parliament, in defiance of Halifax's strong advice, after Munich. Now, just as Baldwin had been in 1935, Chamberlain felt himself hemmed in by events abroad. But this policy of dissimulation carried so high a risk as to cast doubt on its validity. It was one more 'signal' to Germany that Britain would not, if or when the bottom line was reached, intervene in Eastern Europe.

Almost at once Hitler set about creating circumstances which would, on practical as well as diplomatic grounds allow, indeed compel, the British to look away. The mutuality of interest between Germany and the Soviet Union was considerable, and of long standing. Each shared a contempt for the soft and meddlesome countries of the West and their bourgeois mores. Each admired the repressive techniques which the other applied against their own people, and stood in awe of their armed forces.

German troops and airmen had trained in Russia in that decade before the Versailles Treaty had formally been repudiated. From these experiences, as from fighting and killing each other in Spain, the Russians had learned to respect German technical proficiency; while German officers were left with an awesome impression of Soviet mass. Both powers were predatory, and aggressive. For the time being each had a preference for dividing their victim's spoils rather than coming to blows. Russia was the only country that might have given practical effect to 'solidarity' with the Czechs after Prague, and had done nothing. As soon as this was apparent Hitler had instructed Ribbentrop to alter the tone of comment by the Wilhelmstrasse and, by the legation staff in Moscow, of conduct. The topic of a trade agreement was gradually to be approached; and a still greater prize was identified as being within reach.

Neville Chamberlain, meanwhile, was recovering his poise. The eight-gun fighters (Hurricane and Spitfire) were being delivered to the Home Defence squadrons. The destroyer-building programme was gathering momentum. What, after all, could Germany actually *do* to Britain if we kept our nerve? Moreover, rearmament with its ancillary stimulus to the economy was being funded within revenue. If we could go six months without another 'scare' the Prime Minister felt that he might, just, be able to hold an autumn election. At the end-of-term lobby briefing Chamberlain was buoyant:

> Reassure public opinion, he urged us; the worst was over and there would be no more shocks or surprise coups by the dictators – he was convinced of their good intentions. Have a good holiday, he advised us, free from worry and concern.

At this stage Chamberlain and Hitler were working on entirely different assumptions which, as ill-fortune would have it, dove-tailed perfectly with each other. For Chamberlain the fact that it was impossible to defend Eastern Europe without Soviet compliance, if not support – and that opening their frontiers to the Red Army was utterly rejected by the Polish, Baltic and Romanian governments – meant that the whole concept of a 'Front' was unrealistic. That, in the last resort, there would be no parliamentary or electoral support for British involvement, and so, just as at Munich, he would have to draw back at the last moment if the bluff was called.

Hitler from the outset discounted British intentions, for the same reasons as Chamberlain. His anxieties focused on Russia with whom in a matter of months there would, unless a deal was struck, be a collision. Both sides had plenty to offer. Raw materials from Russia; a 'blind eye' to territorial incursion by either power; and a westward advance by the Soviets allowing a broad 'rectification' of the Brest–Litovsk and Versailles treaties. None of these trading counters was in the western portfolio. The two-front war – that sole contingency which Hitler had always promised his General Staff would never recur – might arise unless German and Soviet demarcation lines were clearly agreed before their joint (but not simultaneous) invasion of Poland was to start.

Thus throughout the summer of 1939, and quite unknown to Britain, France, Poland – or even Count Tilea and Princess Bibescu – Soviet–German talks proceeded. On 18 May 'trade' negotiations were officially opened between the two delegations. On 22 July the prospect of a broad agreement covering credit and deliveries was announced by the Russians. A fortnight earlier Henderson had told Cadogan that he 'felt intuitively that the Germans are getting at Stalin'.[10] None the less the Cabinet had dispersed for the holidays, Chamberlain salmon fishing on the Naver in Sutherland when, on 22 August, a non-aggression pact between the two countries was signed by Molotov and Ribbentrop.

Parliament was recalled immediately. On the morning of the emergency debate Joe Kennedy, the American Ambassador, called on Chamberlain. He found him '. . . haggard and downcast. All my work has been to no avail. War could now only be one of revenge . . . would leave Europe in ruins, and our own position in the Far East progressively weakened.'[11]

The Prime Minister opened the debate, on a Motion for the Adjournment that the Emergency Powers (the Defence of the Realm Act of the First World War) be reinstated. In that bleak recitation of preparations for evacuation, ARP, the vesting in unelected civil servants of total discretionary power over many aspects of daily life, there was put in place, almost without demur, by a Conservative government, a densely interwoven web of socialist control that would endure for more than a decade. The bank rate was doubled and 'voluntary' exchange control (until – unsaid – the machinery of restriction could be put in place) was required 'of British citizens generally'.

There was much reference, particularly on the government benches, to 'this period of uncertainty' while Labour, sensing

Chamberlain's weakness, abandoned their pacific stance and argued for 'honouring to the full' the country's obligations to Poland. There was every sign that the situation was slipping out of government control. Many of the speeches on that evening* show the House at its worst. Miss Ellen Wilkinson said that the Soviet Union was an 'anti-Fascist democracy'. Harold Macmillan congratulated her 'very eloquent speech' with which 'I have great sympathy'.[12] And the Communist Willie Gallacher read into the record a large part of Stalin's address to the Party Congress in March.

But the debate was wound up by Aneurin Bevan. He spoke forcefully, yet without deference to the shibboleths of the Left. Bevan pointed out that the guarantee to Poland was meaningless unless we first reached an understanding with Russia. And, by implication, it was now disastrous. He ended with a spectacular assault on Chamberlain:

'... I do not accept the statement that the Prime Minister of Great Britain has a heavier burden upon his shoulders than anybody else. His is the easiest job in the House of Commons.

The more blunders he makes, the more necessity there is for unity and for no criticism to be heard. The bigger the catastrophe of which he is the architect, the safer he is. This is the same Government, its personnel is the same, as that which was the architect of Munich. The suggestion is that the people of my constituency, the colliers, steelworkers and railwaymen, should offer their bodies as a deterrent to German aggression. There is one man over there whom you could offer – offer him.

Let the Conservative party, if it wants to convince us that it is in earnest, call a Carlton Club meeting, and get rid of the Prime Minister...'

An Hon. Member: 'Be British!'

'Yes, talk to us about being British – you Francophiles.'[13]

This may have been an uncomfortable experience for Cham-

* 24 August 1939.

berlain. But, as he was to remind the House the following spring, he had his 'friends'. However depressing was this diplomatic defeat the weight of parliamentary arithmetic would, for the time being at least, prevent it spilling over into domestic politics. On that later occasion there would be impatience, and humiliation. But in the autumn of 1939 only a kind of despair, a bewilderment.

It is likely, and there is testimony supporting this from both their public utterances – of which Eden's speech in the debate of 29 August is the exemplar – and their recorded private conversations, that most senior Conservatives (with the exception of Amery) still clung to the hope that Hitler might be deterred by evidence of our *resolve*, or 'sober resolution' as Eden put it:

> [the German Government] ... appear to believe that as a consequence of the Pact we should go back on our pledge to Poland. That is unthinkable.

Did anyone, except Amery, apply his mind more deeply? If they did not, it can only be for the reason that the further and the longer they did look the more unwelcome were the conclusions. Henderson had telegraphed on 24 August that 'Intimidation will not deter [Hitler] and it is useless to think that it will'.[14] Would anything? By now the majority of 'informed' opinion had got into a state where an attack on Poland was equated with an attack on Britain. This was an unjustified, indeed a reckless, extension of the commitment of 31 March. Certainly it was not what Chamberlain himself had envisaged when, in concluding his speech, he claimed that:

> As far as it is possible for his Majesty's Government to help to restore confidence *by plain words* [AC's italics] we have done our part. I trust that our action ... will prove to be the turning point, not towards war, which wins nothing ... but towards a more wholesome era when reason will take the place of force.

At no point in this speech was there any reference to the direct interest, or even the security of Britain. It is hardly surprising, therefore, that Hitler felt the bluff could be called, and even if it went wrong there would still be plenty of time, while Germany digested her victim, to repair relations. On 27 August, halfway into that short, doomed week that separated the signing of the Soviet pact and the invasion of Poland, Hitler had been telegraphed by the Duke of Windsor – an 'entirely personal, simple though very earnest appeal'. The message was prefaced by 'Remembering your courtesy at our meeting two years ago'. Hitler, punctilious as always, replied instantly:

> You may be sure that my attitude towards England is the same as ever . . . It depends upon England, however, whether my wishes for the future development of Anglo-German relations materialise.[15]

As the Chiefs of Staff had pointed out in their memorandum immediately following the annexation of Prague in March, the prospects for saving Poland by military action were unfavourable in the highest degree *even with Russia as ally*. Any other diplomatic combination was, in strategic terms, valueless. Now Russia had changed sides. Her enmity, even possibly her active hostility, looked unavoidable. Britain had, in an indeterminate and perilous way, 'guaranteed' Polish territory. Had we guaranteed it against incursion by Russia also? And if we were to fight, how were we going to win? Plainly, there was no longer any possibility of succouring Poland by direct operations on her territory. Polish integrity could be restored only by defeating the Germans and forcing restitution. No one could seriously visualise defeating the German Army in head-on battle on the Western Front. So how was this to come about?

The possibility of an effective blockade, as in 1917–18, was extinguished by German access to the raw materials of the Soviet Union. Were there, within the Reich, internal economic or fiscal stresses? Were these so acute as possibly leading to the assassination, or deposition, of the Führer? From time to time this consolatory notion got a tentative airing at the Cabinet table. Chamberlain tried – though in his heart he must have realised that the concept was absurd – to integrate it; if not as an objective, at least as a 'consideration' affecting policy. The Prime Minister's lieutenants spread the word among back-benchers, most of whom were grateful for any 'line' having even a shred of credibility.

So here was the Prime Minister, and Leader of the Conservative Party, dead stuck. He had guaranteed the integrity of an isolated East European power of the second rank. There was no direct British interest – lives, possessions or investments – at stake. The only 'ally' who might have been of assistance was a traditional oppressor of that same victim and had, indeed, just given recognition to its predator status by changing sides.

Chamberlain knew, too, that statesmen who start wars very seldom finish them. The scene, and the atmosphere, change. Apportionment of praise, as of blame, is unpredictable and fickle. All that was certain was that the country would be damaged. And, unless the situation were handled with the very highest combination of cunning and prudence, so would the party. Yet the political pressure on Chamberlain built up daily. Ill-informed, emotional and fuelled by the personal ambitions of those, on both sides of the House of Commons, who sensed personal opportunity.

Each of those last days in August 1939 saw a new attempt to avert the inevitable.

Some were craven in the lowest degree – like the suggestion from Nevile Henderson that Germany be offered a non-aggression pact.[16] Others seemed to contain the seeds of an acceptable compromise, such as the telegram from Berlin which set out German objectives as Danzig, the whole of the Polish Corridor, and 'rectifications' in Silesia. As a preliminary stage (although uncomfortably similar to the cession of Sudetenland and its fortresses) this offered an escape route. And could, if credibility were stretched enough, be construed as within the terms of the British note of 28 August that expressed a readiness to enter into discussions concerning *the safeguarding of Poland's national interests and the securing of the settlement* [sic] *by international guarantee.*

Henderson described his first meeting with the Führer at which Hitler swore that he 'desired British friendship more than anything else in the world'. And certainly this is a sentiment expressed often in the pages of *Mein Kampf*. Goering, justifying the confidence which Lothian and Halifax had expressed concerning his bona fides,* was busy communicating through his chosen intermediary and old friend the Swedish businessman Birger Dahlerus (dismissively referred to by Cadogan and Foreign Office ministers as 'the Walrus'). And certainly this will have been done with the tacit connivance of the Führer. But even if his goodwill were genuine Hitler must have been perplexed, if not contemptuous, at the extraordinary vacillation, and absence of central control, which characterised British foreign policy at this time. To his anxious staff Hitler declared that 'Our enemies are men below average, not men of action, not masters ...'[17] And he will have detected nothing significant to deter him from raising the stakes by resort to force of arms, which duly occurred with invasion of Poland, along its entire frontier, at dawn on 1 September.

Initial British reaction was tepid in the extreme. A 'warning' was drafted and sent – though not until 9.30 in the evening. It called on the Germans to withdraw – though without setting any time-limit. This was wholly unacceptable to the House of Commons ('I have never seen so much drink being consumed before ...' wrote Hankey, after a visit to the smoking room) whose members were boisterous and impatient. The whole of the press, and editorial comment, were now treating a declaration of war as inevitable within hours.

The Cabinet remained uneasy, being almost equally divided between those in favour of an ultimatum (not a 'warning'), and a hard core of appeasers who were apprehensive – as much of the political as of the military consequences. At 12.30 on the morning of 2 September Alec Dunglass† crossed over from Downing Street to the Foreign Office and conversed with Rab Butler. There was still a possibility, he said, of some kind of last-minute settlement that would induce the Germans to retire from Poland. It would have to be 'brokered' by a third party and the Italians were,

---

* See p. 152 above.
† Chamberlain's Parliamentary Private Secretary, the future Prime Minister, Alec Douglas-Home.

according to Count Ciano, Italian Foreign Minister, willing.

It is of course perfectly possible that the Italians, alarmed at the prospect of serious fighting into which they might find themselves drawn, believed that they could repeat their Munich role. In fact we now know the concept to have been utterly unrealistic. Once battle had been joined both Hitler and the Wehrmacht staff were exultant, and determined to 'finish the Poles once and for all'. The only circumstance that might have altered this would have been an effective Polish defence, and of this there was no sign whatever.

In the meantime, alignments within the Cabinet had altered. Sir John Simon, sensing personal advantage, changed his position and came out for the war party. For Chamberlain this tipped the scales. The Prime Minister was now under constant personal pressure from Churchill, who had placed his own interpretation on recent conversations.

> I have not heard anything from you since our talks on Friday, when I understood that I was to serve as your colleague, and when you told me that this would be announced speedily. I really do not know what has happened . . . it seems to me that entirely different ideas have ruled from those which you expressed to me . . .[18]

Chamberlain knew that he could quieten down Churchill with office; Halifax, though weighty, suffered – other than in dire emergency – that handicap which had been made much of when the party had searched for excuses not to take Curzon. But Simon was, or could be, a direct contestant for the premiership. It would be extremely difficult for Chamberlain to sustain an anti-populist policy without Simon's support.

When Chips Channon, who had spent much of the previous day helping his servants 'frantically hanging black curtains', and having heard rumours that 'the brand may yet be snatched from the burning', somewhat nervously inquired of the Chief Whip how things were going, Margesson told him, 'It must be war, old boy. There's no other way out.' And so at 11.15 a.m. on Sunday 3 September in a rather quavery voice, redolent of disappointment and uncertainty, Neville Chamberlain concluded his short broad-cast to the people: '... *So I have to tell you that a state of war exists between this country and Germany.*'

Not since the Angevin kings had responded to mystic revelations from the Divinity, instructing them to call a crusade to arms, can any group of national leaders have taken so momentous a decision on such tenuous assumptions. Nor will there have been many who cannot have echoed, in their heart at least, Goering's comment at the Berghof when news came through that the British ultimatum had expired: '*Wenn wir diesen Krieg verlieren, dann möge uns der Himmel gnädig sein*' (If we lose this war, then Heaven help us).

BOOK TWO

War and
Coalition

THIRTEEN

The Phoney War

A slow start – The RAF learns hard lessons –
Chamberlain's objective – is shared by the Dominions –
Brief reappearance of 'the Walrus' – The industrial
balance sheet – Contrast between Chamberlain and
Churchill – The dismissal of Hore-Belisha – 'Raising
the temperature' – Finland – The Norwegian
expedition – Churchill catches the mood –
and exploits it.

MEMBERS OF PARLIAMENT, SOMEWHAT disconsolate in the
main, although a few seemed to have been excited, poured out of
New Palace Yard and tried to hail taxis after the sirens had wailed
for the first time.

Was this now to be apocalypse? Many took shelter as and
where they could. In Whitehall the tiers of sandbags, sensibly
regimented in their new hessian, marked the entrance to
'designated cellars', sometimes – chillingly, for the concept was
surely harder to accord credibility than the contingency against
which it was intended to protect – Gas-proof Rooms. Some of
the shelters in Westminster, particularly those around Whitehall,
had 'Reserved' notices at their entrance. ARP wardens in tin
hats and dark suits, new gas-mask satchels slung over their
shoulders, enjoyed an officious role. The public were apprehensive. Contemporary Pathé film shows them running for
shelter, their faces white and strained. But there was also some
banter and camaraderie, a foretaste of the spirit that would
sustain the population one year hence, when the German

bombers were coming, from their bases on the French Channel coast, twice or three times in a single night.

That day, and for many months, there were no raids. Single Dorniers on reconnaissance had touched the edge of the radar 'envelope' at the mouth of the English Channel and, overzealous, the Observer Corps stations twice transmitted full 'Red' alarms. The Luftwaffe, in any case, was incapable of carrying more than a token bomb-load from its bases at Sylt or along the Frisian coast – a round trip, without escort, of over 1,000 miles. The Royal Air Force, on the other hand, was more adventurous. After a mission on the evening of 3 September – the very first night of the war – had to turn back owing to failing light and rain squalls one squadron, repeating the flight the following morning, broke through cloud exactly above the German battleship *Scheer* at anchor off the approach to the Kiel Canal. Flying at under a hundred feet with their bombs fused at 11 seconds, the bomb aimers were mortified to see each others' 500-pounders simply bouncing off the armoured decks of their target. The only damage was caused by a single Blenheim flown by the leader of the second attacking formation which, flying in at fifty feet above the water, actually crashed into *Scheer*'s foc'sle, killing nine sailors as well as its own entire crew.

This first raid on the German fleet was greatly exaggerated in its effect by the Ministry of Information, whose film unit quickly scripted and produced a 'docufiction' entitled *The Lion Has Wings* which was doing the rounds of provincial cinemas by Christmas. In reality, heavier and better-directed raids (always against naval targets) continued against a background of rapidly improving German defensive tactics and increasingly heavy casualties.

By the end of the year it had become plain that unescorted daylight sorties by bombers were suicidal.

The Ministry of Information also commandeered, and put at risk, five squadrons of Whitley heavy bombers which were deployed nightly throughout the month of September in dropping leaflets, hastily written in somewhat academic language, assuring the German people that 'we had no quarrel with them'.

★   ★   ★

So now the party was at war. For many Conservatives in the country, and for a good number of MPs, it was a mode into which they could fall naturally. Flags, valour, younger sons in uniform. The apparatus of patriotism was congenial to display. But was their heart in it? Few dared to ask this question, even of each other.

The Poles crumbled in the first week. The French Army put on a ponderous display of march and counter-march using, it seemed, practice ammunition, along the western boundary of the Siegfried Line. Then fell into torpor. The closing agonies of the Polish cavalry were abruptly terminated by a mass invasion in their rear when the Red Army crossed the Byelo-Russian frontier at dawn on 12 September, moving up to a dividing line (plainly a secret annexe to the Molotov–Ribbentrop pact of the previous month) resembling the original 'Curzon Line' boundary of 1919.

What could Britain do about this? Nothing.

> What I have always half foreseen, half feared as a nightmare, is now a possibility, that is, an entire alteration in the European system, with the power of Russia enormously strengthened. There will be, indeed, some sort of Bolshevik regime over most of our continent ... the USA may save us, but our days of power are over for a long time to come.[1]

Thus wrote Sir Henry Channon in his diary for 19 September. No clearer or more succinct contemporary exposé can be found of what the policy of appeasement was designed to avert.

Was everything now lost? Possibly not. But its retrieval would be difficult – not least because a general election was due to be contested within a twelvemonth. And this could be avoided only if, by whatever device, the Government could pose as having become all-party or 'National'. Yet once he entered into the pretence of a coalition, even coalition with his own Conservative dissidents, Chamberlain's grip on policy would be loosened. The Prime Minister's best prospect lay in the probability that public opinion, all in all, might not yet be so bellicose; that a policy of discretion, of avoiding bloodshed, of hoping that newsreels of burning Warsaw and terrified non-combatants, might fade in the memory. And that a 'compromise' could in the fullness of time be recommended – perhaps even be deployed as a source of electoral credit.

The majority of Tory MPs would certainly have accepted this, although by now their mood was stronger than at the same time in 1938. They felt affronted by Hitler's blatant disregard of his undertakings. Most underestimated Germany's military strength and felt that the time had come to 'teach him a lesson'. Paradoxically, the Nazi–Soviet Pact, which had so transformed Germany's strategic position, was now seen as disqualifying Hitler from claiming to be Western Europe's principal defender against Communism. The Dominions, on the other hand, were more hard-headed. On 6 October Hitler had made a public offer of a 'General Settlement' in Europe. It was, admittedly, accompanied by a demand for the return of Germany's African colonies – but this can have been no more than a bargaining ploy. Unlike the Kaiser, Hitler had no interest in Africa, as is testified in *Mein Kampf*. Three days afterwards the Canadian Prime Minister, Mackenzie King, was complaining that Chamberlain's draft reply might be 'slamming the door' on further discussion. And on 11 October Eden reported the Australian misgivings: 'A settlement should not be sought merely on the basis of the status quo of the Versailles Treaty' (a thinly coded reference to the Polish Corridor).

These sentiments were little different from those expressed at the time of Munich. And more was to come. Cabinet on 12 October learned that all the Dominions had endorsed a proposal by General Smuts for a conference of neutral powers to determine the boundaries of any 'restored' Poland or Czechoslovakia.[2] Although to his colleagues on that occasion he may have professed concern, this did in fact strengthen Chamberlain's hand in two ways. First, while stalemate persisted the Empire's preference for negotiations was unlikely to recede. In the fullness of time it could be a useful card to play. Second, Eden, in Government one of the most prominent of the 'war party', was himself Dominions Secretary; and thus the channel through which these views were conveyed. He would surely be unable to ignore their implication.

In the face of these despatches a belligerent attitude was less and less tenable. All that Chamberlain needed was time, and patience. As to the 'war effort' itself, this had slowly to be cranked up to rotation speed. There was little sign of the unemployed total falling. But an emergency Budget, introduced by Sir John Simon on 27 September was, by the standards even of 1917–18 (though not by those of that future decade 1942–52), Draconian. Income tax was raised to 7s 6d in the pound, or 37½ per cent. Surtax, higher still. And excise duties on wine, cigarettes and – bizarrely – sugar, were all increased. These measures, though, were not inconsistent with a policy of seeking a settlement still – if only because the prospect of their moderation or repeal might, without as much being said, contribute to the well-being that should characterise a return to peace.

Diplomatic channels, of a sort, were kept open. On 28 September Dahlerus returned to London. It is not clear whether he had an interview with Halifax. But certainly Cadogan prepared a paper for the Foreign Secretary which Halifax read to the War Cabinet the following day. 'The Walrus' held out the likelihood of a coup in Berlin which would unseat Hitler and install Goering in his place.[3]

How fantastic this seemed at the time is hard to tell. It, and other such contacts, will certainly have been at the back of the minds of those in the Cabinet who asserted that a policy of 'containment', taking, that is to say, no direct military action against Germany, would ultimately lead to the Nazi system imploding. And, in any case, was 'implosion' really to be desired? Any alteration in the *status quo* of which the Communists would be the beneficiary had plainly to be approached with the greatest caution. In the minds of many Conservatives the ideal would be an arrangement with some kind of 'gentleman's' administration – senior officers of the OKH★ General Staff presided over, possibly, by Goering.

★ Oberkommando des Heeres, the High Command of the German Army. See p. 152 above for character appraisals formed of Goering by various senior members of the Government.

On 3 October the German Embassy in Dublin was informed
by the Irish Foreign Office that 'Mr Chamberlain and people
round him wanted peace provided Britain's prestige could be
preserved', and a signal to this effect was also transmitted by
Bastianini, the Italian Under-Secretary for Foreign Affairs, to
Ciano in Rome.[4] Ambassador Kennedy, who had acquired the
habit of telling anyone listening that Britain and France were
'gonna get thrashed', was travelling round the various offices of
members of the Cabinet asking 'what would happen' if Hitler
now offered acceptable peace terms. It was essential, though, if
any advantage were to be drawn from all this, that the temperature
be kept down. If Germany were not 'provoked' then it was possible
that she might stand off from further aggression – at all events in
the west. At least six months would be needed for the initial
fervour – if such it was – to abate, and perplexity to supervene.
And during that period if 'crises' should arise they must needs be
handled with the highest discretion.

By the end of the first week in November it was plain that, as
far as the Western Front was affected, in R. A. Butler's words,
'nothing much is going to happen'. Nor, if the French got their
way, would it. General Brooke, on a courtesy visit of inspection,
noted in his diary his impressions of a 'guard of honour':

> Seldom have I seen anything more slovenly and badly turned out.
> Men unshaven, horses ungroomed, clothes and saddlery that did
> not fit, vehicles dirty and complete lack of pride in themselves or
> their units. What shook me most, though, was the look in the
> men's faces, disgruntled and insubordinate looks, and, although
> ordered to give *Eyes Left* hardly a man bothered to do so.[5]

Chamberlain could take comfort also from the declared neutrality of Japan (that country understandably taking the view that its
anti-Comintern obligations had been vitiated by the Ribbentrop–
Molotov pact) and from Badoglio's* internal warning to Mussolini

* Marshal Pietro Badoglio, Italian conqueror of Abyssinia. Replaced Mussolini
in 1943.

that Italy was in no condition to take on France and Britain simultaneously in the Mediterranean.

The Chiefs of Staff's gloomy prediction, repeated as recently as March of that year, seemed for the present, groundless. But the position of Neville Chamberlain remained an uncomfortable one. He was Prime Minister of a country at war. But he was also leader of the party whose policies, or rather whose erratic and unconfident response to extraneous events, had brought about the country's involvement; and of the party from which (with little significant exception)* the Government had been drawn. There is no doubt that Chamberlain was unshaken in his private belief that the country was not strong enough to fight against Germany. And those who think otherwise should turn to his speech in the House of Commons on 2 September, before the ultimatum, issued the following day, had even been drafted. The text is so convoluted as almost to be – particularly to a nervous and expectant chamber – unintelligible:

> I hope that the issue will be brought to a close at the earliest possible moment so that we may know where we are . . .

and

> I am the last man to neglect any opportunity which I consider affords a serious chance of avoiding the great catastrophe of war even at the last moment.[6]

Chamberlain himself knew, and so should have realised any detached assessor, that we could defend ourselves – just. But to *wage war* on the scale of 1914 was not feasible. The cash, industrial strength and trained manpower (military as well as civilian) were this time inadequate.

In 1939 the population of Germany was almost eighty million, to which had recently been added some fifteen million or so of

---

* Two figures of prominence, Simon and Hore-Belisha, were (respectively) National Liberal and 'National'. But in their attitude, allegiance and ambition they were to all intents Conservative.

unenthusiastic but industrious Czechs. German steel production was over 20 million tons in 1938, now supplemented by an additional six million tons from Skoda and Brno. Germany produced more than twice as many machine tools as Britain.[7] British manufacturing industry was riddled with skills shortages, particularly of toolmakers and operatives. And direction of labour had been explicitly ruled out by the Cabinet on the perfectly legitimate grounds that imbalances 'artificially' created thereby would damage the export drive, and also ran the risk of creating unemployment in the ancillary trades. As long ago as 1936 Lord Swinton had reported, when Air Minister, to the Cabinet that 'if we could "pick the eyes out" of, say, the Singer sewing machine factory we should in a comparatively short time get improved production', but 'the immediate result would be to throw out of employment in such a factory a number of the residue of the workers'. A risk, in other words, of simultaneous damage both to the Government's domestic standing and to the foreign exchange reserves. This gloomy balance sheet could, of course, be offset to some degree by bringing Imperial and (optimistically) French resources into the reckoning. But even then the Allies were materially inferior. In 1938 German production of manufactured goods had exceeded the *combined* annual total of Britain and France.

A succession of committees were charged with looking at the critical question of skilled manpower. In no case were their findings other than pessimistic. There was no short-term solution. Even to put the economy on a full 'war footing' would scarcely satisfy the demands of the armament industry (and did of course carry substantial electoral risks). Certain key weapons and systems, like the Browning aircraft machine-guns, had to be paid for, in cash, to the suppliers in the US, out of a dwindling reserve of convertible currency. And the greater the diversion of labour from the export to the defence industries, the heavier the drain on the reserves. The balance of trade could scarcely cover the cost of basic raw materials – still less the additional demands of technical equipment or 'consumer' imports. The broad conclusions of this arithmetic were inescapable. No amount of bombast from Winston Churchill, or others like Boothby who looked to him for a lead and, in changed circumstances, preferment, could alter it.

But this reality, and its critical interrelation with the national interest – as an objective observer might measure it – was complicated, as has been shown so often in the past and will be seen so many times in the future, by party and, indeed, personal considerations. Because, whatever the provisions of the Emergency Powers Act might allow, Chamberlain was far too experienced a politician not to see that the Labour Party would agitate for a general election as soon as one fell due – if they thought that they had a good chance of winning it. At its crudest, what Chamberlain had to calculate was this: Which in the medium term was most likely to grant the party an electoral advantage: a competent and effective conduct of the war, with periodic, if not final, victory to show as polling day approached? Or a sensible compromise: the 'peace' card played once again – with the relief felt, at the time of Munich, by the majority now heightened by a sense if not of honour then of obligation discharged? This finesse could only be attained if the party showed that 'enough' had been done. It could argue that the RAF had shown its domination of German skies by scattering leaflets; the Royal Navy had gallantly kept the sea-lanes open and sunk a number of U-boats. A 'war party' has little electoral appeal, unless it can claim responsibility for victories. A 'peace party' is likely to be more formidable but it needs a pretence, at least, of having honourably done its best in order to salve the voters' conscience.

Also disconcerting for Chamberlain was the fact that the peacetime political 'rule-book' was now obsolete. Public expectations were higher and more urgent. The language of 'presentation' had coarsened. In this atmosphere the Prime Minister felt himself ill at ease. And not least because he knew that there were others less scrupulous – but burning with a zeal to which he himself could not aspire – who felt that they would be better suited to doing his job than their own. This is of course the congenital situation of most Prime Ministers for most of the time. But Chamberlain was physically exhausted. In twelve months he had fallen from the

highest pinnacle of public acclaim – his triumphant reception on
the tarmac at Heston aerodrome – to a status that was, at least as
far as the body of the daily press was concerned, barely more than
probationary. Less than twelve months distant in the future lay a
serious abdominal operation that would reveal an advanced state
of cancer. By its very nature this will have been affecting already
the Prime Minister's stamina and general health. Winston Churchill, by contrast, was utterly reinvigorated. Although now sixty-
five years old his energy, daily conserved by a long* afternoon
siesta, seems to have been little different from that last period in
wartime government, twenty-five years earlier. His ambition, and
evident intention, was to advance a claim to the premiership so
powerful that, in the fullness of time, it could no longer be resisted.

There were two theatres where Churchill had to perform,
and build credit, both of them different in their intimacy and
expectation – the Cabinet Room, and the chamber of the House
of Commons. These being additional to the arena of the public
domain where, already, he had long been a favourite and the press
would very largely do his bidding.

Churchill was not an easy colleague. He bombarded fellow
ministers with notes, telling them how to run their departments,
and drawing their attention not just to neglect or oversight but to
the demands of policy. Or rather to what he, Churchill, believed
to be the right policy. To Halifax he noted that he proposed 'my
drawing to your attention from time to time points which strike
me in the Foreign Office telegrams as it is so much better' (Halifax
might not have agreed with this) 'than that I should raise them in
Cabinet.'[8] The First Lord also leaked to the press. Sometimes
contributed articles under his own name couched in an exhor-
tatory tone but carrying, too, warnings against torpor or restraint.
On 1 October, with the conflict less than a month old, Churchill
wrote a long memorandum to the Prime Minister expressing

---

* By Churchill's own account, in *The Gathering Storm*, this was seldom more
than ten minutes; other observers – Chamberlain among them – have put it at
two hours.

concern at the size of the Army and of the Royal Air Force
(Services for which he himself had no departmental responsibility).

This was too much for Chamberlain who sent for Churchill
and had a 'very frank talk' with him. Chamberlain drew attention
to 'the similarity between what was in the memorandum and
what was in the newspapers'. Churchill back-pedalled at once.
Fulsomely he apologised. He 'withdrew' the memorandum, saying
that he would write no more. Somewhat ruefully Chamberlain
wrote afterwards to his sister: '. . . we have to pay [a price] for the
asset we have in his personality and popularity; but I do wish we
could have the latter without the former.'[9]

The Prime Minister needed to finesse a particularly awkward
hand. Without Churchill in the War Cabinet it would immediately
be difficult to sustain popular, or editorial, patience. The majority
in the House of Commons would become restive, and dwindle.
But with Churchill now on the inside, to predict his behaviour –
still less to control it – was going to be demanding in the extreme.
Chamberlain busied himself by setting up an administrative structure that would make it difficult and laborious for Churchill to
bother other ministers by intruding on their responsibilities. And
which, by holding information at several removes away, should at
least inhibit Churchill's taking the initiative with policies that were
outwith his own department.

The number of seats in the War Cabinet was restricted to
eight and there is no suggestion from its recorded minutes that
proceedings were especially discursive. Yet Chamberlain arranged
that its deliberations should be first processed by a series of Ministerial Committees and classified by topic. Initially there were
separate bodies for Home Policy, Civil Defence and Priorities (*sic*).
To these almost immediately were added Economic Policy and
Food. All military matters started on the agenda of the Chiefs of
Staff sub-committee which reported direct to the Cabinet. This
procedure was 'streamlined' – in time-honoured Whitehall style –
by interposing, five weeks into the war, an additional intermediate
stage – the Military Co-ordination Committee.

The effect of this was that every operational issue of importance had to be tackled three times: by the Chiefs of Staff, then by the Military Co-ordination Committee, then by the War Cabinet. As Professor Dilks has drily observed: 'Chamberlain *and others*, mistrusting some of the First Lord's enthusiasms and believing him too ready to overrule advice, probably thought that the advantages of such checks outweighed the inconveniences.'[10]

Churchill did possess one especial advantage over his colleagues and rivals – his power of communicating direct to the nation by broadcasts. These combined oratory –

> As they look out tonight from their blatant, panoplied, clattering Nazi Germany, they cannot find one single friendly eye in the whole circumference of the globe. Not one! Russia returns them a flinty stare; Italy averts her gaze; Japan is puzzled, and thinks herself betrayed; Turkey and the whole of Islam have ranged themselves instinctively but decisively on the side of progress...[11]

– with flagrant distortion of the truth, as the assurance that 'the Germany which assaults us today is a far less strongly built and solidly founded organism than that which the Allies and the United States forced to beg for an armistice twenty-one years ago'.

In the meantime Hore-Belisha was irritating Chamberlain. Like many ministers the War Secretary, once he had 'got his feet under the table', started to feed in his own interpretation of policy, which was far from the understanding on which he had been appointed. Belisha wanted a big army. He wanted to be able to posture and boast both at Question Time in the House, and on Movietone News. This was the exact opposite of what Chamberlain had planned. Resources, the Prime Minister believed, were limited and should be directed into the Navy and the Royal Air Force. The last thing he wanted was for a huge British contingent to stand 'shoulder-to-shoulder' with our Allies in northern France. It had always been something of a risk having 'Leslie' at the War Office. He was a useful counterweight, in terms of populist appeal, to Churchill. But this needed watching, also. If the two men should perceive an identity of interest, and combine, it could mean trouble. Belisha was the weaker, he was disposable; Churchill was not, and had to be left to hang himself. Furthermore there had been rumours, and some actual complaint, that Belisha had been irritating the General Staff with his intrusions, and the very free rein that he allowed his 'military adviser', Captain B. H. Liddell Hart.

On 4 January Hore-Belisha was summoned to Downing Street. Ominously, Chamberlain said that no note would be taken of the meeting, 'I have merely a proposal to make to you'. The proposal, stripped of its complimentary wrapping, was that Belisha should be downgraded to the Board of Trade. This was very bad news for Belisha, and he asked for time to consider. Chamberlain pressed for an immediate response.

> *H-B*: I am completely taken aback. I cannot understand why you will not give me a little time to think it over.
> *NC*: I fear it might leak out.
> *H-B*: I assume that you and I are the only two to know?
> *NC*: Yes.
> *H-B*: Then how can it leak out?[12]

That evening Belisha telephoned to Beaverbrook and reported that he was under threat. Beaverbrook, always easily excited by news of a reshuffle, thought that there might be the makings of a coup – of which, if it were properly handled, Churchill would be the beneficiary. The two of them decided to alert Churchill. But the First Lord was in Paris. Beaverbrook managed to contact Bracken★ with a message that Churchill should get in touch immediately, but a response was slow in coming. Much later that night the three men took a telephone call at Belisha's house where they were waiting, confident that 'Neville had gone too far'. But when they explained to Churchill what was in the air he seemed unconcerned, said 'Take Information'.

★ Brendan Bracken, friend of Churchill in his 'wilderness years'. Conservative MP for North Paddington, Churchill's Parliamentary Private Secretary, 1940–1; Minister of Information, 1941–5.

This was strange. '*Information*'? The conversation, plainly at cross-purposes and impeded by a bad telephone line, was brief. But it was clear that Churchill had been told of an intended reshuffle that morning, before he went to Paris (and before the Prime Minister's own meeting with Hore-Belisha). In fact Chamberlain had intended, at the time that he spoke to Churchill, to make Hore-Belisha Minister of Information. But shortly afterwards Chamberlain also discussed the matter with Halifax and it was at the Foreign Secretary's suggestion that the Board of Trade had been substituted.

> H-B at Information ... would have a bad effect on Neutrals both because ... [he] ... was a Jew and because his methods would let down British prestige.[13]

As for Churchill, he was quite content to see a rival demoted – all the more so in a setting that allowed him to demonstrate his own loyalty to the Prime Minister. But Belisha was doomed, and now knew it. Unhappily he presented himself at Number 10 the following morning.

As almost invariably happens (and this must be nearly always a principal reason why Prime Ministers defer changes in their Cabinet beyond the time at which they should be made) there was something of a scene:

> *H-B*: A fortnight ago you were telling me how highly you thought of my work, and you gave me no impression that you had any idea of making a change.
>
> *NC*: That is true, but I have thought the matter over since and I have come to the conclusion that it would be in your best interests to change from the War Office.
>
> *H-B*: Frankly, Neville, I am completely perplexed. On the one hand, I have had throughout every assurance of your confidence in me, and on the other, you are prepared to accede to prejudice against me. You are delivering me to my enemies. I have no ill-will, but logically I can only reach one conclusion. If you are not prepared to support me against prejudice in the office which I now

hold, the same thing might happen to me in the next office. And if I accepted the other office, I should be in a less advantageous position to defend myself.

NC: That would depend on you.

All that remained to be done was for Hore-Belisha to draft his letter of resignation, which he did after the morning Cabinet. When he showed it to the Prime Minister Chamberlain said it was 'a very nice letter'; but could there be 'a sentence or two about there being no difference of policy between us', and this Hore-Belisha meekly inserted. Chamberlain then 'put his hand on my arm in an affectionate way, saying, "Leslie" '; and Hore-Belisha replied 'Goodbye, Neville' and left the room.[14]

Truly an illustration that in politics two years is an eternity.

The time can of course pass barely without remark; same faces, same policies, same 'arithmetic'. Or it can change careers irretrievably, removing personalities and events from recognition and even, all too soon, from memory. Here had been this figure – alert and thrusting – at his side and one of the most formidable specialised intellects in the kingdom; faster on his feet than colleagues and more popular. His department, long due for overhaul, looked to be soon at the eye of the storm. Hore-Belisha had been that most highly valued of political commodities, 'a man whose time has come'. Yet now he had been cast out. A sacrifice? Or a retribution – for diverging from the brief which his sponsor had given to him, and for getting ideas above his station?

Like many dismissed ministers H-B was to hang around for some years, looking for opportunities to make trouble or, better, so to manoeuvre himself that his claims were acknowledged anew. Amery, who had complained to his diary in 1937 about the promotion of 'bouncing Belisha', recorded that for a day or so Westminster was alive with gossip, including a rumour that H-B had agreed to accept Trade if given 'control of economic co-ordination' – but that this had been 'vetoed by Simon'. From what we now know of the timing this seems highly unlikely – unless Chamberlain had himself floated the idea past his Chancellor when discussing (as we know he had done with Churchill) the reshuffle. But the rest of Amery's entry testifies to the steady undermining which Belisha's enemies had practised:

> For a year or more I have heard much of laziness, refusal to see things through . . . plus lack of tact and manners . . . Soldiers already fretting under changes some of which they felt were undermining discipline . . .
>
> [H–B was] more of a showman than an administrator, but showmanship is so big a side of democratic politics that he may come back again.[15]

After their parting, but while still in the corridor at Number 10, Belisha remembered something for which he had to go back to the Cabinet Room. He turned, opened the door and, seeing some colleagues still in conversation (they were, of course, discussing the news of his dismissal), furtively closed it again and tiptoed away. But Kingsley Wood hastily detached himself from the meeting and caught up with Belisha in the street:

> 'It is awful. It is quite a surprise to me. We none of us knew. What strikes me is if this can happen to you, it can happen to me.'[16]

This certainly was the mood of the whole Cabinet. Even, from time to time, including Churchill himself. They were bound together on this uncertain enterprise. If most of them could have put the clock back, they would have done so.

As war-makers they were useless. As party politicians they were now out of their depth. And yet the instinct for personal survival was deeply implanted. Belisha, who had lost, could do no more than make this Delphic reply: '*Precisely, Kingsley.*'

Four months later Wood was to take very good care that 'it' did not.

The ousting of Hore-Belisha allowed Beaverbrook to make mischief – but only briefly. The *Daily Express* of 7 January carried comment in heavy type – 'If Belisha must go, do all the other members of the Government deserve to stay?' – but without

Churchill's support or connivance the episode was soon to be forgotten. The principal distraction, during the first two months of 1940, was the duel, albeit *sotto voce* and with barely a sign for those outside the ring, between the Prime Minister and his First Lord.

Churchill was impatient. It was the Royal Navy who had been scoring the wins, victorious in every encounter: the *Graf Spee*, the U-boats, the blockade interceptions. The First Lord of the Admiralty, beneficiary in the public eye of the Fleet's achievements, wanted to start serious fighting – and against whom it hardly seemed to matter. So when Russia invaded Finland, in November of 1939, Churchill argued in Cabinet that Britain should go to Finland's help. And the longer, and the more effective, the Finns' resistance, the more adaptive and emotional became Churchill's arguments. Halifax's dismissive comment that 'God made Finland much nearer Russia and Germany than England'[17] made not the slightest difference. Ingeniously Churchill devised a plan whereby British troops *en route* to Finland should land at Narvik and move across northern Sweden, at the same time taking into their protection the iron-ore fields at Gallivare. This resource, Churchill claimed, and his acolytes strongly briefed the press, was 'essential to Germany's war effort, and without it the Reich "might well be forced to sue for peace".' Plans were laid, although the Cabinet, and Chamberlain, were doubtful. On 12 March, the Finns finally capitulated and the scheme, though not the concept, was dropped.

This was a remarkable and providential deliverance. The whole episode, the utter absurdity of challenging the largest army in the world while being simultaneously in a condition of hostility with the most efficient, defies belief. How did it come about? First, a strong element of public pressure. Gallant little Finland slipped effortlessly into the role (soon, though with the element of 'gallantry' to be of very short duration indeed, to be revisited) of gallant little Belgium. There was a general belief, founded in equal parts on historic precedent and self-delusion, that 'the Allies' were omnipotent and that their task was to 'punish aggression' wherever it occurred. Second, the fact that Russia, since the Molotov–Ribbentrop pact, was widely regarded as an accomplice of Germany. Her invasion of Poland had, nominally, invited direct hostilities with that country's guarantors (although no one said anything much about this when it happened) and the brilliant tactics of the Finnish Army had seemed to offer a chance of inflicting on the Germans a military defeat by proxy. Third, the French were desperate to ignite conflict at any point so long as it was as far away from their own eastern frontier as possible. In such a situation they were privy to, and supported, the 'war party' in Britain who simply wanted to widen the conflict, and raise the temperature, regardless of location. This group Chamberlain for his own reasons needed to placate but not to concede substance. Primed by Churchill's own lieutenants, supported by the *Daily Mirror* and other journals, they had been advocating in succession that we should force the Baltic, mine the Rhine, seize Heligoland, bomb Baku and – the only plan which had any pretence to being feasible or effective – blockade the iron-ore route from Narvik.

As Liddell Hart (now in the wilderness and, since the dismissal of Hore-Belisha, banned from entering the War Office building) acidly commented,

> The Charge of the Light Brigade was foolish enough as minor tactics. It would be far worse as Grand Strategy.

But sure enough it was to the Narvik scheme, once Finland had sued for peace, that Churchill forced the Cabinet once again to turn its attention. At the Supreme War Council meeting (attended by both French and British Prime Ministers) on 28 March the arguments of those who wanted to 'broaden' the war finally won the day, and Churchill secured, at last, assent to send the Fleet into Norwegian territorial waters and lay mines. From that, as the First Lord well knew, anything might happen. What did, in fact, happen made him, as the Prime Minister's secretary recorded, 'jubilant'. The Germans moved out, without warning, to do battle. And at dawn on 9 April put their own expeditionary force ashore in Oslo while the British were still twelve hours distant. The war had

changed character. No longer was it 'phoney'; nor, in the same
degree as hitherto, could it be susceptible to solution by 'compromise'.

By the middle of April 1940 Neville Chamberlain's time (although
there is no more evidence that he could see this than there is of
Mrs Thatcher's own monitory perception in the summer of 1990)
was drawing to a close.

Nor was Chamberlain to be saved by the paradox (similarly to
be present with his distant successor some fifty years hence) that
he had been entirely right in both his commitment and his
prediction. Although by instinct a maritimist – almost to the point
of isolationism – Chamberlain now saw the Royal Navy as being
no better than impotent in the face of Luftwaffe strength in the
airspace above narrow waters. And suffering not just humiliation –
in a matter of days the remembered gallantry of the River Plate
and the Altmark rescue were at a discount – but soon to be faced
with the nightmare of a thousand-mile overstretch that would give
the U-boats a safe and secret sallyport into the North Atlantic.

An observer is forced to the conclusion that Chamberlain simply
had not the assertiveness to see through the consequences, in
policy implementation, of how right he had been. The Prime
Minister's conduct of the Phoney War must be seen in the context
of his declining health. It is all one with the stumbles, and lost
opportunities, of the whole appeasement decade. But for Chamberlain there was just this one consolation. At every stage of the
campaign in Norway the mistakes – some petty, some fundamental,
some (if one has to be generous) unavoidable – had been the
responsibility of Churchill.

Certainly this was a difficult time for Winston Churchill. Within
forty-eight hours of the campaign opening he must have realised
that the Admiralty's own plan was falling apart. The German
troops were few in number, but highly trained in Arctic and
mountain warfare. Their use of mortars, skis, and mobility recalled
early Finnish victories over the Red Army. In particular the instant
and devastating co-operation with the Luftwaffe created a kind of

combat in which the British troops had no experience whatever. The two principal ports – Bergen and Trondheim – were consolidated immediately by the invaders, who took over, undamaged, their coastal defence forts. Just as there were no proper quays for disembarkation, so there were no airfields; while the Luftwaffe could operate day and night from Stavanger, whose runways were shaved out of solid rock. The ships carrying the expedition having been loaded, unloaded, reloaded at Scapa Flow, their cargo was in complete disorder: guns, radios, ammunition, vehicles being not on different decks but on different vessels and, it was often found, berthed in different harbours. Narvik, the original objective, remained stubbornly in enemy hands in spite of the heroic destroyer actions fought out in the fiord.

Bad enough in strategic terms, but for Churchill's own personal prospects it looked ominous in the extreme. This was to have been the masterstroke that seized the initiative, pre-empted the Germans' own spring battle-map, contrasted glaringly with the torpor and hesitance of his colleagues in Cabinet and established his claim beyond any doubt whatever to the succession.

Disliked as he was by the bulk of the Tory Party in Parliament, the target of constant and dismissive briefing by the Whips under Margesson's direction, Churchill was at this time in a state of equipoise. Not a comfortable one, but on the very edge of the knife's blade. On the one side the plaudits and clamour of the press, the smart acclaim of Lady Colefax's drawing room and the dining clubs of the 'glamour boys'. On the other the abyss – of a scapegoating dismissal for his ill-judged and impetuous extravagance in lives and material. Already, in the lobbies, 'Gallipoli' was being mentioned, and much else besides. This time, for sure, there could be no return.

On the night of 17 April the chamber of the House of Commons was packed and when Churchill entered his reception was a guarded one. Members were withholding their judgement until he had delivered.

[Winston] . . . is not looking well and sits there hunched as usual

with his papers in his hand. When he rises to speak it is obvious
that he is very tired. He starts off by giving an imitation of himself
making a speech ... vague oratory coupled with tired gibes ...
He hesitates, gets his notes in the wrong order, puts on the wrong
pair of spectacles, fumbles for the right pair, keeps on saying
'Sweden' when he means 'Denmark' ... It is a feeble, tired speech
and it leaves the House in a mood of grave anxiety.[18]

For three weeks Churchill's standing diminished. Each day
brought news of sinkings, evacuation, casualties. How could the
first naval power in the world be defeated in an operation put
before it, in terms of strategic opportunity, from Heaven? Even
Narvik, the ore port on whose alleged strategic importance the
whole scheme had depended, remained secure in German hands;
in spite of two spectacular raids (for which the First Lord of the
Admiralty had been keen to take credit) into the fiord by the
British destroyers. Paradoxically, and for a short time, the defeat
in Norway seemed to rally support, not just for the Government
but for Chamberlain's own policy of detachment. The previous
month Beaverbrook, conducting his own private campaign to
detach the ILP from the Labour Party, had entertained James
Maxton and John McGovern. He tried to square them with his
own argument that there was

> ... not any alternative at that time but to negotiate an honourable
> settlement, retire behind our Empire frontiers, arm ourselves to
> the teeth, leave the Continent to work out its own destiny and
> defend the Empire with all our strength.[19]

A more succinct (and persuasive) summary of Chamberlain's
own diffident and hesitant policy could hardly be found. On 6
May Beaverbrook wrote a leader-page article in the *Express*,
entitled '*What is the damage?*'. He dismissed the Norwegian defeat
as 'a minor affair'. He claimed credit for the Government that
London was not being bombed – 'nor is it likely to be'. The defeat
of the U-boats, immense financial resources, the impregnable
Maginot Line. For this flagrant and misleading piece of propaganda

Beaverbrook's reward was an immediate handwritten note from
the Prime Minister – 'When so many are sounding the defeatist
note over a minor setback, it is a relief to read such a courageous
and inspiriting summons to a saner view'.[20] Now the peace party
seemed to be recovering its wind. And Churchill's reputation was
in shadow. The Military Co-ordination Committee, with whose
proceedings Churchill was attempting constantly to bypass the
War Cabinet, was in disarray. Chamberlain recorded that

> it is ... getting into a sad mess, with everyone feeling irritable and
> strained and with a general conviction that Winston had smashed
> the machine that we had so carefully built up[21]

– and he himself took over the chair. The sound of fighting had
died down.

Yet within forty-eight hours everything would change again.
Strange, the chemistry of politics; and of the House of Commons,
its corridors and lobbies. Suddenly in the first week of May the
mood had altered. Partly indignation, a feeling that military defeat
had been undeserved. Far from being 'a minor setback' the failure
in Norway, riddled as it had been with incompetencies, was seen
as a major humiliation of the world's greatest naval power. Partly
an instinct, such as was to afflict the Major Government in 1997,
that the administration was decomposing; that there was personal
and party advantage to be had from laying into it. And partly,
which Members of Parliament always find difficult to resist, a
beckoning opportunity to declaim and strike attitudes and make
imprint on the passage of history.

The long two-day confidence debate of 7–8 May 1940 – 'the
Norway Debate' – was the greatest, and the most portentous, of
all parliamentary occasions in the twentieth century. The Government won – and with a majority of 81. But its standing had
crumbled, and over 100 Conservatives had either abstained, or
voted against their own party. On that night every actor played his
part – and played it to the gallery. Sir Roger Keyes, dressed in full
uniform of Admiral of the Fleet, speaking 'on behalf of some
officers and men of the fighting, sea-going navy who are very

unhappy . . .' Leo Amery, concluding his critique with Cromwell's valediction to the Long Parliament, '. . . in the name of God, go!' and making respectable at an early stage in the debate the notion that the Government might fall, and a new start be made. And Lloyd George, shrewdly isolating Churchill from his other colleagues, but at the same time setting out his own claims as prophet and conciliator. From the first minute of Chamberlain rising to his feet it was clear that the House was against him. The Whips' 'operation', putting pressure on back-bench nonentities to 'speak up for the Prime Minister', was doomed from the outset. One after another the Knights of the Shire – Sir A. Southby, Sir G. Courthope, and their ilk – rose to their feet and were cruelly heckled.

Finally it was the time of the wind-up – to be delivered by the First Lord himself. Where Lloyd George had been overcritical, and laced his comments with foreboding, Churchill judged perfectly the mood of the House. Here were these two statesmen, each replete with experience of military crisis in the Great War – telling different tales. Lloyd George was merciless in his dissection of detail, as in his conclusion – '*We are in the worst strategic position in which this country has ever been placed*'. Churchill, though, combined total loyalty with the holding out of hope. His periodic resort to bluster ('It seems to me that, although Hitler's sudden overrunning of the vast regions of Norway has had astonishing [*sic*] and unwelcome effects, nevertheless, the advantages rest substantially with us') he lightened with the occasional flash of humour. The House, and especially the Conservative Party, did not want a party speech. It did not want a contrite speech.

For several years MPs had gone along, with varying degrees of reluctance and incomprehension, and in conformity with loyalty and discipline, with appeasement. Now, in an atmosphere fevered and yet engendering a nostalgia for invincibility, for winning always 'the last battle', the party abandoned discretion. It wanted to be told that we were going to fight, and going to win. That evening Churchill perfected, and used with devastating result, the formula with which he had been experimenting since entering

the Government. Furthermore, and in the clearest call to be heard
that night, he concluded by inviting a coalition:

> ... let us keep our hatreds for the common enemy. Let Party
> interest be ignored, let all our energies be harnessed, let the whole
> ability and forces of the nation be hurled into the struggle, and let
> all the strong horses be pulling on the collar.[22]

FOURTEEN

The Coalition Government
is Formed

*Excitement at Westminster – Margesson attempts the
impossible – Halifax calculates – Collapse of the Western
Front – Desperate measures – The 'Joint Citizenship'
offer – The Royal Air Force lifts the threat.*

THE DAY FOLLOWING NEVILLE CHAMBERLAIN'S defeat (for
such, notwithstanding his arithmetic 'victory', it had been) was
one of great confusion. Would the Prime Minister survive? How
necessary was it to broaden the administration? What was to be
the attitude of the Labour Party and how, some of the more
excitable MPs asked each other, might they fare in a general
election should one be called, or half-accidentally come about, on
the issue of competence in directing the war effort?

The hero, or at least the personal catalyst for the previous night's
drama, had been Leo Amery. Early on the morning of 9 May he
attended a meeting of Salisbury's Watching Committee. At this
the 'general feeling' was that 'Neville should now resign and either
Halifax or Winston form a real War Cabinet on National lines
...'[1] Salisbury was deputed (though whether the instruction he
received reflected a majority view of the group is unclear) to
convey this feeling to Halifax. But *not*, in the first instance, to
Churchill. At this early point in the day Halifax had a clear lead
in the party's preference.

Chamberlain was also conferring. During the early evening of
the confidence debate the Chief Whip had been privately and
intimately – as his (numerous) confidants were led to believe –
leaking the Prime Minister's willingness 'drastically' to recast the

administration, and his open mind about sacking Hoare, Simon, and any others who had 'lost the confidence of colleagues'. Not, though, to consider inviting Attlee to suggest names. Chamberlain knew that in a cross-party coalition he would no longer be Prime Minister. But he and Margesson still held to the hope that the mass of Conservative MPs would, in a matter of days, calm down and, if he shed enough Cabinet blood, keep him in place.

Barely had Amery arrived at the House of Commons than he found Hore-Belisha at his side. He, Amery, was the man, Hore-Belisha told him. And, what was more, Max Beaverbrook agreed. They had been talking the matter over at breakfast. Hore-Belisha was aggrieved (and remained so for the next several years) by Chamberlain's peremptory behaviour in January: 'what was really wanted was a clean sweep . . .' (together with, it can be assumed, an invitation to themselves to join the administration). His motives were transparent, and Amery saw this. But Beaverbrook was a truly powerful ally; his political antennae were sensitive. Did he now sense impending collapse? Was he casting around for a new protégé? This will have occurred to Amery; who none the less was lukewarm, or affected to be. 'The last thing I wished was that I should be thought to be running for this or trying to steal a march on the party.'

Minutes later, though, Clement Davies* appeared. He said that he had been talking with Arthur Greenwood and others of the Labour front bench. The surprising, but welcome, consensus of these senior Opposition politicians was that the Tory 'under whom they would soonest serve would be myself'. Amery went off and found Archie Sinclair. He inquired of the Liberal Party opinion; then took the chair at a reconvened meeting of the Salisbury Committee, this time amalgamated with Clement Davies's All-Party Action Group. Amery will have made allowance for the transient nature of a House of Commons accolade awarded on the basis of a single episode – however spectacular. Even so, his handling of the meeting does seem to have been over-decorous.

* Liberal MP for Montgomeryshire, 1929–62; later the party's leader.

'A firm refusal to allow any suggestion of personal ambition to creep in'* was certainly out of harmony with the attitude of some other contenders over these crucial forty-eight hours. Only the text of the Group's resolution that they '... would support *any* Prime Minister who would form a truly National government' could be said to have left things open.²

All these manoeuvrings were taking place within the precincts of the Palace of Westminster. At the restaurant tables there was also activity. Winston Churchill was lunching at the Carlton Grill with Eden and Kingsley Wood. To his amazement Eden heard Wood reveal that the Prime Minister intended to ambush Churchill and secure his endorsement of Halifax's candidature, adding the far from loyal advice:

'Don't agree, and don't say anything.'†³

Earlier that morning Churchill had been approached by Beaverbrook. 'I asked – do you intend to serve under Halifax? He answered – I will serve under any Minister capable of prosecuting the War.'⁴ The 'any' can of course be seen as elliptical – particularly when linked with 'capability' – as it had been in the text of the resolution of Amery's group. But Beaverbrook was disappointed. He went out and had lunch with Sam Hoare. Hoare, predictably, said that he 'hoped very much to avoid the collapse ... and was discussing ways and means of protecting Neville against his enemies'.

It was no use. The party was excited, conspiratorial. It smelled blood. All morning Margesson had been telephoning round. While Horace Wilson, in gross violation (at a pitch which was not to be repeated for fifty years, until Charles Powell was running Mrs Thatcher's office) of the Civil Service code, took soundings on possible additions to the Government, including the making of a personal approach to Amery and offering him an unspecified

---

* The description is from Hore-Belisha, 'reporting' to Beaverbrook.
† This is taken from a verbatim account in Eden's diary. David Carlton, Eden's perceptive biographer, attaches a conspiracy theory which cannot lightly be dismissed, and is extended to Halifax himself in discussion below – pp. 209–12.

Cabinet position. Few MPs were so brazen as to tell the Chief
Whip that 'Neville must go'. But the only conditions under which
colleagues would commit themselves to support made it inevitable.
Too many wanted too many different things. Some, like Harold
Nicolson, wanted a 'National' government. Others favoured
Halifax; others Eden; some mentioned Amery; and a hard core,
with Bracken and Boothby the most assiduous, were pushing for
Churchill. Waiting in the wings was Lloyd George, the 'saviour'
of 1917, who had displaced Halifax as the favourite of the Cliveden
Set. On 7 May, the very eve of the Norway debate, he had
been approached by Nancy Astor, but '. . . preferred to await his
country's summons a little longer . . . he expected to receive it as
the peril grew'.[5]

Now Chamberlain, still desperate, as is every leader when
actually he hears the tread of an approaching executioner in the
cell corridor, humiliated himself. Could Labour be persuaded to
come into (yet another) 'National' government? The practice of
taking refuge in coalition, of sharing responsibility but – as far as
possible – not absolute power, was an established conformity with
many Conservatives. 1915, 1931, now 1940? (And, as will be seen,
Churchill himself, Macmillan and Edward Heath would all in
their time yearn for it.) It was the worst season of the year for
trailing this idea with the Labour leaders. Their party was actually
sitting in Annual Conference. The 'smoke-filled room' in which,
perhaps with help from Sir Alexander Hardinge★ and the Palace,
a deal might have been put together was the size of the Winter
Gardens at Bournemouth.

While soundings were being taken Chamberlain made overtures, politics being what it is, without shame towards his bitterest
critics. To Amery he offered Chancellorship of the Exchequer.
Amery refused. The Foreign Office, then? (Did Halifax know of
this conversation, one must ask?) Amery refused again.[6] Practically
no one, it seemed, was purchasable. By mid-morning Margesson

★ The King's private secretary.

had to tell the Prime Minister a most unwelcome truth. On a vote of confidence he would lose.

Meetings continued during the day. The objective of the appeasers – now a diminishing band – was to 'block Winston'. Only one man could do this. As his biographer has written, 'Halifax entered [the room]' (for that last 4.30 meeting with Chamberlain and the Chief Whip) 'in the certain knowledge that the Premiership was safely his for the taking.'[7] Why did he hesitate? Writing to a friend two days later Halifax said, 'I don't think Winston will be a very good PM, though I think the country will think [sic] he gives them a fillip.' To Butler, on his return from Number 10, Halifax confided that 'as Churchill would be "running the war anyway" his own role would 'speedily turn into a sort of honorary Prime Minister'. But there was more to Halifax's calculation – he admitted that he 'felt he could do the job' – than polite self-effacement. Popular demand, and expectation, for Churchill was so strong that any alternative choice would be impossibly handicapped by Churchill's presence at his side. But Churchill was impetuous; he did not seek, or take, advice; he suffered often from self-delusion. In this extraordinarily difficult and dangerous crisis it was almost a certainty that, in a measurable time – months, weeks, possibly only days – these failings would be apparent. And Churchill, who had still no substantial following among Tory MPs, would have to be replaced.[8]

On the morning of 10 May, with the news of the great German attack in the west pouring in from every station, the miserable Neville Chamberlain had one more try. The crisis was so acute that it would, surely, be imprudent to make any drastic change? It was the same argument on which Aneurin Bevan had poured such scorn in the debate of 24 August 1939 on the Nazi–Soviet Pact – '. . . the bigger the catastrophe of which he is the architect, the safer he is'. At the first meeting, 8 a.m., Cabinet colleagues listened in silence. At the second, 11.30 a.m., Kingsley Wood spoke up. It was impossible, he said. No one else commented. Afterwards Sam Hoare noted, 'Edward [Halifax] . . . quite heartless.'[9]

And so on 10 May 1940, against the wishes of the King, the

Queen, the staff at Number 10 Downing Street, and a substantial number of ministers and back-benchers in the Conservative Party, Winston Churchill became Prime Minister.

The military events which followed on immediately from Winston Churchill's accession to the premiership are (at least in the orthodox version) well-known, but it remains necessary to touch on them. If only to illustrate the sheer scale, the urgency, the cascade of defeat and confusion with which Churchill was faced as 'this hour' struck.

Winston Churchill was now leader not of a Tory, but of a truly all-party National Government. His immediate concern had to be the acute peril in which the country found itself. This did, it is true, find its origins, or many of them, in the collapse of the policy followed so imperfectly by the majority political party; and of the assumptions on which that policy was based. And certainly it was the urgency of the peril to which Churchill owed his selection. What had now to monopolise Churchill's energy was the evident disintegration of the platform on which the entire Alliance rested; and, central to that – a strategic decision which, innocuous enough in the ingredients which first presented themselves, was none the less of the very highest importance. The only one indeed, during the entire course of the next five years, that was literally, and for the whole nation, a matter of life or death.

Because in all the chaos, misdirection and defeat in battle that was accumulating on the Continent there shone but one gleam of light. The single-seater eight-gun fighter aircraft of the Royal Air Force were unbeatable. Even from French airfields, with bad fuel, grass runways and complete absence of radar direction, they had proved capable of taking on every type deployed by the Luftwaffe. Where the Hurricanes of the Air Component* flew, the air soon cleared of German bombers. But there were limits. Within days pilots and maintenance staff were exhausted and the machines

---

* RAF units stationed on the French mainland to give close support to the British Expeditionary Force (BEF).

overstressed. On 11, 12 and 13 May reinforcements were flown from airfields in Kent. By 14 May the total of Hurricane squadrons committed to the battle of France was ten, and many of them were already seriously depleted by accident and combat damage, and aircrew fatigue. They were operating without the benefit of radar controllers, and spare parts had to be flown out from England each day. Already the danger limit, set out by Sir Hugh Dowding in July of 1939, had been exceeded:

> the air defence of Great Britain will be gravely imperilled. If 10 Regular Squadrons are withdrawn, the remaining resources would be altogether inadequate for the defence of this country.

Thus the considered opinion of the Commander-in-Chief of Fighter Command. But was this not a narrow, Service-oriented viewpoint? Surely the defence of Great Britain would be not 'imperilled' but put in catastrophic jeopardy if her ally on the mainland were to collapse? For three days the issue was to hang in the balance, and the argument be closely fought.

Churchill had entered Number 10 Downing Street on Friday evening. The mood was one of exhilaration. Reports were pouring in, many of them contradictory – spies and alarms; quislings, parachutists dressed as nuns – but no inkling of catastrophe.

In fact the whole Allied deployment, agreed at successive meetings of the Joint War Council, had played perfectly into the giant trap conceived by General Manstein; a mirror image, and the more effective for that, of the Schlieffen Plan of 1914. The German General Staff had been scrupulous at every level in their attention to detail. The sheer weight in tanks and firepower deployed was never afterwards equalled by the Wehrmacht; not, certainly, in so narrow a concentration as ruptured the French line at Sedan on the Meuse on 13 May. The German objective was not this time Paris; but the Channel coast, and the amputation of the BEF from the main body of Allied troops.

This was not yet apparent in London. Churchill was preoccupied with forming his new administration. And it is true that – apparently – over these first days the Allied war plan was proceeding smoothly, as the BEF and the French divisions on its right flank moved ('advanced', some commentators did optimistically say) into the Low Countries. Battle, or so it seemed, had not yet been joined.

Churchill's distribution of office had been guided by two considerations: The need for party balance, yet without letting the Socialist or Liberal nominees too close to the great departments of State. And a personal wariness concerning possible rivalries or claimants at some future, but not necessarily distant, point.

'You must not underestimate the great reaction ... among Conservative members, among whom you will find over three-quarters who are ready to put Neville back.' This the judgement of Maurice Hely-Hutchinson, Secretary to the 1922 Committee, recorded by Rab Butler three days into Churchill's premiership.

Nor was Chamberlain the only one from whom a threat might materialise. Halifax could not be relegated so soon, although Churchill tried unsuccessfully to tie him down with trivia and ceremonial as Leader of the Lords, and was immediately put on guard when Halifax refused. But Hoare – a person with little following in the parliamentary party, but a potential quisling none the less – was sacked at once. Amery was offered Secretary of State for India, a shameless sidelining of one who had played a key role in the coup, but whose intellect and vision might, if 'things' got difficult, offer an alternative focus. Anthony Eden, to whom many of the same considerations applied, was made War Minister, but still excluded from the War Cabinet. As Churchill, styling himself Minister of Defence as well as Prime Minister, retained overall military direction Eden was, for the time being at least, little more than Churchill's office boy. Some, but not all, of Churchill's cronies got jobs. Beaverbrook would soon be admitted to the War Cabinet but Kingsley Wood, whose last-minute treachery and change of side had played its part in destabilising Chamberlain, was – despite becoming Chancellor of the Exchequer – left out of the War Cabinet until October (an indication of Churchill's indifference to the economic reality).

Halifax had no say in these appointments – an early example of Churchill's ruthlessness and of the hundred leagues that separate a leader and his deputy. When he was grumbling to Butler and was reminded (perhaps tactlessly) of his own failure to grab the crown only a fortnight earlier Halifax snapped, 'You know my reasons, it's no use discussing that – but the gangsters will shortly be in complete control.'[10]

On 16 May, a Thursday and less than a week after Churchill's accession, some most unwelcome and, to some still, incredible news was put on the table at the 10.15 a.m. Chiefs of Staff meeting. The Maginot Line had been ruptured,* and the German armoured columns had broken into open country. The Chief of the Air Staff, Newall, read out a telegram from the French Commander-in-Chief, Gamelin, who said that he must have – *immediately* – another ten squadrons of Hurricanes. Discussion followed. Newall was uneasy. He suggested that four squadrons be 'assigned', but only two actually be sent that day. The other Chiefs could hardly demur, but when Churchill arrived they agreed to *send* four squadrons, and to 'assign' two more.

The two squadrons designated were actually in the line – based in the Orkneys and defending the Home Fleet at Scapa Flow. This was an extraordinary decision. Besides being a monumental strategic error – to leave the Royal Navy's principal base defence-less it was also a gross tactical miscalculation, as the Luftwaffe bombers would have been able to operate without long-range fighter escort, and the Me 110s could have been redeployed in the south. Churchill then went straight into the War Cabinet, where there was general support for his decision, except from Sinclair, the Air Minister – who was being briefed direct by Dowding.

---

* Like most intelligence reports of the time, this was not strictly accurate. The Germans had broken the French front, but at the very point where the line of fortified emplacements stopped.

Halfway through the proceedings Sir John Dill★ was handed a signal advising that the French left flank was being 'folded back' (i.e., withdrawn). This meant, effectively, that a corridor all the way to the Channel coast at Abbeville would be opened for the advancing Panzers.

The War Cabinet immediately assented to the Prime Minister's request that he be given leave to proceed at once to Paris and see things for himself. As soon as Churchill's little group arrived – that very afternoon at four o'clock – it was clear that all was far from well. 'The officers who met us said that the Germans were expected in Paris in a few days at most.'[11] There then followed the celebrated encounter when General Gamelin explained the situation; and when Churchill, asking him where the strategic reserve was deployed, received the answer – '*aucune*'.†

The 16th of May was a very long day. Churchill returned to the Embassy, sent back to the War Cabinet a telegram saying that 'the situation is grave in the last degree'. He added that 'we should send squadrons of fighters demanded [i.e., six more] tomorrow'. This was almost too much for the War Cabinet, meeting in emergency session at 11 p.m. They discussed for over an hour; then reluctantly agreed but with the ingenious reservation devised by Newall that three squadrons should work from airfields in Kent 'from dawn until noon', the other three 'from noon until dusk'. This, Newall claimed – more than speciously – would be the 'same' as if the whole of the six squadrons were sent to work from French aerodromes. Delighted to have found a formula which allowed him to keep up pressure on his ally, Churchill set off, at 1 a.m., to find Paul Reynaud. He and Major-General Ismay found the French Prime Minister's flat '... more or less in darkness, the only sign of life in the sitting room being a lady's fur coat. M. Reynaud emerged ... in his dressing gown ... and Churchill told him the glad news.'[12]

★ Dill had commanded I Corps under Lord Gort in France, but been recalled to be Vice-Chief of the Imperial General Staff in April 1940. On 27 May he succeeded General Ironside as CIGS.

† 'there isn't one'.

For another eight days scarce and precious resources were poured into France. But by the morning of 27 May Churchill found himself announcing to the ten o'clock Cabinet that the capitulation of Belgium was imminent. This would leave the BEF cut off, with neither flank anchored. Dill then clarified the threat. Two hundred and thirty thousand British troops were 'in the most serious peril'. Cabinet was also informed that provision had been made for the gold reserves, and the Royal Family, to be evacuated to Canada, although the dramatic effect was somewhat impaired halfway through the meeting when Lothian revealed that President Roosevelt, while very anxious to get his hands on the British Fleet, felt that Republicans in the US might object if the King and Queen came any further west than Bermuda.

Now, barely a fortnight into his premiership, Churchill seemed to have got into, or at least been overtaken by, exactly the kind of mess predicted by his enemies; and which so clearly had been at the back of Halifax's mind when he had turned away from Chamberlain's offer at the meeting on 9 May.

At four o'clock on the afternoon of Tuesday the 28th, the subject of a possible negotiation came up for the fifth time in three days. Halifax, sitting directly opposite Churchill, his withered hand concealed under the Cabinet table, repeated his advice: 'Provided that we can [secure our independence] we should make it clear that there were certain concessions that we are prepared to make'.[13] Was this not the traditional, pragmatic Tory approach, even *in extremis*? Many around that table, sensing that another upheaval could be on the cards, will have been considering their personal position. Perhaps this would turn out to be no more than a 'caretaker' administration? Chamberlain sat in silence throughout. The Chiefs of Staff were ready to give evidence, but their testimony could not be optimistic. Realising that the meeting was moving against him Churchill adjourned it. Next, displaying that incredible energy and zeal which, so often, alternated with periods of 'black dog', he summoned to Number 10 all the ministers outside the War Cabinet who could quickly be found and harangued them. It was 'dramatic', 'unreal' (and, as it happened,

untruthful because Churchill greatly exaggerated the prospect of
the United States taking action).[14] But as a political tactic it was
guaranteed to succeed. Ministers of the second rank, fancying
their own talents above their superiors', will always vote to supplant
them. The crisis passed, part elbowed off the stage by the sheer
pressure of accumulating events. But the memory remained with
Churchill for the whole of his period as Leader of the Coalition.
It had been one among many 'very close shaves'.

For a few more melancholy days the pretence was sustained that
France might weather the storm. The front appeared briefly to
solidify along the line of the River Somme, then collapsed finally
and utterly. Weygand replaced Gamelin as Commander-in-Chief.
He hated the British, and only wanted to keep the French Army
in being to 'control rioters'. Marshal Pétain, at eighty-five, was
brought back into the Government. He, too, preferred the
Germans to the British. Paris was evacuated.

Churchill followed the remains of the French administration
from one chateau overnight stay to another. At each meeting he
felt himself more resented. Until, at the very end, the British
played (at whose suggestion is still not clear) their last card to try
and save the French Navy and the African colonies: a proposal of
'joint and indissoluble union' between the two countries. The
atmosphere of desperation that lay over these meetings – on this,
or any other topic – is well illustrated by the fact that it was de
Gaulle himself, the very embodiment of nationalist pride and
exclusivity, who, when the proposal of joint citizenship was first
mooted, weighed in against Churchill's own expressed doubts:

> Yes. That means that its realisation would involve a great deal of
> time. But the gesture can be immediate ... As things are now
> nothing must be neglected by you that can support France and
> maintain our alliance.

This bizarre episode – ill thought out, unconstitutional, and
bearing all the marks of panic – is none the less significant in
shedding light on the problems of 'Europe' that were intermittently to blight all periods of Tory governance in the second

half of the century. And so, even while recounting the events of the great crisis of June 1940, it is as well to interrupt and retrace its origins. They are best found in Orme Sargent's exploratory papers and recommendations from the opening months of the year. Yet in its reckless disregard for, omission even to measure, feeling in either House of Parliament; and in the eagerness shown by its protagonists to subordinate the national interest to their own enthusiasms, there can be traced many of the precursors of that great Euro-schism which was to rack the Conservative Party forty years on.

Two fringe members of the Establishment, Professor Arnold Toynbee and Sir Alfred Zimmern, had composed the report which led to the setting up of the Hankey Committee. They were later charged by Rex Leeper (enjoying Butler's active encouragement) with the drafting of a 'short and striking document' summing up a scheme for Anglo-French co-operation. 'Our new order if it embraces the British and French Empires, would provide a real peace aim for the youth of England [sic] and France.'

Short the document was not. But if by 'striking' was meant radical, and far beyond the scope of its well-intentioned – if banal – terms of reference – that it certainly was. Entitled a *Draft Act of Perpetual Association between the United Kingdom and France*, the text opens full tilt. Ignoring the convention that an *Act* is generally understood, certainly in Whitehall documentation, to mean a Bill which has passed through all its stages in Lords and Commons, the authors explain that

> 'Pact', 'Treaty', 'Convention' or 'Covenant' all ... call up associations which it is desirable to avoid ...

But before they had time to settle back, the startled members of the Hankey Committee, to whom this proposal was submitted on 30 April, were told that 'Association' had been rejected 'because it implies an organic connection which stops short of complete fusion'.

> What is proposed is in form a treaty ... but in fact it provides a

framework for a process of integration which has already begun in
the sphere of war-time co-operation between the two governments
and has reached a point where it is ripe for embodiment in
permanent institutions . . . 'Perpetual' provides assurance that there
will be time for the process of growth.

The sophistry of that distinction between 'in form' and 'in fact'
took shape in the Articles, of which numbers 1 to 6 began each
with a 'pledge' to 'pursue a common Policy' in such diverse fields
as external affairs, economics (a common currency was foreseen)
and an agreement 'not to treat each other's nationals as aliens'.[15]

Sargent had ensured that the report was placed at the top of the
Committee's agenda at its first meeting on 30 April. What will,
by most of the participants, have been foreseen as a genial stroll
through a garden of *biens pensées*, abruptly found itself conducting
a preliminary to the COREPER* discussions ahead of the 1991
Maastricht Treaty.

Suave though he may have been, and accomplished in his
powers of persuasion, Sargent had met his match in Hankey.

> Some discussion took place, read the minutes (this being a well
> recognised Whitehall code for 'time was wasted, and no con-
> clusions were either postulated or allowed') as to whether it was
> really necessary to have a comprehensive document of this nature,
> which was somewhat academic. It was suggested that it might be
> better to consider the actual spheres in which collaboration might
> be elaborated. The most that Hankey would concede was that the
> document 'formed a convenient basis for discussion'.

Moreover, consideration of 'the actual spheres' led to as comprehensive a demolition of their arguments as could be fitted into
the time available. Notably, T. K. Bewley, the Treasury representative, rejected outright the concept of a single currency,
doubting that 'we would be able to support the value of the Franc
indefinitely'; Lord de la Warr had minuted that the Board of

---

* The European Union Council of Permanent Representatives.

Education 'could not insist on the compulsory teaching of French in British schools', but that he would 'ask school inspectors to impress upon the teachers the need to give greater emphasis to France in future when teaching history and geography'. Then, drawing on who knows what fund of personal knowledge, de la Warr suggested that 'there are a number of unemployed French chefs in London whom we might get to go round the schools and cook French meals'.

When the next meeting of the Committee came round, it was 21 May and the discussions were looking more and more 'academic' (Sargent's phrase, when he finally suspended it on 22 June). However Sir Arnold Overton, who had been primed by Hankey to consider the question of a customs union between the two countries, had delivered his paper. The subject was 'beset by many and serious political, practical and administrative difficulties'. Success would require a 'fusion' of financial and political relations between the two countries . . . would damage the domestic economies of both. Bewley returned to the attack with the assertion that:

a common currency had never been possible historically without a common government.

The idea must have seemed stone dead and Hankey, of course, was delighted. Having described these rebuttal papers as 'negative' he none the less conceded that they were 'very convincing'. Halifax, and Butler, also, had other things on their minds.

And yet within weeks this reckless concept, still further embellished, was being seriously advanced as a 'historic breakthrough'.

Portrayed at the time as a generous and spontaneous impulse, a last stretching out of hands to a mortally wounded ally, the Joint Citizenship offer can also be seen in a different light. An opportunist move by the Francophiles in the Foreign Office to establish a 'precedent' for their policy, and a basis for its revival at a more auspicious moment. The French reaction combined incredulity and resentment. Reynaud had hoped to surprise his Cabinet colleagues, but they had been warned by Weygand, who was using his own intelligence operatives to tap the Prime Minister's telephone. Pétain said that it would be 'fusion with a corpse'; Jean Ybarnegaray,* articulating the true voice of the collaborator, advised that it would be

> better a Nazi province: at least we know what that means.

Camille Chautemps† and others warned that it was simply a plot to annexe the French colonies. In fact the offer of 16 June had something of all these things. But in essence it was a last desperate attempt to keep France, and French resistance, and particularly the French Navy, alive. A deferral to the one overriding strategic assumption – that any price was worth paying in order to prevent a French surrender that would leave Britain isolated. Its weakness, aside from utter impracticality and transparent motive, was ignorance: of that irreconcilable junction of logic and fantasy that is the French mind, and which found expression in Pétain's own call:

> The revival of France will issue from the soul of the Nation, which soul can be preserved only by staying, rather than reconquering the country with Allied cannons . . . [I] stay, and accept the suffering that will result. The French renaissance will be the fruit of this suffering.[16]

It was then that Churchill, faced with the text which Jean Monnet and Sir Robert Vansittart had spent the morning 'tightening', declared it 'an enormous mouthful'. Yet he too, with the events of 23 May still fresh in his memory, mindful of the possibility that yet another peace initiative could break out in his own Cabinet if France were seen to receive generous terms, had to try anything. The leading academic study[17] concludes – scarcely surprisingly – 'that there can be no doubt that it was the immediate present rather than the distant future with which they [the authors] were concerned'.

While this may be true of the politicians, the episode offers an

---

* French Minister of State.
† Former French Prime Minister.

early indication of an implacable streak at the Foreign Office. The inbuilt preference of its senior officials for the discourse and company of their diplomatic counterparts; an aversion to 'nationalism', and an impatience with the workings of elective politics that amounted almost to contempt. It was the precursor of all the patient work and periodic ambushes of the late 1980s to 1990 which finally would entrap Margaret Thatcher and trigger the collapse of her own premiership.

On the following day, 17 June, 'With a heavy heart' but to (no doubt) a greatly relieved nation, Pétain broadcast that 'I tell you today that we must cease hostilities.'[18]

Britain had now extricated itself, or escaped from, all of its Continental responsibilities. Over the summer of 1940 Fighter Command of the Royal Air Force fought, and was victorious in, one of the great battles of twentieth-century history. So the Government, now a coalition and so with no political opponents, had a breathing space. Within the Conservative Party intrigue and discontent were dormant. The Tories had been granted security – though not of indefinite duration – in which to determine what course of action would best ensure the preservation of the nation state.

FIFTEEN

Wasted Opportunities

The illusion of stalemate – Uncertain relations with de
Gaulle – The seeds of mutual distrust over the long
term – Mers-el-Kebir – The Dakar expedition –
Rapprochement with Vichy? – Disappointments with
FDR – The 'Destroyers for Bases' deal – The dollars
run out – Neville Chamberlain sickens –
The Eden–Halifax dilemma – The stifling of dissent –
Menzies – The unheralded arrival of Hitler's deputy.

ONCE THE LUFTWAFFE TURNED FROM daylight to night raiding
the crisis was past. The battle was no longer for air superiority –
which if conceded would have made a seaborne invasion impossible either to prevent or, once established, to defeat; and thus
meant the loss of the war in a matter of weeks – but a contest of
attrition. The 'Blitz', as the night raids came to be called, was
disagreeable, and debilitating. But it was no more capable of
forcing a decision on its own than was the many times more
formidable offensive sustained by RAF Bomber Command against
the cities of Germany in 1943.

Thus the scale of decision altered. From being urgently tactical
it could, or should, have become strategic and considerative. The
British Empire had survived – but by the breadth of a hair. By
sometimes no more than an ill-calculated reserve in the fuel tank
of a fighter aircraft, a lucky interpretation of changed direction on
a radar screen, an unforecast cloud bank or a target misidentified.

Yet within days of victory in the daylight air war the British
found themselves involved once again in an unnecessary land

battle, and one for which they were unprepared. The ill-organised and incompetently handled Dakar expedition began, eight weeks late, on 23 September 1940. Three days afterwards it was called off; a wholly needless diversion of resources that suffered, among other casualties and humiliation, the torpedoing of the capital ship HMS *Renown*. Strategically the consequences were negligible – save, in all probability, the reinforcement of existing doubt in the minds of the Combined Chiefs as to the efficacy of amphibious operations (which will have rendered them less than enthusiastic on the one occasion when this should have been advocated *à l'outrance*, namely against Tripoli in February of 1941). But politically its effects were ineradicable; would indeed recur on many occasions, finally to undo a Conservative Prime Minister and his policies some twenty-one years later at Rambouillet. So it is right to set out, and examine in some detail, what took place. And, in particular, the complex, erratic and, for most of the time, disreputable nature of relations between the British Government and General Charles de Gaulle.

At the beginning of June 1940, with the land battle already lost, Reynaud had put de Gaulle, the youngest brigadier-general in the French Army, into his Cabinet as Under-Secretary of State for National Defence. It was an attempt, far from full-hearted, at balancing the defeatism of the two senior Marshals, Weygand and Pétain, who would combine at each morning's conference in producing pessimistic assessments of the military situation. Pétain had been annoyed by this appointment, feeling, with some justification, that having been so recently called back into Government his status endowed him with a right of scrutiny over other military nominations:

> His [de Gaulle's] vanity leads him to think that the art of war has no secrets for him ... Not only is he vain ... he is arrogant, ungrateful and spiteful[1]

– and within a couple of days put in a formal request that de Gaulle be excluded from the morning War Council. Reynaud then arranged for de Gaulle to liaise with the British Government, his particular role being to argue the case for urgent reinforcement, particularly in the air. But Churchill, now realising that the game was up, refused point-blank the request that RAF squadrons be diverted to airfields south of the Loire. Before he left, Weygand, whose only concern had been that the Germans would leave him enough men under command 'to maintain internal order', 'looked me in the eyes and said "*When I've been beaten here, England won't wait a week before negotiating with the Reich.*" '² As for Churchill, de Gaulle's judgement was prescient: 'He seemed to me equal to the rudest task, provided that it also had grandeur.'

By the time of the French Government's final disintegration on 16 June 1940, de Gaulle had been still in two minds whether or not to remain in London. His preference would have been for settling in a French possession either in Africa or the Middle East. But he had then been charged with returning to France, and presenting to the Reynaud Cabinet – by then in terminal decline and sitting in Bordeaux – the offer of 'Indissoluble Union'.*

What of de Gaulle's mind at that time? By all accounts he was enthusiastic, messianically so according to some, about the offer. But this can only be because it offered the last chance of keeping France, or a large part at least of her empire, intact. Unless de Gaulle's character changed out of recognition within the space of a year or so he can hardly at that time have been ready to subordinate for ever his country's national identity. Did he think that there was so much innate goodwill that the British people would take the terms of Union seriously? If he thought this, he was soon to be disillusioned.

At all events, once it had become clear that Pétain was in charge and resistance was collapsing de Gaulle turned to General Spears. Over a bad line from London Churchill told them to stay put. But both men, realising that the French were, effectively, changing sides; and that they might be arrested at any moment; and that the aircraft (a communications Dragon Rapide of the RAF) was still

* See pp. 218–23 above.

on the tarmac at Bordeaux airfield, drove out there early in the morning of 17 June. They boarded together and flew to Northolt, practically running out of fuel *en route* and having to put down at St Helier and refuel from cans. It was the very last aircraft to leave Bordeaux.*

De Gaulle had no great seniority in the French Army. Aloof but pushy, he had theorised, along with other bright officers in other armies, on the subject of armoured warfare – but not as an originator. No more than following on the themes set out by Liddell Hart and J. F. C. Fuller. In addition to the obsessive hostility of Pétain who during their briefly shared period in Reynaud's Government would not return de Gaulle's salute, the General was regarded with suspicion by the grander alumni of St-Cyr who commanded, and administered, the distant satrapies of Tunis, Algiers, Casablanca, and Damascus. Most of these senior officers were mildly, some convincedly, fascist. They were also nationalists who resented German dominance, despised the Italians, and disliked the British. If they had a corporate outlook (as indeed did de Gaulle himself) it was as self-regarding trustees of France's ancient glory. Yet taking the view that this would best be protected by consolidating her post-armistice 'neutrality' – at least until the outcome between the remaining combatants became easier to predict.

Thus when de Gaulle arrived in Britain his prospects were bleak. He had no money. No premises (initially the French Embassy was closed to him and de Gaulle had to operate, and broadcast, from the panelled dining room on the first floor of Cartier, the jewellers in Bond Street). And no men – other than a rag-tag of evacuees from Dunkirk, a few sailors, and some others who, from whatever motive, had coaxed a lift on the ship bringing the remnants of 1st Armoured Division out of Cherbourg in the last days before the surrender. Indeed, so unreliable was this group, and so keen to

---

* The biography of General Spears, *Under Two Flags* by Max Egremont (1997), offers the best and most convincing synthesis of the differing and allegedly 'instant' sources on these troubled days.

desert were the majority believed to be, that it was agreed by
Churchill, on CoS recommendation, that they should never be
allowed to go into action on their own.

De Gaulle was brutally humiliated, on his tours of inspection,
by British officers junior in rank to himself. Immediately after his
first visit to the camp at Trentham Park on 29 June the British
officer commanding, a Colonel de Chair, had the units stationed
there, some remnants of the Foreign Legion and Chasseurs Alpins,
brought back on to the parade ground and told them that while
they were perfectly free to serve under General de Gaulle

> ... it is my duty to point out to you, speaking as man-to-man,
> that if you do so decide you will be rebels against your own
> Government.[3]

The following day, when de Gaulle travelled to Haydock, where
several thousand French sailors were quartered, the British Admiral
in charge would not even allow him to enter the precincts.

Thus Churchill had within weeks of taking office to make a
critical judgement, and he did not find it easy. How best was the
still formidable body of French military power and territory –
known, from the run-down spa resort in the foothills of the Massif
Central where the seat of Pétain's Government was now lodged,
as 'Vichy' – to be handled? To what extent might it be possible
for France to re-enlist as a combatant, in one form or another,
even if only with the Fleet and from the North African colonies?
All this would certainly be put in jeopardy by too enthusiastic
sponsorship of an unpopular and insubordinate junior field officer.
Yet there had to be some focus for the allegiance of those French
men and women (fewer in number it can now be admitted
than Churchill's own romanticism would, either at the time or
subsequently, allow) who loathed the humiliation to which they
were being subjected by the collaborationist regime of Pétain and
Laval.

The balancing of these considerations involved considerable,
and at times ludicrous, duplicity. But his experiences, and the
attendant humiliations, were not to be forgotten by de Gaulle.

They would be repeated, times four, after the entry of the United States into the war. And they would colour the General's attitude to the 'Anglo-Saxons' throughout his tenure of supreme and presidential power in the 1960s.

Immediately after his arrival (on 17 June) de Gaulle had asked for the use of the BBC facility in order to 'rally' French public opinion with a broadcast on the following day. The idea appealed to Churchill who, still in a degree of shock at the French collapse,★ assented immediately.

At that morning's Cabinet, however, the general opinion was that

> ... it was undesirable that General de Gaulle, as *persona non grata* to the French Government, should broadcast at the present time so long as it was still possible that the French Government would act in a way conformable [*sic*] to the interests of the alliance

– and the General was told that broadcasting facilities would *not* be available.

De Gaulle was frantic. He had no leverage, no friends – save one. His staff got hold of Spears. Spears approached Churchill urgently. The prohibition was lifted following (as the minutes record) '... *the members of the War Cabinet being consulted again individually, and agreeing*'.

However, the Foreign Office remained implacable. They had set up their own body, chaired by no less a dignitary than Vansittart, to 'examine and co-ordinate all plans for dealing with the continued resistance of France'. And Duff Cooper (hardly the best-chosen emissary) had been despatched to Morocco to try his hand at 'stiffening' resolve in the overseas garrisons. Duff Cooper's purpose was to enlist some, or all, of the names on a list which included Generals Weygand, Mittelhauser and Nogues, Paul Reynaud, Georges Mandel and Jean Monnet. However, with the

---

★ Although the armistice was not signed until 23 June all military resistance had ceased and the remaining RAF aircraft on French soil were being prevented, by the French military, from taking off.

exception of Mandel none of these figures was interested. And
while the Foreign Office team was assembling, Mandel himself,
together with Daladier and a few nonentities, had set sail in an
auxiliary cruiser, the *Massilia*, for Casablanca. By the time Duff
Cooper arrived they had all been put under close arrest. He
pleaded for their release, but was lucky to avoid the same fate
himself and promptly returned to Britain.

At this time Churchill's attitude to the French was driven solely
by considerations of British survival. Personal loyalty, nostalgic
recall of shared ordeals during the Great War, a conditioned respect
for their military skill and 'weight' as Allies – all this had blown
away. All that was left was the bitter memory of their cowardice
and betrayal. Little of this survives in Churchill's contemporary
papers. Although traces can be found, like his sullen rejoinder to
Ismay when, in the aircraft bringing them back from the last and
melancholy conference at Briare, he told his military assistant –
'You and I will be dead in three months.'

And in the days immediately after the French armistice on 25
June much time in Cabinet had been occupied by Churchill
forcing his colleagues to accept the need for immediate action to
cripple the French Navy. This was Churchill at his most ruthless.
Many ministers and, to their lasting shame, some serving officers,
flinched from what was proposed. But Churchill got his way and
on 3 July the fifteen-inch guns of Admiral Somerville's 'Force H'
straddled the French battleships at anchor in Mers-el-Kebir
(Oran), the battleship *Bretagne* and other vessels were sunk and
1,300 sailors were drowned or burnt. It was Nelson at Copenhagen, although sitting far from comfortably with that offer of
'joint and perpetual citizenship' made to the same people barely a
fortnight earlier. The French ships lying in British ports had been
boarded, their crews forcibly removed. The sailors were packed
off on a twelve-hour train journey, without refreshment or water,
to Liverpool, where they wandered about intimidating the popu-
lace, refusing to pay for anything (few of them had British
currency). They stoned British troops sent to round them up, who
in turn wanted to use live ammunition to impose 'discipline'.

Almost overnight the entente had disintegrated. And the immediate consequence of Mers-el-Kebir was to categorise (in the eyes of most Frenchmen) de Gaulle as a traitor, and an English puppet. Yet within a month, planning was put in train to use him as a front for another attack on French colonies in Africa – this time with infantry as well as ships. The port of Dakar, as an objective, offered many attractions. It commanded the South Atlantic, and its military airfield would allow patrols to cover the gap between Simonstown and the Azores. Geographically, it was far enough from the reach of the German military machine to allow uninterrupted deployment. And there were intelligence reports that some £60 million of gold bullion, property of the refugee Polish and Belgian 'governments', was cached in the vaults of the Banque de Senegal et l'Afrique du Nord.

On 5 August 1940 Cabinet agreed the idea of an expedition.[4] The Royal Navy was to provide an escort, the troops would be 'Free French', and the expectation that their compatriots would welcome them with open arms. 'If not, nothing lost, and we're well rid of them.' By the time this proposal reached the Chiefs of Staff it had lost some of its flavour. Their verdict (entirely correct as it was to prove) being that 'The expedition has no reasonable chance of success, and the local French authorities will not defect to de Gaulle'. Three days later Churchill overrode this advice and instructed the Chiefs 'not to interfere in political decisions'.[5] A plan, suspiciously accelerated in its gestation, came before Cabinet on 13 August and was agreed – in spite of the fact that now the assault (as it had come to be termed) was to be by Royal Marines instead of Frenchmen. Once the expedition was at sea, however, the Chiefs of Staff had another attempt at aborting it. Repeating their warnings of 'powerful shore defences' they now recommended that the landing should be made at Conakry, where opposition would be light, and the force march, overland and through equatorial terrain and malaria, a distance of 630 miles to the objective. This plainly amounted to a *de facto* cancellation. Again Churchill forced through agreement for a direct assault – although this time the bombardment was to be preceded by an 'appeal' (delivered by means unspecified) from de Gaulle.

Three days before landfall, however, Churchill changed his mind and, whether intentionally or not, called the bluff of the Chiefs and redirected the force to Conakry. At this the Chiefs panicked, put out a recommendation for a 'peaceful' diversion to Duala. Churchill now agreed to this, and the whole project would have lapsed — had it not been for de Gaulle. At sea, and only forty-eight hours from D-day, he insisted that the assault be pressed. The resulting action was little more, though, than demonstrative. The Dakar garrison were uniformly hostile, the Royal Navy viewfinders were obscured by fog, and a French submarine torpedoed *Resolution*. She was taken in tow by *Barham*, as far as Freetown, where on shore leave most of the crew became afflicted by either malaria, or venereal disease, or both.

Truly, it had been 'Order — Counter-order — Disorder'.

The Dakar expedition, so hesitant in planning and so clumsy in execution, reinforced the mutual suspicion with which de Gaulle and Churchill regarded each other.

The 'Free French' staff and their hangers-on had talked, recklessly; and complained continuously both to one another and to anyone (including the Americans) on the London diplomatic circuit who might be listening. Their fighting ability, still untested, was dubious. The British, equally, had shown indecision and incompetence at every level of their military command structure. While Vichy now appeared, on reflection, to be quite formidable. The French colonial garrisons had fought well; as had their navy. In terms of territorial and economic strength, of administrative cohesion, of geography, France remained a force to be accounted for. While de Gaulle was a tiresome prophet, without a flock. It is hardly surprising that there were voices, to which Churchill found himself listening, advising that de Gaulle be ignored, if not actually put under arrest, and that serious attempts be put in train to open relations with Pétain. In October of 1940 Halifax persuaded George VI (who, most admirably, had very little time for Frenchmen of any political colour) to send a personal note to Pétain:

Reports are reaching me of an attempt by the German Government to secure from you undertakings that would go far beyond the terms accepted by you at the time of the armistice ... I am confident that ... [you will] ... reject proposals that would bring dishonour to France and cause grave damage to a late Ally.[6]

The Marshal replied tersely. He referred both to Mers-el-Kebir and to 'British support for Frenchmen rebel to their country'. Plainly 'sensible' relations with Vichy could only be nurtured if de Gaulle were discreetly sanitised. But Vichy was Fascistic and unreliable; de Gaulle fretful and impotent. No one could have then predicted that within five years the entire Vichy admin-istration would be in detention; within twenty de Gaulle himself would be arbiter of Western Europe. Much later, when the 'Alli-ance' had recovered its poise and swollen somewhat, Churchill – who makes no mention of this dilemma in his papers – seems to have forgotten the whole affair. De Gaulle, though, had not. In his memoirs he recorded:

It must be said that the British authorities did little ... [beyond distributing a leaflet advising members of the French forces that they could choose between repatriation, joining General de Gaulle, or enlisting in His Majesty's forces] ... to help our efforts. The British High Command was inclined by professional decorum and habit to respect the normal order of things – that is to say, Vichy and its missions.[7]

So much for relations with our erstwhile ally. Complicated, awkward, and unprofitable. But with the United States they were simply that of banker and suppliant. Churchill now knew that Britain could not defeat, or even approach the possibility of defeating, Germany on her own. Rejecting the natural Tory role of trustee for the whole Empire he rejected, too, the search for a stalemate settlement; and set about the task of arranging our alternative subjugation – to the United States. This meant that we had to go on fighting, wherever and whenever possible, with the aim of showing our 'resolve' and of drawing the United States towards a military involvement.

Up until November of 1940 Churchill could excuse Roosevelt's coolness by the imminence of the presidential election. On the eve of Roosevelt's victory the Prime Minister sent him a message of congratulation. Its import was plain enough – now we can work together more closely with just one end in view. Roosevelt did not reply. In the meantime Britain's reserves were shrinking fast, and the submarine sinkings in the Atlantic were running ahead of the replacement building rate.

On 2 September the Government had signed an agreement whereby bases in seven West Indian colonies and Bermuda were ceded to the United States. In return the US Navy undertook to hand over some fifty destroyers, none built later than 1919, that were laid up in the Chesapeake. Only nine of these ships were fit for immediate service. The deal, one of the most one-sided ever concluded by a British Government, took some selling – even by a compliant press. It was the first major step along a hard and undulant road, chosen route on a journey that was to last for four years – the steady dismemberment of the British Empire for cash and credit. The ships themselves were almost useless – run-down, unreliable and their hulls so encrusted with barnacles that none could get within ten knots of their designed speed. All required a 'refit' before being committed to the harsh realities of combat in the North Atlantic; and most of this work was to be done in US yards, adding still further to the dollar debt – itself now completely out of control, in any actuarial sense, and being limited solely by hand-to-mouth availability of convertible currency.

The bases deal was redolent of symbolism. It illustrated the strategic weakness of the United Kingdom and her present inability to protect distant possessions. It highlighted Churchill's recurrent ploy – to draw the US 'envelope' further to the east – even at the expense of British sovereignty. And the exchange of real estate and harbour facilities for obsolete rust-buckets in which men would be killed showed up the distinction between those who were fighting the war and those who were profiting from it. A relationship that characterised every aspect of the two countries' economic relations.

Because in terms of the nation state and its survival the economic implications of what the Government was doing were horrific. British trade had never fully recovered from the punishment – equal parts depleted workforce, retrograde and indifferent management and distortive specialisation – suffered during the Great War. The volume of British manufactured exports in 1913 was still, even by 1937, unattainable. And the country's share of world trade had continued steadily to contract. In the 1920s, until the Slump, it had wavered around 24 per cent; reducing to 18 per cent in the last year (when, in spite of a more intensive armament programme, the Germans overtook Britain) before the outbreak of war.

For the whole of the twentieth century the equilibrium, and the periodic surpluses on the country's balance of payments, had depended on 'invisibles'. Banking, insurance, shipping services and, particularly, dividend income on overseas investments were, in 1939, covering 45 per cent of the import bill. Now, at the very moment when the banks were dormant, when insurance and shipping were effectively removed from the ledger by the intrusion of 'war risk', and when the manufacture of civilian goods for export had been reduced to one-tenth of its peacetime volume, the Cabinet had agreed a wholesale disposal of all those overseas assets on which the country's flow of hard currency depended.

'A very nice little list' was Roosevelt's comment when Lord Lothian had shown him the extent of the British portfolio. 'You guys ain't broke yet.' Certainly many of the sectors where British subjects or institutions held large blocks of equity – steel, chemicals, aeronautics – were to appreciate hugely as US Government spending accelerated. Moreover the technique of disposal was grotesquely incompetent. Instead of 'feeding the market', blocks of shares, often larger than the New York Stock Exchange could absorb all at once, were hawked round and the price reduced, and reduced again, 'in the interests of a quick sale'. A small circle of financiers, associates of Bernard Baruch and Henry Morgenthau, closed up to form a cartel which forced the price down and distributed the prize items among themselves. The Kennedy family trusts, tipped off by Ambassador Joseph about what to 'go for', also greatly enriched themselves at 'the best goddam'd fire sale y'll ever see'.

A further irony, and a painful one, was that a number of US manufacturers – the Allison Aero-Engine Corporation, the Packard Motor Company – were actually given outright cash grants to expand their production capacity so as to meet the demands of Royal Air Force procurement teams. Yet the money paid over in this way was coming directly from the sale of stock in US and Canadian industrial manufacturing and natural resource corporations. Had it been recycled into equity subscription, the country would have been doing little more than altering, albeit somewhat crudely, the balance of its overseas assets. But this was precluded, typically, and short-sightedly, by Treasury guidelines.

Still more damaging, over the longer term, was the transfer of intellectual property – the fruits of research in the laboratories of British universities and developing industries. Even while the Battle of Britain was raging Sir Henry Tizard had travelled to Washington with full details and technical drawings for jet-engine design, microwave radar, the cavity magnetron and valve miniaturisation. All this was handed over without receiving back any consideration whatever, simply as a gesture of 'commitment and sincerity'. And in the expectation that American industry, undisturbed by blackout, fuel shortages or night bombing, would be better placed to move into mass production.

There were many Conservatives who felt uneasy: Amery, Beaverbrook, Hore-Belisha; and Lloyd George also, although by now the old Liberal was 'only good for six hours a day – though mind you, that's six hours of pure radium'.

'The Welsh Pétain', though,* spoke for many – at least among those who could see what was happening, when he said:

* The description was Hugh Dalton's.

A protracted war of devastation and starvation stares Britain, and
Europe, in the face. [We have to be ready] to reconsider this war
into which we have blundered without consideration or wisdom.

Back-benchers who heard of what was going on by way of
rumour and gossip complained to each other. But there were
only two Tories of whom Churchill was still fearful, Halifax and
Chamberlain. Chamberlain was now mortally ill. He resigned
from the Cabinet in September, having but two months to live,
and one of his last acts was to prevent Eden – whom he had always
strongly disliked – from being promoted to Foreign Secretary.
Churchill was thought to be planning to get rid of Halifax as soon
as was feasible, and (although this is far from certain, knowing
what we now do of Churchill's long-term apprehensions concerning Eden) inserting Eden. But when Chamberlain let it be
known that '[any] . . . change at the Foreign Office would be taken
to mean a change of policy and thus a condemnation of my
policy'[8] Churchill, not knowing how much longer Chamberlain
might be active, took the view that provoking simultaneously the
hostility of both men would still be too risky. He tried to console
Eden by assuring him that 'the [Prime Ministerial] succession
must be his' and that he would 'not make LlG's mistake of carrying
on after the war'.*[9]

Then, on 10 November, Chamberlain died. Although decrepit
in his last months Chamberlain's opinions were widely respected.
A kind of 'shadow administration', convenable at a few hours'
notice by Margesson – Sir Maurice Hankey, Rab Butler, the
Colonial Secretary Oliver Stanley, Lord Reith (to give cross-bench
support) and including, in all probability, the duplicitous and
resilient Kingsley Wood – all stood ready, should the signal be
given, to move. Now only Halifax had the prestige to activate
them. The man who had said earlier in the year, that 'If it
[Churchill's premiership] fails, we shall all have to boil our broth
again'. But on 12 December Lord Lothian died. This sudden

---

* See, though, Chapter 20 below.

and unexpected vacancy in Washington offered Churchill the opportunity of sending one of the two remaining threats to his premiership into exile. Halifax was most reluctant to go. Twice he refused. He went and saw Eden, urged him to consider Washington himself, promised to 'put in a good word'. Eden, though, knew that this time he would have to get Halifax's job. Primly he responded that 'In wartime everyone must go where they are sent'.[10] Thus in the space of a few weeks the Prime Minister was rid of the presence of his two most formidable (if dormant) political adversaries. Yet no Premier is ever free for long of personal pressures and claimants. The next contender was from an unexpected, though uncomfortably apposite, quarter. Robert Menzies was the Prime Minister of Australia. He arrived in Britain on 20 February 1941, having flown by way of Singapore and the Middle East, and almost immediately found himself the focus of all those who had misgivings about the leadership. This group of people included many politicians, most editors, and the Royal Family. Staying at Windsor on his first weekend Menzies was told by the Duke of Kent that 'Winston . . . has six ideas a day. They can't all be right!'[11] Menzies's original thesis had been that the Singapore base needed urgent reinforcement, that both Australian divisions in the Near East would have to be recalled as soon as they had cleaned up North Africa, and that the whole Pacific empire was in jeopardy. It could only be saved by shutting down operations in the Mediterranean (where at that time there was no German presence, Rommel having only arrived, in civilian clothes, in Tripoli seven days earlier).

None of this was welcome to Churchill. But Menzies enjoyed a uniformly favourable press. '*Amazing Success*' was predicted by the *Sunday Times*. The *Sketch* (and many others) insisted that he be made a permanent member of the War Cabinet; *The Times* termed his visit 'an event of outstanding importance'. Menzies was quite shrewd enough to see that much of his 'support' was a way of criticising Churchill in code. And he was shameless about stoking this in his approaches to ministers and to Service chiefs. Churchill was furious, but he was apprehensive also, recalling the press campaign that had undermined Chamberlain and assured his own succession. Particularly ominous was a leader in the *Daily Herald*, effective mouthpiece of the Labour Party where lay a good measure of Churchill's support in the Coalition, on 27 February, that 'Robert Menzies had risen to the full stature of an Empire Statesman'.[12]

Menzies was benefiting from that most formidable of all political alliances, a combination of opposites. Many of the old appeasers saw him as potential broker of a European 'settlement' that might still save the Empire. While senior serving officers and politicians in the war party, impatient of Churchill's fumbling and late-night vacillations, saw Menzies's incisive style of thought and speech as more likely to produce 'results'. All this acclaim went to Menzies's head, though. He became reckless in his indiscretions, sometimes entertaining groups of journalists to dinner and matching them drink for drink. He made jokes about Lord Beaverbrook at smart dinner parties. He rapidly found himself 'taken up' by Society where, somewhat out of his depth, he splashed about:

> My dinner for the Prime Minister of Australia . . . one of the gayest and most riotous festivals I have ever arranged. There was a round table; too little to eat but much to drink, the three supreme ingredients of gaiety. Menzies told lengthy stories with great gusto . . .[13]

Menzies never seems to have appreciated that many of the people with whom he was consorting – the Astors, Channon, Lloyd George – were already tainted as the Appeasement Opposition-in-Waiting. Others, like Beaverbrook, were quite ready to run Menzies at the front of a campaign to destabilise Churchill, but this was very different from a concerted plan to make him Prime Minister.

Initially, Churchill's position was strong – at least in terms of popular acclaim. The Desert Army had driven the Italians almost from the whole of North Africa and, as the Luftwaffe started to redeploy in the east, the 'Blitz' was abating. Soon, though, the shadows of the Greek decision* began to lengthen. The only effective infantry in the eastern Mediterranean were the two Australian Divisions, and it was they, together with the New Zealanders, who would have to go to Greece. Churchill 'confided' in Menzies at Chequers on the evening of 23 February that this might 'have to' happen. The two men had already dined, each was smoking a cigar, and sipping brandy. It was the classic politician's trap – the communication of a difficult decision in an intimate atmosphere, without formal 'advice' or paperwork changing hands. But already Menzies's *folie de grandeur* was such that he did little more at the time than acknowledge the compliment of being made privy to a momentous strategic decision. Ten days later, sitting in Cabinet, he spoke – although somewhat hesitantly – in support of the expedition. This was the very man who, a month before, had landed in Britain with the particular objective of securing the naval reinforcement of Singapore and the return of the Australian Divisions to the motherland. Now he had been entrapped and, because of the informal way in which he had been told, Menzies did not even advise the War Council in Canberra of what was afoot.

On 11 March Menzies spoke in Westminster at a meeting of the Empire Parliamentary Association. He received a standing ovation from some two hundred MPs who were present, several of whom told him that 'they would not mind my defeat in Canberra if they could get me into the Commons'. Such assurances are often given, in the afterglow of a successful political meeting, but do usually prove empty when followed through. The very next day, and possibly emboldened by his experience at the rally, Menzies decided to contact Arthur Fadden, leader of the Country Party, suggesting that he should 'discreetly' inform the War Council of the plans to fill the 'British' Expeditionary Force with Australian infantry – 'Not showing them the actual telegrams but giving the substance of the proposals'.

The Australian Labour Party, though, refused to accept respon-

* See pp. 247–8 below.

sibility for a decision concerning which it had not been consulted. And shortly afterwards Stanley Bruce, the High Commissioner in London, called Menzies to order. He told Menzies that his political survival '... depended on his wringing substantial concessions from Churchill'. Bruce presented Menzies with the draft text of a letter for presentation to the British Premier, declaring that if these concessions were not forthcoming at once the Menzies Government might fall – 'with the risk that all Australia's overseas forces might be recalled'.

Whether Menzies actually sent this note is unclear. He may well have reflected that Churchill would, by then, have been quite glad to see him cut down to size. His London star was on the wane, and political difficulties were accumulating in Australia. After some false starts and cancellations Menzies finally took his leave of the capital on 2 May, two of the supporting actors playing their part. Hankey entrusted to Menzies a four-page letter to Halifax in Washington, consisting entirely of grumbles about Churchill, and reiterating that Halifax remained the sole alternative leader. And Beaverbrook, who covered himself in a long talk on Menzies's last evening by saying that 'he approves of me, and thinks it absurd that I should go back to Australia!'[14]

Barely had Churchill seen the last of Menzies than another individual arrived, quite uninvited and bearing a most unwelcome gift.

On the night of 11 May 1941 Rudolf Hess, Hitler's own deputy within the constitution of the Third Reich, jumped by parachute from a Messerschmitt, having single-handedly flown and navigated to Scotland from a German airfield. And in his briefcase he brought an offer of peace.

SIXTEEN

The Haemorrhage Continues

Strategic dilemmas – The Cabinet perplexed – The Hess
mission – The Greek decision – Defeats accumulate –
Hood and Crete – Implications for Empire – Germany
invades Russia – Japan intent on conflict – Churchill's
ambivalence – *Repulse* and *Prince of Wales* set sail for
Singapore.

IT IS NECESSARY TO SUBJECT MILITARY operations during the
winter of 1940–41 to close scrutiny. With the Battle of Britain
won, the cockpit had shifted to the Middle East. Here was to be
decided, irrevocably, the fate of Britain as an Imperial power; the
shape in which it would emerge from the war; even its future
independence. And it is soon apparent that the soldiers, the Chiefs
of Staff, however one may categorise them, had no clear idea of
the War Cabinet's strategic purpose. Nor of the fundamentals of
Britain's national interest. Their deportment is wholly responsive;
and the direction and emphasis of military operations alters, sometimes weekly, sometimes even daily, as a result of political pressure.

'Political' means, of course, principally and sometimes exclusively, Winston Churchill. Yet there is little evidence, on these
crucial issues, of dissent being registered either by senior colleagues
or (with the sole exception of Wavell and Longmore⋆) any of the
Service commanders affected. To some extent this may be ascribed
to shock, or traumatic relief, at the narrow escape from utter defeat
in the summer months. Few seem to have recovered their poise

⋆ Air Marshal Arthur Longmore, AOC-in-C, Middle East, 1940–1.

enough to allow objective strategic contemplation. And this failing was compounded fifty-fold by a total deficiency of military intelligence. The wildest predictions are on record. One school, with Beaverbrook its most vocal protagonist, and periodic support from Dill and Newall, believed that the threat of invasion remained dangerous and immediate; and that no diversion of resources to other theatres should be permitted. Others painted extravagant fantasies centring around the creation of a Balkan 'front' and the enlistment of Turkey as an ally. (This utterly unrealistic concept, ignoring as it did the mutual antagonisms of the different Balkan kingdoms and the fact that Turkey was by tradition a friend of Germany and an enemy of Greece, and that her principal concern was to secure her frontiers against the Soviet Union, continued to distort Foreign Office policy papers until 1944.)

At one single Cabinet[1] Churchill – briefed, presumably, by his scientific adviser, Professor Lindemann – contemplated a renewed invasion attempt and warned of 'a gas attack on an immense scale . . .' Speculation then – without, it seems, any intelligence papers being placed on the table – ranged haphazard across other theatres. Perhaps a blow through Spain, or Italy, or to the Mediterranean through (unoccupied) southern France with the intention of occupying the North African coast? Or, 'the easiest one of all', through Bulgaria to Salonika?

Only Halifax queried, almost to himself, one assessment – of a CoS forecast that German armoured divisions might strike through Turkey, down the eastern Mediterranean littoral, across Syria, Lebanon and Palestine to attack Suez from the north. Sceptically the Foreign Secretary minuted, 'Seems an awful long way round'. Earlier, Churchill had told the Cabinet that '. . . the loss of Athens would be as serious a blow to us as the loss of Khartoum'.

Salonika, Khartoum – these are emblems of earlier conflicts, distant in time, unrelated to the present plight of the kingdom. Not one of those distinguished spectators seems to have been detached enough to realise that for Hitler Britain had become an irrelevance. She had effectively been neutered, in European terms

at least. And her Imperial pretensions were of little immediate
concern to the OKH planning staff who were now proceeding at
maximum urgency with setting up the dispositions and logistics
for Operation BARBAROSSA – the invasion of the Soviet Union.

Certainly no one appreciated the scale of opportunity which
this shift in Germany's strategic purpose offered.

On 10 November 1940, following Chamberlain's death, Clementine Churchill had urged her husband to leave the leadership of
the Conservative Party to someone else in order to remain above
party politics.[2] But Churchill himself remembered very well, and
had indeed suffered from, Lloyd George's neglect of bulk party
support. Churchill may have owed his position to Labour votes,
but knew that he could not rely on them. They had served their
purpose – but never again. This made it essential that he take now
the leadership of the Conservative Party.

The principal forum in which this topic must be addressed was
of course the 1922 Committee. Margesson could not be trusted,
and Churchill well knew that his own lieutenants, his son Randolph, Bob Boothby, Brendan Bracken, were disliked. The pressure had thus to come from outside, from the House of Commons
as a whole. On the afternoon of 10 November 1940 every Conservative member of the Coalition was instructed[3] that no statement of tribute, or even of condolence, should go out until
Churchill himself had spoken on the floor of the House. Sir Philip
Goodhart's own published record of the proceedings of the 1922
Committee makes no mention of this embargo. But there were
many who felt it ungracious, others that it showed 'Winston is
not really a Tory'.

This feeling mattered not so much while the war was going
well. And in the late winter of 1940 the British recovery seemed
little short of miraculous. On 11 November 1940 the Italian
battle fleet, lying at anchor in Taranto harbour, was irrecoverably
crippled by a Fleet Air Arm attack. In the first week of December
General Wavell's 'raid' on the Italian forts at Sidi Barrani was
exploited into a rout. The whole of enemy-occupied North Africa
was starting to crumble. The Royal Air Force had proved its

superiority, and photographs of long queues of Italian prisoners fostered the illusion of military prowess on land. No one could see the economic balance sheet; few outside the convoy escorts knew what was happening in the North Atlantic.

What of Churchill's state of mind at this time? He had reached a bifurcation along his destined route. The country, and the Empire, had been saved. Due, almost entirely, to Churchill's own personal vigour and faith. Britain had been reprieved, certainly, from a summary execution. But the melancholy likelihood remained – of lingering death from malnutrition and disease in the prison cell. Every one of those factors which had coerced Chamberlain into formulating, then reactively adapting, the policy of appeasement was still valid. Industrial weakness, overstretched communications, fiscal bankruptcy and a population that was outnumbered two to one by its principal adversary. Even the bravery and technical skill of the Royal Air Force was a wasting asset. The very guns – eight per aircraft – which endowed Hurricane and Spitfire with their lethal sting, were American Brownings. And so still the overriding political priority – never to be mentioned certainly but never, equally, lost to sight – should have been to evaluate, on an almost daily basis, the possibility of a peace treaty.

For at this point, in the last months of 1940 – surely the most portentous year in the whole history of the kingdom – the situation had changed yet again and there were two obtrusive elements – the one obvious and welcome, the other apparent but depressing – to which the Prime Minister should have been giving his attention.

First, it should now have become plain that there was not the slightest likelihood of the United States entering the war of its own volition. Nor would Lend-Lease (as it was not yet called) be put in place until 'every red cent' in the Bank of England had been paid over. Immediately after winning the presidential election in November of 1940 Roosevelt had told the head of the British Purchasing Commission that 'your gold reserves are good for another six months'. In fact, taking over all the outstanding French contracts (a great relief to the American suppliers but much of the equipment turned out to be incompatible with British Service needs) accelerated the depletion rate. On 23 December the Chancellor of the Exchequer pleaded with his US counterpart for 'help in overcoming our temporary [sic] difficulty as the gold reserves run out next week'. No reply came, save a note from Sir Frederick Phillips, the senior Treasury official in Washington, advising that a USN cruiser was to be despatched to Simonstown where it expected to load the last £50 million* in bullion that was being stored in South Africa after extraction. There was 'nothing for it', Phillips added, 'but to acquiesce'.[4]

Yet there remained time, and resources – just – still to alter direction. By a wholly unpredictable combination of circumstances the old Imperial strategy towards which Chamberlain had been conditioned, and Eden was drawn by instinct, was now on offer – for the last time. Because not only was the Empire intact territorially, but the battles in North Africa, and the evident weakness of the Italians, and the German preoccupation with other theatres offered, transiently, the strategic possibility of returning to Imperial isolationism.

All his life Churchill had been steeped in the heroic integrity of the British Empire, of that great institution's right to demand any sacrifice from its retinue. Now good fortune, and coincidence, offered the opportunity to expand and consolidate. Yet this opportunity would not stay alive for long; and if it were not taken there were dark and overpowering forces awaiting their own moment to strike. Churchill's sense of history and his private instincts were far too acute for him not to have perceived all this. But the reality of party politics made it impossible for him to respond, even had he not become obsessed (and such evidence as there is would indicate that this was already the case) with 'Victory ... victory *at all costs*'.

Harold Nicolson has described Churchill's manner and appearance at this time:

---

* Equivalent to more than £1 billion in 1998.

He seems better in health than he has ever seemed. That pale and globular look about his cheeks has gone. He is more solid about the face and thinner. But there is something odd about his eyes. The lids are not in the least weary, nor are there any pouches or black lines. But the eyes themselves are glaucous, vigilant, angry, combative, visionary and tragic. In a way they are the eyes of a man who is much preoccupied and is unable to rivet his attention on minor things (such as me).

But in another sense *they are the eyes of a man faced by an ordeal or tragedy and combining vision, truculence, resolution and great unhappiness.*[5]

So in the month of January 1941 the Government, barely realising what it was doing, moved slowly away from Imperial consolidation and back towards that mirage which had so distracted, and attenuated, the country's strength since 1914. Since, indeed, that fatal, presumptuous and catastrophic recommendation by the Liberal Foreign Secretary Sir Edward Grey, while so many of his colleagues were on holiday in remote locations, finally to be endorsed on 3 August – to yet again commit soldiers of the Empire to armed intervention on the continent of Europe.

On 28 October the Italians had attacked Greece. Immediately the invaders got into difficulties and within a couple of weeks were forced on to the defensive. There were some, Churchill among them, who began to see the possibilities of opening a Balkan 'front'. Had it not been at Salonika that those first symptoms of German military disintegration had been apparent in the autumn of 1918? Memories of 'Salonika' seem to have excluded the unwelcome recollection that whenever German troops had been put into the line to stiffen the Austria-Hungarians the military situation had instantly been transformed.

What coherent picture was drawn of the probable outcome? None, it seems. The Greeks were perfectly capable of defeating the Italians on their own. They had no desire to provoke the Germans. Nor indeed had the Yugoslavs whose ruling Regent, Prince Paul, was friendly with many in English society and politics sympathetic to the 'appeasement' wing of the Tory Party.

In purely military terms the expedition had all the elements of a nightmare. Poor intelligence, blighted by language difficulties. Bad logistics and supply routing. Uncertain chain of command. No overall battle plan agreed between the Greek and Empire forces. The airfields were of poor quality, without defences or radar. And the force against which defence was to be sustained was the Fourth Panzer Army of Von Kleist, one of the most cohesive, effective and battle-hardened units in the Wehrmacht.

The politico-diplomatic factors were barely more impressive. The Greeks were apprehensive that once the conflict widened they might be attacked by Bulgaria. They were nervous of the Turks, and unpersuaded by Churchill's concept of a grand coalition. As for the Americans, whom Churchill hoped to impress with yet one more costly example of British 'resolution', they seem to have been indifferent. Within the Government opinions changed frequently. Eden, Churchill's emissary in the Near East, recommended in favour, then against, then (this time less full-heartedly) in favour.* Churchill, by now himself uneasy, telegraphed to Eden that he should stay on 'until the opening phase of this crisis has matured'.

> No one but you can combine and concert the momentous policy which you have pressed upon us and which we have adopted.[6]

The warning that if there was a political cost to pay over Greece it would be Eden who might have to be sacrificed could hardly have been more clear.

In fact the campaign was another disaster. There was never a moment when the German forces looked like being held, even for a day or so. The evacuation was extravagant in casualties and in equipment abandoned. Almost 12,000 prisoners were left behind. In the last week, from 24 to 30 April, twenty-six ships were sent to the bottom of the Aegean Sea, including four hospital

---

* For a fuller account, see AC's *The Fall of Crete*, chapter 11, 'The Greek Decision'.

ships. And the balance of British deployment in Egypt, which Rommel was now threatening with the Afrika Korps, was critically affected. The most damaging and unnecessary military diversion in Imperial history was soon over. Its tactical effect was felt immediately. Its strategic consequences were still, just for another week or two, in the balance.

On the evening of 11 May 1941 Churchill had been Prime Minister for a year and a day. By his courage and single-mindedness he had saved Britain from the humiliation of an imposed peace treaty, and set an example to the whole of Europe. But in the months that followed Churchill had foolishly and prematurely committed her soldiers again to the European mainland. Recklessly he had spent her treasure. Heedlessly he had stripped the defences of her distant possessions. Her future remained uncertain in the highest degree. And so there can have been few more dramatic, and unexpected, telephone calls than that which the Prime Minister now received, telling him that Rudolf Hess, Hitler's deputy, had arrived in Scotland in the role of suppliant.

The terms which Hess brought will not have been different, in their generality, from Hitler's broad thesis expressed in *Mein Kampf*. And repeated still, and wistfully, in his last conversations with Martin Bormann in 1945:

> Britain should have made peace in 1941. We had each of us triumphed over a Latin race. In the skies over London she had proved her valour. Now she needed to protect her Empire, and concern herself with the Global balance of power, not the narrow European one. Pitt would have seen this – Churchill could not.

The 'free hand' in Eastern Europe which Hitler believed he had been tacitly allowed by Chamberlain and Halifax and to which, in spite of their enforced last-minute change of mind, he had helped himself – was all too apparent. But now Germany was on the point of attacking Soviet Russia. 'When BARBAROSSA begins, the world will hold its breath', Hitler was to say. Better,

more prudent, to first close down hostilities in the west. How
could the British refuse?

There are only two pages devoted to this whole episode out of
the 1,200 comprising Sir Winston Churchill's official biography
for the first year of his premiership. Even forty-eight hours after
Hess's arrival, and interrogation, all that Churchill would tell the
House of Commons was that:

> ... this is one of these cases where imagination is somewhat baffled
> by the facts as they present themselves.[7]

'Imagination' is all that the historian is allowed, as the key documents are closed, indefinitely it seems, to students. But the phrase
'*as they present themselves*' is more than disingenuous. Hess was put
in prison, tried later as a war criminal (a difficult conviction) and,
uniquely, kept in Spandau gaol under a four-power guard until
eventually, at the age of ninety, he was strangled in his cell. And
perforce the affair must be relegated to that historical category –
the fortuitous drowning of Lord Kitchener aboard the *Hampshire*;
the sealed instructions to the Governor of the Falkland Islands in
1982; the tacit conspiracy of Margaret Thatcher's Cabinet in
1990 – (though hugely outranking all of these in historic
implication) where common sense has to substitute for truth. It
was disclosed – let out might be a better term – at the time,
that one of Hitler's conditions was the 'fall' of the Churchill
Government. And certainly this would have been as compelling a
reason as any to inhibit wider discussion, even in Cabinet. One
footnote, though, is illustrative. News of the Hess flight caused an
immediate drop in the Dow Jones index on Wall Street. The
Consul-General in New York telegraphed:

> The most serious result has been the introduction into the minds
> of some industrialists of doubts as to the advisability of vast plant
> expansion lest this rumoured peace negotiation become a reality
> ... there is undoubtedly abroad a widely-held feeling of appre-
> hension and uncertainty[8]

– precursor, here, of that overriding ethic of the multinational:

'apprehension' relates to the notional profit of the corporation rather than to the certain fate of human beings.

The hypotheses extendable from the Hess mission stretch to eternity. But he was rejected, and thereafter the defeats on land and at sea pile one upon the other. The three weeks in May of 1941, following the rejection of Hess's approach, shattered British power to an extent surpassing far the May-time ordeal of the previous year. The island of Crete was the key to the eastern Mediterranean. With hindsight it can be appreciated that this was the location where the radar crews should have been installed, the airfields and harbour improved and fortified, and that no British Service personnel should ever have set foot on the Greek mainland. Far too late, and after the casualties and humiliation of the retreat to Sphakia and the many sinkings (in losses to naval vessels the Greek evacuation was costlier than Dunkirk), a 'garrison', many of them demoralised survivors of those battles, was put in place.

There now intruded a special factor on the impending battle. Churchill became aware, through the 'Ultra' intercepts, that the German Fliegerdivision – 'the very tip of the Nazi lance' – was to spearhead the assault on the island. More than that, the actual landing-sites, the date and route of the seaborne reinforcement convoy were clearly set out. Here surely, with the dice so loaded in our favour, was a battle which could be won. And where victory would erase the stain of our defeat in Greece and the desert. Nothing, though, could raise the hulls or replace the brave seamen drowned off southern Greece. And when Admiral Cunningham received a signal from Churchill instructing him to 'accept whatever risk is entailed ... to operate by day ... although considerable losses might be experienced' he assented, but warned that:

> The experience of three days [operating by daylight in the Aegean] in which two cruisers and four destroyers have been sunk, and one battleship, two cruisers and four destroyers severely damaged shows what losses are likely to be. Sea control in the Eastern Mediterranean could not be retained after another such experience ...

In fact the intercepts were flawless. The drop zones were fully manned by the defenders. The seaborne reinforcement convoy was intercepted and wiped out. But still the remaining parachutists fought with such vigour that within four days Freyberg, the New Zealand commander, was preparing to evacuate.

And on that same day, 23 May, a dreadful and symbolic blow fell on the Royal Navy in northern waters. The great *Hood*, most beautiful, most powerful (as she was believed to be) and fastest warship afloat, entered into battle at 05.52 hours. Eight minutes later, at 6 a.m., straddled by the *Bismarck*'s guns, she blew up and sank, taking her entire crew of 1,400, less only three.

This avalanche of ill fortune falling on Britain who, still utterly alone against the Axis powers, and now bled to the point of anaemia by a neutral United States, moved towards the very last fortnight of her status as an independent Imperial power.

Many in the country, at every level, were deeply unhappy. Censorship prevented, and frequently prosecuted, conduct 'likely to cause fear and despondency'; but in his diary for 9 June Amery noted:

> . . . the wave of feeling against the Government and the leadership in the Services which he [Godfrey Nicholson MP] says permeates the Services themselves as well as the pubs and other places where men congregate.[9]

Then, on 22 June, came the event of which Hess had given notice, and that was irrevocably to transform the war. The German Army invaded Russia. The likelihood of an attack on the Soviet Union can barely be traced at all in any Cabinet or CoS paper. The appreciations are all of them framed around the assumption that the two principal adversaries were Germany and Britain. Yet we now know that German planning started immediately after the fall of France in July 1940. Hitler's own appreciation was that 'If Russia [is defeated] America, too, is lost for Britain because the elimination of Russia would greatly increase Japan's power in the Far East . . .'

Immediately BARBAROSSA began, the Conservative Party

entered doctrinal terrain replete with difficulty. What about the Polish guarantee? We had after all guaranteed Poland against aggression in 1939. In that same year the Russians had invaded and annexed a huge tract of eastern Poland. Many Polish soldiers were held in Soviet prison camps. And Finland? It was only by the grace of God and the narrowest margin of time that we had not declared war on Russia in January of 1940. Romania, guaranteed at the urgent prompting of Count Tilea in 1939, had also been violated, and Bessarabia annexed into the Ukraine. Fast diplomatic footwork was going to be required here. But it also remained true that many Conservatives had always – though keeping quiet in public at the present time – believed Communist Russia to be the greatest threat, ranking even above Nazi Germany. Following the Molotov–Ribbentrop pact, the Communists and their fellow-travellers had agitated against the 'capitalist war', distributed subversive literature and affected industry. Strikes directly attributable to Communist influence had brought three shipyards to a halt in September of 1940, and closed the Avro aircraft factory in Manchester. With the start of BARBAROSSA this ameliorated somewhat, although Communist cells in the trade unions remained responsive to direct orders from Moscow, however contrary to the national interest or however contradictory they may have appeared. The Soviet propaganda machine moved smoothly into gear, depicting Russia as a happy, friendly society addicted to peasant dances, though unflinching in combat. A land of plenty ruled over by a benign, pipe-smoking autocrat – 'Uncle Joe'.

The effectiveness of this image was to bring trouble later.* But after six weeks of battle, in August of 1941 the Soviet armies seemed to be on the point of collapse. How long was there left before, as had happened in April of 1918, the whole weight of the Wehrmacht, and more significantly the night-bomber strength of the Luftwaffe, would be free to turn on Britain?

This certainly was foremost in Churchill's mind above all else.

* See Chapter 22 below.

He and Roosevelt had a meeting on board *Prince of Wales* in Placentia Bay, Newfoundland, to discuss global events. Both men realised that even if not defeated Russia had, as far as the Pacific theatre was concerned, been placed in baulk. There was now no military threat to keep Japan in check save the distant, uncertain and peaceable image of the United States Navy in its spotless tropical whites. From Churchill, though, was demanded finesse of the highest order. He had to ensure that the now inevitable belligerence of the United States was 'full-hearted' and that, more difficult, it was not confined to the Pacific theatre. On frequent occasions the Americans had shown themselves to be uninterested about defending the British colonial possessions. Some show of force and willpower had to be demonstrated, or else the risk loomed that the Americans would defend only the Philippines and Hawaii, possibly the 'White Dominions', and the entire British Imperial structure to the west would fall apart.

On 23 July the Japanese had occupied, without resistance, the whole of French Indo-China (Vietnam). The great harbour of Camranh Bay, and the airfields around it, now put them 3,000 miles closer to Singapore and their intention was plain. Churchill being absent, a Chiefs of Staff Committee considered the situation.

> As a matter of fact this whole business of a Chiefs of Staff Committee with no Chairman is hopeless. None of the three likes to interfere in the others' domain, still less to tell one of the others that he is lacking in courage; so the conclusion is always timid as well as platitudinous.[10]

There was some talk of warning the Japanese off any annexation of the Kra Isthmus.* 'Phillips, for Admiralty, opposed and suggested that "even if they occupied Kra we should do nothing, as we are so helpless at sea out there".'† Three days later a telegram

---

* The narrowest point – technically Thai sovereign territory – of the Malay peninsula to the north of Khota Bharu.
† Amery wrote, 'I would certainly sack Pound and Phillips at once.' In fact Phillips had four months of life left to him. He was to drown on 10 December – in the waters off the Kra Isthmus.

arrived from Churchill: 'President's idea is to procure a moratorium of say thirty days in which we may improve our position in Singapore area ... President considers a month gained will be valuable.'[11]

Sir Dudley Pound and the Naval Staff first came up with a plan to send two of the old R-class battleships, possibly accompanied by an aircraft carrier, plus another two R-class and the sixteen-inch *Rodney* as soon as their refits were complete. But there were two caveats. The second contingent would only be possible if the US Navy took over protection of the Atlantic convoys against surface raiders, and anyway would not be on station until March. Pound's preference was for Trincomalee in Ceylon rather than Singapore – itself a colossal strategic withdrawal before a shot had been fired – but suggested, perhaps, because the RAF strength in Malaya was so attenuated that he judged it incapable of lasting for more than a few days. There were no Spitfires or Hurricanes. The most modern fighter was the Brewster 'Buffalo', an obsolete US carrier monoplane, bought as part of the inane equipment-buying spree that had bankrupted the Treasury the previous year.

On 25 August Churchill weighed in. On the tactically false analogy that because the Royal Navy was dispersed and distracted by one powerful German ship, the *Tirpitz*, Churchill believed – ignoring the fact that in the Far East it was a full-scale fleet action, head-to-head, that would settle the fate of our Imperial possessions – that a couple of fast modern ships would 'deter' the Japanese. The Prime Minister sent a personal memo to the First Sea Lord, asserting that

> This powerful force might show itself in the triangle Aden–Singapore–Simonstown. It would exert a paralysing effect on Japanese naval action.[12]

Pound, always accomplished in delaying Churchill's schemes for as long as he could, accepted 'in principle', then sent a handwritten note to the Director, Tactical Division, Naval Staff:

> Please let me have detailed reasons, based on experience of KG V

and PoW [HMS *King George V* and HMS *Prince of Wales*] why it
would not be sound for a new ship of this class to be sent abroad
before she has had a thorough working up.[13]

The argument, critical to the fate of the Empire, simmered on
for some weeks. Only cursory attention seems to have been paid
in Cabinet, although it came before them several times. Pound's
strategy, as so often in his disagreements with Churchill, was
correct. A naval force heavy enough to compel Japan to split her
own attacking strength might have forced à postponement (or
even deterred Yamamoto from assaulting both navies
simultaneously) but the old R-class battleships, with their slow
sailing time, would have to be despatched immediately. And on
this Churchill's own arguments were supported by Eden:

> From the point of view of deterring Japan from entering the war
> the despatch of one modern ship, such as the *Prince of Wales*, to
> the Far East, would have far greater effect politically than the
> presence in those waters of a number of last war's battleships. If
> the *Prince of Wales* were to call at Cape Town on her way to the
> Far East news of her movements would quickly reach Japan and
> the deterrent effect would begin from that date.[14]

As it was, the 'negotiations' in Washington pursued their
ordained course. On 2 October the American delegation suddenly
raised the stakes by delivering a note stating that the intended
meeting between Roosevelt and Prince Konoye could not take
place unless Japan stated its readiness to accept the 'basic' American
resolutions for a settlement. As these included a Japanese withdrawal from conquered Chinese territory the loss of face was
intolerable and Prince Konoye's (relatively) pacific government
fell. On 2 November Tojo and his war party assumed power, and
war – although its shape and impact could be neither predicted
nor assessed – became inevitable. While there was still not a single
ship of the Royal Navy on station in the Far East with a gun of
heavier calibre than eight inches, Churchill instructed the Admiralty that the two battle-cruisers should sail forthwith. Tom Phillips,

an Admiral hitherto 'desk bound', but with a reputation founded
in earlier years* on equal parts obstinacy and panache, was designated Commander. And flew his pennant in the *Prince of Wales*.
On 17 November the great ship put in at Simonstown on the way
round and into the Indian Ocean. Once round the Cape Phillips
was to join with *Repulse*, and constitute a 'task force'. Of the two
vessels *Repulse* was the best. The only capital ship to get up steam
and leave Invergordon at the time of the mutiny. *Prince of Wales*
had never been 'happy' after her mauling by *Bismarck* in the
Denmark Strait the previous year; and watching the short, four-
minute, combat life-span of *Hood*. In contrast, *Repulse* had one of
the best-disciplined and most proficient crews in the Navy. Sheer
seamanship was to keep her afloat longer than her more heavily
armoured consort until, struck by the fourteenth torpedo, finally
she would capsize and sink some twenty-eight days hence.

The two battle-cruisers were little more than five days' steam-
ing-time from Singapore – hardly longer, it could be claimed,
than it would take a Japanese convoy to move from Okinawa to
Khota Baru – the most obvious, and the most vulnerable point
on the north-eastern coast of the Malayan peninsula. Was the crisis
passing?

But on his second evening ashore, Admiral Phillips had a long
session with Smuts, a statesman whose strategic acumen was as
acute as Churchill's was delusory. Phillips set out the imbalances
that affected his squadron; its hasty assembly, the absence of air
cover, his ignorance of the command and control arrangements,
such as they were, in Malaya.

The two talked into the night. And the following morning at
05.45 hrs the *Prince of Wales* weighed anchor and set off round the
Cape to force her passage, at a continuous 26 knots, on a course
east by north-east, without landfall for 2,000 miles before her
rendezvous with *Repulse* to the south of Trincomalee. Smuts,
deeply uneasy at what he had heard, transmitted an anxious
message to London:

---

* But see Amery's judgement, p. 254n above.

... if Japanese are really nippy there is opening here for a first-class disaster.

What happened to this signal? Was any attention paid? In any case nothing more could now be done, and the probability is that Churchill never set eyes on it. His position was not dissimilar to that of Kitchener in 1915 before the start of the Battle of Loos, which he, Churchill, had himself so percipiently described:

> He had that air of suppressed excitement like a man who has taken
> a great decision of terrible uncertainty, and is about to put it into
> execution.

All Churchill now had to do was wait. On the night of 7 December he had invited Winant, the US Ambassador, to dine at Chequers. Was this fortuitous? Earlier in the day Churchill had telegraphed the Thai Prime Minister, warning him of an attack in twenty-four hours. And to Winant he had repeated, for the umpteenth time, that 'if Japan attacks you in the Far East we will declare war on her'. And once again had received an evasive reply – that only Congress could declare war – when asked what the US would do if it were us and not them to be attacked by the Japanese.

Late in the evening farce supervened when the Chequers butler, Sawyer, came into the room and claimed to have heard on the wireless that the Japanese had attacked 'an American base'. The two men got through to Roosevelt who (according to Churchill) confirmed the news, saying, 'We are all in the same boat now.'[15]

Once again a respite had been delivered. The kingdom's survival, which could earlier that year have been attained through diplomacy, seemed assured by simple arithmetic of the balance of arms.

But even this was not completely certain. And such survival could now only be in severely attenuated form. Moreover, the reality of global conflict meant that there was no longer scope for Britain to conduct an independent policy shaped to advance or even, other than with the greatest difficulty, to protect her separate interest. And soon would be brought home to Churchill the implacable validity of that conclusion which, however erratically, had guided the policies of those whom he had displaced in 1940. And which he would find himself obliged to articulate in the New Year, winding up the confidence debate in the House of Commons on 27 January:

> There never has been a moment, there never could have been a moment, when Great Britain or the British Empire, single-handed could fight Germany and Italy, could wage the Battle of Britain, the Battle of the Atlantic and the Battle of the Middle East – and at the same time stand thoroughly prepared in Burma, the Malay Peninsula, and generally in the Far East . . .'[16]

SEVENTEEN

The Loss of Empire

Collapse in Malaya – Naval losses – India smoulders –
The Dominions 'decouple' – No recovery in the
military situation – *Scharnhorst* in the English Channel –
Bad omens on the home front.

IN 1921 A NUMBER OF CONSERVATIVE ministers had attended
the four-power Naval Conference in Washington. The delegation
had been headed by A. J. Balfour and the conference sat for
seventy-four days. Balfour was often absent, and most of the
negotiating had been conducted, in a style that would today be
described as 'abrasive', by Lord Lee, the First Lord of the Admiralty.
There is a presentation photograph, which the Lees both signed,
showing them emerging in triumph from the conference after its
final session. Lee holds his briefcase, containing the treaty. His
wife strikes the attitude of a fashion beauty of the day. Both smile
radiantly, their demeanour not so much arrogant as insouciant.
But in the background can be seen a member of the Japanese
delegation hastily moving 'out of camera'. He is short of stature,
plainly uncomfortable in Western attire, his face expressionless.
They have lost *face*, he and his colleagues. Britain, the traditional
ally of Japan, on whose Navy the Imperial Fleet had been modelled
and whose gunnery drill (or so it was believed) had smashed the
Russians in the straits of Tsushima, had betrayed them.

The Washington Treaty signalled the start of Britain's decline
as an Imperial power in the Far East. Hitherto Britain and Japan
had been operationally united in their joint exploitation of the
trade, territory and riches of the China seas and estuaries. The

Americans were at a distance, as were the Dutch. The French were a second-class naval power, the Portuguese, colonisers of Macao, rated not in the scale at all. So it should have been for Britain and Japan to settle the balance of power in the region, if necessary between themselves. The interest of the United States was commercially exploitative, certainly. But its posture was anti-colonial. The likelihood of it co-operating with Britain – still less of intervening to help Britain defend her interests – was nil, whatever lip service might be paid to 'shared ideals'. As Stanley Baldwin had warned, '[We] . . .will get nothing out of Washington but words, big words but only words.'

So at Washington the Japanese Navy now found that Britain was siding with the United States. For a long while the Japanese were 'stubbornly determined . . . to reject the ratio of three to five in battleships, as compared to Britain and America'. Finally they yielded to pressure, but with very little intention (as soon became apparent) of keeping to the provisions. In his memoirs Lee described the outcome as

> a common Pact for the preservation of the territorial status quo in
> the Far East, and which rendered a continuation of the Anglo-
> Japanese Alliance superfluous.'

There is no doubt that personal factors were at work also. Lee was a close friend of Theodore Roosevelt. His wife came from a distinguished East Coast family. He was at this time being freely talked of as candidate for the Washington Embassy and Roosevelt did indeed write to Curzon and request his appointment. But the effect of this diplomacy was, over the long term, disastrous.

A year later, the Coalition Government had fallen, and Lee was never heard of again. But the provisions of the treaty remained, to cripple English naval design (just as with the Anglo-German treaty fifteen years later, Britain was the only signatory to observe the provisions) and to blight any flexibility of foreign policy in the region.

While steadily, year on year, British preoccupation with threats in the European theatre intensified, and it became increasingly apparent – particularly to the Japanese – that

> Britain was painfully caught between the scissors of her strategic obligations as the Mother Country of an Empire on the one hand and, on the other, her own inadequate financial and industrial base which made it impossible to afford, or even to build and equip the size of Navy needed to fulfil these obligations.[2]

To which should be added the proviso: '... unless she were prepared to forgo the debilitating and historically unnatural commitment to raise and send into battle on the European mainland a fully equipped standing army'. In fact, in the autumn of 1941 British strength in Malaya, the richest of her possessions, was less even than those other two doomed colonial powers, each of which had already been defeated on their own home territory, Holland and France.

So it was that by the spring of 1942 the apprehensions, expressed now with increasing frequency by the Tory 'centre',★ were coming, all of them, to pass. The Imperial possessions, the entire wealth of the great trading companies that had helped balance the Exchequer books, even, for example, during the 1914–18 war subscribing as a 'gift' the whole cost of *Malaya*, a Queen Elizabeth class 15-inch battleship, had been abandoned.

Indeed, the Malayan 'campaign' (if the terms can dignify such a helter-skelter, tactically inept retreat before a numerically inferior force) had every ingredient attaching to it of a decadent empire in terminal decline. Soft, ill-trained infantry; jealous and quarrelling commanders; unanswered telephones; pink gin and gossip on the veranda of Raffles Hotel; obsolete equipment poorly maintained; unrequited bravery; a curious and top-heavy chain of command with continuous tension between the fatigued and enervated

---

★ The term 'centre' does not of course carry the ideological code stamp, nor implicit approval, that has come to be attached thereto by liberal commentators who write in terms of 'Left' and 'Right'. Rather, it should be taken to mean *core* or *bulk*.

Field-Marshal (Wavell) and the impulsive, snob-ridden and lately-appointed resident minister (Duff Cooper). Had not a Naval Staff consensus agreed that 'Reports on the capability of Japanese air personnel have for a number of years been consistently adverse . . .'?[3]

With all this were mixed the telegrams, increasingly surreal in tone and instruction, from the Prime Minister himself. Come the early days of February 1942 strong overtones are detectable of that panic in June 1940, when a lethal diversion of tanks and aircraft to a beaten, demoralised France was thwarted only by the combined protestation of Dowding and Alan Brooke.

Churchill now, far too late, realised what was going to happen. Singapore was to be 'scorched-earthed'. Everything must be demolished by explosives. There must be 'no question' of surrender until after protracted fighting amid the ruins of Singapore City.[4] Reinforcements were poured in, and as late as 12 February two battalions of the 17th (Indian) Division, and the whole of the 18th British Infantry Division disembarked to hang around the quays dejectedly for a few days before being ordered to surrender their weapons.

General Ismay has recorded that Wavell was instructed to banish 'any thought of saving the troops or . . . the population. The battle must be fought to the bitter end at all costs.' It is hard not to see parallels here with the tenor of those apocalyptic Führer Directives that began to issue from the Rastenburg bunker in 1943. Certainly, as emanating from the comfort of a leather armchair with tobacco and alcohol close at hand, they do not read well. And when, at the end, the Prime Minister sought to transmit an order that Wavell, his staff and all senior officers (but not, it would appear, Duff or Lady Diana Cooper) were to die at their posts, the Chiefs of Staff refused to send the signal.[5] There is argument as to whether this particular signal was transmitted. Certainly it was not obeyed and the total number of British, Indian and Commonwealth personnel to surrender was 85,000. But of these some 57,000 would die in captivity – a loss of life not much different, it must be admitted, than if they had fought on the spot, at Singapore

Island, as Germans did at Cassino, or Russians at Stalingrad or (the most painful comparison) the Japanese themselves at Iwo Jima or Tarawa.

In the event, after an interlude so short almost as to be unseemly, General Percival and his staff, white-kneed and vacuous in appearance, trailed up the Bukit Timah Road to deliver the Union Jack to General Yamashita and his staff. The 'little yellow men in glasses', although outnumbered by three to one and without heavy artillery or regimental transport, other than bicycles, had conquered – absolutely.

There was to be one last battle at sea, itself illustrative of the end of Empire, and of nostalgia also, when gallant *Exeter* which less than three years before had tackled the heavier *Graf Spee* in the South Atlantic, and whose crew – what was left of them – had marched past to a Guildhall lunch and a flowery speech of welcome from Churchill, was now sunk by the Japanese cruiser fleet. Sent to the bottom in that two-day running battle of the Java Sea was a veritable panoply of colonial strength, the whole commanded by a Dutch admiral and including ships – one after the other sunk – from Holland, the United States, Britain and Australia. Truly the placid circle of Imperial complacency delineated by the four-power Naval Conference of 1921–2 had turned into a whirlpool.

What remained of the Fleet was withdrawn, first to Trincomalee in Ceylon. Then, when the Japanese carrier task force reached out even that far across the Indian Ocean to sink *Hermes*, the last and only British aircraft carrier in the Indian Ocean on 5 April, a further 600 miles westward to Addu Atoll, southernmost island group in the Maldives. 'The heat is simply incredible . . . a burning, torturing sort of heat from which there is no escape',[6] complained Admiral Somerville. But as force commander he seems to have kept to himself the reflection that this was the first time since 1670 that the Royal Navy had steamed so far in one direction in order to avoid combat.

What, then, of India? Where Imperial dominion over the subcontinent was recorded – *Ind Imp* – sharing only with the Anglican faith and the Royal Navy depiction on the coinage of the realm? There was much justificatory talk, at Westminster and in the British press, of 'defending' India from 'aggression'. The reality did not accord with this. The bulk of the population, save only for the ruling families, was in covert sympathy with Japan. Indian prisoners were all too ready to enlist in the 'quisling' army of Subhas Chandra Bose.* The spectre of full-scale rebellion, Mutiny of the Sepoys revisited on a scale of times fifty, threatened a nightmare worse even than the fall of Singapore.

In London opinions were varied. The Labour Party, whether from conviction, political expediency or common sense, favoured concession; an immediate grant, if it should be necessary, of Dominion status. Bevin argued on pragmatic grounds – that it would 'allow us to get the fullest war effort from India'. The 'Moderates' in Delhi had appealed for a 'bold stroke' – the instant Dominion was to be governed by an expanded Central Executive, 'an All-Indian National Government responsible directly to the Crown, and with the restoration of popular government in the provinces'.

For Churchill, still carrying at the back of his mind memories of his time as a 'die-hard', this was too much to swallow. His counterproposal was for expansion of the Defence Council into an elective body of 100, representing the provincial assemblies and the princes, and 'extension of its functions to frame [sic] the new constitution after the war'. Characteristically (but ineptly) Churchill believed that he could persuade the Indians to accept this if he broadcast to them direct, and was prepared to fly out to Delhi and do so. Fortunately the Viceroy, Lord Linlithgow, was able to prevent this. Linlithgow was more hard-headed:

India and Burma have no natural association with the Empire,

---

* After the Japanese surrender in 1945 the 'Indian Legion' were returned to captivity, this time with British guards. There was talk of a 'war crimes' trial. But it was plain that public expectation (in India) demanded their release. None was arraigned and the whole process was quietly dropped.

from which they are alien by race, history and religion ... both
are in the Empire because they are conquered countries. What we
have to decide is whether ... whatever the feelings of India, we
intend to stay in this country for our own reasons.[7]

Still more shocking was the military abandonment of two of
the white dominions, Australia and New Zealand. In August 1940
Churchill was desperate to ensure that the Australian infantry
division was directed to the Middle East (where, indeed, it was to
provide the backbone of Wavell's offensive against the Italians,
capturing Bardia, then Tobruk). The Prime Minister telegraphed
to Canberra and Auckland that 'in the event of their being
attacked' ...

> I have explicit authority of Cabinet to assure you that we should
> then cut our losses in the Mediterranean and proceed to your aid
> sacrificing every interest except only the defence position of this
> island on which all else depends.[8]

This extravagant, and possibly not wholly sincere, assurance lasted
less than a year.

By the summer of 1941 the Greek expedition had allowed
Rommel to dominate the Western Desert. The Defence Committee minuted that 'only in the event of a serious major attack'
would Britain abandon everything and come to (the Dominions')
help, but this 'did not mean we would give up our great interests
in the Middle East on account of a few raids by Japanese cruisers'.

When, though, the 'serious major attack' came, the help forthcoming from Britain was barely adequate to deal with 'a few raids
by Japanese cruisers'. Recognition that here, too, a foreign power
was poised to displace Britain came in a statement by the Australian
Labour Party leader that:

> We refuse to accept the dictum that the Pacific struggle must be
> treated as a subordinate segment of the general conflict ... Australia
> looks to America, free of any pangs as to our traditional links with
> the United Kingdom. We ... shall exert all our energies towards

the shaping of a plan, with the United States as its keystone, which
will give to our country some confidence...[9]

On 12 February had fallen another blow – and again upon the
cruelly mutilated shoulders of the Royal Navy. The German
battle-cruiser squadron – *Scharnhorst, Gneisenau* and *Prinz Eugen* –
had sailed from Brest and proceeded easterly up the English
Channel towards their home port of Kiel. The Luftwaffe had
cleared the Channel of British warships in July of 1940. Now, it
seemed, the German Navy could operate there with impunity. A
scratch flotilla of obsolete destroyers, hastily detached from convoy
duty, were unable to close with the battle-cruisers until the
evening, by which time the German ships were already in the
haven of the Scheldt estuary. All that stood in their way in the
Straits of Dover was the valiant 825 Squadron of Swordfish
biplanes, each carrying a single torpedo at 130 mph, commanded
by Lieut. Com. E. Esmonde.

Esmonde had a combat record of remarkable distinction. Before
returning to Britain he and his squadron had been flying intruder
patrols, mostly at night from Larnaka. Esmonde had reported so
high a tonnage of Italian supply shipping sunk that the debrief
commander began to reject his claims. Following an altercation
(which may well have been insubordinate) Esmonde discarded the
gun operated by his observer and substituted on the gun-ring an
Aldis signal light. After scoring a hit he would do one more slow
circuit, at 30 ft altitude from the water, and illuminate the name
and home port on the stern of the sinking ship in order to
substantiate his claim. Naturally, this caused Esmonde to be marked
down as a 'troublemaker'. Instead of receiving a DSC, which was
his due on posting out of the Mediterranean, he got nothing. He
had launched the first torpedo attack on *Bismarck* the previous
year, and still not been decorated. Now, on 12 February 1942, he
knew that the moment had come. Esmonde went first to Mass,
and after take-off flew, on a dead straight course at a very low
altitude, to close with *Scharnhorst*. For the last three minutes
of approach the attackers absorbed tremendous punishment.

Esmonde's lower wing was shot away and still he held on, until at
the very last moment crashing into the water, releasing the torpedo
just before impact. His Victoria Cross was posthumous, as it was
to two others of his squadron. Not one aircraft returned to their
field in Kent.

This tragic episode, an exact replica in many of its elements of
the Fairey Battle attacks on the Maastricht bridges in May of 1940,
seemed to show that nothing had changed. The sacrifice, on that
same altar of military incompetence and myopia of very brave and
committed young men, was in the great and venerated tradition
of Deeds that Won the Empire. It was drawing on a special
reservoir of human quality and courage that had already been
ruthlessly pillaged in 1917. But now the Empire was no longer
being won, but lost. It was falling apart, and the lives of its sons
being wasted. Everything that Neville Chamberlain had feared,
and predicted, was coming to pass.

For those more comfortably situated than in the open cockpit
of a Swordfish this message was reinforced by a scrutiny of the
financial press. 'Empire' stocks – tea and rubber plantations, commodity dealers and investment trusts – had in a few weeks lost
more than half their value. Much of this equity was included in
the share portfolios of the gentry on account of the dividend
yield – always several points above the Stock Exchange average.
In some family trusts their 'weighting' meant that in the first
months of 1942 their value had been catastrophically reduced.
Chinese government bonds, attached to the customs revenue of
the Yangtse ports, and for long one of the highest-yielding secur-
ities in an 'Empire' portfolio, were now worthless.*

It was a bad period for private capitalists. Not only was taxation
punitive, but the quality of life was deteriorating and becoming
less and less responsive to the leverage which wealthy, or even
'well-off', people had become accustomed to regard as natural.

---

* In the 1939 financial year, revenue 'collections' notwithstanding war disturbance and institutionalised corruption amounted to £28,742,625 – over half
a billion in 1990 values – an increase of 36 per cent on 1938.

The financial commentary of *The Times*, even at the start of 1941, had gloomily recorded that

> The hardship of 100% Excess Profits Tax and the heavy burden of taxation generally continue to be the main themes of company chairmen at annual meetings

– somewhat delphically noting:

> in the long run continuance of the ability of the Government to borrow at longer date probably depends now more than ever upon the progressive physical limitation of the opportunities for consumer spending...[10]

The disintegration (as to many Conservatives it seemed) of the social order at home was exemplified by the final demise of the upstairs-downstairs division in their own households. In less than eighteen months domestic servants had all but disappeared, their registered number falling from 1.3 million to under 200,000. Wages in the Women's Land Army and the factories drew away all but the most loyal or decrepit. Mass Observation reports were indicating that the most frequently requested change hoped for after the war was the 'reduction of class distinction'. This emotion was stoked relentlessly by the *Daily Mirror* (favourite reading in the Forces) which daily pursued and inflamed examples of class 'provocation'. Additionally, the reduction in trans-class organisations like the Churches, or voluntary bodies, and the growth of class-based affiliations like the trade unions, actually helped to make class more of a political issue. All this was steadily undermining the long-term position and, ultimately, the electoral prospects of the Conservative Party.

At this point, and for neither the first nor the last time, a peculiar irony of circumstance attaches to the figure of Winston Churchill. In May 1940 his strength of personality had saved Britain. In the spring of the following year, from motives that were mixed and as a result of calculations that were (if, and there is little evidence of this, he applied his mind to the dilemma in any great degree) defective, Churchill had turned away from the opportunity to do so by a wholly different route. Now, another twelve months later, the question of the Prime Minister's dispensability began to run below the outward surface of Cabinet discussion papers, newspaper editorials, and the situation summaries issued daily by the Ministry of Information.

In 1940 Churchill's retention of the premiership (and thus the impossibility of diplomatic negotiation other than at his own initiative) had been assured by a miraculous deliverance in the skies over southern England, turning so soon into glorious Desert victory. In 1942 it was military defeat, on many and widely different battlefields – and not all of them easily explained – that was weakening him.

EIGHTEEN

1942: Churchill's
Difficult Summer

Claimants to the succession – Their differing political
affiliations – The 'Men of Action' – Potential
contenders – The defeats accumulate – The fall of
Tobruk – Machinations in the 1922 Committee –
'The party is a laughing stock' – Churchill's support
from Labour on the wane – Weak position of the
Conservative Party in the country – Military recovery –
Doubts remain.

ALTHOUGH MUCH IMPATIENCE, AND SOME distrust, had been
privately expressed concerning Churchill in 1941 it was not until
the following year that the concept of displacing him could be
uttered freely. And this speculation was always confined to quite
small groups, Members of Parliament, some senior staff officers,
certain London hostesses and conveners of political *salons*. In the
press, never; except occasionally by the time-honoured editorial
ploy of 'denouncing' it.

Who might succeed to the premiership? As always there were
a number, each of whom (and in many cases with some absurdity)
believed themselves to be uniquely fitted. It would no longer be
someone from the old generation. Chamberlain was dead; Lloyd
George was now recognisably infirm; Halifax, although still communicating from time to time with the recusants in London, was
at the Embassy in Washington; Hoare, discredited, was in Madrid;
Simon, strongly disliked and without experience in the coalition
War Cabinet, was isolated as Lord Chancellor. Even to suggest the

names of any of these was to confirm Churchill's own pre-
eminence.

With one exception. The man who, ultimately, was to succeed
him; who could well have done so on many occasions in the
previous decade and whom, by various devices, Churchill kept at
arm's length for as long as he could.

> Further talk today with AE [Eden] about the PM ... AE feels he
> is more and more obstinate and at the same time losing grip. I
> spoke of the rising of public opinion at successive disasters and
> failures which we both agreed was entirely justifiable. There might
> be an explosion which would sweep the whole Government out.
> The War Cabinet is now quite ineffective ...[1]

Some commentators now found a way around the self-denying
ordinance which prevented overt criticism of the Prime Minister.
Pressure began to build for there to be appointed a separate
'Minister of Defence' who would be charged solely with the
direction of the war. Some keen back-benchers went to see Eden.
The plan was in two (highly optimistic, it must be thought) stages.
'A stage with Winston and a separate M of D; and then a later
stage when Winston faded out.' Richard Law (Bonar's son) said
that if Churchill would not create a separate Ministry of Defence
he must be got to go, and Eden later told his private secretary
Oliver Harvey that he agreed. However, as soon as the name of
Erskine Hill, the Chairman of the 1922 Committee, came up,
Eden started to back-pedal. He would not 'lend himself' to any
intrigue. In public, and even in the smoking room, all he proposed
to say was that 'we must all rally round PM and try to strengthen
the Government'.[2] As so often in history, the heir presumptive
was reluctant to anticipate what was to be his, anyway, in the
fullness of time.

Churchill had his own ideas as to how best this 'strengthening'
should be addressed. He invited Attlee to take the title of Deputy
Prime Minister (the only 'Deputy', be it noted, ever to succeed
to full office. No Conservative has ever done so). And decided to
make Stafford Cripps Leader of the House. He would thus, as he

believed, lock in Labour support in the House of Commons as a precaution against losing (as had happened to his predecessor) a significant number of his own back-benchers. Eden, though, seeing what was afoot, protested. That two of the leading Labour politicians should be raised to positions of such eminence in a coalition would be found offensive by many Conservatives. Churchill explained that Attlee had to have something: 'the whole thing is eyewash anyway'. As for Cripps, he was 'only thinking about it'.

The following day, 18 February, Churchill disarmed (as he must have thought) Eden by offering him Leadership of the House *in addition* to his duties as Foreign Secretary. Somewhat to Churchill's alarm Eden did not refuse so enormous a work overload but said that he wanted to think it over. Churchill said he was going to take lunch, then a siesta. He told Eden to return to Downing Street at 5.30.

Back at the House Eden picked up still more restlessness with the Prime Minister. He formed the view that the position of Leader of the Commons would be useful to him in consolidating his claim to succeed – particularly as Attlee was now to be 'Deputy'. Eden was just on the point of leaving to walk over to Number 10 when he ran into Cripps in the lobby. Cripps said he had had a useful talk with Churchill after lunch, and decided to accept his offer to join the Government.

'Good – in what capacity?'

'Leader of the House.'

For once Churchill had skipped his afternoon rest.[3]

Thus the Prime Minister had pre-empted a possible leadership crisis by the traditional method – playing off the leading contestants against each other. There were plenty left, but they were of secondary calibre. Beaverbrook and Hore-Belisha both harboured ambitions although were sensible enough to operate, at least in the earlier stages, behind smoke. Beaverbrook, as has been seen, first wound up, then identified himself with, public enthusiasm for Russia. His 'mission' the previous autumn although nominally to discuss military aid, and additional aircraft to support the Red

Army, was in fact a giant publicity stunt. Beaverbrook's papers depicted him as 'a man the Russians can get on with . . .' – which is hardly surprising, as his highly irresponsible campaign for a 'Second Front – Now!' was completely in line with the Soviets' broad, anti-Western strategy. Beaverbrook, though, suffered from the delusion, which has afflicted many before and since, that a high level of public and press acclaim can, of itself, deliver high office. He had no supporters, or even cronies, in the House of Commons. While Churchill in 1939, benefiting from a noisy demonstration of approval from outside Parliament, could also count on the backing of some thirty or forty followers as a nucleus in the division lobbies.

The route preferred by Hore-Belisha was that of the indirect approach which he would have absorbed – if it was not already instinctive – from his mentor Liddell Hart in the thirties. 'H-B' now realised that he had been betrayed, or at least let down, by Churchill in January of 1940.* He had made critical remarks in a Commons debate after the fall of Crete, and provoked Churchill to the kind of response not usually served by colleagues upon one another: '. . . the state in which our Army was left when [Hore-Belisha] ended his two years and seven months' tenure of the War Office . . . was lamentable'. After the debate, in which Hore-Belisha had tried to defend his reputation, Churchill followed him into the smoking room and, wagging a finger, warned him:

> If you fight me, I shall fight you back. And remember this, Leslie, · you are using a 4.5-inch howitzer, and I am using a 12-inch gun.[4]

Hore-Belisha certainly also believed that a measure of press support (which was still favourable, as it was believed that he had been sacked from the War Office by the 'Blimps') could compensate for a diminished power base in the House of Commons itself. Additionally, he cultivated the press. In conversation with W. P. Crozier of the *Manchester Guardian* on 20 March Belisha trailed that habitual preference of self-important persons who feel

---

* See pp. 195–7 above.

that they 'have something to contribute' but are excluded from the inner loop – the 'Government of All the Talents'. The interview, at Belisha's solicitation, took place after breakfast at his private address in London, 16 Strafford Street. There was much talk of 'all those people who are discontented with the way in which things are going and are anxious to get the war won with more energy and efficiency'. Although plainly of the opinion that he was the person to do this, Belisha claimed that the lead should be taken by Cripps. And that it was deplorable not to make use of the 'immense talents' of Lloyd George also, who 'in spite of his age and difficulties' (sic) was 'a statesman, a very great statesman'.

Of course, 'getting the war won' was a dubious priority for the old Conservative Party. Just as in 1916 they had wanted to get rid of Asquith in order to reassert the primacy of the Conservatives in administration, so, in 1942, they wanted to control or, ideally, to evict, Churchill before he did any more damage. But with the exception of Eden there was, realistically, no longer anyone to put in Churchill's place who was not a Socialist, an adventurer, or an impostor.

There remained a third category, the Men of Action, scattered about and ready to promote themselves. Fortunately for Churchill, most of these figures were in the Labour Party. And as the Tories still commanded a majority in the House of Commons (the date for a general election having come and, by general consent, passed) the possibility of usurpation from the Left was largely unrealistic.

Ernest Bevin and Herbert Morrison were contenders, but neutralised by mutual loathing, and in any case confident that time was on their side. Attlee was too self-effacing – or was it patience? (Churchill's sneer, 'a modest man – and one with much to be modest about.') Only Stafford Cripps remained for some time a threat. Although with potency diminished – as does very rarely occur in politics – by a character where guile was at a discount to personal rectitude. 'His chest,' Churchill told Stalin, 'is a cage where two squirrels, his conscience and his career, are constantly at war.' Yet Cripps's ascetic, punctilious approach to each and every problem, his appetite for paper and briefs, his preference for objective analysis, made him so complete a contrast to Churchill as to be an alternative that was both recognisable and credible. Leo Amery, also, whom Churchill had presciently sidelined in 1940, still commanded a respectful following on the back benches.

Amery's personality was deficient in the 'killer instinct'. As Baldwin had put it, 'Amery's got a season ticket on the Line of Least Resistance.' This may, of course, constitute a good passport to popularity and promotion under normal conditions. But what was contemplated in the summer of 1942 could come about consequently only through a major act of assassination. None the less, just before the House rose for the recess, 'Crowder* drew me aside in the smoking room and told me that the feeling of rest-lessness ... was getting very acute ... [The '22] did not feel that there was anyone inside the Cabinet who stood for the Conservative point of view at all.' Crowder enlarged on the 'considerable regret in many quarters that Winston had been made leader of the Party ...' And when it came to the need for someone who could speak to Winston, and stand up to him, on behalf of the Conservative Party, Amery was quietly pleased to be told that 'there is a widespread feeling that I ought to be in the War Cabinet for that purpose'.[5]

As the bad news piled up and the papers became more inquisi-tive, the Prime Minister having promoted Cripps to Leader of the House came to regret this. And as soon as an opening offered to despatch Cripps into exile he suffered the same fate as Halifax, being sent on a special mission to India – Churchill's dry sense of humour being, as so often, evident in this arrangement to confront one scrawny ascetic (Mahatma Gandhi) with another.

Coincidentally, and by great good fortune, Beaverbrook had also become tired of the game. He felt himself to be losing acclaim and took off to New York, excusing his absence by asthma. For several months the tone of his contributions would be sulky. In reality Beaverbrook enjoyed the company of US businessmen and politicians and was glad to avail himself of his special facility to

* Joint Secretary of the 1922 Committee.

cross the Atlantic and spend dollars on steaks and Chequer cabs away from the blackout. Even Roosevelt preferred his company to that of Churchill. 'Max' would make indecent jokes and give extravagant presents. And Beaverbrook was then in hot pursuit of Pamela Digby, the Prime Minister's 'flame-haired' daughter-in-law, at that time nominally married to Randolph. 'The greatest romance . . .' as declared the New York *Daily News* '. . . since Romeo and Juliet.'

On 21 June Tobruk fell to Rommel and 35,000 prisoners were lost – including the entire South African Division which, the previous year, had led the conquest of Italian Somaliland and Abyssinia. And on 19 August the Canadian Division was thrown into the Dieppe Raid. This strangely ill-conceived operation – was it simply to demonstrate both to British and Russian critics that a 'Second Front Now' was a military impossibility? – failed bloodily, with most of the assault force being cut down on the shingle as they disembarked. Australians in Greece; New Zealanders in Crete; Canadians at Dieppe; South Africans at Tobruk; and Indians deserting by the thousand to the Japanese. It was not just the territory of the Empire but its sons who were being discarded – to buy what?

On 23 July Max Beaverbrook, now returned to London, gave a dinner for some twenty-five MPs, drawn from all parties, invited for him by Beverley Baxter.* After some ritual declamation in praise of the Red Army, Beaverbrook went on to surprise his guests, and quite possibly please some of them, by urging that there should be a general election as soon as possible. The present House of Commons was 'stale, and needed refreshing'. Whether Mr Tom Driberg, who had just been run by Beaverbrook in the Maldon by-election and won that safe Conservative seat, and Mr Frank Owen, one of Beaverbrook's editors, who was also about to stand as an 'anti-government candidate', could be put in the

---

* There is no mention of this occasion in Beaverbrook's official biography by A. J. P. Taylor (1972), but other published sources, including those attending, make reference to it.

'refreshing' category was plainly a matter of taste but for a few weeks it looked as if Beaverbrook was contemplating a break-out from the smoke-filled room – his habitual operational terrain – to the hustings.

Churchill had written a letter of rebuke:

> The fact that Mr Driberg and Mr Frank Owen are standing as Independent candidates in two by-elections will of course be taken by everyone as indicating that you are running election candidates against the Government. This would be a great pity from many points of view[6]

– but Beaverbrook was too powerful, and Churchill in the summer of 1942 too beleaguered for the Prime Minister to do more. He needed to placate, not to antagonise, his old cronies. Already a favourite target of the *Daily Mirror*, Churchill dare not provoke a total breach with the *Daily Express*.

Sir John Wardlaw-Milne who, a month ago, had brought scorn upon his own head and, in the eyes of many parliamentarians, gratuitously lowered the dissentient vote in the confidence debate of 23 June by suggesting that the Duke of Gloucester be made Commander-in-Chief, was quite out of his depth in this pool of carnivores. Wardlaw-Milne and those around him in the Commons, and who backed him in the associations, represented the old style of Conservatism, the essence of whose *raison d'être* was evaporating fast. The 'good' things – full employment, a healthy and adequate, though sparse, diet for all – were supplemented by a virtuous self-effacement. 'Take your place in the queue'; 'don't you know there's a war on?' (being an all-purpose retort to any complaint, or even inquiry, concerning the petty practices of bureaucracy); an equality of drabness which was seen to be 'fair' – all were redolent of the socialist ethic. For many even communism was becoming respectable. 'Uncle Joe', whose image had been sedulously and without shame burnished in the Beaverbrook press at the behest of its mischief-making and erratically ambitious proprietor, personified the Socialist at War. *Reds Smash Hitlerites Again*; *Nazis Lose Hundreds of Tanks, Planes*. Headlines in

the *Express* were indistinguishable from those in the *M.*
even the front page of the *Daily Worker*.

The repetitious message was one of contrast between unyie
Stakhanovite sharpshooters and effete incompetents. Heroe. ̇ ̇
the Soviet Union set alongside Sir John Wardlaw-Milne and the
Duke of Gloucester. Nor was it difficult to identify which political
party benefited from this comparison. Yet, because of the 'Guilty
Men' syndrome, Churchill himself, except for a few personalised
insults in the cartoons of Low and Zec which would drive him to
fury remained, in the popular conception, unscathed. 'Good Old
Winnie' was depicted as doing his best in spite of the 'Blimps'
who surrounded him.

But was it not the Blimps, in their different ways and mani-
festations, both male and female, who energised the Conservative
Party in the country, whose young sons were in uniform and at
risk of their lives? Most of them, still, did probably believe in
victory, as an abstract entity that would automatically bring in its
train a restoration to Britain of her former power and domination,
just as it had seemed to do in 1919. Few realised that a huge deposit
had already been forfeited. That the tranquil and deferential order,
the gently ascendant curve of private prosperity that Baldwin and
Chamberlain had set in place in the thirties, had gone for good.
It could no more be restored than could the apparatus of colonial
administration and responsibility be returned to those cities and
regions that had seen the British run away, tails between their legs.

Within the parliamentary party there were many who saw this,
and disliked it intensely. Churchill was aware of the discontent.
Personally, and by instinct, he will have shared their misery. Did
he not, nearly ten years later, confide in his doctor, Lord Moran,
his continuing visitation by nightmares of the sinking of *Repulse*,
'the day the Empire was lost for ever'?[7] But in the apt phrase of
Von Mellenthin, Churchill was like a hunter who has a wolf by
the ears, and dare not let him go. His purpose was 'victory',
without caring for the cost. So if the cost was irrelevant, why
count it?

★   ★   ★

Still fresh in Churchill's mind will have been his treatment by the Tories, high and low, during the wilderness years of 'failure'.[8] He knew that their sufferance depended on his delivering the goods. 'Some sugar for the birds'. But right across 1942 the 'evacuations', the excuses, the miserable defeats – even at sea – had accumulated. So that by the autumn it had become a race between an eruption in the parliamentary party and the arrival of good news from the desert. 'If Alexandria had fallen, Winston would have fallen also. As it is he will hold his position until we get another major reverse.' So wrote Ivor Thomas to Tom Jones.[9] Churchill originally had as much, if not more, support among the Labour Members of Parliament than from the party of which he was the nominal leader. But now the muttering had spread, and it was sharpened by party-political opportunism.

> Winston has never, owing to his background and record, been able to capture the affections of the working classes as LlG did. Inevitably, there will be a change . . . and Cripps will be PM. The bulk of the Labour Party would prefer Cripps to Attlee . . .[10]

Early in October, Brendan Bracken had an anxious meeting with Moran: Churchill was not sleeping properly, however late he went to bed. 'I want you, my dear doctor, to keep an eye on your patient. There may be trouble ahead. The Prime Minister must win his battle in the Desert, or get out.'[11] Was this a threat? Or was even Bracken, like a majority in the Cabinet, preparing to defect?

On 21 October, the 1922 Committee devoted its entire meeting to a discussion on 'the Position of the Party', a coded title, like 'Difficulties in Presentation', offering the opportunity to criticise the leadership, or at very least the 'advisers'. Every speaker took a pessimistic line. And that evening Lord William Scott, anticipating that the Whip in attendance would probably, in his report of the meeting, have watered down the strength of feeling expressed, himself wrote at length to James Stuart:

> Throughout the country the Conservative Party has become a

cheap joke. The press and the BBC treat us with contempt ...
You must agree that as an effective body of opinion either in the
House or in the country, the Conservative Party have [sic] ceased
to exist.

There followed the customary complaint of those in the lower
echelon of politics who may feel that not enough attention is
being paid to themselves,

... there is no liaison ... between our 'Leaders' in office...

(the inverted commas presumably intended to indicate, at the least,
scepticism)

and the rank-and-file ... depth of feeling of most of the quiet
Conservative members, and of our Associations in the country ...
the sense of frustration is very acute.

Much of the text is stereotypical of what Chief Whips are bothered
with quite regularly when party morale is low. And Scott had the
wits to admit that 'some of the more vocal elements in such a
set-up are bound to be those who are at present disappointed on
personal grounds'. But the real indicator of back-bench resentment
lay in the sentence:

You yourself are well aware of what the PM thinks of the Tory
Rump: he may not say so himself but RC, BB [Randolph Churchill, Brendan Bracken] and his other satellites are not so careful
of their tongues.[12]

Stuart was in a difficult position. There is little doubt that
his personal sympathies lay with the 'Tory Rump' (though not,
perhaps, to the same degree as his predecessor). But he was
now *Government* Chief Whip. And like all Whips he believed his
allegiance to be owed, excluding all other considerations, to the
centre of power. The sentences in Stuart's letter of response can
be regarded as lightly coded – though their meaning will not have
been welcome. As the largest partner [in the All-Party Gov-
ernment] '... and the most loyal, *we have to give the most*'. And,

still less reassuring, 'As soon as we are able to revert to normal
peace-time conditions, the Party will get together again – *whether
in office or in opposition*'.

This was all, for the majority of Tory back-benchers, most
unwelcome. *Opposition?* The party had a majority of 150. What
was it doing in a coalition at all? Stuart had uttered the usual pleas
for unity, concluding with that obligatory *pietas* – 'I only trust that
this will not lead to any split – or to a Party "divided against
itself". This would weaken us, I fear, and might take a lot of
healing.'[13]

At the meeting the heaviest contributions had come from Walter
Elliot, who had openly invited colleagues to consider comparison
with 1922 when the party had indeed split, and left the 'leaders'
high and dry with Lloyd George. And from Oliver Stanley, 'dropped' as War Minister in May 1940; now attending in the uniform
of a colonel in the Coldstream Guards. Stanley did not mince his
words. The 'supposed' bad record of the party before the war was
'a millstone around our necks'. Guilty Men had done a lot of
harm, and should be answered. The party did not know what
its policy was. It had to say what it was aiming to do after the
war. The party could not regain its place in the House of
Commons without reorganisation (a clear rebuke for the Whips)
and there had never been such a gulf between the party and its
leaders.

MPs slapped their desk lids with approval. It was agreed that
the topic should be continued at the next meeting of the Committee. The whole affair now appeared to be moving far outside
the control of the Whips.

Churchill's immediate response, prompted no doubt by Stuart,
was the traditional party reaction to internal pressure once it
crosses a particular threshold of containability – either to arrest
the blackmailers, or to bribe them. Oliver Stanley was brought
back into the administration – as Colonial Secretary. On the other
hand the Socialist Stafford Cripps, who had misplayed his cards
and seen his support in the country (itself never a very hard
currency in the dealing-house that is internal party power-

broking) diminish, was ejected from the War (
Minister of Aircraft Production.

Churchill, though, remained in jeopardy – and
now the great convoys were at sea, to rendezvous at G
the invasion of French North Africa – Operation TORCH
Harvey has recounted how, on one evening *en petit comité* w ...ıs
cronies, Churchill had reflected:

> If TORCH fails, then I'm done for and must go and hand over to
> one of you.[14]

But TORCH did not fail. And in the same week Montgomery
broke through at Alamein and a giant pincer movement, along
the North African coastline, was put in motion. So Churchill,
who then ordered that the church bells be rung to celebrate the
victory, did indeed have much, personally, for which to give
thanks. The parliamentary rebellion smouldered for a few more
weeks. At its next meeting, the 1922 Committee passed a resolution that a deputation should be appointed '... to discuss with
Conservative Ministers, the Chief Whip and the Chairman ...
the question of reorganisation on the lines set out in Colonel
Stanley's speech'. Six prominent back-benchers, three of whom
were now serving officers and including Henry Willink and J. F.
Crowder, were nominated, under the leadership of the amenable
Sir Joseph Nall.

But the moment had passed. Sir Joseph did not report back
until the end of January 1943. After a longish introduction the tail
in his report stung. For by now Churchill felt himself strong
enough to dictate that:

> The suggestion that the Committee should, on occasion, hold
> meetings only of Private Members, from which Ministers would
> be particularly excluded, is not acceptable to the Leader of the
> Party...[15]

A further month would go by, with the military situation improving all the time, and a revised motion went back to the full '22

wherein, effectively, they retracted their position and demands. The leader had reasserted his control.

Put to the vote, though, the majority was only 20 out of 106 attending. Many stayed away in order to convey their reservations. The party remained uneasy. It was the growing prestige and unassailability of the Prime Minister rather than any change of mood among the back-benchers that had restored the appearance of harmony.

For the situation-map had been transformed. With the break-through at Alamein, the start of TORCH, and Zhukov's capture of the Kalatsch bridge over the Don (precursor of victory at Stalingrad) all occurring in the first week of November, it had been in purely military terms as the Prime Minister declared: 'the end of the beginning'.

Politically, Churchill was now safe for just as long as he wished to remain leader (another twelve years, as it was to be). But, politically, the Conservative Party was now in as great a peril as had been, in military terms, the Empire earlier in that year. Not far over the horizon an apparition was gathering substance. One that would test to the utmost the party's powers of adaptation, of evasion and pretence – the Beveridge Report.

NINETEEN

The Conservative Party
and 'Welfare'

The party's ambivalence – 'Thatcherism' goes into
hibernation – The Tory Reform Group makes the
running – The Catering Wages Bill of 1943 – The genesis
of Beveridge – The party is confused – Discussion in
Cabinet – The orthodox view – Debate on the floor –
Conservative stalling tactics – Labour indignation.

IN 1941 THERE HAD BEEN ESTABLISHED a body, at the headquarters of the Conservative Party, entitled the Post-war Problems
Central Committee (PWPCC). And at its head, inevitably, had
been placed Mr R. A. Butler. For some time it had very little to
do.

Although a few self-styled Young Turks on the progressive
wing of the party bothered its secretarial staff with papers which
they wished to see published and in circulation, the factionalist
Tory Reform Committee (later to become, and henceforth
referred to as, 'the Group' or TRG) was not launched until
1943. With the exception of Lord Woolton no senior member
of the Cabinet had much feel for post-war problems (although
some, like Oliver Lyttelton, kept in close touch with trends,
and opinion, in the City). The general view being that the area
was dull, troublesome and generally uncongenial. And these
adjectives were, in private, often extended to include those
figures in the party preoccupied with the topic. Except of
course for 'Rab' whose rich Courtauld wife, friendship with
Chips Channon and the Guinnesses, and propensity to gossip
and entertain ('when Rab let go with one of his famous cackles

we all doubled up'*) gave him a guaranteed entrée to the party's higher echelons. Indeed, there was already a general assumption that Rab's expertise in 'civilian' matters would, in the fullness of time – quite possibly even to the displacement of Anthony Eden – guarantee him the premiership.

So whilst the PWPCC was the main, indeed only major, focal point for 'progressively' minded Conservatives to discuss social reform – with an ill-defined brief, a disunited composition and a desire to avoid a factionalist conclusion, it proved of little significance.[1] The Conservative Research Department had been dissolved for the duration of the war. One consequence being that when exterior concepts needed a response, there was no effective party policy forum to address them. Conservative *ad hoc* committees had to be quickly cobbled together to respond – with all sense of seizing the initiative lost.[2]

However, in recognition of the subject's important – indeed menacing – aspect, the committee on the Beveridge Report was chaired by Ralph Assheton. Assheton was Chairman of the Party, but he was not a politician of great acuity and his amiable but reactionary demeanour, though congenial to colleagues, was hardly suited to navigating through so widely dispersed a minefield. In addition, the committee's findings were secret and for restricted circulation even within the party. This afforded members the chance to speak freely and bluntly – but also ensure that the wider political sphere was entirely denied their counsel and did little to correct the impression that the Party was doing nothing.

In 1943 Conservative Central Office launched its Signpost series of booklets in which broadly sympathetic writers expressed non-socialist ideas about how the post-war country should develop. Two of these writers, Quintin Hogg and Hugh Molson, did (by 1944) feel safe enough to express Tory Reform Group views from

---

* Recorded by Chips Channon of an episode on 2 September 1939 when a group of ministers were waiting in the ante-room outside the Prime Minister's office in the House of Commons while the declaration of war was being composed.

the left of the party. But they were still the exceptions. A majority of authors were expressing right-of-centre arguments.[3] For example, when the City Editor of the *Sunday Times*, Norman Crump, wrote the Signpost booklet, *The Future of Money*, financial orthodoxy was placed before welfarism since:

> Our objective is to ensure that the pound note will have substantially the same purchasing power after the war as it has today. If we light-heartedly embark on all kinds of grandiose and unproductive plans, and still more light-heartedly create fresh money with which to pay for them, then our money will be much less after the war.[4]

The technocratic generation of bureaucrats which accompanied wartime controls, and showed every intention of entrenching itself for the post-war world under the self-advertising slogan '*The Future Must Be Planned*', were dismissed by the Chairman of the 1922 Committee, Alec Erskine-Hill, as

> part of a powerful vested interest, the Government machine, with which they identify their own existence and their own privilege of exercising power.[5]

These were arguments quintessentially Conservative but soon to be driven underground until Keith Joseph and Alfred Sherman began to prepare the way for Margaret Thatcher in the mid-seventies. The lack of convergence between the views floated by the Left in the TRG and those of the traditional Right is, and has always been, endemic. Some claim it to be a source of strength and vitality. Others argue that being an indicator of 'division' it damages the party's electoral standing. Certainly, as late as 1944, in the face of the Coalition being committed to much of the spirit of the Beveridge Report, Conservative Central Office sanctioned another Signpost booklet which used language of a kind soon to be repressed for almost three decades. In preferring 'to order other things from the productive machine', G. L. Schwartz argued that

> the working classes have poor housing and health care because

their judgement, tastes, habits, and morals led them to choose to
spend their money on drink and tobacco instead.[6]

And this view, besides being audible on any day at any table in the
Conservative end of the members' dining room in the House of
Commons, was also staple conversational fare at most college high
tables. Beatrice Webb has recorded in her diary a conversation
with the Master of an Oxford college and prominent technocrat
in which:

> he admitted almost defiantly that he was not personally concerned
> with the condition of the common people. His human sympathies
> were satisfied by the family group at the College and his pleasant
> relations with his fellow dons and his college undergraduates . . .[7]

– unremarkable, except that the Master and technocrat concerned
was William Beveridge himself.

Already by 1942, though, a growing reticence to argue their
case in public was affecting the Right. A feeling was abroad that
the 'future' lay more with the young careerists of the Tory Reform
Committee now so very publicly trying to shift the Conservative
Party to the Left:

> so many of our Party – more especially the younger members –
> are more 'left' than the Labour Party, terribly afraid of being
> thought unprogressive – and nowadays to be thought progressive
> you must be all out for totalitarian methods of administration, no
> matter how much you may condemn such methods in Germany
> or in Italy.[8]

And when Sir Spencer Summers MP set up in November 1943
a group of twenty or so Tory MPs to attempt to hold the line, he
felt it prudent to call it 'The Progress Trust'. The group met
privately once a week to try to influence senior members of the
Government through personal contact. Among its members were
the 1922 Chairman, Alec Erskine-Hill, Henry Willink (then in
the process of taking over the Health portfolio in the Government),
E. C. Cobb, Sir Douglas Thomson, R. A. Brabner, E. R. G. Lloyd

and R. E. Manningham-Buller.[9] Whatever influence they may have had behind the scenes (and judged by results it must be measured as inadequate) the Trust, and other extempore groupings on the Right of the party, were irrelevant to the public debate where all impetus was coming in from the proven record of socialism in co-ordinating the 'war effort'.

In February of 1943 the Catering Wages Bill had come before the Commons. Apparently uncontentious, it was one of those measures which Churchill, and James Stuart the Chief Whip, would periodically endorse as part of the 'share' in legislation due to the minority Labour representation in the Coalition. True, it would not have appeared on a Tory programme. But the stature of Ernest Bevin, its principal sponsor, and his own critical importance as Minister of Labour in maintaining co-operation with the TUC, looked to assure the Bill of Conservative support in the lobbies.

In fact the Catering Wages Bill brought about the largest Tory vote against the Government of the war. It demonstrated Conservative opposition to any measure of state control over enterprise which was not directly applicable to winning the war. Significantly, the debate came only days before the publication of the Beveridge Report. And the experience undoubtedly encouraged a more guarded approach by Tory ministers to the Report's recommendations. Ernest Bevin, speaking at the despatch box as Minister of Labour, recommended the catering legislation as a means 'to extend collective bargaining in an unregulated area of the economy'. This was very far from being a Conservative objective at that time. Tory back-benchers, all of whom, it should be remembered, had won their seats at the 1935 general election, were mobilised by Sir Douglas Hacking MP. The catering employers were naturally suspicious that the proposed appointment of a Catering Commission, with 'powers to make recommendations on the industry's efficiency', was really the back door to its nationalisation.

The latent divisions in the party were all too plain when these fears were condemned as belonging to the 'Manchester school' by

Bevin's close friend and Parliamentary Secretary to the Ministry of Labour, the 'pink' Malcolm McCorquodale, Conservative Member for Epsom. As was to become habitual with the TRG, McCorquodale tried to associate the intended state interference with the 'true Conservatism' of Benjamin Disraeli. The Tory Reform Group members voted for the Bill as a bloc. But of 365 Conservative MPs (43 in the Government, 322 on the back benches), 110 Tories (plus 8 other MPs) voted against. Significantly, a further 139 back-benchers and 9 ministers were, on one excuse or another, absent.[10]

Thus, within days of the most important debate to address a 'post-war', that is to say a social rather than a military, topic it was seen that the 'old' Tory Party, inarticulate and, for most of the time, dormant as it seemed, could suddenly come to life.

Tory suspicions were not soothed by their having so little to do with the Beveridge Report in its formative stages. The 'Inter-Departmental Committee on Social Insurance and Allied Service' was the product of a TUC meeting with Ramsay MacDonald's son, Malcolm, at the Health Ministry in February 1941. Its remit being to find a way in which health insurance (at that time providing workers with fewer and more erratic material assistance than unemployment benefits) might be better integrated into the social insurance system.[11] Three months later the committee was formally launched

> to undertake with special reference to the inter-relation of the schemes, a survey of the existing national schemes, of social insurance and allied services, including workmen's compensation and to make recommendations.[12]

Arthur Greenwood, as Minister without Portfolio, was nominally responsible for reconstruction issues. Bevin, though, saw at once what was at stake. First, the scope for using the remit to put in place a fully socialist system of universal welfare, and claim for the Labour Party exclusive credit. Second, that to gain general acceptance the findings of the 'inquiry' should be presented by someone not of the Left, but with impeccable centrist credentials.

It is sometimes said that Bevin foisted Beveridge on Greenwood's office because he wanted to be rid of an official whom he found patronising and officious. This overlooks the fact that Bevin knew the Report's survival prospects would depend on its Establishment pedigree.

At once an interesting question of Whitehall protocol arose. This was an inquiry, rather than stated government policy. The Civil Service's impartiality might be called into doubt by the promotion of the Report's policy. Greenwood wrote to Beveridge suggesting:

> In view of the issues of high policy which will arise, we think that the departmental representatives should henceforward be regarded as your advisers ... This means that the Report will be your own Report; it will be signed by you alone[13]

– thus was the formula adopted and its title legitimised.

In October 1942, Brendan Bracken who, at the Information Ministry, had been getting 'trailers' of the Beveridge recommendations, warned Churchill about the incipient dangers. In particular that Beveridge and his allies would soon be leaking details in order to start a momentum before the Report's publication. On 16 November, with Churchill's assent, Bracken persuaded the War Cabinet that the publicity surrounding the Report's launch should be in the hands of his department, thus denying Beveridge the opportunity to speak out publicly himself. But soon afterwards Churchill changed his mind, justifying this on the grounds that 'once it is out he [Beveridge] can bark to his heart's content'. The best of a bad job might be made by contriving that its more commendable features should rub off on the Government.

This was a failure of nerve or, more likely, a bout of inattention. It would have been perfectly legitimate to reject Bracken's advice on the grounds that the Conservative Party approached the question in a totally different manner, and could not support its being legitimised as a government policy without a free vote on the floor of the House. Certainly this would have been the response of Neville Chamberlain. Baldwin, more likely, would have gone along with Bracken's plan, but arranging in advance a full consultation with his own back-benchers. It is all the more surprising because Churchill had in fact set up a secret committee.

Another committee of heavy input was made up from six MPs: Ralph Assheton (selected by the Party Chairman to advise him on party feeling towards the Beveridge Report), Sir Archibald Grindley, Sir Herbert Williams, Dr A. B. Herbert, Spencer Summers and Florence Horsburgh, and by a member of the Information Department at Conservative Central Office, the Social Services Administrator who headed the Women's Voluntary Services Evacuation Department, and a representative of an industrial assurance company. The report they returned to Churchill in January 1943 purported to represent 90 per cent of back-bench Conservative MPs – which would mean almost everyone except those who were to form the nucleus of the Tory Reform Group.

The report of the Assheton Committee worked on the assumption that universal unlimited benefits would 'encourage malingering and laziness' and, more fundamentally, that it was not, in any case, the duty of the State to guarantee subsistence income. Sir Arnold Grindley added to this his fears, derived from the Beveridge Report's paragraph 457: 'the plan for Social Security is first and foremost a method of redistributing income'.[14] And here lay the core of the problem for Conservatives. The sheer universality of the proposals, in contrast to the targeting of relief, demonstrated the Report's essentially redistributive aims.[15] And it was the skills and the vagaries of the market that ought, surely, to redistribute wealth? Not the State.

In the absence of a clear lead the result was a policy of confusion. On 26 November, the Cabinet agreed to issue the Report as a White Paper.[16] On the day of its launch, 2 December 1942, the BBC fully covered the scheme in twenty-two different languages. But the Political Warfare Office was told, by Bracken, to give it no publicity whatsoever. The War Secretary, Sir James Grigg, withdrew a pamphlet on the Beveridge Report for the Army

Bureau of Current Affairs (ABCA) allegedly because of its lack of objectivity and the impression it gave that it was already adopted public policy[17] (two heads of argument that did not sit very easily in the same saddle).

The Times tried to soothe its readers. The Report promised no more than:

> a completion of what was begun a little more than thirty years ago when Lloyd George introduced National Health Insurance and Mr Winston Churchill . . . introduced Unemployment Insurance.[18]

Beveridge himself, though, soon let the cat out of the bag (and revealed his burgeoning ego) by announcing:

> My plan is not a plan to develop social insurance: it is a plan to give freedom from Want by securing to each citizen at all times . . . a minimum income sufficient for his subsistence needs and his responsibilities.[19]

The Employers' Confederation, roused by these claims, warned Beveridge that the cost of paying for social security would drive up the cost of production and thus undermine competitiveness. The Confederation's Director declared that:

> We did not start this war with Germany in order to improve our social services; the war was forced upon us by Germany and we entered it to preserve our freedom and to keep the Gestapo outside our houses, and that is what the war means.*[20]

The strength of popular support for Beveridge's recommendations put the Conservative Party in a difficult position. They could hardly be seen to be wholly condemnatory even though, aside from the activists of the TRG, this was the majority view among MPs. In any case, the Report was steadily acquiring

---

* These words were unconsciously reused by Churchill, who, having digested Hayek's *Road to Serfdom* (1944), implied in his election broadcast of 4 June 1945 that socialism to be implemented involved 'some kind of Gestapo' even if 'no doubt very humanely directed in the first instance'; and see p. 312 below.

the mantle of *Government* policy. There were echoes of 1922, with the bulk of the party increasingly uneasy in coalition; but with this significant difference – that they were going to find themselves on the wrong side of public opinion at any future general election. The party line matured – to its habitual posture when policy could not be agreed – that there should for the time being be no unequivocal commitment one way or the other.[21] Churchill granted this indecision respectability in a note to be circulated in Cabinet:

> We must not forget that we are a Parliament in the eighth year, and we have been justified in prolonging our existence only by the physical fact of the war situation and for the purposes of the war. We have no right whatever to tie the hands of future Parliaments in regard to social matters which are their proper province. I could not as Prime Minister be responsible at this stage for binding my successor, whoever he may be, without knowledge of the conditions under which he will undertake his responsibilities.[22]

All this was too much for Lord Salisbury, President of the National Union of Conservative and Unionist Associations. Salisbury condemned Beveridge at source, stating that it was insecurity which was 'a great, if not the greatest, stimulus to effort'.[23] Although coming from the safety of Hatfield House, this observation was an unfortunate hostage to lay before the left-wing press whose editors, reporters and cartoonists were by now stimulating civilian (and Service) morale by propagating class hatred. Conservative Central Office took a more moderate approach. *Onlooker*, the party newssheet, argued that the Report should be implemented if and when the post-war economy boomed and not before. The Chairman of the party organisation pointed out this crucial truth – that the Government's current mobilisation of manpower and the economy could not be achieved in the coming peace since:

> We are not by any means paying for the war out of our own resources. We are paying out of our forefathers' earnings. We have

spent all the capital investment abroad bequeathed to us by former generations and are borrowing astronomical sums on which our sons' sons will have to pay interest.[24]

Unemployment had been the great blight, both on society in general and, increasingly, on the reputation of the Conservative Party itself. By now most senior (Conservative) members of the Government accepted that the country could not revert to its pre-war regime. The Assheton Committee recommended the continuation of a National Assistance programme with the means-testing after six months of applicants who would place 'their services at the disposal of the State, which will be entitled to direct those seeking its aid'. And, subject to an Appeal Tribunal, the reduction of aid to those refusing jobs on such grounds as distance from home and difference of trade.[25] The committee was not opposed to Beveridge's plans for a National Health Service − a provision of last resort for those who could not afford better − hence their advice that those earning above £420 per annum would not be obliged to contribute (they did not wish to see it replacing private health and pension schemes where there was a demand); and that those using the private sector would, likewise, not be obliged to pay contributions to the NHS.[26] The fear was widespread that a service which covered the whole nation would 'so narrow private practice as to virtually destroy it, with an inevitable lowering of standards in the medical profession'.[27]

Central to the Committee's report was the huge cost of the Beveridge proposals. For Conservatives the most urgent consideration was the need to reduce taxation (income tax had risen from 5s 6d in the £ in September 1939 to 10s in the April 1941 Budget). A rising social spending Budget would undermine the taxable sector of the economy whose first duty was not to pay welfare reform but to provide for defence and reduce the National Debt.[28]

Behind the scenes the Chancellor, Kingsley Wood, together with Treasury officials, had from the first been deeply suspicious of the Beveridge Report. Wood had written to Churchill in

to be adequately established), the placing of a time-limit on unemployment and disability benefits to prevent malingering and that the whole package would have to wait in the queue and battle with alternative claims on government resources in the post-war world.[36] This drew approval from the Chairman of the 1922 Committee:

> I listened with the greatest possible pleasure to what the Lord President of the Council had to say, because it seemed clear that the Government realised that there were great dangers in pressing on too hurriedly with a scheme which is essentially controversial[37]

– but most of his colleagues, now sensing the direction of the wind, were more cautious. The line of Tory left-wing MPs (thirty-seven of whom were now enlisted in the Tory Reform Group) was different, seeking to ensure that delay was not a code for burial. Forty-five of them therefore tabled an amendment to the Greenwood motion asking the Government 'to set up forthwith the proposed Ministry of Social Security for the purpose of giving effect to the principles of the Report'.[38] The Labour back bench had decided to go further, however, despite Anderson's assurance that the Government had accepted most of Beveridge 'in principle'. 121 voted against the Government and therefore in favour of implementing Beveridge as quickly as possible (97 Labour, 3 ILP, 1 Communist, 11 Independents and 9 Liberals including Lloyd George). Only two Labour back-benchers voted with their leaders in what was the largest vote against the Government of the war. Bevin, in particular, took this as a personal slight, telling Labour MPs that he was against disturbing doctors' private practices and that this sort of shoddy treatment from foot-soldiers was not what he was used to from the trade union movement. He refused to attend party meetings from that date until May 1944.[39]

Had the Parliamentary Labour Party subsequently not backed down and agreed to accept that the Government would continue to plan on the implementation of the Beveridge Report after the war, a very serious threat to the survival of Labour participation in the Coalition would have been manifest. This worry particularly vexed Hugh Dalton who feared that the action would persuade Churchill to call a snap election on whether winning the war should take precedence over social security benefits, in which scenario 'the Labour Party would be scrubbed out as completely as in 1931'.[40]

In fact the Conservative ministers had gone as far towards embracing the Report as they could reasonably be expected to go. A bedridden Churchill told his PPS that he felt his ministers in the Commons debate 'had gone farther with Beveridge than he would have gone himself'.[41] Apparently for the electorate, however, this was not nearly far enough. According to Mass Observation, whilst only 20 per cent had believed none of the Beveridge Report would be implemented when the Commons debate commenced, this had doubled to 41 per cent thereafter. While during 1941 around a half had been 'satisfied' with the 'Commons' representation of public opinion', this had halved in the aftermath of the fall of Singapore, soared to a clear majority of support after the Beveridge Report and then slumped equally quickly to around a fifth. The proportion optimistic about post-war financial prospects had hovered around a quarter throughout the period, before soaring to around three-quarters with the Report's launch, before falling back to around one-fifth after the Commons debate.[42] 'Sampling' techniques for opinion polls were far from sophisticated in 1943, but the message was plain enough, and seized on by the Tory Left. Their electoral calculation being that the party would do well not to oppose a policy which was apparently so popular. As Quintin Hogg put it with typical rhetorical over-flourish: 'if you do not give the people social reform, they are going to give you social revolution.' Furthermore, he argued that the Beveridge measures were necessary to prevent post-war strikes.[43]

This was all very well coming from someone on the back benches who was keen to advance his personal career and who had by now effected a smooth transition from deferential Chamberlainite to 'hot-head'. But in Cabinet so awkward a subject, so replete with electoral advantage for the unscrupulous to exploit, was dealt with at a more measured pace.

Despite Herbert Morrison's★ pleading, Kingsley Wood and the Treasury view prevailed. The Report was not to be a priority above the other demands on revenue. Lord Cherwell† had argued for making it clear to the public that they could have Beveridge *or* the other schemes for spending, but not both. So the line reverted to 'looking into' plans for the proposals, but seeking to convert nothing into legislation until after the war, when the issue could be decided in the light of the times and by a new Parliament. Attlee naturally pressed for more binding commitments.[44] A war of attrition developed, but with the bulk of the press, and many popular commentators on radio, of whom J. B. Priestley was the most intrusive, openly talking up the Labour Party case.

In November 1943 Churchill appointed Lord Woolton to the Cabinet as Minister for Reconstruction, with the task of relating different departments' proposals to one another but without a department of his own.[45] (The protests of Labour ministers at the prospect of his original preference of Beaverbrook for the job had led him towards the less antagonistic Woolton.[46]) Churchill tried next to get round Labour's presence by deliberately stalling their actions through constant cross-referrals with Beaverbrook in his capacity as Lord Privy Seal and with Bracken at the Information Ministry.

All the Cabinet did come to agree was to accept children's allowances. And entered into more vague commitments to a 'comprehensive health service' and 'the maintenance of employment'. Always, though, with the attendant caveat that 'no firm commitments can be entered into at the present time'.[47] But these stalling tactics were making the Conservatives deeply unpopular in the country.

★ Labour MP, Leader, London County Council 1934–40, Minister of Supply 1940, Home Secretary 1940–5, served in Attlee Government and in 1951 as Foreign Secretary.

† As Churchill's scientific adviser, Professor Lindemann, had become.

Attlee, by January 1945, was moved to compose a hand-typed six-page remonstrance:

> The conclusions agreed upon by a Committee on which have sat five or six members of the Cabinet and other experienced ministers are then submitted with great deference to the Lord Privy Seal and the Minister of Information, two ministers without Cabinet responsibility neither of whom has given any serious attention to the subject. When they state their views it is obvious that they do not know anything about it. Nevertheless an hour is consumed in listening to their opinions. Time and again important matters are delayed or passed in accordance with the decision of the Lord Privy Seal. The excuse is given that in him you have the mind of the Conservative Party. With some knowledge of opinion in the Conservative Party as expressed to me on the retirement from and re-entry into the Government of Lord Beaverbrook, I suggest that this view would be indignantly repudiated by the vast majority.

Churchill replied to this long, and perfectly reasonable, paper from his Deputy with the icy, one-sentence rejoinder: 'You may be sure that I shall always endeavour to profit from your counsels.'[48]

By the late spring of that year the two men would be openly campaigning against each other.

TWENTY

1944: The Coalition in Decline

A discontented nation – The political climate alters –
Labour and the electoral 'truce' – Churchill's personal
standing, and weaknesses – With Beaverbrook at
Marrakesh – The election battle-lines – An unexpected
landslide.

THE PICTURE OF BRITAIN IN 1944 IS not happy. A great war-weariness affected the people. Lassitude, chagrin and discontent. And with a dull fear hanging over – of bereavement or affliction. Beaverbrook, who conducted his own running assessment of public opinion via the letters page of the *Daily Express*, reported to Harry Hopkins that:

> Here in Britain we are passing through a strange phase in public life. For the first time the English are not sure of themselves. They are anxious about their future. And this is in some measure due to the extent to which they have had to rely on outside assistance during the War.

The eleventh of November 1943 – marking the equivalent duration of the Great War of 1914–18 – had come and passed. And still the German Reich was intact, the enemy far distant from its borders. The Russians were bogged down in eastern Poland, the western Allies in Italy. In the Atlantic, and on the hated Arctic convoy route, U-boats were still sinking British merchant ships. While Bomber Command of the RAF, the only force that could strike at enemy cities, was stretched to the point of fracture, suffering an attrition rate on crucial sorties of eight, nine, even eleven per cent in a single night.

Yet the security of the realm was now assured. The mortal threat of military defeat, of subjection to an occupying force, was over. And with it had expired also the exhilaration, the sense of triumph, at having been part of a miracle. Everything was rationed. Queues could be seen at all times of the day, and formed up not just for food but in hope of the most obscure, or mundane, articles – from shoelaces to torch batteries. Buildings and streets, even where undamaged, were shabby and unkempt in appearance. The 'blackout' was still in force.

Only the Americans could offer some taste of another world. Their crisp new uniforms and abundance of ready cash; the extravagance and superfluity of their equipment; the untold riches of their 'PX' stores, where lay bars of Hershey chocolate, nylon stockings and the latest jazz records – all contrived to generate an atmosphere not so much of resentment as of wistful envy. Could we ever get to be as clean, efficient and well-fed as these uncouth but manifestly *classless* visitors? We had been fighting for more than four years. What for? What had we got to show for it? These were questions not easily answered except by dilation on what was in store. Jam tomorrow.

But the form in which this 'jam' would arrive – secure jobs, proper sickness benefits and care, improved housing, decent education – the inference that we were fighting 'for' these things, translated all too easily into the logic of pointing up what we were fighting *against*. Or rather who stood in the way of our achieving these goals.

Labour Party activists, and their sympathisers in journalism and the BBC and in the Civil Service – particularly in the lower reaches of the Ministry of Information – had paid scant regard to the concept of a party truce. They worked and proselytised. At first sulky, and cynical concerning the 'capitalists' war', they were galvanised by the German attack on Soviet Russia and had for three years been spreading their message throughout the ramifications of the 'war effort'. A whole infrastructure of complementary and overlapping organisations, ranging from the Army Bureau of Current Affairs to the Council for the Encouragement of Music and the Arts, was backed and primed across the country by shop-floor, pit-head, dockside meetings, discussion groups and seminars. Always the lecturer's conclusion, direct or subliminal, was the same. The era of 'the Common Man' as depicted by Low, Zec and Strube (cartoonists all, interestingly, of Eastern European origin), as lauded in the BBC Brains Trust and on his hugely popular radio 'talks' by J. B. Priestley, was at hand.

Provided, that is, the 'Men of Munich' did not thwart us.

A useful group pejorative, this. For it could be extended to include every Conservative politician except Churchill and, possibly, Anthony Eden. At the time of Munich there had been nearly two million people out of work, had there not? And yet at the same time our defences were so weak that we had been compelled to fight to, and beyond, the point of exhaustion. Now unemployment was down to 84,000. Only Socialism at home in the shape of wartime *planning*, and abroad in the form of our Soviet ally, had saved the day.

In the summer of 1944 what was left of the German armies in northern France were in headlong retreat. Disappointment (at Arnhem) and unexpected reversal (in the Battle of the Ardennes) lay in the future. Victory might come, it seemed to many observers, in a matter of weeks. And the fashionable topics for discussion were the Post-war Settlement and, in particular, 'Reconstruction', whose urgency was heightened by the still-continuing German bombardment of London with the V-weapons. Moreover, the whole concept of Reconstruction now carried firmly embedded within it a presumption that Socialism, and interventionist techniques, having won the war must now be applied to 'win the peace'. Agreement, though, as to how far, if at all, this approach was valid was far from universal; least of all in the House of Commons.

The *Economist* editorialised that:

The present session of Parliament, like the war, has reached a late and critical stage [but] ... it is legislation that counts, and it is legislation that is still perilously [*sic*] lacking.

A number of White Papers were in the course of preparation. And as each in turn saw the light of day the Coalition atmosphere deteriorated until, by the spring of 1945, the Conservatives were flatly refusing to discuss a proposal to revise the Trade Disputes Act of 1927; while Labour effectively detached itself from any cross-party consensus on 'Medical Reform' and signalled that an incoming Socialist government – at that time thought to be unlikely – would play a free hand on this topic (thereby marking up what was to become the largest and most destabilising single expenditure heading of the post-war decade).

The first of these papers, *Employment Policy*, was composed of input from the Treasury, from Lord Woolton's Reconstruction Committee and, the most advanced or 'Keynesian' of the advisory groups, the War Cabinet's Economic Section. In its final form it represented, in the judgement of one historian, 'the very limits of coalition consensus ... the parties were able to support the document only by agreeing to disagree on future policy'.[1] Conservative advocates, among whom the Chancellor, Sir John Anderson, was the most implacable, succeeded in removing a commitment to *full* employment from the text and replaced it by a call for 'the creation [*sic*] of conditions necessary for a high and stable level of employment'. The ceiling on total unemployment was set at the unexpectedly high level of 8.5 per cent of the labour force – a figure of which sight was soon lost with, in the sixties, most of the Conservative benches in the House of Commons ready to throw up their hands in horror when the total exceeded six per cent.

This paper was debated on 22 July 1944, barely a fortnight after D-Day. Predictable contributions had come from Aneurin Bevan and Sir Herbert Williams. But it was Arthur Greenwood's winding-up speech that presaged a return to full-time party politics:

... while we accept the recognition by the State of a new responsibility which hitherto has been unrecognised and unaccepted by
the State, we do not believe that the machinery in the White Paper
will, as it stands now, solve our problems ... If the predominant
motive in industry is to be private gain we can say goodbye to all
hopes of ending large-scale unemployment. I still must, on behalf
of my honourable friends, re-assert the faith we all hold that the
one way is the way we call Socialism.[2]

Too late, the rank and file of the Conservative Party had woken
up to the unwelcome fact that they were unpopular, and widely
regarded as out of date. They were alarmed. They faced the
prospect of losing power. Most dangerously, this was rampant and,
in the context of the 'war effort', respectable. To whom could
they make complaint?

The Chairman of the Party was Ralph Assheton. He listened
attentively. His instinct was to agree. But the party machinery was
decrepit. Local agents were, many of them, still in uniform. Those
that remained were elderly and set in their ways. Functions were
poorly attended and, in utter contrast to the Labour Party whose
own meetings were in effect little more than extended branch
sessions of the locally dominant trade union, there was a general
reluctance to look beyond ending the war and getting loved ones
'back from the front'.

Were Conservative MPs aware of this deep-running mill-race
in public opinion? Dimly, perhaps, among the back-benchers. In
the Government barely at all. Occasionally the matter would be
raised at the '22 Committee (but not as often as in 1942, when
politically the Conservative parliamentary party disposed of more
power). With each year that passed the party organisation had
degenerated still further. Subscriptions faltered; the money being
pre-empted – to a far greater degree than the income of the
Labour Party which was paid directly out of the trade union levy –
by patriotic appeal funds. This condition could only be reversed
by wholesale changes at the top of the party, a reversion, almost,
to the political demarcation lines of 1939. For some Tories who

felt that an election could only be won outside the Coalition there were parallels with 1922. But the comparison was invalid, because now both the leader and the Chief Whip were from their own ranks. And so often, 'loyalty' and the distant hope of personal advancement rode in double harness. Little attention seems to have been paid to reports from the 'field', even when coming from junior party officials. The agent in West Dorset, a strongly Conservative constituency, reported that:

> ... the anti-political mood in the pub, which was so noticeable in the first years of the war is, however, changing, and this is largely due to the consideration of post-war problems and the publication of various reports.[3]

To a large extent the Labour Party outside Westminster had already discarded any but formal attachment to the Coalition pact. They would run campaigns – providing resources, printing, volunteers to distribute literature and halls for meetings – for candidates from the Commonwealth, or Independent Labour, parties. The language was overtly, and often crudely, anti-Tory. Excusing themselves by the plea that the candidates were not 'official' and the supporters were acting simply 'as individuals'. In February of 1944 there occurred, by chance, an electoral collision between two archetypical candidates in West Derbyshire. This was a traditional Conservative division, long regarded as being in the gift of the Dukes of Devonshire. And as if in confirmation the Tory candidate was the Duke's eldest son, the Marquess of Hartington. Hartington was an amiable, pink cheeked young man with a drawling voice and a commission in the Coldstream Guards. The contest, normally, would have been a formality (in 1935, indeed, the Duke's nominee had been 'unopposed'). This time it was contested by Alderman White, a Labour Party councillor and shop steward from Derby, now pretending to the political neutrality attaching to an 'alderman' but campaigning in the crudest language of the class war.

White took good care, on instructions from the local branch of

the Labour Party, to cover his candidature in terms of the electoral
truce:

> ... the anti-Conservative speakers would make reference to Chur-
> chill's record, and the debt owed him by the people of this country.
> Great and enthusiastic applause always greeted this. Then they
> would go on to say that despite his services to the nation no man,
> Churchill or any other, had the right to dictate to the people of
> the country how they should vote. Invariably this brought even
> louder applause.[4]

Thus Churchill's own position, increasingly unassailable as the
tide of war changed and victories accumulated, seemed to derive
additional benefit from the very weakness in the party's political
strength for which many among them felt him to blame. The
Prime Minister's popularity across the country (as it was believed
to be) was, for the Tories, the best – and soon to be regarded as
the only – guarantee of electoral success. Especially (and certainly
the Labour members of the Coalition believed this) in the first
'khaki' election. After that, Conservative back-benchers consoled
themselves, the necessary changes to the leadership could, indeed
would, have to be made.

As will be seen, there was in fact not the slightest likelihood of
Winston Churchill winning a 'khaki', or any other kind of,
election. Nor is it clear whether, by this stage, either Churchill's
direction of strategy or his diplomatic skill in negotiation were
superior to, say, what Eden might have shown had he taken over
as Prime Minister.

> Winston is to my mind beginning to go downhill a bit even from
> the war leader point of view – at any rate in Cabinet – while the
> dangers arising from his lack of judgement and knowledge in
> many respects and his sheer lack of sanity over India make him
> increasingly dangerous.[5]

In the autumn of 1944, with the battle of Normandy won and
final victory only weeks – it must have seemed – distant, Churchill
was in visible decline. In Cabinet he would utter long, grumbling

monologues, speaking into his cigar. He avoided decisions. He kept proceedings going for an intolerable length of time – sometimes as much as five hours. He seldom maintained order and often there were several people speaking at once.

But this was a time when great energy, and a breadth of vision looking far beyond the simple balance sheet of military success, was needed. What was to be the shape of post-war society, and how could and should Conservatives influence this in order to prevent their alienation? What steps should be put in train so as to avert national bankruptcy? What alterations to Imperial balance and emphasis were now inevitable? What was the ideal shape for a liberated Western Europe to assume? And (had Churchill been a real *Party* Leader this would have been his first preoccupation) how does the interplay of all these different factors relate, and how can it be exploited, to endow party-political advantage in the general election that cannot be more than a twelvemonth distant?

> What makes me so tired at Cabinets is the same feeling that one has in a taxi, wishing to catch a train with a driver who dawdles and misses every green light. I have had a good deal of experience now, what with Lloyd George's brisk if dominating manner of getting through business while at the same time extracting the views of others; Bonar's quiet interjections almost invariably beginning with 'I am afraid . . .' Baldwin's screwing up his lips and twiddling a pencil while taking our views in rotation and acquiescing with the majority except about once a year when he would take the bit between his teeth and announce a very personal decision . . .
>
> Winston neither reads the papers nor tries to collect opinions systematically and is a good deal slower in the uptake than Ll.G, with the consequence that when he is not talking himself the thing is rather a bear garden, everybody, himself more particularly, interrupting everybody else, while the whole purpose of the discussion gets lost sight of and confused.[6]

In the New Year Churchill had been in Marrakesh, convalescing from a chest infection that he had contracted at the Teheran Conference, and Beaverbrook flew out to join him. Beaverbrook was now Lord Privy Seal. Nothing much to do, but a good overview of what was happening and ready access to the Prime Minister. Government business in the Mamounia Hotel was not heavy, and the two men allowed their lunchtime discussions to range widely. Beaverbrook had no more love for the Tories than had Churchill – perhaps even less. What interested him was power. Back in London he drafted a paper setting out how the Coalition Government might be continued into peacetime. The paper was replete with ill-thought-out clichés – a long Opinion-page article for the *Daily Express*. 'Food, Homes, and Work for All' – that was to be the platform on which to contest the election. Under particular subject headings the paper was strongly un-Conservative, pointing up the conclusion that the best way forward was in some kind of 'modified' – modified, that is to say, by the Conservatives making a lot of concessions – Coalition.

Nationalisation of the banks – 'A way out might be found ... whereby money and credit become instruments of Government'. The coalmines – 'Here the Conservatives will have to give way'. Transport – '. . . the Labour Party will press for full nationalisation as registering what they will claim is already an accomplished fact'. Food – 'a programme of equitable food distribution ... the continuance of food rationing as well as of food subsidies'.

In March of 1943, responding to Beaverbrook's paper and other suggestions which, from various quarters, had come in during his illness and convalescence, Churchill had broadcast a long speech on post-war planning. It was, doubtless because the subject bored him, a stilted and discordant performance. Churchill warned his audience 'not to take your eye off the *ball* (i.e., the war) even for a moment . . .' He excused his own dealing with 'some post-war and domestic issues' in the hope that 'I may simplify and mollify political divergences'.

Even a cursory scrutiny of this text points to the conclusion that Churchill did not write, or at least wrote very little of, the passages dealing with 'planning'. The speech was laden with cliché – *Sunlit uplands . . . comradeship of war . . . peering through the mists of the future . . . the bells will clash their peals of victory . . .* But Churchill's real objective, and the extent to which he was prepared to compromise the traditional principles of the party he was leading, and defer to the basic points of Beaverbrook's draft, was revealed when he began to digress on a suggested Four-Year Plan.

> When this plan has been shaped, it will have to be presented to the country, either by a National Government formally representative, as this one is, of the three parties in the state; or by a National Government *comprising the best men in all Parties who are willing to serve.*[7]

Here then was the paradox. And for the Conservatives it was damaging. Churchill was seeking so to order things that he remained leader – not of the party but of the nation. This could most easily come to pass if the 'new' House of Commons was 'freely chosen by the whole electorate including the armed forces wherever they may be' to enact 'a clear policy . . . in the name of an effective and resolute majority' (by implication) above 'the politics and party fights of peacetime'.

For the time being, as was generally thought,

> The Tories can rest more securely in the knowledge that they hold the ace of trumps. And that ace, of course, is the Prime Minister.[8]

But how did Churchill see himself? The last thing he wanted to do was retire to Chartwell and hose out the fishpond.* Churchill will have been well aware of the Mass Observation finding that a majority of the electorate were strongly Labour but 'whatever Party *or group* Winston Churchill heads will win'. And at Cabinet on 4 May 1945, Bevin reproached Churchill for behaving as if the election was imminent, suggesting that 'the Labour Party has never in so many words decided that the Coalition was to be broken up the moment Germany is defeated'. Churchill, though, had been

---

* The activity preoccupying Churchill in early August of 1945 when Leo Amery visited him and found him 'in wonderful heart'.

in politics all his life. Quite possibly his personal preference might have been that the Coalition should continue – 'in some form' – but this could only come following a formal appeal to Attlee, in the national interest, not as a result of a private deal, however much everyone involved wanted to hold on to their jobs. Accordingly, after some preparatory leaking to the press, Churchill wrote to Attlee on 20 May, suggesting that the Coalition should continue 'at least' until the end of the Japanese war.

It was too late. This plan was quite different from the future as seen by the activists of the Labour Party. And at their conference on 21 May continuance of the Coalition was rejected by 1,100 votes to two. Labour were in fact as determined, and in terms of their party machine as strong, as the Conservative Party in 1922 – the last time pressure from rank and file had forced a rupture with the grandees. And on 23 May Churchill went to the Palace and was asked to form a new government, and for Parliament to be dissolved on 15 June.

At a meeting of Conservative ministers at 10 Downing Street on the day following the split it was agreed that 'Winston proposes to do most of the election over the wireless, very wisely'.[9] This judgement had to be revised when at his first broadcast Churchill '. . . jumped straight off his pedestal as world statesman to deliver a fantastical exaggerated assault on Socialism'.[10] The very next day Attlee responded in a banal, matter-of-fact style that drew universal plaudits in the press. The era of the Common Man had arrived.

This was masked from Churchill, and from most of his entourage. On his presidential journey across the land, he was greeted by flowers, bunting and cheering crowds. Only at the very end of the campaign, when the strident warnings of imminent repression: 'the socialist hand over your mouth and around your windpipe' – mainly drafted by Bracken and Beaverbrook – started to irritate people, did Churchill's cortège encounter hostility. He was booed in Walthamstow, and stoned in Ladbroke Grove. Generally, though, Conservatives were optimistic, ascribing the occasional ominous sign to 'exceptional factors', a misreading of events or (possibly in some settings correctly) 'Communist sympathisers'.

The Party Chairman himself (about to lose his seat) wrote a friendly note to Anthony Eden:

> I am just off to my constituency and though I shall be in constant touch with the office I shall not be in London very much. We have got a fine field of candidates and some excellent literature and posters.[11]

Whether or not the literature and posters were 'excellent' they were certainly monotone. Winston Churchill's face was on every poster; it appeared in every election address. A facsimile of Churchill's signature was placed below the message: 'Mr XX is pledged to support me. I ask you to give him your vote'. The word 'Conservative' was seldom anywhere to be seen.

It is hard to find anyone senior who dissented from the general thrust of policy during the election campaign (although there were several who grumbled to each other about Churchill's broadcasts). If senior Tories were tied so closely to Churchill's persona – 'Let Winston finish the job' – then plainly they could not pick and choose. Even when it became clear that this particular slogan, very widely distributed on posters, with 'the job' understood to mean the war against Japan, was actually proving negative in its effect. Amery, at the outset, recorded his belief that it were better to concentrate on 'urgent measures of demobilisation, housing, etc.' rather than the philosophic distinction between socialism and individualism. Rab Butler, whose domestic portfolios had kept him rather closer to the mood of the man in the street, ticked off by Beaverbrook for criticising the Prime Minister in committee – 'Young man, if you speak to Mr Churchill like that you will not be offered a place in the next Conservative Government' – replied, 'There is not going to be a Conservative Government.'[12]

Part of the illusion that continuity of Conservative government was unbreakable may be found in the nature of the 'caretaker' administration which continued to 'govern' even after polling day and while the votes were being counted. This process took, or rather had allotted to it, three weeks. Thus it seemed, once the fervour of the campaign had abated, that the Tories were still in place, and with Churchill at their head. There were now just those three weeks left of calm, not to say lethargic, Conservative government. Even Leslie Hore-Belisha who had been in the sulks since 1940* was brought back as Minister of National Insurance, with instructions to take an immediate look at the Beveridge Report with the object of 'humanising' (*sic*) and 'purging its present traces of Socialism'.[13] It might almost have been the summer of 1935.

Not much, though, was seen of Churchill at this time. The day after polling he left for Hendaye with his paintbox and canvases. Beaverbrook, whose task it was to wind down the campaign, sent him messages. At first Beaverbrook was confident. The Conservatives were going to emerge with an 'adequate' majority. Then things started tightening up. On 15 July (by which time Churchill had moved to Potsdam) Beaverbrook sent him a note warning that the majority might be as low as 10. Then, on 17 June, a further letter grumbling that 'The Tory Party is without spirit ... It has no fighting disposition for the future ... Tory papers are frankly hostile to the administration.'[14]

These views were not widely shared, even in the upper reaches of the Labour Party. Beyond an admission that it was going to be 'close', the only limitation on perpetual Tory rule was suggested as re-forming the Coalition 'to reflect more closely the new numbers in the House'. On the assumption that there would be cause for celebration the two press lords invited guests (drawn from much the same list) to banquets on 26 July. Rothermere chose the Dorchester Hotel, for a great lunch, Beaverbrook the Savoy, for a long-drawn-out dinner, with two orchestras, a dance floor and a 'nightclub'.

Even the lunch barely got started. The science of projecting swings from sample results as they came in was in its infancy; but it was hardly needed. By one o'clock it was plain that a landslide was under way, and many of the City notables had already left the

* See pp. 196–7, 208 above.

dining room to go short of equities on the Stock Exchange.[15] Slowly the manually operated scoreboard (brought down from Wimbledon) filled out, until by nightfall the scale of what had happened sank in. The Conservatives had polled only 189 – a truly terrible result in England if the Ulster Unionists were subtracted from this total along with the 26 Conservatives elected in Scotland. Labour were at 393; the Liberals out of sight at 12.

Beaverbrook's own verdict could well be repeated on the last page of any report on the next occasion – more than half a century distant – when the Conservatives were to suffer a like fate:

> The truth is that the British public have been conceiving for a long time an immense dislike of the Tory Party, the Tory Members of Parliament and many of the Tory ideas. They were bored and wanted a change.[16]

BOOK THREE

The Management
of Decline

TWENTY-ONE

The Party in Defeat

The Conservative Party in shock – The grandees are
dejected – The Young Turks take control of policy-
making – The *Industrial Charter* – The Maxwell-Fyfe
reforms.

THE GREAT LABOUR landslide of 1945 swept away nearly half of
the Conservative parliamentary party* including not a few who
had fancied that their own personal eminence should ensure
survival. These ranged from grandees like Sir Reginald McClarry,
the last of the founding fathers of the 1922 Committee, and the
two immediate past Chairmen, to Cabinet ministers and the
Chairman of the Party, Ralph Assheton. Macmillan was out at
Stockton. Bracken was out at North Paddington. After thirty-four
years of continuous service, Leo Amery was out at Birmingham
Sparkbrook. Indeed in that great city, heart of Midlands Unionism,
the Tories lost ten of the thirteen seats – a turnaround from their
clean sweep of 1931. Nor did the electorate show much respect for
'household' names. An Independent who stood against Churchill
(neither Labour nor the Liberals were so disrespectful as to field a
candidate in his constituency) still managed to receive more than
10,000 votes. Beveridge, hailed less than a year earlier as the most
popular wartime figure in the country after Churchill, lost his seat

---

* 292 Labour MPs were elected, together with 3 Independent Labour members,
2 Communists and 3 Irish Nationalists. 189 Conservatives were returned together
with 9 Ulster Unionists and 13 National Liberals. Fourteen Independents and 12
Liberals were elected.

to an unknown Conservative. While the Liberal Party, once the greatest power in the land, was demolished; only a rump of twelve surviving.

The mood of the Conservative Party in Opposition, and for a year or more after that catastrophic defeat, was one of deep shock. 'Disgusted' of Tunbridge Wells pronounced that 'The people have elected Labour, and the nation won't stand for it'. These were sentiments echoed by some of the Conservative Party's walking wounded. Cuthbert Headlam felt 'ashamed of his countrymen'; Chips Channon, surviving the backlash (to his own personal surprise), was 'stunned and shocked by the country's treachery'. Having observed the scene from Worcestershire where he was well aware that he had outlived his reputation, the former Prime Minister, Baldwin, told Butler that it was 'the classic example of democratic ingratitude'.[1]

Indeed, had it not been for the prolonged and arctic weather of the winter of 1947, which for the first time focused public attention on the administrative inadequacies of doctrinaire socialism, morale would have worsened still further. Such a sense of dejection showed itself in many ways. Torpor and fatalism – a feeling that the tide had turned irreversibly, that the sheer weight of electoral numbers would keep the party out of office for as long as could be foreseen. A nostrum which had been uttered on and off since 1832, that 'Universal suffrage means the end of the Conservative Party', was being re-uttered at the dining tables of the well-to-do. 'Society', in the meantime, made feeble efforts to reform, along the behaviour patterns of the thirties. At a grand wedding reception Lady Cunard was greeted by an excitable fellow guest: 'It's too wonderful. *Everybody* is here! This is what we fought the war for.' To which her Wildean rejoinder, 'Really? Are they all Poles?' pithily summarised the futility of the occasion.

Punitive, indeed confiscatory taxation of income was disagreeable, and looked to be permanent. But capital gains (of which the war had delivered plenty) were still untaxed and allowed conspicuous expenditure by those who wished to defy the trend. The new Bentley cost four times the manufacturer's list price on the black market yet by 1947 five, all owned by Conservative MPs, could be counted in the New Palace Yard car park and there would be scores attending the Royal enclosure at Ascot.

Petrol rationing and exchange control were irritants. But the real deprivation was the severance of that link between the administration and the upper classes which had always in former times allowed the socially prominent, when they had a personal problem or an opinion to air, to operate the 'old boy network'. 'Leave it to me. I'll get hold of ... [for example] ... Oliver'; or Julian; or Anthony. This linkage was no longer operational. The party was now, for the first time in the twentieth century, effectively cut off from power. On all previous occasions when it had been out of office – even after defeat in 1906 and briefly at different points in the twenties – its presence, and particularly the weight of its various personalities, still made themselves felt. When Labour's Hartley Shawcross uttered his celebrated gloat – 'We are the masters now' – it rang more true than was comfortable.

First we must consider the leader.

Churchill, who had intermittently applied his mind to the subject of governing the country (as distinct from winning the war) until July of 1945, did not thereafter focus on it with much enthusiasm. It was the international stage for which he yearned. And this, of course, remained at his disposal. Whenever Churchill wished, the footlights would be switched on. But reminiscence, oratory – even when embracing premonition – and the tributes which these earned, had none of them the same taste attaching as if uttered from the standpoint of continuing executive power. So Churchill wrote. He painted. He could be found in the owners' – and sometimes the winners' – enclosure at race meetings.* He took holidays, often at Max Beaverbrook's villa on Cap d'Ail.

For the parliamentary party this was a source of irritation. And one not moderated by the fact that the electorate at large remained

---

* A portrait in oil of Churchill's favourite race horse 'Colonist II' hangs still above the chimney-piece in his study at Chartwell. Today his racing colours can be found on the scarves of undergraduates at Churchill College, Cambridge.

happy that their wartime leader should thus enjoy himself. Stubbornly, Churchill's personal popularity rating remained above that
of the Conservative Party.

In the House of Commons parliamentary discipline was simultaneously strict and slack. Strict among the 'troops' over whom
Patrick Buchan-Hepburn kept a tight control. Slack at the higher
levels of direction. Three-line whips were common, voting often
went on late into the night. In aid of what? MPs asked themselves
(and each other) when the Labour majorities were habitually in
the high seventies. A peremptory note was circulated, with the
whip, by the 'Chief':

> While the attendance has been very good on other days, I must
> draw attention to the importance of attendance on Fridays by all
> who can arrange to be present in the House.[2]

But what was the point of it all? The question was asked at
the 1922 Committee immediately following this instruction. Mr
David Eccles* said that the Conservative Party had no industrial
policy, or principles. Morale among colleagues was low, and their
minds wandered to fields of reward outside politics. Chairmen of
the various party committees were appointed by the leader – and
thus effectively by the Chief Whip himself – instead of being
elected by the membership of the 1922 Committee. There was to
be no risk of discontent taking shape as it had done in 1942 and
feeding through to either the formulation, or the criticism, of
policy.

Nor, indeed, at this stage is there much sign of any serious
approach to policy – certainly not to significant *alternative* ideas –
being addressed. As almost invariably happens when a party feels
itself to have been the subject of total rejection by the electorate
(and of which the most obvious contemporary example is that of
the Conservatives' defeat by 'New Labour' in the late nineties)
the solution was seen to be in assuming as close a resemblance as

* Minister of Education, 1954–7 and 1959–62; President of the Board of Trade,
1957–9.

possible to the opponents by whom the defeat had been inflicted. To offer little more, that is to say, than a 'new' team, fresher and more amiable, who would maintain continuity but administrate more competently. The *Economist* declared reproachfully that – '. . . the Conservative Party has been so anxious to avoid the odium of opposing the social policies of the present government that they have jettisoned most of the logical grounds for criticising its economic policy'. The whole incubus of Socialist planning and control, put in place to underpin the 'war effort' went, other than in the smallest points of detail, unchallenged. Quite often indeed, should a proposal get as far as Churchill for endorsement, he would reject it on the grounds that it had been originally agreed while he was Coalition Leader and he should therefore feel himself bound to *concur*.

In the five years in which the Attlee Government held power, 347 Acts passed into law. This was a time of intense friction and, at times, severe ill feeling between the two main parties. At one stage, the Conservative Chief Whip, James Stuart, was deliberately blocked by over thirty Labour MPs from passing through the division lobby and had to virtually punch his way through.[3] Nye Bevan's ill-judged comment about the Tories 'being lower than vermin' raised the political temperature and has entered legend. Perhaps more astonishing was the claim in 1948 by the Chancellor of the Exchequer, Sir Stafford Cripps, on the floor of the House of Commons that 'if we cannot get nationalisation of steel by legal means, we must resort to violent methods'. Given the chance to form a future government, the Conservatives, the nation was assured, would turn Britain into a totalitarian state. At the following year's Labour Party Conference, Nye Bevan and Manny Shinwell claimed that if the Conservatives won the next election there could be a civil war.

The election defeat, which had removed so many of the old faces in the parliamentary party and left many of those remaining tagged with the sense of having run off the rails, presented the young progressives with their opportunity, as they thought, to capture the party. By implicating Beaverbrook and Bracken with

the election defeat (regardless of the fact that the result had probably relatively little to do with the campaign that they ran), the
left-progressives were also able to sideline two of the most senior
figures on the party's right wing. Notwithstanding his own rejection by the people of Stockton, Macmillan (quickly re-elected in
a by-election at Bromley) was one of the first off the blocks in this
respect. Inspired by Peel's creation of 'the Conservative Party'
after the old Tories had been blown away by the Great Reform
Act, Macmillan now advocated changing the party's name to
'New Democratic Party'. Bracken wrote to Beaverbrook that at
the 1946 Party Conference:

> The neo-Socialists, like Harold Macmillan, who are in favour
> of nationalising railways, electricity, gas and many other things,
> expected to get great support from the delegates ... It turned out
> that the neo-Socialists were lucky to escape with their scalps. The
> delegates would have nothing to do with the proposal to change the
> party's name. They demanded a real Conservative policy instead of
> a synthetic Socialist one so dear to the heart of the Macmillans and
> the Butlers, and it gave Churchill one of the greatest receptions of
> his life.[4]

The phrase that Eden had popularised in his 1946 Conference
speech, a 'property-owning democracy', was readily taken up, but
little was at first done to articulate what it meant in terms of
legislative proposals. Believing that resistance to the Labour Government would produce better dividends than throwing political
hostages to fortune, Churchill resisted the appeal to set out policy,
protesting that:

> I do not believe in looking about for some panacea or cure-all on
> which we should stake our credit and fortunes, and which we
> should try to sell in a hurry like a patent medicine to all and sundry
> ... We ought not to seek after some rigid symmetrical formula of
> doctrine such as delights the mind of Socialists or Communists.[5]

None the less, presented with the demands of the 1946 Party
Conference that detailed statements of policy were essential, Chur-

chill had to back down and claim that he had also come to this conclusion. He appointed Butler (then chairing the successor to the Post-War Problems Central Committee) to head an 'Industrial Policy Committee' charged with spearheading the agenda. This gave Butler considerable authority, further augmented when Churchill failed to stop him becoming chairman of the Conservative Research Department as well. There he presided over a team which included Iain Macleod, Reginald Maudling and Enoch Powell.

In time, energy, and self-advertisement, the *Industrial Charter* far out-weighed all the other policy pronouncements from the Conservative Party between 1945 and 1951. With the academically-minded Butler as chairman, the committee which drew it up included those considered to be amongst the party's future stars – Harold Macmillan, Oliver Stanley, David Maxwell-Fyfe and Oliver Lyttelton – as well coming men still further distant like Derick Heathcoat-Amory and Reggie Maudling. Touring the country in order to extract evidence, this little group, engaged on what in 1997 was termed 'Listening to Britain', certainly did not lack source material. Following general approval from the Shadow Cabinet (such as it was), at that moment being chaired by Eden, the conclusions were finally released to the public (initial print run – a quarter of a million) in May 1947. Some of the *Charter*'s features represented conventional Tory thinking, tailored only with a few qualifying or emollient sub-clauses. Free collective bargaining should be upheld. Rationing should be ended as soon as it was possible to do so. The share of spending by the State should be scaled down and so, too, taxation with it. Opposition to the trade unions' 'closed shop' policy was restated. Hostility to monopolies and to further nationalisation made a battle cry. These, together with a few of the usual agreeable platitudes about the workforce which politicians are minded to make along with tolerance of existing practices where they persisted or might be spread (such as industrial co-partnerships and joint production councils), made up the core of the policy. To all but the most free thinking of Conservatives they were uncontroversial. However, tucked in between them were a number of statements demonstrating support for a more corporatist approach to economic management. Government would now play a strong role coordinating economic policy in tandem with the trade unions and industrialists. Underlining a commitment which had already been given during the war, the *Charter* also stated that Government would be responsible for retaining 'a high and stable level of employment'. A year after the death of John Maynard Keynes, the Conservative Party now seemed to be sure that it intended laying to rest the ghost of Adam Smith.

Mild in its tone towards the trade unions, the document disappointed the Tory Right. Importantly, it did not suggest that the existing nationalised industries and public utilities should be privatised. And in the ensuing decades any suggestion that this should be considered was branded (by the leadership) as verging on lunacy. But with the 1922 Committee as well as the party's front bench endorsing the *Charter*'s proposals, the right wing was consigned to a long uphill struggle. Sir Waldron Smithers's paper on the subject, which he entitled 'Save England' and duly decorated on its title page with a biblical quotation about the 'oracles of God', was no match for the secular forces ranged against it. Beaverbrook, it is true, also opposed the *Charter*, but this did not in itself sway many minds – or at least not in the direction he hoped. When it came to a vote of delegates at the 1947 Party Conference the dissidents were routed. In his closing speech to the conference, Churchill also felt compelled to give his endorsement to the document. Told beforehand by Maudling what it involved, he had protested that he did not agree with a word of it. But when told that it now had the Conference's stamp of approval, Churchill thought he had better endorse it after all.[6]

The reinvigoration of the party, the adoption of 'new' techniques, and the better working of its organisational operation in the years after 1945 have all been lauded for heralding a revolution in the building of the modern Conservative Party out of the ashes of what went before. But as Dr John Ramsden has pointed out,

Central Office staff and Woolton in particular, who had not served in the party before the war, were really in the position of those who 'having never seen a wheel in action, it was easy to believe that they were inventing one'.[7] Set against the organisational disintegration during the war years, the subsequent turnaround was dramatic. But setting results against the worst possible trough for a benchmark does not necessarily present a balanced picture. In the 1930s, and before, the party – certainly by comparison with its competitors – had been extremely well organised and efficient, and to some extent the post-1945 modernisers were merely regaining ground which had been only temporarily conceded. None the less, this they did – and quickly.

Lord Woolton joined the Conservative Party the day after the 1945 election defeat. However, in September 1946 he began work as the party's Chairman. His popularity as a wartime minister overcame any resentment that his recent conversion might otherwise have spawned. Until Woolton's appointment, Ralph Assheton had reluctantly stayed on as Party Chairman in the immediate aftermath of the election and it is now recognised that much of the accomplishment of his successors' reforms came on top of his spadework in this period. In failing to avert the disintegration of the party mechanism and its very means of operation, the Tories' response to the war years had added to the problems created by the inevitable natural wastage during that period (for a year after the defeat there was still not even a party telephone directory or comprehensive list of Central Office staff). By 1947, however, the General Director, Stephen Pierseené, could report that the essential structures had been re-established and what was now needed was to entice the supporters to fill them. A large increase in the numbers of qualified Conservative Party agents took place from 1946 onwards. Some in Central Office and the National Union Executive wanted to ensure that the best agents were assigned to the marginal constituencies and that, therefore, the pay and appointments of agents should be directed from Central Office. Fearing for local autonomy, opposition was mounted to the attempt to introduce this initiative, so that a decision was deferred until 1948 whereupon the notion of centralised appointment was again put on hold.

The party's membership and funding improved remarkably quickly after 1946 and this was primarily the result of better organisation rather than a different structure from that which had existed before the war. In 1928, 180 people had worked directly in Conservative Central Office; by 1947 the figure was 233 and rising. CCO co-ordinated recruitment campaigns on a scale far above previous efforts and, to this extent, a greater degree of centralised command was created without major institutional alteration needing to take place. In 1947, the party appeared to have in the region of 1.2 million members. Woolton's great fund-raising and membership drives on the back of Labour's unpopularity drove up membership to 2.5 million in 1950 and a summit of 2.8 million in 1952. Courses, like those organised by the Centre for Policy Studies at Lord Swinton's old home in North Yorkshire, improved the training of party hopefuls. The relaunch of the Junior Imperial League as the Young Conservatives, already planned during the war itself, took off quickly from around 50 branches in mid-1945 to 2,129 branches and 149,000 members three years later. Attendances at the National Union's Party Conference also shot up – twice as many delegates attending the 1947 conference as had attended in 1937. Woolton's personal popularity amongst the party rank and file also assisted the fund- and membership-raising campaign although it should be noted that in Scotland, where Woolton's writ did not run (Colonel Blair and James Stuart were the leading lights), the results were every bit as impressive – indeed proportionately more so. The best recruiter was arguably the performance of the Labour Government.

The second period, 1947–9, was that in which reconstruction was followed by reform. The 1947 Party Conference carried resolutions in favour of placing new limits on the amount that prospective candidates and MPs could donate to their constituencies, and on the Central Office's funding from local associations; and discussing the terms and conditions of agents' employment. The last, as described above, got nowhere but the first two were enacted into the 1949 'Maxwell-Fyfe Report' (in which David Maxwell-Fyfe himself in fact played little creative part). The Maxwell-Fyfe Report was the conclusion of work done by sub-committees between October 1947 and May 1948, work in which no front-bench figure was involved at first hand. The report established a comprehensive system in which constituencies were given fund-raising quotas as their target to raise for Central Office. In return, greater openness about the party's finances was promised. To the consternation of many contributing constituencies this openness was largely denied in practice (Conservative Party accounts were not published until 1967). A resolution from one of the branches, requesting that constituencies should have a say in CCO's personnel and finances, was easily quashed by the Central Council.

The placing of limits on MPs' contributions to their own constituencies was intended to reduce the alleged practice in which safe seats were effectively for sale to the highest bidder. An attempt during the war had already been made to tackle this. In 1941 the Central Council supported the removal of any candidate who had been selected having been asked financial questions during his selection (a provision which was difficult to enforce given the ability of informal requests and 'understandings' agreed outside the selection process itself). In 1944 the National Union Executive set a £100 maximum contribution from candidates to their constituency per year (plus half of their election expenses). The Maxwell-Fyfe Report abolished the payment of electoral expenses by candidates/MPs and limited their contribution to that of the maximum annual subscription (£25 for candidates and £50 for MPs). These reforms came against the backdrop of two considerations outside the party's control: a top-rate income tax of 95 per cent, which reduced the amount of money potential candidates were normally likely to have available for large donations; and the Attlee Government's reduction of the maximum election expenses allowable, ensuring that their financing was more within the grasp of the local associations themselves. Great claims were made for the Maxwell–Fyfe Report's 'democratic effect. Judged by the raw statistics, however, the real effect that it had in respect to MPs and their constituency expenses proved at best marginal in changing the background from which selected candidates came.

The Maxwell–Fyfe Report also dealt with the geometry between several party institutions (for example, 1922 Committee representatives were added to the National Union Executive) although little was altered – the changes being outweighed by the predominating spirit of leaving alone. It restated that the National Union's functions were 'primarily deliberative and advisory', its committees designed to 'enable the collective opinion of the party to find expression'. Naturally such remote and mystic procedures as choosing a leader of the party were left at a great distance. Indeed there is no evidence that they were even mentioned in discussion.

TWENTY-TWO

Friction at the Highest Levels

A relaxed high command – The question of succession –
The certainty of Anthony Eden – Churchill is irritated –
He humiliates his deputy – Others play an equivocal
role – Beaverbrook's warning.

AT SHADOW CABINET level things were much slacker than at Conservative Central Office. Indeed, no such body can be said to have existed; no set responsibilities were assigned to senior individuals nor any specialist data on particular subjects made available to them. All that happened was that Churchill would invite some colleagues to lunch at a private room in the Savoy on Wednesdays. There would be a general *tour-de-table* (by all accounts pretty discursive) and it would be agreed who should lead for the Opposition. This group – usually, but not always uniformly, the same individuals – was dignified by the title 'Co-ordinating Committee'. The term 'motivation' is a tiresome one, with its overtones of psychoanalysis. But if it means anything it is an apt description of what the majority of Churchill's colleagues in the committee did not have.

Part of the explanation for this has to be found in the prospects for succession to the leadership. Most of the members – Lyttelton, Salisbury – were too old. Those in the Upper House were disbarred by their being outside the elective process. What were they all doing, anyway, besides enjoying the food, the wine and the brandy in the Savoy at a time when rationing was if anything more astringent than it had been during the war? The prospect of their recovering office seemed remote. The temptation (sometimes the need) to make money in the City held a greater allure.

Besides, the succession was fixed, or so ran the received wisdom, and had been for many years. The loyalty, spotless reputation and public charisma of Anthony Eden could not be matched by any other claimant.

But there one encounters a paradox. Eden's speciality, and the field in which he had enhanced his standing, was that of international affairs. Yet, it was this very subject that still, to the exclusion of all others, preoccupied Churchill's attention; nostalgic yearning for the days when he was one of the arbiters' triumvirate. So it was natural that he should look with a mixture of steadily increasing bitterness at Eden's own credentials, which Churchill, recalling the times when Eden had been his subordinate in office, had long regarded as inferior to his own. If anything, these feelings appear to have intensified rather than diminished once Churchill became again Prime Minister in the autumn of 1951 and was tasting daily the fruits of power.

Here, then, were the ingredients, an uneasy duumvirate of no fixed term, that would slow down the party's evolution in its first years of separate power since 7 May 1940. Churchill's ambivalence towards Eden was of long standing. And some of the illustrative episodes can be seen in the context of, and frequently giving rise to, hesitation in the execution of policy.

As had been seen, Churchill's original reaction to Eden's appointment as Foreign Secretary, in December of 1935, was ill-natured.[1] But at that time Churchill was in the wilderness, and his prospects were poor. Three years later Churchill was recovering credibility as a national figure and so – when he wrote of Eden, in a special article for the *Strand Magazine*, that

> there is no one else of his age and experience who has a greater hold upon the sympathy and imagination of what may, in its widest sense, be called 'the liberal forces in England' . . . It may be that he will lead our country in days when leadership will even more be needed'

– it should be read as much in the context of destabilising Neville

Chamberlain as of soliciting Eden's approval. And it is true that in the first volume of his war memoirs, *The Gathering Storm*, there is a most beautiful and moving passage when Churchill reflects on Eden's resignation in 1938: '... I watched the daylight slowly creep in through the windows and saw before me in mental gaze the vision of Death ...'[2] But this will have been written after the war and during that period when, freshly in Opposition together, their relations were acceptably cordial.

During the Coalition period Eden had behaved impeccably, even when sorely tempted by approaches from others with high influence, and, especially at those times when Churchill felt himself to be under pressure, extreme provocation. But Churchill, right from the start, had known that Eden needed to be kept in play yet at the same time prevented from attaining too high a level of prominence.

Periodically Churchill's irritation, founded often in simple jealousy, would break the surface. As far back as 1944 Eden had told a friend:

> One night, or rather at 2 am one morning Winston was really insulting. He accused me of setting up the Press and the House to hound him, even suggesting that I was trying to force him to resign ...

Sometimes Churchill would display malice little short of spite in trying to embarrass his Foreign Secretary in the presence of others. Eden's biographer has recorded an occasion when Churchill was congratulating Dean Acheson – the US Secretary of State whose relations with Eden were, at best, reserved – on his handsome bearing and sartorial elegance. Then, turning to the convalescent Eden 'now showing distinct signs of becoming middle-aged', Churchill said to him, 'Dean looks like you are supposed to do.'[3]

Eden, at the outset of the new administration, had set great store on being recognised as 'Deputy Prime Minister'. (A strange fixation, this hankering on the part of Conservative ministers for a post that has no recognised status in the constitution – although

Eden would certainly not be alone in suffering from it. Nor was he to know that not one of the subsequent 'Deputies' – Butler, Whitelaw, Howe, Heseltine – would ever succeed.) Yet the omens were hardly promising, as could be seen from the fate of the last Conservative 'Deputy' – the Marquess of Curzon. And in fact 'the Palace' – advised by whom, and by what convoluted route, is not known – objected. And no more was to be heard of the idea.

In June of 1952 Eden married Churchill's niece, Clarissa. The supposedly dynastic nature of the ceremony was underlined by the Prime Minister offering Number 10 for the reception, and when the couple returned from honeymoon Churchill confided in Clarissa that he wanted (sic) to give up. Relaying this piece of news, Clarissa told Eden that he 'must be gentle with Winston'. A little later on Churchill asked Eden to allow (sic) him to retire 'as privately as possible. Only one speech.' Whether or not Churchill was doing anything more than playing for time – he was particularly keen to make another journey to the United States in the New Year – he soon picked up his confidence again, asserting that only he 'had the status to negotiate with Ike as an equal'.

Another example of this goading, the minutiae of protocol to which overworked politicians in positions of high responsibility often attach a disproportionate weight, can be taken from April of 1954. A note from Molotov, in itself predictable and supportive of the status quo, had been delivered, and Attlee had put down a Private Notice Question. As Leader of the Opposition he addressed this to the Prime Minister. But Eden felt that he should answer, said as much to Churchill's office, and Foreign Office officials set about preparing a text.

Halfway through the morning a message was received that the Prime Minister '. . . as it is addressed to him thinks that he should answer it'. Eden, in a high state of indignation went personally across to Number 10 ('my nerves are at breaking point') and won his point. Barely, though, had he got back through the door of his own office when the telephone rang and Colville told Eden that the Prime Minister would rise first, and say that 'I have asked my Right Honourable friend to reply'. Eden could then come in 'behind' Churchill and deliver the prepared answer.

As often in their relations, each had something of a Technically, it could be said that the Prime Minister was ob. to answer. But it was now nearly two years since he had t.d Clarissa that he 'wanted' to resign, and to Eden himself that he wished to make but 'one more' speech. To Eden it seemed as if he was being 'treated as if I needed a nurse'. Question Time was approaching and the Speaker's secretary had still to be advised. Eden would not concede. He sent his own secretary (Evelyn Shuckburgh) over to Number 10 to protest. After some further argument Colville gave in, announced that '... the PM never wanted to make the statement anyway, couldn't care less, etc'.[4]

It is plain that what had started as a reluctance became, with the passing months, an obsession. Churchill was determined that Eden should not succeed him. And it is hard to avoid the view that at least half of Churchill's intention became to postpone the moment of change until Eden had himself become so manifestly infirm and unsuitable that an alternative claimant might slide into the role of heir apparent. The question was – how long would this process take, and who might that individual be?

When the House of Commons rose for the summer recess at the end of July 1954 the Cabinet dispersed for their holidays 'some of them glum, some of them bewildered'.[5] But the reputation of Anthony Eden stood high, although his health was poor. Eden had recorded diplomatic victories in Europe, Indo-China, Egypt and the Gulf. He had most skilfully shifted American policy in Iran away from subservience to their own oil moguls, the 'Seven Sisters', and secured the abasement of 'Doctor' Mossadeq. Eden's staff at the Foreign Office were talking of an *annus mirabilis*. But when was he to enter his inheritance? The time for a general election was approaching fast. Certainly its proximity would soon be so close as to preclude – or at least offer the excuse of pre- cluding – any change in the leadership of the Party. At Chartwell Winston Churchill was getting exceedingly cross, and the focus of his anger was Anthony Eden:

Never had a Prime Minister been treated like this, that he was to be hounded from his place merely because his second-in-command wanted the job.[6]

On 27 August Eden was back in his room at the Foreign Office, where he received two visitors, Rab Butler and Harold Macmillan. The customary seasonal rumours of a reshuffle were in the air. Eden greeted his friends, told them that he feared some of Churchill's changes to the Cabinet 'might be actuated by animus'. Butler, following a disclaimer about his 'divided loyalties', suggested that some way should be found for Eden to take over the home front and leadership of the House, immediately. Naturally, so half-hearted a 'solution' was not to Eden's liking at all. He told Butler that the reshuffle would 'merely be a device [for Churchill] to carry on even longer, while doing even less'. In particular, if Eden took over home affairs there would be 'further scope for Churchill to interfere with the FO, which might have disastrous results'. The only solution was for the Prime Minister to stand down – from every office. Both Butler and Macmillan urged Eden to confront Churchill personally, that very afternoon – although neither offered to accompany him. Eden walked across Downing Street, found Churchill unoccupied. The interview opened 'stiffly' and later became 'emotional'.[7]

Churchill challenged Eden to resign and take however many colleagues there might be, six Churchill suggested, with him. Eden didn't answer, said he would like to discuss the whole question with colleagues, Churchill being present. Very reluctantly Churchill agreed, '– provided it is a discussion of reconstruction and not of [my] resignation'. But a short time later a letter arrived on Eden's desk:

> I am sorry you are not happy about Home Affairs. I must admit I have had a rather trying time myself during the last fifteen months.
>
> During the first part of these I was much troubled by your absence through illness and the uncertainty about whether [sic] and when you wd be able to return.
>
> Since this has happily occurred, I have been distressed by the

continuous pressure of some of yr friends who want me to retire
in yr favour.

I have tried to discharge the duty to which I was appointed by
the Crown and Parliament. I am glad to say I have not missed a
single day's control of affairs in spite of a temporary loss of physical
mobility. *Now I have good reports from my doctors* . . .[8]

Almost immediately Eden was deeply involved in the – successful – negotiations to bring Germany into NATO as a full
member and set up the Western European Union (which would
ultimately become the military committee of the European
Community). Still there was no news of a reshuffle. Was this a
good sign? Perhaps, if Churchill now intended to go promptly
and discreetly, it was being left to his successor.

On the contrary. Churchill sent for Eden, and told him that
'with so many achievements in the air it would be "impossible"
for Eden to leave the FO at the present time'. Cabinets were
becoming increasingly difficult. Churchill's powers of concentration were intermittent; his taste for news increasingly subjective. Colleagues often talked among themselves while Churchill
was summing up. They were no longer in awe of him, and when
he remonstrated – sometimes even saying that he would 'go' if the
majority wished it – there was no response. But during this period
Eden does record in his diary, at what must have been one of their
last meetings, 'the only occasion when Winston warned me about
a colleague':

   ... he asked me how I got on with Harold. I said, 'Very well,
   why?' He replied, 'Oh, he is very ambitious.' I laughed.[9]

TWENTY-THREE

The Rejection of Opportunity

The perceived importance of consensus – Rab Butler
arrives at the Treasury – Sir Edward Bridges and his
tales of woe – Butler thinks things through – ROBOT –
Whitehall takes fright – Eden is nobbled – then
Churchill – ROBOT dies.

THIS UNHAPPY PROGRESSION, often farcical, always frustrating,
deferring the point at which the party could make real progress
in adapting itself to meet the demands of the future, must also be
seen against the background of a particular crisis that had arisen
in the autumn of 1951. There are some half-dozen occasions in
the post-(Great)-War story of Britain, always with the Tories in
charge, when it is possible to identify a real historic watershed.
The first failure of nerve in 1935, when the League of Nations
was left unsupported and Mussolini attacked Abyssinia. The rejection of the Hess terms in 1941. The indifference and obstruction
during those early formative days of the European Community;
Messina in 1955. On all of these occasions, had a contrarian policy
been followed we can now see that the outcome would have led
to a completely different historic evolution. But in these the
context is international. In 1951 the factors were entirely domestic.

Churchill had become Prime Minister again on 26 October
1951. But his majority was narrow. In number of votes cast the
Conservatives were actually behind Labour. Even had he not
been Coalition-minded – and certainly he was 'overlord'-minded,
preferring elderly public servants of distinction to Conservative
Party Turks – Churchill had to be mindful of these restraints. Never

again must the party be associated with large-scale unemployment. Nor should it be suspected of designs on the welfare state.

Nor, or not immediately (and this meant in fact that the moment was postponed *sine die*), should it consider confronting trade union power. The Ministry of Labour, a creation of the wartime administration, was endowed with a bogus 'above party' status and its emollient Secretary of State, Walter Monckton, was even barred for three years from attending the annual Party Conference. Partly, one may assume, this was to sterilise resolutions of a critical nature being tabled by the constituencies, and printed in the conference handbook. Or indignant what's-going-on? speeches being delivered from the rostrum. There may also have been an element of self-protection. Monckton, in his Coalition days, had put his name to the notorious 'What We are Fighting For' statement among whose received aphorisms had been the injunction that:

> We must cease [*sic*] thinking in terms of risk and profit; we must think only in terms of the needs to be met ... For the workers of Great Britain there must be greater security, increased partnership in industry, more fruitful leisure.[1]

Thus there was much ballast, of which Monckton provides an exemplar, that would provide a heavy drag on change or radicalism of any sort.

Possibly the word 'crisis' is misleading. In those first months of Conservative government there was a crisis of opportunity rather than one of ill-fortune. Nor, paradoxically, was either Churchill or Eden aware of, or even capable of understanding, its full dimension. But there was now presented to the government an early chance to break free of the financial constraints to which it had voluntarily submitted in 1941; and which its successor had failed to overcome with the negotiation of the US loan in December 1945, and from which it had failed to break out with the sterling devaluation of 1949.

The problem was simple in outline; complex and unclear in detail. If the pound sterling could be allowed to 'float', and if those with access to the machinery of intervention kept their nerve and

refrained from touching the levers, then the strong likelihood –
the inevitability, indeed – was that after a period of turbulence the
exchange would find a 'natural' level. And that the reserves, not
having been depleted in 'defending' a particular rate, would survive
intact. Furthermore, once it was plain to speculators that the
reserves were not at risk; would not, that is to say, be used up in
buying currency which if the pressure was sustained for long
enough they would be able to buy back for less within a matter
of weeks or days, the pressure would abate. The pound would
recover and, in probability, augment in value. The experience in
the immediate aftermath of the country's exiting the gold standard* was there for the enlightenment of anyone who cared to
look.

To go through with this required nerves of steel. Although the
weight of speculative or 'hot' money was but a fraction of its bulk
forty years on, and there were effectively no more than three
major foreign exchange markets – London, Zurich and New
York – the concept of Real Comparative Purchasing Power was
in its infancy. It was radical in the extreme to argue that any
currency movement that caused a fall from the 'true' RCPP level
would ultimately be self-correcting. And in any case, how long
was 'ultimately'? Even in the 1990s, when technical proficiency
multiplied one hundredfold the speed with which funds
(themselves far larger) could be transferred, the process of natural
correction has often taken months.

And here lay the rub. What was proposed – or so it could be
depicted – was actually to provoke, to induce, that most hor-
rendous of all administrative nightmares – *a run on the pound.*
Never mind the argument that once the rate had been artificially
depressed the traffic would decline in volume as traders flinched
from selling sterling at a punitive level. Or that other central banks,
notably the United States Federal Reserve, might have their own
motives for trying to hold the currency above a certain rate. Or
that the political risks (of the speedy return of a confiscatory

---

* See pp. 111–12 above.

Socialist administration) were minimal. None of these co
accepted without demur by so astutely ambitious a Chancel
R. A. Butler.

Moreover those charged, or likely to be charged, with the
scheme's technical overview had neither the practical experience
nor the theoretical training that should have helped them to keep
their nerve. They could not even decide whether the policy should
be recommended as a 'last resort', deriving from catastrophic
weakness; or as an expression of confidence, founded on sterling's
basic resilience.

First, consider the circumstances of Butler's appointment.
Butler has described how Churchill, as soon as he had returned
from the Palace and accepted the King's Commission, retired to
bed. The Prime Minister had then summoned selected colleagues,
presented them with the list of Cabinet appointments and invited
them to search for their own name. Butler, naturally, had been
delighted to see his at the top of the list opposite 'Chancellor of
the Exchequer'.

He feigned surprise – 'I hadn't expected this. I had very much
looked forward to a job, but . . .'

Did Churchill have any private reservations? There is no means
of knowing, except for the clue in his curious reply to Butler's
protestation – '*Anthony* [Eden] and I think it had better be with
you . . .'[2]

As has been seen, Churchill's level of consultation with Eden on
most topics, including the preferment or rejection of colleagues'
claims, was not high. And it is possible that, at the outset, he was
preparing the ground for distancing himself from too close an
association with someone whom he had always regarded with
suspicion. Because Butler had been out of sympathy with practically every aspect of Churchill's attitude and, after he had acceded
to the premiership, his policy. From reform in India, to Munich,
to his 'wobbling' in the summer of 1940, to the Education Act of
1944 and 'post-war planning' . . . Far from being a crony Butler,
with (in those days) his low resistance to alcohol and 'famous
high-pitched cackle', had been lucky, on a number of occasions,

to keep his job. And Churchill's initial preference for Chancellor had, predictably, been one of his cronies and late-night drinking companions, Oliver Lyttelton. However, the City establishment had cautioned against this; alluding to Lyttelton's record of prowess as a 'dealer'. (In the case of Bracken and others it could be thought that these reservations may have been fuelled by simple jealousy.) Then (although of course on that first afternoon meeting Butler did not know this) the Prime Minister had thought of installing another old War Room crony – emphatically not a drinking companion – Sir John Anderson, as 'Overlord'. This though would have been in total breach of Whitehall convention – not least that former Secretaries of State should never be put in positions of seniority to their successors in the same department. So a third idea had been concocted.

Citing Butler's lack of economic expertise – in fact neither more nor less than any of the other incumbents except, thirty years later in 1983, Nigel Lawson – Churchill told him: 'I am going to appoint the best economist since Jesus Christ to help you.'[3] Whether this reference to the Son of God was calendric, or carried some subliminal association with the miracle of the loaves and fishes, the individual designated as 'Minister of State for Economic Affairs' was remarkably dim.

Sir Arthur Salter was seventy years old, punctilious in matters of detail, and hand-wrote his own memoranda in green ink. After thirteen months in the post he stepped aside, to become Minister of Materials (and the very fact that such a portfolio was still in existence shows how habituated this administration was to the interventionist practices of the wartime Coalition). Salter was in fact to play no significant role in the drama which, almost immediately, was to preoccupy the Treasury.

Nor to any significant degree was a body which, following Anderson's tactful declining of the post of Overlord, Churchill promulgated as 'the Treasury Advisory Committee'. Here, too, lurked old Coalition cronies – Woolton, Swinton and others – who might be expected to keep Churchill informed of what the Treasury was 'up to' and, if necessary, to do his bidding. A third overseer, however, in the person of Lord Cherwell, the friendless but increasingly combative 'Prof', was appointed Paymaster-General, and his role was indeed to prove significant.

Within minutes of settling behind his desk at the Treasury, Butler was greeted – if that be the word – by the Permanent Secretary, Sir Edward Bridges, accompanied by Sir Edwin Plowden. Before entering, the two men had a brief word in the outer office with Butler's (inherited) private secretary, Sir William Armstrong.

A more heavyweight Whitehall triumvirate could scarcely be conceived. Bridges had been in that post since 1946, having come on from eight years as Secretary to the Cabinet; Armstrong had served as private secretary to both Stafford Cripps and Hugh Gaitskell; Plowden was 'Chief Planning Officer', and chairman of a body whose very title was redolent of socialist interventionism – the Economic Planning Board.

Grimly, they presented 'the books'. The deficit on the balance of payments was £700 million;* the rate of erosion was accelerating. Bridges pushed across the desk an 'explanatory' note. What he wanted, at once, was more 'austerity'. He and Armstrong then took Butler round to the Athenaeum where, over lunch, they deployed phrases such as 'blood draining from the system' and 'a collapse greater than had been foretold in 1931'.[4]

Faced with this lurid 'advice' from his most senior officials, Butler showed his mettle. Eden would have panicked. Though not, probably, as completely as would have Macmillan. Churchill, shaken, would have fallen back on rhetoric and baffled inter-locutors with his own particular technique of combining grand-iloquent phrase and impractical suggestion. Butler, though, will have realised that he was in the company of very senior civil servants whose careers, now at their apogee, were entirely con-ditioned by the ethic of interventionism. All had been at their existing posts, and would undoubtedly have preened themselves, when Mr Douglas Jay had first uttered his aphorism that 'The

* Equivalent today to £11.1 billion.

man in Whitehall knows best'. Now they were faced with the prospect of a Conservative government, less than twenty-four hours old. Surely the best way of affirming their ascendancy was by subjecting the incoming Chancellor to an ordeal which would, or should, leave him wholly convinced of their particular expertise and infallibility?

Now Butler was only forty-eight years old. He had enemies in the party, certainly, but he had exceptional qualifications. Highly intelligent, unusually (for a Conservative minister) hard-working, and financially independent. Ahead of him, it is true, lay cruel disappointment: two occasions when his claim to the leadership would be thwarted by lesser men. But in that first week of the first wholly Conservative administration since 1940 Butler found himself in a position of critical importance. He must tread carefully – but not in so tentative a manner that his career lost momentum. The public were sick of 'austerity'. The manifesto, still fresh in people's minds, had hinted at 'sunlit uplands'. It would not be good for Butler if, immediately and as his officials wanted, he were to turn himself into a simulacrum of Sir Stafford Cripps. Butler put some 'emergency' measures in place, like cutting the foreign travel 'allowance', bought time, and set about thinking things through.

This was not, of course, what Bridges had in mind at all. He forced the Second Secretaries, at their weekly meeting on 27 November, to agree a note that

> the Chancellor should be told as soon as possible [i.e., the moment Bridges got back to his office] that the position had deteriorated rapidly since the beginning of the month, and additional action was necessary in order to save the country from early bankruptcy.[5]

Robert Hall, who sat on Bridges's Committee, was more sensible. He was director of the economic section of the Cabinet Office and more politically aware than his colleagues. His view was that this just showed how silly senior Treasury officials could be. Hall told Butler that 'If they are not careful it will be 1931, and another Bankers' ramp'.[6] Even so, there was unwelcome talk of cutting food subsidies. Lord Woolton, during the campaign, had given an assurance that this would not happen. He was a powerful man, and his enmity was to be avoided. Butler conferred around, and it was not long before – as can happen in the upper reaches of every major department in Whitehall – he found some who were ready to argue for the unorthodox. Rapidly the alignment began to fall into place, with both senior officials and political colleagues taking sides.

To both aggravate (and justify) his indecision, there were two schools within the Treasury; and even those in favour of floating were apprehensive of doing so *à l'outrance*. The scheme which took shape was called ROBOT and documents circulated under that title. Did this title designate the automatic pilot – the rise, and fall, and self-correction by which the market mechanism would protect sterling? Or, more ominous for its chances of survival, was it an acronym derived from the three very senior officials most closely associated with it – Sir Leslie ROwan, Sir George Bolton, and OTto Clarke?

The real problem attaching to ROBOT was that it was contrary to the Bretton Woods Agreement, and would irritate (and not only for that reason) the Americans. Professor Harold Robbins was circulating papers saying that what really upset him about the scheme was that it was 'so dishonourable'. (Is Britain the only country in the world, for we can easily imagine an equivalent response arising in similar circumstances today, where senior officials can be found who rate an abstract notion of 'honour' above the national interest?)

Gradually the scheme was reduced in scope. Soon the time-honoured Whitehall formula for extinction started to make its way into the memoranda –

> [following arguments against] it was subject to the overriding condition that matters might so develop that we should have to take action on the lines proposed in two or three months' time . . .[7]

On 19 February Churchill gave dinner to the Governor of the Bank of England, Butler, and Harry Crookshank, Leader of the

House. No firm outcome could have been expected from a meeting which by its nature would have been discursive and convivial rather than analytic. But there was one decision which was urgent. The Budget was to be presented in the House on 4 March. Plainly, if so radical a step as convertibility was imminent, it would be highly improper to make no mention of it in the Budget statement some few days before. The Budget therefore had to be postponed, for a week at least, until 11 March.

By now all Whitehall was in a fever. Cherwell was telephoning to Number 10 twice a day.

The Prime Minister was bemused. What was Eden's attitude? At this time the Foreign Secretary was attending a NATO conference in Lisbon. Normally Eden would not concern himself with such matters, but this very detachment, and his key position in the Cabinet, would give victory to whichever side could enlist Eden's support. How, and by whom, should Eden be approached? Woolton devised the excuse. The strength and reputation of sterling was so central to our international relations that the Foreign Office should be closely involved. A Deputy Secretary, Eric Berthoud, was despatched to Lisbon where he joined up with Plowden. Together they did their best to make Eden's flesh creep. They . . .

> came out from London . . . with very grim news about the UK balance of payments and a really alarming plan worked out by the Bank of England and accepted by the Chancellor for dealing with the situation. In brief the plan, *so far as AE and I could understand it*, was to block the Commonwealth and other sterling balances . . . and to make sterling convertible. The effect and object of this would be to throw the burden of the adverse trade balance off the reserves (which were rapidly running right out) and onto the home economy and the standard of living . . . [8]

The contention concerning 'the effect and object . . .' of the scheme was, of course, grossly one-sided and misleading. But greatly to his credit (and perhaps to the alarm of his informants) Eden first took the view that the scheme, if the majority of his colleagues favoured it, could only be put in place after a general election at which the facts could be explained to the electorate. 'The more he thought about it, however, the more doubtful AE became about the premisses on which it was based.'

A less honourable man contemplating his principal rival for the Leadership of the Party on the verge of some spectacular but perilous operation would have held off for a little while. Certainly Macmillan, who as always was thinking of himself in such a context, would not have put the knife in so early. Perhaps Eden, still the acknowledged favourite, believed that it was better to humiliate Butler in Cabinet immediately and leave himself a clear run.

Without doubt he was genuinely appalled at the version – not uncoloured by prejudice – which Berthoud and Plowden had given him. Eden wrote at once to Churchill, in his own hand, recommending that 'greater thought' be given to the proposal. The Prime Minister no longer had the ability, nor ever would have had the inclination, to focus on so arcane a dispute. Butler's own arguments were increasingly being overlaid by 'the noise of controversy emanating from his own embattled officials'.[9] Coming on top of all those other protests, from many different quarters, Eden's letter ensured that the proposal was effectively dead before even it came to Cabinet. Butler was defeated. And did not again try to tamper with ('sacrifice' was the emotive verb deployed by his opponents) the controlled economy and the policy of full employment.

'Whitehall as a whole,' recorded Shuckburgh, 'was profoundly relieved.' And within the text of Cabinet minutes for 28 9 February 1952 can be found the essence of a political standpoint to which the Conservative Party, still navigating without a compass, was obeisant:

Under democratic government with universal suffrage such violent reversals of policy were hardly practicable. Even if the case for this change were abundantly clear on the merits, there would be very great difficulty in persuading the public to accept it. Moreover,

the adoption of this policy would create an unbridgeable gap
between the Government and the Opposition; and ... it would
be unjustifiable to take at this stage a step which might exclude all
possibility of forming a National Government ... [to handle an
'even more grave economic crisis'].[10]

Practically every element in the party's collective loss of confidence
is listed here – 'universal suffrage' (Conservatives in a permanent
minority); 'violent reversal of policy' (abandonment of consensus);
'unbridgeable [sic] gap between Government and Opposition'.
And lastly, of course, a possible threat to the party's lifeline and
standby for which, from Churchill downwards, there was much
nostalgic hankering over 'the possibility of forming a National
Government to handle the situation'. Seriously to be paying heed
to the concept of a 'National Government' barely three months
after being elected with a working majority to form a Conservative
one is testimony to the extent of the party's fixation that it could
now only preserve its power by a level of self-abasement that
entailed, in effect, a discarding of its real identity.

A further irony is that the 'dash' for convertibility should have
been conceived as an act of desperation. As soon as the reserves
began to pick up – by June of 1952 they stood at $1.7 billion and
rising as compared with the original Treasury forecast which had
started the panic, of $1.3 billion – most of its protagonists lost
interest. Butler's own biographer suggests that 'Rab may well have
felt that his original remedies were beginning to do the trick'.[11]

But a crucially important milestone had been passed. And
almost casually the alternative route, stony-looking indeed, but
leading after a quite short distance to financial and economic
independence, had been rejected. Britain could have been the first
and, with the exception of Switzerland, the only European state
to attain full convertibility since 1939; pre-empting the revalued
Deutschmark by two years.

In mitigation it has to be said that neither the functionaries at
the Bank, nor the senior officials at the Treasury nor, emphatically,
the politicians themselves had any familiarity with the techniques

of management and intervention which were to become routine in the 1980s – and in particular the device of tuning a currency's value by alterations in the interest rate (as was to be perfected in the 1980s by Mr Paul Volcker of the US Federal Reserve).

None the less there is one piece of evidence suggesting that Butler was aware that a great opportunity had been allowed to pass, and that a renewed challenge to the received wisdom was unlikely for many years. In a handwritten note to the Prime Minister, dated August of that year he referred to this

> ... very intricate matter. My view was that if we did not take the plunge early into the freedom of the price mechanism – even in the external field – we should go without the benefits of full planning and of the full discipline of the [exchange] Rate. I further felt that nothing could control the vast spreading leaking sterling area but the Rate. As against my original recommendation there were ranged very powerful arguments, which prevailed. I still regret that decision, since I believe our policy [at present] lies between two stools ...

In fact, 'policy' in the whole field of exchange control, convertibility and floating rates was to drag on virtually unquestioned. To come were another thirty years, or thereabouts, of intermittent crisis, panic and subservience to the US dollar. The perceived need to placate, rather than to ignore, the 'markets' was to load the economy with 'stop-go', the 'Regulator', 'import premiums', hire-purchase controls, and (as their short-term effectiveness came to be discovered) punitively high domestic interest rates. And, in the field of foreign and Imperial policy it was to bring about the greatest national humiliation since the fall of Singapore.

TWENTY-FOUR

The Eden Anachronism

Eden's personal failings – and rivals for the leadership –
Beaverbrook warns against Macmillan – Resounding
success at the general election – A reshuffle – Problems
with the Suez Group – A State Department verdict.

WHEN ANTHONY EDEN finally arrived at his premiership it must
have seemed that a golden age was in prospect for the Conservative
Party. He was popular, and the liking felt for him by ordinary
people transcended, it seems, the normal boundaries of class and
political allegiance. It appeared that he was endowed with that
special gift, or combination, that invariably wins respect (and for
which his successor was to strive with such assiduity, though never
with quite the success that initially favoured Eden) – the 'toff',
whose concern was for the whole nation. The Eden Government
was in truth the first authentic Conservative administration for
fifteen years, since the spring of 1940. It was 'progressive' in
attitude, though conscious of, and having to defer to, tradition;
humane but certainly not radical in its approach to social issues.
Eden himself was committed to One Nation – but in its original
form, as a paternalist rather than a classless concept.

Eden entered Number 10 on 5 April 1955. He dissolved Parliament on 7 May. And on 26 May he was returned with what
was to be the largest percentage of the popular vote recorded by
any Conservative in the second half of the century. He was
handsome, 'glamorous' indeed (the adjective had been attached,
though with pejorative intent, to him in the thirties by Chips
Channon). And with a respectable record of defiance, to the

point of resignation, of the 'Men of Munich'. He had been long recognised as Churchill's right-hand man, seeming by contrast to be younger by a whole generation. Save for a little gossip there had been no general awareness of the petty frustration and bitterness which affected the closing years of their relationship. And had there been, it is likely that public sympathy would have favoured Eden.

Nor was he tainted to any degree by the party's domestic record before the war. Eden's entire career seemed to have been spent 'standing up to the dictators'. But this, both in slogan and substance, although endowing Eden with an instant electoral advantage, was in fact a source of grave political weakness. And as soon as, beset by domestic problems, he tried to revert to that mode – it was to bring disaster.

Eden's handicaps were serious, and his colleagues were aware of them. He had no personal following in the House of Commons – not even the customary group of placemen whose 'loyalty' is a function of their dependence. Indeed there were plenty who, for a variety of motives, wanted to make trouble for him from the start. Ten years earlier (when, of course, Eden's accession might have, through an Act of God, occurred at any time) Oliver Harvey had reflected that while . . .

> The relation of PM to AE is father to son and heir . . . the others are left out in the cold and there is risk of AE himself becoming isolated from his own age group of colleagues . . . for [those] colleagues and the H[ouse] of C[ommons] he has an invincible distaste . . .'

Play has been made of Eden's vanity; and certainly he enjoyed, and felt to be his due, the plaudits heaped on him while Foreign Secretary and the painless glide from one assignment to another within the itinerary of the *corps diplomatique*. Whether or not Eden was markedly vainer than any other prominent politician is arguable. But he was certainly also nervous, and exceptionally sensitive to criticism.

Another source of weakness was Eden's own natural decency.

He had negotiated long and hard in the international field. But of
the party-political smoke-filled room he had – outside the periodic
harangues and disappointments to which he was subjected by
Churchill – very little experience. Thus Eden was not given to
suspecting, or even scrutinising the motives of, those whom he
thought to be 'on the same side'. It was the ethic of the regiment
that shaped his reaction to events. In Flanders, where Eden had
fought, suffered wounds, and been decorated, the enemy was plain
for all to see. Those experiences, formed in early adulthood,
remained with Eden as at the start of his career he enthused for
the League of Nations, argued for Collective Security, strove to
preserve as best he was able the interests of the Empire and the
independence of the United Kingdom.

The two politicians who most wanted his job, however, were
altogether more realistic. It is likely that Eden felt that he had
already taken the measure of Rab Butler. Stepping outside his
departmental brief Eden had forced the Chancellor into a humiliating retreat at a quite early stage in the Churchill premiership
(ROBOT).* Rightly he saw Rab as a tortoise, patiently plodding,
but without teeth. Harold Macmillan, though, was a wholly
different calibre of rival. Macmillan's record as Minister for
Housing, supported by an able team, was what put him on course
for the leadership. He assumed the mantle (although the work had
largely been done by his deputy, Ernest Marples, himself a former
builder and MP for Wallasey) of 'a man who got things done'.
And boasted, in language alternately statesmanlike and genial, of
his achievements at Party Conference. Although it appeared that
the requirement for new houses, a demand swelled by wartime
damage and post-war shortage, had been met, it must be said that
Macmillan's answering of this pressing need – greatly welcomed
at the time – has produced a mixed legacy. In the majority of cases
these were not houses in the meaning of the term understood by
most middle-class Conservatives, but *housing units*. So that the
most tangible remaining monument to the life and work of Harold

* See pp. 345–6 above.

Macmillan, his enemies can now be heard to argue, is the tower block and the sink estate. He eagerly embraced the Britain of the bulldozer and prefabricated concrete. Housing estates seemingly modelled on the morally debasing aesthetics of the Eastern European Communist bloc received Macmillan's enthusiastic backing. He had declared, at the formal opening ceremony, that Park Hill, a monstrous concrete jungle in Sheffield into which 2,000 council-house dwellers were herded, was an estate which would 'draw the admiration of the world'.[2]

Did Eden underestimate Macmillan, or was it simply that he was deluded into thinking that Macmillan's shared experience as a subaltern in the trenches, as a prominent supporter of the 'glamour boys' in the thirties, offered a guarantee of 'loyalty'? Both men shared the same foppish style, the Etonian dialect that communicates by inflection, understatement and the unfinished sentence. The same mannerisms, the same interests, the same world-view. It had been Macmillan, had it not, who put his own career in jeopardy (of course he was doing nothing of the kind) by writing to Churchill advising that he step aside for Eden in 1952?* Eden can be excused for not realising, when he made Macmillan Foreign Secretary in 1955, that in Beaverbrook's words:

> Macmillan will do strange things and he will live to perpetrate a great deal of mischief†

At the very outset of his premiership Eden, in his dealings with Macmillan, made a serious tactical miscalculation. In practically every one of the Cabinet posts which he had inherited from Churchill, Eden confirmed the incumbent. But needing resolution was the question of his own former portfolio. Eden had twenty years of direct and senior experience in foreign affairs; he

---

* See p. 337 above.
† This warning, characteristically prescient, may be read in the context of a personal message sent by telex from the Bahamas, which Macmillan himself was to receive on 19 January 1957, reminding him that 'I have always hoped for, and prophesied, your becoming Prime Minister', from Beaverbrook.

was more accomplished in diplomacy than any other British politician. Plainly there could be scope for frustration and discord if the portfolio were assigned to anyone whose interpretation of the role was likely to be more than consultative and obedient. The nearest comparison that can be made is that of Minister of Defence under Churchill or, looking forward, Chancellor of the Exchequer under Margaret Thatcher. Loyalty was the pre-eminent, indeed the sole, quality required. 'Bobbety' Cranborne, now Lord Salisbury, was Eden's closest friend in politics. The two men had worked together, supported each other, conferred constantly even when out of office, during the black days of Chamberlain's appeasement. They were of the same mind, still, on most issues. The assumption was universal that 'Bobbety will get the FO'.

Eden, though, thought otherwise. Salisbury was too grand, too welcome and too well versed in the chancelleries of the world. With his large personal fortune and genetic arrogance (the Cecils had been advising monarchs since the sixteenth century) Salisbury might suddenly have proved 'difficult'. And then what? Salisbury could never be sacked, not by Eden; he would have been at the Foreign Office for life. Yet Salisbury could not be deprived of his birthright in favour of a nonentity. That would have been humiliating. So, citing 'democratic considerations', Eden put Macmillan at the Treasury with every intention of shuffling him sideways after the general election, and made Salisbury Lord Privy Seal, ranking second only to the premiership. Salisbury took it in good part – he was over sixty, after all. But for Macmillan it was the ox's hide. Now, Macmillan knew, only two men stood between him and the premiership – Butler, and Eden himself.

As for the general election, it was a walkover. Eden was so handsome, and he looked so clearly and directly at his audience, that *The Times* could write:

> the greatest tour-de-force among the television broadcasts was the final one by Sir Anthony Eden. Speaking in a genuinely extempore fashion, summarising the issues of the election, not attacking his

opponents, but presenting the Conservative case with a confident quiet reasonableness. He used no memorable phrases, he said nothing new and, as usual, he was more authoritative on foreign policy than on home affairs. But he won universal praise for the way in which he managed to convey a sense of calmness, optimism, decency and compassion.[3]

This was not quite how Churchill saw it. He told Moran, his doctor, that he thought television was a 'flop' during the campaign. 'This business of just chatting round the fire is all very well, but a candidate should make a pronouncement that will become part of the English language, part of English history. People ought to have to fight to get into his meetings . . .'[4] Churchill had not been invited to take part, although, in theory, he was himself campaigning for re-election. Was Eden apprehensive that he might be upstaged? Hardly likely. Did he think that Churchill's appearance, and impediment of speech, might put off the elector? Possibly. But a quiet and private motive of retaliation for all the disappointment and humiliation to which he personally had been subjected in earlier years cannot wholly be ruled out.

Within a fortnight of taking the premiership Eden had instructed – in his gentle, mellifluent, but always well-informed style – the Chancellor to produce a friendly Budget. Butler was already something of a household name, with his benign, family GP manner, and was glad to oblige. Butler's speech of 19 April set out the first truly generous Budget since 1937. Income tax was cut by 6d and £150 million of tax reliefs were distributed. The Conservative majority five weeks later was 58 over all other parties. It was to be an early illustration of 'stop-go' economic management. The tax concessions had been made against a background of rapid growth, based as much on the return of domestic confidence as the growth of world trade. Rapidly the boom heated up, with wages and inflation breaking away. And in no time Sir Edward Bridges reappeared on the scene in his customary role as Cassandra. Never one to understate a crisis, Bridges told Butler, on 27 July just as MPs began to disperse for their holidays, that

Parliament might have to be recalled, as 'the reserves were running out'.

Butler had experience of Bridges's alarmism since his very first day at the Treasury, and did not even pass on the warning at Cabinet. But by the autumn he had to announce an 'emergency' budget in which practically every one of his election-winning measures (with the exception of the cut in income tax) was reversed. This was a setback for Eden, whose confidence in Butler was further undermined by the Chancellor arguing, from his official brief, that milk and bread subsidies would have to be cut, or even abolished. Eden decided accordingly to shuffle Butler sideways and put Macmillan in his place. Macmillan was adroit. And the problems at the Treasury would keep him busy while allowing the Prime Minister to play his own role, without an ambitious understudy, on the world stage.

Macmillan in all probability was glad to be out of the Foreign Office. He had renewed his personal contacts, both in Europe and in the United States. He had enhanced his reputation for *gravitas* in the chamber – easier to do as Foreign Secretary than as Housing Minister – and now he had moved to the very centre of power next door, literally, to Number 10. On 24 October 1955 Macmillan had set out his 'ideas' for a reforming Chancellorship. As these included a requirement that he should be 'undisputed head [*sic*] of the Home Front'; that he must have the firm support of the Prime Minister at all times; that he must have a position in the Cabinet not inferior to Butler; and that Butler should not be designated as 'Deputy' Prime Minister – it can be appreciated that they were not so much 'ideas' as conditions. It is most unusual, indeed only those who consider themselves to be in a position of great strength will ever essay it, to lay down rules to the Prime Minister about the preferment of Cabinet colleagues. As for the request for 'firm support' this can only have meant, and been intended to read – a blank cheque.

Eden gave his new Chancellor what he wanted. While Macmillan was at the Foreign Office there had already been a hint of friction over policy towards Europe and, more ominously, Egypt.

The Prime Minister now had recovered control of foreign policy, his favourite sector for personal activity. If Macmillan was so keen to be hyperactive at the Treasury, let him get on with it. Butler became Leader of the House and continued to chair Cabinet, as Lord Privy Seal, whenever (which was often) Eden was in the care of doctors.

The Government changes (as so often happens) had little effect on the electorate and none whatever on the economic climate; nor on the international scene where things were going badly. In January of 1956 Eden was forced to agree to a rise in interest rates and the 'broad principle' of further expenditure cuts. Practically all of his advantage at the polls had disappeared. Churchill was watching, and expressed in private, but not in such a manner as would prevent his opinion going into immediate circulation, feelings of scorn. On St Valentine's Day came a particularly bad by-election result, at Taunton. The Tory candidate, a fresh-faced young fellow who had made a reputation for himself in the City selling Unit Trusts, named Edward du Cann, scraped home. But the Conservative majority declined by some 80 per cent, from 5,542 to 657.

Conservative voters were 'staying at home'. They were disappointed with Eden who, it seemed, was letting them down in the one sector where he had the best credentials; where 'it would never have happened under Mr Churchill'. Because quite suddenly the Empire seemed to be falling apart.

The episode which above all others in that fateful year of 1956 symbolised British Imperial decline was the dismissal of Glubb Pasha. Glubb was commander of the Arab Legion, a kind of mechanised successor to the dashing camel corps of *El Orans*. He was based in the most Anglophile and subservient of all the British satellites in Arabia – the Kingdom of Jordan. Glubb flew the Union Jack on his car, and on his tank. He was the military proconsul. Now, without warning – itself a sinister indicator that the intelligence of the bazaars was diminishing in quality – Glubb had been dismissed by the King and, with his two senior aides, given twenty-four hours to leave the country.

Now it must be remembered that barely a decade had passed since the victorious conclusion of the Second World War. Within the living memory of every adult was the image of British military prowess and her overwhelming strength. But there was legend, also, of resistance and guerrilla techniques; of how a native population, black or white, Muslim or Christian, will in the end wear down an army of occupation. This was the new wave. Long-dormant nationalist aspirations could emerge, and assert themselves. In the background were the Soviet agents, always ready to foment rebellion and to supply arms. In Malaya the British had won. And in Kenya, also, where the Mau Mau had been rounded up and shot. Yet already in those two countries, and in spite of the appearance of recent military victory, the pace of evolution towards independence had quickened. There were many, still, in the Conservative Party and in the saloon bars around the country who yearned for General Dyer; the belt-feed Vickers firing into the crowd. But this was no longer feasible. Even the Wehrmacht, ready in the villages of Bosnia to hang every fourth male from a gallows in the market square, had been forced to cede possession. And when, in the spring, Eden had responded to unrest in Cyprus by the arrest and banishment of Archbishop Makarios, the killings by EOKA terrorists had multiplied instantly. Eden's problem, not insoluble at that time (but almost impossible following defeat at Suez), was how to retain and to maximise British commercial and cultural influence in territory where a military presence was being gracefully reduced in scale. It demanded a finesse which few in his party could appreciate. (The loudest applause which Eden was ever to experience came on the afternoon that he announced the deportation of Makarios.)

In the meantime Macmillan had decided to show his muscle. He insisted on the cutting of food subsidies. The same, indeed – bread and milk – for which permission Butler had vainly sought. And one need look no further than the way in which he handled this contentious issue to understand why in the fullness of time Macmillan became Premier and Butler did not. First he threatened

resignation; not in so many words, of course, but by indicating
that he was not afraid of it:

> I don't want to appear to threaten the Cabinet; I have never tried
> such tactics in all my service. But I would not like you to be under
> any misapprehension and afterwards perhaps blame me for not
> letting you know the depth of my feeling . . .[5]

Eden was, or thought he was, equal to this. A face-to-face encounter might be difficult. If Macmillan did not want to 'threaten' the
Cabinet, then it need not go before Cabinet. Eden delegated three
of his own supporters, loyal but 'heavy', to call on Macmillan and
talk things through. Butler did most of the talking. With him
were Peter Thorncycroft and Derrick Heathcoat-Amory (and it
is testimony to the circular ironies of politics that three years later
Heathcoat-Amory would himself be appointed Chancellor of the
Exchequer – by Macmillan, and after Thorneycroft had resigned).
Macmillan himself said very little. When at the end of the meeting
the delegation warned him that 'The PM is absolutely determined
not to give in' Macmillan seized the opening: 'Tell him . . .'
(knowing that this was impossible) 'to get another Chancellor.'

The very next day the matter came before Cabinet. The subsidies were abolished, effectively. Only a tiny fragment was left on
each item so as to save Eden's face. He had been defeated, as was
plain for all to see, and Bracken wrote at once to Beaverbrook:

> Your prophecy that [Macmillan] would make trouble for Eden has
> been swiftly proved. He sent in his resignation yesterday on a
> cunningly contrived issue which would have gravely embarrassed
> his boss and would have given [him] the credit for being the only
> virtuous and strong man in the Government. A truce has been
> patched up . . .
>
> Unfortunately [Eden] has given this man a job which puts him
> plumb in the middle of the political stage, and we may be sure he
> will make the fullest use of his nuisance value.[6]

Promptly Beaverbrook replied with his own advice. 'Be sure that

Macmillan will make trouble if he has the power. As long as he is kept in order he will be all right.'

Over the summer months there was no improvement in morale. One seasoned observer noted that although '... Tory MPs ... are profoundly gloomy about the state of the world and the state of their leadership, they are not now rebellious. But ... another setback to British policy or to the home economy, *coupled with any sign of indecision*, will create an entirely new situation. I don't rule out the sort of rebellion that I watched in late April and early May 1940.'[7] For Eden the problem was of the worst kind that can afflict a Tory leader. He found himself simultaneously under pressure from the Left – for economic incompetence, expectations disappointed, electoral rejection shown up in by-election results – and from his own Right, a clear majority of the parliamentary party, who were deeply suspicious of his Imperial policy.

In June the last British troops left the Canal zone, abandoning prematurely much booty of every kind to which the Egyptians gleefully helped themselves. The 1922 Committee was in uproar. To military humiliation (as it was portrayed) had been added damage to the taxpayer. This withdrawal, peacefully negotiated though it might have been, was taken throughout the Middle East, and gleefully trumpeted by the Americans by every device from *Time* magazine to their own Embassy press release, as 'the Empire on which "the sun never sets" – no more!'

Was there now any point or position on which Britain would make a stand? Here were in combination those most dangerous of all ingredients – evident military weakness, and perceived indecision. The same, although the scale would be different, as led to conflict in the South Atlantic a quarter-century later. Slowly Eden was being drawn into a situation that was going to involve force. More than force – war.

Some years earlier, during his Foreign Secretaryship, in the margins of a four-power conference in Berlin a senior member of the US State Department had observed Eden. And his verdict is so percipient, so central to the whole dilemma of British foreign policy and the manner in which Tory statesmen were compelled to operate from an economic power base with barely any substance whatever, that it should be cited at length:

> Eden was quick, he was skilful, he was eloquent in debate. His rather languid manner concealed a lively, imaginative, perceptive mind ... He had an underlying characteristic which I detected in every British statesman with whom I've had any dealings ... with the sole exception of Winston Churchill: he [Eden] had that almost inbred, instinctive effort, in any conflict, in any collision, great or small, to find a compromise solution ... the British do have and have had, ever since their power quite patently was on the decline, from the battle of the Somme on, I suppose, ... the realisation that their role was not of a determiner, not as a dictator of events but as a negotiator, as a compromiser, as a mediator ... in the crunch Eden was always to be counted on, but it had to be very clearly a true crunch.[8]

Now, in the late summer of 1956, the 'true crunch' was very near. And Eden was soon to find who among his allies, and among his colleagues, could be 'counted on'.

TWENTY-FIVE

Relegation

A very grand dinner at Number 10 – An unwelcome
interruption – The strategic dilemma – The realities of
power – The party is indignant – Macmillan at the
Treasury – A failure to consult – The 'little coalition' –
US vindictiveness – Anthony Eden becomes
dispensable – Rab Butler awaits the call.

ON THE EVENING of 26 July 1956 the Prime Minister was host
to a very grand dinner party at Number 10. It was the last occasion,
we can now see, when all the accoutrement of the British Empire –
insofar as it had survived the Second World War – was in place.
The occasion was social in character, political in motive. The guest
of honour being the youthful monarch of a client state, together
with his powerful and Anglophile Regent. Iraq, and the oil located
there, was of immense strategic importance. British influence was
dominant, but rested as much on force, or the recent memory of
force, as on goodwill. It being but fifteen years since the 'upstart'
Rashid Ali had tried to take advantage of British weakness in the
region and had been roundly defeated by the far smaller, but more
energetic, British garrison at Habbaniyah. On some maps the
country was shaded pink – halfway to the comforting red which
still coloured all Commonwealth territory in the atlases of state
schools. Thus it had been thought appropriate to include all three
Chiefs of Staff, the Lord Chancellor, the Foreign Secretary and
five members of the Cabinet. Even the Leader of the Opposition,
Mr Hugh Gaitskell, had been invited, together with his fashionable
and well-connected mistress Mrs Ian Fleming.

At the halfway point in the meal there was an interruption. A sheaf of telegrams was put before the Prime Minister. They contained excerpts from a two-hour speech by Colonel Nasser in a most inflammatory tone – 'friends of the hated Israel are bent on the ruination of a poor but brave people ... we will take back into our possession what is rightfully ours, and will no longer be slaves in our own country' – concluding with the announcement that Egypt had 'nationalised', that is to say annexed and confiscated, the Suez Canal.

The niceties of coffee and port were curtailed. The dinner came to an end and the guests (with some notable exceptions) departed. On the doorstep the Iraqi regent, Nuri El Said, told Eden that he should 'hit Nasser hard *and quickly*'. Nuri will have known that, in default, the durability of British protection (and in all likelihood his own life expectancy) could now be measured in months.*

This was a most unpleasant blow for Eden. Certainly the telegrams from Cairo had, over recent weeks, been bad. The party had been uneasy. But the House was due to rise in three days' time for the summer recess. The dinner, indeed, had something of an end-of-term celebration about it. Surely this new situation was controllable? A photograph exists† showing Eden in his very last months as Foreign Secretary, immaculately dressed in dinner jacket and black tie and the very picture of debonair vigour. Together with Sir Ralph Stevenson, the Ambassador in Cairo, Eden shows every sign of enjoying the company of Colonel Nasser, who occupies a sofa between the two men. Nasser had recently displaced another colonel, Neguib. It must have seemed at the time that he was just one more of those military 'strong men' so many of whose caricatures can be seen in the margins of the Imperial tapestry; who come and go, and who will be susceptible to a combination of flattery, economic blackmail and military pressure.

* Fourteen, in fact. On 23 June 1958 he was eviscerated by the Baghdad mob and, while still conscious, pulled through the streets attached to the bumper of the Palace Rolls-Royce.
† Included in Sir Robert Rhodes James's biography of Eden.

Anthony Eden had founded his career on a combination of skill and the appearance (not wholly synthetic) of idealism, in diplomacy. The League, sanctions, the principle of Collective Security – it was in these fields that Eden had earned laurels in his youth. But now, as Prime Minister, Eden was having to keep the balance between three influences, all of them in some degree adverse, that were to blight all British policy (be it Conservative or Labour in origin) for thirty-five years after the end of the Second World War, and which in this late autumn of 1956 were joined in malignant combination.

First the uncomfortable and enduring reality that the whole sum of our exertions from 1939 until 1945 had resulted simply in our having substituted, in the field of international relations and European security, one totalitarian threat for another – one that was equally menacing and implacable.

Second, that the old Imperial pattern of economic dependence and military deployment could never in its entirety be recovered and, even in those regions where it could, looked increasingly precarious.

And, third, that the fragility of the country's balance of payments, and reserves of gold and foreign exchange – themselves the result of a congenitally weak industrial performance – were a constant inhibitor on nationalist diplomacy.

Britain was in fact less able to resist Soviet aggression in the 1950s than had been Britain and France together set against Germany in the 1930s. It was absolutely essential that the United States be involved as well, and as our protector. For Churchill this had been natural. It following smoothly on the 'Former Naval Person' correspondence with Roosevelt, the early discussions on the deck of the *Repulse*, and underlay the transition, barely acknowledged, from an experienced military partner to a bankrupt dependant. Because the United States needed Britain still, as the only reliable component of its anti-Communist axis in Europe, the 'unsinkable aircraft-carrier', the illusion spread – and it was in the interest of both to encourage it – that the two countries were 'allies'. But in fact the reciprocity of power and status which characterises a true alliance was missing. For Britain the US was the guarantor of its security, of its very life expectance. But for the US Britain was simply a 'client state'; an enthusiastic remittance man and mercenary.

This relationship, whose crudity was seldom admitted even in private, boded ill for Britain should the commercial interests of the two countries collide – particularly if such collision occurred in a theatre not directly overlaid by the Communist 'menace'. All this was well known to Eden, and will have been at the forefront of his mind when discussion (the remaining diners having moved downstairs to the Cabinet Room) resumed. At once an observer is struck by the similarities with those same urgent meetings that were convened on the morning of Saturday 2 April 1982, when the first reports came in of the Argentine seizure of the Falklands. A cautious and hesitant Staff assessment; a recital from the Foreign Office of the paramount need to consult with allies and particularly with the United States; a general balance of opinion that nothing precipitate could or should be done without testing the diplomatic temperature. All that was different – and it was critical – was the Prime Minister's force of personality.

Britain at this time was spending nine per cent of gross national product on defence. The average for the other countries in the Organisation for European Economic Co-operation was five per cent. Yet when Eden told the Chiefs, that evening, that he wished to respond forcefully and immediately, their response was defeatist (as, indeed, with the exception of Sir Henry Leach, the First Sea Lord, it was to be in 1982).* They needed time to review the position. Technical arguments such as the range of aircraft based in Cyprus and their 'loiter' time; the shortage of armour-piercing ammunition in the region and the delay in shipping it from Portsmouth; even the time needed to paint vehicles based in Britain in sand-coloured camouflage, were all cited.

As the argument proceeded Eden will have felt himself drawing back into that familiar mode of high diplomacy where he felt most

* See pp. 475–6 below.

at ease – but which his successor, in 1982, most despised. To massage world opinion; to assemble a coalition; to secure the good offices of the United States; with all this assured, Eden would be impregnable, surely, and while it was being put in place Nasser might be forced to 'climb down'. Thus when, MPs having deferred their holiday plans, the House met in emergency session the text of Eden's statement was cautious and prosaic.[1] In marked contrast to one of his dinner guests, Hugh Gaitskell, who declared the Egyptian action to be 'high-handed and totally unjustified', Eden emphasised calmness and moderation:

> The action of the Egyptian Government affects the rights and interests of many nations, and consultations are taking place with the other Governments immediately concerned.

Thus within twenty-four hours the Government had publicly ruled out the likelihood of unilateral action. A more gratuitous bonus for Colonel Nasser could hardly have been conceived. Nor a more blatant flouting of that archetypal verdict in Rommel's infantry manual – '*Never forget that a section can do in the first hour what by nightfall will require a company, the following day a battalion, and, by the end of the week, an Army Corps.*'

On 30 July the Foreign Affairs Committee assembled in Room 8 at the House of Commons, its habitual venue. So many back-benchers wished to attend that the meeting adjourned so as to shuffle down the corridor to the much larger Room 14. The Foreign Secretary, Selwyn Lloyd, told colleagues that 'we must force Nasser to accept international control' (this was already a backtracking from a straight pledge – as uttered by Margaret Thatcher on the first day of the Falklands crisis – to recover possession). Lloyd went on to warn that the Reservists would be called up, that other military measures would be put in hand, that 'it will not be pleasant'.[2]

The room cheered long and loud. And colleagues then dispersed for their (delayed) summer vacation. August passed, and September. By the beginning of October it was perfectly clear that no assistance would be forthcoming from the Americans. Harold

Macmillan had travelled to Washington and on 24 September held an hour-long conversation with Eisenhower. Roger Makins, the Ambassador, sat in on the meting. To Makins's great surprise Macmillan made no mention whatever of the Suez Crisis. He chatted amiably, spent most of the time reminiscing about Africa and the leisurely conferences at the Villa Dar al Ayoum.* This must have greatly relieved Eisenhower, who will have been expecting Macmillan to try and cash a cheque on their old and long-standing friendship. After a bit the President took his visitor to the window and showed him the street lamp at which he aimed when practising golf strokes. They parted amiably, but inconclusively.

Why did Macmillan neglect this opportunity? It may be that he was waiting for Eisenhower to say something. Let the horse come to you. If it was tactics, it certainly was not pride, for Macmillan was often shameless and craven in his suppliance when he judged it necessary. More likely was his intention to be seen as an impressive personality. Calm and amiable. Someone with whom in marked, but unstated, contrast to Eden, one could 'do business'. Possibly because Macmillan did not want to deter Eden from swimming out still further from shore, and the President not having mentioned the subject did just allow Macmillan to report back to Eden that the US was supportive. Makins's own despatch was less sanguine. He warned that no 'precipitate' (meaning military) action should be put in hand until after the presidential election in November. But this was Makins's last despatch. Macmillan arranged for him to be recalled a week later to come to the Treasury as the new Permanent Secretary. He was not replaced in Washington until 8 November – an extraordinary and unexplained act of omission which left the United Kingdom under-represented at ambassadorial level for the whole period of the Suez war.

This curious and culpable neglect of United States attitude – ignoring even the obvious constraint of an impending presidential election – may be accounted for by the maturing of plans for the 'little coalition'. If there was to be effective military action there

* Macmillan's HQ in Tunis in 1942–3.

had to be troops on the ground. The British had only a brigade in Cyprus 'and if we move it, there will be an uprising'. The French would be coming by sea from Marseilles, and in no great strength. The only effective army in the region were the Israelis. They would have to do the job. But how was this to be fixed? What repercussions would there be across Arab opinion? British force, if effective, commanded respect. But in alliance with the Jews ... If the operation 'went wrong', we were finished. Far more would be lost than was at stake in July.

And so, somewhat laboriously, for Staff talks between the Services of three separate nations will not be entirely smooth – especially when they have to be conducted by a tiny group in total secrecy – the plans were cobbled together. The intention was to displace Nasser just as, when at one time during the war he had seemed troublesome and about to desert to the Fascists, King Farouk had responded to a brutal show of force by Sir Miles Lampson. The publicly declared objective, convoluted and incredible as it may have seemed, was to 'separate' the combatants (for Israel was to open, by the tiniest of margins, hostilities).

Thus, on 30 October Eden, his face expressionless, told a crowded House of Commons that we had 'urged restraint' on Israel, and that her attack had come as a complete surprise. But in this new situation 'we must put an immediate stop to the war to protect our people and the shipping in the Canal zone'.[3] The House took it quietly. By now the mood was very different from July. When Eden went on to say that an ultimatum had been issued to both sides to withdraw ten miles from the Canal, and if this was not complied with in ten hours British and French forces would intervene to 'separate' them, the news was received in almost total silence.

On the whole, the military operations went well. The Royal Air Force Canberras flying from Akrotiri destroyed most of the Egyptian MiGs on the ground on the first day. Neither against the British nor the French contingent did the Egyptian defenders show much evidence of combat training. While the Israeli armour galloped across the Negev to arrive on the banks of the Canal on

29 October, it was not in terms of firepower, training, or the courage of their men that this little extempore coalition would be found wanting. Its vulnerability lay along that perennially weak flank – the inadequacy of their national currencies and the reserves available to support them.

Macmillan's behaviour as Chancellor during the Suez Crisis might – had it been known at the time – have finished off his chances of the leadership once and for all. In fact, and operating covertly, he exploited his tenure of this key office most unscrupulously to undermine Eden and to advance his own claims to the premiership. Having egged on the expedition, he chose his moment deliberately to sabotage it by grotesque exaggeration of a sudden financial crisis. He told his Cabinet colleagues on 6 November that £100 million had been wiped off Britain's gold reserves. In fact the losses at that time were only £30 million. Despite receiving confirmation of this lower figure, Macmillan deliberately kept the true figure from the Cabinet.[1] And there is strong anecdotal evidence that he encouraged – although his turns of phrase will have been oblique – the US Federal Reserve to sell sterling short in order to intensify the pressure. Certainly Macmillan was adamant in opposition to the one manoeuvre which would have most disconcerted the US authorities – namely to float the pound. Robert Hall, who had so nearly persuaded Butler to essay this five years earlier,* recommended this course as the only way simultaneously to protect the remaining reserves and to concentrate the minds of the Fed. But Macmillan enlisted the Governor of the Bank of England, Cameron Cobbold, who told Cabinet that it would be 'a catastrophe course'.[5]

By one of those grand-scale, and unfortunate, coincidences that occur sometimes in history a rebellion in Hungary was crushed, over a few days, by a cruel, effective and instantaneous Russian response. Bloated with confidence Bulganin, the Soviet Prime Minister, threatened to strike London with nuclear rockets if British 'aggression' continued. There was no formal ultimatum.

* See pp. 344–5 above.

The language, although bellicose, was clearly styled to impress the less sophisticated media of Africa and the Middle East. But as newsreels appeared in the cinemas, showing in the same bulletin British tanks in Port Said and the effects of Red Army shell fire in Budapest, the impression spread of an approaching general conflict. As the situation deteriorated, so did the mood of public support contract, and focus on a narrower spectrum. Hugh Gaitskell, who had been so forthright in his support at the outset, was now feigning indignation. He accused the Government of abandoning the three principles that had guided British foreign policy since the war – namely, solidarity with the Commonwealth; the Anglo-American alliance; and adherence to the Charter of the United Nations. The House of Commons had reverted to division along party lines. And the Conservatives were themselves uneasy – split between 'the weak sisters'* and those like Captain Waterhouse, the MP for South-East Leicester since 1924, who wanted to bomb Cairo. Much of the press, sensing the alteration of mood, changed sides.

Eden himself suffered acute attacks of pain and exhaustion and consulted daily with his medical advisers. He was doomed, though did not yet know it. Of him Butler wrote:

> I admired his courage, his gallantry, his wartime record and his Foreign Office achievements. He seemed thoroughly in character standing up for British rights in the Middle East ... These were deep-seated emotions affecting liberal-minded people, but they . coalesced only too easily with less generous sentiments; the residues of illiberal resentment at the loss of Empire, the rise of coloured nationalism, the transfer of world leadership to the United States. It was these sentiments that made the Suez venture so popular, not least among the supporters of the embarrassed Labour Party.[6]

By now Eisenhower was openly, and gratuitously, hostile. The

---

* Eden's phrase. Nigel Nicolson, who was to be deselected by his Bournemouth constitutents on this account, lists them as Boyle, Nutting, Walter Elliot, Boothby, John Foster, David Price, Jakie Astor and others – including the young and newly elected Keith Joseph. (Nicolson, *Long Life: Memoirs*, 1997, p. 164.)

United States had effected a complete transition – from supportive
ally, to well-intentioned counsellor, to detached arbiter of UN
resolutions. In November of 1956 Eisenhower was directing the
campaign to punish, and in exemplary fashion, the 'aggressor'.
Not content with selling short sterling, and using US influence
to block the loan – which under the Bretton Woods Agreement
should have been forthcoming as of right – from the IMF to
support the currency, the President also let it be known that oil
sanctions were being considered as a punitive 'gesture'. The degree
of humiliation inflicted on Britain by the Americans following
the Suez débâcle is certainly remarkable. Immediately after the
cease-fire was announced Eden had hoped to convene a three-
power meeting in Washington. This would, at least, allow a general
cosmetic overlay, a briefing that the Alliance remained intact and
was working jointly to repair the situation. Eisenhower refused.
And three times in twenty-four hours telephoned to ask when
the British withdrawal would start, concluding the last with a
peremptory warning that no further informal contacts would
occur unless the announcement of withdrawal were issued immediately. The United Nations Emergency Force was to have no
British contingent. British pilots and dredgers were to play no part
in clearing the blockships – even though the crews were present
and in position. This task would be entrusted to Swedes and
Yugoslavs – and, of course, to Egyptians. No face-saving device
of any kind was to be permitted.

It was plain that the United States intended to exploit the crisis
to advance its claim to global suzerainty; to be the sole arbiter, in
the 'free' world, of territorial disputes and to ensure that henceforth there could be no rival centre where unilateral decisions
were made. Overlaying this was the atavistic desire to assist at the
death throes of the British Empire, whose wealth in territory and
natural resources both corporate America and the State Department had so long coveted. And of which the Conservative Party
had for so long regarded itself as the rightful and hereditary
custodian.

★   ★   ★

By the third week in November Tory morale was at its nadir. The Prime Minister was ill. The Americans had deserted us. The armed forces had been humiliated or, at the very least, stabbed in the back. Who was to blame? Nasser? Selwyn? The Israelis? The United Nations? Eisenhower? In the smoking room 'insiders' could be found ready to point the finger at any, or all, of these. The party wanted to vent its anger. An Early Day Motion lay on the Order Paper. It accused the US administration by their actions of 'gravely endangering the Atlantic Alliance', and had attracted over a hundred signatures.

On the morning of Thursday 22 November the Chairman, Secretary and Treasurer of the 1922 Committee paid a call on the Prime Minister. Eden was sitting, propped up by pillows, in his bedroom at Number 10. He was 'much better', he told them. But then the Prime Minister broke the news: his doctor had advised a 'complete rest', he was about to leave for Jamaica, and would be absent for about three weeks.

There was still much goodwill towards Eden. But it overlay a general admission among colleagues that he was too petulant, too frail, too erratic to remain as leader. In any case, the life expectancy of the Government could, it was generally agreed, be measured in no more than weeks. And who should succeed Eden? Plainly it would be Rab. Rab had been a tower of strength. He had chaired many Cabinet meetings. He had been a popular Chancellor and, insofar as there was any fund left of public goodwill towards any member of the Conservative Cabinet, it was for *Mister Butler*. The Downing Street press office had briefed lobby correspondents, only two days earlier, that *'Mr Butler will be in effective charge of affairs so long as Sir Anthony is absent'*.

It was against this background that Butler had accepted an invitation to address not the Executive Council, but the full 1922 Committee, on 22 November immediately after his Commons statement from the despatch box. Understandably, Butler was exhausted. He had been on his feet for almost three hours. First, as Lord Privy Seal, answering for the invalid Prime Minister (it was a Thursday); then, as Leader of the House, taking 'business' questions; then, facing the music with his statement on the Suez withdrawal. Butler was pessimistic, too, about the state of the party and its electoral prospects. The meeting was going to be a difficult one.

Butler had always regarded the 'Suez Group' with distaste and had been warned by the Chief Whip that they might make trouble. So it is likely that he was relieved, as well as surprised, to observe the Chancellor of the Exchequer approaching from the opposite end of the Committee Room corridor; and to have Macmillan join him at the door of Room 14. Together the two men made small talk while they waited for the Chairman to usher them in.

TWENTY-SIX

Macmillan

Rab Butler at the despatch box – and then at the '22 –
Macmillan as virtuoso – Eden returns – and fails his
medical – The Cabinet's verdict – A fair wind – A bad
press – Selwyn Lloyd has his card marked – Night of
the Long Knives – Vassall and Profumo – Rambouillet
and Skybolt – Macmillan is 'unassailable'.

ON 22 NOVEMBER the House had been expecting a statement
on the latest position in the Suez Crisis. Rumours, the majority
of them grounded in wishful thinking, were everywhere. Some
said that we were going to drive on Cairo. Most, that a 'deal' had
been done, though few realised that we would be worse off than
when the whole operation started. The problem for the party
managers, and particularly for R. A. Butler who had to break the
news across the despatch box, was how to present the reality of
military and economic defeat in such language as would, as might,
allow it to be accepted on the Tory back benches. He had already
lied, and lied flagrantly, on the floor of the House, when being
pressed by Gaitskell regarding the degree of collusion with the
Israelis. 'The action we took . . . was to urge restraint.' The solution
now, or so it appeared, was to remove the whole affair out of the
tawdry realm of national self-interest and prestige and place it in
the context of a higher ideal. 'We are witnessing [sic] an attempt
by the United Nations,' Butler told his listeners, 'to organise an
effective intervention in an area which has long threatened the
peace of the world.' Keeping as straight a face as possible he went
on to claim that 'This intervention has been made *possible* by

Franco-British action. If this United Nations intervention succeeds ... a precedent will have been set which will give mankind hope for the future.'¹

The whole affair was really a ploy to enhance the authority of the UN. Or at least that was the 'line'. 'A great act of international constructive statesmanship'. And pretty thin it must have sounded even to an audience who were well-disposed (which the Conservative Party never is) to the United Nations.

Butler took twelve questions, all of them awkward, and no fewer than nine coming from Privy Councillors. He had barely time to sit down on the bench before trudging up the committee floor staircase to his rendezvous first, and unexpectedly,* in the Committee Room doorway with the Chancellor of the Exchequer, then with the '22. At Rab's introduction members slapped, in the traditional manner, their desk-tops. But with no great enthusiasm. Ploddingly Butler took them through the history of the affair. Candidly he spoke of the international situation – 'uncertain'; of the electoral prospect – 'somewhat bleak at the present time'; of the need for all concerned to 'try and get our message across a bit better'.

The minutes of the meeting on 22 November are strangely reticent about this episode which was to determine the style, policy and deportment (not to mention the leadership) of the party for the next decade:

> Mr Butler and Mr Macmillan addressed the meeting on the situation in the Middle East and explained the Government's views. The Lord Privy Seal (Mr Butler) announced the Government's intention to overhaul [its] publicity arrangements.²

Whether or not so attenuated an account is the result of prompting

---

* Some authorities, including Butler's biographer, have it that Macmillan attended at Butler's invitation. If such an invitation was extended in so many words (which I doubt) it will only have been consequent on a suggestion from the '22 Chairman whom Macmillan, knowing him to be a supporter, had solicited that morning. (Interview between the author and the Rt Hon. Peter Morrison MP, 1992.)

from John Morrison, who will have been aware that a collision was rapidly approaching; or simply of that instinctive caution which earns the 'officers' of the 1922 Committee their position, is unclear. But certainly the entry does no justice at all to the virtuosity of Macmillan's performance. He was contrite. He was visionary. He was uplifting. Exhorting colleagues to fresh and confident endeavour, Macmillan's gestures were so expansive that at one point he seemed almost to push Butler (seated next to him) off his chair. Macmillan dwelt on his personal friendship with the US Secretary to the Treasury; he laid claim to a special understanding of French sensitivities and the European dimension. Above all – infallible guide to the approval of back-benchers – he told them that the next election could, and would, be won.

And when Macmillan came to articulate the 'line to take', in much the same words as Butler – 'We intervened to divide, and above all to contain, the conflict. The occasion for our intervention is over. The fire is now out' – he portrayed it as a remarkable and victorious achievement.

Much of this was bogus. Macmillan's contact with George Humphrey* bordered on the treasonable. While his simultaneous deferral to American bullying, and ingratiating self-abasement before Eisenhower's every requirement, confirmed Anglophobes at the Quai d'Orsay in their view that no reliance should ever be placed on Britain where a conflict of interest might arise between Europe and America. De Gaulle, too, had been watching this outcome from his exile at Colombey-les-deux Eglises.

But Macmillan's objective was short-term, and immediate. For him, it was now or never. By including in his speech even what Butler's biographer has called 'a *tremolo* on his own advancing years'[3] Macmillan cunningly planted the seed, invariably fruitful, of opinion that – whether or not his leadership was to be preferred over the longer term – he was willing and competent to serve as a caretaker. The applause was long and hard, and members left the room with their spirits raised for the first time since the summer.

* US Secretary to the Treasury.

Macmillan now set about mobilising his American contacts. Rumours started to circulate that the United States would never resume normal relations with Britain unless there was a change of leadership. Eisenhower – on whose advice it is not known – refused even to accept a visit from Selwyn Lloyd who was in New York attempting to salvage what he could from the United Nations Security Council. The US press, with its customary brutality, had already written off Eden – Britain is the sick man of Europe, with the sick man of Britain at its head.

This was a period of high risk for Macmillan, or so it might have seemed. On 14 December Eden suddenly appeared at Heathrow, looking bronzed. To waiting reporters he seemed ebullient. They were not to know that the statement which Eden read out had been hastily drafted 'for' him by a triumvirate consisting of Butler, Salisbury and (for reasons of form only) Selwyn Lloyd, and hastily pressed into the Prime Minister's hands in the privacy of the VIP lounge. Eden had a brief medical examination at Number 10, then drove on down to Chequers. The assumption spread that he was 'taking stock' and would announce his resignation before Christmas.

This was certainly not the way Eden saw things. On the last Thursday before the recess he insisted on addressing the '22. He thanked the party for their loyalty, and answered questions for forty-five minutes. At the end, although the Chairman expressed to him and Lady Eden the best wishes for Christmas' the applause was not, as the Secretary noted, 'strong enough to sustain the Prime Minister through his illness'.[4]

This was now the accepted code for Eden's impending demise. His health had simply broken down. Meanwhile the *Economist* (whose reputation seems to have been unscathed by a record of political commentary and prediction shown over decades to be almost uniformly defective) wrote that

> If Sir Anthony were to lay down the Premiership tomorrow, there is really [*sic*] no doubt that the Queen would be constitutionally bound to send for Mr Butler[5]

– a verdict which for Rab Butler must have been as reassuring, over Christmas, as the morning press which greeted Curzon on 22 May 1923 as he settled into the first-class railway carriage from Montacute to London.

After the holiday Salisbury and Kilmuir* explained to Eden that in order to allay misgivings in the party he should really submit to a comprehensive medical examination. All three doctors (not chosen by Eden) came up with the same verdict – the Prime Minister should lay aside the seals of office immediately.

Now the die was cast. On 9 January 1957 Eden resigned. The 'selection' process which followed has, in terms at least of minimising division and foreshortening the period of uncertainty, never been bettered. Each member of the Cabinet was summoned singly and in turn to Lord Salisbury's Privy Council office. Beside Salisbury, the traditional kingmaker of the Conservative Party, was seated Kilmuir. One question only was put to the visitor – 'Who is it to be, Rab or Harold?'

It would, of course, have been perfectly possible for another preference to have been named, but none was. Macmillan was driven to the Palace and kissed hands on 10 January. Somewhat uncritically (or, reading between the lines, is there a suggestion of irony?) The Times welcomed him as 'essentially a man of goodwill, and he has a capacity to engender it ... warm emotions ... generous humanity ... he is a man of energy'.[6]

Macmillan was the third leader in a row to have endured a difficult relationship with the pre-war Conservative Party. Indeed, from a position of profoundly 'unhelpful' (by convention the strongest adjective in the Whip's public vocabulary of reproach) dissent, Macmillan had gone much further than had his two more experienced predecessors against the Chamberlain regime. Neither Churchill nor Eden had felt it necessary to resign the party whip as Macmillan had in 1936 (over appeasement of Mussolini's Abyssinian conquest). And no other Conservative MP (certainly not Churchill or Eden) would have found it necessary to make an

---

* As Sir David Maxwell-Fyfe had become.

exhibition of themselves by burning an effigy of their own Party Leader – as Macmillan crudely and youthfully did of Chamberlain at Birch Grove on 5 November 1938. None the less, as far as the public were concerned, Macmillan, like Churchill and Eden, had been on the side of right against his party's pro-appeasement elders and placemen in the 1930s. And upon this the basis of his political credibility now rested. It was the trump card Macmillan held always over Rab Butler, whose commitment to finding an 'accommodation' with Hitler had continued even after Chamberlain had been displaced.

To this day the controversy is unsettled. Was Macmillan a leader in the great tradition of Tory paternalism or a left-wing fellow-traveller seeking redemption through a good tailor and a well developed taste for the *bon mot*? Representing a depressed area like Stockton during the 1930s certainly had its effect on him. His sympathy was genuine and he was not afraid to adopt views at variance with the leadership in pursuit of what he perceived to be his constituents' best interests. This led him into adopting profoundly un-Tory views on economic policy. Indeed, at that time he felt free to tell the press of the Tories that 'a party dominated by second-class brewers and company promoters – a Casino Capitalism – is not likely to represent anybody but itself'.[7] This may have been, in part, a dig at his brother-in-law who was in the beer business. In 1938 Macmillan had written a book, *The Middle Way*, in which he advocated that the stock market should be abolished and replaced by a National Investment Board.

When, during the 1950s, Macmillan was responsible for listing historic buildings, he took as many off the list as he could, so as to facilitate their destruction and replacement with the handiwork of the local authority 'planner' and property developer. This was not 'managing decline', it was the wanton destruction of an architectural civilisation to be replaced by one so shoddy that its only redeeming defect was a speedy biodegradability. Macmillan even had the effrontery to advise his nephew the Duke of Devonshire to abandon Chatsworth, the house which had for centuries been the seat of the Cavendish family. During this period conservationists including Sir John Betjeman★ petitioned Macmillan to halt the orgy of vandalism which he orchestrated in London and the other great cities. The destruction of the Euston Arch, a fine example of the Doric order, became a particular *cause célèbre* amongst conservationists who wondered if the minister even understood the meaning of the term 'Conservative'. But Macmillan proved deaf to such protestations, commenting loftily that 'only dying countries tried to preserve the symbols of their past'.[8]

At this point in his career Macmillan had been striking a modernist (today it would be termed *post*-modernist) posture. It was only later, securely established as the nation's governing elder statesman, that he himself assumed the identity of a 'symbol from the past'. First Macmillan had to distinguish himself from his peers, and his predecessors. Despite being a paternalist by sentiment, Churchill's sympathies, as Dr Paul Addison has pointed out, were extended to the struggles of the 'small man' – the shopkeeper, the tradesman and the clerk.[9] Churchill's post-war agenda, under the slogan '*Set the People Free*', was an attempt to relieve the burdens of state regulation from the lower-middle class. Eden continued this theme, advocating 'a home-owning democracy' whose end result was essentially a middle-class ideal. In contrast, Macmillan, surely, must have been the only Tory leader this century who could exclaim 'What *do* the middle classes want?'[10] in contemptuous exasperation rather than as a strategy to win the general election.

What fuelled Macmillan's apparent disregard, perhaps even contempt, for the interests and values of the British middle class? A different age, be it before or after his time, must have categorised these beliefs as socialistic. Macmillan, however, chose to regard them as Disraelian. As an admirer of the nineteenth-century novel, he was certainly conscious of Disraeli's nightmare vision of 'two nations', the rich (of which he was a representative) and the poor (which he had represented in his Stockton constituency until 1945). The lesson Macmillan drew from this (rather more so than had Disraeli) was to use the apparatus of the State to build a

---

★ Poet, conservationist and broadcaster, subsequently Poet Laureate, 1972–84.

new relationship with the poor. The sector squeezed out by this relationship was the middle class, the sector to whom the Conservatives spent most of the rest of the century appealing.

Furthermore, Macmillan was often quick to ascribe insufficient social class to anyone who stood in his way, a trait that must have been galling for those who had to listen to his frequent recitation of the view (held through thick – 1974 – and thin – 1984) that 'miners are the best people in the world, the salt of the earth'. Thus in later life Macmillan did not take to Thatcherism. And, as will be seen,* made mischief for Mrs Thatcher at every turn.

Now, on 10 January 1957, Macmillan set about rebuilding the Cabinet.

There is no doubt that, from the very first moment at Number 10 Macmillan was also looking ahead (as had done every Prime Minister except Alec Douglas-Home, although not perhaps to the same obsessive degree) to detect the first vapour trails of a potential successor. The night before he had taken to dinner at White's the Chief Whip, Edward Heath, and they consumed a large number of oysters. Heath was only a member of the Carlton, where the oysters (being sent across the street from Wilton's) are not as good as at White's. This was a prudent move by Macmillan. And the following day he sacked Gwilym Lloyd George, Patrick Buchan-Hepburn, Walter Monckton and James Stuart, that small minority in Cabinet who could have been inferred – even without enjoying the Chief Whip's company at dinner – to have voted for Butler. Butler himself presented a problem. He wanted the Foreign Office as consolation prize. But Macmillan insisted that he go to the Home Office remembering, perhaps, that no Conservative Home Secretary has ever become Prime Minister. (This piqued and saddened Rab who put it about that the real reason was that Lloyd's wife had left him for a younger and more sporting lover – '[Selwyn] got into bed with his sweater on!')[11]

For two years all went well. Macmillan cruised to victory in 1959

* See p. 485 below.

having first borrowed, then subsequently disowned, the slogan
'*You never had it so good*'.

But by the spring of 1962 the inflationary seed-corn so liberally
sprinkled during his first term had started to sprout. The polls
were no longer friendly. Macmillan had to turn his attention to
the prospect of his second general election. It was a twelvemonth
distant, of course. Perhaps longer if he chose to eat into the reserves
of time. 'The last year allowed by the Parliament Act should always
be regarded as a *reserve*,' he often said.

The immediate present was unsettling.

On 14 March the Government was roundly defeated in the
Orpington by-election by the Liberal candidate. Nor was this
result alone in predicting a heavy swing away from the party by
its traditional supporters. Summoned to the next meeting of the
1922 Committee on 22 March the Chairman of the Party, Iain
Macleod, was far from reassuring:

> . . . things would get worse before they got better, and some of the
> by-elections to come would be very bad . . .

> The . . . [Pay Pause] . . . policy was wholly right, but very unpopu-
> lar, and unfortunately the Orpington type of constituency was
> worst hit by it. There was a feeling that the very rich and the
> Unions could opt out and the middle classes had been sacrificed.
> *Frankly, they had been.*[12]

This was a strange performance by the Chairman of the Party. It
came, admittedly, at the end of a long and critical session. Perhaps
Macleod felt resentful that the Whips had not organised some
supportive speakers. Perhaps he was not himself wholly disconcerted to see so much disquiet in the parliamentary party
focused on the existing Leadership. But in the complaints made
from the floor it is possible to identify practically every one that
would be repeated on the next occasion, some thirty years later,
when the party was once more deeply unpopular after a very long
period in office. And which, with hindsight, can now be seen as
ineradicable without a purgative period in the wilderness.

They range from Philip Goodhart's – 'There is great boredom with us . . . particularly amongst those under 45 . . . it is no longer avant-garde to vote Tory'; to Geoffrey Hirst's – 'The government had lost its sense of mission . . . a general sense of discontent among the middle classes', and Nigel Fisher's practical point – 'High mortgage interest rates and the cost of season tickets on suburban trains all worry the young married'. More ominous was Douglas Glover – 'The party must have a tighter grip on Ministerial activities from now on'.[13]

Macmillan's preferred strategy was to call polling day – preferably in the early summer of 1963 – with the convergence of a diplomatic triumph and a 'give-away' Budget in March of that year. Both of these objectives demanded a cautious approach. The 'triumph' of acceptance into the European Common Market would be difficult enough to sell unless the concessions demanded as a condition of approval were very slight. And everything that Macmillan was hearing from our posts overseas indicated quite the reverse.* And here, too, there was considerable unease both in the constituencies and Parliament. The Lord Privy Seal was charged with 'explaining' the position. Evidently he adopted the technique (not always reliable) of speaking at such length that the room would slowly empty. The minutes record that '*Mr Edward Heath delivered a very long and complicated speech which had a favourable reception*'. In fact Heath dodged criticism, or even properly focused argument (for neither the first nor last time in the consideration by the Conservative Party of this unremittingly divisive topic) by the simple expedient of lying:

> The Community . . . even take the view that if British problems have not been solved exactly [*sic*] right [during the negotiations] they can easily [*sic*] be adapted once Britain is in.[14]

On the third weekend in June the Prime Minister convened a small group of ministers at Chequers. He lectured them on the

---

* There seems at this stage to have been no trace of a suggestion that the UK might be vetoed altogether.

economic situation. His views were unchanged from those that
he had put to Cabinet on 28 May but he had now thought through
some ideas for 'presentation'. A Consumers Council; a Standing
Commission on Pay (but with recommendatory powers only);
and, even more amorphous, a 'Guiding Light' for steering incomes
policy.

Selwyn Lloyd listened without enthusiasm. Was he in charge
of economic policy, or not? Surely these 'ideas', and they were
barely worthy of the name, should have been first discussed by
the Prime Minister with him? The presence of four colleagues,
all of them part of Macmillan's own private *claque*, was simply
a clumsy device to exert pressure on him. The episode was one
more example, neither the first nor the last in this saga, of
how quickly Prime Ministers and their Chancellors fall out,
and how difficult they find it thereafter to maintain cordial
relations.

Throughout the afternoon Lloyd was uncommunicative, and
waspish in his retorts. But his fate was sealed. On returning to
London the following Monday, Macmillan immediately invited
Butler to a private lunch. Because if anything drastic was to be
done Butler had to be inveigled into granting, even though only
tacitly, his approval. In his diaries Macmillan clearly asserts that
Butler agreed Lloyd should go, while disclaiming any expectation
of returning to the Treasury himself. Butler was highly indiscreet,
and known to be such. And it is possible that Macmillan was, for
that reason, too opaque in his language. Butler has himself since
claimed that the first he heard of suggested Cabinet changes was
on 6 July.

In midsummer the opinion polls remained heavily in deficit. In
such circumstances, to 'sack' a Chancellor may look decisive. Or
(and this often deters Prime Ministers, usually to their tactical
disadvantage) it can risk unexpected, and unwelcome, consequences. Macmillan decided to drown Lloyd's cries of protest
by committing a general massacre. On 13 July he dismissed six
Cabinet ministers, of whom the Chancellor was one, drawing
from Jeremy Thorpe one of the century's wittiest political

aphorisms – that 'greater love hath no man than that he lay down his friends for his life'.

It was drastic. Butchery on this scale was unprecedented in the annals of the party. Not Bonar Law in 1922, nor Baldwin in 1931. Not Chamberlain when he came to power in 1937; nor even Churchill when he reshaped the Cabinet in 1940 to follow the contours of a Coalition administration – had expelled so many colleagues into the wilderness. The Executive Council of the '22 were far from happy. 'The Chancellor goes and we have a new piano, but why are we playing the same tune?' 'If this is a continuation of the Selwyn Lloyd policy, why get rid of Selwyn Lloyd?' 'Wouldn't it have been better if the Ministers had sent proper letters of resignation and not been pushed aside?' 'The country had been given the impression that we [sic] were panicking.' And more.

Macmillan, of course, was entirely equal to this. 'I have the greatest admiration for the work Selwyn did' ... and ... 'a very painful decision to make' ... and ... 'history will show whether it has been right or wrong' ... and 'I was not going to let [things] drift ... I did what I thought was right.' The one passage calculated to make the Executive prick up their ears – 'I felt we needed a new team of younger men ...' was heavily qualified by the Prime Minister's statement that he himself intended to 'carry on for the time being'.[15]

There now opened a long and difficult passage for Macmillan. Watched, one may assume, with quiet satisfaction by his aggrieved colleagues. An accumulation of events, some of them superficial, some portentous, all depicted by the press in the same, 'crisis-size' typeface on the front pages as being evidence of incompetence and loss of grip.

There were scandals, homosexual and hetero. An Admiralty clerk, Vassall, had been entrapped by the KGB. He had been dabbling in secret material, codes had been betrayed; there were rumours of his enjoying 'patronage' from within the middle ranks of the Government. When, though, the Director-General of MI5 reported that Vassall had been caught, Macmillan's spontaneous reaction was memorable. The purest milk of Establishment cynicism. After some grand disclaimer – 'No, I'm not at all pleased. After my gamekeeper shoots a fox he doesn't go and hang it up outside the MFH's drawing room...'

> You can't shoot a spy as you did in the war. You have to try him ... Better to discover him, and then control him, but never catch him.

Macmillan pointed out that in the ensuing

> great public trial ... the security services will not be praised for how efficient they are but blamed for how hopeless they are. There will then be an enquiry [which] will say – like the Magistrate in *Albert and the Lion* – that no one was really to blame. There will be a terrible row in the press, there will be a debate in the House of Commons and the Government will probably fall...[16]

In the early spring another sex scandal, of a more entertaining nature, broke into the news. Practically every ingredient which a sub-editor could ask for was present. The two cuties, one blonde, the other dark, were plainly of easy virtue yet far enough from being professional prostitutes to make their 'adventures' an easy read ... A senior peer (Lord Astor); a great house (Cliveden); a shifty 'physiotherapist' in dark glasses (Stephen Ward); giggles and horseplay around the swimming pool on a summer evening. And especially an element, real or supposed, of a threat to national security. Because the brunette, Christine Keeler, had simultaneously been enjoying the favours of the Soviet military attaché and Jack Profumo, the British War Minister! When the scandal broke, a still further dimension had been added by the conduct of Profumo who most foolishly lied to the House of Commons about the association. As with Vassall an inquiry was set up and, in the fullness of time, found that 'no one was really to blame'. The only enduring legacy from the Profumo affair being the response to Lord Astor's counsel by Mandy Rice-Davies, the blonde, still much quoted in both political and business commentary – '*He would, wouldn't he?*'*

In December of 1962 Macmillan suffered two major blows,
both to his personal reputation and to the policies around which
he was intending to set up the Conservative Party for the next
general election. The British application to join the European
Economic Community (EEC) was, after a long and in large part
humiliating series of concessionary negotiations, vetoed by de
Gaulle. And the cancellation of the Skybolt nuclear weapon,
which forced the British deterrent into a submarine-borne ballistic
rocket system, built by the Americans – Polaris. Whether or not
de Gaulle had heard, or even cared, that in the past Macmillan
had described him as 'that Frenchman with hips like a woman and
a head like a pineapple', there is little doubt that his veto was
fuelled by a deep personal mistrust. France had been repeatedly
humiliated by Britain during the war at, and following, Dunkirk;†
in Syria, North Africa, and at the Peace Conference. She had been
abandoned after Suez and at the very moment of the Rambouillet
conference was being drawn into dependence on US nuclear
technology. Set against this, Macmillan's Thespian claim to *ancien
camaraderie* amounted to very little.

And yet notwithstanding these setbacks, there he would be, still
firmly in position almost a year after putting six of his Cabinet
colleagues to the sword. In the summer of 1963, as the House
prepared to rise for the summer recess, and the year of the general
election cast its shadow – always a cooling relief for beleaguered
Prime Ministers – Macmillan seemed (to employ a notorious
adjective in its correct usage) unassailable. Macmillan's critics have
seen the Night of the Long Knives as indicating a loss of nerve.
Unlikely, it must be suggested, in one who as a twenty-year-old
subaltern had been decorated for gallantry in the main street of
Hulluch village on 24 September 1915. The Prime Minister was

---

* In answer to cross-examination: 'I put it to you that Lord Astor denies having
had sexual intercourse.'

† See pp. 225–30 above.

certainly not diffident about concealing his contempt for erstwhile colleagues. Selwyn Lloyd was no more than 'a little country notary'. And when Lord Kilmuir complained that he had been dismissed 'with less notice than you would give to a cook' Macmillan retorted that '. . . it is easier to find a Lord Chancellor than a good cook'.

Resentment this would cause, to be sure. But fear, also, both among the victims, and in the ranks of their various supporters and acolytes. To the Prime Minister's insouciance and cruelty there must be added a further characteristic – that element of ruthless calculation which is inseparable from effective leadership and can be detected at so many points in Macmillan's career. He had not quelled, as yet, the widespread feeling in the parliamentary ranks that he should be replaced. But who by? There now remained in the Cabinet not one single credible claimant to the succession.

TWENTY-SEVEN

'A Sad Blow for Me'

The end-of-term speech – The grandees are
unconvinced – A quiet autumn at Birch Grove – A
tricky meeting with the Chairman – Preparations for the
Party Conference – 'In the care of doctors' – A change
of mind at Sister Agnes's.

ON THURSDAY 25 JULY 1963, the catalpa trees in New Palace Yard were in full flower – always accepted as an indicator that the rising of the House is overdue. It was time for the last occasion of the 'term' – the leader's speech to the 1922 Committee.

'*Macmillan faces showdown*'. The headlines were unfriendly. Indeed, since the Profumo affair and regardless of the Denning conclusions (which were, of course, to mischievous editors most unwelcome) the press were uniformly hostile and critical. They had tormented him long enough. Now they wanted Macmillan dead. And certainly it is impossible to think of any Leader of the Conservative Party in this century whose departure, *expulsion*, from office the media have not first gleefully anticipated; then tried without scruple to bring about.

Macmillan, though, was a most difficult target. Not petulant and snappy, as became John Major or Stanley Baldwin. Not arrogant in terms of their own invincibility, like Chamberlain and Thatcher and Edward Heath. Not hysterical, as had been Eden, or indifferent as, at all times, seemed to be Douglas-Home. The nearest comparison would be with Winston Churchill's obstinacy in the fifties. But Macmillan had more cunning than Churchill – after half a century in public life – could be bothered to apply. At all times he professed his readiness – sometimes even (particularly when no obvious successor was in sight) – his 'irreversible decision' to stand down. When? Why, when it was the universal view of the party that he should. And until that view was clearly expressed Macmillan would 'put the country first'; rise above, in other words, petty internal conspiracy and scheming.

The Prime Minister had been greatly helped by the announcement, almost as he walked through the doors of Committee Room 14, where the '22 was meeting, of the Test Ban Treaty. When Macmillan rose to his feet the party was almost twenty points behind in the polls. He knew, though, that this would be self-correcting almost as he spoke.* The Prime Minister spoke of 'throwing *up* the sponge' (a characteristic affectation) and openly discussed that very subject which many leaders, before and since, have found painful:

> The transition from one leader to another has got to be smooth, and the Party must know its mind. I tell you, frankly, that I should be most reluctant to lay down my responsibilities until I was sure that the Party, under its new Leader, was going to be more certain, more strong, more united than it was before the change.

Macmillan then moved to his peroration. 'All this . . . [recovery in the ratings] . . . can be perfectly well achieved if, discarding the passions of these last few weeks, you will trust my intention to see that they are done. So much, then, for that. *I say again, my whole concern, whether I stay or go, will be to see that what is done and the method of doing it is in the best interests of the Party.*' Dutifully, and perhaps in some relief, MPs banged their desks to show appreciation. Macmillan knew, of course, that colleagues always acknowledge a 'performance', and this does not necessarily imply support either for policy or the individual propounding it. But the House would now disperse. After a brief jaunt to Scandinavia Macmillan retired to Birch Grove, writing in his diary: '. . . serenely

---

* A 'careful record' – most unusual at the '22' – of the speech shows it to have been both orthodox and highly accomplished. It is reproduced as Appendix III.

out of the . . . House of Commons and all the rest, thinking about my own future . . . I can do this quietly for the next few days here, and then during my fortnight's holiday in Yorkshire. I shall come south at the end of August.'[1]

If Macmillan really had felt 'serene', that is an indicator as much of his imperfect early-warning system as of his sang-froid. After the final '22 meeting there had been a private conclave between Morrison*, the Committee Chairman, and two other heavy-weights. Sir Harry Legge-Bourke and the Vice-Chairman, Charles Mott-Radclyffe, both told Morrison – citing a 'substantial' body of opinion on the executive council – that there was a 'feeling' inclined to the view that the Prime Minister, in spite of his effective performance at the end-of-term meeting, should go very soon. Colleagues were slow to articulate this because they could not agree on the person by whom Macmillan should be replaced.†

A sample poll conducted by Harry Boyne, chief political cor-respondent of the *Daily Telegraph*, had the previous month con-firmed a majority as being of the view that Macmillan should stand down. This mood had to some extent been superseded by events. In any case only fifty would answer questions of detail. But Boyne had then projected these figures across the entire parliamentary party to come up with some figures (which the paper published) that were both mischievous and misleading. Clear favourite appeared to be Maudling, with 147 votes. Next Hailsham, with 56. Followed by Heath, 42; Butler, 28; Powell, 21. Bottom of the list were Macleod and Home, with 7 each. These figures were not at all to the liking of the grandees. Both men told Morrison that their preference (which Morrison himself shared, though for different reasons) was for Home. Morrison undertook to approach Home, which he did promptly. The discussion was evidently so detailed as to extract from Home an undertaking that he would see his doctor in order to get a clean bill of health. Morrison then set off for Islay, the family home in Scotland,

---

* John Morrison, father of Sir Peter Morrison, MP.
† Conversations between the author and Sir Peter Morrison.

having invited to join him there immediately a key figure who
needed squaring: the respected former Chief Whip Edward
Heath.[2] Heath was a bachelor. He did not socialise. For his summer
holiday he preferred to go to Bayreuth and listen to Wagner. But
he was the strongest contender among the 'new' generation. If,
should a vacancy occur, Heath made no move, then neither could
Maudling or Macleod. Before they put things in train the Douglas-
Home camp needed to be sure of Heath's support, offering that
often-used but unenforceable assurance – that his time would
come; but not yet. And so, in the unfamiliar ambience of rock,
heather, peatwater and whisky, Heath was first confided in, then
enlisted.

The Prime Minister was by now back at Birch Grove. Just as
he had predicted, the polls did go into reverse, and on his return
the deficit had shrunk to an entirely manageable six points. But
now a most unwelcome document lay in the Prime Minister's
'urgent' box. It was a memorandum from the Chairman of the
Party.

> The Chief Whip *and*★ the Chairman of the 1922 Committee will
> I am sure advise you that the Parliamentary Party wish for a change
> before the next election ... I am ... doubtful if it is possible to
> delay a decision over the leadership until after the Christmas recess
> without doing irreparable harm to the Party.[3]

Even after discounting the careless hyperbole in Oliver Poole's
letter – '*irreparable harm* ...' – this was a setback. Nor was it
alleviated by the somewhat funereal deportment of Rab Butler
who turned up uninvited at Birch Grove, whither Macmillan had
almost immediately returned. Macmillan did not like Butler –
although Butler himself seems to have been unaware of this. In
his diary Macmillan noted that he '... was rather careful *not* to
give him any idea ... [of what was going through his mind]'.[4] But
after Butler had left, Macmillan noted that his principal (apparent)
rival 'is 60. He likes politics. He doesn't want to go into business,

---

★ AC's italics.

for he has enough money.' After some further thought Macmillan decided to raise the stakes. He would announce his intention to resign. Not immediately, but *sine die*.★ Such an arrangement would be virtually unworkable. People would see this, and a clamour would arise for the Prime Minister to remain fully in charge.

Macmillan even went so far as to tell the Queen, at his weekly audience on 20 September, drawing of course the intended reaction: '– she was very distressed'. That week Denning finally published his report on the Profumo affair. The Prime Minister was cleared, both of complicity and negligence. And the polls continued to improve. The press, though, feeling their quarry about to elude them, intensified their hostility. In a couple of weeks it would be the time of the Party Conference: lions, gladiators, and blood in the arena sawdust. Lobby correspondents were instructed to trawl endlessly across the opinions of back-benchers and local chairmen in search of a thumbs-down majority. Nor would editors print letters of support from the public, although to Macmillan's delight they had begun to arrive in Downing Street. On Saturday 5 October Christopher Soames, just back from his own holiday, burst into Number 10 and said the whole thing hardly mattered as Wilson was almost certain to win the election, regardless.[5]

On Sunday 6 October Macmillan was back at Birch Grove. The company, and the opinions, were more congenial. First his son, Maurice; then his son-in-law, Julian Amery. At dinner, Alec Douglas-Home. On each of them the Prime Minister tried out his new, developed, theme: 'I feel somehow that the tide is turning, that people as a whole will support me . . . I *hate* the feeling that I shall be letting down all those loyal people, from the highest to the lowest, if I give up.' Maurice and Julian agreed. The problem of the speech to Conference on Saturday was to be solved by the Prime Minister delivering first his *tour d'horizon* from a carefully prepared text. Then moving on to an emotional extempore passage setting out his beliefs and hopes for the future, delegating, it might appear, to the body of the hall the decision as to whether he

★ Without setting a fixed date.

should go or stay. It was to be a personal statement in the form of an interrogative – but one clearly intended to elicit the answer 'yes'.

Douglas-Home was perhaps a little less enthusiastic about this device. He talked mainly about the international scene, the prospects for détente, for extending the Test Ban Treaty. (All of which conversation will have played its part in confirming Macmillan's resolve to keep hold of the reins.) Both men agreed, though, that 'Plan A' – Macmillan announcing his intention to retire early in the New Year – was unworkable. 'I am to be PM under (self-imposed) sentence of death. Would not the whole situation disintegrate?'[6]

The atmosphere seemed to be improving. But that night Macmillan again slept badly. Recurrently, phrases from the Conference speech flitted across his consciousness. He was sixty-nine and experiencing, more acutely than in previous months, what in medical parlance is termed 'discomfort'.

Monday was spent in further meetings. Macmillan's car arrived at Number 10 around midday. There were two reporters outside, only one cameraman. Nothing newsworthy appeared immediately to be in prospect. Tim Bligh told the Prime Minister that over the weekend the Cabinet had been 'rallying'. The Chief Whip came in, and said that his office would 'do battle', and the Lord Chancellor was also supportive. Only a tricky passage with the Chairman of the Party spoiled the harmony. In spite of Macmillan – any pretended indecision now having been firmly cast aside – setting out the arguments against standing down in a manner that did not invite compromise:

1) I should seem to be 'deserting' and this would especially affect the 'marginal' seats.
2) I would seem to have yielded to a group of malcontents, who are swayed either by personal or purely reactionary sentiment.
3) I should leave the Party in complete disarray . . .[7]

Familiar, not to say trite, as are these claims coming from the mouth of a leader under pressure to 'make way', they none the less – or so Macmillan has recorded in his diary – had the effect of moving the Chairman to tears. Although this may have been due as much to the developing awkwardness of his task as to any sense of personal grief. Poole recovered his demeanour quickly; then drew from his own armoury of cliché to signal dissent: '... think it my duty ... as Chairman, but still more as a personal friend ... very great affection ... must warn against this course'.

Other than reminding Macmillan of Poole's 'unreliability' this made little difference to his resolve. He spent the evening seeing other ministerial colleagues on whom, for various reasons, he felt he could count, so as to square them in advance of the Cabinet meeting next day. Macmillan was particularly cheered by a personal note from his brother-in-law James Stuart, a former Chief Whip and a person still highly respected in the parliamentary party. 'There is no doubt in my mind that your position is immensely stronger than it was in mid-July. Whether you want to go or not, there is now no serious rival to you as leader who is visible!' So the discussions went well. All that blighted the evening was the Prime Minister's need frequently to interrupt and retire to the lavatory where he was finding it painful, and increasingly difficult, to urinate.

None the less, as his biographer notes, 'Macmillan went to bed that night exhausted, but immensely relieved at having "finally determined to inform the Cabinet that I had now decided to stay on and fight the General Election and to ask for the full support of my colleagues" '.[8]

Fate now took a hand. At three o'clock in the morning the Prime Minister was afflicted by excruciating pain. Spasms shook his body, but he could pass no water at all. Macmillan's own doctor, Sir John Richardson, was on holiday in the Lake District. The locum, a Dr King-Lewis, came round and administered a catheter, returned at 8 a.m. and repeated the treatment. Dr King-Lewis's instant prognosis was gloomy. He arranged for the leading specialist to attend at Number 10 and subject the Prime Minister to a full examination immediately after that morning's Cabinet.

Feeling (and looking) dreadful Macmillan sat at the Cabinet table sipping from a glass that contained a 'milky solution' and speaking in a very low voice. But as the business on the agenda rolled past the Prime Minister began to think his condition improving. He stuck to the plan agreed with key participants the evening before. And, at the halfway stage, when most colleagues, booked on the lunchtime train to Blackpool, would be looking at their watches, asked officials to leave the room. Macmillan expressed his wish to fight the next election, then, 'since there can be no free discussion in my presence', himself withdrew accepting, on the way out, a valium pill from Rab Butler. Most of the Cabinet were fidgety. Just as Macmillan had foreseen they were, many of them, expected on the Conference platform that evening. Still fresh in their minds was the peremptory way in which the Prime Minister had recently punished dissent. 'Discussion' was a formality, with only Enoch Powell expressing doubt, and the meeting adjourned, leaving some business unfinished. Macmillan believed himself to have surmounted the major hurdle. Now came Badenoch's examination. The surgeon found it difficult to tell how serious was the Prime Minister's condition and, in particular, whether malignant or benign. It was agreed that the three doctors should confer among themselves just as soon as Sir John Richardson, at that moment driving down from Windermere, arrived at Number 10.

One last ordeal remained. A staff party, to celebrate the return of the Prime Minister's office from Admiralty House to the redecorated Downing Street. Rab Butler, who had not gone to Blackpool, also attended and recalls Macmillan telling him that the doctors were going to 'patch him up' so as to make the keynote speech on Saturday.[9] To his press secretary Macmillan said that he was 'feeling much better', that the doctors (now assembling on the ground floor) would be able to 'get him through Blackpool', and the two men began to draft the text of a pre-emptive statement. But they were interrupted by Tim Bligh who said that the doctors (Sir John had arrived) wanted to re-examine Macmillan in his bedroom. Fifteen minutes later the medical men imparted their

joint verdict. The Prime Minister was to be operated on immediately. He was booked into Sister Agnes's at nine o'clock.

The drama of Sir John's appearance and the doctor's announcement was matched, *upstaged* indeed, by the Prime Minister. After
his examination Macmillan had put on a set of pale blue pyjamas,
and his old brown cardigan. Over this he wore a dressing gown
with dark red and blue silk brigade facings. To the small group
urgently called into the study he declared, 'I am finished. Perhaps
I shall die.' Turning to his press secretary the Prime Minister said,
'You can say that it is quite clear that I shall be unable to fight the
election.' Harold Evans claims that he then asked, 'Do you *really*
want me to say this?' 'Yes' came the reply.[10] So a new draft
statement was put in hand.

But within an hour or so of coming round from the anaesthetic
in Sister Agnes's Macmillan was told the good, but at the same time
extremely frustrating, news. His prostatic inflammation turned out
to be benign. When the Queen came to receive his resignation
Macmillan was wearing a white silk shirt, though made more
casual by the familiar brown cardigan.

> The Queen said, very kindly, 'What are you going to do?' And I
> said, 'Well, I am afraid I can't go on.' And she was very upset...

Macmillan then, like a conjuror, produced from under the bed-
clothes his prepared letter of resignation and 'advice', which he
read out to the Sovereign. Send for Alec.

The Queen agreed with his recommendation that 'Lord Home
was the most likely choice to gain public support', and undertook,
as Macmillan requested, that his memorandum be placed in the
Royal Archive. She handed the large, white, cartridge-paper envelope to her secretary, Sir Michael Adeane, giving him, short and
plump as he was, the appearance, Macmillan whimsically observed,
of the Tenniel 'Frog Footman'.[11]

The official biography of Harold Macmillan barely addresses its
subject's curious, and abrupt, change of preference in the second
week of October 1963. Originally, as all accounts agree, when
asked his opinion Macmillan had said, 'If you want to win the

election, it has to be Quintin.'* Some versions have the advice
more crudely expressed: '... *hold your nose and vote for Quintin*'.
What made him, in Nigel Birch's phrase, 'swap peers in midstream'? The received version, as with every case when Macmillan
betrayed or assassinated those around him, has the decision being
made reluctantly, and with deep regret. Macmillan, or so his
advocates claim, saw in Hailsham something of his own iconoclasm
during the 1920s, and felt a deep affection. Then suddenly decided
that 'there was a fatal excess of boyishness'.[12]

Now it must be remembered that there can be few more
exhilarating experiences for the middle-aged or elderly than being
told that you have not, after all, got cancer. Macmillan was sitting
up in bed at Sister Agnes's, feeling perfectly all right, and sipping
Glen Morangie whisky and water while colleagues, friends and
distinguished journalists arrived to pay their respects and seek his
general advice. (Also, without doubt, to see for themselves his
condition and potential for recovery.) Yes, he had stood down and
there was no way back – at the moment. But if the party chose
Hailsham, Hailsham would lead it for ever. If Home ... who
could say? And if, particularly, there was a row, even an immediate
row on Home's accession, to whom would it be most congenial
to turn?

This remains the conundrum, the mystery which surrounds
that abrupt change of preference. What Macmillan will not have
realised, any more than did the others holding it, is the extent to
which this preference was so widely shared. And always for the
same reason. Home was seen as a respectable 'caretaker' while the
various groupings around alternative personalities could make
their own preparations.

Macmillan kept his true motivation to himself, and to the grave.

Not the Queen, nor his diary, nor even his habitual confidante
Ava (Lady) Anderson. Although years later he was to write to her
of his disappointment at Douglas-Home's performance – 'he
could not impress himself on Parliament or people enough. He

---

* Quintin Hogg, Viscount Hailsham.

was an Edward Grey, not an Asquith.' And privately, Macmillan's judgement was even harsher – 'Home didn't have enough fire in his belly – he wouldn't say "Bugger Off".' All of which, an objective spectator might reflect, was, or should have been, known to a Prime Minister who had worked so closely with his Foreign Secretary for so long.[13]

Macmillan did soon, though, realise that he had miscalculated (if calculation it had been):

> That illness was a sad blow for me. Without being conceited, it
> was a catastrophe for the Party.

TWENTY-EIGHT

The Short Orthodox Premiership
of Sir Alec Douglas-Home

Jockeying and resentment – Quintin Hogg is cross – Sir Alec is diffident – Powell and Macleod – Heath at the Department of Industry – A general election – William Rees-Mogg pronounces – Rules to govern the election of a leader.

As SOON AS it was plain that Macmillan finally had stood down all pretence of personal loyalty was jettisoned. Something of a free-for-all developed. Macleod was lunching at the Mirabelle, with Maudling and his wife, and the subject of the succession was uppermost in their conversation. Then the first rumours reached their table that the 'circle' was, if not sponsoring then at least proposing, Douglas-Home. Macleod was most indignant. It was derisory. The chances of there being any truth in it were minimal. Why? Because, Macleod told a journalist who 'doorstepped' him as the party left the restaurant, 'it simply is not possible'. Maudling, who knew himself to be one generation distant from the immediate contest, and whose preference extended to the individual in whom he might best repose hopes of patronage, was more circumspect.

Hailsham, on the other hand, was very angry. He telephoned to Carlton Gardens, where Home's 'core' support was in session. The call was taken by Selwyn Lloyd, Douglas-Home being also in the room and within earshot.

> If Alec takes the job it will be a disaster. You realise that I will have to denounce him publicly?[1]

Almost immediately calls came in from Macleod and Powell.

Macleod expressed, or at least pretended to, incredulity. Powell was grave.

Home, Lloyd and Martin Redmayne (the Chief Whip was also in attendance at Carlton Gardens) talked the situation through. Of the three protesters, Hailsham was clearly the most dangerous and Selwyn Lloyd was instructed to ring him back: 'Quintin, I must honestly say that if you make a fuss it will simply look like sour grapes.' Hailsham back-pedalled a little, but Home remained anxious. To Lord Dilhorne, who had now turned up, Home was plaintive:

> Well, I was quite prepared to come forward as the candidate to unify the Party, accepted by everyone; but if it is said that my coming forward would split the Party, that is a different proposition.[2]

Whether Dilhorne knew, or not, that Macmillan had at one point identified him as a possible 'longstop' in case Home's candidacy fell apart, the advice he gave was to 'pay no attention'. In common with many others in the party, or at least in the inner circle, Dilhorne will have felt that Douglas-Home's tenure was unlikely to last very long; but it was important now to maintain continuity, keep out the 'undesirables' and prepare the ground for a more durable candidate later on.

The immediate question for Douglas-Home, as he set about forming his government, was to what extent the parliamentary party had been upset by his 'emergence' and how best to placate its feelings. To reduce the potency, whether by isolation or purchase, of those various individuals who had expressed their disapproval.

Foremost among these was the Party Chairman, Iain Macleod. Macleod refused to serve; and came up with a number of objections to Douglas-Home's appointment, some of which – those derived from a feeling of social inferiority – he publicised assiduously.

Enoch Powell, at that time a figure who commanded within the party considerable respect for his intellectual powers and not a little support based on the calculation that he was 'a man to watch', was more circumspect – or, at all events, more cerebral. Powell argued that it was an affront to the House of Commons that they should have a peer placed over them; and that it was a slight against the decorum of the House of Lords that a bill could be enacted causing one of their number to revert to the status of commoner. (This objection, conveniently, applied also to a more directly personal antagonist of Powell's, Quintin Hogg.) Macleod, in contrast, was arguing that the whole contest had been stage-managed by a group of Old Etonians; that 'the Tory Party, for the first time since Bonar Law, is being led from the Right of Centre'.

Their first target was Rab Butler. If Rab would join with them in refusing to serve, Home would have to stand aside. The pair sought Butler out, and in a considerably agitated state tried to persuade him. They would, of course, themselves endorse his candidature and announce their readiness to enter his Cabinet. Melodramatically, Powell spoke afterwards of handing him the pistol. But Rab declined to pull the trigger. For Butler this was his last chance; and certainly if he had declined a post the party would have to choose someone other than Home. But would it be Butler? Much of the fight had gone out of Rab. Twice he had been outmanoeuvred by Macmillan. His followers in the party were fewer in number than they had been in 1957. The outcome was uncertain. Butler did not want to be humiliated twice and, in any case, there were notional ties of loyalty – just as there were in 1995 when Michael Heseltine would also shy away from a second challenge. Macleod was furious. He would talk to anyone who listened – journalists, society hostesses, colleagues in the smoking room. As his friend Nigel Fisher was to observe, '*Having first cooked his goose he now is stuffing it with sour grapes.*' But the effect of this chatter was damaging to Douglas-Home, at least among those classes who chatter. Mr Richard Ingrams, then editor of *Private Eye*, referred to Home as 'this half-witted Earl who looked and behaved like something out of P. G. Wodehouse'. Mr Bernard Levin, who at that time made a lot of appearances on television, described the Prime Minister, setting his insult in no particular context of performance, as a 'cretin'. In fact his beautiful manners, the attentive technique of a far from negligible mind, and a particular skill in 'defusing' confrontation quite quickly abated the class resentment that greeted Douglas-Home's accession.

One major stumbling block, though, lay in his path. In the closing months of the Macmillan administration Edward Heath had been a junior minister at the Foreign Office. He and his officials had, most of them, their tails between their legs following de Gaulle's brutal rejection of the United Kingdom's application to join the EEC. Much of their time was consumed 'building bridges', or trying to, with their counterparts at the Quai d'Orsay, and other chancelleries, with an eye to reopening Britain's application.

How was this to proceed? Heath was already a figure of considerable importance in the Conservative Party, where MPs and journalists are from habit more concerned with 'buying forward' than contemporary performance. Next time round, it was generally (and, for once, correctly) assumed, the contest would be between Heath and Maudling. Their joint status as Duumvirate-in-Waiting would naturally have demanded that one be at the Treasury, the other at the Foreign Office. The two principal Departments of State have boundaries of responsibility allowing them to live in tranquillity one with another. Each of the two claimants had in any case to vie with the other in demonstrations of loyalty. Until the tide of opinion turned, that is. That was to Home's advantage at the outset of his premiership. Home's own preference for the succession is unknown. And he was too honourable as well as too discreet to manoeuvre or conspire, as Macmillan would have done, to vary the balance between them.

But certainly Home felt strong enough to ignore Heath's claim to the Foreign Office. Instead, he put Heath in charge of the new, enlarged Department of Industry. Its responsibilities included 'Regional Development' and all those formerly pertaining to the Board of Trade. And lying there, somewhat dog-eared and battered but very much, still, apple of the eye of departmental officials who relished the notion of dominating the new legislative programme with a 'lead' item, was a draft Bill. Its purpose was to abolish Retail Price Maintenance (RPM). And its effect, for a distracting and contentious period of many months, to revive, like some dormant malarial infection within the Tory Party, ancient divisions between free-traders and protectionists.

Many Conservative MPs were highly alarmed. This was going to be the end of the 'corner shop'. Their mailbag became heavy, and copiously flavoured with that hackneyed, but always unsettling, opening sentence – 'I have voted Conservative all my life, but never again'. Twice Heath was summoned to the 1922 Committee, where members were treated to a foretaste of the medicine that would be their lot in the seventies. Heath told his colleagues that –

> This is a package deal dealing with monopolies, restrictive practices and mergers as well. In an expanding economy we have to foster competition and help reduce prices wherever possible.[3]

The meeting on 16 January 1964 was the longest in the Committee's history. The secretary recorded that 'Members appeared almost equally divided on the merits of what was proposed'. Some remained apprehensive and found Heath's personality to be irritating. Others thought him 'dynamic'. But back-bench rebellions affected every stage of the Bill's passage and soon critical resolutions from the constituencies began to pile up ahead of the Party Conference.

Meanwhile Reginald Maudling at the Treasury was having problems with his officials – at a very senior level. The concept of the 'Dash for Growth', always unsettling with its undertone of urgency, was becoming increasingly discredited. Now it was being referred to as the 'Maudling Experiment'. The very title implied a distancing from Treasury, or even government, policy. In reality, as Edmund Dell has observed, 'It was not, of course, an 'experiment'. The best that could be said of it was that it was a hallucination.'[4] In the hostile but all too familiar terrain of trade balances and exchange reserves, fearsome monsters were assembling. Maudling advised Home, within days of his assuming the premiership, that he should 'go for' (*dash* for?) an election as soon as practicable. Home rejected the advice. Understandably the Prime Minister took the view that as his Chancellor had made all those predictions of benign consequence they should be allowed as much time as possible to 'work through'.[5]

In spite of having to raise the bank rate in February Maudling told the House of Commons in his presentation of the first, and only, Budget of the Douglas-Home administration, on 14 April 1964, that 'The economy has developed in the last twelve months much as I [then] anticipated'.[6] But while the Chancellor tried to dampen anxiety concerning figures which were available for all to see, claiming that 'provided it – the trade deficit – is only temporary this should give rise neither to alarm nor dismay', he went on to remind the House of the country's 'very large first and second line reserves, and *other borrowing facilities*'.* It was plain that the fair weather, on which the 'experiment' depended, was coming to an end.

The Governor of the Bank of England, Lord Cromer, had already and, in terms of Whitehall convention not entirely correctly, been privately to see the Prime Minister to register his concern. Now he felt obliged to minute the Chancellor directly and personally:

> There are some who argue that it is right and proper for a great industrial power to borrow abroad in order to finance the stock-building phase of the economic cycle. I do not subscribe to this view. As a matter of hard fact, we have no automatic access to the resources or savings of other countries. More important still, the tacit acceptance of dependence on overseas creditors must undermine the political influence that we could exercise in world affairs.[7]

Had the Conservatives won the general election in October 1964 Maudling's position would have been very strong. While Heath would have been remembered by many colleagues for his stubbornness over RPM and as having alienated 'our own people'. But because the election was lost, and so narrowly, the roles were

* AC's italics.

reversed. It was Maudling who had taken unnecessary risks; Heath who had appeared 'steady'. When Home re-formed his team as a Shadow Cabinet the fight had already gone out of Maudling. He was short of money, and wanted to shore up his earnings with sinecures in the City of London. He declined the position of Shadow Chancellor, preferring responsibility for foreign affairs where, in fact, Home's encyclopaedic knowledge and diplomatic reputation meant that Maudling had very little to do. Heath shadowed the Treasury, and made something of a name for himself, especially with the 'new intake', in opposing Callaghan's 1965 budget. (Which makes it all the more surprising that he should have allowed Margaret Thatcher to use exactly the same spring-board for her own challenge, against him, ten years later.)

The campaign itself had been rough, and unexpectedly so. On one occasion Home and his entourage had to escape through the ground-floor windows of a drill hall. Partly this was founded (as it would be in 1997) on impatience with the Tories 'hanging on' to office until the last moment. Wilson, in his prime, was also at his most unpleasant. He gloated and sneered and made much of the difference between himself and Home in terms of age and social origin. Home was dignified. Personally he campaigned on the ground of an essential need to keep Britain's independent deterrent. 'I cannot believe,' Home told a television interviewer quite late in the campaign when the prognosis was not good, 'that the British people would ever allow the final decision regarding their defence to be taken by a foreign power, however friendly ...' Wilson, whenever he got the opportunity, referred to the '*so-called* independent, *so-called* deterrent.' At this point in his career Wilson was still contriving to straddle both the unilateralist and the 'responsible' camps.

W. F. Deedes, then a Deputy Chairman (of the party), rec-ommended that 'The more I study Harold Wilson's form, the more I favour contrast. It suits their book to have a gladiatorial contest. It does not suit ours. The Prime Minister's character is in an entirely different mould.'[8] The media were all too ready to oblige. Deliberately, television producers arranged for their technicians to 'light' Home so that he looked gaunt and skull-like at interviews. His courteous and considerative replies to hectoring interrogation made him seem unassertive. And the impression was reinforced nightly by footage of the Prime Minister being heckled when on the hustings. Once, at Birmingham, being compelled even to close down a meeting altogether. For all those old-fashioned people who preferred good manners to the raucous bullying of the mob this was painful; and in the privacy of the polling booth they might cast their vote accordingly. To their number would be added many who felt themselves to be better off, who were benefiting from the 'dash for growth'. But the tide of modernist inevitability was running strongly. The Tories were jaded; they had been in office for thirteen years; their leader was 'old-fashioned'. Labour were going to win.

Before the last returning officer had stumblingly read out the number of votes cast for each candidate the Conservative Party was deep in speculation. How long, now, can Alec last? The result had been close. The overall Labour majority was four, one less than in 1950. But in that year Labour had been exhausted and on the retreat. Now they were confident. A new era beckoned. On the floor of the House of Commons would soon be found conditions where aggressiveness and speed of reaction were uppermost among the qualities which a leader was going to need.

In no time Mr* William Rees-Mogg, a distinguished commentator then at the height of his influence, came forward with an analogy at the same time ruthless and well-mannered:

> He has in fact played the sort of captain's innings one used to see in county cricket before the war. There were then in most counties good club players ... who were appointed captain because they were amateurs ... [they could] by dint of concentration and a well-coached forward prod survive to make twenty runs or so and see their side past the follow-on.[9]

But Rees-Mogg's title 'The Right Moment to Change', left no

* Later Lord.

room for delay. On 22 July Home, like his predecessor less than two years earlier, was due to give the end-of-term address to the 1922 Committee. Like Macmillan, only more so, he looked 'terribly drawn and ill'. Unlike Macmillan, who was determined to hold on, Home had made up his mind to go. Afterwards in the smoking room a small and embarrassed group gathered round to say how sorry they were, including, and unsurprisingly, those who had been conspiring to bring this about.[10]

Heath's machine, under the direction of his vigorous and plebeian young lieutenant Peter Walker, was ready to go. Had, indeed, been standing by since Heath had been summoned to Islay★ and identified by Morrison and Mott-Radclyffe for 'sponsorship' in 1963. Much was made of the fact that the party had been led, in succession, by three Old Etonians. To confront Wilson's image there had to be chosen not a contrast but, as far as was feasible, a replica.

Now it was time for the new rules to have an airing. They had been approved by the Committee in February – notwithstanding a minuted (but not attributed) complaint that it was 'unwise to give an exactly equal vote in choosing a potential Prime Minister [sic] to a senior Cabinet minister and to the newest recruit to the Parliamentary Party'.[11] Like all attempts to codify a practice that has hitherto depended on assumption and consent the text was not easy to understand. And lying there, at paragraph (6), was the special provision – difficult for the less numerate MP to fully absorb – that in the first round the winner's margin required *both* (the word was italicised in the text) an overall majority and 15 per cent more of the votes cast than any other candidate. Conceived as a device to prevent an incumbent being 'blitzed' it was, in the fullness of time, to bring about the demise of the longest-serving Conservative Prime Minister by a margin of two votes.

Few seem to have realised that a door had opened on to terrain every bit as difficult, uncertain and scattered with pitfalls as that within the old 'Magic Circle'. For the first time, and as on every

★ See pp. 391–2 above.

subsequent occasion, the 'choice' of the public (Maudling ran ahead of Heath by 44 to 28) would be ignored. But there was no way back. Henceforth the party would be committed to electing its leader. Comment on their proceedings, always abundant, would now have an extra edge, for Members of Parliament would find themselves drawn into assessing contenders on the basis of their approval rating in the newspapers. Nor would this any longer be confined principally to those periods of turbulence surrounding an actual or impending vacancy. The form, the arithmetic, the prospects, the timing – all would endlessly recur, whenever the party hit choppy water, and would take too much of its time and attention in the future.

TWENTY-NINE

Heath in Difficulties

Excellent prospects for the Prime Minister – The genesis
of 'Selsdon Man' – Colleagues and protégés – Enoch
Powell – The European vision – Interventionism
multiplies – The Ulstermen are alienated – The TUC
in the ascendant – The Oil Crisis – The miners are
recalcitrant – The election.

EDWARD HEATH ENTERED upon his premiership with a fresh
and amiable disposition (as it appeared), a very large popular vote of
support, and the implied promise of a comfortable 'honeymoon'.
Whether or not he knew that Lord Carrington and others had
been in discussion during the election campaign so as to be ready
with a contingency plan for defeat whose principal component
had been the replacement of Heath as leader – and the presumption
has to be that he did – this should hardly have come as a surprise
to a former Chief Whip. But now the very unexpectedness of his
victory made it unthinkable that any challenge to Heath's authority could come from colleagues.

Furthermore the Labour Party, discomfited and confused, had
been quick to fault-find within their own ranks. The search for
blame – never easy to keep separate from the advancement of
private ambition – was on. When Harold Wilson returned to
Transport House from the Palace there were some who desisted
from even the ragged courtesy cheer that spectators felt honour
bound to offer. 'That man misled us all and picked the wrong
debate. Why should I cheer him?' And in his diaries Tony Benn
has recounted how, already, '[at] the Home Policy Committee ...

where Jim Callaghan got himself dug in as chairman, his power base absolutely everywhere at the moment

The likelihood of a coherent and effective Opposit. House of Commons, at least for some months, was small. the period of the Heath Government, almost from its ᴄ set, remains the most frustrating and melancholy of all interludes in the Conservative Party's twentieth-century history. Many have tried their hand at explaining this. And the reasons proffered have ranged from personal – the sudden removal by death of Iain Macleod less than five weeks after the Government was formed; to doctrinaire – the precipitate abandonment of the Selsdon resolutions. But Conservative administrations should not depend for their effectiveness – still less for their durability – on the life expectancy of political figures in subordinate positions. Nor on a consistent adherence to the doctrinal imperative. The explanation is simpler. With the single exception of 'taking the country into Europe' Edward Heath did not really have the slightest idea of what he wanted to do. He made great play of 'modernisation'. The word is innocuous enough and indeed, evoking Harold Wilson's first appearance on the scene, does have a certain superficial political impact. There is no reason to suppose that Heath was not sincerely committed – to the concept. But Heath's objectives were couched in language so imprecise as to have the effect, as often it seemed, of misleading the author as well as the audience:

> As I go around the country, I find that people are asking for an entirely fresh approach to the country's problems. They are looking for constructive policies, *how* we do things rather than what needs to be done.[1]

With the intention of tightening things up a bit the Shadow Cabinet convened in January 1970 at Selsdon Park, a large hotel near Croydon. It had not been intended as a major news event. The meeting had been conceived as a private weekend at which the front-bench figures would congregate to take stock of policy, and receive instructions to sing in unison when the general election was declared. Whereas previous get-togethers at the Swinton

Conservative College in Yorkshire had involved the whole entourage, Maudling had seen to it that none of the junior spokesmen was invited. The minutiae of policy had already been largely decided. The point of the Selsdon meeting was to 'prioritise' strategy; to draw up a realistic framework for legislation within the first two years of the party's return to power.

But foolishly and opportunistically, when the press caught on to the existence of the meeting, Heath announced to them (on the advice of Macleod who thought it a vote-winner) that they had been discussing law and order – an issue which had in fact been scarcely touched upon. At once Harold Wilson, himself ignorant of what the discussions had really involved, uttered the jibe which was to give the meeting lasting fame:

> Selsdon Man is not just a lurch to the right, it is an atavistic desire
> to reverse the course of 25 years of social revolution. What they
> are planning is a wanton, calculated and deliberate return to greater
> inequality.[2]

Ironically, Wilson's comment did Heath much good: it gave the impression that (at last) there was a coherent substance to his message.[3] A momentum developed that implied the Tories were a government-in-waiting. This, naturally, was welcome to Heath; but it also excited hopes on the Right of the party that he would bring forward some of the policies which Wilson's caricature now associated with the Selsdon Park meeting.

The limits of Selsdon Man should have been clear from the resulting 1970 election manifesto, *A Better Tomorrow*. On examination, this emerged as largely a reprint of the 1966 version. Even membership of the EEC, although mentioned as a possibility, was counterbalanced by the warning that Britain would not join if the asking price was too high. This could hardly be seen as being controversial at the time. The passage on immigration was tightened up, with a commitment to end 'large-scale permanent' immigration. Again, a statement of this kind was to be expected from the party. Much depended on what was meant by those words. But despite the resulting legislation of 1971, immigration continued to increase exponentially during the period of Heath's tenure in Downing Street. On economic policy, the manifesto now committed the Conservatives to replacing Labour's incomes policy and – as with all previous Tory manifestos – opposing further industrial nationalisation. Yet, there was no commitment to any degree of privatisation, simply a bland undertaking 'to open up greater competition to make the state-directed industries more efficient'.

By 1970 the long process of concealed 'accommodation' with the trade unions – unbroken since Churchill's Coalition – the insidious creep of inflationary pressure, and certain chronic industrial weaknesses, of which over-manning was the most general, were omnipresent. The passage on incomes policy in the manifesto should have been the key section in the whole document. In fact it was deliberately misleading. Heath was opposed to Labour's compulsory controls; or judged that, at least, he should adopt that posture. But this was far from meaning that there was now no prospect of any future incomes policy. According to Peter Walker, it had been Macleod who had devised the smokescreen:

> we might have to have an incomes policy, but to explain in a manifesto that you might have to do it in certain circumstances was grey. Manifestos had to be black and white. Either we said we were going to have an incomes policy and it would be superb or that we were not going to have one at all. We should say that we were not going to have one and if in a few years we changed our minds we would have to explain there were special circumstances. As far as the manifesto was concerned it should not be blurred. No 'ifs' or 'buts'.[4]

Peter Walker was a favourite of Heath's. He enjoyed two advantages over most of his colleagues: a social origin that ensured Walker could not (as many senior Conservatives were still prone to do) 'look down on' his boss. Quite the reverse, in fact, as Heath had been a Scholar at Balliol while Walker enjoyed – or affected to enjoy – the joke that he had been educated at the 'University of Life'. Furthermore Walker was a young man of thirty-six years;

being of an age-group where he was cast as a 'future Prime Minister' rather than a potential rival. Even younger was another favourite, David Howell, then only thirty-two. Howell had the misfortune, in the mood of the time, to be an Etonian. But he was possessed of a quite remarkable degree of self-effacement. At the Conservative Political Centre he had written tracts in language that had appealed to Heath. Both men were recommended by political commentators as 'forward buys', highly likely to be sharing between them the posts of Chancellor and Prime Minister in the early eighties.

Heath asked Howell to help him with the introduction to the manifesto. But it still contained language all too redolent of Heath's own communicative style: Labour, the electorate were told, had ensured that 'the long-term objective has gone out of the window'. The Conservatives, though, would only endeavour to 'seek the best advice and listen carefully'. Already, Heath appeared to be asking the question 'Who governs Britain?' – and to be unsure of the answer – before he was even in charge himself. That this Conservative administration would be concerned with gathering advice was one of the manifesto pledges it did manage to carry out. In September 1972, the Heath Government put back in place a major plank of the corporate State by initiating the tripartite convocations between government, the trade unions and the CBI.

The 1970 manifesto further treated its readers to the expectation that, returned to office, the Conservatives would 'use up-to-date techniques for assessing the situation' – but in a process which 'should not rush into decisions'.

However:

> Once a decision is made, once a policy is established, the Prime Minister and his colleagues should have the courage to stick to it. Nothing has done Britain more harm in the world than the endless backing and filling which we have seen in recent years.

This mildly equivocal reference to 'a Prime Minister *and his colleagues*' was not accidental. Enoch Powell has claimed that Heath took exception to his attempts to formulate new ideas whilst in

Opposition.[5] His rigorous intellect showed up the vacuity of Heath's perception of politics, as a correspondence course in management studies. Powell was advocating a floating exchange rate and reduced international commitments. His natural patriotism and formidable acumen were a most dangerous combination in scrutinising the country's relations with the EEC. But Heath resented this intellectual challenge to the settled party consensus – a concept that underpinned his own control of the machine. It was inevitable that the two men should collide and the eventual cause of their parting – Powell's April 1968 'rivers of blood' speech – was a gift to Heath and his acolytes in that it provided the excuse for a public breach that had become inevitable. To the very end Heath feared Powell, and reciprocated his dislike. A *Financial Times* columnist wrote, 'One reason why constituency workers are besotted with Mr Enoch Powell is that he gives the strongest impression of any leading figure in the party of believing that there is more to politics than simply "getting the economy right".'[6]

The Tory case against the Heath administration has been often articulated. Heath's Government was 'wet', in that it failed to overturn the orthodoxy pursued by the previous six years of Labour rule. But it went further, building upon what Wilson had put in place. There was a very small amount of privatisation, the travel agents, Thomas Cook, and the denationalisation of some pubs in Carlisle. But other industries were nationalised, like the Upper Clyde Shipbuilders and Rolls-Royce. On balance, the Heath Government nationalised a larger share of economic activity than had its Labour predecessor. While Tories had criticised the growth in public spending during the Wilson years, over the winter of 1972–3 public spending was accelerated. This coincided with the use of the machinery of State on a level never intended for peacetime conditions. In three-and-a-half years, five states of emergency were declared under the 1920 Emergency Powers Act. Nor, in manpower terms, was the State's authority clipped: the result of the Heath Government was a net increase of 400,000 public-sector officials. Yet none of these drives towards Leviathan

succeeded in implanting the Government's will upon the course
of events. Some 23 million days were lost to strikes in 1972
alone, the highest figure since the General Strike, forty-six years
previously. No wonder otherwise patriotic men and women began
to look to 'Europe' to solve their problems. It was clear that their
own government could not.

On this subject the manifesto for the 1970 campaign had been
clear enough:

> Ministers and Members will listen to the views of their constituents
> and have in mind as is natural and legitimate, primarily the effect
> of entry upon the standard of living of the individual citizens
> whom they represent ... Obviously there is a price we would not
> be prepared to pay ...

(in what currency this 'price' was to be measured was not made
clear)

> ... our sole commitment is to negotiate; no more, no less

– and within ten days of the Conservatives being returned to office
a delegation was installed at Brussels and fresh negotiations were
opened.

At the time there were few indeed who could have predicted
either the degree of contention or the sheer tenacity of the subject
as an adverse influence on the morale, competence and electoral
appeal of the party. Enoch Powell, whose ruthless logic searched
out the small print in drafts and 'discussion papers'; Derek Walker-
Smith and Neil Marten, who responded to and exploited their
constituents' anxieties at least partially in the hope of raising their
own 'profile' and advancing their careers if a change of direction
occurred; Nicholas Ridley, whose objections were all part of
a wider discontent with Heath's economic policy and general
approach to government. These were individuals whose personal
eccentricity was familiar to, and discounted by, the broad mass of
their colleagues. In any case the issue was easier at that time, with
the Conservatives only eighteen months into their first admin-

istration since 1964, to see as divisible along party lines. Europe was open, prosperous and undoctrinaire. Socialist parties, even when they were briefly in power, seemed to shed their ideology and become practical – even 'Christian'. The 'Common Market' (as at that time it was still known) seemed to offer a benign makeweight to the possibility of a Marxist Labour Party ever again getting a free run at Britain. And Conservative Central Office came up with the notion, soon articulating it into a slogan which even at the time caused some uneasiness:

Conservatives – the Party of Europe

The extent to which the rediscovery of *satire* in the 1960s caused damage to the esteem in which the Conservative Party was held has already been discussed.★ *Private Eye*, house magazine of the movement, had rapidly evolved a parodic column entitled 'Heathco' where an unhappy managing director published messages of extreme bathos on the noticeboard in the works canteen. And, as so often happens, nature imitated art. Very soon Heath's pronouncements and exhortations (as exemplified above) would become indistinguishable from the texts of his own parody. And in his first Budget speech Anthony Barber, precipitately installed at the Treasury against (or so he was to claim) his own better judgement or, at least, preference, took his tone dutifully from Heath's instructions.

The Chancellor undertook to

> ... attempt to regulate the level of demand, making changes during the year as necessary in order that the economy should achieve its productive potential ...

Productive potential is a singularly inexact term. If it means anything it has to be an amalgam of industrial capacity (measured how? in square feet?) times size of labour force (with what offset for skills differential?) divided by liquidity available for investment (with

★ See pp. 402–3 above.

what distinction between reserves and borrowing? between funds from the private and the public sector?). The 'Treasury Model' was not yet sophisticated enough, nor its custodians possessed of the temerity, to subject this well-intentioned cliché to close scrutiny.

Furthermore, the concept of 'regulating demand' was already out with the spirit of Selsdon, and epitomised a peremptory withdrawal to the comforting foothills of Keynesian territory. All too soon the irresistible force of inflation would be in collision with the immovable object of rising unemployment. Of all periods in the party's history, that of the Heath administration offers surely the most painful example of ministers (and particularly the Chancellor) being aware, and showing in words their awareness, of dangers, while at the same time walking straight towards them. At first, though, a great impression of activity, intense if not transparently purposeful, was generated. Peter Walker, Keith Joseph and Margaret Thatcher were all entrusted with 'Policy Groups' where ideas (provided that they did not jar with the Leader's own broad inclination) might be churned around.

John Davies, whose short and unhappy tenure of office at the Department of Trade and Industry, ending with him being booed off the rostrum at the Party Conference and retiring from public life with a brain tumour brought on by 'stress', personified both Heath's perpetual hankering for administration by non-party (by which of course he always meant non-*Conservative* Party) figures, and the risks attendant on placing captains of industry in the political firing line.

The Chancellor of the Exchequer, Anthony Barber, was Heath's nominee and, to a far greater extent than any previous (or subsequent) incumbent except Selwyn Lloyd, his subordinate as well as his intellectual inferior. And if, notwithstanding, Treasury officials should demur from policy implications, they would be 'balanced' by the Department of Trade and Industry – now at its all-time zenith. And the Central Policy Review Staff could be expected to provide a rationale, and supporting papers, that would allow the Prime Minister to restrain colleagues who showed signs of independence or restlessness.

Heath was at this time, and indeed throughout his term as Prime Minister at least as far as machinery of government was concerned, 'in charge'. But of what? All too soon this structure – sensible, bureaucratic and utterly lacking in inspiration – was subject to challenge from the cruder political forces of opportunism and self-interest. This was not going to end well. The Government, the *Conservative* Government was still, more than fifty years after the passing of the Emergency Powers Act, promulgating bodies and endowing powers in the spirit of a measure which had been evolved and adapted to a wartime regime.

In addition to their misgivings over the shape and style of the Government a large number of MPs would express their unease (and with good reason) at what was happening in Ulster. On 28–9 March 1972 the Northern Ireland (Temporary Provisions) Bill was rushed through Parliament to take effect the following day. The Bill was in response to the strike and two-day protest organised by William Craig's 'Protestant Vanguard'. Thenceforth the Unionists were in Opposition and subjected to a series of humiliations and betrayals in the province itself. The following month William Whitelaw, the Secretary of State, began freeing internees. His call for the Army to keep a 'low profile' in Catholic areas led to their effective annexation by the IRA. The 'no-go' area was born.

On 2 July 1972 was delivered a further insult to the Unionists: Whitelaw, having always made clear that he would not talk to terrorists, had a 'secret' meeting with the IRA at Paul Channon's house in Chelsea to which the IRA were flown in an RAF aircraft. The IRA delegation, one of whose number was a young hothead named Martin McGuinness, demanded British withdrawal from Ulster, an All-Ireland referendum on Ulster's future sovereignty, and amnesty for 'political' prisoners. This was too much, even for Whitelaw, and the meeting ended as fiasco.

Whatever the long-term prospects for the North (and with hindsight we can understand how, as on every other occasion, there was found to be no escape from the culture of endemic violence) the effect of Heath's policy was to cut twelve votes out of the party's strength in the House of Commons. This was an impossibly risky thing to do, even with a good majority. And there were solid party reasons for objecting. Not only was the traditional head start at every general election being casually discarded, but the historic and visceral links between the complementary elements of the *Unionist* Party were placed in jeopardy. All too soon was this to render impossible a renewal of the Conservative mandate to govern.

By July of 1971 it had been thought possible to claim sufficient 'advance' in the European entry negotiations for a White Paper to be printed. This was accompanied by a glossy brochure published by the Stationery Office. That same evening Heath made a television broadcast and told the public that a great decision was 'at hand'.

Much of the preamble, and many of the reassurances scattered about the document, were reckless, if not deliberately misleading. As:

> When a government considers that vital national interests are involved, decisions are only made if all members agree.
>
> There is no question of Britain losing essential national sovereignty; what is proposed is a sharing and an enlargement of individual national sovereignties in the common interest.

Keen to exploit the initial flush of enthusiasm the Foreign Office strongly recommended that the terms be whipped through Parliament immediately, to get the subject (which was likely to become more rather than less contentious) 'out of the way' before the recess. In so doing that department was merely acting in conformity with its established tradition of Francophilia, and a direct line can be traced to the (grossly unconstitutional) 'Joint Citizenship' offer of June 1940.*

Significant, too – if only in relation to the many reassuring

---

* See p. 218 above.

disclaimers that he was himself to make from the despatch box
some twenty years later as Foreign Secretary – was the role of Mr
Douglas Hurd. From his intimate position in Heath's private
office, and with the fluency of one who had lately served as an
official in that very department, Hurd strongly endorsed their
advice.

And once again – this time more effectively than often had
happened in the past – or, indeed, would apply in the future – the
party was allowed a temporary reprieve, or at least a breathing
space in which to consider its opinion, by the intervention of the
Chief Whip. Francis Pym told Heath, and repeated his advice at
a full meeting of the Cabinet, that 'the ... [Parliamentary] ...
Party wouldn't stand for it'. Carrington, consulted in his role as
Chairman, said as much about the party in the country. Both
dissimulated as to the reasons why. Time was needed not so much
to persuade, as to 'get the case across'. Once all the facts were
known, surely, the arguments in favour would be irresistible and
much credit would accrue to the Government. Against his better
judgement Heath agreed. And so, in February of 1972, there took
place the Second Reading of the 'entry' Bill.

Much was said during this period, on both sides, that would
stalk the party until the millennium. Not least by a bumptious
newcomer, the Member for Rushcliffe, who was anxious to
ingratiate himself with the leadership.

> This new Europe ... will be a very great and important power
> grouping in the world. Economic and monetary union, political
> development, a common foreign policy, a defence policy, inter-
> national contacts – all this lies in the future of the Community.
> This is not just visionary politics or a dream world.[7]

The same man who, fifteen years later as Chancellor of the
Exchequer, would drive the Conservative Party to the very threshold of self-destruction.

The Werner Report's timetable did indeed provide for rapid
progress towards economic and monetary union. Much of the
text – which survived more or less intact for tabling at Maastricht

twenty years later – on developing common industrial, economic and 'social' policies was prepared for the projected Heads of Government meeting in Copenhagen in December 1973. As were recommendations for 'streamlining' (i.e., centralising) the decision-making process. In the debate not much reference was made to this by those speaking in favour. Of those against, few seem to have taken it seriously, and Enoch Powell, who did, was condemned for 'scaremongering'.

The last word, though, had already been uttered by Winston Churchill some twenty years before. Winding up the debate on the Schuman Plan he had warned against any derogation of 'the full rights of power of this House of Commons to judge the final result – *to judge as a whole and not as a party, or as supporters or opponents of a Government'*.

By the time the Bill was through the Commons this precept, and much else besides, had been overridden, or relegated, or concealed. And a huge roller of cast iron, at first very gradual in pace but, over decades, of steadily accruing mass, had started on its journey – with the blessing, albeit hesitant, of Conservative parliamentarians and activists.

On New Year's Day of 1973 Britain thus became a member of the European Economic Community. Foreseeing (rightly) that no one would either notice or bother much, Hurd and Central Office had set up a programme of public events to attract attention grouped under the broad, and somewhat hyperbolic, heading – *'Fanfare for Europe'*.

The programme went on for eleven days, although no real shape is detectable. Cookery demonstrations and tree-planting in the provinces; concerts and firework displays in the urban areas. A gala at Covent Garden attended by the Queen helped convey a message that those in favour were fashionable and 'civilised'; those against of (through no fault of their own) a lower level of culture. Inevitably, also, there were town-twinning ceremonies. And the Environment Department provided money for boroughs to erect notices at their boundaries so that approaching travellers could be informed of this new relationship.

But all too soon the hard realities of a creaking economy and an erratic industrial performance reasserted themselves. Wage claims continued to rise, as did unemployment. Hoping to stimulate investment, in March 1972, Barber announced in his Budget his intention to see output rise by ten per cent in two years. Whilst keeping the basic rate of income tax unchanged, a whole raft of tax concessions were introduced in order to create the necessary incentives. Coming at a time of growing global reflationary pressure, with soaring commodity prices, this initiative was particularly ill-timed. In the words of the economist Sir Alec Cairncross, the Conservative government

> had abandoned incomes policy; now it was abandoning the alternative to incomes policy – rising unemployment. Once it set about reducing unemployment as its first priority it had no option but to go back to incomes policy – and in unpropitious circumstances.[8]

During December, Barber's emergency Budget attempted to shut two stable doors after the horse in each had bolted. Hire-purchase controls (abolished in 1971) were restored and fiscal policy put into reverse. The minimum lending rate (as the bank rate had become since 1972) was increased to 13 per cent. It was plain that the economy was in serious trouble. The attempt to determine growth primarily through fiscal adjustments had seriously unbalanced the books. Reducing tax revenues and increasing public spending could hardly have any other result. State spending as a proportion of GDP had risen to almost 34 per cent under Macmillan. It had then soared during the Wilson administration to nearly 40 per cent before Roy Jenkins's measures had curtailed it back to 37.5 per cent by the time the Conservatives won the general election. Within three years the figure was back nudging 40 per cent. The Government was now borrowing heavily.

Against this background the Government found itself vulnerable to a steady advance of trade union confidence and ambition. Wilberforce. The Relativities Board. Stage Three. The 'Counter-Inflation Policy'. Each in their turn takes centre stage only to

Harold Macmillan on location, and in his prime. The jacket is perhaps fractionally too new looking but Macmillan has compensated by having the pocket flap 'casual'.

Alec Dunglass served as Neville Chamberlain's PPS throughout the
Appeasement period. At Munich Aerodrome in 1938, von Ribbentrop,
the German Foreign Secretary, bids Chamberlain farewell.

On succeeding Macmillan as Prime Minister in October 1963 Lord Home,
as he now was, disclaimed his peerage, took the title Sir Alec Douglas-Home
and his manner became more ingratiating.

The only woman in the cabinet. Margaret Thatcher enjoys a joke in June of 1970. Later she was to lose weight, while Heath put it on. Hailsham stayed the same.

At the 1975 Party Conference Margaret Thatcher photographs as a cross between Pamela Harriman and Eva Peron. But she has not yet won any General Elections, and Sir Richard Webster (left, pretending to clap), Director of Operations at the National Union, is suspending judgement.

Mrs Thatcher displays poise with a bunch of 'monkeys' at very close quarters.

Above Michael Heseltine had a very high opinion of himself indeed, and expected to be Prime Minister.

Right In John Major's final two years as Prime Minister, Heseltine was Deputy PM and First Secretary of State.

Opposite page

Above A propaganda postcard from Conservative Central Office. *The Daily Mirror* excelled in its commitment, but within the Party dissent soon became endemic.

Below The European Community Treaty of Accession has just been signed; but only Mr Geoffrey Rippon looks pleased.

Douglas Hurd, John Major and Jacques Delors at the 1992 Birmingham European Community summit. The month before, Britain had 'left' the ERM.

Michael Portillo lost a safe seat in 1997, and made a dignified speech accepting his fate. Had he survived he would have been strongly placed, and after Heseltine's heart attack a certainty, to lead the Conservative Party.

...?' – thus opening the way to supplementaries framed around his relationship with these two centres of power. No one, it seems, observed the paradox that the head of a democratically elected government should by implication stand constantly in deference to bodies that were both appointed, narrowly drawn and self-serving.

At the halfway stage of the Heath administration the whole body politic, like some middle-aged patient in chronic ill-health, was vulnerable to an unforeseen accident or shock. Only Lord Rothschild, from his 'think-tank' (to whose predictions, being pessimistic, scant regard was now paid), had forecast a steep and imminent rise in the price of crude oil, and stressed that provision urgently be contemplated for such an emergency.

The change occurred with a greater suddenness than the think-tank had predicted. The outbreak of the Arab–Israeli War led not only to a quadrupling of price by the producers' cartel but to an embargo on exports of oil to states, of whom Britain was the most vulnerable, who were thought to have been sympathetic to Israel. Instantly the Government's troubles went into 'fast forward'. What followed, as Dr Ramsden has summarised, '. . . was a re-run of the Government's relationship with the Unions . . . [so far] . . . but in more concentrated form: first, a ministerial intention to avoid a confrontation demonstrated by informal talks with union leaders; second, a serious misinterpretation of what the miners would do; third, a miscalculation of the consequences of standing firm against a coal strike; . . . finally a confused stance that was neither con-frontational nor conciliatory and which lost the benefits that could have arisen from either approach'.[9]

Soon the notion began to spread, in Cabinet as in the press, that the only way 'out' for the Government was to dissolve Parliament. A general election would bestow on them the mandate that they needed. This had worked in the past, had it not? But history does not repeat itself, only its patterns. Overlaying these interminable meetings, reconvening of discussions abruptly broken off, revised draft texts of interim communiqués, was an implacable question to which reference was seldom made. The Arabs had quadrupled the price of oil. They were aliens, ill-disposed and erratic in their behaviour. Yet the miners, British, isolationist indeed to the core, were being penalised. No advantage for them in all this.

Repeatedly the miners were exhorted to stick with Stage Three. But the price of energy, its proportion as a component of industrial costs, was altering for good. A permanent shift in the direction and volume of liquidity flows was boosting as well the profits of the oil companies and their share quotations. Coal, too, was a 'fossil fuel'. Surely, in a true *market* there should be benefits for those who had a monopoly of the extraction process? Yet with each turn of the screw Conservative appeals to the 'patriotism' of the miners, and reproaches for their evident lack of it, became more strident.

There was, of course, a school within the party deeply uneasy at what they saw happening ... Winston Churchill and Harold Macmillan had both in their different ways compensated for, and coped with, the reality of reduced domestic power by drawing on their sense of history and theatrical skills. But Heath's personality was entirely different. He saw himself as a composite of 'public servant', in the Whitehall sense, and fair-minded managing director. Did he in fact (as some have alleged) 'funk' an election? Or did he genuinely and high-mindedly strain himself to avoid what he saw as being needlessly divisive?

In the Prime Minister's last broadcast, announcing the start of the campaign, there was more than an overtone of 'Heathco':

> The issue before you is a simple one ... Do you want a strong Government which has clear authority for the future to take the decisions that will be needed? Do you want Parliament and the elected Government to continue to fight strenuously against inflation?

The extent to which the electorate would be inspired by this was far from certain. Why should they have to vote for a 'strong' government? – because they presently had a weak one? What was it that made the existing government's authority *un*clear? What 'decisions' were 'needed'? As set out by Heath this was hardly a 'simple' issue. The Prime Minister concluded his appeal in almost suppliant tones:

> This time the strife has got to stop. Only you can stop it. It's time for you to speak with your vote. It's time for your voice to be heard, the voice of the moderate and reasonable people of Britain ... 'We've had enough. There's a lot to be done. For heaven's sake let's get on with it.'[10]

Whatever 'moderate and reasonable people' were thinking – and it was far from clear why (or how) 'only they' could 'stop the strife' – the Conservative Party in the country saw the issue very clearly indeed. Worsted by the miners in 1972, they could now take revenge. Fortified by a fresh mandate, they could use the troops, cut off benefit from miners' families, smash – at last – the NUM, and use the opportunity to cut the Labour Party down to size. Their Leader's attitude was bewildering. And while most fell in, loyally, behind his 'above party politics' screen it soon became apparent that this was an uncovenanted gift to the Liberal Party. Liberal spokesmen offered a plague-on-both-their-houses approach that many neutral voters were to find congenial – if only as an excuse from making up their minds.

Moreover, with every move that he made Heath further clouded the issue which he had declaimed as being 'simple'. Practically his first announcement after the dissolution – the opening shot, in other words, of the election campaign – was an assurance that 'even now' the Government was willing to refer the miners' claim to the relativities panel of the Pay Board, and would accept its adjudication. This completely demolished the 'We've had enough ... For heaven's sake let's get on with it' plank in Heath's case. When taken in the context of the lifting of the emergency curfew on television and the general easing, whether by abuse or circumvention, of the three-day week the effect was to bring about a progressive fall in the political temperature just as the campaign got under way. People asked themselves, with some justification: 'What's all the fuss about?' To this day it remains unclear how

strongly, even when finally at the end of his tether, the Prime
Minister really wanted a general election.

Pressures in the Cabinet remained evenly balanced. At one
point Heath will have read in *The Times* that there was a 'move'
building up to replace him with William Whitelaw. But Whitelaw
did not want an election either. He, indeed, did not even favour
it when the NUM 'forced' the Government's hand. But at least
Whitelaw was clear what he *did* want. And nearly always the
Conservative Party, once it feels an uncertain hand on the tiller,
will look round for ways of conferring authority without necessarily questioning how a particular individual may be going to use
it.

In any case there is no evidence, once the decision had been
made (and unlike the plotting that took place during the 1970
election), of any move to displace Edward Heath. Because there
was a general assumption that the Government would win.

It remains curious, this assumption that Conservatives often
make – most spectacularly false in 1945 – that whatever the polls
may read they are understating 'real' support. Yet it was a view
shared, just as it had been in 1945, by many in the Labour Party
and certainly, right up until polling day, by the entire broadsheet
press.

On 20 February, before a large, though carefully controlled
crowd in Manchester Free Trade Hall, Heath made a speech which
his percipient biographer has described as the 'high point' of the
campaign.

> *We* have no single group to represent. We as a Conservative party
> and a Conservative Government represent all the people. We are
> the trades union for the pensioners, and for children. We are the
> union for the disabled, and for the sick. We are the union for those
> who live in slums or for those who want to buy homes.
>
> We are the union for the unemployed and the low paid. We are
> the union for those in poverty and for the hard pressed. We are
> the union of the nation as a whole. We cannot just say 'Give us
> the money and be hanged the rest'. We must balance all the

carefully conflicting claims and reach a just solution.[11]

This eloquent passage must rank as the last *cri de coeur* of the old paternalist Tory tradition. A direct, although not uniformly consistent, line runs back to Macleod, Baldwin, Disraeli. And indeed it should include Winston Churchill; although in Churchill's case it is more obviously rooted in the realities of Coalition, and the assignment of the majority of domestic portfolios to Socialist ministers.

Much of the argument was specious. But the claim that Conservatives should (and by definition would be best suited to) '. . . balance all the carefully conflicting claims and reach a just solution . . .' showed how deeply ingrained in politics had become the ethic of Sir Stafford Cripps. Here was a Conservative Prime Minister actually *fighting* an election on the plank of suspending the right to fix a bargain in a free market and substituting a statutory process of arbitration where the Government, or some body of government appointees, would adjudicate.

The fact that this process had already been tried repeatedly, and had failed, made its offer unconvincing in fact as well as in doctrine. Harold Wilson, on the other hand, was cunning enough to contrast the emptiness of Tory negotiating power with his own ability to 'get on with' the unions. He lost no time in delivering the assurance that Labour would immediately honour whatever recommendation the relativities panel came up with for the miners, and then exploited the leaked (and subsequently contested) allegation that in fact the figures which the National Coal Board had put before the Pay Board were – intentionally or not – misleading.

But while Wilson assumed geniality – a respected statesman in search of a compromise – his henchmen kept up the spirits of the Labour rank and file with intemperate hustings abuse. They, and their canvassers in the cities, portrayed the whole contest as a test of working-class loyalty. Denis Healey even compared Heath's 'treatment' of ordinary trade unionists as being akin to that of the South African Government and its own (black) miners.

Heath was aggrieved. The misrepresentation was cruel. It is

possible, even, that he might have risen above these charges and
persuaded the electorate of his 'moderate' credentials had it not
been for the continuous distraction offered by the genuine article,
most tranquilly on view at a television studio in Barnstaple. Here
Mr Jeremy Thorpe was declaiming, on a daily basis and with wit,
fluency and (towards his opponents) condescension, the virtues of
'Liberalism'. Within a week or so alleged distaste for the party
'slanging match' came to be recognised by activists on the doorstep
as a coded expression of intent to vote for the Liberal candidate.
Soon the Liberal Party was polling in all three agencies, at over 20
per cent. And these votes were being drawn from that very
'moderate majority' with which Heath was trying to identify;
depleting the apolitical reserve battalions of the Conservatives and
many of those who ranked, or pretended to rank, 'fairness' above
'firmness'.

The campaign dragged on, with little to enliven it and the
atmosphere of crisis gradually lifting. Events, such as they were,
seemed to pile up against the fortunes and reputation of the
Conservatives. The trade figures, published on 24 February, were
horrific. Recalling the impact of a (far slighter) adverse movement
in the 1970 campaign, the Central Office machine attempted to
derive advantage by citing the figures as evidence of a mounting
world economic crisis which made it essential that the Government should be given a 'vote of confidence' by the British
people. Heath was that evening making a speech in Bradford and
a passage was quickly inserted into the text in which the Prime
Minister claimed that:

> The trade figures merely confirm what I have said all along ...
> They emphasise the gravity of the situation ... We have got to get
> the problem right.

To this Roy Jenkins, echoing, perhaps unconsciously, Bevan's
devastating critique of Neville Chamberlain in August of 1939,*
retorted drily that '[Heath] ... presumably thinks a still worse

* See p. 173 above.

result would have given him a still stronger claim.'[12] The next day Campbell Adamson* played his part. Like the majority of big businessmen he fancied himself as a public figure. He was fond of seeing his name in print accompanied, where possible, by a photograph. And, preferably, in the news rather than in the 'business' section. Flattered by the attention he had been lately receiving, Adamson started to 'think aloud'. And, at a conference of the Industrial Society he was highly critical of the Industrial Relations Act. Deploying, probably deliberately, 'centrist' language Adamson said that 'we' (sic) must repeal the Act, so that 'we can get proper agreement on how to replace it . . . I [sic] have a feeling that the trade unions, faced with this sort of situation, would be quite ready to talk about it.'[13]

Never mind that Whitelaw would have agreed. Nor that this could have been a model text for a spokesman in that half-baked Coalition Government of All the Talents for which Heath increasingly hankered as a refuge both from his own 'Right' and from having to confront the Socialists head-on – it looked bad.

Equally disconcerting, though perhaps more predictable, was the behaviour of Mr Enoch Powell. On the day of the dissolution Powell announced that he would not be standing. This was a very considerable shock to his constituents and to his natural, and humble, supporters across the Black Country. It was also disconcerting for his followers (few in number) and sympathisers (more numerous) in the parliamentary party. Because, were Heath to be defeated, Powell would have been a powerful candidate to succeed him.

> I personally cannot ask electors to vote for policies which are directly opposite to those we all stood for in 1970 and which I have myself consistently condemned as being inherently impractical and bound to create the very difficulties in which the nation now finds itself.[14]

At first it was not wholly clear whether the 'policies' to which

* Secretary-General of the CBI.

Powell was objecting were those affecting our relations with Europe, or the trade unions, or both.

It was put about by ill-wishers that Powell's description of the election as 'essentially fraudulent' was simply a phrase concealing his chagrin at the apparently inevitable victory of his personal adversary, and his own relegation to the periphery of national politics. But in the last week of the campaign it became clear that Powell was up to something more serious. The 'Get Britain Out' movement was running a series of public meetings and at their last two Powell was the principal speaker. Distributing widely his text in advance, Powell was seen to be telling his audience that neither the miners nor inflation were topics that compared with the scale and menace of our commitment to the EEC. And quite plainly he conveyed to them that the Labour Party was likely to prove a more reliable guardian of their historic liberties as British citizens. Two days before polling Powell, whom the media were now watching as intently as any of the party leaders, announced that he had already delivered his postal vote – for Labour.

How much influence did this have on the outcome? Powell had made his initial impact, certainly, by speaking in the sixties of racial problems in language which no one else dared to use. But his reputation did not depend solely on this. His beautiful English, ascetic manner and lifestyle, commanded respect. And the sheer intensity of his conviction was in such marked contrast to the equivocations of Wilson and Heath, or the frivolousness of Jeremy Thorpe.

Allowance must always be made for this: The extent to which respondents to an opinion pollster actually reflect their intention in the polling booth is highly subjective. NOP found that the day after Powell's speech in Birmingham on 24 February Labour had a lead of two points locally – while a week before the Tories had been, in the same NOP poll, thirteen points ahead. And in their national poll NOP found that 6 per cent of all respondents declared that Powell's speeches had made them 'more likely' to vote Labour. In a very close result (which of course no one at that time anticipated) these figures, even if only fractionally projected, would be of critical importance. Moreover, to the campaign Enoch Powell did contribute the most effective recorded response ever to a heckler, who shouted at him – 'Judas!'

> Judas was paid. I have made a sacrifice.[15]

To no single one of these episodes can Heath's defeat be attributed. But, subliminally perhaps, their cumulative effect was to create the impression of a Government that no longer had confidence in itself or much sense of direction; that no longer commanded the confidence of its natural supporters; and that had lost its single most vital and compelling orator.

Taken singly, these may at the time have seemed no more than irritants. Those who are appealing for a 'doctor's mandate' do not want to be drawn on the subject of detailed variations in the prescribed medication. And so the illusion, even if somewhat tattered, of a large moderate majority that would endorse the Conservative 'stand', persisted at Number 10 just as it did in party Committee Rooms across the land. Polling day was quiet and Heath did not leave Downing Street, where he hung about signing papers and (one may assume) working out draft responsibilities for a fresh Cabinet, until the late afternoon. He then drove down to Bexley accompanied by William Waldegrave and Michael Wolff. The final total, it was generally agreed, might not be as good as had seemed likely at the outset but certainly Heath would be forming the next Government.

However with the very first declarations, even though coming from the safe Conservative seats of Guildford and Billericay, two things were apparent. First, that there had been an enormous turnout of voters; second, that a peculiar result was in prospect. And by the time his own count was complete Heath will already have known that the whole manoeuvre had miscarried disastrously. All through the night the disappointments accumulated. And by the morning the result was apparent – the new Parliament would be 'hung'.

Yet the longer Heath looked at the figures the more puzzling, and frustrating, they seemed. The Conservatives had polled more votes than Labour. They had lost but twelve seats in England and Wales. The diminution of their strength in the Commons was as much accounted for by Ulster, the Scottish Nationalists and the Plaid. The enormous Liberal vote had, surely, been drawn from that same 'great moderate majority of the British people, men and women of all Parties and no Party, who reject extremism in any shape or form . . .' to whom the Conservative manifesto had been addressed? And most of the seats which had changed hands had done so by very small margins and in a substantially increased poll. From this Heath tried to draw comfort. It would guide his actions, and insulate him from the humiliation which he was to suffer, over the next few days. And particularly it would colour his strategy between that time and losing a third general election later in the year.

As a verdict on Heath personally, though, it was a disaster. His biographer wrote:

> they [the British people] . . . had not been prepared to stand up and be counted. When asked to declare themselves firmly . . . against sectional intransigence, they had preferred the easy option and voted, many of them, for a quiet life. *He had counted on the British people to support him and they had let him down.*[16]

Whether or not this judgement is, in its entirety, valid is arguable. But certainly Heath, if he had any sense or recollection of history, should have been put in mind of that by-election at Oxford in November of 1938. When the 'anti-appeasement' candidate to whose cause, as a first-year undergraduate, Heath had been passionately committed had suffered defeat. And for the very reason that the electorate preferred the 'easy option'. The irony, too, that this reverse had been at the hands of his present colleague Quintin Hogg, now serving in the Conservative Cabinet as Lord Chancellor.

THIRTY

1974: The Year of Blunder

Heath's attempts to remain as Prime Minister – Thorpe
goes missing – Heath's discussions with the Liberals
and the Ulstermen – Indiscipline and discontent in the
Commons – A second election approaches – A further
change of tone – A bad campaign.

FOR FIVE PAINFUL days Heath attempted to 'form' an administration. The initial shock of rejection depressed him. But within
hours the Prime Minister had become quietly convinced that
'moderate' opinion expected him to save a situation which had,
he persuaded himself, come about almost by accident.

Cabinet was convened on Friday afternoon and Heath addressed
them crisply and without emotion. Without, indeed, any word of
thanks or even acknowledgement of the effort which all had put
into the campaigning of the previous three weeks. There were a
number of alternatives to consider, he told them – but all should
be seen in the light of Conservatives having polled a majority of
votes, and of the overall national 'moderate' vote (an arbitrary bloc
arrived at by aggregating the entirety of Liberal support with the
Conservative total) being as high as 57 per cent.

Further projection of this fantasy arithmetic suggested that if
the seats had been decided on a basis of 'moderate' versus 'extrem-
ist', the 'moderate' majority in Parliament would have amounted
to more than seventy.

So what, then, if Heath remained as Prime Minister and put
forthwith a 'National' programme into the Queen's Speech? What
of the possibility of defying Labour to vote it down, and (this was

an embellishment suggested by Robert Carr*) thus saddling them with the odium of bringing about immediately another election? Surely, if the manifesto were framed to attract general approval the resulting 'National' Government would, just as in 1931, be strongly placed? Thus ran discussion in the Cabinet Room. Ministers, though, were exhausted. Some had barely yet been to bed. Many were irritated that there had been no agreed line to take on those several occasions when they had been 'doorstepped' by cameras and reporters throughout the morning. All were aware of a general public expectation that Wilson, having 'won', would soon be on his way to the Palace. Privately, most will have regarded the idea of a second election campaign with distaste and several, Margaret Thatcher among them, did not speak at all. Whitelaw, with his customary good sense, pointed out that 'trying to be too clever' might result simply in an immediate increase in the size of the Labour majority.

Heath was adamant, however. He was the Prime Minister in possession and felt it to be his responsibility – his duty, as sometimes he was to claim afterwards – to try and form an administration. (Which must be reckoned an anomalous argument from one who had started three weeks earlier with a perfectly good administration and a workable majority that he had deliberately discarded ahead of its time.) Gloomily the Cabinet assented. The Prime Minister should take 'soundings' where appropriate. But colleagues indicated that they would expect to be kept closely informed.

When the meeting broke up Heath set off immediately to explain to the monarch, herself hastily recalled from an Australian tour, what he was trying to do. Naturally the waiting reporters assumed that he was on his way to hand over the seals of office and there was a considerable sense of anticlimax when Heath re-emerged from the Palace and returned to Downing Street still, apparently, as Prime Minister.

---

* PPS to Anthony Eden, 1951–5; Secretary of State for Employment, 1970–2; Lord President of the Council and Leader of the Commons, 1972. Home Secretary, 1972–4.

In the meantime contact had at last been established with Jeremy Thorpe. Thorpe had not been to bed either. But he was in a state of high elation having for most of the night been carried shoulder high by his supporters around the streets of Barnstaple. On the telephone he was jocular, facetious almost, but agreed to come in to Downing Street on the Saturday morning.

The meeting went on for two hours. The only other person in the room was Robert Armstrong – providing yet another example where the presence of a senior official from private office would cloud the distinction between party and government business. A practice which was to grow exponentially under the duumvirate of Margaret Thatcher and Mr (as he then was) Charles Powell.*

Heath's tactics were mistaken. He appealed personally to Thorpe, massaged the Liberal leader's vanity (scarcely necessary) and offered him by implication, some allege directly, the post of Home Secretary in a coalition.

Had Heath ever paid the slightest attention to what other people were saying – still less listened to gossip – he would have known that Thorpe's own colleagues were already deeply anxious concerning their leader's behaviour. His flamboyance, his impulsiveness, his impatience with matters of detail were failings that a good supporting team could, for most of the time, compensate for; although they were not ideal characteristics in a political leader when patience and subtlety were what was needed. But there were also the rumours, insistent, and some with an uncomfortable degree of substance, of homosexual scandal. In the nature of things this material was going to increase in value – and thus the likelihood of it 'breaking' – the closer that the Liberal Party, and Thorpe himself, approached to the exercise of executive power.

All this was of course in Thorpe's dossier with Special Branch and should have been known to Heath or, at the very least, been

---

* As neither of the participants has (at the time of writing) revealed much of the substance of this discussion it is to be hoped that, at least, Sir Robert's presence will have ensured that a Meetings Note was kept, which should be available to students at the expiry of the statutory period.

drawn to Armstrong's attention by the Cabinet Secretary ahead
of the meeting on 2 March. One must assume that the Prime
Minister thought it to be 'containable'. Heath may also have
calculated that if Thorpe's scandalous behaviour did later become
public knowledge and arouse indignation, this might offer a convenient device for diminishing the Liberal influence in the Coalition, were one to be formed.

Yet it remains quite extraordinary that, of all positions in Government, there should have been any consideration given to
entrusting Thorpe with the secrets and sensitivities of the Home
Office. Nor was it necessary. The price of Liberal co-operation
had to be paid not in the distribution of portfolios but in a
particular emphasis of policy. Whatever Thorpe's own personal
feelings, and his belief that he could continue on the high wire,
improvising his act to suit the demands of the audience below, the
more hard-headed among his party realised that this moment –
apparently of triumphant ascent – was in fact their last chance.
They were never going to recover their ancient strength in the
House of Commons under the existing electoral system. But
with proportional representation (PR) there might come enough
public confidence to assure them, quite possibly and in the present
mood, the status attaching to largest-number-of-seats.

Before boarding the train at Exeter on Friday Thorpe had made
some more telephone calls. By the time of his first meeting with
Heath he was fully aware of his own party's terms for 'propping
up' (as was the contemptuous phrase which Liberal activists had
already minted) the Conservative minority. All Heath could offer,
though, was a Speaker's Conference to examine the whole question of electoral reform. The two men enjoyed each other's
company. Both, personally, were of much the same mind.
But both were constrained by the weight of their own party
members and thus neither had the power to deliver what the
other needed.

Even so, Thorpe agreed to have one last try, although pretty
certain that it would be useless. Heath meanwhile composed his
mind to a tentative approach to the Ulster Unionists – smaller in

number, and whom he detested. So during the afternoon of Friday Heath offered the Conservative whip – a pretty soft currency on that first weekend of March 1974 – to seven of the Unionists, excluding the four Paisleyites. And here an immediate paradox is apparent. Thorpe's terms, the requirement of an immediate change in the voting system, were to a considerable degree acceptable to Heath but not, nor ever could be, to his party. While the demands of the Ulstermen – fresh elections to the Northern Ireland assembly and an effective scrapping of the whole Sunningdale process would surely have been welcomed by a majority of Conservative MPs, but were repugnant to Heath, as well as to Armstrong, his *éminence grise* in all matters relating to Northern Ireland. Seldom indeed can so wide a gulf have separated the personal taste and objective of the leader from the general aspirations of his back-benchers.

An agreement along these lines would also have caused acute embarrassment to Whitelaw, forcing, in all probability, his resignation. Whitelaw was at that time the only credible alternative to Heath for the leadership, and widely recognised as such. And other leaders – Baldwin, Macmillan – would have seen this added advantage in an accommodation with the Unionists: forcing out their principal rival on to what, in party terms, was the low ground. Yet this seems never to have occurred to Heath – perhaps because Whitelaw's own behaviour had at all times been utterly above suspicion of conspiracy. More likely because Heath's dislike of the Ulstermen was so strong that he would have found any excuse to stay away from them. His overtures were in fact purely formal; and made at the behest of colleagues rather than with any serious intention to negotiate. So the meeting was doomed from the start.

Meanwhile, during the evening of 2 March, Thorpe conferred with David Steel (who was eventually to succeed him) and John Pardoe (who wanted to). He also spoke with Jo Grimond (his predecessor) and Lord Beaumont (a direct contemporary at Eton). Grimond told Thorpe that he 'might get it later if he played his cards right'. The others saw, with good reason, that Heath's own tenure of office could well be drawing to a close; that 'the cheque should be cashed at once' and that, in any case, for the mass of the Liberal Party 'the sky's the limit'. Steel drove Thorpe back to Downing Street – or rather to Horse Guards steps so that the Liberal Leader had only a short walk along the pavement from the iron gate at the top of the staircase and could thus evade the small posse of sleepy journalists who were on duty there. Thorpe was under instruction to insist – 'PR now. Or there's no deal.' And Steel remained in the car until he emerged.[1] At this point Heath did not make the same mistake – of 'putting everything on the table' – that he had done in the later stages of his negotiation with the NUM. But what Thorpe needed to take back to his colleagues, who were meeting in his room at the Commons the following morning, was a straightforward offer to put electoral reform into the first Queen's Speech of the Coalition Government. And even with that he could not guarantee their assent. Nor indeed could Heath guarantee the endorsement of his own back-benchers, or even of his Cabinet. Nor could there be any question of 'talks about talks'. The Liberals believed their position to be stronger than it was; while the Conservatives were by now acutely short of time.

At a brief meeting of Cabinet on Monday morning Heath recounted his efforts. None of those attending made any constructive comment. At the same time the Liberals were in conclave. They lost no time in turning down the idea of a coalition with the Tories. But turned the Conservative flank with a call for 'an *all-party* [i.e., including notabilities from the Labour Party] government of National Unity'.

There was nothing (as will be seen) that Heath could have liked more. Particularly as he seems to have nursed, for the whole of 1974 (and, some would say, for the whole of his life thereafter), the illusion that were such an administration to be formed he would be its natural, as well as its rightful, leader. But for it to be *All*-Party the Socialists would have to be involved. And of that happening there was not the slightest likelihood. Even Heath could see this. He called one last Cabinet, in the late afternoon.

'He neither thanked his colleagues for their support nor did they pay any tribute to him.'[2]

Heath then put out a statement in which can easily be detected the theme of his chosen electoral posture – that he would support the new Government '*in whatever realistic measures it takes in the interests of all the people*' and drove, for the third time in three days, to the Palace, and delivered the seals of office. What authority did the Prime Minister – as at the time he had been – derive from Cabinet for issuing this statement? None of those then serving have referred to any discussion taking place, although there will have been some who would have supported this line had they been asked.

It is possible that Heath believed, and certainly some of the advice he was receiving assumed, that Wilson would quite soon get into difficulties. Be forced, that is to say, into dissolving Parliament before Labour plans for the second election were complete. What then should Conservative tactics be?

The delusion, aired at the Cabinet table only the previous Friday, that this would lead to the electorate having second thoughts was fast dispelled. Within days Heath's objective stood on its head and now became to avoid, at almost any price, Labour having the excuse to dissolve. He instructed Humphrey Atkins (who had remained in post as Chief Whip) that while there would be opposition it should be 'responsible' and, whenever possible, 'constructive'. The first test came with the debate on the Queen's Speech on 17 March. Opening for the Opposition, Heath assured Wilson that he would not be 'factious'. He made play of the 'national interest' – though without being very clear where he considered it to lie. Plainly Heath's chosen role was that of states-man-in-waiting.* And it was one in which he felt all too comfortable. Mr Mark Schreiber, reporting the manner of his delivery

---

* Curiously, this prospect also alarmed Harold Wilson because he believed (implausibly) that Heath was still a credible leader of a national government. (See n 3 for the text of a letter from Mr Joe Haines to the author.)

in the *Economist*, described him as 'more mellow than most of his supporters could ever remember...'

Almost immediately a squall blew up. Atkins had been put under pressure by a number of senior colleagues, still fixated by 'Stage Three', to table an amendment condemning the Government's intention to abandon it. Heath was easily persuaded that this would fit with the revised 'responsible' image, and put himself at the head of the list of signatories. And immediate confirmation of the amendment's 'moderate' credentials came with an instant promise of support from the Liberals. The Conservatives were thus faced immediately with the likely prospect of fighting an election. Starting with Liberal support, but with no strategic master plan and every likelihood that any extempore alliance would break down in a matter of days. Worse, the issue would be a policy already shown up as of dubious fairness, largely incomprehensible and, among the majority, highly unpopular. As well as being provocative to what was now recognised as the dominant power bloc in the land, the Trades Union Congress.

A good number of back-benchers could see this. Described, in shorthand, as 'the Selsdon Group', but including many who were not originally part of that faction, they made their opinion known to Atkins and – without inhibition – to other colleagues who listened. Emboldened by the extent of sympathy for their views in the body of the party they raised the stakes by telling Atkins, on the morning of the debate, that they could not vote for the Opposition amendment. This was an early, and most unwelcome, breach of discipline. There was nothing for it but to withdraw the amendment. However, total humiliation was avoided because at the same time Michael Foot decided to insert an assurance in his speech to the effect that the Government would after all be ready to keep Stage Three in place 'for the time being'.

Thus the crisis passed almost before, outside the House of Commons, it had been noticed. But there was a certain portent in the manner of its passing – something lost, it would seem, on Heath himself; the Chief Whip; and most of the Shadow Cabinet. This was the presence of some forty Members of Parliament who were minded to reject the entire received wisdom of economic policy. The Keynesian notion that intervention by Government, regulation by statutory power over market forces, was the secret of 'growth' and (more importantly to many) of full employment.

On that first occasion this group could still with ease be depicted as disparate eccentric theorists, and *refusés*. They were unorganised, and had no leader to whom they could turn. Leadership 'problems' there certainly were in the Conservative Party by this time. But they were related not to fundamentals of policy but to the personal traits of the incumbent and contenders close to him. Heath realised this. And he knew also, as has every leader before and since, that the ability to deliver, or to recover, office was of a distinctly higher value than the proselytising of radical ideas. How was this to be approached?

At first, and for a few weeks, Heath seems to have clung to the view that he had been 'right'. The election result had been an aberration. Something which would be reversed as soon as the results began to be felt of a Government dependent on the unions and with no policy to control inflation. 'He had been right in February. He was still right. And the electorate would quickly come to see that he was right.' Certainly it is remarkable how often a period in the highest office will delude the holder that what matters above all else is to be 'right' (by which, of course, is meant no more than that the incumbent sees no reason to change his, or her, opinion). And an identical set of mind will be observed in Heath's successor as her own premiership drew to a close.

A harsher judgement, learned on the way up but often forgotten in the rarer air of extreme altitude, is aphorised in that ancient ditty of the Wild West:

> There was a young fellow called William Gay
> Who died asserting his rights of way.
> He was right – *dead* right – as he rode along
> – and just as dead as if he'd been wrong.

Predictably, Wilson wasted no time in opening the till and distributing what remained of the contents. Price controls, including a freeze of rents; increased food subsidies and pensions – these were measures that would consolidate voting intention over the short term while further aggravating the inflationary trend.

This was bad for Heath. He was quite realistic enough to see that a third defeat at the polls would put him, personally, in serious jeopardy. He no longer disposed of the assets needed to bribe the electorate, so could not compete with Wilson on that level. His only realistic chance of survival would be as the respected Coalition leader, above party, a rallying icon for 'moderate' opinion whose strength, as has been already illustrated, Heath greatly overrated. Heath, though, had the Whip's natural cynicism regarding both the stamina and the malleability of his colleagues. Managing a Coalition Cabinet is different and in some respects easier than managing one from your own party. Easier still is, or should be, a Cabinet made up of 'independent' (dependent, that is to say, on the leader's patronage) figures from the political fringe. Heath felt that he might need support from respectable heavyweights and his mind turned to Christopher Soames,★ a very senior Conservative but now at a distance from the centre.

At this point there is a brief sighting of James ('Jimmy') Gold-smith. Goldsmith was a member of the international governing class. He was an Etonian, and his father, 'Major Frank', had been a Conservative MP, his mother a French landowner. Old Goldsmith had been ousted from his seat in circumstances that brought little credit to the party, and had ended his days as part-owner of the Carlton Hotel in Cannes. But Frank's humiliation inflicted a lasting psychic bruise on his son and was without doubt one of the motive forces that drove Jimmy in so single-minded a fashion to pursue the creation of an enormous fortune. In 1974 Jimmy Goldsmith was already rich, and being of an impatient nature sought to use his wealth as a lever to make rapid ascent within the Conservative Party. He joined, on an unpaid basis, the Conservative Research Department where, as a rich and young

★ Churchill's son-in-law, MP for Bedford, 1950–66; Ambassador to Paris, 1968–72; Vice-President of the European Commission, 1973–6.

(aged forty) businessman, he caught the eye of Ted Heath. Heath chose Goldsmith, possibly for reasons of security, as his emissary. Jimmy went first to Paris, where already his contacts in both politics and industry were of the first rank, and spoke to Soames. Yes, Soames would endorse Heath, align himself firmly if a squall blew up. His price? The Foreign Office. Heath knew that Soames still fancied himself as a possible Leader of the Party. He had been exerting massive pressure in Central Office to 'find' him a parliamentary seat. 'He'll ask for the Foreign Office,' Heath told Jimmy. 'Tell him "Yes".'[4]

During this period it can be asserted without fear of contradiction that the administration (though not the party) finally abandoned any claim to call itself Conservative. Heath's own biographer has most percipiently remarked that

> He had never, after all, had much love for the Tory Party except
> as a necessary instrument for realising his vision of Britain.[5]

Now he was finding himself confined to measures designed to save his skin. Although in this conviction he shared with his party the outlook that *his* survival was of fundamental importance, rising above particular 'issues' of policy, to the well-being of the country. In a little-remarked move — utterly characteristic of the way in which Heath's mediocrity of aesthetic judgement dovetailed with the Rotarian outlook of Hugh Fraser and senior Central Office advisers — a 'study' was commissioned which found that, over a given week, issues of *The Sun* and the *Daily Mirror* drew on only 2,000 separate words, in contrast to 'the average educated person' who had some 40,000 at their command. The leader's speeches, it was suggested, might attain extra 'punch' if his team of writers confined themselves to that same thesaurus from which the tabloid sub-editors drew their vocabulary.[6] Thus did the great Conservative Party, which in former times had reflected a quiet pride in Churchill's sonorous Macaulayism, or Macmillan's classical allusions, demean itself by substituting for their memorable sentences the *lumpen* monosyllables of a Central Office 'phrase-making group'.

And with each month that passed it became more plain that the Tories were not going to win an election as Tories (Heath, naturally, shrank from the corollary that they were not going to win an election *under him*). The way out of this, it seemed to Heath, was for the Conservative Party to metamorphose as fast as could be done without total loss of credibility into the vanguard of a 'National' administration. Non-confrontational, experienced, 'moderate', best suited to cope with the catastrophic economic crisis that Wilson's irresponsibility was, plainly, going to induce.

The Industrial Relations Act was buried. Prior's Policy Group, recommending moderation in all things, decreed acceptance of the 'fact of life' that the trade unions were 'an important Estate of the Realm'.[7] Still more abjectly, Heath announced that the new Trade Union and Labour Relations Act, which had been the TUC's pay-off for their support of Wilson in and after the February election, would be 'accepted'.

These things were barely noticed, except by bewildered and resentful Tories. The political temperature remained high, and with it the assumption that Wilson would go to the country and ask for a 'real' mandate in the autumn. As the date approached, Heath became unconfrontational to the point of parody. At his first press conference (on 23 September) he was so soft-spoken that journalists at the back of the room could not hear what he was saying. Nor, as this record shows, would they have been much the wiser if they had:

Q: What would be your first action again inflation?
A: To see precisely what the situation is.
Q: What would be your next move?
A: To take appropriate action.

Challenged about his 'soggy' performance Heath replied that he was '. . . adopting the technique you have so often urged upon me of quiet, reasonable conversation'. At an all-ticket rally for Conservatives in Cardiff he spoke for forty minutes without inducing a single round of applause.[8]

With Parliament scattered and MPs isolated in their constituencies there was no likelihood of any dissent from this policy being co-ordinated. Indeed the mood of individual candidates was often to clutch at any straw. Bernard Weatherill, the deputy Chief Whip, was delegated by Atkins to ring round and promote, subliminally or otherwise, the concept of a 'Government of National Unity'. Obediently, Conservative parliamentary candidates repeated over and again the mantra across public address systems of indifferent quality, from the back of Land-Rovers in the freezing wind:

'Firm Government, but Fair Government'

This was a slogan of low intelligibility even had the party been in government, which it was not – nor was likely to be. It stood weakly beside the commitment of the Labour Party to the 'Social Contract', a skilfully packaged assortment of electoral bribes that promised to distribute cash for the 'needy' in every direction, and relied on 'the sense of responsibility of people in the workplace' to ensure that wage negotiations were carried out 'in a responsible manner'.

Whether this amounted, or not, to a 'crisis', Heath invoked the concept of an emergency to justify the text and tone of his last few days' campaigning:

> I have no doubt that the real hope of the British people . . . is that a National Coalition government, involving all the parties, should be formed, and the party differences could be put aside until the crisis is mastered.

This was a curious lurch across into the Centre. Or rather from the Centre, where Heath fancied himself as standing, towards the Liberal Left. If Heath thought seriously that he could separate 'the British people' from the Labour Party he was doing no more than many in (and out of) politics – namely, to propagate the delusion that because they hold to a conviction with particular fervour it must also be held by a 'silent' majority. What Heath chose, apparently, to ignore was the opening sentence of the Labour manifesto – '*There is no meeting point between us and those with quite different philosophies*'.

When asked for his response at the daily Labour Party press conference Wilson's reply had been that this was a 'desperate attempt . . . to get back into power by any means'. Contemptuously he warned that Coalition would mean 'Con policies, Con leadership by a Con Party, for a Con trick. And how long would it last? About as long as it would take to get the country back to last February, back to the other "cons" – confrontation, and conflict.'[9]

Deep gloom, interspersed by occasional bouts of panic, pervaded the Conservative Party. Barely had the campaign started when some of the candidates approached Whitelaw to see if a way could not be found of putting him at its head (and thus, effectively, of the party).* Already there were many talking openly of the need to displace Heath – and at the instant the result was declared. Only victory, as it had four years before in June 1970, could save him. When the result was known, with the Labour majority over the Conservatives having increased from five to forty-two, the party was plunged into recrimination. There were plenty who argued that the short period intervening between the two polls had been wasted, that a forthright return to Conservative policies would have closed the gap. There were others who gave up hope. The country was sick of the Conservatives, ran their argument. Conservatism was out of date. Henceforth it would be the 'special-interest' groups of whom, manifestly, the trade unions were the most significant, who applied policy decisions through their nominees in the Labour Party; and it was with them that the Conservatives should seek accommodation. There were some voices, even, who agreed with Heath's desperate final judgement of 'a need for a "blood transfusion" of practical people with experience

---

* The author recalls a telephone conversation with Whitelaw at his house in Cumberland on 3 October, at which Whitelaw made no comment whatever other than, utilising a particular personal technique of communicating *diminuendo* but in a very loud voice, to repeat his wishes for 'a very great success, a very good success, a good result'.

of the real world' (so long, presumably, as it was not they whom the 'practical people' were going to displace).

This extreme variety of opinion, whose only common factor was an acceptance that the Conservatives were in bad shape – worse, by far, than the raw figures indicated – suggested that the party must now look to its reserves. Those deep instincts – intuitive, historic, radical – from which in the past it had managed to draw when believing its survival to be threatened. Anything, in other words, might happen.

BOOK FOUR

Shock Therapy

THIRTY-ONE

The Varied Roles of Edward du Cann

*The Chairman of the 1922 Committee and his power –
Ill-feeling towards Edward Heath – Willie Whitelaw
does his best – A welcome invitation – The scene
changes – Sir Keith Joseph falls by the wayside – The
Party machine sets out to thwart Margaret Thatcher.*

THE 1922 COMMITTEE is a body where reposes considerable power; but whose inclination to exercise that power is unpredictable. Of particular importance is the persona of Chairman. Of all influential positions in the Conservative Party it is the one most dependent on the personality and force of character of the incumbent. When the party is in government the Chairman, assured by long tradition of a peerage when his term of office comes to an end, plays usually a supportive role. He is, if a military analogy may be introduced, the Battalion Colonel to the Chief Whip's RSM. A gentleman as distinct from a professional. The two men shadow-box a little, largely for effect, but usually they will combine in muffling any unease over policy.

In Mrs Thatcher's time Cranley Onslow was to play such a role. Too well, indeed. So that when she fell, and policy as well as personnel became less certain, he was displaced by Sir Marcus Fox. Then Sir Marcus would find that when the tiller is wobbling the crew do not take kindly to empty reassurance and he, also, was to have notice served upon him by the parliamentary party in 1997. Neither man did, in fact, receive his peerage.

In Opposition the Chairman's role is greatly different. The party itself will be more fractious. Gifts of patronage no longer attach to the leadership. The right of personal access that by tradition the Chairman enjoys is something to which the Leader of the Party has to pay close attention. Unspoken (for most of the time), but in the minds of all, should be the knowledge of a probationary element in the leader's tenure far more pronounced than attaches to a Prime Minister enjoying endorsement from the electorate at large.

Following their second consecutive defeat under the leadership of Edward Heath the Conservative Party was greatly demoralised. Events were to pile one upon the other thick and fast over the winter of 1974–5, and MPs to become first distracted, then inspired. But in those weeks immediately after the October poll spirits were as low as they had been in the autumn of 1945. The electoral arithmetic (a habitual preoccupation of the party when times are bad) seemed to be implacable. And in any case if, as was the lament that could be heard on all sides, the country was 'ungovernable', what was the point of being in government? To many it seemed as if *administration* – a word with fewer overtones of authority – was and would remain in the hands of a kind of triumvirate: the Trades Union Congress, the Civil Service and the Parliamentary Labour Party.

A general unease with the leadership, a feeling of frustration at opportunities missed and Conservatism (of which each had their own separate image) betrayed, was widespread. Thus there existed a good body – if they were all to combine, a majority – of malcontents amongst whom the recruiting sergeants of every leadership contender could operate. Who aspired, in the late autumn of 1974, to lead the Conservative Party? As usual they were many; and the 'front runners' – those, that is to say, who were being tipped by political editors – were among the least likely to succeed.

First, William Whitelaw. He was affable, unexpectedly so for a former Chief Whip. Although he had been Chairman up to and during the second election defeat, Whitelaw had emerged with his reputation unscathed. He was made Shadow Employment Secretary, a position grounded doubtless on Heath's belief that, objectionable and intransigent though they might be, the union bosses were hardly as disagreeable as those Irish factional leaders with whom, after a fashion, Whitelaw had 'got on' while he was Viceroy at Stormont. Also, Whitelaw had guile, and he was safe. Under Whitelaw there would be no radical changes. There were some who thought him to be a candidate who might hold the party together while they watched Wilson burn out.

But did Whitelaw really want it? Not, certainly, hard enough to challenge Heath directly – for this he had been several times urged to do by different party notables, even in the run-up to the second election that October.

Then there were two contenders of the old school, John Peyton and Hugh Fraser. Their chances were talked up (not least by themselves) in the smoking room. Fraser was reactionary. Peyton a liberal. Both, though, had plummy voices and shared the mannerisms characteristic of an earlier decade. The party was in no mood to go backwards.

So was it to be a Young Turk? Geoffrey Howe had the advantage (or handicap) that many already expected that 'in the end' he would be leader. These people envisaged, of course, the 'end' to be a good ten years away from the present crisis; but some none the less (including Ian Gow, later to become Margaret Thatcher's principal aide) felt it prudent, at such a time of uncertainty, to take out insurance by quietly letting it be known that they were supporting Howe.

Jim Prior, too, was a beneficiary of this approach. He was clever, laid back, and almost ludicrously bucolic in appearance. Everyone's second choice, Prior would have become leader under the Alternative Vote system.

None of these characters, though (except Whitelaw), was a heavyweight. And in the first weeks after their defeat most MPs, feeling that they ought to choose a heavyweight, focused, albeit reluctantly, on Sir Keith Joseph.

Sir Keith had served in the Cabinet with distinction. As Health Secretary he had been a vigorous and profligate dispenser of taxpayers' money. Now, with the zeal of the convert, he declaimed that those very policies '... had done huge harm to the Conservative Party and to the country'. He gestured wildly, often (literally) beating his breast during a speech; and he glared at his audience. At close quarters Joseph was not easy company. To choose him in place of Heath would, warned one former Cabinet Minister '... be like going from the 'fridge into the freezer'. In the Members' dining room the Deputy Chief Whip, Sir John Stradling Thomas, would mock Joseph and refer to him as 'the mad monk'. Any assault by Sir Keith would be very far from a walkover.

All these antics were being closely watched by the Chairman of the 1922 Committee. Edward du Cann had never been in Cabinet, but he had served as a junior minister, and he knew how government worked. He had also done a stint as Chairman of the Party. He was popular with the staff at Smith Square, and had circulated generously among the party organisation in the country, being on Christian-name terms with many of the local chairmen. So there was much useful colouring at the back of the canvas. But du Cann's real advantage derived from his weekly access to those individuals who comprised the electoral college itself. As Chairman, du Cann was witty, sympathetic and authoritative. He was adept both at accelerating tedious business and, by echoing in a subtly embellished tone the views of those who approached him, at flattery. In the corridors du Cann would address colleagues as 'dear boy', and fall into step beside them while putting his arm around their shoulder. He possessed just a trace of self-parody. 'What time would you *like* it to be, dear boy?' du Cann once answered a new and nervous back-bencher who asked him the time of day. While on his feet in the chamber du Cann harried Labour from a stance that combined homespun thrift and high patriotism.

But from his long experience and natural instinct du Cann knew that he could not declare his candidacy. Not yet, at least. It was well known that, in Jim Prior's (only slightly exaggerated) words, 'He can't stand Ted; and Ted can't stand him'.[1] The basis for this was historic. The two men had fallen out at the Board of

Trade where they were both ministers in 1964. Du Cann had backed Maudling for the leadership in the following year. He was a useful ally for 'Reggie' who himself welcomed du Cann's influence, depicting him as one of the young and self-made Tories whom Heath's supporters were claiming as their exclusive constituency. After Maudling lost, du Cann offered to resign (knowing that it could not be so soon accepted). Then, in the months following, whenever Heath had been minded to get rid of him du Cann would pre-empt the move by leaking it to the press. Finally he went of his own accord having, or so he claimed, extracted the assurance that he would be offered a post as soon as the Conservatives were back in power.

No such thing happened, of course. But now du Cann was back, with the authority of having been elected by colleagues – and at the very fulcrum of power. As Chairman of the '22, responsible for all the machinery of any contest and the continuing supervision of all 'developments', it was essential that du Cann should maintain the carapace of impartiality. Let every other candidate fall, or trip, by the wayside. Even in the quiet and apparently reluctant destabilisation of Heath himself, timing was critical. Until finally, at a given moment, (du Cann's hope was that) the Party would have to turn to him.

Heath, though, knew what was up. He had been a former Chief Whip after all. His antennae, though somewhat dulled by the years of deference, still functioned. Whitelaw would never challenge. Nor anyone else from within the Cabinet. The party would never take Keith Joseph; as for Margaret Thatcher, she will never have crossed Heath's mind. Du Cann was the threat.

As soon as the result of the general election was known, on 10 October 1974, both men moved fast – but each behind his own smokescreen. Du Cann convened a meeting of the 1922 Executive Council at his private address (the House of Commons had not yet even opened its doors). Members of the Executive had seen two elections, in quick succession, lost 'unnecessarily'. They were in an indignant, and disrespectful, frame of mind; the perfect foil to du Cann's statesmanlike restraint in attributing 'blame'. Calmly, he appealed for 'patience'. This had no effect. Du Cann was instructed to confront at once (although not simultaneously) Whitelaw — at that time still Chairman of the Party; Humphrey Atkins, the Chief Whip; and Heath himself. The message —

> that it is the unanimous opinion of the Officers and Executive of the 1922 Committee that the Leader of the Party should resign.

Du Cann told the Council that their views were not his. That he believed them to be 'making a mistake'. They listened. But the instruction was repeated.

First du Cann spoke to Atkins, who was 'upset at the news'.[2] That evening du Cann invited Whitelaw to dinner, and for most of the meal the two men fenced one with another (for it is safe to assume that both Whitelaw and Heath had been telephoned by Atkins the instant that du Cann had left his company). Whitelaw did his best to prevent du Cann bringing the subject up at all. He told his host — a time-honoured card, habitually kept in reserve for such a situation — that he 'believed du Cann to have been treated very badly by the Party in the past ...'. Strongly did Whitelaw imply (though not actually say) that 'Ted badly needs your help ...'; that a Shadow post was in the offing. Du Cann paid no attention, finally got his message through, and drew from Whitelaw the comment that he was 'unsurprised'.

Next came the meeting with Heath. 'Don't they realise what they are doing to our party?' Heath asked him. Only too well, du Cann might have responded. Instead the 1922 Chairman confined himself to reminding Heath that he had been leader for ten years, that he had lost three elections, that it was surely reasonable that colleagues might want to 'review the position'. Heath said little. He knew, as did du Cann, that under the existing (Douglas-Home) rules there was no provision for a challenge, only for regulating the terms of a contest arising out of a vacancy.

There was no discord in the Cabinet. They sank, or swam, together. A poll of constituency chairmen was shortly to show that a very large majority remained loyal to the leader. And of those who had voted Conservative at the election more than half wanted Heath to stay. It was the MPs, the rank and file, who were troublesome. There were ways, though, of handling that. Had Heath not during earlier 'difficult' times bullied the 'Suez Group', and the Rhodesia Rebels, and the 'Monday Club'* into submission? The atmosphere in the room deteriorated. Du Cann next moved on to difficult terrain. He told Heath that the committee which had devised the original rules should be re-established, and be given the remit of putting in place a 'revision' which would allow for an election to be held 'as a matter of routine' at the beginning of each new Parliament.

For Heath this was, of course, a most unwelcome suggestion. But he was in a situation without precedent. He, the Leader of the Party, had been formally told by the 1922 Chairman that he had lost the confidence of colleagues and was required to step down immediately. Heath had to make time. Both, he hoped, to put his own men on the party committees and, ideally, to displace du Cann at the impending 1922 Committee elections; also simply to let the atmosphere cool, allow a normality of tedium and discipline to reassert itself. Heath told du Cann that he would think it over, and the two men parted.

As soon as du Cann reported back to his Executive – a matter of hours – they agreed to send Heath a further message. He was invited to attend and address the first meeting of the full 1922 Committee on 30 October. Just as promptly, Heath responded. The Executive Council had no legitimacy, he said – ignoring the inherent paradox – until they had stood for re-election. He would await that, and come to the newly confirmed body as soon as it met.

Battle was now joined, and Heath's acolytes busied themselves in trying to 'organise' the outcome of the internal vote for Committee chairs, and places on the Executive Council. They portrayed it as a straight contest between Left and Right. Heath himself was encouraged by Hailsham, Whitelaw and Peter Walker

---

* A right-wing splinter group within the Conservative Party under the aegis of the Marquess of Salisbury that included some serving parliamentarians.

to 'sit tight'. He went on television and declared that 'the unity
of the Conservative Party is my particular responsibility *as its
leader*'. His office arranged for the *Sunday Telegraph* to carry some
paragraphs in their City pages casting oblique doubt on du Cann's
financial probity. Other lobby correspondents were primed to
write critical pieces about the 'Milk Street Mafia', and to empha-
sise that '... the 1922 Committee were out of touch with the
feeling of Conservatives in the country'.[3]

It was no use. The existing Executive Council was returned *en
bloc*, and no one could be found to run against du Cann for the
position of Chairman. For Heath this was a very bad sign. Patronage in the Conservative Party is based on a combination of fear
and expectation of future reward, and it was plain that the majority
of MPs felt that Heath, being himself in some jeopardy, disposed
of neither. Du Cann was unopposed, and returned to Committee
Room 14 accompanied by prolonged and noisy applause. Pon-
derously, Heath shifted his position. He agreed to promulgate a
committee which would rewrite the rules, allowing a challenge;
then sent for du Cann and offered him a position in the Shadow
Cabinet (whichever loyal existing member was to be sacrificed is
not clear). Du Cann refused, announced that nominations would
close on 30 January (1975) and the first round of balloting would
come the following Tuesday, 4 February. At the next full meeting
of the 1922 Committee Mr Kenneth Lewis, the Member for
Rutland, coined a phrase which was to blight – from their aspect
at least – not just Heath but every Leader of the Party who was to
follow him, namely that:

> The position of Leader of the Conservative Party is a leasehold,
> not a freehold.

In the meantime Keith Joseph had been making a fool of
himself. In all probability du Cann had foreseen this, when making
his very generous timetable for the lodging of nominations,
although he may not have anticipated it coming so quickly.

The flaws and unpredictability in Joseph's make-up rendered
him easy prey to any smear or 'spin' with which the various

factions should choose, at the given moment, to entrap him. In fact, none was necessary. Speaking at Edgbaston in what he saw as 'an attempt to provide a background for Conservative social policy' founded on 'the remoralisation of Britain', Joseph argued that

> ... the balance of our population, our human stock, is threatened ... [on account of] ... the high and rising proportion of children being born to mothers 'least fitted to bring children into the world', having been 'pregnant in adolescence in social classes 4 and 5'.[4]

There was uproar. Not less deafening for being contrived and founded, largely, in discomfort at hearing the truth. Now it began to seem that, with the exception of du Cann, there really were no credible contenders. The majority of MPs were on the right of the party. They did not welcome the idea of Willie Whitelaw leading them, particularly remembering his 'appeasement' of Sinn Fein; although in all probability they would have put up with him. Was there really no one else? Suggestions became more far-fetched. Lord Hailsham, possibly? Or Christopher Soames, still only fifty-four years old, although without a seat in Parliament. Other soundings were put in train.

It must have seemed to du Cann that his moment was now approaching, and a letter was received by him before the House rose for the Christmas recess:

> For some time it has been increasingly obvious to a number of us that you have the qualities which are required in a new leader: Your warmth, your ability to present our case forcefully and sympathetically, your skill as chairman and, above all, the affection in which you are held by your colleagues make it essential, as we see it, that you should offer yourself for the leadership of our Party. Indeed we consider it is your duty to do so.
>
> We know that it has not been your wish to stand for election, but during the space for reflection that the Christmas recess will bring, we ask you to consider your position and what we have

said, and we earnestly hope that you will allow your name to go
forward on the first ballot when nominations are made.[5]

Sir Keith Joseph's error of judgement in articulating an uncomfortable truth had disqualified him. But Joseph had absorbed much
revisionist wisdom. Alfred Sherman, Alan Walters, thinkers and
academics of distinction, had found their monetarist theories given
most effective expression by a prominent politician. And many
Conservative MPs latched on to the new thinking. Some, quite
possibly, simply as a means of discomfiting Heath; some in desperation; some from conviction.

One who would have been motivated by elements of all three
of these factors was the new Shadow Treasury Minister, Margaret
Thatcher. Thatcher had been Education Secretary in Heath's last
administration, where she had got on his nerves. But Heath
realised, particularly in Opposition, that he must display a 'statutory woman'. Who was that to be? Heath felt ill at ease, with very
few exceptions, in the company of women. And although he
might have preferred to put Mrs Charles Morrison or the Countess
of Harewood in his team, there were practical difficulties. Margaret
Thatcher had already done damage to her prospects by getting
depicted as the 'milk-snatcher'. She was irritating; but unlikely
ever to become of any great consequence. So Heath kept Mrs
Thatcher on in his team, giving to her the post of Shadow Financial
Secretary under his mild-mannered and subservient crony –
Robert Carr. He may well have thought that, being a woman, her
grasp of macroeconomics would be unsure. That faced with the
complexities of an assault on the first Labour Budget Margaret
Thatcher would be seen as inadequate, and in the fullness of time
could justifiably be relegated to a 'woman's' portfolio and then,
after a decorous interval, be sacked.

This understandable error of judgement gave to Margaret
Thatcher her first opportunity, which most effectively she seized.
Robert Carr was an archetypal consensus politician. He found it
almost impossible to do anything unless everyone agreed. And as,
in politics, this happens very seldom Carr spent most of his time

doing nothing. Holding the position of Shadow Chancellor, Carr was entirely content to fall in with Heath's general approach, searching for 'consensus' wherever it might be found and never to oppose measures that could be depicted as 'in the national interest'. As inflation was by now fluctuating at around 20 per cent and the *Financial Times* Stock Exchange index was at 174 the atmosphere of crisis could justify, indeed demanded, 'responsible' (nonexistent, in other words) Opposition.

The attitude of Margaret Thatcher was very different. She threw herself into the task of demolishing the Finance Bill. Well-briefed and passionate, she poured scorn on every line. Saying often – and without any prior authority from Carr or Heath – 'We will repeal this clause!' With this assurance ringing in their ears as they dispersed into 'No' lobbies each evening, MPs soon began to talk, even though in the first instance couched in disclamatory language, of her leadership potential. Not, of course, at the very pinnacle. But as a fiery and hyperactive Number Two to either 'Keith' or 'Edward'.

Then, on the very day when Joseph had ruled himself out, Margaret Thatcher decided to run. Joseph had telephoned her in the morning. Neither he nor his wife, he told Thatcher, could stand the persecution and the pillorying to which they were being subjected by the press. The standard treatment, 'staking out' his house, flash-guns on motordrive in the certainty of catching at least one shot – and no more than one was needed – of a face contorted by distaste and self-doubt; was this to be the prospect for the next five years? In addition, as a distinguished and observant member of the Jewish community, Joseph had been wounded bitterly by Tony Benn's charge that his arguments were covert eugenics – 'the same flag as that which flew over Auschwitz'.

The extent to which Mrs Thatcher's response was spontaneous or whether for some weeks she had been in waiting for just such a critical moment, cannot be known.*[6] But there was no hesitation:

* Somewhat lamely, Lady Thatcher asserts in her autobiography, *The Path to*

'Look, Keith, if you're not going to stand, I will, because someone who represents our viewpoint *has* to stand.'[7]

It was a Friday. Heath himself was nowhere around. The weekend press abounded with speculation. And on the Monday Mrs Thatcher went to the room of the Leader of the Opposition, behind the chair in the House of Commons, and a very, very brief exchange took place. Heath was sitting at his desk.

'I must tell you,' she said, 'that I have decided to stand for the leadership.'
'If you must,' he answered.

Heath rose and walked over to the window. Without turning round he told his visitor:

'You'll lose.'*

As soon as Margaret Thatcher left the room Heath was in touch with Michael Fraser, the Director of Operations at Central Office. This was good news, the two agreed. A sustained campaign of vilification and innuendo directed against Edward du Cann had already gone some way towards undermining his position. Du Cann owed money. He had substantial borrowings outstanding against the security of shares which had plunged in value. His directorships were of the second rank, and many of the 'financial

---

Power (1995): 'I did think that by entering the race, I would draw in other stronger candidates who, even if they did not think like Keith and me, would still be open to persuasion about changing the disastrous course on which the Party was set.' (p. 267)

* The two were not destined to exchange another word until, on 13 February, Mrs Thatcher called on Heath at his house in Wilton Street – this time sitting down without being invited to do so. This second exchange was equally brief, but the very obverse of that meeting on 27 November. Thatcher invited Heath to join the Shadow Cabinet. He refused. If anything, the encounter was of even shorter duration. But Margaret Thatcher loitered in the hall on her way out, making conversation with Tim Kitson MP, in order that the meeting should not have seemed to waiting press to have been unduly abrupt.

service' and property sector were in considerable difficulty. This was apparent for all to see, and offered an easy background for rumours of impending 'trouble' to circulate in the smoking-room corridor.

Now had come the diversion of Margaret Thatcher's candidacy. Something that ought to be so easily dismissed that no second round would take place. 'Mrs Thatcher', wrote the *Economist*, '. . . is precisely the sort of candidate who ought to be able to stand, and lose, harmlessly.'[8] Reassuringly for Heath, a poll of constituency chairmen across the country showed a substantial majority for 'no change'.

What was the principal reservation that unsettled most Conservative MPs regarding Margaret Thatcher? Why, that she was a woman. So Heath had best defend himself by allowing attention to be drawn towards the failings, as many held them to be, attaching to female politicians. They were small-minded, erratic, overcautious but unpredictable. Their response to the great affairs and challenges of global statecraft would be tuned to the imperatives of the homestead, of the *scullery*.

Almost immediately an incident was contrived and, by assiduous and selective briefing from senior officials at Central Office, was imbued with a media life of its own. A strenuous search of the cuttings library for 'quotes' that might be taken out of their context and used to portray Margaret Thatcher in an unfavourable light – a no more than routine operation when the Establishment needs to discredit a 'target' – yielded instantly a prize. Two months previously, in an interview with the not widely read *Pre-Retirement Choice*, she had said that it made sense for old people, when they had the spare cash, to buy several tins of food at one time in case (as was happening almost weekly) the price went up.[9] *Hoarding!* There is practically no figure (possibly because the image is so antipathetic to that of the typical journalist) whom the press would rather vilify than the wise virgin. An unpleasant, spiteful and highly coloured series of commentaries followed. In no time reports had effected the transition from truth to deliberate falsehood. The advice, itself perfectly sensible, was no longer mentioned. The 'story' was now that a wealthy married woman MP was herself hoarding tins of food at a time of impending shortage. The Birmingham Labour Party – to the delight, it can safely be assumed, of Conservative Central Office – convened a deputation of impoverished housewives who proposed to travel to London and, 'confronting' Mrs Thatcher, would ask her to hand over the tins. And a former Chief Whip, Lord Redmayne, was put on television to say that 'any sort of inducement to panic-buying was . . . against the public interest'.[10]

Soon the temperature had risen to such a pitch that a team of reporters and photographers claimed the right of insisting on admission to the Thatchers' larder – 'to put the record straight . . .' – where they filmed the shelves and asked clumsy, but provocative, questions. As the shelves were found to be almost empty, and as, in any case, the polls were beginning to show that most people thought the advice to be prudent, Fraser's team tried again. They put a 'spin' on the story by telling the press that Mrs Thatcher had been seen buying sugar (a sugar shortage was rumoured to be imminent) in unnaturally large quantities.

Where had she been 'seen'? In her constituency. Where in her constituency? In the Finchley Road. Suddenly the case collapsed. The shop described did not exist; neither in the Finchley Road nor anywhere else. The whole episode had much about it that was farcical. Although well illustrating (not that this is ever needed) the clumsy and unscrupulous nature of the Conservative Party machine and the preference in Fleet Street for discreditable anecdote over mundane fact. But the effect on Margaret Thatcher was enduring. To two of her supporters she said, 'I saw how they destroyed Keith. Well, they're not going to destroy me.' Already she was entering that crucible where the stamina of acceptable leaders is tested in the flame.

Privately, Thatcher recorded:

> It showed many people from modest backgrounds like mine how close to the surface of the Tory grandees lay an ugly streak of contempt for those they considered voting fodder.[11]

This conclusion would remain, its validity unimpaired, throughout Mrs Thatcher's period as Leader of the Party in Opposition; and then as Prime Minister; and was at last to find exemplification in the manner of her going.

THIRTY-TWO

Mrs Thatcher's First Government

A leader on probation – A 'balanced' Cabinet – A resolute Chancellor – War in the South Atlantic – and at the colliery gates – Doubts at Buckingham Palace – Enemies and favourites – A touch of hubris – A full decade in power.

WHEN ON THE evening of 13 February 1975 Margaret Thatcher took her seat, at the centre of the table in the Leader's Room, and watched her colleagues troop in to their assigned places she could have been pardoned for taking an informal head count of her supporters. It would not have taken long. The name was Keith Joseph. Her majority in the parliamentary party, in the final round of the election at which she was victorious, was 146 against 76 for Whitelaw, and some 50 in total for the various contenders of the second rank. But in the Shadow Cabinet Margaret Thatcher was outnumbered by seventeen to one.

Present were five of the six challengers:* Carr, Peyton, Prior, Howe and Whitelaw. Of these, only Whitelaw was now (in terms of personal ambition) 'dead'. Carr had already signalled his distance by calling at an early stage and saying that the only Shadow post that he would accept would be Foreign Secretary. Prior was biding his time in the quiet expectation that when the 'experiment' failed the party would revert to the Left-of-Centre mode established by Heath. When this happened Prior would be in contention with

---

* Hugh Fraser, the 'misogynist' candidate at the first round who had scored sixteen votes, was not a member of the Shadow Cabinet.

Geoffrey Howe, his direct contemporary; although Howe probably had a vested interest in keeping the show together for a little longer, before emerging as the legitimate heir of the 'moderate' Right. Hailsham congratulated Thatcher on her victory, and pledged the loyalty and co-operation of all his colleagues, but there cannot have been many in the room who were not asking themselves – for how long?

In 1945 the Conservative Opposition had scarcely been recognised as an alternative government; though more so, perhaps, than after its drubbing in the election of March 1966. But in 1975 the narrowness of the Labour margin in many constituencies, the divisive and unpopular character of much of their policy and especially their subservience to the unions gave to the 276 Conservative MPs in the House of Commons a particular status. The Shadow Cabinet was an administration-in-waiting; and a place therein gave a clear recognition of seniority and potential. Thus it was of particular importance that while she herself was on probation Margaret Thatcher should maintain the balance, both of doctrine and personal commitment, within it.

On the night of her election Thatcher (as had Macmillan twenty years before) dined with the Chief Whip. Humphrey Atkins was someone to whom, in a particular manner, she deferred. He was a Whip in the ancient Tory tradition – cagey, ruthless, and with a veneer of affability. He was also a 'ladies' man'. So that the mutual confidence between Atkins and Thatcher aroused groundless muttering – 'Elizabeth and Essex', and more.* Atkins had been Chief Whip to Heath. Certainly he had played a part in conditioning colleagues to support Heath. If he held views at all, they would be Left-inclined. So the degree to which he was allowed an advisory role in the composition of the Shadow Cabinet was remarkable. Atkins could do nothing to save Carr, nor Peter Walker. But undoubtedly he was responsible for the inclusion of Michael Heseltine, whom Thatcher already distrusted.† Ian

* The analogy was raised by Sir Richard Body, MP for Holland with Boston.
† Heseltine, or so the Chairman (Airey Neave) maintained, had come close to

Gilmour, as she somewhat ungenerously noted, 'lacked the
support or standing which might have made him politically costly
to dispense with. But I valued his intelligence.'[1]

The most substantial achievement of the centrists was to block
the appointment to the Chancellorship, as should have been
natural, of Sir Keith Joseph. The party argument – that Geoffrey
Howe was 'owed' the post on account of his loyally switching
allegiance, his moderation on social issues and his (alleged) following among younger colleagues – is credible. It is also likely
that Thatcher herself flinched from risk of an impetuous 'thinking
aloud' as in the notorious Birmingham speech.* Certainly the
effusive compliments – 'original thinker – best mind in politics –
philosopher in action – humility, open-mindedness and unshakeable principle – deeply sensitive to people's misfortunes' – paid to
Joseph by Margaret Thatcher ought to have put him on guard that
all was not going to be as it should. Her own justification for this
act of ingratitude to one who, effectively, brought about her
selection by withdrawing in her favour is elliptical: '... such a
combination of personal qualities may create difficulties in the
cruel hurly-burly of political life which Chancellors above all must
endure'.[2] When turning her attention to Conservative Central
Office, only two choices were open to Margaret Thatcher. Drastic
vengeance – or circumspection. She chose the latter. And, in fact,
Smith Square was never subordinated – nor has it ever been since
Neville Chamberlain was leader – to the Prime Minister. As
Chairman, Thatcher chose '... that fellow who looks like a butler,
with a pretty Italian wife – can't remember his name'.† Although
in her own (hindsighted) version this choice was influenced by
Thorneycroft's combination of doctrinal orthodoxy and self-

lying when he testified as the newly promoted Minister for Aerospace in the
Heath Government to the Aviation Select Committee, of which Neave was
chairman in 1972. Neave repeatedly warned Thatcher about Heseltine, and
was instrumental in preventing his being made Chairman of the Party in
1978.

* See pp. 465–7 above.

† As described by Harold Macmillan.

sacrifice in resigning when Chancellor to Harold Macmillan, it was well calculated. She herself had written that

> [my election] ... had delivered a shattering blow to the Conservative establishment. They had fought me unscrupulously all the way. I felt no sympathy for them.

The appointment of Thorneycroft was plainly intended to reassure this 'establishment'. He would be a steady hand on the tiller at Central Office, and offset any notion in the voluntary sector that the party was overzealous.* Although there is evidence that during the years of doubt his own commitment wavered. His memorable announcement at the critical point in the 1979 general election, as the party lead shrank below the margin of statistical error, that 'Whatever happens [sic] I ask for no complacency and no despair', as Margaret Thatcher noted in her own memoirs, 'indicated all too accurately the feeling of its author *and his advisers*'.[3]

During the first three years of her leadership, Margaret Thatcher's tenure was far from secure. She never enjoyed a majority support in her own Cabinet, nor, it would seem, in the party organisation – still less at its headquarters in Smith Square. It is more than possible, it is likely, that the Labour Party would have won the autumn general election of 1978, had Callaghan's nerve not failed him almost at the point of dissolving Parliament. Margaret Thatcher, with no achievement to her name except that of displacing Ted Heath (now being remembered, as evicted statesmen so often are, and not only in their own party, with affection), was easily depicted as 'strident'. As 'nagging'. As 'woman driver'. It is not easy now to recall that 'Thatcherism' was coined first as a term of dismissal, a kind of Selsdon Female – but without experience. So different from 'Uncle Jim'. A cartoon in the *Daily Mirror* depicted Callaghan over the inscription: '*If you must have a Conservative Prime Minister, I'm your man*'. For still to come was the

---

* 'Too much ideas-stuff,' this Chairman said, in censoring an article from AC for *Conservative News* in 1978.

Winter of Discontent, that illustration of Labour's total subservience to union militancy, and of the party's disregard for
ordinary non-unionised citizens.

Had the Conservatives been defeated in 1978 Margaret
Thatcher would have been gone by Christmas. As to who might
have taken her place, the contest would have been fought out
between Prior and Howe. But Conservative policy would have
hardened around the text of the 1978 (contingency) manifesto –
'too long, diffuse, and chock-full of costly spending commitments'[4] (and written in the main by Mr Christopher Patten).
And indeed it is Mr Patten who reappears in 1981 as author of a
pamphlet, entitled *Changing Gear*, which set out a consensus
approach to moderating the revised, 1979, version of economic
policy.

Because, two years into her first Parliament, Margaret Thatcher
was already cruelly beleaguered. Polls showed that she was more
unpopular than any previous Prime Minister. Scarcely one person
in her Cabinet had a good word to say of her, and all of these
characters would conclude by telling their interlocutor – and each
other – 'I told you so'. The year 1981 was marked by the monthly
issue of unemployed totals which, net of the various departmental
'schemes' to keep claimants off the Register, was well into three
million. There were street riots in Brixton and Toxteth. At the
Party Conference in October Mr John Biffen, Trade Secretary
(and notionally one of Thatcher's few supporters in Cabinet), told
a fringe meeting that the party was 'in touching distance of the
débâcles of 1906 and 1945'.

Of all her ordeals, at the hands of feeble subordinates and
perverse circumstance, the year 1981 must be reckoned the most
arduous as well as the most long-drawn-out. It was her will-power,
founded on an extraordinary sense of uniquely being *right*, that
sustained Margaret Thatcher through that most difficult of periods.

Had she not, after all, told a startled Sir Anthony Parsons* that

---

* At that time (1978) British Ambassador to Iran. During the Falklands War he
served as Ambassador to the United Nations.

she regarded people who believe in consensus politics as 'quislings and traitors'?[5] One of these, pre-eminently, was Jim Prior. But he was also the original persona to whom attached the scornful dismissive – 'They're not called wets for nothing', allowing himself to be shuffled from the key post of Employment Secretary to the remote proconsulship of Belfast after twice telling reporters that he would resign rather than be moved. Prior was at least right in his percipience that however much pressure might be brought to bear on Thatcher (off and on throughout the year there was the customary talk of delegations of party heavyweights charged with the task of inviting her to 'step down') she '... would hang on until the whole show came crashing round her. That woman's got a Joan of Arc complex.' Not far off was the clash of arms that would indulge this instinct. A battle of almost designer perfection to enhance the standing of its commander.

The Falkland Islands were distant, but their inhabitants were fiercely British. Suddenly they were invaded and   as was luridly depicted in the tabloid press – by a bunch of dagos, responding to the inflammatory exhortations of a bemedalled dictator. The Argentine army was heavily equipped but poorly trained and more used to hunting down and shooting in cold blood its own civilians. It was irresistible for the entire population of Britain not only to see the conflict in such terms, but absolutely to identify with the families of those shepherds and fishermen whose little white-washed bungalows and green roofs of corrugated tin matched exactly with their own aspiration for an idyllic 'second home' in Devon or Windermere.

The sheer effrontery of Galtieri in attempting to seize by force territory rightfully belonging to, and inhabited by, British people had also a unifying effect which buried party allegiance. On Saturday 2 April 1982, Margaret Thatcher had to leave Downing Street and descend to the House of Commons where MPs in Emergency Session were excitedly waiting for enlightenment. Already a large crowd had assembled behind the crush barriers. As the Prime Minister emerged from the door of Number 10 she was roundly booed. The crowd were furious at the humiliation which had been visited on Britain, and her armed forces (Argentine television was quick to send round the world pictures of British Marines lying in the main street of Port Stanley, unwounded but having thrown down their arms). 'Go on, Maggie, get them back'; 'What are you waiting for?'; 'Nuke them'; and so on. The BBC tape of this episode is not often seen. But it must remain on archive as a valuable reminder of what will have been uppermost in the Prime Minister's mind as she made the very short motor journey from Downing Street to New Palace Yard, and went through her speech notes in the back of the official car.

In Washington there was always a considerable lobby whose purpose it was to frustrate the recapture by Britain of the Falkland Islands from Argentina. As at Suez thirty years earlier, US State Department (and some White House) opposition was founded in a combination of jealousy and commercial interest. There was the broad question – how congenial, how appropriate was it to the pyramidic and deferential character of the Western Alliance at whose summit sits the United States, that one of the allies should, quite independently, be engaged in a major military expedition? And the secondary issue, heavily declaimed by senior diplomats – notably Jean Kirkpatrick and Tom Enders – was that the intrusion of a European colonial power into the Southern Hemisphere was something with which the US could not afford to be associated – which, indeed, under the traditional obligations of the Monroe Doctrine of 1823 it should be resisting.

Additionally, there existed the politico-economic case. It was fanciful, but alarming. If war broke out the British would win and a coup in Buenos Aires would displace Galtieri, and probably the entire Junta. The possibility then arose of a domino reaction, with populist governments rapidly coming to power in the majority of Latin-American capitals. Not only would these regimes be less dependent on, and responsive to, the United States. But there was the question of their national debt. Hundreds of billions of dollars of borrowing, most of it from Wall Street banks at 'commercial' rates, was in 1982 'non-performing' and its future under nego-tiation. But if that debt should be repudiated – and who knows what scale this might take once an example were set? – then the effect on the banks' own balance sheets would be so damaging that they would have to be re-rated on the Standard and Poor scale. The matter was less technical than at first it seemed. Because, were this to happen, then all those trusts and fiduciary corporations holding stock in the affected banks would – under Federal law – have to divest their portfolios. The effect on the Dow Jones index, on sentiment in Wall Street, could be catastrophic.

Hence the desperate 'shuttle diplomacy' of Al Haig, the American Secretary of State, and the various compromises – 'trusteeship', dual presence, joint governors, flags flown side by side and so forth which, in the early stages, the US tried to 'sell' to both sides. As the imminence of conflict hardened Haig became more desperate. He repeatedly claimed to detect a 'change of heart' among the Argentine Junta, and urged Margaret Thatcher 'not to be too rigid about sovereignty'.

Finally, Haig dropped the mask. The South American desk at the State Department drafted a statement, little different from the sort of text Dulles and Eisenhower were putting out at the time of Suez:

> Since the outset of the crisis the United States has not acceded to requests that would go beyond the customary patterns of co-operation. [This] will continue to be its stand while peace efforts are under way. Britain's use of US facilities on Ascension Island has been restricted accordingly.[6]

The arrogance of claiming to 'restrict' Britain's access to her own sovereign territory; the combination of bullying and callousness implicit in this text, is memorable. And all too clearly illustrates how, within that amalgam of corporation imperialism and Tammany Hall politics that governs policy formulation in the White House, Britain, in the wrong circumstances, was as disposable as Taiwan.

Unlike 1956, though, the pound sterling was a petro-currency, and immune to speculative pressure. Margaret Thatcher was of tougher fibre than Anthony Eden. And she knew that if the Task

Force, under whatever pretext, returned without fighting – her own days as Prime Minister would be numbered.

And so at every stage in the prelude Margaret Thatcher chose the hard solution. The *Belgrano* was torpedoed; the last-minute plan of the UN Secretary-General for a compromise was so tampered with as to be impossible for Galtieri to accept; even Reagan's personal plea that the defeated Argentine 'garrison' at Port Stanley might be allowed to leave 'with honour' and bearing their weapons was contemptuously brushed aside.

The whole country was delighted. The war was short, heroic and, against hugely superior numbers, victorious. The return of the troopship *Canberra* to the Solent was marked by celebration as prolonged and uninhibited as the relief of Mafeking in 1900. Small wonder, then, that in the general election of the following year the Conservatives – as commented one lugubrious 'Progressive' – were returned 'unopposed'.

Now was the stage set for the final, and to some Conservatives the most sweet-tasting, of all Margaret Thatcher's achievements. Revenge exacted on the party's traditional enemy, the National Union of Mineworkers. Yet even this epic struggle, so often depicted in terms of confrontational simplicity, was subject at times to the influence of chance, and was throughout interwoven with the personal motivation and opportunism of the leading participants.

Margaret Thatcher had chosen her ground well. For almost a year Nigel Lawson, at that time in the middle ranks of government* and more amenable than he was to become when filling the office of Chancellor of the Exchequer, had been stockpiling enormous reserves of coal at the power stations. The Prime Minister was fortunate in her adversary. Like her, Arthur Scargill was infected by more than a trace of megalomania. But he had no guile whatever; nor patience, nor sense of tactics. Scargill's

---

* He served from September 1981 to June 1983 as Secretary of State for Energy. His successor was Peter Walker.

weapons were intimidation and, like some general commanding in the Great War – mass. And, also in common with those commanders, he could think only in terms of the previous conflict (in which he had been victorious) at Saltley Gate in 1972:

> The shutting of [that] depot was living proof that the working class had only to flex its muscles and it could bring governments, employers – *Society* – to a total standstill.[7]

In contrast Ian MacGregor, the Chairman of the National Coal Board, was a United States citizen, though Scottish born and bred. He was tough, and energetic, and tended to see any problem only in its primary colours. MacGregor was distrustful of his Secretary of State; sometimes even disappointed in his Prime Minister; and was on record as saying (along with much else) that he '. . . wished I had a bunch of good untidy American cops out there. Because, whatever else you can say about them, if someone points out to them a law is being broken, then they go and *do* something about it.'[8]

Thus the three principal adversaries were noteworthy for their garish warpaint. But there were others who calculated more deviously. For Mr Peter Walker, the Energy Secretary, the miners' strike offered a double opportunity and at the same time an impossible challenge. This was his last, and his most spectacular, chance to recover momentum. For almost four years he had played his cards – at the start, anyway, a pretty poor hand – with considerable discretion. Walker had leaked very little and, in contrast to others among his Cabinet colleagues, conducted few hostile briefings. How was he now to balance the apparently conflicting objectives of an outcome that would rebound to his personal credit, and yet not be so absolute as to still further consolidate the power of the Prime Minister? Walker will have been of the same mind as Francis Pym, and Robert Carr, now angrily in the wilderness; and of Jim Prior, in distant exile. Was the Government on a disaster course? Possibly at the very back of their minds there was a secret thrill that this might be the case. The ideal solution would be consensual, non-confrontational. An opportunity to display that magnanimity which had been so cruelly rebuffed by Mick McGahey in 1974. And which – was this too much to hope? – as part of the deal might involve the displacement of Margaret Thatcher.

As for the minister nominally in charge (the strike was, after all, an 'industrial dispute'), he could scarcely believe his eyes. Tom King had served his ministerial apprenticeship in Ted Heath's last government. Both from experience and from personal inclination his preference was to avoid confrontation, to search for consensus. Like so many of his contemporaries King was scarred by the recollection of the dispute of 1973, and the election defeat which followed, the cutting short of their political careers in midstream, and an opening of the field to new ideas and new faces. In conversation with Prior, and with Whitelaw, and Heseltine, and with Walker himself King could find tacit, cautious, but increasingly apprehensive concurrence with his view.

Still more ominous for Margaret Thatcher was (or might be if the situation became truly critical) the attitude of the 'Palace'. This body (as convention obliges it to be termed) was already thoroughly disconcerted by Mrs Thatcher's whirlwind disregard for protocol and convention; being the more irritated by her scrupulous conformity, and low curtsey, when in personal contact with the Sovereign.

An additional irritation was that after her double victory over the Argentine military, and then the Labour Party, Thatcher was widely regarded as, and in many instances accorded the privileges of, a Head of State. It became necessary for the Palace to request of the Foreign Office that British posts overseas be reminded, and draw to the attention of host bodies, that the playing of the national anthem was inappropriate as a form of ceremonial greeting to the Prime Minister. Naturally very few chancelleries, even when reminded of this, paid the slightest attention.* As the intensity of the conflict rose, and the turbulence in the mining communities

---

* An incident (at the Maggiore Summit) is recalled by the author on p. 230 of his published *Diaries*.

increased, the Palace started to let it be known where its sympathies lay. Surely the time was approaching for a compromise? Somehow it got out that Her Majesty had taken to the Leader of the Opposition and found him to be 'nice'.

'Nice Mr Kinnock', though, had his own difficulties. His sympathies were with the miners. It was in his blood. Was he not a son of the Valleys, who had spoken so eloquently of working-class struggle in seconding the gracious speech a decade earlier, when a new Labour government owed its election to a miners' strike? This time, though, the strike – due to Scargill's bungling – was not official. Much of it was indeed, under the new Tory legislation, illegal. And how should Kinnock react to daily accounts, nightly portrayals on the television screen, of violence? In 1973 the effect had been to intimidate the voter. In 1984 the electorate, taking their cue from the Iron Lady, decided that it should stop. It was a complete turnaround from the ignominious failure of will under Edward Heath. And by March of 1985 all resistance ceased, and the 'industrial action' came to an end.

During her decade at the head of the Conservative Party Margaret Thatcher had consummated three extraordinary victories, each one in a separate, but critically interdependent, field. The feat of arms in the Falkland Islands had restored the morale of the whole nation. The shattering of militant trade unionism had at last cleared the scene for an industrial revival. And the victory at the polls in May of 1987 was the first, and only, time in British history that the same party, under the same leader, had won three consecutive general elections.

Thatcher had even, by a combination of luck, courage and brazen self-confidence, flushed out of the Cabinet her principal adversary, and claimant to the position of heir presumptive. The details of the Westland 'crisis' like the Profumo 'affair' or, under the Labour Government of 1945, the groundnut 'scandal' have receded into the source-books of history. To examine them now is to emerge with a feeling of amazement that an established government with a comfortable majority in Parliament could

actually have been threatened by collapse at the time. The real
interest attaches to what is disclosed, or can be surmised, about
the intentions of the main participants. In particular, was Heseltine
set up, as he contended? Or did, as his sympathisers have subsequently claimed, Margaret Thatcher temporarily lose her head
and find herself in contemplation of lying to a crowded chamber?

Heseltine was already established, by his performances at Party
Conference and popularity in the constituencies, as the principal
claimant, over the long term, to the succession. So it would be
difficult for him summarily to be dismissed. Matters had to be so
contrived that his lack of judgement, and impetuosity, caused him
to fall into the pit. But the whole affair was messy. And the largely
innocuous Trade Secretary, Leon Brittan, suffered as penalty for
his pliant assent to what was happening: a permanent exclusion
from British public life. What is certain also is that the Westland
affair consolidated the relationship of the Prime Minister and
her two principal (though unelected) supporters. Both Bernard
Ingham* and Charles Powell† were implicated – if not in con-
ceiving of the scheme then at least in its extempore handling. And
both would henceforth be bonded to their mistress; objects at the
same time of awe and resentment felt, on differing occasions, by
back-benchers as well as by colleagues in the Cabinet.

None of this mattered very much while Thatcher continued to
deliver, as it was believed could no one else, what the party needed:
power, and the electoral approval from which it derives. Some
statistics from the election result of 1987 illustrate how much the
party owed to her. For the first time since the Great Depression
(and then, the Conservative vote, though huge, was subsumed
within the 'National' label and is thus less easy to compute) the
Tory share of the manual workers' vote was 36 per cent. And
within that national average there was a total domination of the
skilled workers in the South – 46 per cent to 28 per cent. Still
more impressive was the preponderance – 76 per cent – in the

* The Chief Press Officer at Downing Street 1979–90.
† The Prime Minister's Private Secretary 1984–91.

'new' middle class. Voters, that is, without further education who now ranked themselves in that group purely on the basis of their own material advancement.

Within this analysis only a very few cautionary trace elements could be detected. Among the 'intelligentsia'* and the government salariat, even at its higher earning levels, the proportion of Conservative voters continued to fall.[9] Here, if any of them had any courage left, were the critical statistics for the 'consolidators' to deploy. Having forced Labour back into its northern fastness the Tories could now afford the time, and the amelioration of policy, needed to recover their traditional supporters; to remind them of a shared dedication to *public* service.

What was needed from Thatcher in her hour of triumph was a subtle re-annexation of the 'One Nation' ethic. So contrived that the Establishment could return to its natural Conservative allegiance instead, simply, of recruiting from that narrower catchment of those motivated principally by greed and careerism. Quite the reverse, though, was happening. Nicholas Ridley, never the most even-tempered although certainly now one of the most trusted of Thatcher's confidants, was touring the country proclaiming the need for still more radical 'solutions'. And others, without even Ridley's intellectual grasp of the argument, were seeking their mistress's favour by echoing the theme.

What was needed may not even have been considered by Margaret Thatcher. But at this point there disappeared over the horizon a particular opportunity. It was one of those high watersheds, several of which the party would scale in this century and thereafter follow a misguided route. The rejection of Empire Free Trade by Baldwin in the twenties; Chamberlain's appeasement of Italian Fascism in the thirties; the Polish guarantee of 1939; and Churchill's refusal to allow Butler to float sterling in 1951. In all probability Thatcher's own innate hostility and contempt for the universities, and the Civil Service and, indeed, anyone on the state payroll except for the police and the armed forces, made this

* The description accorded by Mr Hugo Young to university graduates.

impossible. But its neglect was a breach of the first rule of Conservative politics – that the pursuit of power is the criterion against which all policy decisions should in the last resort be judged. Only two members of the Cabinet – Joseph and Whitelaw – might have argued this case with the Prime Minister. But both were past their prime. Joseph in all likelihood himself unconvinced; Whitelaw incapable of arguing the dialectic in persuasive tone.

On 8 May 1988 Thatcher herself uttered a sentiment so hubristic, so utterly discordant with the traditional theme of Conservative leaders in the past, as to indicate that the seeds of her own destruction were now firmly planted:

> I shall hang on until I believe there are people who can take the banner forward with the same commitment, belief, vision, strength and singleness of purpose.[10]

Not only was this corporately insulting to her own immediate colleagues – the use of the plural noun 'people' implying that not even one of them was worthy of consideration – but it was replete with abstractions which do not sit comfortably within the Conservative ethic. The concept of a 'banner' and Margaret Thatcher's frequent reference to her 'crusade' was high-denomination rhetoric. But not easy to sustain. Nor, indeed, was the position of leader within Thatcher's exclusive gift although, as do many incumbents, she behaved as if it were, teasing and tempting a succession of favourites. In their day Geoffrey Howe (briefly), Cecil Parkinson, John Moore, Norman Tebbit and David Young enjoyed that identity. And each one of them when they felt themselves to have been displaced became sulky, and allowed it to show. Moore and Young disappeared into the glass-and-concrete forest of private finance; Tebbit and Parkinson hung about, tearful and pining but neither ever to recover their former influence and intimacy. Nor can there be any doubt that the same fate would have befallen John Major, whose very favourite status caused him to be promoted, in rapid succession, from junior Treasury Minister to Foreign Secretary and then to Chancellor of the Exchequer, had not the music stopped, in November 1990, while he was still apparently the chosen heir.

As Margaret Thatcher's tenth anniversary in power approached there was some talk of a spectacular gesture, a 'standing down', leaving open, of course, the possibility of a return if the 'call' should come. But although this was mooted, to be stage-managed either on the anniversary itself or at the Party Conference of that year, it seems not to have been closely considered by the subject herself. Nor was anyone bold enough seriously to recommend it. And in any case, who had ever achieved this? De Gaulle, yes. Other than him only a few Italian politicians who shuttled in and out of gerrymandered coalitions. For all to see there was the example of David Lloyd George. At the very height, it seemed, of his powers and prestige he had slipped, and fallen, and never once afterwards come – or been allowed to come – near the centre of power. *Been allowed to come.* That is the cautionary phrase; for no serious politician will ever believe, with more than half of him at least, that he is truly indispensable. Indeed it is these pretensions to indispensability that most alarm colleagues, and unite them in a conspiracy to exclude. And it is this which explains the widening gap between the devotion of the voluntary worker, the party member in the constituencies, and a very large number – soon to reach the point of constituting a majority – in Parliament. There is a longing to clear the decks, to throw overboard much encumbrance (and not a few individuals) who stand in the way of personal advancement or against whom a score has to be settled.

After a very long term in office a leader has practically no solution to this, excepting ever more spectacular provision of electoral bounty. And almost immediately after the 1987 election this cornucopia seemed suddenly to have been emptied of all content, blown to the winds by the great hurricane which stripped the roofs and parks in southern England in October of that year, and tore through the financial markets of London and New York. The good fortune, as well as the authority, of the leadership seemed not to recover fully from that difficult winter.

I was present at the anniversary lunch in the Savoy Hotel in

May 1989, a great occasion with three former leaders, and Prime
Ministers, seated at the top table. It was to be a rerun of the
Falklands victory parade, though in a domestic context and with
each separate encounter being commemorated in speeches rather
than by the tramp of feet and the applause of crowds lining the
pavement. But I can illustrate the mood of the majority among
her Cabinet, as they now freely expressed it, from personal recollection – not diminished in value, I suggest, by its seeming triviality.
My table being adjacent to the top where Margaret Thatcher and
her predecessors, and other dignitaries, were seated, we had among
our number the personal bodyguard.

On leaving the dining room I fell into step beside a friend from
my schooldays, not long since a member of the Cabinet, and
making light conversation told him, 'We had a man with a gun at
our table.'

'Oh really', came the reply, 'why didn't he use it?'

THIRTY-THREE

The Year of Discontent

Exposure on two flanks – The breadth of discontent –
An invitation from Lord Carrington – Margaret
Thatcher's opinion of her colleagues – Differing
interpretations of the 1922 rules – Autocracy is
combined with negligence – Resignation of Sir Geoffrey
Howe – Heseltine challenges – Weaknesses in the Prime
Minister's position – Her departure.

BY THE EARLY spring of 1990 the concept of *changing* the Leader
of the Party for another (displacing, that is to say, a sitting Prime
Minister and installing in her place a former Cabinet colleague) was
assuming a gradually widening acceptance among Conservative
Members of Parliament. Margaret Thatcher had exposed both
flanks simultaneously. In the field of international affairs her isolation at the Councils of the European Community was portrayed
less now as heroic than as precarious. While domestic policy was
blighted by the poll tax; widely misrepresented but disastrously
unpopular and heavily overloading the postbag of all MPs and the
resilience of those holding down marginal constituencies. Harold
Macmillan administered by drip-feed his own particular potion of
toffish scorn, decrying the Cabinet (always a popular topic among
those who have been dismissed or feel themselves wrongly to have
been excluded) as suffering from 'more Estonians than Etonians*
and that Mrs Thatcher had redecorated Downing Street – the

---

* Both Leon Brittan and Lord Young had Baltic parenthood. Nigel Lawson,
Malcolm Rifkind and Michael Howard (not in the Cabinet) were Jewish.

height of middle-class aspiration – 'to look like Claridge's'.

Thus what had, initially, been no more than a form of words for expressing indignation or discontent, confined to a few who felt themselves to have been slighted or overlooked, now began to assume the status of a topic that could, if an appropriate tone of *gravitas* were sustained, be discussed at length, even in public. One Sunday evening in April Lord Carrington, the very personification (now that Viscount Whitelaw was in semi-retirement) of the Conservative establishment, had invited Margaret Thatcher to an intimate dinner at his private house. Carrington's diplomatic skills, a courteous manner equal parts flattery, heartiness and cajolery, were deployed. But his message – that the party '. . . wanted me to leave office both with dignity and at a time of my own choosing . . .'[1] – was no more welcome than it had been when relayed in the fifties to Winston Churchill, or in 1974 to Edward Heath. And the principal reason, or rather the excuse in which all of these Conservative Prime Ministers had in their time genuinely believed, was that there was no worthy, or even suitable, successor.

A photograph, taken in her anniversary year but less than six months before Carrington's dinner invitation, shows the Prime Minister seated at her desk in Number 10.[2] Certainly it is a formal study, with Charles Powell at her side. Together the two of them are looking at official papers. Margaret Thatcher is composed, glossy and utterly in control. This is a woman who has Britain's oldest political party at her feet. All Europe is in awe of her. Had she not dared, after visiting France to celebrate the bicentenary of the Revolution of '89, to express the opinion that their great national festival commemorated '. . . an attempt to overthrow a traditional order in the name of abstract ideas, formulated by vain intellectuals, which collapsed not by chance but through weakness and wickedness into purges, mass murder and war'?[3] Across the United States, and in Washington, she truly enjoys a 'special' position. Small wonder that she has recorded: 'For various reasons I did not believe that any of my own political generation were suitable . . . [to succeed me]'. There followed a perfunctory, dismissive and largely unsubstantiated résumé of the various reasons –

'Cecil Parkinson had been damaged in the eyes of the old Guard';
'Michael Heseltine was not a team player' (both of these, it may
be thought, pre-eminently personal characteristics which they
shared with Margaret Thatcher herself); while 'Something had
happened to Geoffrey . . . his clarity of purpose and analysis had
dimmed'.

At that time Margaret Thatcher's eye was on John Major. It is
usual for long-established autocrats, when they cannot designate
an heir from their own blood, subconsciously to select from a
generation some years distant. How long John Major would have
lasted as the leader's favourite boy is not possible to predict.
Perhaps no longer than did John Moore but it was his good fortune
to be still the beneficiary when events moved, as in the autumn
of 1990 they were to do, with alarming speed.

To leave office 'with dignity' had implied two assumptions.
First, that this departure would occur before a general election;
second, that it would be in advance of, rather than consequent to,
a challenge under the leadership rules. With the reshuffle complete, but many of its scars unhealed, Margaret Thatcher has
written that:

> The 1965 procedure for electing the Tory Leader was, by unwritten
> convention, not intended for use when the Party was in office.[4]

The basis for this assertion is unclear. In politics, especially where
crude power is at stake, it cannot be safe to rely on the strength
of an 'unwritten convention'. Indeed she herself has said that
'theoretically [sic] I had to be re-elected every year; but . . . no one
else stood . . .'

There had, in fact, been a challenge in November of 1989. Sir
Anthony Meyer was an opinionated Eurofederalist on the far Left
of the party. Personal irritation with Margaret Thatcher, and at
her behaviour, drove Meyer to act. And for a little while loyalists
had been made anxious. There was much discontent and frustration in the parliamentary party. Supposing they were to treat
the contest as a 'by-' rather than a 'general' election? A high
adverse vote – after some discussion the danger level was fixed at

eighty – might induce (whatever the rules provided) a demonstrative intrusion by Michael Heseltine. At the price of considerable, and specious, assurances from Ian Gow and others on the Prime Minister's team (she played no part herself in the campaign) that 'Things would improve' Meyer's vote was restricted to a total of thirty-three. There were three abstentions and, more ominously, twenty-five 'spoilt' ballot papers.

But in the spring of 1990 this seemed already to have been in the distant past. It was only, after all, a month or two since the roof of the Blackpool Conference Hall had shaken from the reverberations of enthusiastic constituency activists and their chanted '*Ten More Years*'. The party workers who expressed their support with such fervour were not to realise that the Prime Minister's authority within her own government was at last being seriously eroded. In her aversion to the monetary disciplines of Europe she was alone, save for Nicholas Ridley. And he was soon to be dismissed after the disclosure to the daily press of what he had believed to be a private conversation with the editor of the *Spectator*. A series of altercations with the Chancellor of the Exchequer, increasingly public in their context, had led to his resignation. Finally Sir Geoffrey Howe, already the subject of public humiliation (the Prime Minister's press secretary had told journalists that the position of Deputy Prime Minister 'didn't amount to anything', and there had been an unseemly public squabble concerning his official residence), resigned. Howe had taken umbrage at a spirited extempore dismissal of the Federalist concept which Thatcher was goaded into uttering when taking questions from the floor – after reading from a statement whose text, concerning the European Council meeting in Rome, had been agreed with the Foreign Office.

At once there was a welter of speculation, most of it gloating, in the press. Would this bring down the Government or, at the very least, the Prime Minister? It was the season, under the rules of the 1922 Committee, for a challenge. That Sunday, 4 November, the broadsheets devoted their entire political space to speculation as to the intentions of Mr Michael Heseltine. Thatcher conferred with her advisers. In order to pre-empt a bandwagon starting to roll she persuaded, or instructed, the Chairman of the '22, Cranley Onslow, to bring forward by a week the date of a contest (if in fact there was to be one). At the same time, a most foolhardy step, Bernard Ingham challenged Heseltine to 'put up or shut up'. On this occasion, and in marked contrast to the occasion of their last encounter at the time of Westland (although perhaps fortified by its recollection), Ingham's touch was less sure. In the full knowledge of Heseltine's impetuous character, Ingham attempted to provoke him. That central device of the Westland crisis – the leaked letter – was deployed once again. Leaked by whom? It hardly mattered. Leak was followed by counter-leak. One dignitary of the Henley association was read as asserting that their Member of Parliament had no following among his constituents. Another declared that he was greatly respected and had their full support. Did Thatcher realise how precarious her position was becoming? The tactical mistiming, so that the temperature was raised during the very fortnight when a leadership challenge was permitted, was itself unnecessarily reckless. Her absence in Paris not just for the closing days of the 'campaign' but for the count itself would seem needlessly disdainful of her parliamentarian constituency. While the general public mood, with the poll tax on the statute book and inflation rising fast, was fickle. Even the Lord Mayor's Banquet at the Guildhall, normally an uncritical audience, had listened in silence to the Prime Minister's jokes,[5] most of them within the cricketing metaphor – of which she was shortly, and catastrophically, to be reminded.

Thus when Geoffrey Howe finally delivered his resignation speech, on 13 November (and after conferring on the telephone with Michael Heseltine),[6] he was already certain of a sympathetic audience. Two of his sentences were to enter history. Of trying to negotiate in European Councils:

> It is rather like sending your opening batsmen to the crease only for them to find the moment the first balls are bowled, that their bats have been broken before the game by the team captain.

And effectively signalling a green light to Heseltine by implicitly removing himself from any contest:

> The time has come for others to consider their own response to the tragic conflict of loyalties with which I have myself wrestled for perhaps too long...[7]

Heseltine 'declared' immediately and the arena was cleared for a fight to the death.

For the next week or so the Conservative Party in the House of Commons shed any pretence of being the natural governing party, or even of concern for the day-to-day incidents of administration. It had become completely introverted. The power of the electoral college which Douglas-Home had brought into being, which had conducted itself with some decorum in the contest between Maudling and Heath and which, flexing its muscles with greater abandon, had replaced Heath with Thatcher, now showed many of the symptoms of decadence.

MPs were so consumed by their own importance, so indulgent of the pleasures of gossip, intrigue and – in not a few cases – sweet retaliation, that they lost sight of their two principal *raisons d'être* – the good of the country and the interests of their constituents. It may well be that both would be served by a change of leadership. Or not. But MPs saw things only from their own aspect. The Parliament had run but half its course; few had yet announced their intention to retire at the next election even though a good number may privately have resolved to do so. Eighteen months lay ahead and promised now an atmosphere greatly altered. Many had foreseen defeat – for such in reality it was to be, even with that arithmetical majority – for the Prime Minister. It is probably true that a majority even, although voting for her in that first ballot, had not done so with any special goodwill or fervent hope of her sweeping success.

But very few realised that this defeat was irretrievable. Immediately following the statement from the courtyard – few settings could have been so charged with irony – of the Ambassador's residence in Paris, a number of loyalists and others whose personal survival was closely linked to Mrs Thatcher, set about trying to improvise a campaign machine for the second ballot. Gerald Neale made contact with David Davis, and other 'first-generation' Thatcherites. On the assumption (itself quite tenuous) that all those who had supported her in the first ballot would do so again, they set about the corralling of 'just' twenty more votes. In the Commons dining room that night there were some loyalist tables to be found that regarded the outcome of the second vote as a foregone conclusion.

At this point a rather closer look is required at the party, its conduct in adversity and its motives – conscious or instinctive. The first consideration that preoccupies MPs except on those very rare occasions of absolute national crisis (all of them in this chronicle at least – Norway, Suez, the Falklands – being associated with armed conflict) is the balance of probability in their retaining their parliamentary seats. Self-centred this may be, but it above all else accounts for that strange ability of the Tory Party to sleepwalk the path to whichever tactical decision will keep it in power. In the case of Mrs Thatcher, it was not easy to know whether she was, by November of 1990, an electoral liability. Certainly the polls said so. And, most discouragingly for Mrs Thatcher's supporters, the polls also showed that a substantially larger percentage of the electorate would vote Conservative if the party were led by Michael Heseltine instead of by her. This kind of 'snapshot' may not have been wholly valid, but it was an unpromising background against which to mount a defence.

There were a number of other factors special to this case – all of them to the disadvantage of Margaret Thatcher. Her intelligence system was defective in the highest degree. The Chief Whip, Tim Renton, was a placeman of Geoffrey Howe, installed as part of the concessionary dealing on which Howe had insisted when he was sacked as Chancellor. His private preference was that she should lose, and at an early stage he had put the Whips' Room into a neutral mode (of which all that could be said was that from Mrs Thatcher's point of view this was an improvement on 1975 when they had been actually working against her). Mrs Thatcher's own private office, which had operated so effectively under Ian Gow, had been in steady decline since 1983 and by 1990 was in a state of virtual atrophy.

To some extent this was a natural consequence of her own standing in the House of Commons. From 1979, and most particularly in 1981, Mrs Thatcher's survival had depended on the full and enthusiastic support of her own back-benchers, whom she could invoke against that majority in Cabinet – the 'Wets' – who not only disagreed with, but wished to displace, her. These MPs were most ably cultivated, with every appearance of deferential attention, by Ian Gow. He had taken over the Prime Minister's private office after the murder of Airey Neave. But following the 1983 general election the Prime Minister was (to deploy the adjective in its correct usage, as distinct from when she herself used it in referring to her Chancellor in 1989) *unassailable*. Executive problems were more likely to originate in Whitehall than at Westminster and increasingly, against the background of the international role which the Prime Minister had assumed and with which she had become so deeply preoccupied, with the Foreign Office.

Here the most 'helpful' and very soon the most powerful, figure at the Prime Minister's court was Mr Charles Powell. And for the presentation of policies, as for the periodic 'dirty trick', Mrs Thatcher had come increasingly to rely on Mr Bernard Ingham. Always (and understandably) mistrustful of Conservative Central Office since their hostile behaviour at the time of her own assault on the leadership in 1975, and deeply suspicious of senior civil servants, the Prime Minister came to operate directly, short-circuiting the conventional channels, through her personal staff at Number 10. This practice led almost to as much resentment in the parliamentary party as it did inside the machinery of government. Some MPs used it as a convenient cover for more deeply rooted antipathy – whether personal or doctrinal or both. But most back-benchers felt the change. The illusion of approachability which Ian Gow had so expertly developed was no more. And when to this was added a stark and immediate threat to their own seats – most cruelly exemplified by the result of the Eastbourne by-election in Gow's very own constituency, following his murder in July 1990 – it became plain that the core loyalty of the back-bench majority was no longer infinitely durable.

The reader of Margaret Thatcher's own account of this time will be struck by her preoccupation with securing, and locking in, assurances of support from her Cabinet. And contrast this with the confidence that allowed her to put them to flight in 1981, or indeed when she had invoked the back-benchers – the Peasants' Revolt, as Sir Julian Critchley was later to term it – against the party establishment in 1975. Certainly among the many factors accounting for this is her neglect of both the mechanism, and the personalities, needed to operate an effective House of Commons intelligence and mobilisation system.

It is remarkable, in terms of raw politics, this complete failure by Margaret Thatcher to plan strategically, still less tactically, for her own personal defence. An unusual weakness, not normally found among those at the head of the Conservative Party.

Macmillan, as we have seen, was also believed by many, in the spring of 1963 if not before, to be eligible for replacement. Yet he fought to the bitter end having, at a strategic level, dismissed from the Cabinet practically every member who might have been seen as a contender, on the Night of the Long Knives. And, tactically, even down to such minutiae as to order Cabinet business on the basis of when the last train guaranteeing a place on the Conference platform would be leaving for Blackpool Chamberlain remained, until his very last hours, in the closest contact both with the Chief Whip, David Margesson and with his right-hand man at Central Office, Sir Joseph Ball. Churchill, while ready to allow others to depict him as being 'above' such considerations, was adept at the pre-emption, both on the floor of the House or on the international stage, of his enemies' devices.

Margaret Thatcher was certainly a victim of her own self-confidence. Her opinion of all those who might contest for her own job was so low that she thought it incredible that the party could, seriously and after due reflection, prefer to put some one of them in her place. The superficialities of her situation gave welcome reinforcement to this view. The Cabinet was sulky, to be sure. But in session it gave still the appearance of docility. Sir Geoffrey Howe, like some unhappy beast of burden, would simply lower his head deeper and deeper into his brief as the blows rained on him. Their eyes never met; but none of Howe's colleagues would interrupt these vituperative assaults. The order of Cabinet business did not change, so that the Prime Minister (unlike either her predecessors or John Major) would open the discussion giving, often in uncompromising tones, her opinion on the subject before them. Effective though this may have been in expediting proceedings in the good times, it was a technique that excluded any measurement of the strength of opinion, or of the nuances of personal alignment, around the table. A leader better informed would surely have found it easier to divide and rule – this being, for the moment at least, her only chance of avoiding serious trouble.

On the broader stage the Prime Minister had become accustomed to total adulation. A decade of motorcades, in every capital city in the world; of dominating in most cases the main Conference, and always the press conference which followed it;* the direct telephone link to the White House. In contrast the tearoom of the House of Commons must have seemed squalid, petty and unimportant. This error of judgement was compounded by a perilously inadequate parliamentary private office. Neither of her two secretaries was of any use at what should always be the primary function of the Prime Minister's principal aide – the gathering of information. Both left that task to the Whips' Office, in ignorance of the fact that this body had long since developed its own far from amiable motivation. Sir Michael Alison was an Old Etonian who in his youth had served in the Coldstream Guards. In later life he became a devout Christian, and was reluctant to believe ill

* A copy of Mr Bernard Ingham's notes for the Maggiore Summit is included as Appendix IV.

of anybody. Sir Peter Morrison was also an Etonian. In the past he had served as a Whip, and been responsible for the approval of 'pairing'; a role in which enmity is both suffered and aroused. The two men contented themselves with being pleasant (not always even that in the case of Sir Peter) and escorting the Prime Minister when she moved about the place.

Nor had Margaret Thatcher made any attempt to recruit into the Cabinet from the various pools of support that remained loyal to her in the parliamentary party. She allowed the Whips to talk her out of promoting Nicholas Ridley to Chancellor, preferring John Major in whose 'loyalty' she believed because he had been her protégé; and thus ignoring one of the basic rules of politics – that the pluperfect tense annuls historic obligation. Was the Thatcher intelligence system so defective that no one reported to her Major's verdict – six months before the coup, and recorded in the diary of Judith Chaplin, a detached and observant official – that she was 'finished'?[8]

Thatcher had made no attempt to fill even the middle and lower ranks with her committed supporters. The '92 Group, a right-wing dining club of some forty members whose efficiency in dominating the elections to party committees was a byword, and which was to become one of the centres of internal opposition to John Major, she almost completely neglected. Now the Prime Minister was to find that an annual visit as guest of honour, on which occasion she would gush her appreciation of their '*true loyalty*', was not enough. There was never (or not, at least, since the deaths each at the hand of the IRA – of Airey Neave and Ian Gow) a true Praetorian Guard; a devoted body, that is, properly armed with the keys of departmental office, and access to policy.

From time to time (and there is no evidence that it caused her anything but pleasure) Margaret Thatcher would be compared with Joan of Arc.* It is unlikely that she appreciated the full irony of how apposite this comparison was to become. The Maid of Orleans, having delivered France from her enemies, had afterwards

---

* See p. 473 above.

found herself first plotted against, then abandoned, by the French nobility who came to believe that her incongruity was threatening. Just as soon as news was brought of Heseltine's declaration of intent to challenge, Sir Peter Morrison put together a team of prominent senior Conservatives who would 'work' for the Prime Minister: a former Chairman of the Party; a former Chief Whip; the 'manager' of her campaign the previous year; one of her most favoured protégés.

Alas, this seems to have amounted to little more than putting the names down on a sheet of paper. Sir Norman Fowler claimed that his friendship (of which few people had been aware until that moment) with Geoffrey Howe would 'make his position impossible'. Mr Michael Jopling (a curious choice by Morrison as Jopling had been sacked from his position as Agriculture Minister by Thatcher in 1987) made his excuses immediately. George Younger was amiable in his encouragement but explained that his duties as Chairman of the Royal Bank of Scotland placed too many demands on his time. Mr John Moore disclaimed a role on the grounds that he was 'out of the country so often'. (It was not anticipated that the campaign would last for longer than six days.) A further unwelcome augury was the behaviour of Mr Peter Lilley, notionally a cerebral Thatcherite, who had replaced Nicholas Ridley a few months earlier at the Department of Trade and Industry. Asked to lend his help to the composition of a speech which the Prime Minister was to make in the confidence debate the following week he declined on the somewhat crudely expressed grounds that 'There's no point. She's finished.'[9]

On Sunday 17 November, the Prime Minister convened a small dinner party – it was to be her last – at Chequers. The guest list is instructive. There were but two members of the Cabinet present. Kenneth Baker, a man deeply unpopular with colleagues and with an indifferent record of achievement in office, whose career was entirely bound up with her fate; and John Wakeham. All the rest – Alistair McAlpine, Tim Bell, Peter Morrison, Gordon Reece, Michael Neubert and his wife, John Whittingdale – were hangers-on or nonentities. Thatcher's two children, Carol and Mark, also sat around the table. This was not a purposeful occasion. Forced heartiness and competitive essays in reassurance were the predominant themes.[10] The central subject was seldom referred to, although most diners will by now have become uneasy concerning the result. This ominous 'distancing' by the senior figures in the party was a foretaste of the wholesale change in declared attitude that followed the first count.

Certainly the trust, if in reality she believed it, that Margaret Thatcher had reposed in her Cabinet was misplaced. Whose idea was it, once the result was known, that these senior but very far from devoted colleagues should be called into the Prime Minister's room singly in order to give their opinion? It is possible, although highly unlikely, that the Prime Minister might have extracted a grudging authority from her Cabinet, had she addressed them fully assembled – as Macmillan had done in October 1963. One by one they entered (having of course first conferred among themselves in small like-minded groups and agreed their 'line'). Some, notably Malcolm Rifkind and Christopher Patten, were clear that she should go. All that had to be determined was the emollience of their language. Others were more concerned to take out insurance – in every direction – but their innate pessimism was unmistakable. As the evening wore on Margaret Thatcher, if the medieval analogy may be pursued, came increasingly to resemble a fourteenth-century monarch who summons allegiance from distant earldoms and margravates within her fief; tragically being compelled to face a reality, not so much of betrayal as of indifference.

Elsewhere in the Palace of Westminster a regiment of loyalists spontaneously assembled. Neale, Forsyth, Portillo – and others – pursued her to Number 10. Singly and in little groups they came to the door insisting on an audience. Beyond the midnight hour they argued for a second round. This was the body to which, over the last eighteen months, Margaret Thatcher should have turned to draw support, placing them in the junior ranks of her Cabinet. Now it was too late. Energy they possessed in abundance, to be sure; but neither standing nor experience.

For Thatcher to re-form her battle line, cut adrift from the grandees whose 'ugly streak of contempt' she had first identified when, herself, battling for the leadership in 1975* might have been in character a decade earlier. Now, though, she was dejected and more cautious. The risk of losing to Heseltine – of all people – was one that she dared not run, being driven by a lethal mix of personal dislike for her challenger and protective zeal for the policies to which her name had become attached.

There is a certain grandiose innocence about the manner in which Margaret Thatcher met her end. The Conservative Party had dismissed in succession five of its six preceding leaders. Only Macmillan (and that by falling suddenly ill) had cheated the execution squad. Sometimes their fate had been abrupt, as with Chamberlain and Heath. Sometimes dressed with a contrived courtesy, as in the 'resignation' of Churchill and – more heartfelt – of Douglas-Home. But in every case once a certain mood and intention had taken hold of the party, there was no stopping it.

And yet right up until the evening of 21 November 1990 Margaret Thatcher could not *believe* that she was doomed. For six more days she remained in limbo, conducting government business at an exiguous level, preoccupied now with her single remaining obsession – the thwarting of Heseltine. And when the news came through, first of John Major's lead at the opening ballot, then of Heseltine's conceding defeat, accounts have it that the Prime Minister (as still she would remain for a few more hours) danced on the landing at the head of the main staircase in Number 10.

All too soon, though, Sir Tim Bell noticed that the crowd around her thinned – '. . . as people left her side and gravitated to Major'.[11] Truly recognition of the transfer of power is, at the epicentre of its vortex, instantaneous.

* See p. 466 above.

THIRTY-FOUR

The Beginning of the End

A very short honeymoon – The Prime Minister travels
to Bonn – Maastricht – A personal victory at the polls –
The Maastricht time bomb detonates – Heseltine takes
revenge on the Nottingham miners – 'Sleaze', and the
forfeiture of respect.

THE ABRUPT EXPULSION of Mrs Thatcher from the office of
Prime Minister seemed, at first, to have achieved the impossible –
a complete reversal in the electoral fortunes of the Conservative
Party. Measured by every opinion poll John Major managed,
within the space of a few weeks, to attain a higher approval rating
than any Prime Minister since Winston Churchill.

Slowly though, yet gradually increasing in severity, certain
symptoms became apparent. There had been implanted in the
party's body politic a malignant condition. It was caused (if the
medical analogy may be pursued) by the coming together of
several incompatible strains of chromosome.

First, a certain covert triumphalism among the parliamentary
party at large; unspoken but, henceforth, ineradicable. 'Deselection', the most dreaded word in the back-benchers' glossary when
used as a threat, was now all too obviously a power which they
themselves held in their own hands. Here, just as with the constituencies, it must be only a matter of time before *L'appétit
s'aggrand en manger.* The deed having been perpetrated so flagrantly
and with so little regard for decorum; the concepts of loyalty and
honour having been so crudely relegated; it was plain that the

tenure of leaders in the future – the Lewis 'leasehold'* – would be henceforth precarious.

As always, the primary concern of MPs was for their own tenure. Their postbag on the poll tax had been huge; there were graffiti of protest everywhere in their constituencies – on garage doors, smooth walls, flat surfaces. At last the old Left had found receptive terrain for agitation while memories of those violent riots that had marked the closing months of the Thatcher period were still disturbingly fresh.

And as the euphoria of the 'honeymoon' polls subsided MPs became fearful again – the very emotion which had contributed so powerfully to their discontent with Margaret Thatcher. Major addressed this immediately. He let it be known that the poll tax would go, be altered in effect so as to revive, with a different title, the old rating system.

Quite quickly, in a matter of months only, the party's lead in the opinion polls shrank. Soon it disappeared altogether and the ratings of both the Conservatives and their leader went into deficit. Now considerable numbers of MPs announced their intention to retire, and the feeling spread that the Government's life expectancy was precarious.

But there was another subject that needed to be handled with a greater finesse. It was Europe, which had in fact been the undoing of Mrs Thatcher; which had led to her personal isolation, caused Geoffrey Howe finally to turn on her in public and, even in her last month as Prime Minister, had required her attention at the CSCE† Conference in Paris when she should have remained in London personally to defend her position in the smoke-filled committee rooms of the House of Commons.

Within a very short time of entering on the premiership John Major made a remark that was to blight his diplomacy – both internal and external – for the whole of the rest of his period.

---

* See p. 460 above.
† Conference on Security and Co-operation in Europe.

Attending a CDU conference in Bonn (hardly the most tactful setting as far as his own parliamentary colleagues were concerned) Major, after addressing the audience as '*meine Damen und Herren*' said that he wanted Britain to be '... where we belong, at the very heart of Europe, working with our partners ...' Since the German press paid not the slightest attention, the speech being barely reported, as a diplomatic overture it was useless. But it served notice on the Thatcherite wing of Major's own party that they might not have 'bought' quite what they thought when they voted him into the leadership. And the impression was deepened when the Party Chairman, Mr Christopher Patten, a notorious 'Wet' who had played a significant role in undermining Margaret Thatcher in her last hours, declared himself to be a 'Christian Democrat' rather than a Conservative. Patten even encouraged the Tory Euro-MPs to join the European People's Party in the Strasbourg Parliament on a platform which included '*the institutional development of the Community into a European Union of a federal type*'.

For most of the year the party was more concerned about its falling total in the opinion polls than with the detail of European policy. The shadow of the Maastricht Conference in December lay long on the political landscape and some of the old Thatcher coterie – Norman Tebbit, Teddy Taylor, Margaret Thatcher herself – sounded notes of warning. But most were preoccupied with the approach, and then the passing, of the date for an October election. The Labour lead seemed to be irreducible. The assumption that this would be the last Conservative Parliament gained strength as sitting MPs announced, in great numbers, their intention to retire.

There now occurred the first of John Major's many evasionist *coups*. He returned from the Maastricht Summit claiming to have 'confirmed' the country's right to opt out of the single currency, and to have blocked EU moves to impose the social charter. *The Times* echoed the euphoria:

John Major returned from Maastricht to a hero's welcome from

Conservative MPs yesterday, optimistic that he had struck a deal
to lay the European ghost that has dogged his party and destroyed
the career of several senior ministers

– although only a year away was the paper's portentous editorial
headed '*The Maastricht vice*'. For the time being the party quietened
down and began to prepare for the election. Even Margaret
Thatcher, it was noted, had 'smiled and nodded' throughout the
Prime Minister's statement. Only seven MPs voted against the
Government in the Commons debate★ a week after Major's
return.

Now came Major's second remarkable achievement. He won
the general election. And this he did in the face of much mockery
and denigration, a unanimous prediction of failure in the Conservative press, and a high degree of private disloyalty among
individual MPs who found it convenient, during the campaign
and almost to the end, to excuse their own failings by reference
to John Major not being well received 'on the doorstep'.[1] In fact
the very reverse was true. Major's personal likeability; his readiness
to mix informally (the 'soap-box'); the contrast with Neil
Kinnock, alternately bombastic and whingeing, persuaded people
that they would be safer in returning to the Tories.

So, on 15 April 1992, John Major arrived at his peak moment,
never to be repeated, of personal authority. *Personally* it could be
said, just as it used to be claimed of Margaret Thatcher, he had
delivered victory. Many colleagues 'owed' their seats to him.
Gratitude, certainly, is a highly perishable commodity in politics,
but if ever there was a time to consolidate his grip on the party
this was it. This was an extraordinary opportunity, without precedent since 1931 and unlikely ever to be repeated, for the party
to set its stamp not just on the century but on the millennium.
The Labour Party was in great confusion. Kinnock was a liability,
to be disposed of as rapidly as was decent. His successor would be
safe, plodding, 'old' in doctrine if not in years. Most commentators

★ A further three abstained: Margaret Thatcher, Gerald Howarth and Teresa
Gorman.

assumed a Tory administration in perpetual office, developing perhaps its own 'factions' in the manner of the Japanese Social Democrats.

Unlike, though, the two predecessors whom he professed at different times to admire most, Baldwin and Chamberlain,* Major seems to have had no concept of a broad policy objective. Stanley Baldwin had a political objective – the destruction of the Liberal Party and the personal humiliation of Lloyd George. Baldwin had a national goal, also: to bring about and maintain a decent and tranquil society which would allow the wounds inflicted by the Great War – social and economic – to heal. Neville Chamberlain no longer bothered about the Liberals. Unlike Baldwin, who at least pretended to have a 'soft spot' for Labour, in Chamberlain's case it was Labour whom he feared and disliked. Chamberlain's National goal, in which ultimately he was unsuccessful and which brought about his political downfall, was to keep the British Empire out of a European war.

Now, at the end of the century, it was Europe which again cast a long shadow, and the shadow was sombre indeed. Having humiliated one Prime Minister (Macmillan) and destroyed a second (Thatcher), it was Major's lasting apprehension that Europe would do the same for him unless, by whatever dissimulation and sleight of hand might be necessary, he kept the Conservative Party in one piece.

Upon his return to the Cabinet Room, now as Prime Minister incumbent, Major experienced one, accidental, surprise. A pile of papers awaited him. And that which was uppermost, a general briefing on engagements for the immediate future, caught his eye.

The pace at which 'submissions' from officials fill the prime ministerial box during an election campaign slackens. This is particularly true when, as was the case in 1992, there is a broad

---

* John Major would not pretend to be much of a scholar concerning these two statesmen, and it is more than possible that he simply identified them (on different occasions) as a way of disclaiming too close a link with Margaret Thatcher.

expectation in Whitehall that the Government will be changing. '*Who'll help Neil rule?*' had asked (in red typeface) the cover of Labour's house magazine, the *New Statesman*. And the article within made mention of a number of distinguished civil servants, and other putative members of a new establishment. 'There will be a lot of people in Whitehall who will be longing for a change' was the quoted opinion of Lady Blackstone.[2] Even so, Major was disconcerted to see the injunction, attached to his next engagement in the European Community,

> On this occasion, you will wish to notify your partners that you intend to sign up to the Social Chapter.[3]

The 'advice', worded in this instance more as an instruction, had been intended for Kinnock, and there had been not time to effect a substitution. But here, at a very early stage, was the clearest evidence of that submerged, almost unanimous, force of opinion in the Civil Service – which mirrored, sometimes even in enhanced form, the enthusiasm of their official counterparts in Brussels – that an accelerated move towards a Federal Europe was now urgent.

Within a month, though, as the small print of the Maastricht Treaty began to emerge, there were twenty-two Eurosceptics who voted against the Bill. Only a fortnight later the Danes voted by referendum not to ratify the Treaty. This, under a strict interpretation of the Treaty text itself, rendered the whole project null and void. And eighty-two Conservative MPs, a significant number indeed, signed a motion calling for a 'fresh start'.

Worse was to follow. After an uneasy summer of hesitance and recrimination, speculation against the pound sterling reached such a pitch that, on 'white' Wednesday, 16 September, Britain quit the Exchange Rate Mechanism to which originally the then Chancellor subscribed on the basis that it offered a refuge from currency turbulence. Major subsequently argued that, having given his word in international negotiation, he could not go back on it and take advantage of the 'loophole' offered by the result of the Danish referendum. Certainly this begs the question as to whether the honouring of an undertaking made to a group of foreign powers should rank above majority opinion in his own country. Instead Major conspired with the other EU ministers to bully and cajole the Danes into holding a second vote the following year; and in the intervening period to carry on as if the episode had never taken place.

Major has since claimed that he saw the ERM as necessary to protect the pound against speculators. But whatever validity this argument may have had at the time of the Bretton Woods Agreement it was now, and had for many years been, entirely specious. Fixed-rate systems were effective at 'ironing out' minor fluctuations and were convenient for businessmen. But as a defence mechanism to protect against the exploitation of fundamental imbalances they were worse than useless – affording, simply, extra time during which the speculators could enrich themselves. And in fact it was the speculators from *within* the system, including especially the Bundesbank, that had started the run. By now the majority of Conservatives were deeply uneasy. The Party Conference was in uproar with the sceptics, led by Norman Tebbit, being cheered to the rafters. Emboldened, MPs were voting regularly against the Government. On 4 November 1992 the 'Paving' resolution of the Maastricht Bill scraped through by three votes. But on 8 March 1993, with the Conservative majority now seriously eroded by 'wastage' and lost by-elections, the Government were defeated by 314 to 296 with 26 of their own side voting against. In July came, at last and after much rancour, the motion to ratify the Treaty and the Government were again defeated by 324 to 316. Immediately Major declared a vote of confidence, and scraped home – probably the last time that this could have been guaranteed. Only five days later the Prime Minister was caught on a 'live' microphone referring to his Eurosceptic ministers as 'bastards'. Such divisions had not been seen in the Conservative Party since the days of Tariff Reform (or, a better illustration, of Munich) – if then. Practically the whole of the Conservative press were stridently, and regularly and, often, prejudicially critical of Major. Talk in the parliamentary party of his replacement was continuous – and not confined to the 'Right'. It was clear that a challenge would come, under the rules of the 1922 Committee – all that was uncertain being when, and from whom?

In the five years of life that remained to it the Conservative administration was to suffer a number of setbacks, none of them singly apocalyptic, but whose cumulative effect was to render the party virtually unelectable. Some were macroeconomic, like the ERM fiasco. Some called into question either their competence – like the BSE affair – or, with the handgun legislation, the steadiness of their nerve under pressure. Some were the result of defective internal management – like the steadily rising level of bitterness over 'Europe'. Others, most notably the argument over the single currency, arose from a simultaneous failure either to explain the issues or to assert prime ministerial authority in the House of Commons – or even in Cabinet. The impression of fatigue was heightened by the tendency among ministers – many of whom had been in Whitehall for more than a decade – to prefer the esteem and, in 'speeches', to echo the exact formulae, of their own civil servants (which was hardly surprising as it was usual for the civil servants to write the text, and all, on most occasions, that the minister had to do was to read it out).

A particularly damaging episode was the pigheaded and tactless closure of the Nottingham pits. Many suggestions have been offered to explain, even to excuse, its mishandling. Michael Heseltine, whose responsibility this was, had just been reconfirmed, after a most nervous opening, as the favourite of the Party Conference. He will have felt that his personal prestige was now fully recovered, and that (not an easy argument to reconcile with having contested an election against him) Major 'owed' his premiership to Heseltine's 'sacrifice' in November of 1990.[4] As the pressure mounted, Heseltine refused to give way. Over 20,000 letters were received at Number 10. The Chairman of the 1922 Committee said that the closures were 'unacceptable'.[5] All Conservatives were furious because it was the Nottingham Union of Democratic

Mineworkers whose loyalty had undermined the NUM strike of 1985 and saved Margaret Thatcher's battle plan. (Possibly also for this reason Heseltine felt that he owed them very little.) At the end an expensive U-turn was put into place. But Arthur Scargill was able to say, 'I told you so.' The Conservative Government of John Major could now be depicted as equally harsh as that of Margaret Thatcher (though markedly less competent).

But of all the factors the most tiresome, the hardest to eradicate, and (on this scale) the most novel, was the image of 'sleaze'. Tiresome, because in essence it was superficial in content. Not central, that is to say, to the effective governance of the country and certainly completely distinct from the personal conduct and image of the Prime Minister. Tiresome, also, because it seemed impossible for the public (and certainly they were not encouraged in this by the media, who used the term at random to describe any conduct that merited a headline) to distinguish between financial corruption and sexual impropriety.

To some extent the Conservatives brought this latter confusion upon themselves by trumpeting (the concept was very soon dropped) the idea of *Family Values*. Whatever that meant it was inevitable that editors should interpret it in their own way and then publicise cases where, in their opinion, those 'values' were being flouted. In fact, as the Party Chairman did at an early instance comment, 'This is no more than you may find in any large group or corporation'. But the analogy was not an entirely comfortable one. Nor was the case in question – that of an obscure back-bencher who had been found strangled by an electric flex while dressed in female underwear and with, lodged in his gullet, an orange impregnated with amphetamines – particularly promising ground on which to make a stand. Certainly, mention of the 'sado-masochistic *community*' was scarcely well-chosen at a time when many people in the party were having difficulty enough coming to terms with the European one.

As for financial corruption, the number of MPs 'on the take' was not large. Fewer, probably, than the number who were leading irregular private lives. Directorships, 'consultancies', the acquisition of tangential benefits, had long been part of the advantage attaching to back-benchers in the party of government. And, provided that they were declared on the Register of Members' Interests, and tax duly paid, were not regarded as improper. These perks were seldom a reflection of the recipient's acumen; more of his or her ability to pick up the telephone and get straight through to a minister or a senior official.

But then a new, and more disreputable, element began to break the surface. It appeared that Members of Parliament were accepting money, or money's worth, to ask questions of ministers, and elicit information that would be of advantage to their paymasters. This struck at the very root of a Member's relations with his constituency, the protection and advancement of whose interests was traditionally the motivation for detailed questioning. Several Conservatives were actually entrapped, caught on tape, by a national newspaper, discussing terms with an impostor 'lobbyist'. Worse, Mr Mohammed Al Fayed, the owner of Harrods and a man of considerable ruthlessness and determination who (probably with some reason) nurtured a grudge against the Conservatives on account of their refusal to process his naturalisation papers had, apparently, put a number of back-benchers on his payroll. In one case the cruder traditions of the corporate hospitality room were applied at the Ritz Hotel in Paris; where two guests emptied into their suitcase the entire contents of the bedroom mini-bar before leaving the premises. Al Fayed's scale of reward was munificent. And the manner of its transmission – in high-denomination used banknotes in brown-paper envelopes – implied at the very least a certain laxity in book-keeping.

Perhaps this misconduct was dealt with by Major in too measured a style. There are times when setting up an inquiry is a useful device that allows Government to muffle discordance until public outrage (or curiosity) has abated. But in the mid-nineties two phenomena aggravated the general indignation. The majority of people had suffered from the recession. Many had seen their own assets diminish in value. Some were seriously in debt through little fault of their own other than (it seemed to them) taking government assurances at face value. Yet now a separate class, immune to economic privation, seemed to have come into being. The directors of the newly privatised monopolies were awarding themselves colossal salary increases while, at the same time, raising the cost of the commodity that they were supplying beyond any reasonable expectation. Share-option schemes proliferated, endowing their beneficiaries, overnight in some cases, with sums to the value of several 'ordinary' people's houses. And yet it seemed that the very people who should be monitoring this, the MPs themselves, had switched their allegiance to become part of the process of private enrichment. They, too, aspired to be 'fat cats'.

Was there any way out of this? One solution put privately[6] to Major was that he might require all of his colleagues to lodge, in their constituency office, a full register of their extra-parliamentary receipts, so that their own electors could inspect it on demand at any time. Only thus would complete 'transparency' be restored.

'If I did that', was his reply without much humour, one must suspect, 'they'd have me for breakfast'.[7]

The Prime Minister might, of course, have insisted; appealed over the heads of his parliamentary party to the country as a whole where, still, he commanded personal respect. This comment came in the month that Major was to contrive, and after a fashion win, a leadership election. The combination of authority renewed, on a platform of asceticism, could have been strengthened by a clear-cut attitude to Europe. In all probability it mattered not very much what this attitude was – as long as it could be clearly understood. Europe did not figure high among the concerns of the electorate. This was John Major's last opportunity to put up a real fight. But it involved taking a huge risk also. And to have conducted himself in this way would have been wholly out of character. Because then, as throughout the period, the profile of the opinion polls was bad. A snap election, particularly if seeming to arise from a total rupture within the party, would be lost. Although probably not lost badly. Major's national reputation might well have been enhanced; although the party would never have forgiven him – as is always the case when its leaders miscalculate the timing of a dissolution.

And it is this uncertainty that blighted the whole process of decision and leadership throughout Major's second term. Always there was the hope, justifying compromise and delay but diminishing most painfully as the months and years passed, that there might be first an improvement; then, as in 1992, a deliverance. This never came about. And even in the very last weeks, after the promulgation of the Downey Inquiry (into MPs' earnings) did to a large extent defuse the corruption crisis, a whole series of personal 'scandals' came thick and fast.

An MP was discovered to have enjoyed a 'relationship' with a married woman whom he had met at an alcohol dependency clinic. Another was set up by a tabloid newspaper which photographed him embracing a seventeen-year-old 'hostess', whom he had invited to help canvassing, in a public park in his constituency. A backbench MP suffered the indignity of seeing his 'love' letters to a male researcher published in the press. Another very senior party dignitary felt suddenly obliged to resign in circumstances that remain unexplained, and the resultant by-election was catastrophically lost.

Essentially these episodes were completely trivial. Redolent, indeed, of slapstick more than disrepute. But they were presented in the media as further instalments of a 'sleaze' that had come to be seen as exclusively, and characteristically, Tory. Gloomily a former minister mused, 'Is the Labour Party made up of two hundred virgins?' Alas, that was to miss the point. The British public are very easygoing. And certainly the conduct of which they were reading was a useful antidote to the argument (no one quite liked to deploy this case) that MPs should be 'more like ordinary people'. What was felt to be demeaning was the absurdity of it all. Combined with their evident incompetence, and their staleness, it caused the Conservative Party to forfeit that most valuable of all political currencies in a democratic society – respect.

THIRTY-FIVE

A Trial of Leadership

The Prime Minister is dejected – The likelihood of a
challenge – and his decision to pre-empt – John
Redwood declares – Shifting factions – The 'deal' with
Michael Heseltine – The party remains uneasy.

THE MANNER IN which John Major conducted himself both
during and immediately after the contrived leadership contest of
July 1995 illustrates to perfection both the nature of his character,
and the difficulties of subjecting it to definition.

Here is this man incapable, or so it seems, of making any
pronouncement of a public nature – still less a formal speech –
without taking refuge in the repetitious qualification and cliché
of the Whitehall briefing note (only a year hence when invited to
wish the English football team well, in advance of their match
against Germany, he would express his hope for a *satisfactory*
result). And yet in private, or before a very small group, Major is
witty, clear-headed and incisive. Are the inhibitions which blight
(or so it appears) his style and deportment on formal occasions
grounded in shyness, and insecurity? Or is it a camouflage that
allows him to operate without at any time exposing his true self,
or his private objectives? In seeking to answer this conundrum art,
as often can happen, is a better guide than science. And just as
Vicky's mocking depiction of Harold Macmillan as 'Supermac'
conceived at first in irony was soon accorded, by friend and foe
alike, the status of a 'brand name', so the portrayal of John Major
by the *Guardian* cartoonist Steve Bell wearing, absurdly, a set of
'briefs' outside his suit, even at international conferences, has

subliminally illustrated a particular, recurrent (and to Major's enemies unwelcome) truth. Namely that whatever trapdoors, explosions or custard pies may affect his colleagues, when the smoke clears Major is standing, and still in charge.

So, it can be asked, was the decision to call a contest, itself of dubious validity within the Douglas-Home rules – not that there was the least likelihood of Sir Marcus Fox objecting on these grounds – a tactical masterstroke, pre-empting the carefully planned timetable of his enemies? Or was it an act of impulse, founded in a combination of petulance and fatigue?

Certainly John Major, in the last weeks of June 1995, had been apprehensive. At that time it appeared inevitable that there would be a leadership challenge when the rules allowed it, in November. Would this challenge come from a nonentity? Mr John Carlisle had let it be known that his name would without fail go forward. Would it come from the Salon des Refusés, of whom the most prominent, and the person most frequently canvassed by malcontents, was Mr Norman Lamont? Or might it come from within the Cabinet itself? There were rumours, or traces of rumour (although none broke in the press), that Mr John Redwood was planning to resign just ahead of the Budget, and publish simultaneously his own proposals for taxation and expenditure. The Welsh Secretary, Major was warned, was working on his own 'manifesto'.*

These apprehensions were compounded by exhaustion, and a depressive feeling that nothing could go right for Major, that everyone was 'discounting' him. The shadowy figure of that erstwhile Whip, the Member for Watford,† in his habitual role as

---

* Mr Hywel Williams, who was working at this time as 'political adviser' to Redwood, has published as appendix to his book *Guilty Men: Conservative Decline and Fall 1992–1997* (1998, pp. 263–72) three papers on taxation and general policy which were allegedly sent to the Policy Unit in 1995, one of them 'undated and unsigned'. Whether or not these were actually seen by Major, their style of presentation, plainly intended for a wider audience, may have formed the basis for these rumours.

† Mr Tristan Garel-Jones.

the bearer of ill-tidings, can be seen at the back of the stage. The night before Major went to Nova Scotia for the G7 Conference he told, apparently as an aside, Ms Sue Tinson of ITN that he was 'thinking of throwing in the towel'.*

Had the Prime Minister been minded to subject his situation to a more objective assessment – and it seems to have been the case that from time to time he did so† – it would surely have proceeded at two levels.

A contest – any contest – carries an element of risk. It is possible that the arithmetic could 'go wrong'; that, as a result either of accident or tactical voting, the adverse number on the first ballot would put him in jeopardy. Nor should this number necessarily (to bring about such a result) be at, or even close to, the total required under the rules to trigger a second ballot. It would depend on the status and identity of the challenger, the manner in which the result, in its immediate aftermath, was depicted in the media and understood by the back benches. And how effective, if it came to that, would be the Prime Minister's own coterie at managing the presentation?

Ordinarily, the Chief Whip would have had a role in such a situation. But the incumbent, Richard Ryder, was also exhausted. He had been suffering from back pain for a long time. And, after five years in the job, had let it be known (others, too, played their part in disseminating the news) that he wished to stand down. If it were the Prime Minister's intention to use the result to 'clear the air' then the advice he received about colleagues' feelings would not – formally at least – be coming from Ryder.

Yet this element of risk would be present whenever the contest

---

* Dame Sue – as she became – relayed this news to the author that same evening (15 June) in the inapposite setting of the *Times* summer party at the Reform Club. AC went round immediately to Number 10 and sought to persuade the Prime Minister to change his mind. The substance of this conversation remains private; but it was plain that Major had already decided to call an election immediately on his return from Halifax.

† In her own book *Too Close to Call* (1995) Ms Sarah – now Lady – Hogg claims that she also put these arguments to the Prime Minister.

took place. The probability was that by pre-emption the Prime Minister could disrupt the planning of his personal enemies. How promising, though, were the chances of avoiding a contest altogether? There were those who argued, and put the case to Major,[1] that the summer recess was only three weeks away; that in fact the temperature starts to fall after even the first fortnight in July; that the next important political fixture was the Party Conference – the easiest of all events at which, by stage management, to enhance the leader's standing. A little luck or, at least, the avoidance of ill-fortune; some smooth presentation of plans and policies sharpened by an implied threat of ground being lost if the party were deliberately to divide itself – all this might just carry Major past that dangerous Thursday in early November when a challenger, having collected the names of his thirty sponsors, must present them to the Chairman of the 1922 Committee. In the event and for neither the first nor the last time in his long and resilient tenure of the premiership, Major was assisted by the errors of colleagues who wished him ill.

First, those on the 'Left'. 'Not called "wets" for nothing' did, as was usual, characterise their behaviour. The Chancellor Kenneth Clarke, who had several times threatened – or at all events huffed and puffed about – resignation, was stuck. How could he challenge at the first ballot? On policy grounds? Surely not. There was at that time no policy issue, save the remote and somewhat amorphous question of 'joining' a single currency. Subordinate, and indistinctly dependent on it lay the question of a 'commitment' to a referendum. These, in any case, were subjects that had not (like the decision to join the ERM) even come forward for any *in extenso* discussion in Cabinet. The relationship between the Chancellor and the Governor of the Bank of England; the disagreements – sometimes triangular when the Prime Minister had himself taken a political view – over interest rates, were neither sharp enough nor easily enough understood to offer grounds for a breach.

There remained the justification – time-honoured in its usage to obscure the nakedness of personal ambition – *pro bono publico.*

Pressed by colleagues; the good of the party; more in sadness than in anger – these protestations would, coming from the Chancellor, have sounded thin. At that time Clarke's own standing was weak. He had made careless errors, muddling names, places and facts in public;* he had been unnecessarily rude and impatient to colleagues with whom he disagreed. The likelihood was that Kenneth Clarke had already lost the support of the Centre (except for a few desperate to preserve their majorities). His total vote might be no more than twenty-five, plus the additional ballast of some twenty or thirty votes cast in 'protest'.

In any case the reason, if not the excuse, to change the leadership lay in the party's miserable rating in the opinion polls. And there was no evidence that Major's substitution with any other member of the Cabinet – subject only to one exception – would make the slightest difference.

Michael Heseltine alone enjoyed advantages over his colleagues. A high media profile and 'recognition factor'; a talent for the packaging and presentation of the 'initiatives' (most of them insubstantial – but what did that matter?) emanating from his own Department of Trade and Industry; and a reputation for aggression and hyperactivity. It was true that Heseltine's reception at the Party Conference the previous year had been less enthusiastic than formerly. But Margaret Thatcher no longer commanded the adulation of former years. With each fresh expression of irritability – 'disloyalty' – on her part, the odium attaching to her displacement when Prime Minister waned a little. The ordinary elector knew Heseltine's face and, whether out of mischief or conformity, would often tell the pollster that he, or she, would be more likely to vote Conservative if the party was led by Heseltine than by Major. It would have been possible for Heseltine to 'package' a bid – to mute, that is to say, his appeal to the naked self-interest of Members of Parliament who believed themselves

---

* A few weeks earlier on a trip to the North of England he had referred to 'a very splendid factory you've got here . . .' – the factory had been closed three years earlier.

likely to lose their seats and his exploitation of this to further his own ambition – as follows:

> *The Party is drifting. We have two years to get it back on course. Do not question me closely about matters of policy. We have and are suffering from too much argument and self-doubt. Trust me. I alone can tell the electorate what they want to hear.*

Heseltine could no more challenge on policy grounds – less indeed – than the Chancellor. But there was no reason why his supporters could not have canvassed for him – in the American parlance – to be *drafted*. And this drafting, of course, could only occur in the context of a second round. First, there had to be an opening, not directly of the challenger's making. Why did Heseltine's nerve fail? Age, uncertain health, family pressures, have all been cited. Perhaps a feeling at the back of his mind that he might, even then, lose – suffering the final humiliation of polling fewer votes than he had in the first ballot against Margaret Thatcher.

These factors were certainly not present in Major's own calculations. He knew that the Trade Secretary had readjusted his sights on the premiership from that very moment in December 1990 when he had announced his intention not to contest a second ballot. Heseltine had maintained his own staff, driver, Jaguar, public relations advisers on a scale quite outwith the customary apparatus of a Cabinet minister. A small coterie of back-benchers, the core body of Heseltine's attempted coup in 1990 and, some of them, former ministers had persisted quietly in briefing colleagues on their sponsor's attitude and distinction whenever the occasion offered. Heseltine was indeed the only protagonist whose intervention was utterly unpredictable, and in there lay a considerable element of risk. His attractions made him formidable. His defects, vanity and low intellect (Heseltine was cunning but not clever) were known to the Prime Minister. How should Major play to them? In the week following the local election results, which for Major had been disappointing but not catastrophic, the two men had a private meeting. Major told the Trade Secretary that he felt exhausted, and saddened. But for the time being he was determined to carry on and attempt to keep the party in one piece. None the less Heseltine's loyalty, which Major appreciated greatly, and his personal status in the country and the party made him due some special recognition. How would he feel about the position (vacant since the unhappy tenure of Howe) of Deputy Prime Minister? With this would go a comprehensive supervisory role over many Cabinet committees. And a broadening of Heseltine's position in Whitehall which would be unequalled by any other possible contender should 'anything' happen.

It is hard not to see a trace, in this episode, of Churchill's periodic teasing of Eden. Possibly Heseltine sensed a trap. But what was it? The Trade Secretary said that he still had important work to see through his department, and that he would think it over. At the time each party to these negotiations may have believed himself to have strengthened his hand thereby. Neither had an interest in leaking them, not immediately at least, to a wider audience. There were not even rumours.

The menacing noises were coming, as always, from the Right. But although the 'bastards' could cause trouble in Cabinet they could never have taken a large enough proportion of the electoral college to win, outright, a leadership ballot. Their problem, or rather their handicap, was that they were simply not convincing as winners of a general election. Heseltine was the only man who could claim this pretence; and even he would not become formidable unless he could enrol at least some support from the more gullible, or apprehensive, MPs whose habitual domicile was on the Right.

On this territory the skills of political manoeuvre were at a premium. If Heseltine could be deflected from challenging directly, or allowing himself to be 'drafted' (a trick which could all too easily go wrong) then he had to wait until the second round. As it was inevitable that the contest be triggered, and the first round contested by a challenger — of what calibre remained to be seen — from the Right, Heseltine was going to depend on some of those votes switching to himself.

The nearest thing to a bloc was the '92 Group; some eighty strong, of whom up to sixty would probably follow the recommendation of their Chairman, Sir George Gardiner. Gardiner disliked Major, and, as has been seen, felt that he had a score to settle over his humiliation when leading a delegation to discuss European policy the previous year.* For the first six months of 1995 Gardiner had been badgering Norman Lamont to stand. He had done much preparatory work. He had ensured that the thirty names would be to hand immediately the contest was declared. Lamont for his part was preoccupied much of the time with his own reselection problems and then, following his rejection by Kingston-upon-Thames, with finding a new constituency. He considered the matter carefully and often, but made no commitment. But Lamont had already set out his credentials as a radical thinker, and gone some way towards clearing the stigma of those repetitious defensive pleas for the ERM in 1991–2, by stating the case, in analytical terms, for complete withdrawal from the EU. This he had first done at a Conference fringe meeting in Bournemouth the previous year, and he would now return to it from time to time.

So as soon as Major had announced his resignation on the lawn at Number 10 Downing Street Lamont asked Gardiner to meet him in one of the St Stephen's Hall committee rooms. 'What about it?'

Lamont found Gardiner evasive.† Tread carefully. We (that is to say the '92) don't yet see our way. We will be having a meeting. And so on.

This surprised Lamont. He felt himself disconcerted. But at the same time, in all honesty, relieved. Like so many before him – one could cite a dozen names, and there had then been only three elections under the Douglas-Home rules – Lamont felt that the moment was not quite ripe, that his chances might improve as the situation developed.

---

* This account is taken from a much later conversation the author had with Norman Lamont which is recorded in AC's (unpublished) diary.
† Conversation recorded in AC's (unpublished) diary, July 1997.

Gardiner, of course, had covertly switched his support to Redwood. Although now the original plan, for a formal challenge under the rules in November, had been pre-empted. Yet Redwood still had more credibility than Lamont. Credibility, that is, in the context of causing the maximum disruption to Major – and by this stage Gardiner was completely obsessed with ousting Major, to the extent that he had lost sight of the wider policy objectives. With thorough preparation Redwood might even – just – go 'all the way'. As it was, he had still to be given preference over an ex Chancellor who had been sacked – not following a disagreement over policy but because he had become an electoral liability. Redwood was an outside chance. But at least he was a serious candidate. Lamont could never be more than a stalking horse.

Even Redwood, though, was not the true candidate of the Right at this time. He had intellect (too much, in fact, for the party ever to be at its ease with him); charisma also, but of so peculiar a nature that it was on the verge of being negative. Much of the voluntary sector regarded Redwood as being slightly barmy; others felt that he was disloyal, although in ways that they could not pin down. The one man who might, if he went all out, challenge Major successfully was Michael Portillo. He was a more capable minister, a cooler customer, a more popular Conference star. Redwood's great weakness, the most crippling of all handicaps, was that the majority of Conservative MPs felt that he could not possibly, under any circumstances, win a general election. A MORI poll that week showed Redwood to suffer a two-to-three-point deficit compared to Major. With Portillo as leader it was just – unlikely, but *just* – possible. Would Portillo win in a straight fight against Heseltine? Impossible to say. But Heseltine's own premium, in that same poll, was no more than 2 per cent. And Portillo, surely, could match this?

For many, myself included, the risks attendant on displacing Major were too high. But on that first weekend his position looked precarious in the highest degree. On the morning of Friday 23

June the temperature was further raised by an announcement that Douglas Hurd had resigned; the timing being so inept as, surely, to have some higher significance. The loss of a Foreign Secretary? And at this critical moment in the fortunes of the administration? Hurd's motives remain mysterious.*² But the two men to whom he was closest – Clarke and Heseltine – each had their private reasons for seeing advantage therein. The funeral of Gordon Greig, political editor of the *Daily Mail*, was held that morning at Brookwood Crematorium. A good number of politicians† and every editor and commentator of influence made the journey. The general view, drawn as journalists so often do, from reading each other's headlines, was that 'Major is finished'.

Major, meanwhile, was in Cannes attending – as had been Thatcher in November five years earlier – an EU summit. The British press dominated the turgid question-and-answer period at the end of each session, and sent back reports that the Prime Minister seemed 'lacklustre'. And who could blame him? Just as with his predecessor less than five years before, his fate depended on a 'good' vote – more than a majority under the rules, a dominant total. If over a hundred colleagues withheld support, his continuing premiership would be no stronger than formerly.

This, now, looked to be inevitable. The *Economist* proclaimed that Heseltine was 'worth fifty seats'. Yet the Right seemed oblivious to this threat. On 30 June I motored to Reigate where I was guest of honour at the annual dinner of the Conservative Association. Before the meal I spoke privately to George Gardiner, my host, MP for the division and Chairman of the '92. I told him that the group (of which I was still a member) had to support Major. 'The choice is between Michael Howard as Foreign Secretary, or Michael Heseltine as Prime Minister.'³ Gardiner was

* Major's biographer, Anthony Seldon, somewhat opaquely records that 'Major tried to dissuade him, but saw the force of the argument about having a new Foreign Secretary in place well before the next general election' (*Major: A Political Life*, 1997, p. 577).

† AC was present and records the event in his (unpublished) diary.

unrelenting. Major had to go. What followed scarcely mattered.

To this day it is impossible to separate rumour from conflicting account. To what extent (if at all) did Redwood and Portillo confer after Major's resignation? Was there a secret agreement between Heseltine and Portillo for a 'dream ticket' with Portillo as Foreign Secretary or – more likely – Chairman of the Party and heir presumptive? Discussion, often between subordinates, is one thing. Commitment by the principals is quite another. What is incontestable, as it shows on the BT worksheets, is the installation of an additional forty telephone lines for Portillo's personal use at 11 Lord North Street. These would hardly have been needed if Portillo was going to ride in the second round on Heseltine's 'ticket'. And yet Portillo remains the only challenger who might have brought Major down in the first round. Once this had passed so, for good, had Portillo's chance of leading the Conservative Party.

In the event Major secured 218 votes, Redwood a surprisingly high 89, and 20 colleagues abstained. The whole affair, unlike the contest of 1990, had brought no advantage in the national polls. There were no discernible issues of policy at stake. It had been focused from start to finish on 'personalities' and their alleged failings. So in the immediate aftermath of the contest the party remained unhappy. A large number among them had wanted, and others had deluded themselves that they wanted, to displace John Major. But who with? They were never agreed.

Now Major was safe. Immediately he arranged with Sir Marcus Fox that there should be a ruling from the Executive Council of the 1922 Committee stating that the July vote had, in fact, 'been' the annual election. So there was no other one due until November of 1996. In all probability this would come the far side· of the general election. If the old Parliament was still sitting it could only mean that the start of the campaign was but weeks away. A leadership contest at such a time would be out of the question.

Among the Right there was a degree of resentment bordering on panic. Part of the compact – implied rather than expressed – which had reserved Centre-Right votes to the Prime Minister

was that Michael Howard would take the place of Douglas Hurd
as Foreign Secretary. Was this considered? Certainly it did not
happen. Howard and others around him believed that Michael
Heseltine had been consulted on Cabinet appointments. And in
those first few weeks, the ones remaining before the parliamentary
recess, Heseltine's own powers and 'empire' seemed steadily to
be extending. He embarked on the practice of sending for the
Permanent Secretaries of other departments and demanding verbal
briefs on 'where they were going'. He usurped the Chair of the
'No. 12 Committee' – a powerful body of informal constitution
midway between party and official status – from the Chief Whip.
And, unlike any of his predecessors, he insisted on being both
addressed and referred to as 'First Secretary of State' as well as
Deputy Prime Minister.

Some of this – the commandeering of a set of enormous rooms
in the Cabinet Office, the ordering of new expensive furniture
and redecoration – was mildly absurd. But in the short term at
least it enhanced the 'image' of Michael Heseltine. It was put
about, in both Westminster and Fleet Street, that if the next set of
local elections – in May of 1996 – were 'bad' the Prime Minister
would simply stand aside and allow his Deputy to take over.*

At the same time some junior ministers who had felt themselves
to be close to Major and who had worked, for the second time in
four years, to ensure his re-election felt aggrieved. They appeared
to have been shut out from promotion. And the Prime Minister
by appointing a new Chief Whip in the traditional mould, and
consulting daily with the Leader of the Party in the House of
Lords, seemed to be reversing the party into an image that was
not so much pre-Thatcher as pre-Heath.

As for the Prime Minister himself, he was victorious – but

* The notion that this could be done outwith the leadership rules of the 1922
Committee *by acclaim* was pretty far-fetched although, in the immediate aftermath
of Heseltine's becoming Deputy, widely believed. It is more than likely that
Heseltine believed enough of it himself, having thought that he understood as
much from his conversation with the Prime Minister in May of 1995 (before the
'snap' leadership election).

isolated. His strength resided in two factors, one constant, the other uncertain. Constant was the fact that more than half of his Cabinet believed that they, individually, could perform the role of Prime Minister better than he. The likelihood of them combining – although it could not be excluded – was remote. What was uncertain was the extent to which the party's ratings in the country might improve. If they did, the episode would all soon be forgotten – save as another example of Major's skill in tactics and management. But if they did not, the Prime Minister would increasingly have difficulty in sustaining his personal following and reputation.

The minutiae of this squabbling barely matter. But they serve to illustrate a consequence – unforeseen but damaging – of the Douglas-Home rules. The purpose of the formula had been to make the party appear more 'democratic'. (Although whether this could be claimed of a process that, in a party of many tens of thousands, extended power of selection from four or five individuals to some three hundred, was arguable.) What happened was that a process – the 'Magic Circle' – which had been the very embodiment of continuity, of a calm and united authority endowed with these traditional gifts of good judgement and discrimination that made it best suited to govern the country, had been discarded. In its place there were now offered in terms of media coverage a series of gladiatorial battles, with net and sword, before an arena of jeering spectators.

It may be that this was inevitable. Certainly the signs of *personalising* can already be seen in Hailsham's intemperate demonstration at the 1963 Party Conference. The first contest under the rules, between Maudling and Heath, had maintained the public decorum which concealed earlier 'processes'. But thereafter whether real, or pretended for reasons of propriety and appearance, policy statements had to be declared by the various contenders. It became all too easy for commentators to depict the party as being divided. That fine line between debate and altercation would soon, at the urging of excitable colleagues and the encouragement of the media, be transgressed; with lasting damage to the party's reputation.

THIRTY-SIX

The Party Hits the Reef

A gloomy prognosis – Acrimony and depression –
The Referendum Party – Postponing the election – A
shapeless campaign – Landslide – 'Hats' into the ring –
Michael Heseltine is afflicted – The end of the Tories.

BY THE LATE autumn of 1996 the Conservative Party in Parliament and, to a very large degree, in the voluntary organisation –
the 'activists' – was completely obsessed by the subject of Europe.
Never mind that the opinion polls gave the topic a very low rating
in public awareness, or in the extent to which it governed people's
voting intention; nor that the rancour and distraction to which it
gave rise was perpetuating that most unfamiliar (and, by traditional
repute, lethal) image of a *divided party*. Most MPs could think and
talk of little else. They saw the 'right' decision – i.e., that which
they favoured – providing the key to electoral success and, almost
as important, as being the determinant of succession to the leadership – and thus of the personality with whom, discreetly, they
should be aligning themselves.

Mr John Redwood seems to have overestimated his strength.
There is no recorded case (certainly not in this history) of an
erstwhile 'favourite', or even a formal challenger, coming round
for a second, and successful, attempt on the leadership. Often,
though, such persons believe themselves to be 'knocking on the
door'; that, perversely, they have been strengthened by the original
rebuff. Redwood got into the habit of convening, every Wednesday evening, a group of his own parliamentary supporters.
They would discuss their reaction to, even their 'line to take' on,

the events of the previous week. It is possible that Redwood saw himself as did Winston Churchill in 1938 in his relation with the 'Focus' group.* He would write at very short notice for any newspaper editor who invited him, and found himself in favour with the *Daily Mail* who, having originally supported his candidature in the previous year's leadership contest as a device for inserting Michael Heseltine, were now simply using Redwood – in common with most of Fleet Street – as the easiest way of adding to the Prime Minister's difficulties. Redwood told one of his staff that:

> Churchill commanded popular opinion through the *Express* when he was out of office, and that's what I am going to do with the newspapers now.[1]

One difference from 1938, though, was the level generated of personal abuse and opprobrium. There is no record, even when in the company of Bracken and Beaverbrook, of Winston Churchill being personally insulting or cruel to Neville Chamberlain – or even to Sir Samuel Hoare. And although there was much covert briefing by Margesson and the 1938 Whips' Office against the 'glamour boys', Anthony Eden and his ilk, nothing was ever published comparable to the 'bastards' aside of the Prime Minister; or Kenneth Clarke's intemperate comment at a lunch (one of many) with two reporters from the BBC. His leader's remarks in an interview with the editor of the *Daily Telegraph* had been, the Chancellor said, 'a boomerang laden with high-explosive'. And in the will-he/won't-he resign furore that followed (itself utterly artificial, there never at any time being the slightest risk of the Chancellor, who wanted the premiership and was not happy about having to wait, resigning) Clarke's 'friends' – a collective term by now universally accepted as a formula for unattributably identifying the subject himself – boasted of having told the Party Chairman: 'Tell your kids to get their scooters off my lawn.'[2]

* See p. 134 above – 'Focus' at that time being a title and not, as it is today, a generic term.

Some of these incidents occurred late in the life of the Government, when tempers were frayed, and stamina exhausted. But
the very fact that their authors were so senior, and the context of
their issuing – often reckless, but sometimes deliberate – so varied,
raised the level of disunity far above that of periodic back-bench
dissent. Just as in Margaret Thatcher's closing period the parliamentary party at every level, within and outside the administration, was embittered. There was a lethal combination of
personal dislike, policy disagreement, and apprehension of seats in
jeopardy.

The strength, and likely following, of the Referendum Party
was an additional and highly unsettling factor. Would its votes be
drawn off that fast-diminishing pool of Conservative supporters?
Most MPs assumed that this is what would happen, although
bluster about equal or even negative effect (picking up disillusioned
Labour voters) could be heard. Some Conservatives, backed in a
few instances by Eurosceptic hotheads in their associations, even
thought about enlisting in the new and populist movement. In
the spring of 1996 I travelled, at his invitation, to Sir James
Goldsmith's villa at Cuixmala. It was an easy journey in the private
Boeing with long-range tanks which allowed completion of the
flight from Heathrow to the western Pacific coastline of Mexico
without once putting down. Before departing I had consulted
with the Prime Minister about possible 'terms'. The price, that is
to say, of securing Goldsmith's undertaking simultaneously to
dissolve his own party and endorse the Conservatives. This was
an unrealistic concept. John Major, as he on several occasions told
me and as will certainly have been known to others, was terrified
of losing his Chancellor. Major believed that Margaret Thatcher's
own fate had been sealed not, as was the received wisdom, by the
Howe speech in October of 1990 but exactly twelve months earlier
when Nigel Lawson resigned. And so I listened to a dissertation,
expressed in the most courteous manner but without clear rationale, on the impossibility of repudiating Monetary Union outright,
and the impracticality of holding a referendum before the election.

Goldsmith, by contrast, was overexcited. He had written to

every Tory candidate, whether at that time in or out of the House of Commons, and also to a good number of Labour MPs, telling them that the only way to avoid a Referendum candidate standing in their constituency at the election would be to commit themselves, quite privately and by exchange of letters in the first instance, in favour of an immediate referendum (on a question whose exact wording remained to be determined. Even during the period of my own stay at Cuixmala a number of differing texts were put into draft). Goldsmith claimed to have had a large number of pledges already – including some 'from the most surprising quarters'. He, too, greatly overestimated his strength, and believed himself to be in the position of *demandeur*.

Thus it soon became apparent that there no longer existed any opportunity for co-operation, or even coexistence. Whether or not such a moment had existed earlier is academic. But the fact remains that in at least fifteen seats (some allege as many as thirty) the thousand or so votes cast for the Referendum candidate were to be of critical importance. Although Goldsmith would make no difference to the outcome of the election his presence may well have been responsible for keeping the Conservative strength in the new Parliament below the level – around 200 seats – of critical mass.* Yet even if this be true, it remains a commentary on the plight of the Tory Party in 1996 – that its survival should be in any way dependent on the whims of a millionaire expatriate, issuing his encyclicals at 6,000-mile range from a replica Ruritanian *palacio*.

Goldsmith did in fact come to London himself a few weeks later. On 14 April Sir James announced that he would commit £20 million of his own fortune and field 600 candidates. But by then, although this was apparent to few, his peak moment of influence had already passed. Nor was either target met. Redwood visited Goldsmith at Claridge's and foolishly allowed his acolytes to publicise the 'discussion'. This was a strangely tactless move, to

---

* Even in 1945 there were 213 Conservatives returned – although this figure included nine Ulster Unionists and thirteen National Liberals.

consort with a political adversary so soon after he had announced his hostile intentions; and may well have been remembered by the constituency activists when their leadership votes (of 'approval' only) were cast in June the following year.

The months passed. The predictions of the opinion polls remained implacable. At each favoured or orthodox point when Parliament could be dissolved, and an election called, the polls never wavered. The 'feel-good' factor – a convergence of benign economic statistics that would, some believed, raise Conservative support and morale – slowly accumulated weight. Though without, it seemed, any parallel enhancement of public approval. And even this factor came to be perceived as having a sinister downside. Perhaps the electorate would soon be 'feeling good' to such an extent that they could afford to take the risk (as they had not dared to do in the recession year of 1992) of voting Labour?

As each date approached it was allowed to pass. The party organisation, which had been on provisional standby since the Bournemouth Conference the previous October, remained expectant; though very far from ready or, to use the phrase which the unfortunate Major had coined after winning the election of 1992 – 'at ease with itself'. On 13 December 1996 the Dublin EU summit passed in relative tranquillity – save for one unfortunate development. The European Commission Press Office chose that moment to release facsimiles of the new euro banknotes in their various denominations. The unfamiliar, but so obviously foreign, appearance made many people uneasy. Polls showed that the electorate, for most of the time indifferent to European squabbling, whose technicalities they could not be bothered to master, disliked the removal of their Sovereign's head from the currency of the realm. The sceptics took fresh heart and the likelihood of the dispute fading – even for the short duration of the election campaign itself – became still more remote.

Over Christmas Major consulted closely on the timing of the dissolution. Some – Howard, Mawhinney, Shephard – wanted to jump before they were pushed. Others, including the Chancellor and the Deputy Prime Minister, wanted to hold on until the very last moment, as had done Douglas-Home in 1964, believing that the steadily improving economy must – at the very least – diminish the number of seats lost. Major's own preference, which waxed and waned according to passing fortune, was for 20 March.

As the dissolution date approached ill-fortune, some of it trivial, some of it highly disconcerting, accumulated. Disaster at the Wirral by-election (itself postponed until the very last permitted day); cases of 'sleaze' that came thick and fast; conflicting advice as to how the Downey Report on MPs' financial misdemeanours should be handled; conflicting opinions as to the efficacy of the party's opening advertisement campaign – not a day seems to have passed without at least one episode, unforeseen but damaging, that demanded the Prime Minister's urgent attention. At one point Major left on a jaunt to India. He liked Indians and claimed to enjoy their company. It was hoped that Major could take advantage of the confined space in the aircraft to brief the accompanying journalists. In fact he lost his temper several times, and the only photograph that got back to the press at home showed the Prime Minister looking decidedly ill at ease in an ethnic head-dress. To the considerable relief of MPs in marginal seats, whose severance pay went up if the Parliament sat into the new financial year, the election date was agreed finally as 1 May – the latest, again, which the constitution could allow.

There followed a long and disconsolate approach march. There was some doubt about the Prime Minister's own commitment. It was spread about – and not only by those who had a vested interest in competing for his position – that Major had forsaken any idea of victory as a Party Leader but wanted, simply, 'to ensure his place in History'.[3] The Right were far from happy with the Chancellor's assertion that he would not countenance 'a narrow Nationalist campaign'; nor with Major's public denunciation of an apparently neutral stance on race relations by Nicholas Budgen ('The Prime Minister deserves congratulation,' Tony Blair had said). Nor even with a spontaneous declaration of personal commitment in an unscripted speech at Bath: 'I dream of a People's [sic] Britain in which the have-nots become the haves.' Comments

like these certainly provided the justification, as thought many on
the Right, for drafting their own election addresses and in particular, with the overt support of the *Daily Mail*, of declaring their
opposition to the single currency. The image of a Conservative
Party irretrievably divided, that had been to a large extent contrived and imaginary in Major's first years, now loomed dominant
over the whole scene. 'There are two Conservative Parties fighting
this election', had said Blair at his morning press conference on
17 April. 'John Major is in charge of neither of them.'[4]

All this time the press were continuing to entertain their readers
with accounts of Tory malfeasance, both sexual and financial; both
real and invented; both actual and historic. Beside these eye-
catching headlines 'policies' – if they could be dignified by such a
title – on 'basic pension plus' or 'transferable family tax' were of
no relevance whatever. Major's behaviour became erratic. More
and more he made off-the-cuff speeches, telling his somewhat
apprehensive staff that he would give his personal credo 'hot and
strong'. Not that it by now could make the slightest difference.
Any more than the vast amount of thrashing and churning that
governed the schedule (composed, as is so often the case, by
competing desks each of whom will take mortal umbrage if their
own suggestion is left out or played down) of the Prime Minister
and his team. On 7 April, for example, the Prime Minister travelled
from Downing Street to Northolt airport (12 miles); flight
to Manchester (185 miles); 'battlebus' to Bury to visit and
speak at an opt-out school (17 miles); helicopter to a factory in
Andover (195 miles *due south*); helicopter to Aintree (213 miles
due north); helicopter to Cheltenham (142 miles *due south*), plus
car to an out-of-town Tesco store; helicopter to Chelsea barracks
landing pad (113 miles); speech at dinner in London, and
back to Number 10 for a meeting and campaign report at midnight.[5]

It was not until the very last Sunday of the campaign that the
Conservative leadership found themselves admitting – although
still only to themselves, and never even in front of subordinates –
that a serious defeat was in prospect. Received wisdom was that

the deficit would be 'about' thirty seats. Some said sixty. No one is on record, or could even be found subsequently to admit, suggesting that the outcome might be a catastrophe. There is a certain analogy with the general election of 1945 when the polls (such as they were, being a digest founded on the – at that time rudimentary – techniques of Gallup and Mass Observation) equally did predict a Labour victory. But Churchill's prestige, the cheering throng that crowded his triumphal tour of the countryside and the regimented optimism of the Beaverbrook press fostered a belief that the 'real' result would be different. And in 1997 the comparison was drawn with the bad predictions that most polling teams had made in 1992. Many candidates were reporting that their experience 'on the doorstep' – disregarding that all too often these encounters were with what analysts would call a *flawed sample* – was friendly. The party organisation had in many districts atrophied and so, with polling station exits unmanned and committee rooms understrength, it was only from the 'good' wards in the constituency that canvass returns were available.* These results were then in many cases projected, or 'averaged', onto marginal return cards to induce a wholly misleading 'profile'.[6]

What defence mechanism of the psyche allowed, combined in, otherwise sensible and hard-headed men and women to induce this illusion? Every single device for *measuring* (as distinct from estimating) popular opinion was pointing consistently in the same direction. All four polling organisations, plus a range of special samples, follow up inquiries, specially selected 'marginal' groups, were in agreement: the Labour Party was not far from twenty points ahead. And as the body of Conservative candidates trudged disconsolately across the last defile of their election campaign a vast cornice of melting snow, a great overhang made up by equal parts of discontent, sulky recollection, impatience and (concerning

---

* A fact ignored by the many congratulatory, and self-congratulatory, speeches made at Conference later that year on the '*Whoever-lost-the-election-it-wasn't-you/us*' lines.

'New' Labour) curiosity, was poised to crash down, and bury more than half their number.

The brutal truth could in fact, by the last weekend in April, no longer be avoided. The Chairman of the Party was privy to the findings of certain 'private' polls that his research department were running, and on the Sunday he told Major that the picture 'looked bad'.

'How bad?'

'We could lose by as much as fifty.'

Like the Imperial German Army in 1914 the party was the prisoner of its timetables. One day, for example, had been designated, by the faceless – but far from diffident – 'wonks' in Central Office as 'Inward Investment Day', with the Prime Minister instructed to travel a further 900 miles on a circuit of foreign-owned factories. The last three days of the campaign had been scheduled for an assault on the 'High Ground'. The party would promote itself as defender of the constitution, under threat from Labour's ill-thought-out plans for devolution. The electoral impact of this tactic was doubtful. It was true that Sir Alec Douglas-Home had come within an ace of winning in 1964, fighting similarly on the high ground (above, that is to say, the day-to-day preoccupation with living standards and prospects) of retaining an independent nuclear deterrent. But the plight of the Major Government in 1997 was more serious. Too many people wanted rid of it, and for too broad a spectrum of reasons, to be distracted by some last-minute foray.

Major, though, persisted doggedly with his schedule. Returning from Wales, in the late afternoon of Wednesday 30 April the Prime Minister was immediately hustled by aides into a last 'command' ('*contrived*' might be truer) performance of his favourite act – the soap-box impromptu. The 'box' – actually a welded platform of aluminium slats – was carried quickly from the campaign bus, parked outside 32 Smith Square, and set up on College Green. And here, at the very location where for months past detractors in his own parliamentary party had made the most of their open invitation from the media to opinionate, Major put on his very last act. Coverage was assured. The cameras and sound equipment had to travel only the eighty or so yards from the studios at Millbank. The senior commentators – Brunson, Vine, Oakley – could walk across from their offices in the House of Commons. And in order that there should be the semblance of an enthusiastic crowd the agents at the Chelsea and Westminster association offices were telephoned by headquarters and instructed to down tools immediately, present themselves on the Green, and applaud. When Major's armoured Jaguar drew up at the pavement Mawhinney detached himself from the crowd and walked over to greet him. The Prime Minister was a long time dismounting. He listened to Mawhinney through a half-lowered window, turning round from time to time and speaking to Norma. Three, five, eight minutes went past and the 'crowd', being mainly paid or voluntary party workers, whiled away the time telling each other★ that they had a 'hunch' that the results 'might be far better than expected'. When at last the Prime Minister climbed up on to his portable scaffold he had recovered poise. He was friendly, fluent, confident. A few planted questions were gently lobbed in his direction, then he made off. None of the very senior commentators bothered to make any attempt at securing an 'exclusive', or even a throwaway line. It was a waste of time. As indeed had been a long conference that Tuesday evening (no others were present) with Lord Cranborne.

The two men faced facts. Defeat was certain. Only its scale was indeterminate. Cranborne had a harder agenda than Major. He was a Cecil. His ancestor had arranged the accession to the English throne of James VI of Scotland in 1603 and his forebears had played their part in the governance of the country ever since. Cranborne's objective, founded on a proper Tory assessment of what would be best for country and party, was to thwart the ambitions of Michael Heseltine. Cranborne had been working with the Deputy Prime Minister and formed a low opinion of his present abilities. But he had served also in the Commons; he

★ AC being one of their number.

knew all too well the self-serving motivation of the majority of colleagues and their tendency, in crisis, to respond as a herd. If a vacuum opened Heseltine would fill it. What was important was that Major should remain at his post, at least until the summer had passed. Thus the various contenders to the succession should get time to prove themselves in the very different climate of Opposition; and the Party Conference could, also, pronounce its verdict.

Major concurred.* Or at least that was the impression with which he left Cranborne. But the Prime Minister was utterly exhausted. Heseltine had in fact over the last few months saved him a lot of trouble. The 'Deputy' had kept (though from realism as much as loyalty) to the deal which the two men had struck in the summer of 1995. It is likely that Major, privately knowing he was going to lose and in no special mood of gratitude towards his colleagues, hardly cared for 'blocking' Heseltine with the same ardour as Cranborne. Whatever the reality, this was to be the very last occasion on which the Prime Minister would listen attentively to a visitor or complainant and lead them to believe that he was in agreement with what they were saying.

On the evening of polling day Tony Garrett, the Director of Organisation, gave Major some figures based on the Conservative tellers' own returns at the polling stations. They were, in many cases, still hard to believe. But a Labour landslide, a true landslide on the scale of Churchill's defeat in 1945, was now in prospect. For more than six years Major had been at the helm. He had zigzagged brilliantly and not one torpedo (save only eviction from the ERM) had struck. Personally, he remained popular. But some while back the ship had run out of fuel. Now every differing type and weight of ordnance were landing on target. As he realised this Major became clear in his mind, and a great weight slipped from him. At once he told Cranborne that the circumstances had altered

---

* The participants are not unanimous in their agreement concerning the events, conversations and encounters over this period. AC is satisfied, from his own evaluation of the sources, that the version recounted here is the correct one.

so drastically that he could no longer feel himself bound (if 'bound' he had been) by their agreement of Tuesday evening. And so, both at his own 'count' at Huntingdon, and later outside the door of Number 10, Major announced his intention of standing down immediately. The statement was dignified, and utterly without rancour or reproach. The timing of his exit was plainly to be foreshortened. Within hours it became clear that it would be, to all intents and purposes, immediate. The Prime Minister's action was calculated, and in full awareness of the likely and disruptive consequences. Yet he could hardly be blamed if he felt that the party should stew in its own juice. Now followed a sequel that none could have predicted.

Early on the Friday morning Major personally telephoned to Michael Heseltine and confirmed that he intended to announce his retirement immediately. Heseltine took the call on his car phone; he was already *en route*, with his wife, to Oxfordshire. The news should have pleased Heseltine, as at that point he was, in terms of loyalty, prestige, and achievement so recently acquired during the campaign, well ahead of any possible rival to the succession. But he too was physically exhausted. And, with adrenalin ebbing as the scale of the party's defeat, and the likely duration of its sentence in the wilderness, sank in, the former Deputy Prime Minister felt dreadfully fatigued. On the Friday night, although Heseltine had been awake all through Thursday and now for nigh on thirty-six hours, and should have been replenishing his reserves, he barely slept at all. His right arm was sore, perhaps from over-expansive gestures at the hustings. He discussed with his wife, and from early on Friday morning with his lieutenants, what he should do and how he should do it. Mrs Heseltine was doubtful whether her husband should run at all. His aides in Parliament, two of whom had held on to their seats,* urged Heseltine to declare instantly. And this time, they told him, the bandwagon would be unstoppable.

* Messrs Ottaway (Croydon South) and Mates (East Hampshire); Dr Keith Hampson failed to hold Leeds North West.

Heseltine disagreed with both his interlocutors. He wanted to run; he *had* to run, it was his destiny. But, in spite of the disadvantages (that had so soon become apparent) of holding back in June of 1995, Heseltine believed that even on this occasion he should not seem too eager. What were the chances, he asked Richard Ottaway, of being 'drafted'? The party after all, was no more than 160 strong. Thirty or forty names was no longer the statutory ten per cent which the rules of the 1922 Committee required, but a formidable bloc greater, it seemed, than any other candidate (among the numerous motley at that time gathering) could assume. Might there even be a possibility of securing the prize, although the history of events in the spring of the previous year was scarcely encouraging, by *acclaim*? Heseltine did not tell his supporters – or at least not in so many words – that he had also, in reserve, a private agreement with Kenneth Clarke. Clearly the two men could not stand against each other. Clarke would make the running. Until, that is, he hit rock with the charge of 'splitting' the party. Then Heseltine could materialise, on the basis of his recent flirtation with some of the 'sensible' Right, as the *unity* candidate. Together, operating from the Left, they would take charge. But it needed to be handled smoothly. Better, all things considered, if a spontaneous 'acclaim' could be induced.

The answers were optimistic, but imprecise. More time was needed.

But that very afternoon the former Chancellor, Heseltine's old crony and supporter in the Europhile 'resistance', had been a guest on the BBC *World at One* programme. Clarke had declared – whether deliberately or by a slip of the tongue – his intention of standing. This would trigger a free-for-all. Soon, like a bodged start to the Grand National, there would be riders and horses all over the course. Mr Peter Lilley booked prime space for an interview in the *Sunday Telegraph*; Mr John Redwood said 'I am very close to announcing . . .'; Mr Michael Howard told reporters, via his 'friends', that he 'would definitely be a candidate'; Mr Stephen Dorrell, also through 'friends', was ready to try and *unify* – but from the Left. Indeed speculation was already running that

Dorrell might himself end up with the crown on the third round, having seen Heseltine pick up the running from Clarke but being still unable to command the statutory majority.

It is in retrospect curious, this urgent obsession with personalities. The party had been routed. Its administrative structure, patronage, career prospects, 'Policy Units' were in ruins. Yet within hours of receiving the electorate's verdict there were half a dozen individuals (and if some of the contestants had not lost their seats in Parliament it is safe to assume that there might have been at least three more) openly jockeying for a position where, none too covertly, they had sought to promote their chances at intervals over the preceding three years.

Allowance should be made, of course, for the fact that the noise of the campaign had barely died down. That the *habit* of both operating and enjoying the machinery of government was congenital. None seem to have come to terms with the reality, and implications, of their expulsion – after so long – from office. Some indeed continued for a few more precious hours to negotiate, and to issue statements from their official residence. But the brutal fact could not be avoided. The great Conservative Army, once so formidable – but over the years become shabby, ill-disciplined and complacent – had been utterly defeated on the field of battle. Now the criteria, as well as the rewards, for successful leadership would be altogether different.

At Thenford Heseltine and his wife were walking on the lawn. And the former Deputy Prime Minister began to feel ill. The pain in his right arm seemed now to be invading his rib-cage. It was a symptom concerning which he had been warned by his specialist, and an ambulance was called.

Not since Harold Macmillan had miserably stood shaking in the downstairs lavatory at Number 10 on the morning of Thursday 13 October 1963 had the sudden onset of a disagreeable ailment impacted so dramatically on a politician's career. The statement, issuing from Conservative Central Office before even a full diagnosis had been made at Horton Hospital, was certainly of a kind from which there can be no drawing back:

MICHAEL HESELTINE

Michael Heseltine suffered mild angina pains this morning and is now in hospital having tests. He has not had a heart attack and hopes to be home in a few days. He would like to confirm that he will not be a candidate in the leadership campaign for the Conservative Party

– and it must be said that there are more than one who claim to have had a hand in both the composition and the urgent issuing of the text to the Press Association. Mrs Heseltine, arriving at the hospital, told the press that:

It was my statement and was put out by them* for me. I am delighted that they did so and I thought it would end any form of query.[7]

But 'a senior official' at Central Office said: 'I think he was sort of bounced.'[8]

John Major sent flowers to Horton Hospital. Curious, that. Men seldom send flowers to each other when they are ill. Although it is of course usual to place them at a grave. Major also put out a statement. His said that it was 'not true' that Mrs Heseltine was behind her husband's decision not to run for the leadership. 'Michael's decision is sad for the Conservative Party but emphatically it is a joint decision.' After a period of 'tests' Heseltine was discharged and said to waiting reporters, as he was driven away, that he 'felt fine'. Another statement was issued, though now accorded little prominence, that 'Mr Heseltine is looking forward to resuming his political career'.

The reality could not be avoided. The assassin of Margaret Thatcher, twice robbed – by force of circumstance or personal deficiency – of what should have been his due, had now suffered a final and irredeemable forfeiture of the crown. And, once again,

---

* 'them' can be taken to mean Conservative Central Office.

could be suspected intervention by those very household gods of the Conservative Party that had so often, so unpredictably, and – most usually at times of crisis – so undeservedly, attended on its fortunes.

Extracts from the Diary of Neville Chamberlain

5 November 1924
Today at S.B.'s request I went to see him at Palace Chambers at 3
p.m. He began by saying, needless to say I want you to go back to
the Treasury. I made no comment and he went on to say that he
had offered [Sir Robert] Horne the Ministry of Labour and was
awaiting his reply. Horne was not as well thought of in the City
as he imagined. At this moment a letter was brought in from
Horne and S.B. read it and said, 'He won't take it'. He mentioned
that Austen [Chamberlain] had told him that he wd take the
Exchequer if it were offered him but he did not say why he had
not offered it [illegible words] . . . He said he had decided to take
Winston in at once – 'He would be more under control inside
than out' – and he thought of putting him at Health. He then
asked me what I should like and I said I had given the matter full
consideration and would like to go back to Health. But who then
could be Chancellor, he asked. I enquired whether he had thought
of S. Hoare. He said No, and I concluded the idea did not appeal
to him. He mentioned Winston but said he supposed there would
be a howl from the party. I said I thought there would but that
would be so if he came in at all, and I did not know if it would
be much louder if he went to the Treasury than to the Admiralty.
On the whole I was inclined to say that W. for the Treasury was
worth further consideration. We then discussed a good many other
posts and I suggested Steel-Maitland for Labour and the Duchess of
Atholl as Under-Secretary for Education. Both these suggestions
seemed to appeal to him. Presently he said he had another visitor
but didn't say who he was and [illegible word] was very particular
that we shouldn't meet showing me out by another door. However

I went up to see Jackson who I had met before and who had asked me to come and see him and he pointed to <u>Winston's</u> hat and coat on a chair which gave the show away. In fact going downstairs I met W. coming up arm-in-arm with Sidney Herbert and so intent on his conversation that he didn't see me.

The impression left on my mind was that S.B. had seen Austen in the morning and ascertained from him that I wanted Health. That he had postponed his final decision till he had seen me but that he offered me the Exchequer expecting that I should decline and that he had determined in that case to offer it to Winston. I must see Austen and ascertain whether in fact he did discuss me with S.B. S.B. said he had had a painful interview with the Marquess [Curzon] who wept at being denied the F.O.

6 November 1924
This morning Austen rang me up and wanted to know if W[inston] was Chancellor. He was evidently in a state of intense irritation saying that S.B. was a maddening person. Horne was bitterly and deeply hurt and offended. S.B. had never mentioned the Treasury to him nor even suggested that the M. of Labour should be anything more as to status and salary than it had ever been. I interrupted that S.B. in his account to me said he had told Horne that the salary w<u>d</u> be £5000. 'So he said to me' said A. 'but he had forgotten to mention it to Horne.' A. said S.B. had told him he wanted the Treasury for me and that was why he wouldn't give it to Horne and A. had [illegible words] with me and said I sh<u>d</u> be quite happy at Health if Horne were Chancellor. He supposed that the Treasury had not been offered to me but I corrected him on that and he seemed much astonished at my having let it go. But he said Winston w<u>d</u> have been delighted to go to Health and he thought his appointment w<u>d</u> cause consternation and indignation in the party.

[later...]
... I had no idea that S.B. would appoint him [Steel-Maitland to the Ministry of Labour] without consulting any more than I had

conceived the possibility of his making Winston Chancellor the moment my back was turned.

Later in the morning Geoffrey Fry S.B.'s P.S. rang me up about something else and I told him the fat was in the fire. In the afternoon Sam Hoare came to see me. He said Horne had rung him up at 3 a.m. this morning 'in a state of dementia'. He was convinced from S.B.'s manner that he had put the offer in order that it might be refused. S.H. was in despair saying that S.B. had made every mistake possible. He had never said a word to any of the peers he was leaving out in the cold – Balfour, Devonshire, Derby or Peel. The City would be intensely alarmed over Winston's appointment. 'Anyone but him' they would say, and all over the country confidence would be shaken.

For myself I feel thoroughly depressed. By his incredible bungling S.B. has already thrown away much of what we had gained by the election. Why on earth he should be in such a desperate hurry to rubbish his Cabinet at once I can't think. Why he should act on his own initiative in such delicate affairs without a word to people like Austen is a mystery. He is unfit to be leader, that is the long and short of it and I foresee splits in the Cabinet, resignations and the destruction of our great power before long!

20 November 1924
Things have gone better than I expected. The app[ointment] of W.C. to the Treasury has been well received and the Horne incident has blown over. . . .

Munich Abstentions

*Names and constituencies of MPs who abstained from
both their government's motion and the Labour amendment
on the Munich Agreement (see Chapter Twelve).*

Vyvyan Adams: Leeds West since 1931.
Rt. Hon. Leopold Amery: Birmingham Sparkbrook since
    1911.
Cdr Robert Bower: Cleveland since 1931.
Brendan Bracken: North Paddington since 1929.
Ronald Cartland: King's Norton since 1935.
Rt. Hon. Winston Churchill: MP 1900–1923 and for Epping
    since 1924.
Rt. Hon. Alfred Duff Cooper: MP 1924–9 and for Westminster
    St George's since 1931.
Viscount Cranborne: South Dorset since 1929.
Anthony Crossley: MP 1931–5 and for Stretford since 1935.
H. J. Duggan: Acton since 1931.
Rt. Hon. Anthony Eden: Warwick and Leamington since 1923.
Paul Emrys-Evans: South Derbyshire since 1931.
Capt. Sir Derrick Gunston: Thornbury since 1924.
Capt. Sir Sidney Herbert: MP 1922–31 and for Westminster
    Abbey since 1932.
Rear-Adm. Sir Roger Keyes: Portsmouth since 1934.
Richard Law: South West Hull since 1931.
Harold Macmillan: Stockton-on-Tees 1924–9 and since 1931.
Duncan Sandys: Norwood since 1935.
Brig.-Gen. E. L. Spears: MP 1922–4 and for Carlisle since 1931.
J. P. L. Thomas: Hereford since 1931.

Harold Nicolson: Leicester West (National Labour Party) since
1935.
Rt. Hon. Viscount Wolmer: MP 1910–18 and for Aldershot
since 1918.

Extract of Speech by Harold Macmillan to the 1922 Committee, 25 July 1963

With hindsight, it is easy to think, or for the critics to say, that [the Profumo scandal] should have been handled differently. Whether that is true or not, or whether, in fact, it is not a greater virtue to believe the word of a colleague, is now irrelevant. What matters is that the disclosure of the truth was a great shock to the Party and that its timing, coming as it did during the Whitsun recess, and being debated immediately there-after, was just as difficult as it could be. This shock to the system has put a great strain on us all.

I am well aware that, under the stress of these conditions, many of you have said that it is time for a change in the leadership, and in respect of that let me say, straightly, that any decision which I may reach will be based wholly on my assessment of what is right and good for the Party and for the nation.

What we have got to do is to win the next election. In order to win the next election, we must be poised as a united party under the strongest leadership available to us. Our policies must be forward-looking, well presented, highly political in content and, if possible, strongly contrasted to those of the Socialists. Further, the public appreciation of them must not be distracted by irrelevancies of rumour and scandal.

I can tell you that when the pressures against me were at their highest, I was sorely tempted to throw up the sponge. Had I done so, I would have been guilty of a crime against the Conservative Party and against my colleagues. My first responsibility, whatever may follow, is to see that this bogey of rumour and scandal, which has pursued us throughout the whole of this year, and particularly during the last few months, is finally destroyed. It would be unthinkable that I should allow any successor to be saddled with this additional burden.

If one is to consider change, one must consider also the timing of it. It is a nice thought that one can change a Prime Minister, reform a Government, recast policies and press on through a full parliamentary year to assured electoral success. I have been in this game a long time, and believe me it does not work out that way. Admittedly, you have got to build up the image of your new man. I am not sure that my image, in my turn, in the years leading up to 1959 was not *too* well presented. 'Super Mac' is a splendid illusion, but a difficult position to maintain through seven long years. You might well think, therefore, that if the timing is to be right, it ought to be based first on a decision as to when an election should be held, and then, by working back from that, to take account of the optimum period required to build up the image of a new man. The time can be unduly exaggerated or, on the other hand, damaged by some unavoidable misfortune. This is worth consideration.

Another factor is the choice itself. The transition from one leader to another man has got to be smooth, and the Party must know its mind. I tell you, frankly, that I should be most reluctant to lay down my responsibilities until I was sure that the Party, under its new Leader, was going to be more certain, more strong, more united than it was before the change.

Various theories have been voiced as to how certainty of choice is to be achieved. I do ask you to consider carefully the constitutional effects of some of them. No one in this room can deny that it is The Queen who has the right of choice, and although it may seem an attractive proposition that she should be guided by foreknowledge of what man would be acceptable to the Party, if we were to insist too firmly on such procedure, we might well do damage, which in the years to come could lead to the destruction of the Monarchy. What is guidance to-day might be dictatorship by a political party to-morrow, and, at a time when the balance of political power was very much more extreme than it is to-day, there could be real danger that The Queen might be forced by these procedures to send for a man whose political beliefs could put the whole safety of the Nation at stake.

Nevertheless, I appreciate that where there is not an heir apparent, I must be sure that in due course one is forthcoming, and I give you my word that I shall not give up until I know that, by the various proper methods of communications which are open to us, the Party will accept a man who may be called as my successor, and accept him with goodwill and with the certain knowledge that their views have been fully assessed and fully taken into account. All this can be perfectly well achieved if, discarding the passions of these last few weeks, you will trust my intention to see that they are done. So much, then, for that. I say again, my whole concern, whether I stay or whether I go, will be to see that what is done and the method of doing it is in the best interests of the Party.

Bernard Ingham's Briefing to the
Prime Minister, 21 October 1988

PRIME MINISTER
YOUR PRESS CONFERENCE

Your joint press conference with Mr De Mita is to be held in the press centre within the Villa complex. You will need to clear with him whether you or he will give the first account of the bilateral. We rather think he may invite you to speak first.

So far as the British press is concerned, their sole interest in this bilateral is to take forward the reaction to your Bruges speech, as sharpened up this week by Kohl, Lubbers, Martens and Santer, evidently with De Mita's full support.

The media objective will be to drive a wedge between you and De Mita – thereby ranging virtually half the Community against you.

There is nothing to be gained from ignoring the issue in your opening remarks. The attached speaking note (Annexe 1) makes the point while at the same time stressing the degree of common ground.

The most likely story tomorrow – and put in its most positive terms – is that you are standing firm against Community enthusiasm for European political and economic union and a human rights conference in Moscow. The negative translation is 'Thatcher out of step again – on Moscow as well as on Europe'.

However your talk with Chancellor Kohl yesterday – which is mentioned in the attached speaking note – enables you to cloud the issue:

– you did not discuss the Bruges issue with him; so much for its dominance;

– Chancellor Kohl agreed with your conditions for any Moscow conference – i.e. concrete improvement in Soviet human rights performance.

In terms of stressing Anglo-Italian cooperation the attached speaking note mentioned:
– *terrorism*, including maritime terrorism;
– hope for treaty to *confiscate drug trafficking proceeds*;
– hope for confirmation of draft *extradition treaty*.

You could add in the course of the press conference:
Double Taxation: agreement signed today.
Defence: EH 101; European fighter aircraft; A129 helicopters; Tornado; Operation Clean Sweep.
Industrial and scientific: Italy soon to sign agreement on participation in ISIS (spallation neutron source) in the United Kingdom; EC R & D and EUREKA programmes; links between British and Italian companies.
Trade: Italy and the UK each the other's fifth largest supplier.
Cultural: look forward to major exhibition of modern Italian art at the Royal Academy in London in January; Glyndebourne, to pay first visit to Italy next year.
Ministerial exchanges: intensive, and in diary – Treasury Minister Amato visiting Chancellor in November; Home Secretary visits Rome, January; Foreign Secretary welcomes Andreotti to Royal Academy exhibition, January; Minister Ruberti in London soon for talks on scientific collaboration.

OTHER ISSUES
It is possible that you will be asked to comment on:
Barlow Clowes (anything you say, and you can't advance on Lord Young, will detract from coverage of the bilateral).
Public expenditure: bilateral negotiations continue; too early to say whether Star Chamber will be required.

Chancellor's Mansion House forecasts: inflation to turn down next year; trade deficit in 1990.

BERNARD INGHAM
21 October 1988

Senior Figures in Conservative Governments
1922–1997 (with dates of assuming office)

LAW'S GOVERNMENT
OCTOBER 1922–MAY 1923

Prime Minister	Andrew Bonar Law	23 October 1922
Chancellor	Stanley Baldwin	24 October 1922
Foreign Secretary	Marquess Curzon	24 October 1922
Home Secretary	William Bridgeman	24 October 1922
Party Chairman	Sir George Younger	1 January 1917
	Francis Stanley Jackson	13 March 1923
Chief Whip	Leslie Wilson	1 April 1921
Chair, 1922 Committee	Gervais Rentoul	23 April 1923

BALDWIN'S FIRST GOVERNMENT
MAY 1923–JANUARY 1924

Prime Minister	Stanley Baldwin	22 May 1923
Chancellor	Stanley Baldwin	24 October 1922
	Neville Chamberlain	27 August 1923
Foreign Secretary	Marquess Curzon	24 October 1922
Home Secretary	William Bridgeman	24 October 1922
Party Chairman	Francis Stanley Jackson	13 March 1923
Chief Whip	Leslie Wilson	1 April 1921
	Bolton Eyres-Monsell	25 July 1923
Chair, 1922 Committee	Gervais Rentoul	23 April 1923

BALDWIN'S SECOND GOVERNMENT
NOVEMBER 1924–JUNE 1929

Prime Minister	Stanley Baldwin	4 November 1924
Chancellor	Winston Churchill	6 November 1924
Foreign Secretary	Austen Chamberlain	6 November 1924
Home Secretary	Sir William Joynson-Hicks	6 November 1924
Party Chairman	Francis Stanley Jackson	13 March 1923
	J. C. C. Davidson	4 November 1926
Chief Whip	Bolton Eyres-Monsell	25 July 1923
Chair, 1922 Committee	Gervais Rentoul	23 April 1923

MACDONALD'S NATIONAL GOVERNMENT
AUGUST 1931–JUNE 1935

Prime Minister	Ramsay MacDonald (National Labour)	24 August 1931
Lord President	Stanley Baldwin	25 August 1931
Chancellor	Philip Snowden (National Labour)	25 August 1931
	Neville Chamberlain	5 November 1931
Foreign Secretary	Marquess of Reading (Liberal)	25 August 1931
	Sir John Simon (Liberal National)	5 November 1931
Home Secretary	Sir Herbert Samuel (Liberal)	25 August 1931
	Sir John Gilmour	28 September 1932
Party Chairman	Lord Stonehaven	14 April 1931
Chief Whip	Sir Bolton Eyres-Monsell	25 July 1923
	David Margesson	10 November 1931
Chair, 1922 Committee	Sir Gervais Rentoul	23 April 1923
	William Morrison	5 December 1932

BALDWIN'S NATIONAL GOVERNMENT
JUNE 1935–MAY 1937

Prime Minister	Stanley Baldwin	7 June 1935
Chancellor	Neville Chamberlain	5 November 1931
Foreign Secretary	Sir Samuel Hoare	7 June 1935
	Anthony Eden	22 December 1935
Home Secretary	Sir John Simon	7 June 1935
	(Liberal National)	
Party Chairman	Lord Stonehaven	14 April 1931
	Douglas Hacking	2 March 1936
Chief Whip	David Margesson	10 November 1931
Chair, 1922	William Morrison	5 December 1932
Committee	Sir Hugh O'Neill	16 December 1935

CHAMBERLAIN'S NATIONAL GOVERNMENT
MAY 1937–MAY 1940

Prime Minister	Neville Chamberlain	28 May 1937
Chancellor	Sir John Simon	28 May 1937
	(Liberal National)	
Foreign Secretary	Anthony Eden	22 December 1935
	Viscount Halifax	21 February 1938
Home Secretary	Sir Samuel Hoare	28 May 1937
	Sir John Anderson	3 September 1939
	(National)	
Party Chairman	Sir Douglas Hacking	2 March 1936
Chief Whip	David Margesson	10 November 1931
Chair, 1922	Sir Hugh O'Neill	16 December 1935
Committee	Sir Annesley Somerville	20 September 1939
	William Spens	6 December 1939

CHURCHILL'S COALITION GOVERNMENT
MAY 1940–MAY 1945

Prime Minister	Winston Churchill	10 May 1940
Chancellor	Sir Howard Kingsley Wood	12 May 1940
	Sir John Anderson (National)	24 September 1943
Foreign Secretary	Viscount Halifax	21 February 1938
	Anthony Eden	22 December 1940
Home Secretary	Sir John Anderson	3 September 1939
	Herbert Morrison (Labour)	3 October 1943
Party Chairman	Sir Douglas Hacking	2 March 1936
	Thomas Dugdale	6 March 1942
	Ralph Assheton	29 October 1944
Chief Whip	David Margesson	10 November 1931
	James Stuart	14 January 1941
Chair, 1922	William Spens	6 December 1939
Committee	Alexander Erskine-Hill	11 December 1940
	John McEwen	12 December 1944

CHURCHILL'S 'CARETAKER' GOVERNMENT
MAY 1945–JULY 1945

Prime Minister	Winston Churchill	10 May 1940
Chancellor	Sir John Anderson (National)	24 September 1940
Foreign Secretary	Anthony Eden	22 December 1940
Home Secretary	Sir Donald Somervell	25 May 1945
Party Chairman	Ralph Assheton	29 October 1944
Chief Whip	James Stuart	14 January 1941
Chair, 1922 Committee	John McEwen	12 December 1944

CHURCHILL'S CONSERVATIVE GOVERNMENT
OCTOBER 1951–APRIL 1955

Prime Minister	Winston Churchill	26 October 1951
Chancellor	R. A. Butler	28 October 1951
Foreign Secretary	Anthony Eden	28 October 1951
Home Secretary	Sir David Maxwell-Fyfe	28 October 1951
	Gwilym Lloyd George	18 October 1954
Party Chairman	Lord Woolton	1 July 1946
Chief Whip	Patrick Buchan-Hepburn	4 July 1948
Chair, 1922 Committee	Sir Arnold Grindley	31 October 1945
	Derek Walker-Smith	29 November 1951

EDEN'S GOVERNMENT
APRIL 1955–JANUARY 1957

Prime Minister	Anthony Eden	6 April 1955
Chancellor	R. A. Butler	28 October 1951
	Harold Macmillan	20 December 1955
Foreign Secretary	Harold Macmillan	7 April 1955
	Selwyn Lloyd	20 December 1955
Home Secretary	Gwilym Lloyd George	18 October 1954
Party Chairman	Viscount Woolton	1 July 1946
	Oliver Poole	1 November 1955
Chief Whip	Patrick Buchan-Hepburn	4 July 1948
	Edward Heath	30 December 1955
Chair, 1922 Committee	Derek Walker-Smith	29 November 1951
	John Morrison	1 November 1955

MACMILLAN'S FIRST GOVERNMENT
JANUARY 1957–OCTOBER 1959

Prime Minister	Harold Macmillan	10 January 1957

Chancellor	Peter Thorneycroft	13 January 1957
	Derrick Heathcoat-Amory	6 January 1958
Foreign Secretary	Selwyn Lloyd	20 December 1955
Home Secretary	R. A. Butler	13 January 1957
Party Chairman	Oliver Poole	1 November 1955
	Viscount Hailsham	18 September 1957
Chief Whip	Edward Heath	30 December 1955
Chair, 1922 Committee	John Morrison	1 November 1955

MACMILLAN'S SECOND GOVERNMENT
OCTOBER 1959–OCTOBER 1963

Prime Minister	Harold Macmillan	10 January 1957
Chancellor	Derrick Heathcoat-Amory	6 January 1958
	Selwyn Lloyd	27 July 1960
	Reginald Maudling	13 July 1962
Foreign Secretary	Selwyn Lloyd	20 December 1955
	Earl of Home	27 July 1960
Home Secretary	R. A. Butler	13 January 1957
	Henry Brooke	13 July 1962
Party Chairman	R. A. Butler	14 October 1959
	Iain Macleod	10 October 1961
	Iain Macleod and Lord Poole	17 April 1963
Chief Whip	Martin Redmayne	14 October 1959
Chair, 1922 Committee	John Morrison	1 November 1955

DOUGLAS-HOME'S GOVERNMENT
OCTOBER 1963–OCTOBER 1964

Prime Minister	Sir Alec Douglas-Home	18 October 1963

Chancellor	Reginald Maudling	13 July 1962
Foreign Secretary	R. A. Butler	20 October 1963
Home Secretary	Henry Brooke	13 July 1962
Party Chairman	Viscount Blakenham	21 October 1963
Chief Whip	Martin Redmayne	14 October 1959
Chair, 1922 Committee	John Morrison	1 November 1955

HEATH'S GOVERNMENT
JUNE 1970–MARCH 1974

Prime Minister	Edward Heath	19 June 1970
Chancellor	Iain Macleod	20 June 1970
	Anthony Barber	25 July 1970
Foreign Secretary	Sir Alec Douglas-Home	20 June 1970
Home Secretary	Reginald Maudling	20 June 1970
	Robert Carr	18 July 1972
Party Chairman	Anthony Barber	11 September 1967
	Peter Thomas	31 July 1970
	Lord Carrington	7 April 1972
Chief Whip	Francis Pym	20 June 1970
	Humphrey Atkins	2 December 1973
Chair, 1922 Committee	Sir Henry Legge-Bourke	16 July 1970
	Edward du Cann	16 November 1972

THATCHER'S FIRST GOVERNMENT
MAY 1979–JUNE 1983

Prime Minister	Margaret Thatcher	4 May 1979
Chancellor	Sir Geoffrey Howe	5 May 1979
Foreign Secretary	Lord Carrington	5 May 1979
	Francis Pym	6 April 1982
Home Secretary	William Whitelaw	5 May 1979
Party Chairman	Lord Thorneycroft	27 February 1975

	Cecil Parkinson	14 September 1981
Chief Whip	Michael Jopling	5 May 1979
Chair, 1922 Committee	Edward du Cann	16 November 1972

THATCHER'S SECOND GOVERNMENT
JUNE 1983–JUNE 1987

Prime Minister	Margaret Thatcher	4 May 1979
Chancellor	Nigel Lawson	11 June 1983
Foreign Secretary	Sir Geoffrey Howe	11 June 1983
Home Secretary	Leon Brittan	11 June 1983
	Douglas Hurd	2 September 1985
Party Chairman	Cecil Parkinson	14 September·1981
	John Selwyn Gummer	14 September 1983
	Norman Tebbit	2 September 1985
Chief Whip	John Wakeham	10 June 1983
Chair, 1922 Committee	Edward du Cann	16 November 1972
	Cranley Onslow	15 November 1984

THATCHER'S THIRD GOVERNMENT
JUNE 1987–NOVEMBER 1990

Prime Minister	Margaret Thatcher	4 May 1979
Chancellor	Nigel Lawson	11 June 1983
	John Major	26 October 1989
Foreign Secretary	Sir Geoffrey Howe	11 June 1983
	John Major	24 July 1989
	Douglas Hurd	26 October 1989
Home Secretary	Douglas Hurd	2 September 1985
	David Waddington	26 October 1989
Party Chairman	Norman Tebbit	2 September 1985
	Peter Brooke	2 November 1987
	Kenneth Baker	24 July 1989
Chief Whip	David Waddington	13 June 1987
	Timothy Renton	27 October 1989

Chair, 1922 Committee	Cranley Onslow	15 November 1984

MAJOR'S FIRST GOVERNMENT
NOVEMBER 1990–APRIL 1992

Prime Minister	John Major	28 November 1990
Chancellor	Norman Lamont	28 November 1990
Foreign Secretary	Douglas Hurd	26 October 1989
Home Secretary	Kenneth Baker	28 November 1990
Party Chairman	Chris Patten	28 November 1990
Chief Whip	Richard Ryder	28 November 1990
Chair, 1922 Committee	Cranley Onslow	15 November 1984

MAJOR'S SECOND GOVERNMENT
APRIL 1992–MAY 1997

Prime Minister	John Major	28 November 1990
Chancellor	Norman Lamont	28 November 1990
	Kenneth Clarke	27 May 1993
Foreign Secretary	Douglas Hurd	26 October 1989
	Malcolm Rifkind	6 July 1995
Home Secretary	Kenneth Clarke	11 April 1992
	Michael Howard	27 May 1993
Party Chairman	Chris Patten	28 November 1990
	Sir Norman Fowler	10 May 1992
	Jeremy Hanley	21 July 1994
	Brian Mawhinney	6 July 1995
Chief Whip	Richard Ryder	28 November 1990
	Alastair Goodlad	6 July 1995
Chair, 1922 Committee	Cranley Onslow	15 November 1984
	Sir Marcus Fox	14 May 1992

NOTES

1: The Carlton Club and the New Conservatives (PP. 3–16)

1 Charles Loch Mowatt, *Britain Between the Wars 1918–1940* (1955), p. 9.

2 George Dangerfield, *The Strange Death of Liberal England* (1936; 1965 edn), p. 60.

3 Headlam diary, 28 February 1924, in Stuart Ball, *Parliament and Politics in the Age of Baldwin and MacDonald: The Headlam Diaries 1923–1935* (1992), p. 39.

4 Macready, Annals II, p. 549, in Mowatt, *Britain Between the Wars*, pp. 79–80.

5 John Campbell, *F. E. Smith, First Earl of Birkenhead* (1983), pp. 588–9.

6 Younger to Austen Chamberlain, 24 December 1921, Campbell, *F. E. Smith*, p. 587.

7 Davidson to Stamfordham, Robert Rhodes James (ed.), *Memoirs of a Conservative: J. C. C. Davidson's Memoirs and Papers* (1969), p. 103.

8 Birkenhead to Churchill, 17 November 1920, Campbell, *F. E. Smith*, pp. 592–3.

9 Lady Lee diary, 16 October 1922, in Alan Clark (ed.), *A Good Innings: The Private Papers of Viscount Lee of Fareham* (1974), pp. 230–1.

10 Lord Beaverbrook, *The Decline and Fall of Lloyd George* (1963), p. 190.

11 Rhodes James, *Memoirs of a Conservative*, p. 134.

12 Beaverbrook, *Decline and Fall*, p. 225.

13 Ibid., p. 221.

14 Ibid., p. 226.

2: Bonar Law Comes to Grief (PP. 17–28)

1. Lady Lee diary, 2 February 1923, in Clark (ed.), *A Good Innings*, p. 236.
2. Robert Blake, *The Unknown Prime Minister: The Life and Times of Andrew Bonar Law 1858–1923* (1955), p. 496.
3. Younger to Bonar Law, 15 January 1923, in Blake, *Unknown Prime Minister*, p. 496.
4. Bonar Law to Lord Edmund Talbot, 24 January 1923, in Blake, *Unknown Prime Minister*, p. 497 (AC's italics).
5. Rhodes James, *Memoirs of a Conservative*, p. 139.
6. Rothermere to Beaverbrook, 26 April 1923, in A. J. P. Taylor, *Beaverbrook* (1972), p. 207.
7. Bonar Law/Curzon correspondence, 25 April 1923, in Blake, *Unknown Prime Minister*, pp. 510–11.
8. Beaverbrook to Sir Robert Borden, 10 May 1923, in Taylor, *Beaverbrook*, p. 207.
9. Rhodes James, *Memoirs of a Conservative*, p. 151 (AC's italics).
10. Ibid., p. 151.
11. Ibid., pp. 154–5.
12. David Gilmour, *Curzon* (1994), p. 584.

3: Stanley Baldwin Finds His Feet (PP. 29–42)

1. Gilmour, *Curzon*, p. 583.
2. Lady Lee diary, 27 May 1923, in Clark (ed.), *A Good Innings*, p. 238.
3. Worthington-Evans to Austen Chamberlain, 22 May 1923, in Campbell, *F. E. Smith*, p. 629.
4. Baldwin's speech, recorded 28 March 1929, issued on Columbia 5338.
5. Ibid.
6. Rhodes James, *Memoirs of a Conservative*, p. 180.
7. Ibid., p. 182.
8. Alan Coles and Ted Briggs, *Flagship* Hood, *the Fate of Britain's Mightiest Warship* (1985), pp. 35–6.
9. Rhodes James, *Memoirs of a Conservative*, pp. 184–5.
10. Maurice Cowling, *The Impact of Labour* (1971), p. 294.
11. Ibid., p. 309.

[12] Baldwin to Tom Jones, September 1935, in Keith Middlemas and John Barnes, *Baldwin, a Biography* (1969), p. 212.

[13] Cowling, *Impact of Labour*, p. 314.

[14] Ibid., p. 318.

[15] Robert Blake, *The Conservative Party from Peel to Thatcher* (1970; 1985 edn), pp. 220–2.

[16] Cowling, *Impact of Labour*, pp. 305–6.

[17] Ibid., p. 327.

4: An Unhappy Ship (PP. 43–54)

[1] Martin Pugh, *The Making of Modern British Politics 1867–1939* (1982), p. 242.

[2] Campbell, *F. E. Smith*, pp. 651–2; Cowling, *Impact of Labour*, p. 337.

[3] Cowling, *Impact of Labour*, p. 337.

[4] Ibid., p. 364.

[5] Ibid., pp. 410–11.

[6] Birkenhead to Sir Robert Houston, 31 October 1924, in Campbell, *F. E. Smith*, pp. 673–4.

[7] Curzon to Baldwin, 31 October 1924, in Gilmour, *Curzon*, p. 595.

[8] Neville Chamberlain diary, 5 November 1924, Neville Chamberlain Papers 2/21.

[9] Gilmour, *Curzon*, p. 596.

[10] *The Times*, 2 October 1924, in Campbell, *F. E. Smith*, pp. 670–1.

[11] Ibid., p. 689.

[12] Ibid., p. 678.

[13] Birkenhead to Sir Robert Houston, 31 October 1924, in Campbell, *F. E. Smith*, p. 679.

[14] Keith Middlemas (ed.), *Tom Jones, Whitehall Diary*, vol. 1: *1916–1925* (1969), p. 304.

[15] Neville Chamberlain diary, Neville Chamberlain Papers 2/21.

[16] Martin Gilbert, *Winston S. Churchill*, vol. V: *1922–1939*, (1976), p. 60 (AC's italics).

[17] Neville Chamberlain diary, Neville Chamberlain Papers 2/21.

[18] Ibid.

5: The Gold Standard and its Consequences (PP. 55–68)

1 Churchill to the Commons, 28 April 1925, Hansard 183 H.C. Deb. 5s, col. 53.

2 Motion before the Commons, 4 May 1925.

3 Churchill to the Commons, 5 August 1925, Robert Rhodes James (ed.), *Winston S. Churchill: His Complete Speeches 1897–1963*, vol. IV (1974), pp. 3741–2.

4 Frances Spalding, *Vanessa Bell* (1983), p. 187.

5 Peter Clarke, *The Keynesian Revolution in the Making 1924–1936* (1988), p. 34.

6 Leith-Ross, quoted in D. E. Moggridge, *The Return to Gold, 1925* (1969), p. 67.

7 Boothby's recollection, quoted in John Charmley, *Churchill: The End of Glory* (1993), p. 207.

8 Memo from Churchill, undated (early 1925), Treasury: T171/246, quoted in Paul Addison, *Churchill on the Home Front 1900–1955* (1992), pp. 246–7.

9 Churchill to Niemeyer, 22 February 1925, Chartwell Papers, in Martin Gilbert, *Winston S. Churchill*, Companion vol. V, pt. 1, pp. 411–12.

10 As indeed he was to do, on justification more slender still in 1945.

11 P. J. Grigg, *Prejudice and Judgement* (1948), pp. 182–4.

12 Keynes in *The Nation*, quoted by Churchill to the Commons, 4 May 1925, Hansard 183 H.C. Deb. 5s, col. 667.

13 Horne to the Commons, ibid., col. 640.

14 Churchill to Niemeyer, 2 January 1925, Chartwell Papers in Gilbert, *Churchill*, Companion vol. V, pt. 1, p. 329.

15 Churchill to the Commons, 4 May 1925, Hansard 183 H.C. Deb. 5s, cols 673–4.

16 Churchill to the Commons, 5 August 1925, Rhodes James (ed.), *Churchill: Complete Speeches*, vol. IV, p. 3742.

17 Horne to the Commons, 4 May 1925, Hansard 183 H.C. Deb. 5s, col. 639.

18 *The Times*, 29 April 1925, p. 17.

19 Grigg's recollection of Lord Bradbury's case at Churchill's March 1925 dinner party, Grigg, *Prejudice and Judgement*, p. 183.

20 N. H. Dimsdale, 'The British Economy and the Age of Gold', in *Twentieth Century British History*, vol. 6, no. 1 (1995), p. 114; Moggridge, *Return to Gold*, p. 67.

21 Quoted in Clarke, *Keynesian Revolution*, p. 40.

22 Churchill to the Commons, 4 May 1925, Hansard 183 H.C. Deb. 5s, cols 671–2. This point is brought out by Addison, *Churchill on the Home Front*, p. 250.

23 Alan Sked, *Britain's Decline: Problems and Perspectives* (1987), pp. 22–3.

6: The General Strike (PP. 69–85)

1 Headlam diary, 28 July 1925, in Stuart Ball (ed.), *Parliament and Politics in the Age of Baldwin and MacDonald: The Headlam Diaries 1923–1935* (1992), p. 69.

2 Headlam diary, 31 July 1925, ibid., p. 70 (AC's italics).

3 Campbell, *F. E. Smith*, p. 767.

4 Birkenhead to Reading (Viceroy of India), 8 October 1925, ibid., p. 768.

5 Geoffrey McDonald, 'The Defeat of the General Strike' in Chris Cook and Gillian Peele (eds), *The Politics of Reappraisal, 1918–39* (1975), p. 65.

6 Headlam diary, 3 August 1925, in Ball (ed.), *Parliament and Politics in the Age of Baldwin and MacDonald*, p. 70.

7 John Barnes and Richard Cockett, 'The Making of Party Policy', in Anthony Seldon and Stuart Ball (eds), *Conservative Century: The Conservative Party since 1900* (1994), p. 358.

8 McDonald, 'Defeat of the General Strike', pp. 70–1.

9 A. J. P. Taylor, *English History 1914–1945* (1965), p. 243.

10 McDonald, 'Defeat of the General Strike', p. 66.

11 Middlemas (ed.), *Tom Jones, Whitehall Diary*, vol. 2: *1926–1930* (1969), p. 32.

12 Neville Chamberlain diary, May 1926, Neville Chamberlain Papers 2/22.

13 Sidney Pollard, *The Development of the British Economy 1914–1990* (4th edn, 1992), p. 141.

14 Middlemas (ed.), *Tom Jones, Whitehall Diary*, vol. 2, p. 36.

15 McDonald, 'Defeat of the General Strike', p. 73.

[16] Taylor, *English History*, p. 250.

[17] Headlam diary, 4 May, 5 May, 7 May 1926, in Ball (ed.), *Parliament and Politics in the Age of Baldwin and MacDonald*, pp. 86–7; Middlemas (ed.), *Tom Jones, Whitehall Diary*, vol. 2, p. 37.

[18] Taylor, *English History*, p. 245.

[19] Campbell, *F. E. Smith*, p. 774.

[20] McDonald, 'Defeat of the General Strike', p. 77.

[21] Birkenhead to Lord Irwin, 16 August 1926, in Campbell, *F. E. Smith*, p. 778.

[22] Headlam diary, 6 May 1926, in Ball (ed.), *Parliament and Politics in the Age of Baldwin and MacDonald*, p. 87.

[23] McDonald, 'Defeat of the General Strike', pp. 77–8.

[24] Middlemas (ed.), *Tom Jones, Whitehall Diary*.

[25] Birkenhead to Lord Irwin (later Halifax), 20 May 1926, in Campbell, *F. E. Smith*, p. 777.

[26] Quoted in Andrew Taylor, 'The Party and Trade Unions', in Seldon and Ball, *Conservative Century*, p. 507.

[27] Ibid., p. 509.

[28] Ibid., p. 510.

[29] Campbell, *F. E. Smith*, p. 782.

7: Stanley Baldwin Survives (PP. 86–100)

[1] Rhodes James, *Memoirs of a Conservative*, p. 294.

[2] Ibid., p. 296.

[3] Ibid., p. 300.

[4] Letter to Mimi Davidson, 20 May 1929, ibid., p. 303 (AC's italics).

[5] Rhodes James, *Memoirs of a Conservative*, p. 287.

[6] Ibid., p. 304.

[7] Ibid., p. 311.

[8] Ibid.

[9] Stuart Ball, *Baldwin and the Conservative Party: The Crisis of 1929–31* (1988), p. xvii.

[10] Anne Chisholm and Michael Davie, *Beaverbrook* (1992), p. 282.

[11] Rhodes James, *Memoirs of a Conservative*, p. 331.

[12] Quoted in S. R. Ball, 'Failure of an Opposition? The Conservative

Party in Parliament 1929–1931' in *Parliamentary History*, vol. 5 (1986), p. 90.

[13] Chisholm and Davie, *Beaverbrook*, p. 298.

[14] Amery diary, 9 October 1930, in John Barnes and David Nicholson (eds), *The Empire at Bay: The Leo Amery Diaries, vol. 2: 1929–1945* (1988), p. 82.

[15] Quoted in Gilbert, *Churchill*, vol. V, p. 390.

[16] Ball, *Baldwin and the Conservative Party*, pp. 137–8.

[17] Chisholm and Davie, *Beaverbrook*, p. 304.

8: Economic Crisis and 'National' Government (PP. 101–16)

[1] See Phillip Williamson, *National Crisis and National Government* (Cambridge 1992), pp. 299–303, 322–5.

[2] Ibid., p. 389.

[3] Coles and Briggs, *Flagship* Hood, p. 51.

[4] Ibid., p. 55.

[5] Ibid., p. 62.

[6] Ibid., p. 63.

[7] Ibid., p. 68.

9: Foreign Affairs (PP. 117–26)

[1] Keith Middlemas and John Barnes, *Baldwin: A Biography* (1969), p. 745.

[2] Thomas Jones, *Diary with Letters*, 1936, pp. 180–1 (Tom Jones to Lady Grigg, 8 March 1936).

[3] Rhodes James, *Memoirs of a Conservative*, p. 396.

[4] Earl Winterton, *Orders of the Day* (1953), p. 217.

[5] Rhodes James, *Memoirs of a Conservative*, p. 411.

[6] Davidson to Baldwin, 30 June 1936, ibid., p. 411.

[7] Baldwin to Mrs Davidson, 3 August 1936, ibid., p. 412.

10: The Abdication (PP. 127–43)

[1] Philip Ziegler, *King Edward VIII* (1990), p. 192.

[2] Lady Lee diary, 5 January 1929, in Clark (ed.), *A Good Innings*, p. 289.

[3] Ziegler, *Edward VIII*, p. 206.

[4] Ibid., p. 215.

[5] Ibid.

[6] Edward to Freda Dudley Ward, 16 February 1922, and Lord Reading to Edwin Montagu, 24 November 1921, ibid., p. 143.

[7] Ibid., p. 209.

[8] 6 December 1928, ibid., p. 193.

[9] Channon diary, 17 January 1935, Robert Rhodes James, *Chips: The Diaries of Sir Henry Channon* (1967), p. 22.

[10] In the words of his official biographer. Ziegler, *Edward VIII*, p. 219.

[11] Aird diary, 14 April 1934, ibid., p. 229.

[12] Lascelles Papers, ibid., p. 291.

[13] Duff Cooper diary, 30 November 1936, ibid., p. 316.

[14] Ibid., p. 250.

[15] Ibid., p. 244.

[16] Tony Benn diary, 11 January 1977, Tony Benn, *Conflicts of Interest: Diaries 1977–1980* (1990), pp. 2–3.

[17] Gilbert, *Churchill*, vol. V, pp. 818–19.

[18] Ziegler, *Edward VIII*, p. 319.

[19] Nigel Nicolson (ed.), *Harold Nicolson: Diaries and Letters 1930–39* (1966), pp. 282, 284.

[20] Baldwin to the Commons, 10 December 1936, Hansard 318 H.C. Deb. 5s, col. 2177.

[21] Gallacher to the Commons, 11 December 1936, ibid., col. 2215.

11: Diplomatic Disappointments (PP. 144–61)

[1] Robert Rhodes James (ed.), *Churchill: His Complete Speeches 1897–1963*, vol. VI (1974), p. 5857.

[2] Amery diary, 8 April 1937, in Barnes and Nicholson (eds), *Empire at Bay*, vol. 2, p. 439.

[3] Ibid., 27 May 1937, p. 442.

[4] Ibid., 2 June 1937, p. 443.

[5] Ibid., p. 444.

[6] Ibid., 25 May 1937, p. 441.

[7] Ibid.

[8] Channon diary, 6 August 1936, in Rhodes James (ed.), *Chips*, p. 107.

⁹ Halifax Papers, in Andrew Roberts, *The Holy Fox: A Biography of Lord Halifax* (1991), p. 73.

¹⁰ Lady Lee diary, Chequers Papers, 29 November 1936.

¹¹ Alan Clark (ed.), *A Good Innings: The Private Papers of Viscount Lee of Fareham* (1974). Lady Lee diary, October 1936.

¹² Page-Croft to the Commons, 29 October 1936, Hansard 316 H.C. Deb. 5s, cols 72–3.

¹³ 14 April 1937, Hansard 322 H.C. Deb. 5s, col. 1063.

¹⁴ Quoted in John Charmley, *Chamberlain and the Lost Peace* (1989), p. 107.

¹⁵ Robert Rhodes James, *Churchill: A Study in Failure* (1969), p. 338.

¹⁶ FO 800/269 Halifax to Henderson, 19 March 1938, in Charmley, *Chamberlain*, p. 74.

¹⁷ Cecil of Chelwood MSS 51081 fol. 142, ibid., p. 146.

¹⁸ Rhodes James, *Churchill: A Study in Failure*, p. 339.

¹⁹ Richard Law to Emrys Evans, 30 December 1939, in Charmley, *Chamberlain*, p. 147.

²⁰ Cadogan diary, 9 October 1938, in David Dilks (ed.), *The Diaries of Sir Alexander Cadogan 1938–1945* (1971), p. 114.

12: Munich to Outbreak of War (PP. 162–80)

¹ PRO FO 371/22951, C2861, 8/18. Report on British exports to Germany, 9 March 1939, in Scott Newton, *Profits of Peace: The Political Economy of Anglo-German Appeasement* (1996), p. 91.

² *The Times*, 15 March 1939.

³ Cadogan diary, 18 March 1939, in Dilks (ed.), *Diaries of Sir Alexander Cadogan*, p. 160.

⁴ Cadogan diary, 19 March 1939, ibid., p. 161.

⁵ Chamberlain to the Commons, 31 March 1939, Hansard 345 H.C. Deb. 5s, col. 2415.

⁶ Cadogan diary, 30 March 1939, in Dilks (ed.), *Diaries of Sir Alexander Cadogan*, p. 165.

⁷ Churchill to the Commons, 3 April 1939, Hansard 345 H.C. Deb. 5s, col. 2501.

⁸ *The Times*, 1 April 1939.

[9] Richard Cockett, *Twilight of Truth: Chamberlain, Appeasement and the Manipulation of the Press* (1988), p. 109.

[10] Henderson to Cadogan, 4 July 1939, FO 800/294, C2/39/23, in Charmley, *Chamberlain*, p. 195.

[11] US Emb. file 23.8.39. Telegram 1221.

[12] Wilkinson and Macmillan to the Commons, 24 August 1939, Hansard 351 H.C. Deb. 5s, cols 51–2.

[13] Bevan to the Commons, 24 August 1939, Hansard 351 H.C. Deb. 5s, col. 58.

[14] FO 800/316 H/XV/268.

[15] Ziegler, *Edward VIII*, pp. 400–1.

[16] Henderson to Halifax, 29 August 1939, Vansittart minute, Charmley, *Chamberlain*, p. 203. Cadogan diary, 28 August 1939, in Dilks (ed.), *Diaries of Sir Alexander Cadogan*, p. 203.

[17] IMT Doc PS-1014 in John W. Wheeler-Bennett *The Nemesis of Power – The German Army in Politics 1918–1945* (1953), p. 447.

[18] Churchill to Chamberlain, 3 September 1939, in Gilbert, *Churchill*, vol. V, p. 1110.

13: The Phoney War (PP. 183–206)

[1] Channon diary, 19 September 1939, in Rhodes James (ed.), *Chips*, p. 221.

[2] Cab 65/1, David Carlton, *Anthony Eden: A Biography* (1981), pp. 154–5.

[3] Cadogan diary, 29 September 1939, in Dilks (ed.), *Diaries of Sir Alexander Cadogan*, p. 220.

[4] Bastianini to Ciano. no. 550, 2 October; It. Emb. 1054. It should be noted that the FO 371/22985, no less that 45 pages spanning October 3–4, is 'closed'. So also are the Chamberlain–Horace Wilson Papers (PREM 1/333) and Hankey's October and November files CAB 63, 84–5. Students have to assume, therefore, that the topics illuminated therein are of considerable moment.

[5] Alistair Horne, *To Lose a Battle: France 1940* (1969), pp. 160–1.

[6] Chamberlain to the Commons, 2 September 1939, Hansard 351 H.C. Deb. 5s, col. 285.

[7] B. R. Mitchell, *European Historical Statistics* (1975), table E9.

[8] Churchill to Halifax, 10 September 1939, Martin Gilbert, *Winston S. Churchill*, vol. VI: *Finest Hour 1939–1941* (1983), p. 23.

[9] Iain Macleod, *Neville Chamberlain* (1961), p. 284.

[10] David Dilks, *The Twilight War and the Fall of France: Chamberlain and Churchill in 1940*, in *Transactions of the Royal Historical Society*, 5th series, vol. 28, 1978, p. 65.

[11] Churchill's broadcast of 18 December 1939, in Martin Gilbert, *Finest Hour, Winston S. Churchill 1939–41*, 1989 ed., p. 80.

[12] Hore-Belisha diary, 4 January 1940, in R. J. Minney, *The Private Papers of Hore-Belisha* (1960), pp. 269–70.

[13] Chamberlain to his sister, 7 January 1940, Charmley, *Chamberlain*, p. 286.

[14] Hore-Belisha diary, 5 January 1940, in Minney, *Hore-Belisha*, pp. 276–7.

[15] Amery diary, 5 January 1940, in Barnes and Nicholson (eds), *Empire at Bay*, vol. 2, p. 579.

[16] Hore-Belisha diary, 5 January 1940, in Minney, *Hore-Belisha*, p. 277.

[17] Cazalet diary, 13 April 1940, quoted in Roberts, *Holy Fox*, p. 190.

[18] Nicolson diary, 11 April 1940, in Nigel Nicolson (ed.), *Harold Nicolson: Diaries and Letters 1939–1945* (1967), p. 70.

[19] Taylor, *Beaverbrook*, p. 405.

[20] Ibid., p. 408.

[21] Chamberlain to his sister, 20 April 1940, in Charmley, *Churchill: End of Glory*, p. 387.

[22] Churchill to the Commons, Hansard 360 H.C. Deb. 5s, col. 1360.

14: The Coalition Government is Formed (PP. 207–23)

[1] Amery diary, 9 May 1940, in Barnes and Nicholson (eds), *Empire at Bay*, vol. 2, p. 611.

[2] Ibid.

[3] (Lord Avon) Anthony Eden, *The Reckoning, The Eden Memoirs*, vol. 2 (1965), pp. 96–7.

[4] Taylor, *Beaverbrook*, p. 409.

[5] Thomas Jones, *A Diary with Letters 1931–56* (1954), p. 457.

[6] Roberts, *Holy Fox*, p. 198.

[7] Ibid., p. 203.

[8] Ibid., p. 199.

[9] Templewood Papers XII 3; Roberts, *Holy Fox*, p. 207.

[10] Roberts, *Holy Fox*, p. 209.

[11] Notes of meetings of the Supreme War Council between 16 May and 16 June 1940, in Gilbert, *Churchill: Finest Hour*, p. 349.

[12] Ismay to Churchill, 20 May 1946; ibid., p. 553.

[13] CAB 65/13 WM 145.

[14] Roberts, *Holy Fox*, p. 225.

[15] FO 371/24299, 26 April 1940, also FO 371/24298.

[16] Herbert R. Lottman, *Pétain, Hero or Traitor? The Untold Story* (1985), p. 169.

[17] Avi Shlaim, 'Prelude to Downfall: the British offer of Union to France, June 1940' in *Journal of Contemporary History*, vol. 9, no. 5, July 1974.

[18] Lottman, *Pétain*, p. 175.

15: Wasted Opportunities (PP. 224–41)

[1] Lottman, *Pétain*, p. 165.

[2] Charles de Gaulle, *War Memoirs*, vol. I: *The Call to Honour* (1953), p. 61.

[3] Ibid., p. 94.

[4] War Cab. 304 of 1940. Meeting of the War Cabinet, 5 August 1940.

[5] Cab 79/6 253.

[6] Lottman, *Pétain*, p. 207.

[7] De Gaulle, *War Memoirs*, pp. 93–4.

[8] Quoted in Carlton, *Eden*, p. 167.

[9] Ibid.

[10] Roberts, *The Holy Fox*, p. 275.

[11] David Day, *Menzies and Churchill at War* (1986), p. 66.

[12] Ibid., pp. 67–8.

[13] Channon diary, 3 March 1941, in Rhodes James, *Chips*, p. 293.

[14] Day, *Menzies and Churchill*, p. 171.

16: The Haemorrhage Continues (PP. 242–59)

[1] WM (40) 306 CAB 65/16.

[2] Mary Soames, *Clementine Churchill* (1979), p. 299.

[3] Amery diary, 10 November 1940, Barnes and Nicholson (eds), *Empire at Bay*, vol. 2, p. 666.

[4] Gilbert, *Churchill: Finest Hour*, pp. 970–1.

[5] Nicolson (ed.), *Harold Nicolson: Diaries and Letters 1939–1945* (1967), 20 November 1940, p. 127.

[6] PM's personal telegrams, Ismay Papers vi/i KC.

[7] Churchill to the Commons, 12 May 1941, Hansard 371 H.C. Deb. 5s, col. 1085.

[8] Prem 3/219/1 fol. 43.

[9] Amery diary, 9 June 1941, in Barnes and Nicholson (eds), *Empire at Bay*, vol. 2, p. 693.

[10] Amery diary, 8 August 1941, in Barnes and Nicholson (eds), *Empire at Bay*, vol. 2, p. 701.

[11] ROSK 4/79.

[12] Correlli Barnett, *Engage the Enemy More Closely: The Royal Navy in the Second World War* (1991), p. 394.

[13] ADM 205/10, 26 August 1941.

[14] Barnett, *Engage the Enemy*, p. 398.

[15] Gilbert, *Churchill: Finest Hour*, pp. 1266–8.

[16] Churchill to the Commons, 27 January 1942, Hansard 377 H.C. Deb. 5s, col. 601.

17: The Loss of Empire (PP. 260–70)

[1] See Clark (ed.), *A Good Innings*, chapters 19 and 20.

[2] Barnett, *Engage the Enemy*, p. 380.

[3] Ibid.

[4] Richard Lamb, *Churchill as War Leader – Right or Wrong?* (1991), p. 193.

[5] Ibid.

[6] Barnett, *Engage the Enemy More Closely*, p. 864.

[7] Barnes and Nicholson, *Empire at Bay*, p. 728.

[8] David Day, *The Great Betrayal: Britain, Australia and the Onset of the Pacific War 1939–1941* (1988), p. 75.

[9] John Curtin in the *Melbourne Herald*, 27 December 1941, in Winston S. Churchill, *The Second World War*, vol. IV: *The Hinge of Fate* (1951), pp. 7–8.

[10] *The Times*, 3 January 1941.

18: 1942: Churchill's Difficult Summer (PP. 271–84)

[1] Harvey diary, 12 February 1942, in J. Harvey (ed.), *The War Diaries of Oliver Harvey 1941–1945* (1978), p. 94.

[2] Harvey diary, 16 February 1942 (Harvey Papers), in Carlton, *Eden*, pp. 202–3.

[3] Harvey diary, ibid., p. 203.

[4] Minney, *Hore-Belisha*, pp. 293–4.

[5] Amery diary, 18 December 1941, in Barnes and Nicholson (eds), *Empire at Bay*, vol. 2, p. 754.

[6] Churchill to Beaverbrook, 14 June 1942, Taylor, *Beaverbrook*, p. 536.

[7] Moran diary, in Lord Moran, *Winston Churchill: The Struggle for Survival 1940–1965* (1966), pp. 101, 496.

[8] The title used to describe the first half of Churchill's career by Rhodes James, in *Churchill: A Study in Failure*.

[9] Ivor Thomas to Tom Jones, 14 August 1942, in Paul Addison, *The Road to 1945, British Politics and the Second World War* (1975; 1994 edn), p. 208 9.

[10] Ibid.

[11] Moran, *Churchill: Struggle for Survival*, p. 72.

[12] Philip Goodhart with Ursula Branston, *The 1922: The Story of the Conservative Backbenchers' Parliamentary Committee* (1973), pp. 124–5.

[13] Ibid., pp. 125–6 (AC's italics).

[14] Harvey, *War Diaries*, p. 165.

[15] Goodhart, *The 1922*, p. 128.

19: The Conservative Party and 'Welfare' (PP. 285–301)

[1] Kevin Jefferys, *The Churchill Coalition and Wartime Politics 1940–1945* (1991 edn), p. 116.

[2] Richard Cockett, *Thinking the Unthinkable: Think-Tanks and the Economic Counter-Revolution 1931–1983* (1994), p. 75.

[3] Hartmut Kopsch, 'The Approach of the Conservative Party to Social Policy During World War II', unpublished University of London PhD thesis, 1970, p. 65.

[4] Norman Crump, *The Future of Money*, Signpost Booklet, 1943, p. 9, quoted in Kopsch PhD, p. 67.

[5] A. G. Erskine-Hill, *The Future of the Small Trader*, Signpost Booklet, 1944, quoted in Kopsch PhD, p. 68.

[6] G. L. Schwartz, *Why Planning?*, Signpost Booklet, 1944, pp. 25–6, quoted in Kopsch PhD, p. 69.

[7] Beatrice Webb diary, 10 August 1938, in Addison, *Road to 1945*, p. 213.

[8] Headlam diary, 11 February 1943, in John Ramsden, *A History of the Conservative Party: The Age of Churchill and Eden 1940–1957* (1995), pp. 45–6.

[9] Kopsch PhD, pp. 71–2, 71n.

[10] Kopsch PhD, pp. 80–5.

[11] Addison, *Road to 1945*, pp. 168–9.

[12] (Beveridge Report) HMSO, Cmnd. 6409, 1942, para. 1.

[13] Greenwood to Beveridge, 27 January 1942, quoted in Beveridge Report, para. 40, and Kopsch PhD, p. 91n.

[14] Kopsch PhD, p. 119.

[15] Cockett, *Thinking the Unthinkable*, p. 61.

[16] Correlli Barnett, *The Audit of War: The Illusion and Reality of Britain as a Great Nation* (1986), p. 28.

[17] Kopsch PhD, p. 125.

[18] Beveridge's radio broadcast, *The Listener*, vol. xxviii, 28 December 1942, p. 742, quoted in Kopsch PhD, p. 98n.

[19] Beveridge, 'Real Freedom from Want', *The Observer*, 28 February 1943, p. 99, quoted in Kopsch PhD, p. 99.

[20] Quoted in Addison, *Road to 1945*, p. 214.

[21] Kopsch PhD, pp. 103–4, 105.

[22] Reproduced in Churchill, *Second World War*, vol. IV, Appendix F, p. 862.

[23] Salisbury, *Post-War Conservative Policy*, September 1942, p. 11, quoted in Kopsch PhD, p. 108.

[24] T. L. Dugdale in *Onlooker*, January 1943, p. 5, quoted in Kopsch PhD, p. 108.

[25] Kopsch PhD, p. 113.

[26] Addison, *Road to 1945*, p. 221; Kopsch PhD, p. 113.

[27] Assheton Committee report, quoted in Jefferys, *Churchill Coalition*, p. 131.

[28] Quoted from the Assheton Committee report in Addison, *Road to 1945*, p. 221.

[29] Ibid., p. 220.

[30] Jefferys, *Churchill Coalition*, p. 114.

[31] Ibid., p. 115.

[32] Addison, *Road to 1945*, p. 363.

[33] Butler's speech in Glasgow, reported in the *Western Mail*, 23 February 1943, quoted in Kopsch PhD, p. 121.

[34] G. S. Harvie-Scott, *Most of My Life* (1980), p. 117.

[35] Note by Churchill to the Cabinet, 12 January 1943, in Churchill, *Second World War*, vol. IV, Appendix F, p. 861.

[36] Kopsch PhD, pp. 128–30.

[37] Hansard 386 H.C. Deb. 5s, col. 1682.

[38] Ibid., col. 1613.

[39] Addison, *Road to 1945*, p. 225.

[40] Dalton diary, 18 February 1943, in Jefferys, *Churchill Coalition*, pp. 120–1.

[41] Harvie-Scott, *Most of My Life*, p. 117.

[42] Kopsch PhD, pp. 135–6.

[43] Hansard 386 H.C. Deb. 5s, col. 1818.

[44] Addison, *Road to 1945*, p. 223.

[45] Jefferys, *Churchill Coalition*, p. 124.

[46] Addison, *Churchill on the Home Front*, p. 372.

[47] GAB 87/13 PR (43) 13, 11 February 1943, in Barnett, *Audit of War*, p. 30.

[48] Barnett, *Audit of War*, p. 33; quotes from Addison, *Churchill on the Home Front*, p. 378.

20: 1944: The Coalition in Decline (PP. 302–16)

[1] Jefferys, *Churchill Coalition*, p. 171.

[2] 22 June 1944, Hansard 401 H.C. Deb. 5s, cols 363–5.

[3] Quoted in Ramsden, *Age of Churchill and Eden*, p. 67.

[4] Ibid., pp. 68–9.

5 Amery diary, 12 August 1944, in Nicholson and Barnes (eds), *Empire at Bay*, vol. 2, p. 995.

6 Ibid., 23 November 1944, p. 1020.

7 Churchill's broadcast on post-war planning, 21 March 1943, Rhodes James (ed.), *Churchill: Complete Speeches*, vol. IV (1974), p. 6759 (AC's italics).

8 Beaverbrook to J. P. Bickell, 18 November 1943, in Taylor, *Beaverbrook* (1943), p. 553.

9 Amery diary, 22 May 1945, in Barnes and Nicholson (eds), *Empire at Bay*, vol. 2, p. 1043.

10 Amery diary, 4 June 1945, ibid., p. 1046.

11 Quoted in Ramsden, *Age of Churchill and Eden*, p. 78.

12 Ibid., p. 75.

13 Minney, *Hore-Belisha*, p. 299.

14 Beaverbrook to Churchill, 17 July 1945, in Taylor, *Beaverbrook*, p. 568.

15 Personal recollection of the author who attended the party on 'long leave' from school.

16 Beaverbrook to J. P. Bickell, 31 July 1945, in Taylor, *Beaverbrook*, p. 568.

21: The Party in Defeat (PP. 319–30)

1 Ramsden, *Churchill and Eden* (1995), pp. 86–7.

2 Goodhart, *The 1922*, p. 141.

3 James Stuart, *Within the Fringe: an Autobiography* (1967), p. 141.

4 Quoted in Alistair Horne, *Macmillan 1894–1956*, vol. 1 (1988), p. 299.

5 Quoted in Ramsden, *Churchill and Eden*, pp. 142–3.

6 Ibid., pp. 158–68.

7 Ibid., p. 95.

22: Friction at the Highest Levels (PP. 331–7)

1 Carlton, *Eden*, p. 135.

2 Winston Churchill, *The Second World War*, vol. 1, *The Gathering Storm* (1948), p. 201.

3 Rhodes James, *Anthony Eden* (1986), p. 56.

4 Carlton, *Eden*, p. 295.

5 John Colville, *The Fringes of Power: Downing Street Diaries 1939–1955* (1985), p. 703.
6 Ibid.
7 Eden diary, Rhodes James, *Eden*, p. 385.
8 Eden correspondence, ibid., p. 386 (AC's italics).
9 Eden diary, 22 December 1955, ibid., p. 392.

23: The Rejection of Opportunity (PP. 338–49)

1 Andrew Roberts, *Eminent Churchillians* (1994), p. 248.
2 Anthony Howard, *RAB: The Life of R. A. Butler* (1987), p. 178.
3 Lord Butler, *The Art of the Possible* (1971), p. 156.
4 Ibid., p. 157.
5 Edmund Dell, *The Chancellors: A History of the Chancellors of the Exchequer 1945–1990* (1996), p. 165.
6 Ibid.
7 Ibid., p. 179.
8 Diary of Sir Evelyn Shuckburgh, quoted in Carlton, *Eden*, p. 296 (AC's italics).
9 Dell, *Chancellors*, p. 175.
10 Ibid., p. 181.
11 Howard, *RAB*, p. 188.

24: The Eden Anachronism (PP. 350–61)

1 Harvey diary, 24 July 1942, J. Harvey (ed.), *War Diaries*, pp. 143 4.
2 Quoted in *The Times*, 31 August 1996.
3 David Butler, *The British General Election of 1955* (1955).
4 Moran diary, 29 May 1955, Moran, *Churchill: Struggle for Survival*, pp. 657–8.
5 Macmillan to Eden, 11 February 1956, Carlton, *Eden*, p. 396.
6 Beaverbrook Papers BBK C58, in Carlton, *Eden*, pp. 396–7.
7 Middleton to Aldrich, 9 March 1956, in Carlton, *Eden*, p. 399 (AC's italics).
8 Recollections of Livingston Merchant, Carlton, *Eden*, p. 339.

25: **Relegation** (PP. 362–73)

1 Rhodes James, *Eden*, p. 455.
2 Nigel Nicolson, *Long Life: Memoirs* (1997), p. 161.
3 Nicolson, *Long Life*, p. 162.
4 See Diane Kunz, *The Economic Diplomacy of the Suez Crisis* (1991).
5 Dell, *Chancellors*, p. 219.
6 Lord Butler, *The Art of the Possible* (1971), pp. 188–9.

26: **Macmillan** (PP. 374–88)

1 22 November 1956, Hansard 560 H.C. Deb. 5s, cols 1943–4 (AC's italics).
2 Minutes of the 1922 Committee, 22 November 1956, in Goodhart, *The 1922*, p. 174.
3 Howard, *RAB*, p. 241.
4 Goodhart, *The 1922*, pp. 174–5.
5 *Economist*, 22 December 1956, in Howard, *RAB*, p. 243.
6 *The Times*, 11 January 1957, in Alistair Horne, *Macmillan*, vol. 2 (1989), p. 5.
7 Horne, *Macmillan*, vol. 1, p. 105.
8 Peter Mandlet, 'Saving the heritage from ourselves', *The Times*, 16 August 1996.
9 Addison, *Churchill on the Home Front*, p. 436.
10 Simon Heffer, 'Centenary of a Double-Crosser', *Spectator*, 5 February 1994.
11 Horne, *Macmillan*, vol. 2, p. 7.
12 Goodhart, *The 1922*, pp. 183–4 (AC's italics).
13 Ibid., pp. 182–3.
14 Minutes of the 1922 Committee, ibid., p. 184.
15 Minutes of the 1922 Executive, 19 July 1962, ibid., pp. 185–6.
16 Horne, *Macmillan*, vol. 2, p. 461.

27 **'A Sad Blow for Me'** (PP. 389–99)

1 Macmillan diary, 16 August 1963, Horne, *Macmillan*, vol. 2, p. 530.
2 John Campbell, *Edward Heath: A Biography* (1992), p. 293.
3 Horne, *Macmillan*, vol. 2, p. 531.
4 Macmillan diary, 11 September 1963, ibid., p. 532.

[5] Ibid., p. 535.
[6] Macmillan diary, 6 October 1963, ibid., p. 537.
[7] Macmillan diary, 7 October 1963, ibid., p. 538.
[8] Ibid., p. 539.
[9] Howard, *RAB*, p. 309.
[10] Sir Harold Evans, *Downing Street Diary* (1981), pp. 296–7, in Horne, *Macmillan*, vol. 2, p. 544.
[11] Macmillan diary, 18 October 1963, Horne, *Macmillan*, vol. 2, p. 566.
[12] John Ramsden, *The Winds of Change: Macmillan to Heath 1957–1975* (1996), p. 280.
[13] Horne, *Macmillan*, vol. 2, p. 582.

28: The Short Orthodox Premiership of Sir Alec Douglas-Home (PP. 400–9)

[1] D. R. Thorpe, *Alec Douglas-Home* (1996), p. 312.
[2] Ibid.
[3] Goodhart, *The 1922*, p. 197.
[4] Dell, *Chancellors*, p. 292.
[5] Sir Alec Cairncross, in Dell, *Chancellors*, p. 298.
[6] Maudling to the Commons, 14 April 1964, Hansard 693 H.C. Deb. 5s, col. 239.
[7] Cromer to Maudling, 24 July 1964, Dell, *Chancellors*, p. 299.
[8] Ramsden, *Winds of Change*, p. 216.
[9] *Sunday Times*, 18 June 1965, in Thorpe, *Douglas-Home*, p. 387.
[10] His biographer alleges, on the basis of 'private information'. Ibid., p. 388.
[11] Goodhart, *The 1922*, p. 203.

29: Heath in Difficulties (PP. 410–34)

[1] John Ramsden, 'The Prime Minister and the Making of Policy', in Stuart Ball and Anthony Seldon (eds), *The Heath Government: A Reappraisal* (1996), pp. 26–7.
[2] Campbell, *Heath*, p. 265.
[3] Ibid.
[4] Peter Walker, *Staying Power: An Autobiography* (1991), p. 52, quoted by Ramsden in Ball and Seldon (eds), *Heath Government*, p. 30.

[5] Campbell, *Heath*, p. 239.

[6] Ibid., pp. 244–5.

[7] Kenneth Clarke to the Commons, Hansard, 22 July 1971, col. 1781.

[8] Cairncross, in Ball and Seldon (eds), *Heath Government*, p. 117.

[9] Ramsden, *Winds of Change*, p. 368.

[10] Campbell, *Heath*, pp. 596–7.

[11] Ibid., p. 605.

[12] Ibid., p. 606.

[13] Ibid., p. 608.

[14] Ibid., p. 607.

[15] Robert Shepherd, *Enoch Powell: A Biography* (1996), p. 447.

[16] Campbell, *Heath*, p. 619 (AC's italics).

30: 1974: The Year of Blunder (PP. 435–49)

[1] Conversation between the author and Jo Grimond, 1985.

[2] Campbell, *Heath*, p. 618.

[3] Letter from Mr Joe Haines to the author:

'February 10, 1999

I've just finished reading your splendid book on the Tories, but there was one point on which I thought I could add to your knowledge – the issue of a vote on the Queen's Speech debate in March, 1974.

At the time, Wilson was convinced that Heath intended to try to defeat the Government at the end of the debate in the belief that the Queen would then send for him and ask him to form a Government. We would then be back on the National Government track which Wilson always believed was possible.

Wilson did not want to put the hypothetical question directly to the Queen about what she would do in the event of the Government's defeat. He therefore asked the Lord Chancellor, Elwyn-Jones, to inquire at the Palace (presumably of the Queen's private secretary) whether she would grant him a Dissolution if he requested it after a defeat on the Speech. The reply was that she would. Wilson then asked Elwyn-Jones to convey the news to Quintin Hogg. Shortly afterwards, we heard that a division wouldn't be forced.'

[4] Conversation between the author and Sir James Goldsmith, February

1994 (at which Sir James minted that enduring aphorism – 'Assurances bind only those who receive them').
5 Campbell, *Heath*, p. 650.
6 Ramsden, *Winds of Change*, p. 413.
7 Ibid., p. 414.
8 Campbell, *Heath*, p. 645.
9 Ibid., pp. 650–2.

31: The Varied Roles of Edward du Cann (PP. 453–67)

1 James Prior, *A Balance of Power* (1986), p. 48.
2 Edward du Cann, *Two Lives* (1995), p. 200.
3 Ibid., pp. 202–3.
4 Margaret Thatcher, *The Path to Power* (1995), p. 262.
5 Du Cann, *Two Lives*, p. 205.
6 Thatcher, *Path to Power*, p. 267.
7 Ibid., pp. 266–7.
8 *Economist*, 30 November 1974, unsigned but presumably by Mr Mark Schreiber.
9 Thatcher, *Path to Power*, p. 268.
10 Ibid.
11 Ibid., p. 269.

32: Mrs Thatcher's First Government (PP. 468–84)

1 Margaret Thatcher, *Path to Power*, p. 286.
2 Margaret Thatcher, *The Downing Street Years* (1993), p. 26.
3 Thatcher, *Path to Power*, p. 458 (AC's italics).
4 Ibid., p. 435.
5 This anecdote, all too credible, is unfortunately unsourced in Hugo Young's biography of Margaret Thatcher, *One of Us* (1990), p. 223.
6 Quoted in Thatcher, *Downing Street Years*, p. 200.
7 Arthur Scargill writing in *New Left Review*, April, 1975 (AC's italics).
8 Ian MacGregor, *The Enemies Within: The Story of the Miners' Strike, 1984–5* (1986), p. 192.
9 Hugo Young, *One of Us*, p. 526.
10 *Sunday Times*, 8 May 1988.

33: The Year of Discontent (PP. 485–98)

[1] Thatcher, *Downing Street Years*, p. 832.
[2] Reproduced in Thatcher, *Downing Street Years*, p. 754.
[3] Ibid., p. 753.
[4] Thatcher, *Downing Street Years*, p. 829.
[5] Diary for 12 November 1990, in Alan Clark, *Diaries*, p. 344.
[6] Seldon, *Major*, p. 120.
[7] Quoted in Thatcher, *Downing Street Years*, p. 839.
[8] Seldon, *Major*, p. 121.
[9] Thatcher, *Downing Street Years*, p. 846.
[10] Alan Clark's (unpublished) diary: conversation with Peter Morrison.
[11] Seldon, *Major*, p. 128.

34: The Beginning of the End (PP. 499–510)

[1] AC's personal experience canvassing in NW Norfolk, and generally anecdotal.
[2] *New Statesman*, 27 March 1992.
[3] Sarah Hogg and Jonathan Hill, *Too Close to Call: Power and Politics – John Major in No. 10* (1995), p. 1. The author of the paper is not identified, but he or she will not have been of middle rank.
[4] Alan Clark's (unpublished) diary for 26 September 1992; conversation with Gordon Greig, political editor of the *Daily Mail*.
[5] Seldon, *Major*, pp. 332–3.
[6] Conversation between Alan Clark and John Major.
[7] Alan Clark's (unpublished) diary note, 19 June 1995.

35: A Trial of Leadership (PP. 511–23)

[1] Alan Clark's (unpublished) diary, 30 June 1995.
[2] Seldon, *Major*, p. 577.
[3] Alan Clark's (unpublished) diary, 1 July 1995.

36: The Party Hits the Reef (PP. 524–39)

[1] Hywel Williams, *Guilty Men: Conservative Decline and Fall 1992–1997* (1998), p. 148.
[2] Seldon, *Major*, p. 687.
[3] Ibid., p. 703.

[4] Ibid., p. 723.

[5] The distances and destinations are compiled from Seldon, *Major*, p. 719.

[6] AC in conversation with Sir Mark Lennox-Boyd, October 1997, whose experience in Blackpool North was typical, a Conservative majority of 10,500 transforming into an adverse margin of 6,000 on a swing of 16 per cent.

[7] Conservative Party News (CCO Press Release), Saturday 3 May 1997, 1026/97.

[8] *The Times*, 5 May 1997.

Diaries and memoirs

Ball, Stuart (ed.), *Parliament and Politics in the Age of Baldwin and Mac-Donald: The Headlam Diaries 1923–1935*, 1992.

Barnes, John and Nicholson, David (eds), *The Empire at Bay: The Leo Amery Diaries 1929–1945*, 1988.

Benn, Tony, *Conflicts of Interest: Diaries 1977–1980*, 1990.

Butler, R. A., *The Art of the Possible*, 1971.

Churchill, Winston S., *The Second World War*, vol. I: *The Gathering Storm*, 1948; vol. IV: *The Hinge of Fate*, 1951.

Clark, Alan (ed.), *A Good Innings: The Private Papers of Viscount Lee of Fareham*, 1974.

Colville, John, *The Fringes of Power: Downing Street Diaries 1939–1955*, 1985.

Dilks, David (ed.), *The Diaries of Sir Alexander Cadogan 1938–1945*, 1971.

Du Cann, Edward, *Two Lives*, Upton-upon-Severn, 1995.

De Gaulle, Charles, *War Memoirs*, vol. I: *The Call to Honour*, 1955.

Evans, Harold, *Downing Street Diary: The Macmillan Years 1957–63*, 1981.

Grigg, P. J., *Prejudice and Judgement*, 1948.

Harvey, J. (ed.), *The War Diaries of Oliver Harvey 1941–1945*, 1978.

Harvie-Scott, G. S., *Most of My Life*, 1980.

James, Robert Rhodes (ed.), *Chips: The Diaries of Sir Henry Channon*, 1967.

James, Robert Rhodes (ed.), *Memoirs of a Conservative: J. C. C. Davidson's Memoirs and Papers*, 1969.

James, Robert Rhodes (ed.), *Churchill: His Complete Speeches, 1897–1963*, vols. IV and VI, New York, 1974.

Lawson, Nigel, *The View From No. 11: Memoirs of a Tory Radical*, 1992.

Middlemas, Keith (ed.), *Tom Jones, Whitehall Diary*, vol. 1: *1916–1925*; vol. 2: *1926–1930*; Oxford, 1969.

Minney, R. J. (ed.), *The Private Papers of Hore-Belisha*, 1960.

Moran, Lord, *Winston Churchill: The Struggle for Survival 1940–1965*, 1966.

Nicolson, Nigel (ed.), *Harold Nicolson: Diaries and Letters 1930–1939*, 1966; *1939–1945*, 1967.

Nicolson, Nigel, *Long Life: Memoirs*, 1997.

Stuart, James, *Within the Fringe: An Autobiography*, 1967.

Thatcher, Margaret, *The Downing Street Years*, 1993.

Thatcher, Margaret, *The Path to Power*, 1995.

Winterton, Earl, *Orders of the Day*, 1953.

Biography

(Lord Avon) Anthony Eden, *The Reckoning: The Eden Memoirs*, vol. 2, 1965.

Blake, Robert, *The Unknown Prime Minister: The Life and Times of Andrew Bonar Law 1858–1923*, 1955.

Campbell, John, *F. E. Smith, First Earl of Birkenhead*, 1983.

Campbell, John, *Edward Heath: A Biography*, 1992.

Carlton, David, *Anthony Eden: A Biography*, 1981.

Charmley, John, *Churchill: The End of Glory*, 1993.

Chisholm, Anne and Davie, Michael, *Beaverbrook*, 1992.

Egremont, Max, *Under Two Flags: The Life of Major-General Sir Edward Spears*, 1997.

Gilbert Martin, *Winston S. Churchill, 1922–1939*, vol. V, 1976; vol. VI, *Finest Hour 1939–1941*, 1983.

Horne, Alistair, *Macmillan 1894–1956*, vol. I, 1988; *1957–1986*, vol. II, 1989.

Howard, Anthony, *RAB: The Life of R. A. Butler*, 1987.

James, Robert Rhodes, *Churchill: A Study in Failure*, 1969.

James, Robert Rhodes, *Anthony Eden*, 1986.

Kunz, Diane, *The Economic Diplomacy of the Suez Crisis*, New Haven, CT, 1991.

Lamb, Richard, *The Failure of the Eden Government*, 1987.

Lottman, Herbert R., *Pétain: Hero or Traitor? The Untold Story*, 1985.

Macleod, Iain, *Neville Chamberlain*, 1961.

Middlemas, Keith and Barnes, John, *Baldwin: A Biography*, 1969.

Roberts, Andrew, *The Holy Fox: A Biography of Lord Halifax*, 1991.

Seldon, Anthony, *Major: A Political Life*, 1997.

Shepherd, Robert, *Enoch Powell: A biography*, 1996.

Soames, Mary, *Clementine Churchill*, 1979.

Spalding, Frances, *Vanessa Bell*, 1983.

Taylor, A. J. P., *Beaverbrook*, 1972.

Thorpe, D. R., *Alec Douglas-Home*, 1996.

Walker, Peter, *Staying Power: An Autobiography*, 1991.

Young, Hugo, *One of Us: A Biography of Margaret Thatcher*, 1990.

Ziegler, Philip, *King Edward VIII*, 1990.

General studies

Addison, Paul, *The Road to 1945: British Politics and the Second World War*, 1975; 1994 edn.

Addison, Paul, *Churchill on the Home Front 1900–1955*, 1992.

Ball, Stuart, *Baldwin and the Conservative Party: The Crisis of 1929–31*, New Haven, CT, 1988.

Ball, Stuart and Seldon, Anthony, (eds), *The Heath Government: A Reappraisal*, 1996.

Barnett, Correlli, *The Audit of War: The Illusion and Reality of Britain as a Great Nation*, 1986.

Barnett, Correlli, *Engage the Enemy More Closely: The Royal Navy in the Second World War*, 1991.

Barnett, Correlli, *The Lost Victory, British Dreams, British Realities 1945–1950*, 1995.

Beaverbrook, Lord, *The Decline and Fall of Lloyd George*, 1963.

Blake, Robert, *The Conservative Party from Peel to Thatcher*, 1970; 1985 edn.

Butler, David, *The British General Election of 1955*, 1955.

Charmley, John, *Chamberlain and the Lost Peace*, 1989.

Charmley, John, *Churchill's Grand Alliance: The Anglo-American Special Relationship 1940–57*, 1995.

Charmley, John, *A History of Conservative Politics 1900–1996*, 1996.

Clark, Alan, *The Fall of Crete*, 1961, repr. 1999.

Clarke, Peter, *The Keynesian Revolution in the Making 1924–1936*, Oxford, 1988.

Clarke, Peter, *A Question of Leadership: Gladstone to Thatcher*, 1991.

Cockett, Richard, *Twilight of Truth: Chamberlain, Appeasement and the Manipulation of the Press*, 1989.

Cockett, Richard, *Thinking the Unthinkable: Think-Tanks and the Economic Counter-Revolution 1931–1983*, 1994.

Coles, Alan and Briggs, Ted, *Flagship Hood*, 1985.

Cook, Chris and Peele, Gillian (eds), *The Politics of Reappraisal, 1918–39*, 1975.

Cowling, Maurice, *The Impact of Labour*, Cambridge, 1971.

Dangerfield, George, *The Strange Death of Liberal England*, 1936; 1965 edn.

Day, David, *Menzies and Churchill at War*, 1986.

Day, David, *The Great Betrayal: Britain, Australia and the Onset of the Pacific War 1939–1941*, 1988.

Dell, Edmund, *The Chancellors: A History of the Chancellors of the Exchequer 1945–1990*, 1996.

Gilmour, David, *Curzon*, 1994.

Gilmour, Ian, *Dancing with Dogma: Britain Under Thatcherism*, 1992.

Goodhart, Philip, *The 1922: The Story of the Conservative Backbenchers' Parliamentary Committee*, 1973.

Hogg, Sarah and Hill, Jonathan, *Too Close to Call: Power and Politics – John Major in No. 10*, 1995.

Horne, Alistair, *To Lose a Battle: France 1940*, 1969.

Jefferys, Kevin, *The Churchill Coalition and Wartime Politics 1940–1945*, Manchester, 1991 edn.

Lamb, Richard, *Churchill as War Leader – Right or Wrong?*, 1991.

Lamb, Richard, *The Macmillan Years, 1957–1963: The Emerging Truth*, 1995.

MacGregor, Ian, *The Enemies Within: The Story of the Miners' Strike, 1984–5*, 1986.

Mitchell, B. R., *European Historical Statistics*, 1975.

Moggridge, D. E., *The Return to Gold, 1925*, Cambridge, 1969.

Mowatt, Charles Loch, *Britain Between the Wars 1918–1940*, 1955.

Newton, Scott, *Profits of Peace: The Political Economy of Anglo-German Appeasement*, Oxford, 1996.

Parker, R. A. C., *Chamberlain and Appeasement: British Policy and the Coming of the Second World War*, 1993.

Pollard, Sidney, *The Development of the British Economy 1914–1990*, 4th edn 1992.

Pugh, Martin, *The Making of Modern British Politics 1867–1939*, 1982.

Ramsden, John, *A History of the Conservative Party: The Age of Churchill and Eden 1940–1957*, 1995; *The Winds of Change: Macmillan to Heath 1957–1975*, 1996.

Roberts, Andrew, *Eminent Churchillians*, 1994.

Seldon, Anthony, *Churchill's Indian Summer: The Conservative Government 1951–55*, 1981.

Seldon, Anthony and Ball, Stuart (eds), *Conservative Century: The Conservative Party since 1900*, Oxford, 1994.

Sked, Alan, *Britain's Decline: Problems and Perspectives*, Oxford, 1987.

Taylor, A. J. P., *English History 1914–1945*, Oxford, 1965.

Wheeler-Bennett, John, *The Nemesis of Power: The German Army in Politics 1918–1945*, 1953.

Williams, Hywel, *Guilty Men: Conservative Decline and Fall 1992–1997*, 1998.

Williamson, Philip, *National Crisis and National Government*, Cambridge, 1992.

Willmott, H. P., *Empires in the Balance: Japanese and Allied Pacific Strategies to April 1942*, 1982.

Unpublished sources

Neville Chamberlain Papers, Birmingham University Library.

Clark, Alan, *Diary 1992–97*.

Woolton Papers, Bodleian Library, Oxford.

Kopsch, Hartmut, 'The Approach of the Conservative Party to Social Policy during World War II', unpublished University of London PhD, 1970.

Stewart, Graham S., 'Winston Churchill and the Conservative Party 1929–1937', unpublished University of Cambridge PhD, 1995.

INDEX